TAKING SIDES

Clashing Views on Controversial

Issues in Race and Ethnicity

FIFTH EDITION

Selected, Edited, and with Introductions by

Raymond D'Angelo
St. Joseph's College

Herbert Douglas
Rowan University

D0161905

McGraw-Hill/Dushkin
A Division of The McGraw-Hill Companies

For our parents

Cover image:
Corbis

Cover Art Acknowledgment
Charles Vitelli

Library of Congress Cataloging-in-Publication Data
Main entry under title:
Taking sides: clashing views on controversial issues in race and ethnicity/selected, edited, and with introductions by Raymond D'Angelo and Herbert Douglas.—5th ed.
Includes bibliographical references and index.
1. Race awareness, 2. Ethnicity. I. D'Angelo, Raymond, *comp*. II. Douglas, Herbert, *comp*.
305.8

0-07-291735-0
95-83858

Printed on Recycled Paper

Preface

This edition of *Taking Sides: Clashing Views on Controversial Issues in Race and Ethnicity* offers 18 selected issues and 36 readings dealing directly with race and ethnic relations in America. We have selected from historians, sociologists, political scientists, and others to reflect a wide range of perspectives. The interdisciplinary nature of the selections provides students with much-needed different perspectives on issues. At the same time, the issues will be attractive to the different disciplines in colleges and universities that teach courses in race and ethnic relations. We anticipate that this edition may be used in history, sociology, political science, ethnic studies, and psychology courses. We have followed the standard *Taking Sides* format, which includes an issue introduction and postscript. The introduction to each issue prepares the student with a brief background and questions to be considered when reading the selections. The postscript summarizes the debate, and suggests additional sources for research on the topic.

This reader is intended to supplement other texts or case studies in college courses dealing with race and ethnicity. As such, it is designed to provide a range of readings within a framework.

Students are encouraged to develop and structure their own ideas about race and ethnicity. The introductions and postscripts of each issue intentionally do not contain definitive answers. Students should consider the selections along with our editorial comments, and then formulate responsible thinking and discussion.

Changes to this Edition Most of the issues in this edition are new to the *Taking Sides: Race and Ethnicity* series. Very much like a first edition, the only repeated issues from the previous edition deal with immigration, college admissions, Hispanic progress, and reparations. Reflecting a constantly changing culture, we tried to include the most central and historically relevant questions that affect race and ethnic relations in America today. These issues include questions about American identity, race progress, race as skin color, race prejudice, political definitions of race, self-segregation, model minority, resegregation, multicultural curriculum in colleges, affirmative action, the permanence of racism, racial profiling, and public policy in the twenty-first century. We feel that each of these issues is of major significance in the study of race and ethnic relations in contemporary American society.

The issues have been organized into four parts. Part 1 deals with classical issues in race and ethnicity. Part 2 addresses specific problems of race, prejudice, and racial minorities. Part 3 contains some of the social and political issues of education and multiculturalism. Part 4 deals with relevant issues for the twenty-first century.

Supplements An *Instructor's Manual with Test Questions* is available from the publisher for instructors who have adopted *Taking Sides: Clashing Views on Controversial Issues in Race and Ethnicity* for their course. Also, a general guidebook offers information on methods and techniques for using the debate format in a classroom setting. Interested instructors should contact the publisher. There is an online version of *Using Taking Sides in the Classroom* along with a correspondence service for adopters at http://www.dushkin.com/usingts/.

Taking Sides: Clashing Views on Controversial Issues in Race and Ethnicity is only one title of many in the series. Any readers interested in viewing the table of contents for any other titles in the Taking Sides series should visit the Web site at http://www.dushkin.com/takingsides/.

Acknowledgements   This book would not have been possible without many stimulating discussions about race and ethnicity that we have had with students, colleagues, and family members over the years. We wish to recognize the many students we have taught over the years at St. Joseph's College and Rowan University. It is their interest and curiosity that helped stimulate our research in this area. One incident stands out. After spending much time copying reserve materials, a student, in frustration, suggested that a collection of readings in book form should be put together for the class instead of complaining about the existing available textbooks. At about the same time, Ted Knight, the former list manager of the *Taking Sides* series inquired about an interest in doing the new edition for race and ethnicity. The timing was good, and about a year ago we started this project on race and ethnicity. So, a thanks is extended to Ted Knight as well as Juliana Gribbins, developmental editor from the Connecticut office of McGraw-Hill/Dushkin.

Raymond D'Angelo is indebted to former professors Eugene Schneider, Judith Porter, and Robert Washington of Bryn Mawr College, all of whom provided the intellectual structure that has enabled me to teach and do research in the fields of race relations and ethnic studies. Thanks also to Connie Curry of Emory University, Frank Wu of the Howard University School of Law, Alan Richard of *Education Week*, and Greg Freeland of California Lutheran University. At St. Joseph's, departmental colleagues Kenneth Bauzon and John Hazzard offered advice and support mixed in with important criticism.

A special thanks goes to my wife, Susan for her support and patience throughout the project. Also, my children, Adam and Olivia, deserve thanks for their questions about the multicultural world they experience. As always, I received unqualified support from my parents who in their own determined way have shed light and understanding on the many controversial issues in race and ethnicity.

Herb Douglas acknowledges the late Gary Hunter, professor of history; Corann Okorodudu, coordinator of African American Studies; and Harold Luciucs and Habte Behre-Giorgis, professors of marketing at Rowan University, for their stimulation and support and encouragement. Nadim Bitar, professor of sociology, University of Toledo, is recognized for the mentoring, guidance and support he has provided over the years. Lastly, Roy Silver, professor of sociology at Southeast Community College of the University of Kentucky, offered his comments and support. A special thanks is extended to Margaret "Peg" Brown, also of Rowan University, whose clerical support was invaluable to this project.

We both appreciate the assistance, diligence, and patience of Jill Peter, Senior Developmental Editor and Jane Mohr, Project Manager in the McGraw-Hill/Dushkin Iowa office. We extend our thanks to them.

Most importantly, we wish to acknowledge the contributions our parents have made to any successes we have achieved in our academic lives and careers. Without the values that they instilled in us, including a commitment to life-long learning, this project would not have been possible for us to achieve.

Raymond D'Angelo
St. Joseph's College

Herbert Douglas
Rowan University

Contents In Brief

Contents

Preface   iii
Introduction   xiii

Arthur Schlesinger, Jr., historian, asserts that America needs a common identity. In that context he views multiculturalism as an attack on the basic values that have made America what it is today. Michael Walzer, professor at the Center of Advanced Study Princeton, makes the pluralist argument that America cannot avoid its multicultural identity. He explores the ways in which citizenship and nationality are compatible with the preservation of one's ethnic identity, culture, and community.

David Cole, law professor, critically examines and rebuffs significant myths alleging substantial destructive sociocultural and economic impacts of immigrants and policies in this field. Peter Brimelow, Senior Editor at *Forbes* and *National Review* magazines, argues that the United States is being overrun by a growing tide of aliens who are changing the character and composition of the nation.

Booker T. Washington, the premier black leader of the period 1896–1915, argues that with the embrace of significant norms of the white culture, the race could make progress in the American South. W.E.B. DuBois, the leading black intellectual and progressive social activist of the first half of the twentieth century, viewed Washington's program as too limited for blacks to progress in the United States.

Lillian B. Rubin, senior research fellow at the Institute for Study of Social Change at Berkeley, contrasts current immigrants who are mostly non-white with nineteenth-century European immigrants, almost all of whom were white. She notes that among many descendants of European immigrants currently there is a fear of whites becoming a minority. For these descendants, American identity has always been associated with being white. Ellis Cose, an African American journalist, argues that the traditional boundaries that determine race and skin color are not what they once were. Although he does not specifically cite ethnicity, Cose furthers the claim that American identity today is an expanding category.

PART 2   RACE, PREJUDICE, AND RACIAL MINORITIES   77

Howard Zinn, eminent historian, asserts that the black skin of the earliest African American was employed by whites to differentiate and establish them as members of a separate, distinct, and inferior race. Marvin Harris, a leading anthropologist, views skin color as a biological phenomenon, and thus he explains differences in skin color as a biological adaptation of humans for dealing with the potentially harmful solar radiation that we face.

Herbert Blumer, a sociologist, asserts that prejudice exists in a sense of group position rather than as an attitude based on individual feelings. Gordon Allport, a psychologist, makes the case that prejudice is the result of a three-stage learning process.

Lawrence Wright, a writer for *The New Yorker,* demonstrates the influence of politics upon census categories of race and ethnicity. In the 1990s, multiracial groups who did not fit into the government's traditional categories of race and ethnicity began to challenge them as too narrow and inaccurate. Clara Rodriguez, a professor of sociology at Fordham University, and Hector Cordero-Guzman, an associate professor and chair of the Department of Black and Hispanic Studies at Baruch College of the City University of New York, suggest that race is a much more complex concept. Using responses by Puerto Ricans to questions about racial identity, they argue that racial identity is "more contextually influenced, determined and defined."

Beverly Daniel Tatum, an African-American psychologist, examines identity development among adolescents, especially black youths, and the behavioral outcomes of this phenomenon. She argues that black adolescents' tendency to view themselves in racial terms is due to the totality of personal and environmental responses that they receive from the larger society. Peter Beinart, Senior Editor for *The New Republic,* in contrast, examines the complexity of the issues of multiculturalism and diversity on the nation's campuses and he asserts that one examine how a broad spectrum of groups responds to the challenges of identity and "fitting in" within increasingly multicultural and diverse communities.

David A. Bell agrees that Asian Americans are a "model minority" and expresses a great appreciation for the progress and prominence they have achieved within the nation. Frank H. Wu, Howard University law professor, rejects the characterization of Asian Americans as a "model minority" based on the belief that this characterization tends to obscure problems facing Asians in America.

Linda Chavez, writer and former political candidate, argues that Hispanics are making economic progress in America. Robert Aponte, a social scientist, argues that Hispanics are not making economic progress. He presents significant disaggregated data to show that certain Hispanic groups are becoming increasingly poor.

Gary Orfield, professor of education and social policy at the Harvard Graduate School of Education, and Susan E. Eaton, author, demonstrate that America's public schools are resegregating. Their argument is based on a series of legal decisions beginning in the 1970s that have successfully reversed the historic *Brown* decision. Ingrid Gould Ellen, writer for *The Brookings Review*, argues that neighborhood racial integration is increasing. She thinks researchers must balance their pessimistic findings of resegregation with increased integration.

William G. Bowen, former President of Princeton University, and Neil L. Rudenstine, former president of Harvard University, make the case for race-sensitive admissions in higher education. With a focus on selective colleges, they cite empirical data that demonstrate the success of beneficiaries of race-sensitive admission policies. Dinesh D'Souza, John M. Olin Scholar at the American Enterprise Institute, questions the racial preference argument and argues that merit should decide admission to any organization.

Gary B. Nash, a historian, sketches the development of American history over the past century, as the research of a new generation of historians sheds light on issues such as class conflict, labor relations, gender roles, and race relations. Nash views the teaching of history with a multicultural emphasis as a positive step in American education. Diane Ravitch, historian of education, fears the incipient weakening of a common knowledge base in American history that is taught in American public schools. This is caused by a particularistic multiculturalism, not the pluralistic multiculturalism that promotes a broad interpretation of a common American culture.

Robert Staples, an African-American sociologist, views affirmative action as a positive policy designed to provide equal economic opportunities for women and other minorities. Patrick A. Hall, an African-American librarian, is opposed to affirmative action based on the belief that it promotes negative stereotypes of African Americans and other minorities, and that it perpetuates the perception that minorities are not advancing based on merit.

Derrick Bell, a prominent African-American scholar and authority on civil rights and constitutional law, argues that the prospects for achieving racial equality in the United States are "illusory" for blacks. Dinesh D'Souza, media commentator and writer, believes that racial discrimination against blacks has substantially eroded within American society and that lagging progress among them is due to other factors, such as culture, rather than racism.

Richard Kahlenberg, fellow at the Center for National Policy, argues that class-based policies would provide a basis for attacking the problems of poverty and disadvantage that are experienced by members of all groups within society. Amy Gutmann, a political scientist, believes that racial injustices are a continuing reality of society and that class-based preferences tend to dilute their necessary focus on racism and their effects on society.

Robert L. Allen, professor and senior editor of *The Black Scholar,* argues that reparations for African Americans are necessary to achieve an economically just society within the United States. Staff writers from *The Economist* oppose reparations and question whether such a policy is appropriate in a nation where the victims of slavery are difficult to identify and the perpetrators of past racial oppressions are no longer among us.

John Derbyshire, political commentator for *National Review,* views racial profiling as a "common sense policy" and a valid response to crime control and national security concerns. David A. Harris, law professor and leading authority on racial profiling, argues that racial profiling is ineffective and damaging to our diverse nation.

Introduction

Raymond D'Angelo and Herbert Douglas

"The problem of the Twentieth Century is the problem of the color-line."

—W.E.B. DuBois

"Neither the life of an individual nor the history of a society can be understood without understanding both."

—C. Wright Mills

History

Immigration

From its inception, America emerged as a multi-ethnic nation. The Anglo-Saxons and other European ethnic groups who came to America during the Colonial Era were met by aboriginal people who had been residing on these lands for thousands of years prior to their arrival. As the colonies developed and their economies began to emerge, African slaves were imported to provide labor for the agrarian economy that would emerge. As the economy of the new nation evolved from agrarian pursuits to industrial capitalism, more and more ethnic groups were attracted to these shores to expand the ranks of labor and to pursue their American dream. Over time, the United States experienced multiple waves of immigration, from the old immigration of pre–Civil War times to the new immigrants of the post–Reconstruction Era, extending to include the most recent immigration of Asians and Hispanics that the nation experienced during the 1990s. So, America has developed as a nation of diverse ethnicities and races derived from virtually every corner of the known world. How does one accommodate the interests and the goals of these diverse ethnic and racial groups while maintaining a unified society? What is an American? How is one to define American identity? (See Issues 1 and 2.)

The United States gained its reputation in the world as a land of freedom and justice for all who arrived on its shores. This quality of the nation's experience has made America a magnet for peoples seeking liberty, justice, and opportunity for improving the quality of their lives.

In the shifting sands of vocabulary that describe the race and ethnic components of American culture, one contemplates "diversity" and "multiculturalism." Public discourse on these matters takes us on a conceptual journey to explain who we are and who we are not. For all who are in America—the most recent arrivals together with descendants of the very first to arrive—the meaning of what is an American requires us to reflect upon and analyze the history of race and ethnicity.

Political authority and control of the means of economic production by a dominant Anglo group presented challenges to new immigrants, and later in the nineteenth century, former slaves along with other people of color, especially Native Americans. The popular notion of the American melting pot was problematic. The dominant group demonstrated a sense of superiority over subordinate groups. Ethnocentrism, xenophobia, and nativism were common in early American culture and soon resulted in policy efforts to restrict opportunities for those who did not look like white, Anglo-Saxon Protestants or practice their values. What price would a non-Anglo have to pay to "become" an American?

An early twentieth century effort to control American identity can be seen in the Immigration Act of 1924. The Act created immigration quotas based on the percentage of each ethnic group present in America at that time. This legislation had the effect of restricting the immigration of less-favored European ethnic groups such as the Italians and the Poles and created space for the great migration of African Americans from the South to the urban, industrial centers of the North.

We see the struggle for American identity encompassing European ethnics and American blacks as remarkably similar. Both groups were attracted to the northern industrial centers of the United States seeking economic opportunity that was shrinking in their rural backgrounds. Both groups were deeply religious and anchored by the church in a new urban environment. At the same time, both were vulnerable to being exploited within the labor markets in which they were competing. The competition among racial and ethnic groups within prevailing labor markets is a significant feature of capitalist economies, and the United States was no exception.

Race Segregation

Segregation emerged as the social and legal framework of race relations at the end of the nineteenth century. In the legal arena, the 1896 *Plessy v. Ferguson* became the law of the land and therefore public policy in race relations. The resulting race segregation that proliferated throughout American cities isolated blacks from European ethnic immigrants. It is in this context that an understanding of early twentieth century race and ethnic relations should be framed. Hence, the early notion of American identity for the most part excluded blacks. Consequently, the late nineteenth to early twentieth century debate within the black community emerged between Booker T. Washington and W.E.B. DuBois (Issue 3). These leaders were concerned with issues of racial advancement, and they offered competing philosophies and strategies for African Americans to achieve these goals.

The intensity and divisiveness of the race issue in American life was manifested in thousands of lynchings of blacks, forced labor camps, and an ideology of white supremacy. This ideology extended to other peoples of color as seen when Japanese Americans were isolated in internment camps during World War II. Increasingly, blacks and other people of color resided in segregated barrios and ghettos within the core cities of the country. Douglas Massey and Nancy Denton, in *American Apartheid and the Urban Underclass,* refer to this housing segregation as American apartheid.

The Civil Rights Movement and Desegregation

During the slave era, some questioned whether this peculiar institution was compatible with important American values such as those of the Christian religion and the nation's democratic ethos. The abolitionists were among the first to raise such questions, and their movement was a significant historical precursor to the civil rights movement of the post–World War II period. Indeed, the war itself contributed to changing race relations in the states. It was Executive Order #1199 issued by President Harry S. Truman that integrated the armed forces. This was significant in that it is an early example of the employment of an egalitarian principal to effect the racial reform of an American institution. Black soldiers receiving equal treatment while fighting the war would return home to face segregation.

During the 1940s, the NAACP's legal defense team under the leadership of Charles Hamilton Houston mapped out a strategy to dismantle Jim Crow. Public education became the battleground to overturn the "separate but equal" law of the land. Eventually, in 1954 the Supreme Court overturned *Plessy* in the *Brown v. Board of Education* decision. This decision was a watershed of progress in American race relations. Soon, the civil rights movement would address many issues including public accommodations and perhaps, most importantly, voting rights among others.

Gunnar Myrdal's *An American Dilemma* (1944), a landmark critique of American race relations, contributed significantly to the depth and breath of knowledge on race in that it argued that America lacked the will to change and enforce its creed of equality and justice within the common life of society, C. Vann Woodward's *The Strange Career of Jim Crow* (1955) became a classic study of segregation.

In the 1960s and beyond, the civil rights movement forced America to recognize and confront the phenomenon of institutional racism. There was more to the problem of racial injustice than just individual attitude and behavior. The Civil Rights Act of 1964 along with the Voting Rights Act of 1965 and the Fair Housing Act of 1968 were key legislative initiatives advanced to address racial inequality.

Multiculturalism

With new immigrants of color arriving in significant numbers in the 1990s—coming together with existing minorities within desegregated America—an emphasis on multiculturalism and diversity emerged. So, for example, the 2000 U.S. Census shows a population breakdown of 12% Hispanic, 12% African American, 3% Asian American, and 70% white. This contrasts with the demographic profile of the mid-twentieth century, in which the minority population consisted primarily of 12% black.

Today, we see a country with an increasing minority population. In this context, multicultural and diversity concerns are affecting a broad spectrum of American institutions extending from the private corporate sector to public education. Further, this calls into question traditional definitions of race and ethnicity (Issue 7). American demographers predict that increasing diversification of the population of the Unites States will continue unabated for the foreseeable future. Thus the challenges to the institutional leaders of America to manage diversity properly will be a major challenge of the twenty-first century.

Trends in the Study of Race and Ethnicity

Race and ethnicity were not focal concerns of American scholarship prior to the dawn of the twentieth century; thus, there was a dearth of course offerings on this subject matter within American colleges and universities. The Chicago School of Sociology is credited with introducing the formal study of race relations in American colleges and universities in the 1920s. Beginning with Robert Park, a journalist turned sociologist, along with Ernest Burgess and their colleagues, the study of race and ethnic groups emerged as a primary area in twentieth century history and sociology due to their introduction of such courses at the University of Chicago. Park's race relations cycle and the idea of assimilation served the country well in terms of policy, as immigrants believed they, and especially their children, would eventually be accepted in their new culture.

Much later in the twentieth century, a pluralist perspective emerged that offered a challenge to the notion of assimilation. Cultural pluralism, a concept noted by Milton Gordon in 1964, refers to the many different cultural systems within the framework of the larger society. When contrasted to assimilation theory, pluralism offers an explanation for the lack of mixing and merging of cultural groups.

It should be noted that Ulrich B. Phillip's *American Negro Slavery* and William Dunning's (*Reconstruction, Political and Economic: 1865–1877*) work on Reconstruction were the primary influences of research and teaching on race prior to the 1950s. The revisionist/reformist scholars who followed them consider both as apologists for slavery and racism. African American intellectuals whose scholarship challenged the perspectives on race presented by Phillips and Dunning found it very difficult to secure publication of their own works. Despite these challenges, black scholars such as Rayford Logan (*The Betrayal of the Negro: From Rutherford B. Hayes to Woodrow Wilson*) and E. Franklin Frazier (*The Negro Family in the United States*) were able to publish works that challenged the traditional notions of race promoted by white scholars of the earlier period.

Some of the most significant challenges to the scholarship and teaching of race that prevailed during the Segregation Era came from white scholars of a leftist orientation. Two prime examples of this scholarly tradition are the multiple-volume work, *A Documentary History of the Negro People in the United States* by the Marxist historian Herbert Aptheker, and Philip Foner's *Mrs. Lincoln and Mrs. Keckly: The Remarkable Story of the Friendship between a First Lady and a Former Slave.*

Immigrants who came to the United States often received an "industrial welcome." This positive participation in certain labor markets was facilitated by existing shortages of labor within certain sectors of the economy dominated by menial jobs of law status and offering minimal remuneration. A good example of this orientation toward low-wage workers can be seen in the situation faced by immigrant labor from Latin America in agriculture. Workers from the existing American labor markets tend to find farm labor as undesirable and thus they are quite willing for Mexicans and other Latinos to do this "dirty work" of society. However, when immigrants begin to compete with native-born workers for higher status jobs in pursuit of upward mobility, the result is social conflict between and among such groups.

Social conflict theories offer us important insights into significant areas of race and ethnic relations. Theories of economic competition and cultural conflict are important theoretical perspectives for examining such inter-group relations. Also, Herbert Blumer's theory of group position became another important analytical construct that can be profitably employed to examine competition and conflict within race and ethnic relations (Issue 6).

The inevitable conflicts between and among the new ethnic, immigrant groups and racial minorities living in a new country were examined by the emerging social sciences. Theodore Adorno, Gordon Allport, Robert Merton, and others applied social scientific thought to prejudice, discrimination, and racism. Many of these problems and issues are explored in this edition (see Issues 6, 7, and 8).

In the wake of the landmark decision of the United States Supreme Court of 1954 and the Civil Rights Movement, new opportunities for advancing the study of race and ethnicity emerged. In the wake of this opening, other scholars including Eric Foner, John Hope Franklin, Thomas Pettigrew, Thomas F. Gossett, and Cornel West and many others proliferated within the academic community to advance this interdisciplinary area of scholarly concern. Emerging in academia now were new programs and college majors whose primary focus is on the unique history and experiences of racial and ethnic groups.

Renewed interest in immigration has emerged in response to the changing American demographics. Consider that recent immigration trends show significant growth of the Asian and Hispanic components of the American population (Issues 9 and 10). The increasing racial and ethnic diversity of America today is not without its controversy. What is the role of race in an increasingly multicultural society? How does the shift in dominant-subordinate relations affect members of the dominant group? These questions are reviewed in the book under the following issues: resegregation (Issue 11), who gets into college? (Issues 12 and 14), and how is the curriculum of higher education reflective of the changes? (Issue 13).

More recent developments concerning public policy revolve around the issue of class and race (Issue 16). Relatively new are issues concerning racial profiling (Issue 18) and reparations for black Americans (Issue 17). Given the resegregation argument is the question of the permanence of racism (Issue 15).

To the Student

It is our hope that, in the end, students will gain a greater understanding of the diversity that is the American experience. Further, we hope that students will develop the skills to elevate the discourse of race and ethnic issues through reading, respectful discussion, and critical analysis. These issues need sociological scrutiny because without critical thinking, they are so often determined by popular culture and media-influenced ideas. At the same time the student is assessing American culture, he or she can then grasp the individual issue of identity. Without theory and historical perspective, one essentially has no context for ideas that otherwise may reflect a narrow, incomplete picture of the culture.

Some limitations in this didactic approach of study, which positions one selection against another for the purpose of "debate," must be recognized. At times, one side of the issue is clearly and articulately stated, while the opposite position lacks these qualities. We have tried to find scholarly representations of different points of view. In the process, however, we have found this to be easier said than done. Also, we are aware that the issues may have greater complexity than the two positions offered. Clearly, we run the risk of creating a false dichotomy. It is our expectation that the positions included in the reader will generate interest and insight for the student. Indeed, issues should be explored more comprehensively.

Some of the analytical questions may strike the reader as simplistic or even trivial. For example, how can scholars evaluate the condition of Hispanics in America with the question, "Are Hispanics Making Economic Progress?" Clearly, a definitive "yes" or "no" ignores a growing body of scholarship dealing with the issue. Further, it ignores the extensive diversity of the Hispanic community. Thus, we seek to further understanding by placing the issue in a format that enables the student to organize and express his or her ideas while, at the same time, addressing the given points of view.

Despite the potential limitations, the *Taking Sides* format serves as an introduction to the student as he or she tries to structure thoughts and ideas in these controversial areas. We consider America as a society whose unifying identity is rooted in ethnic and racial diversity. How the diversity plays out—that is, the structures and the forms it takes—is of sociological interest to us. In sum, we want students to explore critically the historical and contemporary experiences of racial and ethnic groups in America.

Issues in this New Edition

This edition builds on the work of Richard Monk in previous editions of *Taking Sides: Clashing Views on Controversial Issues in Race and Ethnicity,* and seeks to move the treatment of these issues more in the direction of public issues that have scholarly merit. Thus, we have expanded and deepened some of the principal issues in the study of race and ethnic relations. The student or professor familiar with previous editions will notice that the issues contained in this edition all focus on America. Clearly, in the larger picture, the study of race and ethnicity benefits from a cross-national approach. However, it is our decision based on the judgment that race and ethnicity are fundamental to understanding the American experience and that unresolved issues on these fronts continue to challenge us in the twenty-first century.

This edition is organized around four concepts: (1) classical issues in race and ethnicity; (2) race, prejudice, and racial minorities; (3) social and political issues of education and multiculturalism; and (4) issues for the twenty-first century.

Part 1, "Classical Issues in Race and Ethnicity," introduces the student to the historical questions of race and ethnicity. From the early years of the new nation, immigration and the question of slavery confronted both newcomers and those who preceded them. Students should develop a broad historical perspective of these issues, which are still with us today.

Part 2, "Race, Prejudice, and Racial Minorities," deals with the issues of how race is defined, and some of the consequences of prejudice and race conscious behavior. It is imperative for students to grasp the understanding of prejudice and its consequences on subordinate groups. Along with this, the inclusion of issues dealing with Asians and Hispanics offers students the opportunity to critically examine race and ethnic concepts beyond the black-white paradigm.

Part 3, "Social and Political Issues of Education and Multiculturalism," raises critical and contemporary questions that reflect current trends in race and ethnic relations. Each issue in this part deals directly or indirectly with education. College admissions and mandatory curricular requirements do not stand alone. They reflect demographic changes in higher education and are hotly contested public policy issues today. Students in higher education should benefit from exposure to these issues since they are primarily educationally oriented concerns. Further, the work of the Harvard Civil Rights Project has brought to light the late twentieth century resegregation trend of many American communities.

Part 4, "Issues for the twenty-first Century," is focused on racism and its continuing effects within twenty-first century society. How long will racism last? What new forms will it take? What policies should be supported in efforts to deal with continued racism? Students can develop a perspective on the race versus class issue in terms of public policy.

Editors' Note

We have been engaged in what is a fascinating and endless four-decade dialogue about race and ethnic relations in American society. Putting together this reader has given us an opportunity to examine and frame some of the critical problems and issues in the field. We welcome feedback from our readers. E-mail responses to rdangelo@sjcny.edu.

United States Census Bureau

The U.S. Census Bureau Web site presents useful demographic information on ancestry, citizenship, and foreign-born citizens. The links to Hispanic and Asian minority data are extensive. This site is a very good starting point for the serious student to gain background information on race and ethnicity.

www.uscensus.gov

American Ethnic Studies: Yale Library Research Guide

At Yale University, this site provides sources for researching ethnic identity including research guides in African American, Latino, Native American, Asian American, and American studies. It is a valuable site for students to begin research in race and ethnic relations, offering multiple links to college libraries and scholarly journals. Includes links to guides, encyclopedias, and dictionaries, along with connections to museums, centers, institutes, and databases.

www.library.yale.edu/rsc/ethnic/internet.html

United States Citizenship and Immigration Services

This is the home page of the United States Citizenship and Immigration Services (USCIS). It offers up-to-date information on U.S. immigration law and policy.

http://uscis.gov/graphics/index.htm

Ellis Island Foundation

The Web site of the Ellis Island Foundation enables almost everyone a chance to research his or her family history. It contains an American family immigration history center.

http://www.ellisisland.org/

Scholastic Magazine

This is the Web site of *Scholastic Magazine,* a publication for teachers. It is recommended here as an introduction to young students of first-hand accounts of immigrating to the United States. The future teacher will find information and activities for students of all ages.

http://teacher.scholastic.com/activities/
  immigration/

Immigration History Research Center: University of Minnesota

The University of Minnesota Immigration Research Center, with a focus on research sources for European immigrants, seeks to promote the history of the American immigrant experience. It offers an extensive bibliography of manuscripts and monographs on European immigrant groups.

http://www.ihrc.umn.edu/

PART 1

Classical Issues in Race and Ethnicity

*T*here are a number of concerns that have challenged the American nation throughout its history. Given the fact that immigration has been a significant factor in shaping the nation significant concerns with immigration and immigration policies have confronted the American body politic over time. Immigration has challenged the traditional notion of American identity and raises serious issues concerning the maintenance of an American unum. The diversity of the American population to which immigration has been a major contributor has brought substantial issues of race relations to the fore. Racial minorities have challenged the nation to live up to the true meaning of its creed where issues of equity and social justice are concerned and these issues and concerns have been illuminated within the experiences of African Americans and those of the peoples of color that have swelled the ranks of America's immigrant populations. The efforts of these peoples to advance within the institutional domains of the American society have been ongoing challenges to our national experience.

- Do We Need a Common American Identity?

- Is Immigration Good for America?

- Race Relations in the Nineteenth Century: Will Accommodation Insure Progress?

- Does White Identity Define America?

ISSUE 1

Do We Need a Common American Identity?

YES: Arthur M. Schlesinger, Jr., "E Pluribus Unum?," *The Disuniting of America: Reflections on a Multicultural Society* (New York: W.W. Norton Co. 1992)

NO: Michael Walzer, "What Does It Mean to Be an American?" *Social Research* (Fall 1990)

ISSUE SUMMARY

YES: Arthur Schlesinger, Jr., historian, asserts that America needs a common identity. In that context he views multiculturalism as an attack on the basic values that have made America what it is today. For him, Western-rooted values, whether we like it or not, form the fabric of American society. The values of democracy, freedom, rule of law, human rights and so forth are unfairly challenged under the guise of multiculturalism. He makes the argument for continuing the assimilation creed.

NO: Michael Walzer, professor at the Center of Advanced Study Princeton, makes the pluralist argument that America cannot avoid its multicultural identity. He explores the ways in which citizenship and nationality are compatible with the preservation of one's ethnic identity, culture, and community.

Given the varied background differences of the many groups of people who have become Americans, the question of a common identity is inevitable. What is an American? When does an immigrant become an "American"? This edition of *Taking Sides, Race and Ethnicity* begins with the complex issue of American identity. Indeed, the parallel issues of race and ethnicity are at the heart of the American experience. Hence, to understand American identity is to consider the uniqueness of American culture along with what holds it together. A common American identity began as a European immigrant culture that dealt with racial differences through the institution of slavery and isolating Native Americans on reserve land. Throughout American history, the idea of a common American culture has constantly changed. Central to the changes is, on one hand, the firm notion that there must be a common American identity, while on the other is the recognition of several different, sometimes competing, cultural groups who are part of the same culture. This dilemma has emerged conceptually in the form of the assimilation versus pluralism debate.

Arthur Schlesinger, Jr., is concerned about what he sees as an attack on the common American identity, which was initially launched by European immigrants of non-British origin, and continued by later immigrants of non-European origin. For Schlesinger, a common American identity is based on values that originated in Europe and developed fully in America. Values such as individual freedom, tolerance, liberty, equality, and human rights are part of Western culture. They have become the core of a common American identity.

How are racial and ethnic differences included in American culture? The dominant culture is rooted in Anglo-Saxon foundations. Nevertheless, the different immigrant groups ("a nation of immigrants") reflect many different cultures. Culturally, what does an immigrant experience to become an American? How much assimilation is possible? And, what are the perceived costs and rewards of assimilation?

In the same context that Schlesinger critiques the interest in multiculturalism, he cites the democratic principle of tolerance. He assumes that all races are included in the common American identity.

Michael Walzer argues that America has no singular national identity. Further, he writes, that to be an American is "to know that and to be more or less content with it." Using the ideas of Horace Kallen, Walzer furthers the argument that the United States is less a union of states than a union of ethnic, racial, and religious groups.

Walzer maintains that these "unrelated natives" constitute a permanent "manyness." A dissimilation or unique cultural consciousness does not threaten American culture. Given the tremendous diversity of American people, the common culture of the nation is seen through its citizenship. Hence, the need for a common American identity is limited.

As you read this issue, keep in mind that each new wave of immigrants raises the question of American identity. Again and again, the culture and contributions of new immigrants pushes America to ask, should we stress our similarities or encourage diversity? Should we insist on a common American identity or celebrate our differences? Consider Schlesinger's critique of multiculturalism and contrast it with Walzer's ideas of pluralism. Is Schlesinger trying to protect and preserve a dominant group culture? Or is he intolerant of cultural differences? Does Walzer truly favor pluralism? Or does he think a common American identity is impossible?

Arthur M. Schlesinger, Jr.   ➡ **YES**

E Pluribus Unum?

The attack on the common American identity is the culmination of the cult of ethnicity. That attack was mounted in the first instance by European Americans of non-British origin ("unmeltable ethnics") against the British foundations of American culture; then, latterly and massively, by Americans of non-European origin against the European foundations of that culture. As Theodore Roosevelt's foreboding suggests, the European immigration itself palpitated with internal hostilities, everyone at everybody else's throats— hardly the "monocultural" crowd portrayed by ethnocentric separatists. After all, the two great "world" wars of the twentieth century began as fights among European states. Making a single society out of this diversity of antagonistic European peoples is a hard enough job. The new salience of non-European, nonwhite stocks compounds the challenge. And the non-Europeans, or at least their self-appointed spokesmen, bring with them a resentment, in some cases a hatred, of Europe and the West provoked by generations of Western colonialism, racism, condescension, contempt, and cruel exploitation.

꿍

Will not this rising flow of non-European immigrants create a "minority majority" that will make Eurocentrism obsolete by the twenty-first century? This is the fear of some white Americans and the hope (and sometimes the threat) of some nonwhites.

Immigrants were responsible for a third of population growth during the 1980s. More arrived than in any decade since the second of the century. And the composition of the newcomers changed dramatically. In 1910 nearly 90 percent of immigrants came from Europe. In the 1980s more than 80 percent came from Asia and Latin America.

Still, foreign-born residents constitute only about 7 percent of the population today as against nearly 15 percent when the first Roosevelt and Wilson were worrying about hyphenated Americans, Stephan Thernstrom doubts that the minority majority will ever arrive. The black share in the population has grown rather slowly—9.9 percent in 1920, 10 percent in

1950, 11.1 percent in 1970, 12.1 percent in 1990. Neither Asian-Americans nor Hispanic-Americans go in for especially large families; and family size in any case tends to decline as income and intermarriage increase. "If today's immigrants assimilate to American ways as readily as their predecessors at the turn of the century—as seems to be happening," Thernstrom concludes, "there won't be a minority majority issue anyway."

America has so long seen itself as the asylum for the oppressed and persecuted—and has done itself and the world so much good thereby—that any curtailment of immigration offends something in the American soul. No one wants to be a Know-Nothing. Yet uncontrolled immigration is an impossibility; so the criteria of control are questions the American democracy must confront. We have shifted the basis of admission three times this century—from national origins in 1924 to family reunification in 1965 to needed skills in 1990. The future of immigration policy depends on the capacity of the assimilation process to continue to do what it has done so well in the past: to lead newcomers to an acceptance of the language, the institutions, and the political ideals that hold the nation together.

⚜

Is Europe really the root of all evil? The crimes of Europe against lesser breeds without the law (not to mention even worse crimes—Hitlerism and Stalinism—against other Europeans) are famous. But these crimes do not alter other facts of history: that Europe was the birthplace of the United States of America, that European ideas and culture formed the republic, that the United States is an extension of European civilization, and that nearly 80 percent of Americans are of European descent.

When Irving Howe, hardly a notorious conservative, dared write, "The Bible, Homer, Plato, Sophocles, Shakespeare are central to our culture," an outraged reader ("having graduated this past year from Amherst") wrote, "Where on Howe's list is the *Quran*, the *Gita*, Confucius, and other central cultural artifacts of the peoples of our nation?" No one can doubt the importance of these works nor the influence they have had on other societies. But on American society? It may be too bad that dead white European males have played so large a role in shaping our culture. But that's the way it is. One cannot erase history.

These humdrum historical facts, and not some dastardly imperialist conspiracy, explain the Eurocentric slant in American schools. Would anyone seriously argue that teachers should conceal the European origins of American civilization? or that schools should cater to the 20 percent and ignore the 80 percent? Of course the 20 percent and their contributions should be integrated into the curriculum too, which is the point of cultural pluralism.

But self-styled "multiculturalists" are very often ethnocentric separatists who see little in the Western heritage beyond Western crimes. The Western tradition, in this view, is inherently racist, sexist, "classist," hegemonic; irredeemably repressive, irredeemably oppressive. The spread of

Western culture is due not to any innate quality but simply to the spread of Western power. Thus the popularity of European classical music around the world—and, one supposes, of American jazz and rock too—is evidence not of wide appeal but of "the pattern of imperialism, in which the conquered culture adopts that of the conqueror."

Such animus toward Europe lay behind the well-known crusade against the Western-civilization course at Stanford ("Hey-hey, ho-ho, Western culture's got to gol"). According to the National Endowment for the Humanities, students can graduate from 78 percent of American colleges and universities without taking a course in the history of Western civilization. A number of institutions—among them Dartmouth, Wisconsin, Mt. Holyoke—require courses in third-world or ethnic studies but not in Western civilization. The mood is one of divesting Americans of the sinful European inheritance and seeking redemptive infusions from non-Western cultures.

⋯◈⋯

One of the oddities of the situation is that the assault on the Western tradition is conducted very largely with analytical weapons forged in the West. What are the names invoked by the coalition of latter-day Marxists, deconstructionists, poststructuralists, radical feminists, Afrocentrists? Marx, Nietzsche, Gramsci, Derrida, Foucault, Lacan, Sartre, de Beauvoir, Habermas, the Frankfurt "critical theory" school—Europeans all. The "unmasking," "demythologizing," "decanonizing," "dehegemonizing" blitz against Western culture depends on methods of critical analysis unique to the West—which surely testifies to the internally redemptive potentialities of the Western tradition.

Even Afrocentrists seem to accept subliminally the very Eurocentric standards they think they are rejecting. "Black intellectuals condemn Western civilization," Professor Pearce Williams says, "yet ardently wish to prove it was founded by their ancestors." And, like Frantz Fanon and Léopold Senghor, whose books figure prominently on their reading lists, Afrocentric ideologues are intellectual children of the West they repudiate. Fanon, the eloquent spokesman of the African wretched of the earth, had French as his native tongue and based his analyses on Freud, Marx, and Sartre. Senghor, the prophet of Negritude, wrote in French, established the Senegalese educational system on the French model and, when he left the presidency of Senegal, retired to France.

Western hegemony, it would seem, can be the source of protest as well as of power. Indeed, the invasion of American schools by the Afrocentric curriculum, not to mention the conquest of university departments of English and comparative literature by deconstructionists, poststructuralists, etc., are developments that by themselves refute the extreme theory of "cultural hegemony." Of course, Gramsci had a point. Ruling values do dominate and permeate any society; but they do not have the rigid and monolithic grip on American democracy that academic leftists claim.

Radical academics denounce the "canon" as an instrument of European oppression enforcing the hegemony of the white race, the male sex, and the capitalist class, designed, in the words of one professor, "to rewrite the past and construct the present from the perspective of the privileged and the powerful." Or in the elegant words of another—and a professor of theological ethics at that: "The canon of great literature was created by high Anglican assholes to underwrite their social class."

The poor old canon is seen not only as conspiratorial but as static. Yet nothing changes more regularly and reliably than the canon: compare, for example, the canon in American poetry as defined by Edmund Clarence Stedman in his *Poets of America* (1885) with the canon of 1935 or of 1985 (whatever happened to Longfellow and Whittier?); or recall the changes that have overtaken the canonical literature of American history in the last half-century (who reads Beard and Parrington now?). And the critics clearly have no principled objection to the idea of the canon. They simply wish to replace an old gang by a new gang. After all, a canon means only that because you can't read everything, you give some books priority over others.

Oddly enough, serious Marxists—Marx and Engels, Lukacs, Trotsky, Gramsci—had the greatest respect for what Lukacs called "the classical heritage of mankind." Well they should have, for most great literature and much good history are deeply subversive in their impact on orthodoxies. Consider the present-day American literary canon: Emerson, Jefferson, Melville, Whitman, Hawthorne, Thoreau, Lincoln, Twain, Dickinson, William and Henry James, Henry Adams, Holmes, Dreiser, Faulkner, O'Neill. Lackeys of the ruling class? Apologists for the privileged and the powerful? Agents of American imperialism? Come on!

It is time to adjourn the chat about hegemony. If hegemony were as real as the cultural radicals pretend, Afrocentrism would never have got anywhere, and the heirs of William Lyon Phelps would still be running the Modern Language Association.

❧

Is the Western tradition a bar to progress and a curse on humanity? Would it really do America and the world good to get rid of the European legacy?

No doubt Europe has done terrible things, not least to itself. But what culture has not? History, said Edward Gibbon, is little more than the register of the crimes, follies, and misfortunes of mankind. The sins of the West are no worse than the sins of Asia or of the Middle East or of Africa.

There remains, however, a crucial difference between the Western tradition and the others. The crimes of the West have produced their own antidotes. They have provoked great movements to end slavery, to raise the status of women, to abolish torture, to combat racism, to defend freedom of inquiry and expression, to advance personal liberty and human rights.

Whatever the particular crimes of Europe, that continent is also the source—the *unique* source—of those liberating ideas of individual liberty, political democracy, the rule of law, human rights, and cultural freedom that constitute our most precious legacy and to which most of the world today aspires. These are *European* ideas, not Asian, nor African, nor Middle Eastern ideas, except by adoption.

The freedoms of inquiry and of artistic creation, for example, are Western values. Consider the differing reactions to the case of Salman Rushdie: what the West saw as an intolerable attack on individual freedom the Middle East saw as a proper punishment for an evildoer who had violated the mores of his group. Individualism itself is looked on with abhorrence and dread by collectivist cultures in which loyalty to the group overrides personal goals—cultures that, social scientists say, comprise about 70 percent of the world's population.

There is surely no reason for Western civilization to have guilt trips laid on it by champions of cultures based on despotism, superstition, tribalism, and fanaticism. In this regard the Afrocentrists are especially absurd. The West needs no lectures on the superior virtue of those "sun people" who sustained slavery until Western imperialism abolished it (and, it is reported, sustain it to this day in Mauritania and the Sudan), who still keep women in subjection and cut off their clitorises, who carry out racial persecutions not only against Indians and other Asians but against fellow Africans from the wrong tribes, who show themselves either incapable of operating a democracy or ideologically hostile to the democratic idea, and who in their tyrannies and massacres, their Idi Amins and Boukassas, have stamped with utmost brutality on human rights.

Certainly the European overlords did little enough to prepare Africa for self-government. But democracy would find it hard in any case to put down roots in a tribalist and patrimonial culture that, long before the West invaded Africa, had sacralized the personal authority of chieftains and ordained the submission of the rest. What the West would call corruption is regarded through much of Africa as no more than the prerogative of power. Competitive political parties, an independent judiciary, a free press, the rule of law are alien to African traditions.

It was the French, not the Algerians, who freed Algerian women from the veil (much to the irritation of Frantz Fanon, who regarded deveiling as symbolic rape); as in India it was the British, not the Indians, who ended (or did their best to end) the horrible custom of *suttee*—widows burning themselves alive on their husbands' funeral pyres. And it was the West, not the non-Western cultures, that launched the crusade to abolish slavery—and in doing so encountered mighty resistance, especially in the Islamic world (where Moslems, with fine impartiality, enslaved whites as well as blacks). Those many brave and humane Africans who are struggling these days for decent societies are animated by Western, not by African, ideals. White guilt can be pushed too far.

The Western commitment to human rights has unquestionably been intermittent and imperfect. Yet the ideal remains—and movement toward it has been real, if sporadic. Today it is the *Western* democratic tradition that attracts and empowers people of all continents, creeds, and colors. When the Chinese students cried and died for democracy in Tiananmen

Square, they brought with them not representations of Confucius or Buddha but a model of the Statue of Liberty.

◦◦◉◦◦

The great American asylum, as Crèvecoeur called it, open, as Washington said, to the oppressed and persecuted of all nations, has been from the start an experiment in a multiethnic society. This is a bolder experiment than we sometimes remember. History is littered with the wreck of states that tried to combine diverse ethnic or linguistic or religious groups within a single sovereignty. Today's headlines tell of imminent crisis or impending dissolution in one or another multiethnic polity—the Soviet Union, India, Yugoslavia, Czechoslovakia, Ireland, Belgium, Canada, Lebanon, Cyprus, Israel, Ceylon, Spain, Nigeria, Kenya, Angola, Trinidad, Guyana. . . . The list is almost endless. The luck so far of the American experiment has been due in large part to the vision of the melting pot. "No other nation," Margaret Thatcher has said, "has so successfully combined people of races and nations within a single culture."

But even in the United States, ethnic ideologues have not been without effect. They have set themselves against the old American ideal of assimilation. They call on the republic to think in terms not of individual but of group identity and to move the polity from individual rights to group rights. They have made a certain progress in transforming the United States into a more segregated society. They have done their best to turn a college generation against Europe and the Western tradition. They have imposed ethnocentric, Afrocentric, and bilingual curricula on public schools, well designed to hold minority children out of American society. They have told young people from minority groups that the Western democratic tradition is not for them. They have encouraged minorities to see themselves as victims and to live by alibis rather than to claim the opportunities opened for them by the potent combination of black protest and white guilt. They have filled the air with recrimination and rancor and have remarkably advanced the fragmentation of American life.

Yet I believe the campaign against the idea of common ideals and a single society will fail. Gunnar Myrdal was surely right: for all the damage it has done, the upsurge of ethnicity is a superficial enthusiasm stirred by romantic ideologues and unscrupulous hucksters whose claim to speak for their minorities is thoughtlessly accepted by the media. I doubt that the ethnic vogue expresses a reversal of direction from assimilation to apartheid among the minorities themselves. Indeed, the more the ideologues press the case for ethnic separatism, the less they appeal to the mass of their own groups. They have thus far done better in intimidating the white majority than in converting their own constituencies.

"No nation in history," writes Lawrence Fuchs, the political scientist and immigration expert in his fine book *The American Kaleidoscope*, "had proved as successful as the United States in managing ethnic diversity. No nation before had ever made diversity itself a source of national identity and unity." The second sentence explains the success described in the first, and the mechanism for translating diversity into unity has been the American Creed, the civic culture—the very assimilating, unifying culture that is today challenged, and not seldom rejected, by the ideologues of ethnicity.

A historian's guess is that the resources of the Creed have not been exhausted. Americanization has not lost its charms. Many sons and daughters of ethnic neighborhoods still want to shed their ethnicity and move to the suburbs as fast as they can—where they will be received with far more tolerance than they would have been 70 years ago. The desire for achievement and success in American society remains a potent force for assimilation. Ethnic subcultures, Stephen Steinberg, author of *The Ethnic Myth,* points out, fade away "because circumstances forced them to make choices that undermined the basis for cultural survival."

Others may enjoy their ethnic neighborhoods but see no conflict between foreign descent and American loyalty. Unlike the multiculturalists, they celebrate not only what is distinctive in their own backgrounds but what they hold in common with the rest of the population.

The ethnic identification often tends toward superficiality. The sociologist Richard Alba's study of children and grandchildren of immigrants in the Albany, New York, area shows the most popular "ethnic experience" to be sampling the ancestral cuisine. Still, less than half the respondents picked that, and only one percent ate ethnic food every day. Only one-fifth acknowledged a sense of special relationship to people of their own ethnic background; less than one-sixth taught their children about their ethnic origins; almost none was fluent in the language of the old country. "It is hard to avoid the conclusion," Alba writes, "that ethnic experience is shallow for the great majority of whites."

If ethnic experience is a good deal less shallow for blacks, it is because of their bitter experience in America, not because of their memories of Africa. Nonetheless most blacks prefer "black" to "African-Americans," fight bravely and patriotically for their country, and would move to the suburbs too if income and racism would permit.

As for Hispanic-Americans, first-generation Hispanics born in the United States speak English fluently, according to a Rand Corporation study; more than half of second-generation Hispanics give up Spanish altogether. When *Vista,* an English-language monthly for Hispanics, asked its readers what historical figures they most admired, Washington, Lincoln, and Theodore Roosevelt led the list, with Benito Juárez trailing behind as fourth, and Eleanor Roosevelt and Martin Luther King Jr. tied for fifth. So much for ethnic role models.

Nor, despite the effort of ethnic ideologues, are minority groups all that hermetically sealed off from each other, except in special situations, like colleges, where ideologues are authority figures. The wedding notices in any newspaper testify to the increased equanimity with which people these days marry across ethnic lines, across religious lines, even, though to a smaller degree, across racial lines. Around half of Asian-American marriages are with non-Orientals, and the Census Bureau estimates one million interracial—mostly black-white—marriages in 1990 as against 310,000 in 1970.

⋅≺◊≻⋅

The ethnic revolt against the melting pot has reached the point, in rhetoric at least, though not I think in reality, of a denial of the idea of a common culture and a single society. If large numbers of people really accept this, the republic would be in serious trouble. The question poses itself: how to restore the balance between *unum* and *pluribus?*

The old American homogeneity disappeared well over a century ago, never to return. Ever since, we have been preoccupied in one way or another with the problem, as Herbert Croly phrased in 80 years back in *The Promise of American Life,* "of preventing such divisions from dissolving the society into which they enter—of keeping such a highly differentiated society fundamentally sound and whole." This required, Croly believed, an "ultimate bond of union." There was only one way by which solidarity could be restored, "and that is by means of a democratic social ideal. . . . "

The genius of America lies in its capacity to forge a single nation from peoples of remarkably diverse racial, religious, and ethnic origins. It has done so because democratic principles provide both the philosophical bond of union and practical experience in civic participation. The American Creed envisages a nation composed of individuals making their own choices and accountable to themselves, not a nation based on inviolable ethnic communities. The Constitution turns on individual rights, not on group rights. Law, in order to rectify past wrongs, has from time to time (and in my view often properly so) acknowledged the claims of groups; but this is the exception, not the rule.

Our democratic principles contemplate an open society founded on tolerance of differences and on mutual respect. In practice, America has been more open to some than to others. But it is more open to all today than it was yesterday and is likely to be even more open tomorrow than today. The steady movement of American life has been from exclusion to inclusion.

Historically and culturally this republic has an Anglo-Saxon base; but from the start the base has been modified, enriched, and reconstituted by transfusions from other continents and civilizations. The movement from exclusion to inclusion causes a constant revision in the texture of our culture. The ethnic transfusions affect all aspects of American life—our politics, our literature, our music, our painting, our movies, our cuisine, our customs, our dreams.

Black Americans in particular have influenced the ever-changing national culture in many ways. They have lived here for centuries, and, unless one believes in racist mysticism, they belong far more to American culture than to the culture of Africa. Their history is part of the Western democratic tradition, not an alternative to it. Henry Louis Gates Jr. reminds us of James Baldwin's remark about coming to Europe to find out that he was "as American as any Texas G.I." No one does black Americans more disservice than those Afrocentric ideologues who would define them out of the West.

The interplay of diverse traditions produces the America we know. "Paradoxical though it may seem," Diane Ravitch has well said, "the United States has a common culture that is multicultural." That is why unifying political ideals coexist so easily and cheerfully with diversity in social and cultural values. Within the overarching political commitment, people are free to live as they choose, ethnically and otherwise. Differences will remain; some are reinvented; some are used to drive us apart. But as we renew our allegiance to the unifying ideals, we provide the solvent that will prevent differences from escalating into antagonism and hatred.

One powerful reason for the movement from exclusion to inclusion is that the American Creed facilitates the appeal from the actual to the ideal. When we talk of the American democratic faith, we must understand it in its true dimensions. It is not an impervious, final, and complacent orthodoxy, intolerant of deviation and dissent, fulfilled in flag salutes, oaths of allegiance, and hands over the heart. It is an ever-evolving philosophy, fulfilling its ideals through debate, self-criticism, protest, disrespect, and irreverence; a tradition in which all have rights of heterodoxy and opportunities for self-assertion. The Creed has been the means by which Americans have haltingly but persistently narrowed the gap between performance and principle. It is what all Americans should learn, because it is what binds all Americans together.

Let us by all means in this increasingly mixed-up world learn about those other continents and civilizations. But let us master our own history first. Lamentable as some may think it, we inherit an American experience, as America inherits a European experience. To deny the essentially European origins of American culture is to falsify history.

Americans of whatever origin should take pride in the distinctive inheritance to which they have all contributed, as other nations take pride in their distinctive inheritances. Belief in one's own culture does not require disdain for other cultures. But one step at a time: no culture can hope to ingest other cultures all at once, certainly not before it ingests its own. As we begin to master our own culture, then we can explore the world.

Our schools and colleges have a responsibility to teach history for its own sake—as part of the intellectual equipment of civilized persons—and not to degrade history by allowing its contents to be dictated by pressure groups, whether political, economic, religious, or ethnic. The past may sometimes give offense to one or another minority; that is no reason for rewriting history. Giving pressure groups vetoes over textbooks and courses betrays both history and education. Properly taught, history will convey a sense of the variety, continuity, and adaptability of cultures, of the need for understanding other cultures, of the ability of individuals and peoples to overcome obstacles, of the importance of critical analysis and dispassionate judgment in every area of life.

Above all, history can give a sense of national identity. We don't have to believe that our values are absolutely better than the next fellow's or the next country's, but we have no doubt that they are better *for us,* reared as we are—and are worth living by and worth dying for. For our values are not matters of whim and happenstance. History has given them to us. They are anchored in our national experience, in our great national documents, in our national heroes, in our folkways, traditions, and standards. People with a different history will have differing values. But we believe that our own are better for us. They work for us; and, for that reason, we live and die by them.

It has taken time to make the values real for all our citizens, and we still have a good distance to go, but we have made progress. If we now repudiate the quite marvelous inheritance that history bestows on us, we invite the fragmentation of the national community into a quarrelsome spatter of enclaves, ghettos, tribes. The bonds of cohesion in our society are sufficiently fragile, or so it seems to me, that it makes no sense to strain them by encouraging and exalting cultural and linguistic apartheid.

The American identity will never be fixed and final; it will always be in the making. Changes in the population have always brought changes in the national ethos and will continue to do so; but not, one must hope, at the expense of national integration. The question America confronts as a pluralistic society is how to vindicate cherished cultures and traditions without breaking the bonds of cohesion—common ideals, common political institutions, common language, common culture, common fate—that hold the republic together.

Our task is to combine due appreciation of the splendid diversity of the nation with due emphasis on the great unifying Western ideas of individual freedom, political democracy, and human rights. These are the ideas that define the American nationality—and that today empower people of all continents, races, and creeds.

"What then is the American, this new man? . . . Here individuals of all nations are melted into a new race of men." Still a good answer—still the best hope.

Michael Walzer   ← **NO**

What Does It Mean to Be an "American"?*

There is no country called America. We live in the United States *of America,* and we have appropriated the adjective "American" even though we can claim no exclusive title to it. Canadians and Mexicans are also Americans, but they have adjectives more obviously their own, and we have none. Words like "unitarian" and "unionist" won't do; our sense of ourselves is not captured by the mere fact of our union, however important that is. Nor will "statist," even "united statist," serve our purposes; a good many of the citizens of the United States are antistatist. Other countries, wrote the "American" political theorist Horace Kallen, get their names from the people, or from one of the peoples, who inhabit them. "The United States, on the other hand, has a peculiar anonymity."[1] It is a name that doesn't even pretend to tell us who lives here. Anybody can live here, and just about everybody does—men and women from all the world's peoples. (The *Harvard Encyclopedia of American Ethnic Groups* begins with Acadians and Afghans and ends with Zoroastrians.[2]) It is peculiarly easy to become an American. The adjective provides no reliable information about the origins, histories, connections, or cultures of those whom it designates. What does it say, then, about their political allegiance?

Patriotism and Pluralism

American politicians engage periodically in a fierce competition to demonstrate their patriotism. This is an odd competition, surely, for in most countries the patriotism of politicians is not an issue. There are other issues, and this question of political identification and commitment rarely comes up; loyalty to the *patrie,* the fatherland (or motherland), is simply assumed. Perhaps it isn't assumed here because the United States isn't a *patrie.* Americans have never spoken of their country as a fatherland (or a motherland). The kind of natural or organic loyalty that we (rightly or wrongly) recognize in families doesn't seem to be a feature of our politics. When American politicians invoke the metaphor of family

From *Social Research,* vol. 57, no. 3, Fall 1990, pp. 591–614. Copyright © 1990 by Social Research. Reprinted with permission.

they are usually making an argument about our mutual responsibilities and welfarist obligations, and among Americans, that is a controversial argument.[3] One can be an American patriot without believing in the mutual responsibilities of American citizens—indeed, for some Americans disbelief is a measure of one's patriotism.

Similarly, the United States isn't a "homeland" (where a national family might dwell), not, at least, as other countries are, in casual conversation and unreflective feeling. It is a country of immigrants who, however grateful they are for this new place, still remember the old places. And their children know, if only intermittently, that they have roots elsewhere. They, no doubt, are native grown, but some awkward sense of newness here, or of distant oldness, keeps the tongue from calling this land "home." The older political uses of the word "home," common in Great Britain, have never taken root here: home counties, home station, Home Office, home rule. To be "at home" in America is a personal matter: Americans have homesteads and homefolks and hometowns, and each of these is an endlessly interesting topic of conversation. But they don't have much to say about a common or communal home.

Nor is there a common *patrie,* but rather many different ones—a multitude of fatherlands (and motherlands). For the children, even the grandchildren, of the immigrant generation, one's *patrie,* the "native land of one's ancestors," is somewhere else. The term "Native Americans" designates the very first immigrants, who got here centuries before any of the others. At what point do the rest of us, native grown, become natives? The question has not been decided; for the moment, however, the language of nativism is mostly missing (it has never been dominant in American public life), even when the political reality is plain to see. Alternatively, nativist language can be used against the politics of nativism, as in these lines of Horace Kallen, the theorist of an anonymous America:

> Behind [the individual] in time and tremendously in him in quality are his ancestors; around him in space are his relatives and kin, carrying in common with him the inherited organic set from a remoter common ancestry. In all these he lives and moves and has his being. They constitute his, literally, *natio,* the inwardness of his nativity.[4]

But since there are so many "organic sets" (language is deceptive here: Kallen's antinativist nativism is cultural, not biological), none of them can rightly be called "American." Americans have no inwardness of their own; they look inward only by looking backward.

According to Kallen, the United States is less importantly a union of states than it is a union of ethnic, racial, and religious groups—a union of otherwise unrelated "natives." What is the nature of this union? The Great Seal of the United States carries the motto *E pluribus unum,* "From many, one," which seems to suggest that manyness must be left behind for the sake of oneness. Once there were many, now the many have merged or, in Israel Zangwell's classic image, been melted down into one. But the Great Seal presents a different image: the "American" eagle holds a sheaf of arrows. Here there is no merger or fusion but only a fastening, a putting together: many-in-one. Perhaps the adjective "American" describes this kind of oneness. We might say, tentatively, that it points to the citizenship, not the nativity or nationality, of the men and women it designates. It is a political adjective, and its politics is liberal in the strict sense: generous, tolerant, ample, accommodating—it allows for the survival, even the enhancement and flourishing, of manyness.

On this view, appropriately called "pluralist," the word "from" on the Great Seal is a false preposition. There is no movement from many to one, but rather a simultaneity, a coexistence—once again, many-in-one. But I don't mean to suggest a mystery here, as in the Christian conception of a God who is three-in-one. The language of pluralism is sometimes a bit mysterious—thus Kallen's description of America as a "nation of nationalities" or John Rawls's account of the liberal state as a "social union of social unions"—but it lends itself to a rational unpacking.[5] A sheaf of arrows is not, after all, a mysterious entity. We can find analogues in the earliest forms of social organization: tribes composed of many clans, clans composed of many families. The conflicts of loyalty and obligation, inevitable products of pluralism, must arise in these cases too. And yet, they are not exact analogues of the American case, for tribes and clans lack Kallen's "anonymity." American pluralism is, as we shall see, a peculiarly modern phenomenon—not mysterious but highly complex.

In fact, the United States is not a "nation of nationalities" or a "social union of social unions." At least, the singular nation or union is not constituted by, it is not a combination or fastening together of, the plural nationalities or unions. In some sense, it includes them; it provides a framework for their coexistence; but they are not its parts. Nor are the individual states, in any significant sense, the parts that make up the United States. The parts are individual men and women. The United States is an association of citizens. Its "anonymity" consists in the fact that these citizens don't transfer their collective name to the association. It never happened that a group of people called Americans came together to form a political society called America. The people are Americans only by virtue of having come together. And whatever identity they had before becoming Americans, they retain (or, better, they are free to retain) afterward. There is, to be sure, another view of Americanization, which holds that the process requires for its success the mental erasure of all previous identities—forgetfulness or even, as one enthusiast wrote in 1918, "absolute forgetfulness."[6] But on the pluralist view, Americans are allowed to remember who they were and to insist, also, on *what else they are.*

They are not, however, bound to the remembrance or to the insistence. Just as their ancestors escaped the old country, so they can if they choose escape their old identities, the "inwardness" of their nativity. Kallen writes of the individual that "whatever else he changes, he cannot change his grandfather."[7] Perhaps not; but he can call his grandfather a "greenhorn," reject his customs and convictions, give up the family name, move to a new neighborhood, adopt a new "life-style."

He doesn't become a better American by doing these things (though that is sometimes his purpose), but he may become an American simply, an American and nothing else, freeing himself from the hyphenation that pluralists regard as universal on this side, though not on the other side, of the Atlantic Ocean. But, free from hyphenation, he seems also free from ethnicity: "American" is not one of the ethnic groups recognized in the United States census. Someone who is only an American is, so far as our bureaucrats are concerned, ethnically anonymous. He has a right, however, to his anonymity; that is part of what it means to be an American.

For a long time, British-Americans thought of themselves as Americans simply—and not anonymously: they constituted, so they would have said, a new ethnicity and a new nationality, into which all later immigrants would slowly assimilate. "Americanization" was a political program designed to make sure that assimilation would not be too slow a process, at a time, indeed, when it seemed not to be a recognizable *process* at all. But though there were individuals who did their best to assimilate, that is, to adopt, at least outwardly, the mores of British-Americans, that soon ceased to be a plausible path to an "American" future. The sheer number of non-British immigrants was too great. If there was to be a new nationality, it would have to come out of the melting pot, where the heat was applied equally to all groups, the earlier immigrants as well as the most recent ones. The anonymous American was, at the turn of the century, say, a place-holder for some unknown future person who would give cultural content to the name. Meanwhile, most Americans were hyphenated Americans, more or less friendly to their grandfathers, more or less committed to their manyness. And pluralism was an alternative political program designed to legitimate this manyness and to make it permanent—which would leave those individuals who were Americans and nothing else permanently anonymous, assimilated to a cultural nonidentity.

Citizens

But though these anonymous Americans were not better Americans for being or for having become anonymous, it is conceivable that they were, and are, better American *citizens*. If the manyness of America is cultural, its oneness is political, and it may be the case that men and women who are free from non-American cultures will commit themselves more fully to the American political system. Maybe cultural anonymity is the best possible grounding for American politics. From the beginning, of course, it has been the standard claim of British-Americans that their own culture is the best grounding. And there is obviously much to be said for that view. Despite the efforts of hyphenated Americans to describe liberal and democratic politics as a kind of United Way to which they have all made contributions, the genealogy of the American political system bears a close resemblance to the genealogy of the Sons and Daughters of the American Revolution—ethnic organizations if there ever were any![8] But this genealogy must also account for the flight across the Atlantic and the Revolutionary

War. The parliamentary oligarchy of eighteenth-century Great Britain wasn't, after all, all that useful a model for America. When the ancestors of the Sons and Daughters described their political achievement as a "new order for the ages," they were celebrating a break with their own ethnic past almost as profound as that which later Americans were called upon to make. British-Americans who refused the break called themselves "Loyalists," but they were called disloyal by their opponents and treated even more harshly than hyphenated Americans from Germany, Russia, and Japan in later episodes of war and revolution.

Citizenship in the "new order" was not universally available, since blacks and women and Indians (Native Americans) were excluded, but it was never linked to a single nationality. "To be or to become an American," writes Philip Gleason, "a person did not have to be of any particular national, linguistic, religious, or ethnic background. All he had to do was to commit himself to the political ideology centered on the abstract ideals of liberty, equality, and republicanism."[9] These abstract ideals made for a politics separated not only from religion but from culture itself or, better, from all the particular forms in which religious and national culture was, and is, expressed—hence a politics "anonymous" in Kallen's sense. Anonymity suggests autonomy too, though I don't want to claim that American politics was not qualified in important ways by British Protestantism, later by Irish Catholicism, later still by German, Italian, Polish, Jewish, African, and Hispanic religious commitments and political experience. But these qualifications never took what might be called a strong adjectival form, never became permanent or exclusive qualities of America's abstract politics and citizenship. The adjective "American" named, and still names, a politics that is relatively unqualified by religion or nationality or, alternatively, that is qualified by so many religions and nationalities as to be free from any one of them.

It is this freedom that makes it possible for America's oneness to encompass and protect its manyness. Nevertheless, the conflict between the one and the many is a pervasive feature of American life. Those Americans who attach great value to the oneness of citizenship and the centrality of political allegiance must seek to constrain the influence of cultural manyness; those who value the many must disparage the one. The conflict is evident from the earliest days of the republic, but I will begin my own account of it with the campaign to restrict immigration and naturalization in the 1850s. Commonly called "nativist" by historians, the campaign was probably closer in its politics to a Rousseauian republicanism.[10] Anti-Irish and anti-Catholic bigotry played a large part in mobilizing support for the American (or American Republican) party, popularly called the Know-Nothings; and the political style of the party, like that of contemporary abolitionists and free-soilers, displayed many of the characteristics of Protestant moralism. But in its self-presentation, it was above all republican, more concerned about the civic virtue of the new immigrants than about their ethnic lineages, its religious critique focused on the ostensible connection between Catholicism and tyranny. The legislative program of the Know-Nothings had to do largely with questions of citizenship at the national level and of public education at the local level. In Congress, where the party had 75 representatives (and perhaps another 45 sympathizers, out of a total of 234) at the peak of its strength in 1855, it seemed more committed to restricting the suffrage than to cutting off immigration. Some of its members would have barred "paupers" from entering the United States, and others would have required an oath of allegiance from all immigrants immediately upon landing. But their energy was directed mostly toward revising the naturalization laws.[11] It was not the elimination of manyness but its disenfranchisement that the Know-Nothings championed.

Something like this was probably the position of most American "nativists" until the last years of the nineteenth century. In 1845, when immigration rates were still fairly low, a group of "native Americans" meeting in Philadelphia declared that they would "kindly receive [all] persons who came to America, and give them every privilege except office and suffrage."[12] I would guess that the nativist view of American blacks was roughly similar. Most of the northern Know-Nothings (the party's greatest strength was in New England) were strongly opposed to slavery, but it did not follow from that opposition that they were prepared to welcome former slaves as fellow citizens. The logic of events led to citizenship, after a bloody war, and the Know-Nothings, by then loyal Republicans, presumably supported that outcome. But the logic of republican principle, as they understood it, would have suggested some delay. Thus a resolution of the Massachusetts legislature in 1856 argued that "republican institutions were especially adapted to an educated and intelligent people, capable of *and accustomed to* self-government. Free institutions could be confined safely only to free men. . . . "[13] The legislators went on to urge a twenty-one-year residence requirement for naturalization. Since it was intended that disenfranchised residents should nonetheless be full members of civil society, another piece of Know-Nothing legislation would have provided that any alien free white person (this came from a Mississippi senator) should be entitled after twelve months residence "to all the protection of the government, and [should] be allowed to inherit, and hold, and transmit real estate . . . the same manner as though he were a citizen."[14]

Civil society, then, would include a great variety of ethnic and religious and perhaps even racial groups, but the members of these groups would acquire the "inestimable" good of citizenship only after a long period of practical education (but does one learn just by watching?) in democratic virtue. Meanwhile, their children would get a formal education. Despite their name, the Know-Nothings thought that citizenship was a subject about which a great deal had to be known. Some of them wanted to make attendance in public schools compulsory, but, faced with constitutional objections, they insisted only that no public funding should go to the support of parochial schools. It is worth emphasizing that the crucial principle here was not the separation of church and state. The Know-Nothing party did not oppose sabbatarian laws.[15] Its members believed that tax money should not be used to underwrite social manyness—not in the case of religion, obviously, but also not in the case of language and culture. Political identity, singular in form, would be publicly inculcated and defended; the plurality of social identities would have to be sustained in private.

I don't doubt that most nativists hoped that plurality would not, in fact, be sustained. They had ideas, if not sociological theories, about the connection of politics and culture—specifically, as I have said, republican politics and British Protestant culture. I don't mean to underestimate the centrality of these ideas: this was presumably the knowledge that the Know-Nothings were concealing when they claimed to know nothing. Nonetheless, the logic of their position, as of any "American" republican position, pressed toward the creation of a politics independent of all the ethnicities and religions of civil society. Otherwise too many people would be excluded; the political world would look too much like Old England and not at all like the "new order of the ages," not at all like "America." Nor could American nativists challenge ethnic and religious pluralism directly, for both were protected (as the parochial schools were protected) by the constitution to which they claimed a passionate attachment. They could only insist that passionate attachment should be the mark of all citizens—and set forth the usual arguments against the seriousness of love at first sight and in favor of long engagements. They wanted what Rousseau wanted: that citizens should find the greater share of their happiness in public (political) rather than in private (social) activities.[16] And they were prepared to deny citizenship to men and women who seemed to them especially unlikely to do that.

No doubt, again, public happiness came easily to the nativists because they felt so entirely at home in American public life. But we should not be too quick to attribute this feeling to the carry-over of ethnic consciousness into the political sphere. For American politics in the 1850s was already so open, egalitarian, and democratic (relative to European politics) that almost anyone could feel at home in it. Precisely because the United States was no one's *national* home, its politics was universally accessible. All that was necessary in principle was ideological commitment, in practice, a good line of talk. The Irish did very well and demonstrated as conclusively as one could wish that "British" and "Protestant" were not necessary adjectives for American politics. They attached to the many, not to the one.

For this reason, the symbols and ceremonies of American citizenship could not be drawn from the political culture or history of British-Americans. Our Congress is not a Commons; Guy Fawkes Day is not an American holiday; the Magna Carta has never been one of our sacred texts. American symbols and ceremonies are culturally anonymous, invented rather than inherited, voluntaristic in style, narrowly political in content: the flag, the Pledge, the Fourth, the Constitution. It is entirely appropriate that the Know-Nothing party had its origin in the Secret Society of the Star-Spangled Banner. And it is entirely understandable that the flag and the Pledge continue, even today, to figure largely in political debate. With what reverence should the flag be treated? On what occasions must it be saluted? Should we require school children to recite the Pledge, teachers to lead the recitation? Questions like these are the tests of a political commitment that can't be assumed, because it isn't undergirded by the cultural and religious commonalities that make for mutual trust. The flag and the Pledge are, as it were, all we have. One could suggest, of course, alternative and more practical tests of loyalty—responsible participation in political life, for example. But the real historical alternative is the test proposed by the cultural pluralists: one proves one's Americanism, in their view, by living in peace with all the other "Americans," that is, by agreeing to respect social manyness rather than by pledging allegiance to the "one and indivisible" republic. And pluralists are led on by the logic of this argument to suggest that citizenship is something less than an "inestimable" good.

Hyphenated Americans

Good it certainly was to be an American citizen. Horace Kallen was prepared to call citizenship a "great vocation," but he clearly did not believe (in the 1910s and '20s, when he wrote his classic essays on cultural pluralism) that one could make a life there. Politics was a necessary, but not a spiritually sustaining activity. It was best understood in instrumental terms; it had to do with the arrangements that made it possible for groups of citizens to "realize and protect" their diverse cultures and "attain the excellence appropriate to their kind."[17] These arrangements, Kallen thought, had to be democratic, and democracy required citizens of a certain sort—autonomous, self-disciplined, capable of cooperation and compromise. "Americanization" was entirely legitimate insofar as it aimed to develop these qualities; they made up Kallen's version of civic virtue, and he was willing to say that they should be common to all Americans. But, curiously perhaps, they did not touch the deeper self. "The common city-life, which depends upon like-mindedness, is not inward, corporate, and inevitable, but external, inarticulate, and incidental . . . not the expression of a homogeneity of heritage, mentality, and interest."[18]

Hence Kallen's program: assimilation "in matters economic and political," dissimilation "in cultural consciousness."[19] The hyphen joined these two processes in one person, so that a Jewish-American (like Kallen) was similar to other Americans in his economic and political activity, but similar only to other Jews at the deeper level of culture.[20] It is clear that Kallen's "hyphenates," whose spiritual life is located so emphatically to the left of the hyphen, cannot derive the greater part of their happiness from their citizenship. Nor, in a sense, should they, since culture, for the cultural pluralists, is far more important than politics and promises a more complete satisfaction. Pluralists, it seems, do not make good republicans—for the same reason that republicans, Rousseau the classic example, do not make good pluralists. The two attend to different sorts of goods.

Kallen's hyphenated Americans can be attentive and conscientious citizens, but on a liberal, not a republican model. This means two things. First, the various ethnic and religious groups can intervene in political life only in order to defend themselves and advance their common interests— as in the case of the NAACP or the Anti-Defamation League—but not in order to impose their culture or their values. They have to recognize that the state is anonymous (or, in the language of contemporary political theorists, neutral) at least in this sense: that it can't take on the character or the name of any of the groups that it includes. It isn't a nation-state of a particular kind and it isn't a Christian republic. Second, the primary political commitment of individual citizens is to protect their protection, to uphold the democratic framework within which they pursue their more substantive activities. This commitment is consistent with feelings of gratitude, loyalty, even patriotism of a certain sort, but it doesn't make for fellowship. There is indeed *union* in politics (and economics) but union of a sort that precludes intimacy. "The political and economic life of the commonwealth," writes Kallen, "is a single unit and serves as the foundation and background for the realization of the distinctive individuality of each *natio*."[21] Here pluralism is straightforwardly opposed to republicanism: politics offers neither self-realization nor communion. All intensity lies, or should lie, elsewhere.

Kallen believes, of course, that this "elsewhere" actually exists; his is not a utopian vision; it's not a case of "elsewhere, perhaps." The "organic groups" that make up Kallen's America appear in public life as interest groups only, organized for the pursuit of material and social goods that are universally desired but sometimes in short supply and often unfairly distributed. That is the only appearance countenanced by a liberal and democratic political system. But behind it, concealed from public view, lies the true significance of ethnicity or religion: "It is the center at which [the individual] stands, the point of his most intimate social relations, therefore of his intensest emotional life."[22] I am inclined to say that this is too radical a view of ethnic and religious identification, since it seems to rule out moral conflicts in which the individual's emotions are enlisted, as it were, on both sides. But Kallen's more important point is simply that there is space and opportunity *elsewhere* for the emotional satisfactions that politics can't (or shouldn't) provide. And because individuals really do find this satisfaction, the groups within which it is found are permanently sustainable: they won't melt down, not, at least, in any ordinary (noncoercive) social process. Perhaps they can be repressed, if the repression is sufficiently savage; even then, they will win out in the end.

Kallen wasn't entirely unaware of the powerful forces making for cultural meltdown, even without repression. He has some strong lines on the effectiveness of the mass media—though he knew these only in their infancy and at a time when newspapers were still a highly localized medium and the foreign-language press flourished. In his analysis and critique of the pressure to conform, he anticipated what became by the 1950s a distinctively American genre of social criticism. It isn't always clear whether he sees pluralism as a safeguard against or an antidote for the conformity of ethnic-Americans to that spiritless "Americanism" he so much disliked, a dull protective coloring that destroys all inner brightness. In any case, he is sure that inner brightness will survive, "for Nature is naturally pluralistic; her unities are eventual, not primary. . . . "[23] Eventually, he means, the American union will prove to be a matter of "mutual accommodation," leaving intact the primacy of ethnic and religious identity. In the years since Kallen wrote, this view has gathered a great deal of ideological, but much less of empirical, support. "Pluralist principles . . . have been on the ascendancy," writes a contemporary critic of pluralism, "precisely at a time when ethnic differences have been on the wane."[24] What if the "excellence" appropriate to our "kind" is, simply, an American excellence? Not necessarily civic virtue of the sort favored by nativists, republicans, and contemporary communitarians, but nonetheless some local color, a brightness of our own?

Peripheral Distance

This local color is most visible, I suppose, in popular culture—which is entirely appropriate in the case of the world's first mass democracy. Consider, for example, the movie *American in Paris,* where the hero is an American simply and not at all an Irish- or German- or Jewish-American. Do we drop our hyphens when we travel abroad? But what are we, then, without them? We carry with us cultural artifacts of a quite specific sort: "*une danse americaine,*" Gene Kelly tells the French children as he begins to tap dance. What else could he call it, this melted-down combination of Northern English clog dancing, the Irish jig and reel, and African rhythmic foot stamping, to which had been added, by Kelly's time, the influence of the French and Russian ballet? Creativity of this sort is both explained and celebrated by those writers and thinkers, heroes of the higher culture, that we are likely to recognize as distinctively American: thus Emerson's defense of the experimental life (I am not sure, though, that he would have admired tap dancing), or Whitman's democratic inclusiveness, or the pragmatism of Peirce and James.

"An American nationality," writes Gleason, "does in fact exist."[25] Not just a political status, backed up by a set of political symbols and ceremonies, but a full-blooded nationality, reflecting a history and a culture—exactly like all the other nationalities from which Americans have been, and continue to be, recruited. The ongoing immigration makes it difficult to see the real success of Americanization in creating distinctive types, characters, styles, artifacts of all sorts which, were Gene Kelly to display them to his Parisian neighbors, they would rightly recognize as "American." More important, Americans recognize one another, take pride in the things that fellow Americans have made and done, identify with the national community. So, while there no doubt are people plausibly called Italian-Americans or Swedish-Americans, spiritual (as well as political) life—this is Gleason's view—is lived largely to the right of the hyphen: contrasted with real Italians and real Swedes, these are real Americans.

This view seems to me both right and wrong. It is right in its denial of Kallen's account of America as an anonymous nation of named nationalities. It is wrong in its insistence that America is a nation like all the others. But the truth does not lie, where we might naturally be led to look for it, somewhere between this rightness and this wrongness—as if we could locate America at some precise point along the continuum that stretches from the many to the one. I want to take the advice of that American song, another product of the popular culture, which tells us: "Don't mess with mister in-between."[26] If there are cultural artifacts, songs and dances, styles of life and even philosophies, that are distinctively American, there is also an idea of America that is itself distinct, incorporating oneness and manyness in a "new order" that may or may not be "for the ages" but that is certainly for us, here and now.

The cultural pluralists come closer to getting the new order right than do the nativists and the nationalists and the American communitarians. Nonetheless, there is a nation and a national community and, by now, a very large number of native Americans. Even first- and second-generation Americans, as Gleason points out, have graves to visit and homes and neighborhoods to remember *in this country,* on this side of whatever waters their ancestors crossed to get here.[27] What is distinctive about the nationality of these Americans is not its insubstantial character—substance is quickly acquired—but its nonexclusive character. Remembering the God of the Hebrew Bible, I want to argue that America is not a jealous nation. In this sense, at least, it is different from most of the others.

Consider, for example, a classic moment in the ethnic history of France: the debate over the emancipation of the Jews in 1790 and '91. It is not, by any means, a critical moment; there were fewer than 35,000 Jews in revolutionary France, only 500 in Paris. The Jews were not economically powerful or politically significant or even intellectually engaged in French life (all that could come only after emancipation). But the debate nonetheless was long and serious, for it dealt with the meaning of citizenship and nationality. When the Constituent Assembly voted for full emancipation in September 1791, its position was summed up by Clermont-Tonnerre, a deputy of the Center, in a famous sentence: "One must refuse everything to the Jews as a nation, and give everything to the Jews as individuals. . . . It would be repugnant to have . . . a nation within a nation."[28] The Assembly's vote led to the disestablishment of Jewish corporate existence in France, which had been sanctioned and protected by the monarchy. "Refusing everything to the Jews as a nation" meant withdrawing the sanction, denying the protection. Henceforth Jewish communities would be voluntary associations, and individual Jews would have rights against the community as well as against the state: Clermont-Tonnerre was a good liberal.

But the Assembly debate also suggests that most of the deputies favoring emancipation would not have looked with favor even on the voluntary associations of the Jews, insofar as these reflected national sensibility or cultural difference. The future Girondin leader Brissot, defending emancipation, predicted that Jews who became French citizens would "lose their particular characteristics." I suspect that he could hardly imagine a greater triumph of French *civisme* than this—as if the secular Second Coming, like the religious version, awaited only the conversion of the Jews. Brissot thought the day was near: "Their eligibility [for citizenship] will regenerate them."[29] Jews could be good citizens only insofar as they were regenerated, which meant, in effect, that they could be good citizens only insofar as they became French. (They must, after all, have some "particular characteristics," and if not their own, then whose?) Their emancipators had, no doubt, a generous view of their capacity to do that but would not have been generous in the face of resistance (from the Jews or from any other of the corporate groups of the old regime). The price of emancipation was assimilation.

This has been the French view of citizenship ever since. Though they have often been generous in granting the exalted status of citizen to foreigners, the successive republics have been suspicious of any form of ethnic pluralism. Each republic really has been "one and indivisible," and it has been established, as Rousseau thought it should be, on a strong national oneness. Oneness all the way down is, on this view, the only guarantee that the general will and the common good will triumph in French politics.

America is very different, and not only because of the eclipse of republicanism in the early nineteenth century. Indeed, republicanism has had a kind of afterlife as one of the legitimating ideologies of American politics. The Minute Man is a republican image of embodied citizenship. Reverence for the flag is a form of republican piety. The Pledge of Allegiance is a republican oath. But emphasis on this sort of thing reflects social disunity rather than unity; it is a straining after oneness where oneness doesn't exist. In fact, America has been, with severe but episodic exceptions, remarkably tolerant of ethnic pluralism (far less so of racial pluralism).[30] I don't want to underestimate the human difficulties of adapting even to a hyphenated Americanism, nor to deny the bigotry and discrimination that particular groups have encountered. But tolerance has been the cultural norm.

Perhaps an immigrant society has no choice; tolerance is a way of muddling through when any alternative policy would be violent and dangerous. But I would argue that we have, mostly, made the best of this necessity, so that the virtues of toleration, in principle though by no means always in practice, have supplanted the singlemindedness of republican citizenship. We have made our peace with the "particular characteristics" of all the immigrant groups (though not, again, of all the racial groups) and have come to regard American nationality as an addition to rather than a replacement for ethnic consciousness. The hyphen works, when it is working, more like a plus sign. "American," then, is a name indeed, but unlike "French" or "German" or "Italian" or "Korean" or "Japanese" or "Cambodian," it can serve as a second name. And as in those modern marriages where two patronymics are joined, neither the first nor the second name is dominant: here the hyphen works more like a sign of equality.

We might go farther than this: in the case of hyphenated Americans, it doesn't matter whether the first or the second name is dominant. We insist, most of the time, that the "particular characteristics" associated with the first name be sustained, as the Know-Nothings urged, without state help—and perhaps they will prove unsustainable on those terms. Still, an ethnic American is someone who can, in principle, live his spiritual life as he chooses, *on either side of the hyphen.* In this sense, American citizenship is indeed anonymous, for it doesn't require a full commitment to American (or to any other) nationality. The distinctive national culture that Americans have created doesn't underpin, it exists alongside of, American politics. It follows, then, that the people I earlier called Americans simply, Americans and nothing else, have in fact a more complicated existence than those terms suggest. They are American-Americans, one more group of hyphenates (not quite the same as all the others), and one can imagine them attending to the cultural aspects of their Americanism and refusing the political commitment that republican ideology demands. They might still be good or bad citizens. And similarly, Orthodox Jews as well as secular (regenerate) Jews, Protestant fundamentalists as well as liberal Protestants, Irish republicans as well as Irish Democrats, black nationalists as well as black integrationists—all these can be good or bad citizens, given the American (liberal rather than republican) understanding of citizenship.

One step more is required before we have fully understood this strange America: it is not the case that Irish-Americans, say, are culturally Irish and politically American, as the pluralists claim (and as I have been assuming thus far for the sake of the argument). Rather, they are culturally Irish-American and politically Irish-American. Their culture has been significantly influenced by American culture; their politics is still, both in style and substance, significantly ethnic. With them, and with every ethnic and religious group except the American-Americans, hyphenation is doubled. It remains true, however, that what all the groups have in common is most importantly their citizenship and what most differentiates them, insofar as they are still differentiated, is their culture. Hence the alternation in American life of patriotic fevers and ethnic revivals, the first expressing a desire to heighten the commonality, the second a desire to reaffirm the difference.

At both ends of this peculiarly American alternation, the good that is defended is also exaggerated and distorted, so that pluralism itself is threatened by the sentiments it generates. The patriotic fevers are the symptoms of a republican pathology. At issue here is the all-important ideological commitment that, as Gleason says, is the sole prerequisite of American citizenship. Since citizenship isn't guaranteed by oneness all the way down, patriots or superpatriots seek to guarantee it by loyalty oaths and campaigns against "un-American" activities. The Know-Nothing party having failed to restrict naturalization, they resort instead to political purges and deportations. Ethnic revivals are less militant and less cruel, though not without their own pathology. What is at issue here is communal pride and power—a demand for political recognition without assimilation, an assertion of interest-group politics against republican ideology, an effort to distinguish this group (one's own) from all the others. American patriotism is always strained and nervous because hyphenation makes indeed for dual loyalty but seems, at the same time, entirely American. Ethnic revivalism is also strained and nervous, because the hyphenates are already Americans, on both sides of the hyphen.

In these circumstances, republicanism is a mirage, and American nationalism or communitarianism is not a plausible option; it doesn't reach to our complexity. A certain sort of communitarianism is available to each of the hyphenate groups—except, it would seem, the American-Americans, whose community, if it existed, would deny the Americanism of all the others. So Horace Kallen is best described as a Jewish (-American) communitarian and a (Jewish-) American liberal, and this kind of coexistence, more widely realized, would constitute the pattern he called cultural pluralism. But the different ethnic and religious communities are all of them far more precarious than he thought, for they have, in a liberal political system, no corporate form or legal structure or coercive power. And, without these supports, the "inherited organic set" seems to dissipate— the population lacks cohesion, cultural life lacks coherence. The resulting "groups" are best conceived, John Higham suggests, as a core of activists and believers and an expanding periphery of passive members or followers, lost, as it were, in a wider America.[31] At the core, the left side of the (double) hyphen is stronger; along the periphery, the right side is stronger, though never fully dominant. Americans choose, as it were, their own location; and it appears that a growing number of them are choosing to fade into the peripheral distances. They become American-Americans, though without much passion invested in the becoming. But if the core doesn't hold, it also doesn't disappear; it is still capable of periodic revival.

At the same time, continued large-scale immigration reproduces a Kallenesque pluralism, creating new groups of hyphenate Americans and encouraging revivalism among activists and believers in the old groups. America is still a radically unfinished society, and for now, at least, it makes sense to say that this unfinishedness is one of its distinctive features. The country has a political center, but it remains in every other sense decentered. More than this, the political center, despite occasional patriotic fevers, doesn't work against decentering elsewhere. It neither requires nor demands the kind of commitment that would put the legitimacy of ethnic or religious identification in doubt. It doesn't aim at a finished or fully coherent Americanism. Indeed, American politics, itself pluralist in character, *needs* a certain sort of incoherence. A radical program of Americanization would *really* be un-American. It isn't inconceivable that America will one day become an American nation-state, the many giving way to the one, but that is not what it is now; nor is that its destiny. America has no singular national destiny—and to be an "American" is, finally, to know that and to be more or less content with it.

Notes

1. Horace M. Kallen, *Culture and Democracy in the United States* (New York: Boni & Liveright, 1924), p. 51.

2. *Harvard Encyclopedia of American Ethnic Groups,* ed. Stephan Thernstrom (Cambridge, Mass.: Harvard University Press, 1980).

3. Mario Cuomo's speech at the 1984 Democratic party convention provides a nice example of this sort of argument.

4. Kallen, *Culture and Democracy,* p. 94.

5. *Ibid.,* p. 122 (cf. 116); John Rawls. *A Theory of Justice* (Cambridge, Mass.: Harvard University Press, 1971), p. 527.

6. Quoted in Kallen, *Culture and Democracy,* p. 138; the writer was superintendent of New York's public schools.

7. Kallen, *Culture and Democracy,* p. 94.

8. See Kallen's account of how British-Americans were forced into ethnicity: *Culture and Democracy,* pp. 99f.

9. Philip Gleason. "American Identity and Americanization," in *Harvard Encyclopedia,* p. 32.

10. On the complexities of "nativism," see John Higham, *Send These to Me: Jews and Other Immigrants in Urban America* (New York: Atheneum, 1975). pp. 102–115. For an account of the Know-Nothings different from mine, to which I am nonetheless indebted, S.M. Lipset and Earl Raab, *The Politics of Unreason: Right-wing Extremism in America, 1790–1970* (New York: Harper & Row, 1970), ch. 2.

11. Frank George Franklin, *The Legislative History of Naturalization in the United States* (New York: Arno Press, 1969), chs. 11–14.

12. *Ibid.,* p. 247.

13. *Ibid.,* p. 293.

14. Ibid.

15. Lipset and Raab, *Politics of Unreason,* p. 46.

16. Jean-Jacques Rousseau, *The Social Contract,* trans. G. D. H. Cole (New York: E. P. Dutton, 1950), bk. III, ch. 15, p. 93.

17. Kallen, *Culture and Democracy,* p. 61.

18. *Ibid.,* p. 78.

19. *Ibid.,* pp. 114–115.

20. It is interesting that both nativists and pluralists wanted to keep the market free of ethnic and religious considerations. The Know-Nothings, since they thought that democratic politics was best served by British ethnicity and Protestant religion, set the market firmly within civil society, allowing full market rights even to new and Catholic immigrants. Kallen, by contrast, since he understands civil society as a world of ethnic and religious groups, assimilates the market to the universality of the political sphere, the "common city-life."

21. Kallen, *Culture and Democracy,* p. 124.

22. *Ibid.,* p. 200.

23. *Ibid.,* p. 179.

24. Stephen Steinberg, *The Ethnic Myth: Race, Ethnicity, and Class in America* (Boston: Beacon Press, 1981), p. 254.

25. Gleason, "American Identity," p. 56.

26. The song is "Accentuate the Positive," which is probably what I am doing here.

27. Gleason, "American Identity," p. 56.

28. Quoted in Gary Kates, "Jews into Frenchmen: Nationality and Representation in Revolutionary France," *Social Research* 56 (Spring 1989): 229. See also the discussion in Arthur Hertzberg, *The French Enlightenment and the Jews: The Origins of Modern Anti-Semitism* (New York: Schocken, 1970), pp. 360–362.

29. Kates, "Jews into Frenchmen," p. 229.

30. The current demand of (some) black Americans that they be called African-Americans represents an attempt to adapt themselves to the ethnic paradigm—imitating, perhaps, the relative success of various Asian-American groups in a similar adaptation. But names are no guarantees; nor does antinativist pluralism provide sufficient protection against what is all too often an *ethnic*-American racism. It has been argued that this racism is the necessary precondition of hyphenated ethnicity: the inclusion of successive waves of ethnic immigrants is possible only because of the permanent exclusion of black Americans. But I don't know what evidence would demonstrate *necessity* here. I am inclined to reject the metaphysical belief that all inclusion entails exclusion. A historical and empirical account of the place of blacks in the "system" of American pluralism would require another paper.

31. Higham, *Send These to Me*, p. 242.

POSTSCRIPT

Do We Need a Common American Identity?

The classic issue of American identity—assimilation versus pluralism—is alive and well today with the issue of multiculturalism. Today's emphasis on diversity is the latest manifestation of the issue.

Who is eligible to become an American? Until the Civil War, only European American males who owned property could exercise full citizenship. People of color living in the United States were isolated. Africans were isolated as slaves on southern plantations while Native Americans were confined to areas of land reserves. The abolishment of slavery led to an immediate—and temporary—citizenship inclusion for former slaves, but the brief historical period known as the Reconstruction Era soon gave way to a century of Jim Crow culture. Native Americans continued to be sequestered on reservations. Clearly, racial minority groups were separated from whites. So an honest treatment of African Americans escaped us until the 1950s. To what extent did a common American identity ever exist? Does Schlesinger confuse the dominant Anglo-Saxon culture of the past with a common American identity?

Neither Walzer nor Schlesinger address the question of a common American identity in terms of race and racism. Walzer refers to the difficulties of racial minorities in becoming part of the *unum*. But both positions are challenged when we consider the legacy of slavery and the long Jim Crow period of American history. The complexity of an American identity is illuminated when we recognize the divergence of the immigrant experience with that of African Americans.

Arthur Schlesinger, Jr., laments the development of race-conscious politics and public policies due to their impact of promoting divisions within society. These concerns are buttressed by the assumption that significant unity of blacks and whites had been achieved prior to the development and implementation of affirmative action programs. This proposition is not supported by evidence. In contrast, Walzer's approach views race and ethnic-conscious politics as an inevitable and important part of American identity.

It is interesting to observe ethnic holiday celebrations in America. It would appear that the concern with core values and identity emerges substantially in response to African American gains. Do celebrations such as St. Patrick's Day and Columbus Day threaten a common American identity? In the same context, what can we say about the celebration of Martin Luther King Day or Black History Month?

Both Walzer and Schlesinger employ the Great Seal of the United States along with the motto *E pluribus unum* to illustrate different positions on a common American identity. The title of Schlesinger's selection, "E Pluribus Unum?" suggests that the concern of minority group racial and ethnic issues is at the expense of unity. For Walzer, the motto is questioned differently. His emphasis is on the question mark. In contrast, "from many, one" suggests "that manyness must be left behind for the sake of oneness." Are differences melted down into one? Here, Walzer offers another look. The American eagle holds a sheaf of arrows—many in one. "On the pluralist view, Americans are allowed to remember who they were and to insist, also, on *what else they are.*"

Oscar Handlin's classic study, *The Uprooted* (1951), is a good place to begin further reading on this issue. He explains how a new American culture replaced immigrant values. *The Ordeal of Assimilation,* edited by Stanley Feldstein and Lawrence Costello (Anchor Books, 1974), presents more on the rise of ethnic consciousness. A pictorial history of immigration can be found in Bernard Weisberger's *The American People* (American Heritage, 1971). More scholarly information appears in *International Migration Review, The Population Bulletin,* and *Migration Today.*

For further classic reading on Schlesinger's perspective, one can explore Milton Gordon's *Assimilation in American Life* (Oxford University Press, 1964) and Robert Park's noted essay "On Assimilation" in *Race and Culture: Essays on the Sociology of Contemporary Man* (Free Press, 1950). Gordon's *Human Nature, Class, and Ethnicity* (Oxford U. Press, 1978) looks at conflict and cooperation found in all human societies. It is relevant to the question of an American identity in that the reader is exposed to more general issues of racial and ethnic group conflict. *Beyond the Melting Pot* by Nathan Glazer and Daniel Patrick Moynihan (MIT Press, 1970) became a classic when it was first written. It represents a close look at race and ethnic issues in New York City. A useful discussion of the current tension of ethnic identity and a common American identity can be found in Mary Waters' *Ethnic Options: Choosing Identities in America* (University of California Press, 1990).

Michael Novak's *The Rise of the Unmeltable Ethnics: Politics and Culture in the Seventies* (Collier, 1973) is an assessment of the American identity issue. He notes the rise of "ethnic consciousness" in America. Stephen Steinberg's *The Ethnic Myth* offers a labor analysis of immigration and American identity using both assimilation and pluralism. Michael Parenti's essay, "Assimilation and Counter-Assimilation" in Philip Green and Stanford Levison's collection, *Power and Community: Dissenting Essays in Political Science* (Vintage Books, 1970) is an interesting assessment of the assimilation dilemma.

ISSUE 2

Is Immigration Good for America?

YES: David Cole, "The New Know-Nothingism: Five Myths About Immigration," *The Nation* (October 17, 1994)

NO: Peter Brimelow, *Alien Nation: Common Sense About America's Immigration Disaster* (Random House, 1995)

ISSUE SUMMARY

YES: David Cole, law professor, critically examines and rebuffs significant myths alleging substantial destructive sociocultural and economic impacts of immigrants and policies in this field.

NO: Peter Brimelow, Senior Editor at *Forbes* and *National Review* magazines, argues that the United States is being overrun by a growing tide of aliens who are changing the character and composition of the nation in manners that are threatening and destructive to its well-being and prospects for future advancement.

Despite the fact that virtually all members of the current population of the United States are either immigrants or their descendants, concerns with immigrants and immigration policies have confronted the nation throughout history. These issues wax and wane over time, but they never dissipate completely. One reason for this reality is the fact that the United States has promoted the imagery within the world that the nation is a welcoming bastion of freedom and democracy and a land of virtually unlimited economic opportunities. Not surprisingly, this nation has served as a magnet for peoples seeking freedom from tyranny and oppression and opportunities to improve the material circumstances of their lives. Thus, the United States has experienced continuing waves of immigration throughout its history, and these influxes of new peoples have raised concerns within segments of the public and political leadership over the potential for deleterious impacts of these foreigners upon American culture and society.

David Cole offers a critical examination of five significant myths that are presented within the discourse over immigrants and immigration policies in the United States. He presents empirical evidence to refute the claim that the United States is being overrun by first generation, foreign-born people. Cole presents evidence gained from numerous studies, including a 1994 report of the American Civil Liberties Union's Immigrants' Rights Project, a 1994 report of the Urban Institute, and a study of the Council of Economic Advisors, to demonstrate that immigrants are net creators of jobs within the economy and that rather than being a drain on society's budgets for human resources, they generate a surplus in tax revenues over the costs of services that they incur.

Cole disagrees with those who view immigrants as unassimilable permanent aliens, a status of their own choosing, and views assimilation in the form of "Americanization" as powerful sociocultural forces transforming the descendants of immigrants in the succeeding generations. He also decries the tendencies of the U.S. government to extend the basic protections of the Constitution to immigrants as is prescribed in that document, a policy that is inconsistent with the nation's claims to support liberty and justice throughout the world.

In contrast, Peter Brimelow is disturbed by the current immigration policies of the U.S. government and, according to his view, the self-inflicted problems they present to the nation. Among his concerns are the increasing numbers of predominately Hispanics and Asians, who are exerting a negative impact upon the demographic composition and character of the American society and its culture. Brimelow also expresses more traditional concerns that tend to link immigrant populations to crime and expanding prison populations, and to the rising costs of the health care, education, and other human services that these newcomers require.

Peter Brimelow views the nation's current immigration policies as out of control and permitting millions of foreign-born persons, both legal and illegal, to arrive on America's shores. He views immigrants as persons who are distorting the demographic composition of society and requiring increasing levels of financial expenditures to support human services and other social support systems while contributing little or nothing economically beneficial or required to the nation. Thus, Brimelow advocates substantial reform of current immigration policy with an emphasis on restricting newcomers from the global South.

In evaluating this issue, readers are urged to balance the country's historical immigrant past with contemporary patterns of immigration. At the same time, readers should note that there has always been a native reaction to immigration, whether it was nineteenth century nativism or twenty-first century new nativism. Why do some support immigration? Why do others oppose it? What differences have emerged over the past two centuries?

David Cole

YES

The New Know-Nothingism: Five Myths About Immigration

For a brief period in the mid-nineteenth century, a new political movement captured the passions of the American public. Fittingly labeled the "Know-Nothings," their unifying theme was nativism. They liked to call themselves "Native Americans," although they had no sympathy for people we call Native Americans today. And they pinned every problem in American society on immigrants. As one Know-Nothing wrote in 1856: "Four-fifths of the beggary and three-fifths of the crime spring from our foreign population; more than half the public charities, more than half the prisons and almshouses, more than half the police and the cost of administering criminal justice are for foreigners.

At the time, the greatest influx of immigrants was from Ireland, where the potato famine had struck, and Germany which was in political and economic turmoil. Anti-alien and anti-Catholic sentiments were the order of the day, especially in New York and Massachusetts, which received the brunt of the wave of immigrants, many of whom were dirt-poor and uneducated. Politicians were quick to exploit the sentiment: There's nothing like a scapegoat to forge an alliance.

I am especially sensitive to this history: My forebears were among those dirt-poor Irish Catholics who arrived in the 1860s. Fortunately for them, and me, the Know-Nothing movement fizzled within fifteen years. But its pilot light kept burning, and is turned up whenever the American public begins to feel vulnerable and in need of an enemy.

Although they go by different names today, the Know-Nothings have returned. As in the 1850s, the movement is strongest where immigrants are most concentrated: California and Florida. The objects of prejudice are of course no longer Irish Catholics and Germans; 140 years later, "they" have become "us." The new "they"—because it seems "we" must always have a "they"—are Latin Americans (most recently, Cubans), Haitians and Arab-Americans, among others.

But just as in the 1850s, passion, misinformation and shortsighted fear often substitute for reason, fairness and human dignity in today's immigration debates. In the interest of advancing beyond know-nothingism, let's look at five current myths that distort public debate and government policy relating to immigrants.

America Is Being Overrun with Immigrants

In one sense of course, this is true, but in that sense it has been true since Christopher Columbus arrived. Except for the real Native Americans, we are a nation of immigrants.

It is not true, however, that the first-generation immigrant share of our population is growing. As of 1990, foreign-born people made up only 8 percent of the population, as compared with a figure of about 15 percent from 1870 to 1920. Between 70 and 80 percent of those who immigrate every year are refugees or immediate relatives of U.S. citizens.

Much of the anti-immigrant fervor is directed against the undocumented, but they make up only 13 percent of all immigrants residing in the United States, and only 1 percent of the American population. Contrary to popular belief, most such aliens do not cross the border illegally but enter legally and remain after their student or visitor visa expires. Thus, building a wall at the border, no matter how high, will not solve the problem.

Immigrants Take Jobs from U.S. Citizens

There is virtually no evidence to support this view, probably the most widespread misunderstanding about immigrants. As documented by a 1994 A.C.L.U. Immigrants' Rights Project report, numerous studies have found that immigrants actually *create* more jobs than they fill. The jobs immigrants take are of course easier to see, but immigrants are often highly productive, run their own businesses and employ both immigrants and citizens. One study found that Mexican immigration to Los Angeles County between 1970 and 1980 was responsible for 78,000 new jobs. Governor Mario Cuomo reports that immigrants own more than 40,000 companies in New York, which provide thousands of jobs and $3.5 billion to the state's economy every year.

Immigrants Are a Drain on Society's Resources

This claim fuels many of the recent efforts to cut off government benefits to immigrants. However, most studies have found that immigrants are a net benefit to the economy because, as a 1994 Urban Institute report concludes, "immigrants generate significantly more in taxes paid than they cost in services received." The Council of Economic Advisers similarly found in 1986 that "immigrants have a favorable effect on the overall standard of living."

Anti-immigrant advocates often cite studies purportedly showing the contrary but these generally focus only on taxes and services at the local or state level. What they fail to explain is that because most taxes go to the federal government, such studies would also show a net loss when applied to U.S. citizens. At most, such figures suggest that some redistribution of federal and state monies may be appropriate; they say nothing unique about the costs of immigrants.

Some subgroups of immigrants plainly impose a net cost in the short run, principally those who have most recently arrived and have not yet "made it." California, for example, bears substantial costs for its disproportionately large undocumented population, largely because it has on average the poorest and least educated immigrants. But that has been true of every wave of immigrants that has ever reached our shores; it was as true of the Irish in the 1850s, for example, as it is of Salvadorans today. From a long-term perspective, the economic advantages of immigration are undeniable.

Some have suggested that we might save money and diminish incentives to immigrate illegally if we denied undocumented aliens public services. In fact, undocumented immigrants are already ineligible for most social programs, with the exception of education for schoolchildren, which is constitutionally required, and benefits directly related to health and safety, such as emergency medical care and nutritional assistance to poor women, infants and children. To deny such basic care to people in need, apart from being inhumanly callous, would probably cost us more in the long run by exacerbating health problems that we would eventually have to address.

Aliens Refuse to Assimilate, and Are Depriving Us of Our Cultural and Political Unity

This claim has been made about every new group of immigrants to arrive on U.S. shores. Supreme Court Justice Stephen Field wrote in 1884 that the Chinese "have remained among us as a separate people, retaining their original peculiarities of dress, manners, habits, and modes of living, which are as marked as their complexion and language." Five years later, he upheld the racially based exclusion of Chinese immigrants. Similar claims have been made over different periods of our history about Catholics, Jews, Italians, Eastern Europeans and Latin Americans.

In most instances, such claims are simply not true; "American culture" has been created, defined and revised by persons who for the most part are descended from immigrants once seen as anti-assimilationist. Descendants of the Irish Catholics, for example, a group once decried as separatist and alien, have become Presidents, senators and representatives (and all of these in one family, in the case of the Kennedys). Our society exerts tremendous pressure to conform, and cultural separatism rarely survives a generation. But more important, even if this claim were true, is this a legitimate rationale for limiting immigration in a society built on the values of pluralism and tolerance?

Noncitizen Immigrants Are not Entitled to Constitutional Rights

Our government has long declined to treat immigrants as full human beings, and nowhere is that more clear than in the realm of constitutional rights. Although the Constitution literally extends the fundamental protections in the Bill of Rights to all people, limiting to citizens only the right to vote and run for federal office, the federal government acts as if this were not the case.

In 1893 the executive branch successfully defended a statute that required Chinese laborers to establish their prior residence here by the testimony of "at least one credible white witness." The Supreme Court ruled that this law was constitutional because it was reasonable for Congress to presume that nonwhite witnesses could not be trusted.

The federal government is not much more enlightened today. In a pending case I'm handling in the Court of Appeals for the Ninth Circuit, the Clinton Administration has argued that Permanent resident aliens lawfully living here should be extended no more First Amendment rights than aliens applying for first-time admission from abroad—that is, none. Under this view, students at a public university who are citizens may express, themselves freely, but students who are not citizens can be deported for saying exactly what their classmates are constitutionally entitled to say.

Growing up, I was always taught that we will be judged by how we treat others. If we are collectively judged by how we have treated immigrants—those who appear today to be "other" but will in a generation be "us"—we are not in very good shape.

Immigration:
Dissolving the People

There is a sense in which current immigration policy is Adolf Hitler's posthumous revenge on America. The U.S. political elite emerged from the war passionately concerned to cleanse itself from all taints of racism or xenophobia. Eventually, it enacted the epochal Immigration Act (technically, the Immigration and Nationality Act Amendments) of 1965.

And this, quite accidentally, triggered a renewed mass immigration, so huge and so systematically different from anything that had gone before as to transform—and ultimately, perhaps, even to destroy—the one unquestioned victor of World War II: the American nation, as it had evolved by the middle of the 20th century.

Today, U.S. government policy is literally dissolving the people and electing a new one. You can be for this or you can be against it. But the fact is undeniable.

"Still," *Time* magazine wrote in its fall 1993 "Special Issue on Multiculturalism," "for the first time in its history, the U.S. has an immigration policy that, for better or worse, is truly democratic."

As an immigrant, albeit one who came here rather earlier than yesterday and is now an American citizen, I find myself asking with fascination: What can this possibly mean? American immigration policy has always been democratic, of course, in the sense that it has been made through democratic procedures. Right now, as a matter of fact, it's unusually undemocratic, in the sense that Americans have told pollsters long and loudly that they don't want any more immigration; but the politicians ignore them.

The mass immigration so thoughtlessly triggered in 1965 risks making America an alien nation—not merely in the sense that the numbers of aliens in the nation are rising to levels last seen in the 19th century; not merely in the sense that America will become a freak among the world's nations because of the unprecedented demographic mutation it is inflicting on itself; not merely in the sense that Americans themselves will become alien to each other, requiring an increasingly strained government to arbitrate between them; but, ultimately, in the sense that Americans will no longer share in common what Abraham Lincoln called in his first inaugural address "the mystic chords of memory, stretching from every battlefield and patriotic grave, to every living heart and hearth stone, all over this broad land."

Alexander James Frank Brimelow is an American, although I was still a British subject and his mother a Canadian when he shot into the New York delivery room, yelling indignantly, one summer dawn in 1991. This is because of the 14th Amendment to the U.S. Constitution. It states in part:

"All persons born or naturalized in the United States, and subject to the jurisdiction thereof, are citizens of the United States and of the State wherein they reside."

The 14th Amendment was passed after the Civil War in an attempt to stop Southern states denying their newly freed slaves the full rights of citizens. But the wording is general. So it has been interpreted to mean that any child born in the United States is automatically a citizen. Even if its mother is a foreigner. Even if she's just passing through.

I am delighted that Alexander is an American. However, I do feel slightly, well, guilty that his fellow Americans had so little choice in the matter.

But at least Maggy and I had applied for and been granted legal permission to live in the United States. There are currently an estimated 3.5 million to 4 million foreigners who have just arrived and settled here in defiance of American law. When these illegal immigrants have children in the United States, why those children are automatically American citizens too.

And right now, two-thirds of births in Los Angeles County hospitals are to illegal-immigrant mothers.

All of which is just another example of one of my central themes:

The United States has lost control of its borders—in every sense. A series of institutional accidents, of which birthright citizenship is just one, has essentially robbed Americans of the power to determine who, and how many, can enter their national family, make claims on it—and exert power over it.

In 1991, the year of Alexander's birth, the Immigration and Naturalization Service reported a total of over 1.8 million legal immigrants. That was easily a record. It exceeded by almost a third the previous peak of almost 1.3 million, reached 84 years earlier at the height of the first great wave of immigration, which peaked just after the turn of the century.

The United States has been engulfed by what seems likely to be the greatest wave of immigration it has ever faced. The INS [Immigration and Naturalization Service] estimates that 12 million to 13 million legal and illegal immigrants will enter the United States during the 1990s. The Washington, D.C.-based Federation for American Immigration Reform (FAIR), among the most prominent of the groups critical of immigration policy, thinks the total will range between 10 million and 15 million.

It's not just illegal immigration that is out of control. So is legal immigration. U.S. law in effect treats immigration as a sort of imitation civil right, extended to an indefinite group of foreigners who have been selected arbitrarily and with no regard to American interests.

The American immigration debate has been a one-way street. Criticism of immigration, and news that might support it, just tends not to get through.

For example, the United States is in the midst of a serious crime epidemic. Yet almost no Americans are aware that aliens make up one-quarter of the prisoners in federal penitentiaries—almost three times their proportion in the population at large.

Indeed, many problems that currently preoccupy Americans have an unspoken immigration dimension.

Two further instances:

- The health care crisis. Americans have been told repeatedly that some 30 million to 40 million people in the country have no health insurance at any one point in time. Typically, nobody seems to know how many are immigrants. But immigrants certainly make up a disproportionate share—particularly of the real problem: the much smaller hard core, perhaps 6 million, that remains uninsured after two years.
- The education crisis. Americans are used to hearing that their schools don't seem to be providing the quality of education that foreigners get. Fewer of them know that the U.S. education system is also very expensive by international standards. Virtually none of them know anything about the impact of immigration on that education system.

Yet the impact of immigration is clearly serious. For example, in 1990 almost one child in every 20 enrolled in American public schools either could not speak English or spoke it so poorly as to need language-assistance programs. This number is increasing with striking speed: Only six years earlier, it had been one child in 31.

Current law is generally interpreted as requiring schools to educate such children in their native language. To do so, according to one California estimate, requires spending some 65 percent more per child than on an English-speaking child. And not merely money but, more importantly, teacher time and energy are inevitably being diverted from America's children.

My thesis is that the immigration resulting from current public policy:

- Is dramatically larger, less skilled and more divergent from the American majority than anything that was anticipated or desired.
- Is probably not beneficial economically—and is certainly not necessary.
- Is attended by a wide and increasing range of negative consequences, from the physical environment to the political
- Is bringing about an ethnic and racial transformation in America without precedent in the history of the world—an astonishing social experiment launched with no particular reason to expect success.

Some of my American readers will be stirring uneasily at this point. They have been trained to recoil from any explicit discussion of race.

Because the term "racist" is now so debased, I usually shrug off such smears by pointing to its new definition: anyone who is winning an argument with a liberal. Or, too often, a libertarian. And, on the immigration issue, even some confused conservatives.

This may sound facetious. But the double standards are irritating. Anyone who has got into an immigration debate with, for example, Hispanic activists must be instantly aware that some of them really are consumed by the most intense racial animosity—directed against whites. How come what's sauce for the goose is not sauce for the gander?

I have indeed duly examined my own motives. And I am happy to report that they are pure. I sincerely believe I am not prejudiced—in the sense of committing and stubbornly persisting in error about people, regardless of evidence—which appears to be the only rational definition of "racism." I am also, however, not blind.

Race and ethnicity are destiny in American politics. And, because of the rise of affirmative action quotas, for American individuals too.

My son, Alexander, is a white male with blue eyes and blond hair. He has never discriminated against anyone in his little life (except possibly young women visitors whom he suspects of being baby-sitters). The sheer size of the so-called "protected classes" that are now politically favored, such as Hispanics, will be a matter of vital importance as long as he lives. And their size is basically determined by immigration.

For Americans even to think about their immigration policy, given the political climate that has prevailed since the 1960s, involves a sort of psychological liberation movement. In Eugene McCarthy's terms, America would have to stop being a colony of the world. The implications are shocking, even frightening: that Americans, without feeling guilty, can and should seize control of their country's destiny.

If they did, what would a decolonized American immigration policy look like? The first step is absolutely clear:

The 1965 Immigration Act, and its amplifications in 1986 and 1990, have been a disaster and must be repealed.

It may be time for the United States to consider moving to a conception of itself more like that of Switzerland: tolerating a fairly large foreign presence that comes and goes, but rarely if ever naturalizes. It may be time to consider reviving a version of the bracero program, the agricultural guest-worker program that operated from the 1940s to the 1960s, allowing foreign workers to move in and out of the country in a controlled way, without permanently altering its demography and politics.

This new conception may be a shock to American sensibilities. Many Americans, like my students at the University of Cincinnati Law School, are under the charming impression that foreigners don't really exist. But they also tend to think that, if foreigners really do exist, they ought to become Americans as quickly as possible.

However, the fact is that we—foreigners—are, in some sense, all Americans now, just as Jefferson said everyone had two countries, his own and France, in the 18th century. That is why we are here, just as the entire world flocked to Imperial Rome. The trick the Americans face now is to be an empire in fact, while remaining a democratic republic in spirit. Avoiding the Romans' mistake of diluting their citizenship into insignificance may be the key.

POSTSCRIPT

Is Immigration Good for America?

A Common reference concerning the nature of American society is to characterize it as a nation of immigrants. Virtually all of the people of the United States are either immigrants of their descendants. So, immigration is a significant theme of the American experience. These newcomers have made innumerable contributions to the creation and development of the American nation. The earliest European immigrant populations converted the lands that they colonized into viable Western-style political and economic entities, which were transformed by the American Revolution into an independent republic, the United States of America Foreign-born peoples explored the West, broke the sod of the prairie lands by the sweat of their brows, and contributed to those developments that resulted in the establishment of agriculture as a vital component of economic progress while expanding the frontiers/boundaries of this emergent and dynamic nation.

As capitalist industrial and commercial developments emerged to dominate the U.S. economy, immigrants and their children provided the requisite labor to extract the resources necessary to operate the factories producing the goods and services of this emergent economy. Ultimately, "Americanized" children of immigrants made significant contributions to the building of modern American institutions while exerting leadership to move this nation forward to achieve a preeminent position in the world.

The anti-immigration position taken by descendants of immigrants is revealing of the American experience. At what point does an immigrant, or his descendants, identify more with the dominant culture than with his immigrant culture? Perhaps an answer to this question will aid in understanding the immigration issue. Are those who are already here fearful of losing jobs? Is there a perceived cultural threat in terms of language, customs, and values? We need to address these questions in order to understand people, like Peter Brimelow, who oppose immigration.

Brimelow is concerned that America is becoming an "alien nation." He believes that mass immigration is out of control and inflicting harm on the nation. In this context, Brimelow raises concern for American social problems that are heavily affected by immigrants, such as crime, health care, and education. For him, the benefits of immigration do not outweigh the social costs.

Cole, in contrast to Brimelow, points out that despite their labor and other significant contributions to American life, immigrants have had to struggle for recognition and acceptance in this land. They have been subjected to every conceivable bigotry that has evolved and festered within society, including racism, religious bias, classism, anti-Semitism, nativism, and other forms of ethnocentric prejudice and discrimination. Cole argues that each significant episode of immigration has been attended by suspicions and concerns emanating from the resident American population and their leaders who question the ability of these newcomers to fit in to the prevailing culture and their loyalty to the nation, among other reservations. Despite these disabilities, Cole is impressed with the contributions of immigrants.

This is an important issue in that immigration is a major policy concern of American government. The public debate has entertained topics such as border patrol, quotas, English-only demands, labor competition, national security, and cost-benefit analysis. These issues have been the source of controversy throughout history and are likely to continue.

Oscar Handlin's *The Uprooted: The Epic Story of the Great Migrations That Made the American People* (Grossett and Dunlap, 1951) is a good starting point for further research on immigration to America. A general understanding can be found in *A History of Immigration and Ethnicity in American Life* (Harper Perrennial, 1990) by Roger Daniel. A recent issue of *CQ Journal* was devoted to contemporary immigration. It presents a factual comparison of immigration in the 1990s to immigration of the 1890s. *The Emigration Dialectic* (1980) by J. Maldonado Denis provides an interesting examination of the dynamic of Puerto Rican immigration to the mainland United States.

A comprehensive reference book on immigrants and ethnic groups is the *Harvard Encyclopedia of American Ethnic Groups* (Harvard University Press, 1980) by Stephan Thernstrom. *We Are the People: An Atlas of America's Ethnic Diversity* (Macmillan, 1988) by James Paul Allen and Eugene James Turner shows the settlement patterns of immigrants with over 100 maps. A useful pamphlet, *Ethnicity and Immigration* (American Historical Association 1997), by James P. Shenton and Kevin Kenny, provides an overview and an extensive bibliography. An article that deals with Asians, immigration, and assimilation can be found in *Commentary* (July–August 2000), "In Asian America" by Tamar Jacoby.

ISSUE 3

Race Relations in the Nineteenth Century: Will Accommodation Insure Progress?

YES: Booker T. Washington, "The Atlanta Exposition Address," from *Atlanta Letter* (September 18, 1895)

NO: W.E.B. DuBois, "Of Mr. Booker T. Washington and Others," from *Souls of Black Folk* (New York: Fawcett, 1968)

ISSUE SUMMARY

YES: Booker T. Washington, the premier black leader of the period 1896–1915, argues that with the embrace of significant norms of the white culture, the pursuit of an economic program featuring vocational education, practical labor, and the ownership of land and other property, the assumption of a non-threatening approach to the development of race relations, the race could make progress in the American South.

NO: W.E.B. DuBois, the leading black intellectual and progressive social activist of the first half of the twentieth century, viewed Washington's program as too limited and emphasized the need for blacks to vigorously pursue voting rights and political empowerment, civil rights, and higher education as bases for black progress in the United States.

Booker T. Washington was born a slave and his personal advancement in life was facilitated by the education he received at Hampton Institute, Virginia, a vocational school established for the education of black youth. His experiences there had a profound influence on his life as reflected in his advocacy of industrial education as a primary proposal for the advancement of the lives of African Americans.

Washington firmly believed that blacks must exhibit a willingness to work hard, defer gratification, practice frugality, acquire land and property and thus establish a solid economic foundation on which any quest for political and civil rights and social equality would rest. Such a demonstration of economic progress by blacks would be expected to impress white America and facilitate a gradual tendency to include blacks as fully participating citizens of the United States. Washington held that black workers had to establish themselves as a critical and dependable component of the working masses of American society.

Washington strongly emphasized the need for blacks to exhibit conservatism in manners and morals, and to cultivate patience as a virtue in dealing with the deprivations that they faced. This black leader was keen to stress the need for members of the race to utilize nonthreatening approaches when dealing with whites, thus neutralizing any fears that they might develop and employ in support of policies promoting the subordination and exclusion of blacks within the institutional life of the American society.

As the leading black intellectual of his time, the first of the race to earn the Ph.D. from Harvard University, W.E.B. DuBois embraced the idea that education was a sine qua non for African American progress in the United States. An emphasis upon education as a basis for economic, political, and social progress is a core value of the black community that evolved in the post–Civil War period. However, DuBois criticized Washington's educational program, with its emphasis on manual training, as too narrow in focus and serving to restrict black labor to the lowest stratum of American society with few prospects for upward mobility. Additionally, DuBois took Washington to task for his failure to push for educational programs of a more academic focus that would provide higher educational opportunities for the more aspiring and talented black youth. Blacks' acceptance of the industrial education paradigm advanced by Washington would be detrimental according to DuBois. He asserted that it served to reinforce the prevailing notions of white supremacy and innate black inferiority.

DuBois was also concerned that while Washington was promoting the economic advancement and material prosperity of blacks as workers and property owners, he was neglecting to advocate the need to acquire the political rights and empowerment to defend and protect their gains.

DuBois viewed Washington's leadership and the program he advocated for achieving progress for black Americans as seriously flawed. While he did not reject the notion that many blacks could profit from industrial education and that such a venture could assist blacks in their quest for material prosperity, DuBois insisted that higher education, the ballot, and insistent demands presented within organizations for civil rights, equality, and social justice were fundamental to the fuller achievement of progress for America's black citizens.

The Washington-DuBois controversy serves to illuminate the fact that black leaders and organizations have not been monolithic regarding their perspectives concerning the nature and challenges of race and racism within the American experience. This is also true of the programs and methods for improving the prospects of African Americans in achieving equal rights, economic advancement and social justice within the United States. Both African American leaders differed significantly with regards to these matters, though there was an overlapping of their views concerning both the methodology and goals for advancing African Americans.

➡ **YES**

The Atlanta Exposition Address

Cast down your bucket where you are.

One-third of the population of the South is of the Negro race. No enterprise seeking the material, civil, or moral welfare of this section can disregard this element of our population and reach the highest success. I but convey to you, Mr. President and Directors, the sentiment of the masses of my race when I say that in no way have the value and manhood of the American Negro been more fittingly and generously recognized than by the managers of this magnificent Exposition at every stage of its progress. It is a recognition that will do more to cement the friendship of the two races than any occurrence since the dawn of freedom.

Not only this, but the opportunity here afforded will awaken among us a new era of industrial progress. Ignorant and inexperienced, it is not strange that in the first years of our new life we began at the top instead of at the bottom; that a seat in Congress or the State Legislature was more sought than real estate or industrial skill; that the political convention or stump speaking had more attractions than starting a dairy farm or truck garden.

A ship lost at sea for many days suddenly sighted a friendly vessel. From the mast of the unfortunate vessel was seen a signal: "Water, water, we die of thirst." The answer from the friendly vessel at once came back, "Cast down your bucket where you are." A second time the signal, "Water, water, send us water," ran up from the distressed vessel and was answered, "Cast down your bucket where you are." And a third and fourth signal for water was answered "Cast down your bucket where you are." The captain of the distressed vessel, at last heeding the injunction, cast down his bucket and it came up full of fresh, sparkling water from the mouth of the Amazon River.

To those of my race who depend on bettering their condition in a foreign land, or who underestimate the importance of cultivating friendly relations with the Southern white man who is their next-door neighbor, I would say: Cast down your bucket where you are; cast it down in making friends, in every manly way, of the people of all races by whom we are

From "Atlanta Letter", September 1895.

surrounded. Cast it down in agriculture, mechanics, in commerce, in domestic service, and in the professions. And in this connection it is well to bear in mind that whatever other sins the South may be called upon to bear, when it comes to business pure and simple, it is in the South that the Negro is given a man's chance in the commercial world, and in nothing is this Exposition more eloquent than in emphasizing this chance. Our greatest danger is that, in the great leap from slavery to freedom, we may overlook the fact that the masses of us are to live by the productions of our hands and fail to keep in mind that we shall prosper in the proportion as we learn to dignify and glorify common labor, and put brains and skill into the common occupations of life; shall prosper in proportion as we learn to draw the line between the superficial and the substantial, the ornamental gewgaws of life and the useful. No race can prosper till it learns that there is as much dignity in tilling a field as in writing a poem. It is at the bottom of life we must begin, and not at the top. Nor should we permit our grievances to overshadow our opportunities.

To those of the white race who look to the incoming of those of foreign birth and strange tongue and habits for the prosperity of the South, were I permitted I would repeat what I say to my own race, "Cast down your bucket where you are." Cast it down among the 8,000,000 Negroes whose habits you know, whose fidelity and love you have tested in days when to have proved treacherous meant the ruin of your firesides. Cast down your bucket among these people who have, without strikes and labor wars, tilled your fields, cleared your forests, builded your railroads and cities, and brought forth treasures from the bowels of the earth and helped make possible this magnificent representation of the progress of the South. Casting down your bucket among my people, helping and encouraging them as you are doing on these grounds, and, with education of head, hand and heart, you will find that they will buy your surplus land, make blossom the waste places in your fields, and run your factories.

While doing this, you can be sure in the future, as in the past, that you and your families will be surrounded by the most patient, faithful, law-abiding, and unresentful people that the world has seen. As we have proved our loyalty to you in the past, in nursing your children, watching by the sickbed of your mothers and fathers, and often following them with tear-dimmed eyes to their graves, so in the future, in our humble way, we shall stand by you with a devotion that no foreigner can approach, ready to lay down our lives, if need be, in defense of yours; interlacing our industrial, commercial, civil, and religious life with yours in a way that shall make the interests of both races one. In all things that are purely social we can be as separate as the fingers, yet one as the hand in all things essential to mutual progress.

There is no defense or security for any of us except in the highest intelligence and development of all. If anywhere there are efforts tending to curtail the fullest growth of the Negro, let these efforts be turned into stimulating, encouraging and making him the most useful and intelligent citizen. Effort or means so invested will pay a thousand percent interest.

These efforts will be twice blessed—"blessing him that gives and him that takes."

There is no escape, through law of man or God, from the inevitable:

> The laws of changeless justice bind
> Oppressor with oppressed,
> And close as sin and suffering joined
> We march to fate abreast.

Nearly sixteen million hands will aid you in pulling the load upward, or they will pull against you the load downward. We shall constitute one-third and more of the ignorance and crime of the South, or one-third its intelligence and progress; we shall contribute one-third to the business and industrial prosperity of the South, or we shall prove a veritable body of death, stagnating, depressing, retarding every effort to advance the body politic.

Gentlemen of the Exposition: As we present to you our humble effort at an exhibition of our progress, you must not expect overmuch. Starting thirty years ago with ownership here and there in a few quilts and pumpkins and chickens (gathered from miscellaneous sources), remember: the path that has led us from these to the invention and production of agricultural implements, buggies, steam engines, newspapers, books, statuary, carving, paintings, the management of drugstores and banks, has not been trodden without contact with thorns and thistles. While we take pride in what we exhibit as a result of our independent efforts, we do not for a moment forget that our part in this exhibition would fall far short of your expectations but for the constant help that has come to our educational life, not only from the Southern states, but especially from Northern philanthropists who have made their gifts a constant stream of blessing and encouragement.

The wisest among my race understand that the agitation of questions of social equality is the extremest folly, and that progress in the enjoyment of all the privileges that will come to us must be the result of severe and constant struggle rather than of artificial forcing. No race that has anything to contribute to the markets of the world is long in any degree ostracized. It is important and right that all privileges of the laws be ours, but it is vastly more important that we be prepared for the exercise of those privileges. The opportunity to earn a dollar in a factory just now is worth infinitely more than the opportunity to spend a dollar in an opera house.

In conclusion, may I repeat that nothing in thirty years has given us more hope and encouragement and drawn us so near to you of the white race as this opportunity offered by the Exposition; and here bending, as it were, over the altar that represents the results of the struggles of your race and mine, both starting practically empty-handed three decades ago, I pledge that, in your effort to work out the great and intricate problem which God has laid at the doors of the South, you shall have at all times the patient, sympathetic help of my race. Only let this be constantly in mind that, while from representations in these buildings of the product of field, of forest, of mine, of factory, letters and art, much good will come—yet by far above and beyond material benefits, will be that higher good, that let us pray God will come, in a blotting out of sectional differences and racial animosities and suspicions, in a determination to administer absolute justice, in a willing obedience among all classes to the mandates of law. This, coupled with material prosperity, will bring into our beloved South a new heaven and a new earth.

Note

Booker T. Washington (1856–1915) was an educator and reformer who became an important spokesman for African Americans after the turn of the century. He was the founder of Tuskegee Institute, an industrial school for blacks in Alabama.

Of Mr. Booker T. Washington and Others

From birth till death enslaved; in word, in deed, unmanned!
Hereditary bondsmen! Know ye not
Who would be free themselves must strike the blow?

Byron

Easily the most striking thing in the history of the American Negro since 1876 is the ascendancy of Mr. Booker T. Washington. It began at the time when war memories and ideals were rapidly passing; a day of astonishing commercial development was dawning; a sense of doubt and hesitation overtook the freedmen's sons,—then it was that his leading began. Mr. Washington came, with a simple definite programme, at the psychological moment when the nation was a little ashamed of having bestowed so much sentiment on Negroes, and was concentrating its energies on Dollars. His programme of industrial education, conciliation of the South, and submission and silence as to civil and political rights, was not wholly original; the Free Negroes from 1830 up to wartime had striven to build industrial schools, and the American Missionary Association had from the first taught various trades; and Price and others had sought a way of honorable alliance with the best of the Southerners. But Mr. Washington first indissolubly linked these things; he put enthusiasm, unlimited energy, and perfect faith into this programme, and changed it from a by-path into a veritable Way of Life. And the tale of the methods by which he did this is a fascinating study of human life.

It startled the nation to hear a Negro advocating such a programme after many decades of bitter complaint; it startled and won the applause of the South, it interested and won the admiration of the North; and after a confused murmur of protest, it silenced if it did not convert the Negroes themselves.

To gain the sympathy and cooperation of the various elements comprising the white South was Mr. Washington's first task; and this, at the time Tuskegee was founded, seemed, for a black man, well-nigh impossible.

From "The Souls of the Black Folk: Essays and Sketches Chapter III," 1905.

And yet ten years later it was done in the word spoken at Atlanta: "In all things purely social we can be as separate as the five fingers, and yet one as the hand in all things essential to mutual progress." This "Atlanta Compromise" is by all odds the most notable thing in Mr. Washington's career. The South interpreted it in different ways: the radicals received it as a complete surrender of the demand for civil and political equality; the conservatives, as a generously conceived working basis for mutual understanding. So both approved it, and to-day its author is certainly the most distinguished Southerner since Jefferson Davis, and the one with the largest personal following.

Next to this achievement comes Mr. Washington's work in gaining place and consideration in the North. Others less shrewd and tactful had formerly essayed to sit on these two stools and had fallen between them; but as Mr. Washington knew the heart of the South from birth and training, so by singular insight he intuitively grasped the spirit of the age which was dominating the North. And so thoroughly did he learn the speech and thought of triumphant commercialism, and the ideas of material prosperity, that the picture of a lone black boy poring over a French grammar amid the weeds and dirt of a neglected home soon seemed to him the acme of absurdities. One wonders what Socrates and St. Francis of Assisi would say to this.

And yet this very singleness of vision and thorough oneness with his age is a mark of the successful man. It is as though Nature must needs make men narrow in order to give them force. So Mr. Washington's cult has gained unquestioning followers, his work has wonderfully prospered, his friends are legion, and his enemies are confounded. To-day he stands as the one recognized spokesman of his ten million fellows, and one of the most notable figures in a nation of seventy millions. One hesitates, therefore, to criticise a life which, beginning with so little, has done so much. And yet the time is come when one may speak in all sincerity and utter courtesy of the mistakes and shortcomings of Mr. Washington's career, as well as of his triumphs, without being thought captious or envious, and without forgetting that it is easier to do ill than well in the world.

The criticism that has hitherto met Mr. Washington has not always been of this broad character. In the South especially has he had to walk warily to avoid the harshest judgments,—and naturally so, for he is dealing with the one subject of deepest sensitiveness to that section. Twice—once when at the Chicago celebration of the Spanish-American War he alluded to the color-prejudice that is "eating away the vitals of the South," and once when he dined with President Roosevelt—has the resulting Southern criticism been violent enough to threaten seriously his popularity. In the North the feeling has several times forced itself into words, that Mr. Washington's counsels of submission overlooked certain elements of true manhood, and that his educational programme was unnecessarily narrow. Usually, however, such criticism has not found open expression, although, too, the spiritual sons of the Abolitionists have not been prepared to acknowledge that the schools founded before Tuskegee, by men of broad ideals and self-sacrificing spirit, were wholly failures or worthy of ridicule. While, then, criticism has not failed to follow Mr. Washington, yet the prevailing public opinion of the land has been but too willing to deliver the solution of a wearisome problem into his hands, and say, "If that is all you and your race ask, take it."

Among his own people, however, Mr. Washington has encountered the strongest and most lasting opposition, amounting at times to bitterness, and even to-day continuing strong and insistent even though largely silenced in outward expression by the public opinion of the nation. Some of this opposition is, of course, mere envy; the disappointment of displaced demagogues and the spite of narrow minds. But aside from this, there is among educated and thoughtful colored men in all parts of the land a feeling of deep regret, sorrow, and apprehension at the wide currency and ascendancy which some of Mr. Washington's theories have gained. These same men admire his sincerity of purpose, and are willing to forgive much to honest endeavor which is doing something worth the doing. They cooperate with Mr. Washington as far as they conscientiously can; and, indeed, it is no ordinary tribute to this man's tact and power that, steering as he must between so many diverse interests and opinions, he so largely retains the respect of all. . . .

Mr. Washington represents in Negro thought the old attitude of adjustment and submission; but adjustment at such a peculiar time as to make his programme unique. This is an age of unusual economic development, and Mr. Washington's programme naturally takes an economic cast, becoming a gospel of Work and Money to such an extent as apparently almost completely to overshadow the higher aims of life. Moreover, this is an age when the more advanced races are coming in closer contact with the less developed races, and the race-feeling is therefore intensified; and Mr. Washington's programme practically accepts the alleged inferiority of the Negro races. Again, in our own land, the reaction from the sentiment of war time has given impetus to race-prejudice against Negroes, and Mr. Washington withdraws many of the high demands of Negroes as men and American citizens. In other periods of intensified prejudice all the Negro's tendency to self-assertion has been called forth; at this period a policy of submission is advocated. In the history of nearly all other races and peoples the doctrine preached at such crises has been that manly self-respect is worth more than lands and houses, and that a people who voluntarily surrender such respect, or cease striving for it, are not worth civilizing.

In answer to this, it has been claimed that the Negro can survive only through submission. Mr. Washington distinctly asks that black people give up, at least for the present, three things,—

- First, political power,
- Second, insistence on civil rights,
- Third, higher education of Negro youth,—

and concentrate all their energies on industrial education, the accumulation of wealth, and the conciliation of the South. This policy has been courageously and insistently advocated for over fifteen years, and has been triumphant for perhaps ten years. As a result of this tender of the palm-branch, what has been the return? In these years there have occurred:

1. The disfranchisement of the Negro.
2. The legal creation of a distinct status of civil inferiority for the Negro.
3. The steady withdrawal of aid from institutions for the higher training of the Negro.

These movements are not, to be sure, direct results of Mr. Washington's teachings; but his propaganda has, without a shadow of doubt, helped their speedier accomplishment. The question then comes: Is it possible, and probable, that nine millions of men can make effective progress in economic lines if they are deprived of political rights, made of servile caste, and allowed only the most meagre chance for developing their exceptional men? If history and reason give any distinct answer to these questions, it is an emphatic *No*. And Mr. Washington thus faces the triple paradox of his career:

1. He is striving nobly to make Negro artisans business men and property-owners; but it is utterly impossible, under modern competitive methods, for workingmen and property-owners to defend their rights and exist without the right of suffrage.
2. He insists on thrift and self-respect, but at the same time counsels a silent submission to civic inferiority such as is bound to sap the manhood of any race in the long run.
3. He advocates common-school and industrial training, and depreciates institutions of higher-learning; but neither the Negro common-schools, nor Tuskegee itself, could remain open a day were it not for teachers trained in Negro colleges, or trained by their graduates.

This triple paradox in Mr. Washington's position is the object of criticism by two classes of colored Americans. One class is spiritually descended from Toussaint the Savior, through Gabriel, Vesey, and Turner, and they represent the attitude of revolt and revenge; they hate the white South blindly and distrust the white race generally, and so far as they agree on definite action, think that the Negro's only hope lies in emigration beyond the borders of the United States. And yet, by the irony of fate, nothing has more effectually made this programme seem hopeless than the recent course of the United States toward weaker and darker peoples in the West Indies, Hawaii, and the Philippines,—for where in the world may we go and be safe from lying and brute force?

The other class of Negroes who cannot agree with Mr. Washington has hitherto said little aloud. They deprecate the sight of scattered counsels, of internal disagreement; and especially they dislike making their just criticism of a useful and earnest man an excuse for a general discharge of venom from small-minded opponents. Nevertheless, the questions involved are so fundamental and serious that it is difficult to see how men like the Grimkes, Kelly Miller, J. W. E. Bowen, and other representatives of this group, can much longer be silent. Such men feel in conscience bound to ask of this nation three things:

1. The right to vote.
2. Civic equality.
3. The education of youth according to ability.

They acknowledge Mr. Washington's invaluable service in counselling patience and courtesy in such demands; they do not ask that ignorant black men vote when ignorant whites are debarred, or that any reasonable restrictions in the suffrage should not be applied; they know that the low social level of the mass of the race is responsible for much discrimination against it, but they also know, and the nation knows, that relentless color-prejudice is more often a cause than a result of the Negro's degradation; they seek the abatement of this relic of barbarism, and not its systematic encouragement and pampering by all agencies of social power from the Associated Press to the Church of Christ. They advocate, with Mr. Washington, a broad system of Negro common schools supplemented by thorough industrial training; but they are surprised that a man of Mr. Washington's insight cannot see that no such educational system ever has rested or can rest on any other basis than that of the well-equipped college and university, and they insist that there is a demand for a few such institutions throughout the South to train the best of the Negro youth as teachers, professional men, and leaders.

This group of men honor Mr. Washington for his attitude of conciliation toward the white South; they accept the "Atlanta Compromise" in its broadest interpretation; they recognize, with him, many signs of promise, many men of high purpose and fair judgment, in this section; they know that no easy task has been laid upon a region already tottering under heavy burdens. But, nevertheless, they insist that the way to truth and right lies in straightforward honesty, not in indiscriminate flattery; in praising those of the South who do well and criticising uncompromisingly those who do ill; in taking advantage of the opportunities at hand and urging their fellows to do the same, but at the same time in remembering that only a firm adherence to their higher ideals and aspirations will ever keep those ideals within the realm of possibility. They do not expect that the free right to vote, to enjoy civic rights, and to be educated, will come in a moment; they do not expect to see the bias and prejudices of years disappear at the blast of a trumpet; but they are absolutely certain that the way for a people to gain their reasonable rights is not by voluntarily throwing them away and insisting that they do not want them; that the way for a people to gain respect is not by continually belittling and ridiculing themselves; that, on the contrary, Negroes must insist continually, in season and out of season, that voting is necessary to modern manhood, that color discrimination is barbarism, and that black boys need education as well as white boys. . . .

The South ought to be led, by candid and honest criticism, to assert her better self and do her full duty to the race she has cruelly wronged and is still wronging. The North—her co-partner in guilt—cannot salve her conscience by plastering it with gold. We cannot settle this problem by diplomacy and suaveness, by "policy" alone. If worse come to worst, can the moral fibre of this country survive the slow throttling and murder of nine millions of men?

The black men of America have a duty to perform, a duty stern and delicate,—a forward movement to oppose a part of the work of their greatest leader. So far as Mr. Washington preaches Thrift, Patience, and Industrial Training for the masses, we must hold up his hands and strive with him, rejoicing in his honors and glorying in the strength of this Joshua called of God and of man to lead the headless host. But so far as Mr. Washington apologizes for injustice, North or South, does not rightly value the privilege and duty of voting, belittles the emasculating effects of caste distinctions, and opposes the higher training and ambition of our brighter minds,—so far as he, the South, or the Nation, does this,—we must unceasingly and firmly oppose them. By every civilized and peaceful method we must strive for the rights which the world accords to men, clinging unwaveringly to those great words which the sons of the Fathers would fain forget: "We hold these truths to be self-evident: That all men are created equal; that they are endowed by their Creator with certain unalienable rights; that among these are life, liberty, and the pursuit of happiness."

Note

W. E. Burghardt Du Bois (1868–1963), author of The Souls of Black Folk, *was a sociologist, writer, scholar, and civil rights activist. He was one of the founders of the NAACP and editor of its publication,* the Crisis.

POSTSCRIPT

Race Relations in the Nineteenth Century: Will Accommodation Insure Progress?

The Washington-DuBois controversy occurred at a time when American society was being transferred in an irrevocable manner by the dynamic commercial/industrial capitalist revolution and the flood of European and Asian immigrants who came here to provide the muscle required to build this emergent economic system. African Americans represented a substantial component of a domestic American stream of migrants who voted against oppressive conditions of the racist American South to relocate within the North. During and after Reconstruction, the American South was recast in its old racist image, beliefs, and practices.

While the XIII, XIV, and XV amendments of the Reconstruction Era ended formal slavery and established a constitutional basis for citizenship, these reforms proved to be inadequate to the challenges involved in transforming emancipated blacks into fully participating citizens. Education and land ownership as a basis for establishing an economic foundation upon which African Americans' citizenship would rest, were critical to this transformation process. However, neither of these challenges were met adequately to provide a solid foundation for the African American quest to secure freedom and justice in America. Additionally, terrorism emerged from the Klan and similar organizations suppressing black's quest for freedom. Booker T. Washington's paradigm for black progress emphasized conciliation and accommodation. He was opposed to confrontation as a basis for black progress.

During the post–Reconstruction Era, African Americans saw their quest for freedom increasingly challenged. The capstone of these tragic developments was the infamous decision of the United States Supreme Court in the *Plessy v. Ferguson* case, which affirmed the constitutionality of racial segregation based upon the spurious separate but equal doctrine.

As the black Americans' struggle for equality developed during the twentieth century, the influence of W.E.B. DuBois looms very large. His is a powerful legacy of intellectual excellence and a persistent struggle of African Americans for citizenship rights and social justice DuBois' belief was based on effective organizations led by charismatic leaders and utilizing the law and variants of social protest to advance the race. In contrast with Washington's industrial model, DuBois believed that blacks needed more comprehensive educational options.

56

Booker T. Washington had a different approach. His advocacy of such values as the work ethic, achievement orientation, land/property ownership, morality, and material accumulation still resonate within black society/ culture. Washington's emphasis, was for a non-threatening approach to white Americans in building race relations? Some believe this was alienating to increasing numbers of black Americans.

A historical overview that will enable the student to place this issue in context can be found in the classic *From Slavery to Freedom: A History of Negro Americans* (Alfred A. Knopf, 1988) by John Hope Franklin and Alfred A. Moss, Jr. It is an authoritative history of African Americans. DuBois' position is elaborated in *The Souls of Black Folk* (1903). David Levering Lewis' two volume biography of DuBois, *W.E.B. DuBois: Biography of a Race, 1868–1919* (Henry Holt, 1993) and *W.E.B. DuBois: The Fight for Equality and The American Century, 1919–1963* (Henry Holt, 2000) is a complete account of his life and time. More of the work of DuBois can be found in *On Sociology and the Black Community* by DuBois (edited by Dan Green and Edwin Driver) (University of Chicago Press, 1978). Henry Louis Gates and Cornel West's *The Future of the Race* (Knopf, 1996) re-examines DuBois' idea of leadership.

Booker T. Washington's *Up From Slavery: An Autobiography* (A. L. Burt, 1900) further develops the accommodation position. An examination of the Washington-DuBois Conference of 1904, where their different ideas were debated, can be found in Herbert Aptheker's *Afro American History: The Modern Era* (The Citadel Press, 1973). In 1905, the popular novelist, Thomas Dixon (author of *The Clansmen* that later became the basis for the motion picture, *Birth of a Nation*) wrote "Booker T. Washington and the Negro," in *The Saturday Evening Post* (August 19, 1905), in which he argued that Washington's idea would offer false hope to blacks. Dixon believed that blacks had no place in America.

ISSUE 4

Does White Identity Define America?

YES: Lillian B. Rubin, "Is This a White Country, or What?" in *Families on the Fault Line* (Harper Perennial, 1995)

NO: Ellis Cose, "What's White Anyway?" *Newsweek* (September 18, 2000)

ISSUE SUMMARY

YES: Lillian B. Rubin, senior research fellow at the Institute for Study of Social Change at Berkeley, contrasts current immigrants who are mostly non-white with nineteenth-century European immigrants, almost all of whom were white. She notes that among many descendants of European immigrants currently there is a fear of whites becoming a minority. For these descendants, American identity has always been associated with being white. In spite of ethnic differences, a white identity insured inclusion. Recent immigration patterns have led to a (neo) nativist reaction. For Rubin, ethnicity often becomes a cover for white.

NO: Ellis Cose, an African American journalist, argues that the traditional boundaries that determine race and skin color are not what they once were. Although he does not specifically cite ethnicity, Cose furthers the claim that American identity today is an expanding category. The boundaries of whiteness have expanded and are no longer hard and fast.

A recent issue of the *Population Bulletin* devoted to immigration cites recent U.S. Census data that over 1 million immigrants came to the United States in 2001. Over half of these immigrants came from Latin America, while 30% came from Asia. Thus, 81% of recent immigrants are classified as non-white. What are the implications of this trend? Along with the social and demographic issues is the question of race and American identity. Americans have always been concerned with strangers and new immigrants. In one sense, the current concern about white identity and American culture repeats history. Lillian B. Rubin's description of the fears of descendants of European immigrants can be seen as a new nativism.

Clearly, one of the consequences of recent immigration patterns is a renewal of the question of American identity. Issue 1 in this book deals with the historic question of the need for a common American identity. This issue involves the contemporary tensions of how to incorporate non-European immigrants within an American identity. The question posed by Rubin, "Is This a White Country, or What?" is better understood in terms of majority–minority relations. Although European immigrants adjusted to minority (ethnic) group status, the assimilationist promise of inclusion was perceived as within reach. Hence the immigrant dream of becoming part of American culture. Racial considerations were largely ignored when it came to Europeans. For the most part, the immigrant was a member of a minority group as well as white and, thus, part of a majority group.

For example, with all the subcultural variations exhibited by European immigrants, race was not an issue. Yet, the term "race" was used selectively to apply to European ethnic groups. However, it did not refer to skin color. For example, the American public did not see early nineteenth-century Irish immigrants as white. The Irish insisted that they were white. More definitive racial categories such as "Negroes" and "Asians" separated European descendants from non-Europeans. They did not fear that other races in total would be counted together as one and render their "race" a minority. Indeed, it was common to refer to the "Irish race" or the "Jewish race."

The late twentieth and early twenty-first centuries' reaction to the preponderance of non-European immigrants to America has been seen by many as a threat to majority status. Race, however the concept is defined today, is assumed to be included in an American identity. Specifically, whites tend to take for granted that the majority status of whiteness is synonymous with American identity. Demographically, that has always been easy to ascertain. For example, as recently as the 1950s, blacks were 12% of the population, while Hispanics were 3%, and Asians were less than 1%. America was, statistically speaking, nearly 85% white. In contrast, today whites constitute approximately 70% of the population with blacks and Hispanics both at approximately 13% and Asians approaching 5%.

Lillian B. Rubin points to a growing concern among some whites with a changing American population and its potential effect on American identity. Out of this expressed concern she argues that ethnic consciousness masks a white identification that is perceived to be a shrinking majority and soon to be minority.

Beginning with his citation of the McCarran-Walter Act of 1952, Ellis Cose argues that non-white immigrants no longer have to "paint themselves white in order to become Americans." His position is that American identity increasingly is no longer defined by whiteness. Rather, American identity is slowly changing as the definition of what is white expands its boundaries.

The reader should first try to connect Issue 1 with the contemporary ideas of Rubin and Cose. Does Rubin further the assimilation argument, or does she challenge it? How accurate is Cose in his position that for recent immigrants race means less than in the past? Does he make the case for a modern pluralist argument?

Lillian B. Rubin  **YES**

Is This a White Country, or What?

They're letting all these coloreds come in and soon there won't be any place left for white people," broods Tim Walsh, a 33-year-old white construction worker. "It makes you wonder: Is this a white country, or what?"

It's a question that nags at white America, one perhaps that's articulated most often and most clearly by the men and women of the working class. For it's they who feel most vulnerable, who have suffered the economic contractions of recent decades most keenly, who see the new immigrants most clearly as direct competitors for their jobs.

It's not whites alone who stew about immigrants. Native-born blacks, too, fear the newcomers nearly as much as whites—and for the same economic reasons. But for whites the issue is compounded by race, by the fact that the newcomers are primarily people of color. For them, therefore, their economic anxieties have combined with the changing face of America to create a profound uneasiness about immigration—a theme that was sounded by nearly 90 percent of the whites I met, even by those who are themselves first-generation, albeit well-assimilated, immigrants.

Sometimes they spoke about this in response to my questions; equally often the subject of immigration arose spontaneously as people gave voice to their concerns. But because the new immigrants are predominantly people of color, the discourse was almost always cast in terms of race as well as immigration, with the talk slipping from immigration to race and back again as if these are not two separate phenomena. "If we keep letting all them foreigners in, pretty soon there'll be more of them than us and then what will this country be like?" Tim's wife, Mary Anne, frets. "I mean, this is *our* country, but the way things are going, white people will be the minority in our own country. Now does that make any sense?"

Such fears are not new. Americans have always worried about the strangers who came to our shores, fearing that they would corrupt our society dilute our culture, debase our values. So I remind Mary Anne, "When your ancestors came here, people also thought we were allowing too many foreigners into the country. Yet those earlier immigrants were successfully integrated into the American society. What's different now?"

FAMILIES ON THE FAULTLINE, 1994, pp. 464–474. Copyright © 1994 by Lillian B. Rubin. Originally published by HarperCollins. Reprinted by the permission of Dunham Library, Inc. as agent for the author.

"Oh, it's different, all right," she replies without hesitation. "When my people came, the immigrants were all white. That makes a big difference."

"Why do you think that's so?"

"I don't know; it just is, that's all. Look at the black people; they've been here a long time, and they still don't live like us—stealing and drugs and having all those babies."

"But you were talking about immigrants. Now you're talking about blacks, and they're not immigrants."

"Yeah, I know," she replies with a shrug. "But they're different, and there's enough problems with them, so we don't need any more. With all these other people coming here now, we just have more trouble. They don't talk English; and they think different from us, things like that."

Listening to Mary Anne's words I was reminded again how little we Americans look to history for its lessons, how impoverished is our historical memory. For, in fact, being white didn't make "a big difference" for many of those earlier immigrants. The dark-skinned Italians and the eastern European Jews who came in the late nineteenth and early twentieth centuries didn't look very white to the fair-skinned Americans who were here then. Indeed, the same people we now call white—Italians, Jews, Irish—were seen as another race at that time. Not black or Asian, it's true, but an alien other, a race apart, although one that didn't have a clearly defined name. Moreover, the racist fears and fantasies of native-born Americans were far less contained then than they are now, largely because there were few social constraints on their expression.

When, during the nineteenth century, for example, some Italians were taken for blacks and lynched in the South, the incidents passed virtually unnoticed. And if Mary Anne and Tim Walsh, both of Irish ancestry, had come to this country during the great Irish immigration of that period, they would have found themselves defined as an inferior race and described with the same language that was used to characterize blacks: "low-browed and savage, grovelling and bestial, lazy and wild, simian and sensual."[1] Not only during that period but for a long time afterward as well, the U.S. Census Bureau counted Irish as a distinct and separate group, much as it does today with the category it labels "Hispanic."

But there are two important differences between then and now, differences that can be summed up in a few words: the economy and race. Then, a growing industrial economy meant that there were plenty of jobs for both immigrant and native workers, something that can't be said for the contracting economy in which we live today. True, the arrival of the immigrants, who were more readily exploitable than native workers, put Americans at a disadvantage and created discord between the two groups. Nevertheless, work was available for both.

Then, too, the immigrants—no matter how they were labeled, no matter how reviled they may have been—were ultimately assimilable, if for no other reason than that they were white. As they began to lose their alien ways, it became possible for native Americans to see in the white ethnics of yesteryear a reflection of themselves. Once this shift in perception occurred, it was possible for the nation to incorporate them, to take them in, chew them up, digest them, and spit them out as Americans—with subcultural variations not always to the liking of those who hoped to control the manners and mores of the day, to be sure, but still recognizably white Americans.

Today's immigrants, however, are the racial other in a deep and profound way. It's true that race is not a fixed category, that it's no less an *idea* today than it was yesterday. And it's also possible, as I have already suggested, that we may be witness to social transformation from race to ethnicity among some of the most assimilated—read: middleclass—Asians and Latinos. But even if so, there's a long way to go before that metamorphosis is realized. Meanwhile, the immigrants of this era not only bring their own language and culture, they are also people of color—men, women, and children whose skin tones are different and whose characteristic features set them apart and justify the racial categories we lock them into.[2] And integrating masses of people of color into a society where race consciousness lies at the very heart of our central nervous system raises a whole new set of anxieties and tensions.

It's not surprising, therefore, that racial dissension has increased so sharply in recent years. What is surprising, however, is the passion for ethnicity and the preoccupation with ethnic identification among whites that seems suddenly to have burst upon the public scene. . . .

◦◈◦

What does being German, Irish, French, Russian, Polish mean to someone who is an American? It's undoubtedly different for recent immigrants than for those who have been here for generations. But even for a relative newcomer, the inexorable process of becoming an American changes the meaning of ethnic identification and its hold on the internal life of the individual. Nowhere have I seen this shift more eloquently described than in a recent op-ed piece published in the *New York Times*. The author a Vietnamese refugee writing on the day when Vietnamese either celebrate or mourn the fall of Saigon, depending on which side of the conflict they were on, writes:

> Although I sometimes mourn the loss of home and land, it's the American landscape and what it offers that solidify my hyphenated identity. . . . Assimilation, education, the English language, the American 'I'—these have carried me and many others further from that beloved tropical country than the C-130 ever could. . . . When did this happen? Who knows? One night, America quietly seeps in and takes hold of one's mind and body, and the Vietnamese soul of sorrows slowly fades away. In the morning, the Vietnamese American speaks a new language of materialism: his vocabulary includes terms like career choices, down payment, escrow, overtime.[3]

A new language emerges, but it lives, at least for another generation, alongside the old one; Vietnamese, yes, but also American, with a newly developed sense of self and possibility—an identity that continues to grow stronger with each succeeding generation. It's a process we have seen repeated throughout the history of American immigration. The American world reaches into the immigrant communities and shapes and changes the people who live in them.[4] By the second generation, ethnic identity already is attenuated; by the third, it usually has receded as a deeply meaningful part of life.

Residential segregation, occupational concentration, and a common language and culture—these historically have been the basis for ethnic solidarity and identification. As strangers in a new land, immigrants banded together, bound by their native tongue and shared culture. The sense of affinity they felt in these urban communities was natural; they were a touch of home, of the old country, of ways they understood: Once within their boundaries, they could feel whole again, sheltered from the ridicule and revulsion with which they were greeted by those who came before them. For whatever the myth about America's welcoming arms, nativist sentiment has nearly always been high and the anti-immigrant segment of the population large and noisy.

Ethnic solidarity and identity in America, then, was the consequence of the shared history each group brought with it, combined with the social and psychological experience of establishing themselves in the new land. But powerful as these were, the connections among the members of the group were heightened and sustained by the occupational concentration that followed—the Irish in the police departments of cities like Boston and San Francisco, for example, the Jews in New York City's garment industry, the east central Europeans in the mills and mines of western Pennsylvania.[5]

As each ethnic group moved into the labor force, its members often became concentrated in a particular occupation, largely because they were helped to find jobs there by those who went before them. For employers, this ethnic homogeneity made sense. They didn't have to cope with a babel of different languages, and they could count on the older workers to train the newcomers and keep them in line. For workers, there were advantages as well. It meant that they not only had compatible workmates, but that they weren't alone as they faced the jeers and contempt of their American-born counterparts. And perhaps most important, as more and more ethnic peers filled the available jobs, they began to develop some small measure of control in the workplace.

The same pattern of occupational concentration that was characteristic of yesterday's immigrant groups exists among the new immigrants today, and for the same reasons. The Cubans in Florida and the Dominicans in New York,[6] the various Asian groups in San Francisco, the Koreans in Los Angeles and New York—all continue to live in ethnic neighborhoods; all use the networks established there to find their way into the American labor force.[7]

For the white working-class ethnics whose immigrant past is little more than part of family lore, the occupational, residential, and linguistic chain has been broken. This is not to say that white ethnicity has ceased to be an observable phenomenon in American life. Cities like New York, Chicago, and San Francisco still have white ethnic districts that influence their culture, especially around food preferences and eating habits. But as in San Francisco's North Beach or New York's Little Italy, the people who once created vibrant neighborhoods, where a distinct subculture and language remained vividly alive, long ago moved out and left behind only the remnants of the commercial life of the old community. As such transformations took place, ethnicity became largely a private matter, a distant part of the family heritage that had little to do with the ongoing life of the family or community.

What, then, are we to make of the claims to ethnic identity that have become so prominent in recent years? Herbert Gans has called this identification "symbolic ethnicity"—that is, ethnicity that's invoked or not as the individual chooses.[8] Symbolic ethnicity, according to Gans, has little impact on a person's daily life and, because it is not connected to ethnic structures or activities—except for something like the wearing of the green on St. Patrick's Day—it makes no real contribution to ethnic solidarity or community.

The description is accurate. But it's a mistake to dismiss ethnic identification, even if only symbolic, as relatively meaningless. Symbols, after all, become symbolic precisely because they have meaning. In this case, the symbol has meaning at two levels: One is the personal and psychological, the other is the social and political.

At the personal level, in a nation as large and diverse as ours—a nation that defines itself by its immigrant past, where the metaphor for our national identity has been the melting pot—defining oneself in the context of an ethnic group is comforting. It provides a sense of belonging to some recognizable and manageable collectivity—an affiliation that has meaning because it's connected to the family where, when we were small children, we first learned about our relationship to the group. As Vilma Janowski, a 24-year-old first-generation Polish-American who came here as a child put it: "Knowing there's other people like you is really nice. It's like having a big family, even if you don't ever really see them. It's just nice to know they're there. Besides, if I said I was American, what would it mean? Nobody's just American."

Which is true. Being an American is different from being French or Dutch or any number of other nationalities because, except for Native Americans, there's no such thing as an American without a hyphen somewhere in the past. To identify with the front end of that hyphen is to maintain a connection—however tenuous, illusory, or sentimentalized—with our roots. It sets us apart from others, allows us the fantasy of uniqueness— a quest given particular urgency by a psychological culture that increasingly emphasizes the development of the self and personal history. Paradoxically, however, it also gives us a sense of belonging—of being one with others like ourselves—that helps to overcome some of the isolation of modern life.

But these psychological meanings have developed renewed force in recent years because of two significant sociopolitical events. The first was the civil rights movement with its call for racial equality. The second was the change in the immigration laws, which, for the first time in nearly half a century, allowed masses of immigrants to enter the country.

It was easy for northern whites to support the early demands of the civil rights movement when blacks were asking for the desegregation of buses and drinking fountains in the South. But supporting the black drive to end discrimination in jobs, housing, and education in the urban North was quite another matter—especially among those white ethnics whose hold on the ladder of mobility was tenuous at best and with whom blacks would be most likely to compete, whether in the job market, the neighborhood, or the classroom. As the courts and legislatures around the country began to honor some black claims for redress of past injustices, white hackles began to rise.

It wasn't black demands alone that fed the apprehensions of whites, however. In the background of the black civil rights drive, there stood a growing chorus of voices, as other racial groups—Asian Americans, Latinos, and Native Americans—joined the public fray to seek remedy for their own grievances. At the same time that these home-grown groups were making their voices heard and, not incidentally, affirming their distinctive cultural heritages and calling for public acknowledgment of them, the second great wave of immigration in this century washed across our shores.

After having closed the gates to mass immigration with the National Origins Act of 1924, Congress opened them again when it passed the Immigration Act of 1965.[9] This act, which was a series of amendments to the McCarran-Walter Act of 1952, essentially jettisoned the national origins provisions of earlier law and substituted overall hemisphere caps. The bill, according to immigration historian Roger Daniels, "changed the whole course of American immigration history" and left the door open for a vast increase in the numbers of immigrants.[10]

More striking than the increase in numbers has been the character of the new immigrants. Instead of the large numbers of western Europeans whom the sponsors had expected to take advantage of the new policy, it has been the people of Asia, Latin America, and the Caribbean who rushed to the boats. "It is doubtful if any drafter or supporter of the 1965 act envisaged this result," writes Daniels.[11] In fact, when members of Lyndon Johnson's administration, under whose tenure the bill became law, testified before Congress, they assured the legislators and the nation that few Asians would come in under the new law.[12]

This is a fascinating example of the unintended consequences of a political act. The change in the law was sponsored by northern Democrats who sought to appeal to their white ethnic constituencies by opening the gates to their countrymen once again—that is, to the people of eastern and southern Europe whom the 1924 law had kept out for nearly half a century. But those same white ethnics punished the Democratic Party by defecting to the Republicans during the Reagan-Bush years, a defection that was at least partly related to their anger about the new immigrants and the changing social balance of urban America.

During the decade of the 1980s, 2.5 million immigrants from Asian countries were admitted to the United States, an increase of more than 450 percent over the years between 1961 and 1970, when the number was slightly less than half a million. In 1990 alone, nearly as many Asian immigrants—one-third of a million—entered the country as came during the entire decade of the 1960s. Other groups show similarly noteworthy increases. Close to three-quarters of a million documented Mexicans crossed the border in the single year of 1990, compared to less than half a million during all of the 1960s. Central American immigration, too, climbed from just under one hundred thousand between 1961 and 1970 to more than triple that number during the 1980s. And immigrants from the Caribbean, who numbered a little more than half a million during the 1960s, increased to over three-quarters of a million in the years between 1981 and 1989.[13]

Despite these large increases and the perception that we are awash with new immigrants, it's worth noting that they are a much smaller proportion of the total population today, 6.2 percent, than they were in 1920, when they were a hefty 13.2 percent of all U.S. residents.[14] But the fact that most immigrants today are people of color gives them greater visibility than ever before.

Suddenly, the nation's urban landscape has been colored in ways unknown before. In 1970, the California cities that were the site of the original research for *Worlds of Pain* were almost exclusively white. Twenty years later, the 1990 census reports that their minority populations range from 54 to 69 percent. In the nation at large, the same census shows nearly one in four Americans with African, Asian, Latino, or Native American ancestry, up from one in five in 1980.[15] So dramatic is this shift that whites of European descent now make up just over two-thirds of the population in New York State, while in California they number only 57 percent. In cities like New York, San Francisco, and Los Angeles whites are a minority—accounting for 38, 47, and 37 percent of residents, respectively. Twenty years ago the white population in all these cities was over 75 percent.[16]

The increased visibility of other racial groups has focused whites more self-consciously than ever on their own racial identification. Until the new immigration shifted the complexion of the land so perceptibly, whites didn't think of themselves as white in the same way that Chinese know they're Chinese and African Americans know they're black. Being white was simply a fact of life, one that didn't require any public statement, since it was the definitive social value against which all others were measured. "It's like everything's changed and I don't know what happened," complains Marianne Bardolino. "All of a sudden you have to be thinking all the time about these race things. I don't remember growing up thinking about being white like I think about it now. I'm not saying I didn't know there was coloreds and whites; it's just that I didn't go along thinking, *Gee, I'm a white person.* I never thought about it at all. But now with all the different colored people around, you have to think about it because they're thinking about it all the time."

"You say you feel pushed now to think about being white, but I'm not sure I understand why. What's changed?" I ask.

"I told you," she replies quickly, a small smile covering her impatience with my question. "It's because they think about what they are, and they want things their way, so now I have to think about what I am and what's good for me and my kids." She pauses briefly to let her thoughts catch up with her tongue, then continues. "I mean, if somebody's always yelling at you about being black or Asian or something, then it makes you think about being white. Like, they want the kids in school to learn about their culture, so then I think about being white and being Italian and say: What about my culture? If they're going to teach about theirs, what about mine?"

To which America's racial minorities respond with bewilderment. "I don't understand what white people want," says Gwen Tomalson. "They say if black kids are going to learn about black culture in school, then white people want their kids to learn about white culture. I don't get it. What do they think kids have been learning about all these years? It's all about white people and how they live and what they accomplished. When I was in school you wouldn't have thought black people existed for all our books ever said about us."

As for the charge that they're "thinking about race all the time," as Marianne Bardolino complains, people of color insist that they're forced into it by a white world that never lets them forget. "If you're Chinese, you can't forget it, even if you want to, because there's always something that reminds you," Carol Kwan's husband, Andrew, remarks tartly. "I mean, if Chinese kids get good grades and get into the university, everybody's worried and you read about it in the papers."

While there's little doubt that racial anxieties are at the center of white concerns, our historic nativism also plays a part in escalating white alarm. The new immigrants bring with them a language and an ethnic culture that's vividly expressed wherever they congregate. And it's this also, the constant reminder of an alien presence from which whites are excluded, that's so troublesome to them.

The nativist impulse isn't, of course, given to the white working class alone. But for those in the upper reaches of the class and status hierarchy—those whose children go to private schools, whose closest contact with public transportation is the taxicab—the immigrant population supplies a source of cheap labor, whether as nannies for their children, maids in their households, or workers in their businesses. They may grouse and complain that "nobody speaks English anymore," just as working-class people do. But for the people who use immigrant labor, legal or illegal, there's a payoff for the inconvenience—a payoff that doesn't exist for the families in this study but that sometimes costs them dearly.[17] For while it may be true that American workers aren't eager for many of the jobs immigrants are willing to take, it's also true that the presence of a large immigrant population—especially those who come from developing countries where living standards are far below our own—helps to make these jobs undesirable by keeping wages depressed well below what most American workers are willing to accept.[18]

Indeed, the economic basis of our immigration policies too often gets lost in the lore that we are a land that says to the world, "Give me your tired, your poor, your huddled masses, yearning to breathe free."[19] I don't mean to suggest that our humane impulses are a fiction, only that the reality is far more complex than Emma Lazarus' poem suggests. The massive immigration of the nineteenth and early twentieth centuries didn't just happen spontaneously. America may have been known as the land of opportunity to the Europeans who dreamed of coming here—a country where, as my parents, once believed, the streets were lined with gold. But they believed these things because that's how America was sold by the agents who spread out across the face of Europe to recruit workers—men and women who were needed to keep the machines of our developing industrial society running and who, at the same time, gave the new industries a steady supply of hungry workers willing to work for wages far below those of native-born Americans.

The enormous number of immigrants who arrived during that period accomplished both those ends. In doing so, they set the stage for a long history of antipathy to foreign workers. For today, also, one function of the new immigrants is to keep our industries competitive in a global economy. Which simply is another way of saying that they serve to depress the wages of native American workers.

It's not surprising, therefore, that working-class women and men speak so angrily about the recent influx of immigrants. They not only see their jobs and their way of life threatened, they feel bruised and assaulted by an environment that seems suddenly to have turned color and in which they feel like strangers in their own land. So they chafe and complain: "They come here to take advantage of us, but they don't really want to learn our ways," Beverly Sowell, a 33-year-old white electronics assembler, grumbles irritably. "They live different than us; it's like another world how they live. And they're so clannish. They keep to themselves, and they don't even *try* to learn English. You go on the bus these days and you might as well be in a foreign country; everybody's talking some other language, you know, Chinese or Spanish or something. Lots of them have been here a long time, too, but they don't care; they just want to take what they can get."

But their complaints reveal an interesting paradox, an illuminating glimpse into the contradictions that beset native-born Americans in their relations with those who seek refuge here. On the one hand, they scorn the immigrants; on the other, they protest because they "keep to themselves." It's the same contradiction that dominates black–white relations. Whites refuse to integrate with blacks but are outraged when they stop knocking at the door, when they move to sustain the separation on their own terms—in black theme houses on campuses, for example, or in the newly developed black middle-class suburbs.

I wondered, as I listened to Beverly Sowell and others like her, why the same people who find the lifeways and languages of our foreign-born population offensive also care whether they "keep to themselves."

"Because like I said, they just shouldn't, that's all," Beverly says stubbornly. "If they're going to come here, they should be willing to learn our ways—you know what I mean, be real Americans. That's what my grandparents did, and that's what they should do."

"But your grandparents probably lived in an immigrant neighborhood when they first came here, too," I remind her.

"It was different," she insists. "I don't know why; it was. They wanted to be Americans; these here people now, I don't think they do. They just want to take advantage of this country."

She stops, thinks for a moment, then continues, "Right now it's awful in this country. Their kids come into the schools, and it's a big mess. There's not enough money for our kids to get a decent education, and we have to spend money to teach their kids English. It makes me mad. I went to public school, but I have to send my kids to Catholic school because now on top of the black kids, there's all these foreign kids who don't speak English. What kind of an education can kids get in a school like that? Something's wrong when plain old American kids can't go to their own schools.

"Everything's changed, and it doesn't make sense. Maybe you get it, but I don't. We can't take care of our own people and we keep bringing more and more foreigners in. Look at all the homeless. Why do we need more people here when our own people haven't got a place to sleep?"

"Why do we need more people here?"—a question Americans have asked for two centuries now. Historically, efforts to curb immigration have come during economic downturns, which suggests that when times are good, when American workers feel confident about their future, they're likely to be more generous in sharing their good fortune with foreigners. But when the economy falters, as it did in the 1990s, and workers worry about having to compete for jobs with people whose standard of living is well below their own, resistance to immigration rises. "Don't get me wrong; I've got nothing against these people," Tim Walsh demurs. "But they don't talk English, and they're used to a lot less, so they can work for less money than guys like me can. I see it all the time; they get hired and some white guy gets left out."

It's this confluence of forces—the racial and cultural diversity of our new immigrant population; the claims on the resources of the nation now being made by those minorities who, for generations, have called America their home; the failure of some of our basic institutions to serve the needs of our people; the contracting economy, which threatens the mobility aspirations of working-class families—all these have come together to leave white workers feeling as if everyone else is getting a piece of the action while they get nothing. "I feel like white people are left out in the cold," protests Diane Johnson, a 28-year-old white single mother who believes she lost a job as a bus driver to a black woman. "First it's the blacks; now it's all those other colored people, and it's like everything always goes their way. It seems like a white person doesn't have a chance anymore. It's like the squeaky wheel gets the grease, and they've been squeaking and we haven't," she concludes angrily.

Until recently, whites didn't need to think about having to "squeak"— at least not specifically as whites. They have, of course, organized and squeaked at various times in the past—sometimes as ethnic groups, sometimes as workers. But not as whites. As whites they have been the dominant group, the favored ones, the ones who could count on getting the job when people of color could not. Now suddenly there are others—not just individual others but identifiable groups, people who share a history, a language, a culture, even a color—who lay claim to some of the rights and privileges that formerly had been labeled "for whites only." And whites react as if they've been betrayed, as if a sacred promise has been broken. They're white, aren't they? They're *real* Americans, aren't they? This is their country, isn't it?

Notes

1. David R. Roediger, *The Wages of Whiteness* (New York: Verso, 1991), 133.

2. I'm aware that many Americans who have none of the characteristic features associated with their African heritage are still defined as black. This is one reason why I characterize race as an idea, not a fact. Nevertheless, the main point I am making here still holds—that is, the visible racial character of a people makes a difference in whether white Americans see them as assimilable or not.

3. *New York Times,* 30 April 1993.

4. For an excellent historical portrayal of the formation of ethnic communities among the east central European immigrants in Pennsylvania, the development of ethnic identity, and the process of Americanization, see Ewa Morawska, For *Bread with Butter* (New York: Cambridge University Press, 1985).

5. Ibid.

6. Alejandro Portes and Ruben G. Rumbaut, *Immigrant America* (Berkeley: University of California Press, 1990).

7. One need only walk the streets of New York to see the concentration of Koreans in the corner markets and the nail care salons that dot the city's landscape.
    In San Francisco the Cambodians now own most of the donut shops in the city. It all started when, after working in such a shop, an enterprising young Cambodian combined the family resources and opened his own store and bakery. He now has 20 shops and has been instrumental in helping his countrymen open more, all of them buying their donuts from his bakery.

8. Herbert Gans, "Symbolic Ethnicity: The Future of Ethnic Groups and Cultures in America," *Ethnic and Racial Studies* 2 (1979):1–18.

9. Despite nativist protests, immigration had proceeded unchecked by government regulation until the end of the nineteenth century. The first serious attempt to restrict immigration came in 1882 when, responding to the clamor about the growing immigration of Chinese laborers to California and other western states, Congress passed the Chinese Exclusion Act. But European immigration remained unimpeded. In the years between 1880 and 1924, twenty-four million newcomers arrived on these shores, most of them eastern and southern Europeans, all bringing their own language and culture, and all the target of pervasive bigotry and exploitation by native-born Americans. By the early part of the twentieth century, anti-immigration sentiments grew strong enough to gain congressional attention once again. The result was the National Origins Act of 1924, which established the quota system that sharply limited immigration, especially from the countries of southern and eastern Europe.

10. Roger Daniels, *Coming to America: A History of Immigration and Ethnicity in American Life* (New York HarperCollins, 1990), 338–44.

11. Daniels, *Coming to America,* 341, writes further, "In his Liberty Island speech Lyndon Johnson stressed the fact that he was redressing the wrong

done [by the McCarran-Walter Act] to those 'from southern or eastern Europe,' and although he did mention 'developing continents,' there was no other reference to Asian or Third World immigration."

12. For a further review of the Immigration Act of 1965, see chapter 13 (pp. 328–49) of *Coming to America*.

13. *Statistical Abstract,* U.S. Bureau of the Census (1992), Table 8, p. 11.

14. Ibid, Table 45, p. 42.

15. Ibid., Table 18, p. 18, and Table 26, p. 24.

16. U.S. Bureau of the Census, *Population Reports,* 1970 and 1990. Cited in Mike Davis, "The Body Count," *Crossroads* (June 1993). The difference in the racial composition of New York and San Francisco explains, at least in part, why black–white tensions are so much higher in New York City than they are in San Francisco. In New York, 38 percent of the population is now white, 30 percent black, 25 percent Hispanic, and 7 percent Asian. In San Francisco, whites make up 47 percent of the residents, blacks 11 percent, Hispanics 14 percent, and Asians 29 percent. Thus, blacks in New York reflect the kind of critical mass that generally sparks racial prejudices, fears, and conflicts. True, San Francisco's Asian population—three in ten of the city's residents—also form that kind of critical and noticeable mass. But whatever the American prejudice against Asians, and however much it has been acted out in the past, Asians do not stir the same kind of fear and hatred in white hearts as do blacks.

17. Zoë Baird, the first woman ever to be nominated to be attorney general of the United States, was forced to withdraw when it became known that she and her husband had hired an illegal immigrant as a nanny for their three-year-old child. The public indignation that followed the revelation came largely from people who were furious that, in a time of high unemployment, American workers were bypassed in favor of cheaper foreign labor.

18. This is now beginning to happen in more skilled jobs as well. In California's Silicon Valley, for example, software programmers and others are being displaced by Indian workers, people who are trained in India and recruited to work here because they are willing to do so for lower wages than similarly skilled Americans (*San Francisco Examiner,* 14 February 1993).

19. From Emma Lazarus' "The New Colossus," inscribed at the base of the Statue of Liberty in New York's harbor, the gateway through which most of the immigrants from Europe passed as they came in search of a new life.

Ellis Cose

NO

What's White, Anyway?

In Argentina, where he was born, my acquaintance had always been on solid taxonomic ground. His race was no more a mystery than the color of the clouds. It was a fact, presumably rooted in biology, that he was as white as a man could be. But his move to the United States had left him confused. So he turned to me and sheepishly asked in Spanish, "Am I white or am I Latino?"

Given his fair complexion and overall appearance, most Americans would deem him white, I replied—that is, until he opened his mouth, at which point his inability to converse in English would become his most salient feature. He would still be considered white, I explained, but his primary identity would be as a Latino. For his U.S.-raised children, the relevant order will likely be reversed: in most circles they will simply be white Americans, albeit of Argentine ancestry, unless they decide to be Latino. At any rate, I pointed out, the categories are not exclusive—although in the United States we often act as if they are.

He said he understood, though something in his manner told me he was more confused than ever. Playing the game of racial classification has a way of doing that to you. For though the question—*who is white?*—is as old as America itself, the answer has often changed. And it is shifting yet again, even as the advantages of whiteness have become murkier than ever.

In the beginning, the benefits were obvious. American identity itself was inextricably wrapped up in the mythology of race. The nation's first naturalization act (passed during the second session of the first Congress in March 1790) reserved the privilege of naturalization for "aliens being free white persons." Only after the Civil War were blacks allowed to present themselves for citizenship, and even then other suspect racial groups were not so favored. Thus, well into the 20th century persons of various ethnicities and hues sued for the purpose of proving themselves white.

In 1922 the case of a Japanese national who had lived in America for two decades made its way to the Supreme Court. Takao Ozawa argued that the United States, in annexing Hawaii, had embraced people even darker than the Japanese—implicitly recognizing them as white. He also made the rather novel, if bizarre, claim that the dominant strain of Japanese were "white persons" of Caucasian root stock who spoke an "Aryan tongue." The high court disagreed. Nonetheless, the following year a high-caste Hindu,

Bhagat Singh Thind, asked the same court to accept him as a white Aryan. In rejecting his claim Justice George Sutherland, writing for the court, declared: "It may be true that the blond Scandinavian and the brown Hindu have a common ancestor in the dim reaches of antiquity, but the average man knows perfectly well that there are unmistakable and profound differences between them today." While the children of Europeans quickly became indistinguishable from other Americans, "it cannot be doubted that the children born in this country of Hindu parents would retain indefinitely the clear evidence of their ancestry," concluded Sutherland.

The McCarran-Walter Act, passed in 1952, finally eliminated racial restrictions on citizenship. No longer were East Indians, Arabs and assorted other non-Europeans forced, in a figurative sense, to paint themselves white in order to become Americans.

Today such an exercise seems weird beyond words. But it's worth recalling that even Europeans were not exempt from establishing their racial bona fides. The great immigration debates of the first part of the 20th century were driven in large measure by panic at the prospect of American's gene pool becoming hopelessly polluted with the blood of inferior European tribes. Many of the leading scientists and politicians of the day worried that immigrants from Eastern and Southern Europe—people considered intellectually, morally and physically inferior—would debase America's exalted Anglo-Saxon-Germanic stock. Such thinking was influenced, among other things, by the rise of eugenics. "The Races of Europe," a book published in 1899 by sociologist William Z. Ripley, was a typical text. Ripley classified Europeans into three distinct races: blond, blue-eyed Teutonics (who were at the highest stage of development); stocky, chestnut-haired Alpines, and dark, slender Mediterraneans. No less a personage than Stanford University president David Starr Jordan bought into the scheme, along with some of the leading lights of Congress. And though "undesirable" European races were never flatly prohibited from eligibility for citizenship, American immigration laws were crafted to favor those presumed to be of finer racial stock. While all whites might be deemed superior to those who were black, yellow or brown, all white "races" were not considered equal to each other.

Gradually America learned to set aside many of its racial preconceptions. Indeed, much of American history has been a process of embracing previously reviled or excluded groups. At one time or another, various clans of Europeans—Poles, Italians, Jews, Romanians—were deemed genetically suspect; but they were subsequently welcomed. They were all, in essence, made white. The question today is whether that process will extend to those whose ancestors, for the most part, were not European.

To some extent it certainly will. That reality struck me some years ago when, in a moment of unguarded conversation, a radio host observed that "white Asians" were in demand for certain jobs. Initially I had no idea what the man was talking about, but as he rattled on I realized he was saying that he considered some Asian-Americans (those with a lighter complexion) to be, for all intents and purposes, as white as himself. In his mind at least, the definition of whiteness has expanded well beyond its old parameters. And I suspect he is far from alone. This is not to say that Takao Ozawa would be better able today than in 1922 to convince a court that he is Aryan; but he almost certainly could persuade most Americans to treat him like a white person, which essentially amounts to the same thing. America's cult of whiteness, after all, was never just about skin color, hair texture and other physical traits. It was about where the line was drawn between those who could be admitted into the mainstream and those who could not.

Those boundaries clearly are no longer where they once were. And even as the boundaries of whiteness have expanded, the specialness of whiteness has eroded. Being white, in other words, is no longer quite what it used to be. So if Ozawa and his progeny have not exactly become white, they are no longer mired in America's racial wasteland. Indeed, even many Americans with the option of being white—those with, say, one Mexican parent or a Cherokee grandfather—are more than ever inclined to think of themselves as something else. And those for whom whiteness will likely never be an option (most blacks and many darker Hispanics, for instance) are freer to enjoy being whatever they are.

Society, in short, has progressed much since the days when Eastern Europeans felt it necessary to Anglicize their names, when Arabs and East Indians went to court to declare themselves white and when the leading scientists of the day had nothing better to do than to link morality and intelligence to preconceived notions of race. But having finally thrust aside 19th-century racial pseudo-science, we have not yet fully digested the science of the 21st, which has come to understand what enlightened souls sensed all along: that the differences that divided one race from another add up to a drop in the genetic ocean.

Recognizing the truth of that insight is only part of society's challenge. The largest part is figuring out what to do with it, figuring out how, having so long given racial categories an importance they never merited, we reduce them to the irrelevance they deserve—figuring out how, in short, to make real the abstraction called equality we profess to have believed in all along.

POSTSCRIPT

Does White Identity Define America?

The racial and ethnic diversity of the United States in 2004 is obvious to anyone. Large metropolitan areas such as Los Angeles and New York, along with hundreds of other cities and suburbs, are becoming increasingly diverse. The diversity is marked by demographic changes in both race and ethnic groups. The most recent wave of immigrants from Latin America and Asia have added to the multicultural character of American identity. What has it added? How will the new groups reflect on their racial identity? How will these additions change our notion of minority groups?

Controversy is not new to immigration history. Nineteenth century reactions to "new" immigrants gave rise to nativism that opposed Roman Catholic and Chinese immigrants. The sentiment eventually produced a social and political reaction that led to the National Origins System, a highly restrictionist immigration policy directed at the growing immigration from southern Europe. The dominance of a white, Anglo-Saxon, Protestant culture asserted itself. Other European groups would be accommodated but in limited numbers so as to protect the majority culture rooted in Northern and Western European background.

Similarly today, Asian and Latin American immigration raises the question of American identity. With this contemporary immigration pattern, does race emerge as a major factor? Should the paradigm for looking at race relations extend beyond the black-white and include ethnicity? With all the issues surrounding nineteenth and early twentieth century immigration and its impact on a common American identity, race was never an issue. European immigrants and their descendants assimilated to the dominant group, and in the process, distanced themselves from the non-whites such as the Native Americans and African-Americans.

Just as certain segments of the population reacted to "new" immigrants in the two centuries past, today the reaction continues. Whiteness enables them to assimilate. The question of white identity (as American identity) is reflected in the shifting percentages of majority-minority groups. Once again the phrase, "They are not like us," manifests itself to distinguish resident groups from new immigrants.

A history of non-Anglo groups in the United States is found in *A Different Mirror: A History of Multicultural America* by Ronald Takaki (Little, Brown & Co., 1993).

On the Internet . . .

Southern Poverty Law Center

This is the Web site of the Southern Poverty Law Center. It offers educational and community programs to teachers and others interested in dismantling bigotry. Further, it contains a current events news section and advice on how to deal with hate in the schools. Also available are an e-newsletter and an online version of the magazine, *Teaching Tolerance,* which is published twice each year.

www.teachingtolerance.org

NAACP

This Web site offers information, news, and trends dealing with African Americans. The 50th year commemoration of the 1954 decision, *Brown v. Board of Education,* is explored in detail on the site. The official NAACP publication, *The Crisis,* is available, as are past issues through the site's archives section. Additional information revolving around race relations is presented daily, including a Congressional Report.

www.naacp.org

Museum of Racist Memorabilia

This is the Web site for the Jim Crow Museum of Racist Memorabilia located in Michigan. It contains information and illustrations on popular cultural racist memorabilia. The site promotes the scholarly examination of historical and contemporary expressions of racism. The virtual tour reveals several caricatures and an informative essay on racist images.

http://www.ferris.edu/news/jimcrow/menu.html

MIT: Asian American Resources

The Massachusetts Institute of Technology (MIT) offers this site for Asian American resources. It lists links to Asian American organizations, activities, media, and art resources. Students researching Asian American life in the United States will be able to connect to sites that are mostly sponsored by colleges and universities.

http://www.ai.mit.edu/people/irie/aar

Latin American Network Information Center: University of Texas

The Latin American Network Information Center sponsors this Web site. It seeks to facilitate access to Internet-based information to, from, or on Latin America. It provides information about Latin America for students, teachers, and researchers, and potential research links to hundreds of sites on Hispanics in the United States.

http://www1.lanic.utexas.edu/

PART 2

Race, Prejudice, and Racial Minorities

W.E.B. DuBois, the distinguished African American scholar and social activist, reminded us that the color line would be the primary challenge to the American nation of the twentieth century. Issues of race have challenged the nation from the Colonial Era to the present. Traditionally, race developed as a biological concept. The criteria that were established to place human beings within distinct racial categories were biological in nature and included such features as skin color, prognathism, and cranial configuration, among others. As a result of research and scientific discovery, including the human genome project that is currently underway, the biological basis of racial categories has been destroyed. Yet, race has been retained as a social construction that provides a basis for distinguishing and treating human groups other than one's own. A proper understanding of the evolution of "race" within society is important for developing one's understanding of race in today's America.

- Is Skin Color a Proper Determinant of Racial Identity?

- Is Race Prejudice a Product of Group Position?

- Are Definitions of Race Political?

- Do Minorities Engage in Self-Segregation?

- Are Asian Americans a Model Minority?

- Are Hispanics Making Economic Progress?

ISSUE 5

Is Skin Color a Proper Determinant of Racial Identity?

YES: Howard Zinn, "Drawing the Color Line" from *A people's History of the United States* (HarperCollins, 1980)

NO: Marvin Harris, "How Our Skins Got Their Color" from *Our Kind: Who We Are. Where We Came From and Where We Are Going* (HarperCollins, 1989)

ISSUE SUMMARY

YES: Howard Zinn, eminent historian, asserts that the black skin of the earliest African American was employed by whites to differentiate and establish them as members of a separate, distinct, and inferior race.

NO: Marvin Harris, a leading anthropologist, views skin color as a biological phenomenon, and thus he explains differences in skin color as a biological adaptation of humans for dealing with the potentially harmful solar radiation that we face.

T he formation of racial consciousness and its impact upon society is a vital area of scholarly investigation in a world characterized by nations of increasing racial/ethnic diversity. America is a nation in which color-consciousness was employed to separate whites from African Americans and members of other races within the evolving institutional frameworks of slavery and segregation that prevailed throughout the nation's history.

A critical question involved in a scholarly analysis of racial formations is the following: Is skin color an adequate criterion for separating human beings into distinct racial categories?

Howard Zinn, a noted American historian, argues in favor of such a proposition. In his article, he presents evidence to support a claim that the color line between blacks and whites was drawn almost as soon as the first group of twenty Africans arrived on these shores. From the beginning, Zinn believes it was likely that these African slaves were viewed as different and inferior to white servants and were treated accordingly. So according to Zinn, the color line within the American experience was established in the 1600s.

As the colonial economies developed and grew, the need for a stable and secure labor force became transparent. Attempts to subjugate the Native Americans into forced labor or slavery were largely futile, and there was simply insufficient white servants to supply the need. As Zinn points out, African slavery, a racial institution in which membership is defined by one's color, was the answer to this American dilemma. Zinn argues that despite negative cultural preconditioning and socialization concerning racial differences within the American experience, white elites have developed color-coded laws and policies in order to maintain the color line of emergent American apartheid.

Marvin Harris, in contrast, emphasizes the biological and cultural influences upon the development of skin color and its emphasis and significance within society. Harris views skin color as a visible and inherited human characteristic whose biogenic origin reflects the need to protect human populations from potentially destructive solar radiation and nothing more. He assumes that today's black and white peoples shared common brown-skinned ancestors who lived during the early Neolithic Period—a view consistent with the claim that our ancestors emerged on the savannahs of Africa and through on-going processes of migration and diffusion of human populations spread throughout the earth.

As humans settled in the various latitudes of the planet, their skins had to adapt to different threats from the potentially damaging ultraviolet radiation of the sun. According to Harris, skin color is a biological adaptation designed to protect our bodies from the destructive rays of sunlight by altering the amount of melanin a person contains in their skins. Melanin is the chemical particle that provides human skin with protection from the potentially damaging effects of ultraviolet rays. The greater the melanin content, the darker is one's skin, and it is the dark skin of the peoples of the earth's equatorial zone that provides the greatest protection from dangerous solar radiation. Conversely, the people of the more northerly latitudes have less melanin content within their skins due to the lesser threats which they face from the sun's ultraviolet rays, and thus their skins are distinctly lighter in complexion than the peoples of our planet's equatorial regions. It is Harris' contention that the colors of humans' skins are due to a combination of the influences of natural selection and cultural selection.

Drawing the Color Line

A black American writer, J. Saunders Redding, describes the arrival of a ship in North America in the year 1619:

> Sails furled, flag drooping at her rounded stern, she rode the tide in from the sea. She was a strange ship, indeed, by all accounts, a frightening ship, a ship of mystery. Whether she was trader, privateer, or man-of-war no one knows. Through her bulwarks black-mouthed cannon yawned. The flag she flew was Dutch; her crew a motley. Her port of call, an English settlement, Jamestown, in the colony of Virginia. She came, she traded, and shortly afterwards was gone. Probably no ship in modern history has carried a more portentous freight. Her cargo? Twenty slaves.

There is not a country in world history in which racism has been more important, for so long a time, as the United States. And the problem of "the color line," as W. E. B. Du Bois put it, is still with us. So it is more than a purely historical question to ask: How does it start?—and an even more urgent question: How might it end? Or, to put it differently: Is it possible for whites and blacks to live together without hatred?

If history can help answer these questions, then the beginnings of slavery in North America—a continent where we can trace the coming of the first whites and the first blacks—might supply at least a few clues.

Some historians think those first blacks in Virginia were considered as servants, like the white indentured servants brought from Europe. But the strong probability is that, even if they were listed as "servants" (a more familiar category to the English), they were viewed as being different from white servants, were treated differently, and in fact were slaves. In any case, slavery developed quickly into a regular institution, into the normal labor relation of blacks to whites in the New World. With it developed that special racial feeling—whether hatred, or contempt, or pity, or patronization—that accompanied the inferior position of blacks in America for the next 350 years—that combination of inferior status and derogatory thought we call racism.

Everything in the experience of the first white settlers acted as a pressure for the enslavement of blacks.

The Virginians of 1619 were desperate for labor, to grow enough food to stay alive. Among them were survivors from the winter of 1609–1610, the "starving time," when, crazed for want of food, they roamed the woods for nuts and berries, dug up graves to eat the corpses, and died in batches until five hundred colonists were reduced to sixty.

In the *Journals* of the House of Burgesses of Virginia is a document of 1619 which tells of the first twelve years of the Jamestown colony. The first settlement had a hundred persons, who had one small ladle of barley per meal. When more people arrived, there was even less food. Many of the people lived in cavelike holes dug into the ground, and in the winter of 1609–1610, they were

> ... driven thru insufferable hunger to eat those things which nature most abhorred, the flesh and excrements of man as well of our own nation as of an Indian, digged by some out of his grave after he had lain buried three days and wholly devoured him; others, envying the better state of body of any whom hunger has not yet so much wasted as their own, lay wait and threatened to kill and eat them; one among them slew his wife as she slept in his bosom, cut her in pieces, salted her and fed upon her till he had clean devoured all parts saving her head. ...

A petition by thirty colonists to the House of Burgesses, complaining against the twelve-year governorship of Sir Thomas Smith, said:

> In those 12 years of Sir Thomas Smith, his government, we aver that the colony for the most part remained in great want and misery under most severe and cruel laws. ... The allowance in those times for a man was only eight ounces of meale and half a pint of peas for a day ... mouldy, rotten, full of cobwebs and maggots, loathsome to man and not fit for beasts, which forced many to flee for relief to the savage enemy, who being taken again were put to sundry deaths as by hanging, shooting and breaking upon the wheel ... of whom one for stealing two or three pints of oatmeal had a bodkin thrust through his tongue and was tied with a chain to a tree until he starved. ...

The Virginians needed labor, to grow corn for subsistence, to grow tobacco for export. They had just figured out how to grow tobacco, and in 1617 they sent off the first cargo to England. Finding that, like all pleasurable drugs tainted with moral disapproval, it brought a high price, the planters, despite their high religious talk, were not going to ask questions about something so profitable.

They couldn't force Indians to work for them, as Columbus had done. They were outnumbered, and while, with superior firearms, they could massacre Indians, they would face massacre in return. They could not capture them and keep them enslaved; the Indians were tough, resourceful, defiant, and at home in these woods, as the transplanted Englishmen were not.

White servants had not yet been brought over in sufficient quantity. Besides, they did not come out of slavery, and did not have to do more than contract their labor for a few years to get their passage and a start in the New World. As for the free white settlers, many of them were skilled craftsmen, or even men of leisure back in England, who were so little inclined to work the land that John Smith, in those early years, had to declare a kind of martial law, organize them into work gangs, and force them into the fields for survival.

There may have been a kind of frustrated rage at their own ineptitude, at the Indian superiority at taking care of themselves, that made the Virginians especially ready to become the masters of slaves. Edmund Morgan imagines their mood as he writes in his book *American Slavery, American Freedom:*

> If you were a colonist, you knew that your technology was superior to the Indians'. You knew that you were civilized, and they were savages. . . . But your superior technology had proved insufficient to extract anything. The Indians, keeping to themselves, laughed at your superior methods and lived from the land more abundantly and with less labor than you did. . . . And when your own people started deserting in order to live with them, it was too much. . . . So you killed the Indians, tortured them, burned their villages, burned their cornfields. It proved your superiority, in spite of your failures. And you gave similar treatment to any of your own people who succumbed to their savage ways of life. But you still did not grow much corn. . . .

Black slaves were the answer. And it was natural to consider imported blacks as slaves, even if the institution of slavery would not be regularized and legalized for several decades. Because, by 1619, a million blacks had already been brought from Africa to South America and the Caribbean, to the Portuguese and Spanish colonies, to work as slaves. Fifty years before Columbus, the Portuguese took ten African blacks to Lisbon—this was the start of a regular trade in slaves. African blacks had been stamped as slave labor for a hundred years. So it would have been strange if those twenty blacks, forcibly transported to Jamestown, and sold as objects to settlers anxious for a steadfast source of labor, were considered as anything but slaves.

Their helplessness made enslavement easier. The Indians were on their own land. The whites were in their own European culture. The blacks had been torn from their land and culture, forced into a situation where the heritage of language, dress, custom, family relations, was bit by bit obliterated except for the remnants that blacks could hold on to by sheer, extraordinary persistence.

Was their culture inferior—and so subject to easy destruction? Inferior in military capability, yes—vulnerable to whites with guns and ships. But in no other way—except that cultures that are different are often taken as inferior, especially when such a judgment is practical and profitable. Even militarily, while the Westerners could secure forts on the African coast, they were unable to subdue the interior and had to come to terms with its chiefs.

The African civilization was as advanced in its own way as that of Europe. In certain ways, it was more admirable; but it also included cruelties, hierarchical privilege, and the readiness to sacrifice human lives for religion or profit. It was a civilization of 100 million people, using iron implements and skilled in farming. It had large urban centers and remarkable achievements in weaving, ceramics, sculpture.

European travelers in the sixteenth century were impressed with the African kingdoms of Timbuktu and Mali, already stable and organized at a time when European states were just beginning to develop into the modern nation. In 1563, Ramusio, secretary to the rulers in Venice, wrote to the Italian merchants: "Let them go and do business with the King of Timbuktu and Mali and there is no doubt that they will be well-received there with their ships and their goods and treated well, and granted the favours that they ask. . . ."

A Dutch report, around 1602, on the West African kingdom of Benin, said: "The Towne seemeth to be very great, when you enter it. You go into a great broad street, not paved, which seemeth to be seven or eight times broader than the Warmoes Street in Amsterdam. . . . The Houses in this Towne stand in good order, one close and even with the other, as the Houses in Holland stand."

The inhabitants of the Guinea Coast were described by one traveler around 1680 as "very civil and good-natured people, easy to be dealt with, condescending to what Europeans require of them in a civil way, and very ready to return double the presents we make them."

Africa had a kind of feudalism, like Europe based on agriculture, and with hierarchies of lords and vassals. But African feudalism did not come, as did Europe's, out of the slave societies of Greece and Rome, which had destroyed ancient tribal life. In Africa, tribal life was still powerful, and some of its better features—a communal spirit, more kindness in law and punishment—still existed. And because the lords did not have the weapons that European lords had, they could not command obedience as easily.

In his book *The African Slave Trade,* Basil Davidson contrasts law in the Congo in the early sixteenth century with law in Portugal and England. In those European countries, where the idea of private property was becoming powerful, theft was punished brutally. In England, even as late as 1740, a child could be hanged for stealing a rag of cotton. But in the Congo, communal life persisted, the idea of private property was a strange one, and thefts were punished with fines or various degrees of servitude. A Congolese leader, told of the Portuguese legal codes, asked a Portuguese once, teasingly: "What is the penalty in Portugal for anyone who puts his feet on the ground?"

Slavery existed in the African states, and it was sometimes used by Europeans to justify their own slave trade. But, as Davidson points out, the "slaves" of Africa were more like the serfs of Europe—in other words, like most of the population of Europe. It was a harsh servitude, but they had rights which slaves brought to America did not have, and they were "altogether different from the human cattle of the slave ships and the American plantations." In the Ashanti Kingdom of West Africa, one observer noted that "a slave might marry; own property; himself own a slave; swear an oath; be a competent witness and ultimately become heir to his master. . . . An Ashanti slave, nine cases out of ten, possibly became an adopted member of the family, and in time his descendants so merged and intermarried with the owner's kinsmen that only a few would know their origin."

One slave trader, John Newton (who later became an antislavery leader), wrote about the people of what is now Sierra Leone:

> The state of slavery, among these wild barbarous people, as we esteem them, is much milder than in our colonies. For as, on the one hand, they have no land in high cultivation, like our West India plantations, and therefore no call for that excessive, unintermitted labour, which exhausts our slaves: so, on the other hand, no man is permitted to draw blood even from a slave.

African slavery is hardly to be praised. But it was far different from plantation or mining slavery in the Americas, which was lifelong, morally crippling, destructive of family ties, without hope of any future. African slavery lacked two elements that made American slavery the most cruel form of slavery in history: the frenzy for limitless profit that comes from capitalistic agriculture; the reduction of the slave to less than human status by the use of racial hatred, with that relentless clarity based on color, where white was master, black was slave.

In fact, it was because they came from a settled culture, of tribal customs and family ties, of communal life and traditional ritual, that African blacks found themselves especially helpless when removed from this. They were captured in the interior (frequently by blacks caught up in the slave trade themselves), sold on the coast, then shoved into pens with blacks of other tribes, often speaking different languages.

The conditions of capture and sale were crushing affirmations to the black African of his helplessness in the face of superior force. The marches to the coast, sometimes for 1,000 miles, with people shackled around the neck, under whip and gun, were death marches, in which two of every five blacks died. On the coast, they were kept in cages until they were picked and sold. One John Barbot, at the end of the seventeenth century, described these cages on the Gold Coast:

> As the slaves come down to Fida from the inland country, they are put into a booth or prison . . . near the beach, and when the Europeans are to receive them, they are brought out onto a large plain, where the ship's surgeons examine every part of everyone of them, to the smallest member, men and women being stark naked. . . . Such as are allowed good and sound are set on one side . . . marked on the breast with a red-hot iron, imprinting the mark of the French, English, or Dutch

companies. . . . The branded slaves after this are returned to their former booths where they await shipment, sometimes 10–15 days. . . .

Then they were packed aboard the slave ships, in spaces not much bigger than coffins, chained together in the dark, wet slime of the ship's bottom, choking in the stench of their own excrement Documents of the time describe the conditions:

> The height, sometimes, between decks, was only eighteen inches; so that the unfortunate human beings could not turn around, or even on their sides, the elevation being less than the breadth of their shoulders; and here they are usually chained to the decks by the neck and legs. In such a place the sense of misery and suffocation is so great, that the Negroes . . . are driven to frenzy.

On one occasion, hearing a great noise from belowdecks where the blacks were chained together, the sailors opened the hatches and found the slaves in different stages of suffocation, many dead, some having killed others in desperate attempts to breathe. Slaves often jumped overboard to drown rather than continue their suffering. To one observer a slave-deck was "so covered with blood and mucus that it resembled a slaughter house."

Under these conditions, perhaps one of every three blacks transported overseas died, but the huge profits (often double the investment on one trip) made it worthwhile for the slave trader, and so the blacks were packed into the holds like fish.

First the Dutch, then the English, dominated the slave trade. (By 1795 Liverpool had more than a hundred ships carrying slaves and accounted for half of all the European slave trade.) Some Americans in New England entered the business, and in 1637 the first American slave ship, the *Desire*, sailed from Marblehead. Its holds were partitioned into racks, 2 feet by 6 feet, with leg irons and bars.

By 1800, 10 to 15 million blacks had been transported as slaves to the Americas, representing perhaps one-third of those originally seized in Africa. It is roughly estimated that Africa lost 50 million human beings to death and slavery in those centuries we call the beginnings of modern Western civilization, at the hands of slave traders and plantation owners in Western Europe and America, the countries deemed the most advanced in the world.

In the year 1610, a Catholic priest in the Americas named Father Sandoval wrote back to a church functionary in Europe to ask if the capture, transport, and enslavement of African blacks was legal by church doctrine. A letter dated March 12, 1610, from Brother Luis Brandaon to Father Sandoval gives the answer:

> Your Reverence writes me that you would like to know whether the Negroes who are sent to your parts have been legally captured. To this I reply that I think your Reverence should have no scruples on this

point, because this is a matter which has been questioned by the Board of Conscience in Lisbon, and all its members are learned and conscientious men. Nor did the bishops who were in Sao Thome, Cape Verde, and here in Loando—all learned and virtuous men—find fault with it. We have been here ourselves for forty years and there have been among us very learned Fathers . . . never did they consider the trade as illicit. Therefore we and the Fathers of Brazil buy these slaves for our service without any scruple. . . .

With all of this—the desperation of the Jamestown settlers for labor, the impossibility of using Indians and the difficulty of using whites, the availability of blacks offered in greater and greater numbers by profit-seeking dealers in human flesh, and with such blacks possible to control because they had just gone through an ordeal which if it did not kill them must have left them in a state of psychic and physical helplessness—is it any wonder that such blacks were ripe for enslavement?

And under these conditions, even if some blacks might have been considered servants, would blacks be treated the same as white servants?

The evidence, from the court records of colonial Virginia, shows that in 1630 a white man named Hugh Davis was ordered "to be soundly whipt . . . for abusing himself . . . by defiling his body in lying with a Negro." Ten years later, six servants and "a negro of Mr. Reynolds" started to run away. While the whites received lighter sentences, "Emanuel the Negro to receive thirty stripes and to be burnt in the cheek with the letter R, and to work in shackle one year or more as his master shall see cause."

Although slavery was not yet regularized or legalized in those first years, the lists of servants show blacks listed separately. A law passed in 1639 decreed that "all persons except Negroes" were to get arms and ammunition—probably to fight off Indians. When in 1640 three servants tried to run away, the two whites were punished with a lengthening of their service. But, as the court put it, "the third being a negro named John Punch shall serve his master or his assigns for the time of his natural life." Also in 1640, we have the case of a Negro woman servant who begot a child by Robert Sweat, a white man. The court ruled "that the said negro woman shall be whipt at the whipping post and the said Sweat shall tomorrow in the forenoon do public penance for his offense at James citychurch. . . ."

This unequal treatment, this developing combination of contempt and oppression, feeling and action, which we call "racism"—was this the result of a "natural" antipathy of white against black? The question is important, not just as a matter of historical accuracy, but because any emphasis on "natural" racism lightens the responsibility of the social system. If racism can't be shown to be natural, then it is the result of certain conditions, and we are impelled to eliminate those conditions.

We have no way of testing the behavior of whites and blacks toward one another under favorable conditions—with no history of subordination, no money incentive for exploitation and enslavement, no desperation for survival requiring forced labor. All the conditions for black and white in seventeenth-century America were the opposite of that, all powerfully directed toward antagonism and mistreatment. Under such conditions even the slightest display of humanity between the races might be considered evidence of a basic human drive toward community.

Sometimes it is noted that, even before 1600, when the slave trade had just begun, before Africans were stamped by it—literally and symbolically—the color black was distasteful. In England, before 1600, it meant, according to the Oxford English Dictionary: "Deeply stained with dirt; soiled, dirty, foul. Having dark or deadly purposes, malignant; pertaining to or involving death, deadly; baneful, disastrous, sinister. Foul, iniquitous, atrocious, horribly wicked. Indicating disgrace, censure, liability to punishment, etc." And Elizabethan poetry often used the color white in connection with beauty.

It may be that, in the absence of any other overriding factor, darkness and blackness, associated with night and unknown, would take on those meanings. But the presence of another human being is a powerful fact, and the conditions of that presence are crucial in determining whether an initial prejudice, against a mere color, divorced from humankind, is turned into brutality and hatred.

In spite of such preconceptions about blackness, in spite of special subordination of blacks in the Americas in the seventeenth century, there is evidence that where whites and blacks found themselves with common problems, common work, common enemy in their master, they behaved toward one another as equals. As one scholar of slavery, Kenneth Stampp, has put it, Negro and white servants of the seventeenth century were "remarkably unconcerned about the visible physical differences."

Black and white worked together, fraternized together. The very fact that laws had to be passed after a while to forbid such relations indicates the strength of that tendency. In 1661 a law was passed in Virginia that "in case any English servant shall run away in company of any Negroes" he would have to give special service for extra years to the master of the runaway Negro. In 1691, Virginia provided for the banishment of any "white man or woman being free who shall intermarry with a negro, mulatoo, or Indian man or woman bond or free."

There is an enormous difference between a feeling of racial strangeness, perhaps fear, and the mass enslavement of millions of black people that took place in the Americas. The transition from one to the other cannot be explained easily by "natural" tendencies. It is not hard to understand as the outcome of historical conditions.

Slavery grew as the plantation system grew. The reason is easily traceable to something other than natural racial repugnance: the number of arriving whites, whether free or indentured servants (under four to seven years contract), was not enough to meet the need of the plantations. By 1700, in Virginia, there were 6,000 slaves, one-twelfth of the population. By 1763, there were 170,000 slaves, about half the population.

Blacks were easier to enslave than whites or Indians. But they were still not easy to enslave. From the beginning, the imported black men and women resisted their enslavement. Ultimately their resistance was controlled, and slavery was established for 3 million blacks in the South. Still, under the most difficult conditions, under pain of mutilation and death, throughout their two hundred years of enslavement in North America, these Afro-Americans continued to rebel. Only occasionally was there an organized insurrection. More often they showed their refusal to submit by running away. Even more often, they engaged in sabotage, slowdowns, and subtle forms of resistance which asserted, if only to themselves and their brothers and sisters, their dignity as human beings.

The refusal began in Africa. One slave trader reported that Negroes were "so wilful and loth to leave their own country, that they have often leap'd out of the canoes, boat and ship into the sea, and kept under water till they were drowned."

When the very first black slaves were brought into Hispaniola in 1503, the Spanish governor of Hispaniola complained to the Spanish court that fugitive Negro slaves were teaching disobedience to the Indians. In the 1520s and 1530s, there were slave revolts in Hispaniola, Puerto Rico, Santa Marta, and what is now Panama. Shortly after those rebellions, the Spanish established a special police for chasing fugitive slaves.

A Virginia statute of 1669 referred to "the obstinacy of many of them," and in 1680 the Assembly took note of slave meetings "under the pretense of feasts and brawls" which they considered of "dangerous consequence." In 1687, in the colony's Northern Neck, a plot was discovered in which slaves planned to kill all the whites in the area and escape during a mass funeral.

Gerald Mullin, who studied slave resistance in eighteenth-century Virginia in his work *Flight and Rebellion,* reports:

> The available sources on slavery in 18th-century Virginia—plantation and county records, the newspaper advertisements for runaways—describe rebellious slaves and few others. The slaves described were lazy and thieving; they feigned illnesses, destroyed crops, stores, tools, and sometimes attacked or killed overseers. They operated blackmarkets in stolen goods. Runaways were defined as various types, they were truants (who usually returned voluntarily), "outlaws" . . . and slaves who were actually fugitives: men who visited relatives, went to town to pass as free, or tried to escape slavery completely, either by boarding ships and leaving the colony, or banding together in cooperative efforts to establish villages or hide-outs in the frontier. The commitment of another type of rebellious slave was total; these men became killers, arsonists, and insurrectionists.

Slaves recently from Africa, still holding on to the heritage of their communal society, would run away in groups and try to establish villages of runaways out in the wilderness, on the frontier. Slaves born in America, on the other hand, were more likely to run off alone, and, with the skills they had learned on the plantation, try to pass as free men.

In the colonial papers of England, a 1729 report from the lieutenant governor of Virginia to the British Board of Trade tells how "a number of

Negroes, about fifteen . . . formed a design to withdraw from their Master and to fix themselves in the fastnesses of the neighboring Mountains. They had found means to get into their possession some Arms and Ammunition, and they took along with them some Provisions, their Cloths, bedding and working Tools. . . . Tho' this attempt has happily been defeated, it ought nevertheless to awaken us into some effectual measures. . . ."

Slavery was immensely profitable to some masters. James Madison told a British visitor shortly after the American Revolution that he could make $257 on every Negro in a year, and spend only $12 or $13 on his keep. Another viewpoint was of slaveowner Landon Carter, writing about fifty years earlier, complaining that his slaves so neglected their work and were so uncooperative ("either cannot or will not work") that he began to wonder if keeping them was worthwhile.

Some historians have painted a picture—based on the infrequency of organized rebellions and the ability of the South to maintain slavery for two hundred years—of a slave population made submissive by their condition; with their African heritage destroyed, they were, as Stanley Elkins said, made into "Sambos," "a society of helpless dependents." Or as another historian, Ulrich Phillips, said, "by racial quality submissive." But looking at the totality of slave behavior, at the resistance of everyday life, from quiet noncooperation in work to running away, the picture becomes different.

In 1710, warning the Virginia Assembly, Governor Alexander Spotswood said:

> . . . freedom wears a cap which can without a tongue, call together all those who long to shake off the fetters of slavery and as such an Insurrection would surely be attended with most dreadful consequences so I think we cannot be too early in providing against it, both by putting our selves in a better posture of defence and by making a law to prevent the consultations of those Negroes.

Indeed, considering the harshness of punishment for running away, that so many blacks did run away must be a sign of a powerful rebelliousness. All through the 1700s, the Virginia slave code read:

> Whereas many times slaves run away and lie hid and lurking in swamps, woods, and other obscure places, killing hogs, and commiting other injuries to the inhabitants . . . if the slave does not immediately return, anyone whatsoever may kill or destroy such slaves by such ways and means as he . . . shall think fit. . . . If the slave is apprehended . . . it shall . . . be lawful for the county court, to order such punishment for the said slave, either by dismembering, or in any other way . . . as they in their discretion shall think fit, for the reclaiming any such incorrigible slave, and terrifying others from the like practices. . . .

Mullin found newspaper advertisements between 1736 and 1801 for 1,138 men runaways, and 141 women. One consistent reason for running away was to find members of one's family—showing that despite the attempts of the slave system to destroy family ties by not allowing marriages and by separating families, slaves would face death and mutilation to get together.

In Maryland, where slaves were about one-third of the population in 1750, slavery had been written into law since the 1660s, and statutes for controlling rebellious slaves were passed. There were cases where slave women killed their masters, sometimes by poisoning them, sometimes by burning tobacco houses and homes. Punishments ranged from whipping and branding to execution, but the trouble continued. In 1742, seven slaves were put to death for murdering their master.

Fear of slave revolt seems to have been a permanent fact of plantation life. William Byrd, a wealthy Virginia slaveowner, wrote in 1736:

> We have already at least 10,000 men of these descendants of Ham, fit to bear arms, and these numbers increase every day, as well by birth as by importation. And in case there should arise a man of desperate fortune, he might with more advantage than Cataline kindle a servile war . . . and tinge our rivers wide as they are with blood.

It was an intricate and powerful system of control that the slaveowners developed to maintain their labor supply and their way of life, a system both subtle and crude, involving every device that social orders employ for keeping power and wealth where it is. As Kenneth Stampp puts it:

> A wise master did not take seriously the belief that Negroes were natural-born slaves. He knew better. He knew that Negroes freshly imported from Africa had to be broken into bondage; that each succeeding generation had to be carefully trained. This was no easy task, for the bondsman rarely submitted willingly. Moreover, he rarely submitted completely. In most cases there was no end to the need for control—at least not until old age reduced the slave to a condition of helplessness.

The system was psychological and physical at the same time. The slaves were taught discipline, were impressed again and again with the idea of their own inferiority to "know their place," to see blackness as a sign of subordination, to be awed by the power of the master, to merge their interest with the master's, destroying their own individual needs. To accomplish this there was the discipline of hard labor, the breakup of the slave family, the lulling effects of religion (which sometimes led to "great mischief," as one slaveholder reported), the creation of disunity among slaves by separating them into field slaves and more privileged house slaves, and finally the power of law and the immediate power of the overseer to invoke whipping, burning, mutilation, and death. Dismemberment was provided for in the Virginia Code of 1705. Maryland passed a law in 1723 providing for cutting off the ears of blacks who struck whites, and that for certain serious crimes, slaves should be hanged and the body quartered and exposed.

Still, rebellions took place—not many, but enough to create constant fear among white planters. The first large-scale revolt in the North American colonies took place in New York in 1712. In New York, slaves were 10 percent of the population, the highest proportion in the northern states, where economic conditions usually did not require large numbers of field slaves. About twenty-five blacks and two Indians set fire to a building, then killed nine whites who came on the scene. They were captured by soldiers, put on trial, and twenty-one were executed. The governor's report to England said: "Some were burnt, others were hanged, one broke on the wheel, and one hung alive in chains in the town. . . ." One had been burned over a slow fire for eight to ten hours—all this to serve notice to other slaves.

A letter to London from South Carolina in 1720 reports:

> I am now to acquaint you that very lately we have had a very wicked and barbarous plot of the designe of the negroes rising with a designe to destroy all the white people in the country and then to take Charles Town in full body but it pleased God it was discovered and many of them taken prisoners and some burnt and some hang'd and some banish'd.

Around this time there were a number of fires in Boston and New Haven, suspected to be the work of Negro slaves. As a result, one Negro was executed in Boston, and the Boston Council ruled that any slaves who on their own gathered in groups of two or more were to be punished by whipping.

At Stono, South Carolina, in 1739, about twenty slaves rebelled, killed two warehouse guards, stole guns and gunpowder, and headed south, killing people in their way, and burning buildings. They were joined by others, until there were perhaps eighty slaves in all and, according to one account of the time, "they called out Liberty, marched on with Colours displayed, and two Drums beating." The militia found and attacked them. In the ensuing battle perhaps fifty slaves and twenty-five whites were killed before the uprising was crushed.

Herbert Aptheker, who did detailed research on slave resistance in North America for his book *American Negro Slave Revolts,* found about 250 instances where a minimum of ten slaves joined in a revolt or conspiracy.

From time to time, whites were involved in the slave resistance. As early as 1663, indentured white servants and black slaves in Gloucester County, Virginia, formed a conspiracy to rebel and gain their freedom. The plot was betrayed, and ended with executions. Mullin reports that the newspaper notices of runaways in Virginia often warned "ill-disposed" whites about harboring fugitives. Sometimes slaves and free men ran off together, or cooperated in crimes together. Sometimes, black male slaves ran off and joined white women. From time to time, white ship captains and watermen dealt with runaways, perhaps making the slave a part of the crew.

In New York in 1741, there were ten thousand whites in the city and two thousand black slaves. It had been a hard winter and the poor—slave and free—had suffered greatly. When mysterious fires broke out, blacks and whites were accused of conspiring together. Mass hysteria developed against the accused. After a trial full of lurid accusations by informers, and forced confessions, two white men and two white women were executed, eighteen slaves were hanged, and thirteen slaves were burned alive.

Only one fear was greater than the fear of black rebellion in the new American colonies. That was the fear that discontented whites would join black slaves to overthrow the existing order. In the early years of slavery, especially, before racism as a way of thinking was firmly ingrained, while white indentured servants were often treated as badly as black slaves, there was a possibility of cooperation. As Edmund Morgan sees it:

> There are hints that the two despised groups initially saw each other as sharing the same predicament. It was common, for example, for servants and slaves to run away together, steal hogs together, get drunk together. It was not uncommon for them to make love together. In Bacon's Rebellion, one of the last groups to surrender was a mixed band of eighty negroes and twenty English servants.

As Morgan says, masters, "initially at least, perceived slaves in much the same way they had always perceived servants . . . shiftless, irresponsible, unfaithful, ungrateful, dishonest. . . ." And "if freemen with disappointed hopes should make common cause with slaves of desperate hope, the results might be worse than anything Bacon had done."

And so, measures were taken. About the same time that slave codes, involving discipline and punishment, were passed by the Virginia Assembly,

> Virginia's ruling class, having proclaimed that all white men were superior to black, went on to offer their social (but white) inferiors a number of benefits previously denied them. In 1705 a law was passed requiring masters to provide white servants whose indenture time was up with ten bushels of corn, thirty shillings, and a gun, while women servants were to get 15 bushels of corn and forty shillings. Also, the newly freed servants were to get 50 acres of land.

Morgan concludes: "Once the small planter felt less exploited by taxation and began to prosper a little, he became less turbulent, less dangerous, more respectable. He could begin to see his big neighbor not as an extortionist but as a powerful protector of their common interests."

We see now a complex web of historical threads to ensnare blacks for slavery in America: the desperation of starving settlers, the special helplessness of the displaced African, the powerful incentive of profit for slave trader and planter, the temptation of superior status for poor whites, the elaborate controls against escape and rebellion, the legal and social punishment of black and white collaboration.

The point is that the elements of this web are historical, not "natural." This does not mean that they are easily disentangled, dismantled. It means only that there is a possibility for something else, under historical conditions not yet realized. And one of these conditions would be the elimination of that class exploitation which has made poor whites desperate for small gifts of status, and has prevented that unity of black and white necessary for joint rebellion and reconstruction.

Around 1700, the Virginia House of Burgesses declared:

> The Christian Servants in this country for the most part consists of the Worser Sort of the people of Europe. And since . . . such numbers of Irish and other Nations have been brought in of which a great many have been soldiers in the late warrs that according to our present Circumstances we can hardly governe them and if they were fitted with Armes and had the Opertunity of meeting together by Musters we have just reason to fears they may rise upon us.

It was a kind of class consciousness, a class fear. There were things happening in early Virginia, and in the other colonies, to warrant it.

References

Aptheker, Herbert, ed. 1974. *A Documentary History of the Negro People in the United States.* Secaucus, NJ: Citadel.

Boskin, Joseph. 1966. *Into Slavery: Radical Decisions in the Virginia Colony.* Philadelphia: Lippincott.

Catterall, Helen. 1937. *Judicial Cases Concerning American Slavery and the Negro.* 5 vols. Washington, DC: Negro University Press.

Davidson, Basil. 1961. *The African Slave Trade.* Boston: Little, Brown.

Donnan, Elizabeth, ed. 1965. *Documents Illustrative of the History of the Slave Trade to America.* 4 vols. New York: Octagon.

Elkins, Stanley. 1976. *Slavery: A Problem in American Institutional and Intellectual Life.* Chicago: University of Chicago Press.

Federal Writers Project. 1969. *The Negro in Virginia.* New York: Arno.

Franklin, John Hope. 1974. *From Slavery to Freedom: A History of American Negroes.* New York: Knopf.

Jordan, Winthrop. 1968. *White over Black: American Attitudes Toward the Negro, 1550–1812.* Chapel Hill: University of North Carolina Press.

Morgan, Edmund S. 1975. *American Slavery, American Freedom: The Ordeal of Colonial Virginia.* New York: Norton.

Mullin, Gerald. 1974. *Flight and Rebellion: Slave Resistance in Eighteenth-Century Virginia.* New York: Oxford University Press.

Mullin, Michael, ed. 1975. *American Negro Slavery: A Documentary History.* New York: Harper & Row.

Phillips, Ulrich B. 1966. *American Negro Slavery: A Survey of the Supply, Employment and Control of Negro Labor as Determined by the Plantation Regime.* Baton Rouge: Louisiana State University Press.

Redding, J. Saunders. 1973. *They Came in Chains.* Philadelphia: Lippincott.

Stampp, Kenneth M. 1956. *The Peculiar Institution.* New York: Knopf.

Tannenbaum, Frank. 1963. *Slave and Citizen: The Negro in the Americas.* New York: Random House.

How Our Skins Got Their Color

Most human beings are neither very fair nor very dark, but brown. The extremely fair skin of northern Europeans and their descendants, and the very black skins of central Africans and their descendants, are probably special adaptations. Brown-skinned ancestors may have been shared by modern-day blacks and whites as recently as 10,000 years ago.

Human skin owes its color to the presence of particles known as melanin. The primary function of melanin is to protect the upper levels of the skin from being damaged by the sun's ultraviolet rays. This radiation poses a critical problem for our kind because we lack the dense coat of hair that acts as a sunscreen for most mammals. . . . Hairlessness exposes us to two kinds of radiation hazards: ordinary sunburn, with its blisters, rashes, and risk of infection; and skin cancers, including malignant melanoma, one of the deadliest diseases known. Melanin is the body's first line of defense against these afflictions. The more melanin particles, the darker the skin, and the lower the risk of sunburn and all forms of skin cancer. This explains why the highest rates for skin cancer are found in sun-drenched lands such as Australia, where light-skinned people of European descent spend a good part of their lives outdoors wearing scanty attire. Very dark-skinned people such as heavily pigmented Africans of Zaire seldom get skin cancer, but when they do, they get it on depigmented parts of their bodies—palms and lips.

If exposure to solar radiation had nothing but harmful effects, natural selection would have favored inky black as the color for all human populations. But the sun's rays do not present an unmitigated threat. As it falls on the skin, sunshine converts a fatty substance in the epidermis into vitamin D. The blood carries vitamin D from the skin to the intestines (technically making it a hormone rather than a vitamin), where it plays a vital role in the absorption of calcium. In turn, calcium is vital for strong bones. Without it, people fall victim to the crippling diseases rickets and osteomalacia. In women, calcium deficiencies can result in a deformed birth canal, which makes childbirth lethal for both mother and fetus.

Vitamin D can be obtained from a few foods, primarily the oils and livers of marine fish. But inland populations must rely on the sun's rays and their own skins for the supply of this crucial substance. The particular color of a human population's skin, therefore, represents in large degree a trade-off between the hazards of too much versus too little solar radiation: acute sunburn and skin cancer on the one hand, and rickets and osteomalacia on the other. It is this trade-off that largely accounts for the preponderance of brown people in the world and for the general tendency for skin color to be darkest among equatorial populations and lightest among populations dwelling at higher latitudes.

At middle latitudes, the skin follows a strategy of changing colors with the seasons. Around the Mediterranean basin, for example, exposure to the summer sun brings high risk of cancer but low risk for rickets; the body produces more melanin and people grow darker (i.e., they get suntans). Winter reduces the risk of sunburn and cancer; the body produces less melanin, and the tan wears off.

The correlation between skin color and latitude is not perfect because other factors—such as the availability of foods containing vitamin D and calcium, regional cloud cover during the winter, amount of clothing worn, and cultural preferences—may work for or against the predicted relationship. Arctic-dwelling Eskimo, for example, are not as light-skinned as expected, but their habitat and economy afford them a diet that is exceptionally rich in both vitamin D and calcium.

Northern Europeans, obliged to wear heavy garments for protection against the long, cold, cloudy winters, were always at risk for rickets and osteomalacia from too little vitamin D and calcium. This risk increased sometime after 6000 B.C., when pioneer cattle herders who did not exploit marine resources began to appear in northern Europe. The risk would have been especially great for the brown-skinned Mediterranean peoples who migrated northward along with the crops and farm animals. Samples of Caucasian skin (infant penile foreskin obtained at the time of circumcision) exposed to sunlight on cloudless days in Boston (42°N) from November through February produced no vitamin D. In Edmonton (52°N) this period extended from October to March. But further south (34°N) sunlight was effective in producing vitamin D in the middle of the winter. Almost all of Europe lies north of 42°N. Fair-skinned, nontanning individuals who could utilize the weakest and briefest doses of sunlight to synthesize vitamin D were strongly favored by natural selection. During the frigid winters, only a small circle of a child's face could be left to peek out at the sun through the heavy clothing, thereby favoring the survival of individuals with translucent patches of pink on their cheeks characteristic of many northern Europeans. (People who could get calcium by drinking cow's milk would also be favored by natural selection.)

If light-skinned individuals on the average had only 2 percent more children survive per generation, the changeover in their skin color could have begun 5,000 years ago and reached present levels well before the beginning of the Christian era. But natural selection need not have acted alone. Cultural selection may also have played a role. It seems likely that whenever people consciously or unconsciously had to decide which infants to nourish and which to neglect, the advantage would go to those with lighter skin, experience having shown that such individuals tended to grow up to be taller, stronger, and healthier than their darker siblings. White was beautiful because white was healthy.

To account for the evolution of black skin in equatorial latitudes, one has merely to reverse the combined effects of natural and cultural selection. With the sun directly overhead most of the year, and clothing a hindrance to work and survival, vitamin D was never in short supply (and calcium was easily obtained from vegetables). Rickets and osteomalacia were rare. Skin cancer was the main problem, and what nature started, culture amplified. Darker infants were favored by parents because experience showed that they grew up to be freer of disfiguring and lethal malignancies. Black was beautiful because black was healthy.

POSTSCRIPT

Is Skin Color a Proper Determinant of Racial Identity?

W.E.B. DuBois has reminded us of the centrality of skin color for the establishment of distinct racial categories when he noted that issues of color would dominate human relations of the twentieth century. In the United States, African American children tend to develop a keen understanding of the impact of color in social/race relations when they state the following:

> If you're White, you're alright!
> If you're Brown, stick around!
> And, if you're Black, get back!

This was a statement that was uttered routinely by black children during their developmental years within America. It reminds us of the salience of skin color for racial identity.

There is a consensus view among scholars that racial distinctions were not a primary factor influencing human relations in the pre-modern world. The more substantial influence of race within society tends to be a more recent phenomenon influencing modern cultures and civilizations. Is skin color essential for human identity and classification?

In its traditional formulation, race developed as a biological construct within which human beings were established separate and distinct categories based on certain biogenic characteristics, including skin color, hair texture, nasal construction, and cranial construction among others. However, over time these racial classification schemes have been challenged by more advanced understanding of these matters resulting from on-going research and discovery within modern science. It is now clearly understood that from a purely biogenic perspective the genetic composition of human beings is fundamentally the same due to the fact that the genetic makeup of all homosapiens is basically the same. This fact of human existence has just been confirmed by the recently published results of the Human Genome Project. Qualities such as skin color, hair texture, and others represent superficial differences among us and none of these characteristics represent the essence of what comprises a human being.

However, despite the fundamental challenge that science has presented to the biological conceptualization of race, it is retained as a social construction. Essentially, this is Zinn's position. He argues that a color line between blacks and whites was established without regard to other characteristics of race. Thus Zinn supports the idea that "race" has significant utility as a social construction for separating people into distinct categories as a basis for subjecting members of out-groups to differential and unequal treatment.

On the other hand, Marvin Harris seemingly states the obvious when he argues that skin is a proper determinant of race (see Issue 4). For most Americans this appears to be the case. Only recently in American history is this notion being challenged. Why? Are racial categories overinclusive or underinclusive? Volumes have been written about race in terms of people of color. Indeed, laws have determined who is black. But what do we mean by the white race? How do we classify those who are mixed race? Is it by ancestry or by skin color? Increasing diversity and modern scientific discovery have forced these questions upon us.

A history of race and race theory can be found in *Race: The History of an Idea in America* (Oxford University Press, 1997) by Thomas F. Gossett. New ideas about race can be found in "Whiteness Studies: The New History of Race in America," (*American Journal of History,* June 2002) by Peter Kolchin. The anthropological classic, *Almost White,* by Brewton Berry is a study of America's mixed blood minorities and racial classification. In another classic, *The Leopard's Spots: Scientific Attitudes Toward Race in America, 1815–1859* (University of Chicago, 1960) William Stanton shows how time-bound prevailing ideas of race can be. Contemporary studies of race that reflect a social, rather than biological, context for understanding includes *Love and Theft: Black Minstrelsy and the American Working Class* (Oxford University Press, 1993) by Eric Lott; *Color Blind: Seeing Beyond Race in a Race-Obsessed World* (HarperCollins, 1997) by Ellis Cose; and *Seeing a Color-Blind Future: The Paradox of Race* (Noonday Press, 1998) by Patricia J. Williams.

Further reading using the idea of race as skin color and reflecting the idea of biology is the controversial *The Bell Curve: Intelligence and Class Structure in American Life* (The Free Press, 1994) by Richard J. Herrnstein and Charles Murray. Although the book is about intelligence, its use of race is a fixed, biological one. The book along with its argument that blacks have lower IQs than whites became popular in the early 1990s. *The Bell Curve Wars: Race, Intelligence, and the Future of America* (Basic Books, 1995) edited by Steven Fraser critiqued *The Bell Curve* but it did not challenge biological-based racial categories. In her article, "Do Races Differ? Not Really, Genes Show," (*New York Times,* August 22, 2000), Natalie Angier challenges conventional wisdom about race differences.

The reader is strongly urged to see a three-part video, *Race: The Power of An Illusion* (California Newsreel, 2003) produced by Larry Adelman. The first episode looks at the role of DNA in determining race.

ISSUE 6

Is Race Prejudice a Product of Group Position?

YES: Herbert Blumer, "Race Prejudice as a Sense of Group Position," *The Pacific Sociological Review* (Spring 1958)

NO: Gordon W. Allport, "The Young Child," *The Nature of Prejudice* (Perseus Books, 1979)

ISSUE SUMMARY

YES: Herbert Blumer, a sociologist, asserts that prejudice exists in a sense of group position rather than as an attitude based on individual feelings. The collective process by which a group comes to define other racial groups is the focus of Blumer's position.

NO: Gordon Allport, a psychologist, makes the case that prejudice is the result of a three-stage learning process.

Where does prejudice come from? When do we learn it? What are its characteristics? Is prejudice an individual personality trait or, is it a product of structural factors such as group position or economic factors? Ill feelings and overt hostility can reflect prejudice, but so can quiet benign beliefs. The many theories that explain prejudice can be categorized into those that attribute prejudice to individual personality, and those theories that see prejudice resulting from larger structural factors.

Blumer begins his group position argument in the context of dominant-subordinate group analysis. Members of the dominant group will, in addition to feelings of superiority, "feel a proprietary claim to certain areas of privilege and advantage." Suspicions of subordinate group members exist because of a fear that the minority group "harbors designs on the prerogatives of the dominant race." Although Blumer uses psychological concepts such as feelings, superiority, and distinctiveness, his focus is not on the individual. Rather it rests on the process of image formation. Image formation takes place in public domain including newspapers, film, and other media. "Careless ignorance of the facts" is often part of the image formation. Surely Blumer believes that prejudice is learned. Nevertheless, his analysis transcends mere "learning." The analysis of the collective process through which one group defines another involves a historical process. Group position is formed in a process defined by the dominant group and redefines subordinate groups. Hence, attitudes are formed from the dominant group perspective.

When the position of the dominant group is challenged, race prejudice emerges. According to Blumer this may occur in different ways. For example, it may be an affront to feelings or an attempt to transgress racial boundaries. Reaction to interracial marriage or the racial integration of a neighborhood may provoke a "defensive reaction" on the part of the dominant group. Generalizations of the minority group that often lead to fear emerge. Disturbed feelings are marked by hostility. Thus, Blumer suggests that race prejudice becomes a protective device. Prejudice is associated with the belief that gains for other (racial and ethnic) groups will result in losses for one's own—a zero sum game.

Examining how prejudice is learned, Gordon Allport stresses the first six years of a child's life, especially the role of the parents in transferring ideas as creating an atmosphere in which the child "develops prejudice as his style of life." The psychological factors exhibited during child rearing, including how the child is disciplined, loved, and threatened, translate into fear or hatred that may ultimately be directed at minorities. A rigid home environment in which parents exercise strict control is more likely to lead to prejudice among the children than a less rigid upbringing. Tolerance results from a less strict child-rearing style.

Allport explains that there are three stages of learning prejudice. In the first stage, the pre-generalized learning period, the child learns linguistic categories before he is ready to apply them. For example, ethnic and racial slurs are not yet applied to specific groups. Nevertheless, the categories are learned. The second stage in learning prejudice, the period of total rejection, occurs when children connect the labels of groups to be rejected with the individuals in minority groups. For example, Allport argues, by the fifth grade, children tend to choose their own racial group. However, as children grow older and mature, they lose the tendency to overgeneralize minorities. The third stage, differentiation, sets in often during the latter years of high school. By then, the "escape clauses" or exceptions to stereotypes are incorporated into the individual's attitude. So, the limited early learning experiences are replaced by the wider experiences that come with adolescence.

This selection from Allport is part of this more comprehensive social psychological account of how prejudice is learned. The emphasis on personality traits formed during early childhood contrasts with Blumer's group position thesis. We recommend that the student consider both positions to complete a study of prejudice. In this issue we urge students to search for similarities, along with the differences, between Allport and Blumer. Does Blumer reject the notion that prejudice is learned? Does Allport ignore the collective process? If your answer is "no" to these two questions, then how can you build a theory of prejudice?

101

Herbert Blumer  **YES**

Race Prejudice as a Sense of Group Position

In this paper I am proposing an approach to the study of race prejudice different from that which dominates contemporary scholarly thought on this topic. My thesis is that race prejudice exists basically in a sense of group position rather than in a set of feelings which members of one racial group have toward the members of another racial group. This different way of viewing race prejudice shifts study and analysis from a preoccupation with feelings as lodged in individuals to a concern with the relationship of racial groups. It also shifts scholarly treatment away from individual lines of experience and focuses interest on the collective process by which a racial group comes to define and redefine another racial group. Such shift, I believe, will yield a more realistic and penetrating understanding of race prejudice.

There can be little question that the rather vast literature on race prejudice is dominated by the idea that such prejudice exists fundamentally as a feeling or set of feelings lodged in the individual. It is usually depicted as consisting of feelings such as antipathy, hostility, hatred, intolerance, and aggressiveness. Accordingly, the task of scientific inquiry becomes two-fold. On one hand, there is a need to identify the feelings which make up race prejudice—to see how they fit together and how they are supported by other psychological elements, such as mythical beliefs. On the other hand, there is need of showing how the feeling complex has come into being. Thus, some scholars trace the complex feelings back chiefly to innate dispositions; some trace it to personality composition, such as authoritarian personality; and others regard the feelings of prejudice as being formed through social experience. However different may be the contentions regarding the make-up of racial prejudice and the way in which it may come into existence, these contentions are alike in locating prejudice in the realm of individual feeling. This is clearly true of the work of psychologists, psychiatrists, and social psychologists, and tends to be predominantly the case in the work of sociologists.

Unfortunately, this customary way of viewing race prejudice overlooks and obscures the fact that race prejudice is fundamentally a matter of relationship between racial groups. A little reflective thought should

From *The Pacific Sociological Review,* Spring 1958. Copyright © 1957 by Pacific Sociological Association. Reprinted with permission.

make this very clear. Race prejudice presupposes, necessarily, that racially prejudiced individuals think of themselves as belonging to a given racial group. It means, also, that they assign to other racial groups those against whom they are prejudiced. Thus, logically and actually, a scheme of racial identification is necessary as a framework for racial prejudice. Moreover, such identification involves the formation of an image or a conception of one's own racial group and of another racial group, inevitably in terms of the relationship of such groups. To fail to see that racial prejudice is a matter (a) of the racial identification made of oneself and of others, and (b) of the way in which the identified groups are conceived in relation to each other, is to miss what is logically and actually basic. One should keep clearly in mind that people necessarily come to identify themselves as belonging to a racial group; such identification is not spontaneous or inevitable but a result of experience. Further, one must realize that the kind of picture which a racial group forms of itself and the kind of picture which it may form of others are similarly products of experience. Hence, such pictures are variable, just as the lines of experience which produce them are variable.

The body of feelings which scholars, today, are so inclined to regard as constituting the substance of race prejudice is actually a resultant of the way in which given racial groups conceive of themselves and of others. A basic understanding of race prejudice must be sought in the process by which racial groups form images of themselves and of others. This process, as I hope to show, is fundamentally *a collective process*. It operates chiefly through the public media in which individuals who are accepted as the spokesmen of a racial group characterize publicly another racial group. To characterize another racial group is, by opposition, to define one's own group. This is equivalent to placing the two groups in relation to each other, or defining their positions *vis-à-vis* each other. It is the *sense of social position* emerging from this collective process of characterization which provides the basis of race prejudice. The following discussion will consider important facets of this matter.

I would like to begin by discussing several of the important feelings that enter into race prejudice. This discussion will reveal how fundamentally racial feelings point to and depend on a positional arrangement of the racial groups. In this discussion I will confine myself to such feelings in the case of a dominant racial group.

There are four basic types of feeling that seem to be always present in race prejudice in the dominant group. They are (1) a feeling of superiority, (2) a feeling that the subordinate race is intrinsically different and alien, (3) a feeling of proprietary claim to certain areas of privilege and advantage, and (4) a fear and suspicion that the subordinate race harbors designs on the prerogatives of the dominant race. A few words about each of these four feelings will suffice.

In race prejudice there is a self-assured feeling on the part of the dominant racial group of being naturally superior or better. This is commonly shown in a disparagement of the qualities of the subordinate racial group.

Condemnatory or debasing traits, such as laziness, dishonesty, greediness, unreliability, stupidity, deceit and immorality, are usually imputed to it. The second feeling, that the subordinate race is an alien and fundamentally different stock, is likewise always present. "They are not of our kind" is a common way in which this is likely to be expressed. It is this feeling that reflects, justifies, and promotes the social exclusion of the subordinate racial group. The combination of these two feelings of superiority and of distinctiveness can easily give rise to feelings of aversion and even antipathy. But in themselves they do not form prejudice. We have to introduce the third and fourth types of feeling.

The third feeling, the sense of proprietary claim, is of crucial importance. It is the feeling on the part of the dominant group of being entitled to either exclusive or prior rights in many important areas of life. The range of such exclusive or prior claims may be wide, covering the ownership of property such as choice lands and sites; the right to certain jobs, occupations or professions; the claim to certain kinds of industry or lines of business; the claim to certain positions of control and decision-making as in government and law; the right to exclusive membership in given institutions such as schools, churches and recreational institutions; the claim to certain positions of social prestige and to the display of the symbols and accoutrements of these positions; and the claim to certain areas of intimacy and privacy. The feeling of such proprietary claims is exceedingly strong in race prejudice. Again, however, this feeling even in combination with the feeling of superiority and the feeling of distinctiveness does not explain race prejudice. These three feelings are present frequently in societies showing no prejudice, as in certain forms of feudalism, in caste relations, in societies of chiefs and commoners, and under many settled relations of conquerors and conquered. Where claims are solidified into a structure which is accepted or respected by all, there seems to be no group prejudice.

The remaining feeling essential to race prejudice is a fear or apprehension that the subordinate racial group is threatening, or will threaten, the position of the dominant group. Thus, acts or suspected acts that are interpreted as an attack on the natural superiority of the dominant group, or an intrusion into their sphere of group exclusiveness, or an encroachment on their area of proprietary claim are crucial in arousing and fashioning race prejudice. These acts mean "getting out of place."

It should be clear that these four basic feelings of race prejudice definitely refer to a positional arrangement of the racial groups. The feeling of superiority places the subordinate people *below;* the feeling of alienation places them *beyond;* the feeling of proprietary claim excludes them from the prerogatives of position; and the fear of encroachment is an emotional recoil from the endangering of group position. As these features suggest, the positional relation of the two racial groups is crucial in race prejudice. The dominant group is not concerned with the subordinate group as such but it is deeply concerned with its position *vis-à-vis* the subordinate group. This is epitomized in the key and universal expression that a given race is all right in "its place." The sense of group position is the very heart of the relation of the dominant to the subordinate group. It supplies the dominant group with its framework of perception, its standard of judgment, its patterns of sensitivity, and its emotional proclivities.

It is important to recognize that this sense of group position transcends the feelings of the individual members of the dominant group, giving such members a common orientation that is not otherwise to be found in separate feelings and views. There is likely to be considerable difference between the ways in which the individual members of the dominant group think and feel about the subordinate group. Some may feel bitter and hostile, with strong antipathies, with an exalted sense of superiority and with a lot of spite; others may have charitable and protective feelings, marked by a sense of piety and tinctured by benevolence; others may be condescending and reflect mild contempt; and others may be disposed to politeness and considerateness with no feelings of truculence. These are only a few of many different patterns of feeling to be found among members of the dominant racial group. What gives a common dimension to them is a sense of the social position of their group. Whether the members be humane or callous, cultured or unlettered, liberal or reactionary, powerful or impotent, arrogant or humble, rich or poor, honorable or dishonorable—all are led, by virtue of sharing the sense of group position, to similar individual positions.

The sense of group position is a general kind of orientation. It is a general feeling without being reducible to specific feelings like hatred, hostility or antipathy. It is also a general understanding without being composed of any set of specific beliefs. On the social psychological side it cannot be equated to a sense of social status as ordinarily conceived, for it refers not merely to vertical positioning but to many other lines of position independent of the vertical dimension. Sociologically it is not a mere reflection of the objective relations between racial groups. Rather, it stands for "what ought to be" rather than for "what is." It is a sense of where the two racial groups *belong*.

In its own way, the sense of group position is a norm and imperative—indeed a very powerful one. It guides, incites, cows, and coerces. It should be borne in mind that this sense of group position stands for and involves a fundamental kind of group affiliation for the members of the dominant racial group. To the extent they recognize or feel themselves as belonging to that group they will automatically come under the influence of the sense of position held by that group. Thus, even though given individual members may have personal views and feelings different from the sense of group position, they will have to conjure with the sense of group position held by their racial group. If the sense of position is strong, to act contrary to it is to risk a feeling of self-alienation and to face the possibility of ostracism. I am trying to suggest, accordingly, that the locus of race prejudice is not in the area of individual feeling but in the definition of the respective positions of the racial groups.

The source of race prejudice lies in a felt challenge to this sense of group position. The challenge, one must recognize, may come in many different ways. It may be in the form of an affront to feelings of group superiority; it may be in the form of attempts at familiarity or transgressing the boundary line of group exclusiveness; it may be in the form of encroachment at countless points of proprietary claim; it may be a challenge to power and privilege; it may take the form of economic competition. Race prejudice is a defensive reaction to such challenging of the sense of group position. It consists of the disturbed feelings, usually of marked hostility, that are thereby aroused. As such, race prejudice is a protective device. It functions, however shortsightedly, to preserve the integrity and the position of the dominant group.

It is crucially important to recognize that the sense of group position is not a mere summation of the feelings of position such as might be developed independently by separate individuals as they come to compare themselves with given individuals of the subordinate race. The sense of group position refers to the position of group to group, not to that of individual to individual. Thus, *vis-à-vis* the subordinate racial group the unlettered individual with low status in the dominant racial group has a sense of group position common to that of the elite of his group. By virtue of sharing this sense of position such an individual, despite his low status, feels that members of the subordinate group, however distinguished and accomplished, are somehow inferior, alien, and properly restricted in the area of claims. He forms his conception as a representative of the dominant group; he treats individual members of the subordinate group as representative of that group.

An analysis of how the sense of group position is formed should start with a clear recognition that it is an historical product. It is set originally by conditions of initial contact. Prestige, power, possession of skill, numbers, original self-conceptions, aims, designs and opportunities are a few of the factors that may fashion the original sense of group position. Subsequent experience in the relation of the two racial groups, especially in the area of claims, opportunities and advantages, may mould the sense of group position in many diverse ways. Further, the sense of group position may be intensified or weakened, brought to sharp focus or dulled. It may be deeply entrenched and tenaciously resist change for long periods of time. Or it may never take root. It may undergo quick growth and vigorous expansion or it may dwindle away through slow-moving erosion. It may be firm or soft, acute or dull, continuous or intermittent. In short, viewed comparatively, the sense of group position is very variable.

However variable its particular career, the sense of group position is clearly formed by a running process in which the dominant racial group is led to define and redefine the subordinate racial group and the relations between them. There are two important aspects of this process of definition that I wish to single out for consideration.

First, the process of definition occurs obviously through complex interaction and communication between the members of the dominant group. Leaders, prestige bearers, official, group agents, dominant individuals and ordinary laymen present to one another characterizations of the subordinate group and express their feelings and ideas on the relations. Through talk, tales, stories, gossip, anecdotes, messages, pronouncements, news accounts, orations, sermons, preachments and the like definitions are presented and feelings are expressed. In this usually vast and complex interaction separate views run against one another, influence one another, modify each other, incite one another and fuse together in new forms. Correspondingly, feelings which are expressed meet, stimulate each other, feed on each other, intensify each other and emerge in new patterns. Currents of view and currents of feeling come into being; sweeping along to positions of dominance and serving as polar points for the organization of thought and sentiment. If the interaction becomes increasingly circular and reinforcing, devoid of serious inner opposition, such currents grow, fuse and become strengthened. It is through such a process that a collective image of the subordinate group is formed and a sense of group position is set. The evidence of such a process is glaring when one reviews the history of any racial arrangement marked by prejudice.

Such a complex process of mutual interaction with its different lines and degrees of formation gives the lie to the many schemes which would lodge the cause of race prejudice in the make-up of the individual—whether in the form of innate disposition, constitutional make-up, personality structure, or direct personal experience with members of the other race. The collective image and feelings in race prejudice are forged out of a complicated social process in which the individual is himself shaped and organized. The scheme, so popular today, which would trace race prejudice to a so-called authoritarian personality shows a grievous misunderstanding of the simple essentials of the collective process that leads to a sense of group position.

The second important aspect of the process of group definition is that it is necessarily concerned with *an abstract image* of the subordinate racial group. The subordinate racial group is defined as if it were an entity or whole. This entity or whole—like the Negro race, or the Japanese, or the Jews—is necessarily an abstraction, never coming within the perception of any of the senses. While actual encounters are with individuals, the picture formed of the racial group is necessarily of a vast entity which spreads out far beyond such individuals and transcends experience with such individuals. The implications of the fact that the collective image is of an abstract group are of crucial significance. I would like to note four of these implications.

First, the building of the image of the abstract group takes place in the area of the remote and not of the near. It is not the experience with concrete individuals in daily association that gives rise to the definitions of the extended, abstract group. Such immediate experience is usually regulated and orderly. Even where such immediate experience is disrupted the new definitions which are formed are limited to the individuals involved. The collective image of the abstract group grows up not by generalizing from experiences gained in close, first-hand contacts but through the transcending characterizations that are made of the group as an entity.

Thus, one must seek the central stream of definition in those areas where the dominant group as such is characterizing the subordinate group as such. This occurs in the "public arena" wherein the spokesmen appear as representatives and agents of the dominant group. The extended public arena is constituted by such things as legislatives assemblies, public meetings, conventions, the press, and the printed word. What goes on in this public arena attracts the attention of large numbers of the dominant group and is felt as the voice and action of the group as such.

Second, the definitions that are forged in the public arena center, obviously, about matters that are felt to be of major importance. Thus, we are led to recognize the crucial role of the "big event" in developing a conception of the subordinate racial group. The happening that seems momentous, that touches deep sentiments, that seems to raise fundamental questions about relations, and that awakens strong feelings of identification with one's racial group is the kind of event that is central in the formation of the racial image. Here, again, we note the relative unimportance of the huge bulk of experiences coming from daily contact with individuals of the subordinate group. It is the events seemingly loaded with great collective significance that are the focal points of the public discussion. The definition of these events is chiefly responsible for the development of a racial image and of the sense of group position. When this public discussion takes the form of a denunciation of the subordinate racial group, signifying that it is unfit and a threat, the discussion becomes particularly potent in shaping the sense of social position.

Third, the major influence in public discussion is exercised by individuals and groups who have the public ear and who are felt to have standing, prestige, authority and power. Intellectual and social elites, public figures of prominence, and leaders of powerful organizations are likely to be the key figures in the formation of the sense of group position and in the characterization of the subordinate group. It is well to note this in view of the not infrequent tendency of students to regard race prejudice as growing out of the multiplicity of experiences and attitudes of the bulk of the people.

Fourth, we also need to perceive the appreciable opportunity that is given to strong interest groups in directing the lines of discussion and setting the interpretations that arise in such discussion. Their self-interests may dictate the kind of position they wish the dominant racial group to enjoy. It may be a position which enables them to retain certain advantages, or even more to gain still greater advantages. Hence, they may be vigorous in seeking to manufacture events to attract public attention and to set lines of issue in such a way as to predetermine interpretations favorable to their interests. The role of strongly organized groups seeking to further special interest is usually central in the formation of collective images of abstract groups. Historical records of major instances of race relations, as in our South, or in South Africa, or in Europe in the case of the Jew, or on the West Coast in the case of the Japanese show the formidable part played by interest groups in defining the subordinate racial group.

I conclude this highly condensed paper with two further observations that may throw additional light on the relation of the sense of group position to race prejudice. Race prejudice becomes entrenched and tenacious to the extent the prevailing social order is rooted in the sense of social position. This has been true of the historic South in our country. In such a social order race prejudice tends to become chronic and impermeable to change. In other places the social order may be affected only to a limited extent by the sense of group position held by the dominant racial group. This I think has been true usually in the case of anti-Semitism in Europe and this country. Under these conditions the sense of group position tends to be weaker and more vulnerable. In turn, race prejudice has a much more variable and intermittent career, usually becoming pronounced only as a consequence of grave disorganizing events that allow for the formation of a scapegoat.

This leads me to my final observation which in a measure is an indirect summary. The sense of group position dissolves and race prejudice declines when the process of running definition does not keep abreast of major shifts in the social order. When events touching on relations are not treated as "big events" and hence do not set crucial issues in the arena of public discussion; or when the elite leaders or spokesmen do not define such big events vehemently or adversely; or where they define them in the direction of racial harmony; or when there is a paucity of strong interest groups seeking to build up a strong adverse image for special advantage—under such conditions the sense of group position recedes and race prejudice declines.

The clear implication of my discussion is that the proper and the fruitful area in which race prejudice should be studied is the collective process through which a sense of group position is formed. To seek, instead, to understand it or to handle it in the arena of individual feeling and of individual experience seems to me to be clearly misdirected.

Gordon W. Allport

↜ NO

The Young Child

How is prejudice learned? We have opened our discussion of this pivotal problem by pointing out that the home influence has priority, and that the child has excellent reasons for adopting his ethnic attitudes ready-made from his parents. We likewise called attention to the central role of identification in the course of early learning. In the present chapter we shall consider additional factors operating in preschool years. The first six years of life are important for the development of all social attitudes, though it is a mistake to regard early childhood as alone responsible for them. A bigoted personality may be well under way by the age of six, but by no means fully fashioned.

Our analysis will be clearer if at the outset we make a distinction between *adopting* prejudice and *developing* prejudice. A child who adopts prejudice is taking over attitudes and stereotypes from his family or cultural environment. Most of the cases cited in the previous chapter are instances in point. Parental words and gestures, along with their concomitant beliefs and antagonisms, are transferred to the child. He adopts his parents' views. Some of the principles of learning discussed in this and the following chapter will help explain further how this transfer comes about.

But there is also a type of training that does not transfer ideas and attitudes directly to the child, but rather creates an atmosphere in which he *develops* prejudice as his style of life. In this case the parents may or may not express their own prejudices (usually they do). What is crucial, however, is that their mode of handling the child (disciplining, loving, threatening) is such that the child cannot help acquire suspicions, fears, hatreds that sooner or later may fix on minority groups.

In reality, of course, these forms of learning are not distinct. Parents who *teach* the child specific prejudices are also likely to *train* the child to develop a prejudiced nature. Still it is well to keep the distinction in mind, for the psychology of learning is so intricate a subject that it requires analytical aids of this type.

Child Training

We consider now the style of child training that is known to be conducive to the *development* of prejudice. (We shall disregard for the time being the learning of specific attitudes toward specific groups.)

One line of proof that a child's prejudice is related to the manner of his upbringing comes from a study of Harris, Gough, and Martin.[1] These investigators first determined the extent to which 240 fourth, fifth, and sixth grade children expressed prejudiced attitudes toward minority groups. They then sent questionnaires to the mothers of these children, asking their views on certain practices in child training. Most of these were returned with the mothers' replies. The results are highly instructive. Mothers of prejudiced children, *far more often* than the mothers of unprejudiced children, held that

> Obedience is the most important thing a child can learn.
>
> A child should never be permitted to set his will against that of his parents.
>
> A child should never keep a secret from his parents.
>
> "I prefer a quiet child to one who is noisy."
>
> (In the case of temper tantrums) "Teach the child that two can play that game, by getting angry yourself."

In the case of sex-play (masturbation) the mother of the prejudiced child is much more likely to believe she should punish the child; the mother of the unprejudiced child is much more likely to ignore the practice.

All in all, the results indicate that pervasive family atmospheres do definitely slant the child. Specifically, a home that is suppressive, harsh, or critical—where the parents' word is law—is more likely to prepare the groundwork for group prejudice.

It seems a safe assumption that the mothers who expressed their philosophies of child training in this questionnaire actually carried out their ideas in practice. If so, then we have strong evidence that children are more likely to be prejudiced if they have been brought up by mothers who insist on obedience, who are suppressive of the child's impulses, and who are sharp disciplinarians.

What does such a style of child training do to a child? For one thing it puts him on guard. He has to watch his impulses carefully. Not only is he punished for them when they counter the parents' convenience and rules, as they frequently do, but he feels at such times that love is withdrawn from him. When love is withdrawn he is alone, exposed, desolate. Thus he comes to watch alertly for signs of parental approval or disapproval. It is they who have power, and they who give or withhold their conditional love. Their power and their will are the decisive agents in the child's life.

What is the result? First of all, the child learns that power and authority dominate human relationships—not trust and tolerance. The stage is thus set for a hierarchical view of society. Equality does not really prevail.

The effect goes even deeper. The child mistrusts his impulses: he must not have temper tantrums, he must not disobey, he must not play with his sex organs. He must fight such evil in himself. Through a simple act of projection . . . the child comes to fear evil impulses in others. They have dark designs; their impulses threaten the child; they are not to be trusted.

If this style of training prepares the ground for prejudice, the opposite style seems to predispose toward tolerance. The child who feels secure and loved whatever he does, and who is treated not with a display of parental power (being punished usually through shaming rather than spanking), develops basic ideas of equality and trust. Not required to repress his own impulses, he is less likely to project them upon others, and less likely to develop suspicion, fear, and a hierarchical view of human relationships.[2]

While no child is always treated according to one and only one pattern of discipline or affection, we might venture to classify prevailing home atmospheres according to the following scheme:

Permissive treatment by parents

Rejective treatment
> suppressive and cruel (harsh, fear-inspiring)
> domineering and critical (overambitious parents nagging and dissatisfied with the child as he is)

Neglectful

Overindulgent

Inconsistent (sometimes permissive, sometimes rejective, sometimes overindulgent)

Although we cannot yet be dogmatic about the matter, it seems very likely that rejective, neglectful, and inconsistent styles of training tend to lead to the development of prejudice.[3] Investigators have reported how impressed they are by the frequency with which quarrelsome or broken homes have occurred in the childhood of prejudiced people.

> Ackerman and Jahoda made a study of anti-Semitic patients who were undergoing psychoanalysis. Most of them had had an unhealthy homelife as children, marked by quarreling, violence, or divorce. There was little or no affection or sympathy between the parents. The rejection of the child by one or both parents was the rule rather than the exception.[4]

These investigators could not find that specific parental indoctrination in anti-Semitic attitudes was a necessary element. It is true that the parents, like the children, were anti-Semitic, but the authors explain the connection as follows:

> In those cases where parents and children are anti-Semitic, it is more reasonable to assume that the emotional predispositions of the parents

created a psychological atmosphere conducive to the development of similar emotional dispositions in the child, than to maintain the simple imitation hypothesis.[5]

In other words, prejudice was not *taught* by the parent but was *caught* by the child from an infected atmosphere.

Another investigator became interested in paranoia. Among a group of 125 hospital patients suffering from fixed delusional ideas he found that the majority had a predominantly suppressive and cruel upbringing. Nearly three-quarters of the patients had parents who were either suppressive and cruel or else domineering and overcritical. Only seven percent came from homes that could be called permissive.[6] Thus may paranoia in adult years be traceable to a bad start in life. We cannot, of course, equate paranoia and prejudice. Yet the rigid categorizing indulged in by the prejudiced person, his hostility, and his inaccessibility to reason are often much like the disorder of a paranoiac.

Without stretching the evidence too far, we may at least make a guess: children who are too harshly treated, severely punished, or continually criticized are more likely to develop personalities wherein group prejudice plays a prominent part. Conversely, children from more relaxed and secure homes, treated permissively and with affection, are more likely to develop tolerance.

Fear of the Strange

Let us return again to the question whether there is an inborn source of prejudice. . . . [We] reported that as soon as infants are able (perhaps at six months of age) to distinguish between familiar and unfamiliar persons, they sometimes show anxiety when strangers approach. They do so especially, if the stranger moves abruptly or makes a "grab" for the child. They may show special fear if the stranger wears eyeglasses, or has skin of an unfamiliar color, or even if his expressive movements are different from what the child is accustomed to. This timidity usually continues through the preschool period—often beyond. Every visitor who has entered a home where there is a young child knows that it takes several minutes, perhaps several hours, for the child to "warm up" to him. But usually the initial fear gradually disappears.

We reported also an experiment where infants were placed alone in a strange room with toys. All of the children were at first alarmed and cried in distress. After a few repetitions they became entirely habituated to the room and played as if at home. But the biological utility of the initial fear reaction is obvious. Whatever is strange is a potential danger, and must be guarded against until one's experience assures one that no harm is lurking.

The almost universal anxiety of a child in the presence of strangers is no more striking than his rapid adaptability to their presence.

In a certain household a Negro maid came to work. The young children in the family, aged three and five, showed fear and for a few days were reluctant to accept her. The maid stayed with the family for five or six years and came to be loved by all. Several years later, when the children were young adults, the family was discussing the happy period of Anna's services in the household. She had not been seen for the past ten years, but her memory was affectionately held. In the course of the conversation it came out that she was colored. The children were utterly astonished. They insisted that they had never known this fact, or had completely forgotten it if they ever knew it.

Situations of this type are not uncommon. Their occurrence makes us doubt that instinctive fear of the strange has any necessary bearing upon the organization of permanent attitudes.

Dawn of Racial Awareness

The theory of "home atmosphere" is certainly more convincing than the theory of "instinctive roots." But neither theory tells us just when and how the child's ethnic ideas begin to crystallize. Granted that the child possesses relevant emotional equipment, and that the family supplies a constant undertone of acceptance or rejection, anxiety or security, we still need studies that will show how the child's earliest sense of group differences develops. An excellent setting for such a study is a biracial nursery school.

In investigations conducted in this setting, it appears that the earliest age at which children take any note of race is two and a half.

> One white child of this age, sitting for the first time beside a Negro child, said, "Dirty face." It was an unemotional remark, prompted only by his observing a wholly dark-skinned visage—for the first time in his life.

The purely sensory observation that some skins are white, some colored, seems in many cases to be the first trace of racial awareness. Unless there is the quiver of fear of the strange along with this observation, we may say that race difference at first arouses a sense of curiosity and interest—nothing more. The child's world is full of fascinating distinctions. Facial color is simply one of them. Yet we note that even this first perception of racial difference may arouse associations with "clean" and "dirty."

The situation is more insistent by the age of three and a half or four. The sense of dirt still haunts the children. They have been thoroughly scrubbed at home to eradicate dirt. Why then does it exist so darkly on other children? One colored boy, confused concerning his membership, said to his mother, "Wash my face clean; some of the children don't wash well, especially colored children."

> A first grade teacher reports that about one white child in ten refuses to hold hands during games with the solitary Negro child in the classroom. The reason apparently is not "prejudice" in any deep-seated sense. The rejective white children merely complain that Tom has dirty hands and face.

Dr. Goodman's nursery school study shows one particularly revealing result. Negro children are, by and large, "racially aware" earlier than are white children.[7] They tend to be confused, disturbed, and sometimes excited by the problem. Few of them seem to know that they are Negroes. (Even at the age of seven one little Negro girl said to a white playmate, "I'd hate to be colored, wouldn't you?")

The interest and disturbance take many forms. Negro children ask more questions about racial differences; they may fondle the blond hair of a white child; they are often rejective toward Negro dolls. When given a white and Negro doll to play with, they almost uniformly prefer the white doll; many slap the Negro doll and call it dirty or ugly. As a rule, they are more rejective of Negro dolls than are white children. They tend to behave self-consciously when tested for racial awareness. One Negro boy, being shown two baby dolls alike save for color, is asked, "Which one is most like you when you were a baby?"

> Bobby's eyes move from brown to white; he hesitates, squirms, glances at us sidewise—and points to the white doll. Bobby's perceptions relevant to race, feeble and sporadic though they are, have some personal meaning—some ego-reference.

Especially interesting is Dr. Goodman's observation that Negro children tend to be fully as active as white children at the nursery school age. They are on the whole more sociable—particularly those who are rated as high on "racial awareness." A larger proportion of the Negro children are rated as "leaders" in the group. Although we cannot be certain of the meaning of this finding, it may well come from the fact that Negro children are more highly stimulated by the dawning awareness of race. They may be excited by a challenge they do not fully understand, and may seek reassurance through activity and social contacts for the vague threat that hangs over them. The threat comes not from nursery school, where they are secure enough, but from their first contacts with the world outside and from discussions at home, where their Negro parents cannot fail to talk about the matter.

What is so interesting about this full-scale activity at the nursery school age is its contrast to the adult demeanor of many Negroes who are noted for their poise, passivity, apathy, laziness—or whatever the withdrawing reaction may be called. . . . [We] noted that the Negro's conflicts sometimes engender a quietism, a passivity. Many people hold that this "laziness" is a biological trait of Negroes—but in the nursery school we find flatly contradictory evidence. Passivity, when it exists as a Negro attribute, is apparently a learned mode of adjustment. The assertive reaching out of the four-year-old for security and acceptance is ordinarily doomed to failure. After a period of struggle and suffering the passive mode of adjustment may set in.

Why is there, even in the dawning race-awareness of four-year-olds, a nebulous sense of inferiority associated with dark skin? A significant part of the answer lies in the similarity between dark pigmentation and dirt.

A third of Dr. Goodman's children (both Negro and white) spoke of this matter. Many others no doubt had it in their minds, but did not happen to mention it to the investigators. An additional part of the answer may lie in those subtle forms of learning—not yet fully understood—whereby value-judgments are conveyed to the child. Some parents of white children may, by word or act, have conveyed to their children a vague sense of their rejection of Negroes. If so, the rejection is still only nascent in the four-year-old, for in virtually no case could the investigators find anything they were willing to label "prejudice" at this age level. Some of the Negro parents, too, may have conveyed to their children a sense of the handicaps of people with black skin, even before the children themselves knew their own skin was black.

The initial damage of associated ideas seems inescapable in our culture. Dark skin suggests dirt—even to a four-year-old. To some it may suggest feces. Brown is not the aesthetic norm in our culture (in spite of the popularity of chocolate). But this initial disadvantage is by no means insuperable. Discriminations in the realm of color are not hard to learn: a scarlet rose is not rejected because it is the color of blood, nor a yellow tulip because it is the color of urine.

To sum up: four-year-olds are normally interested, curious, and appreciative of differences in racial groups. A slight sense of white superiority seems to be growing, largely because of the association of white with cleanness—cleanliness being a value learned very early in life. But contrary associations can be, and sometimes are, easily built up.

> One four-year-old boy was taken by train from Boston to San Francisco. He was enchanted by the friendly Negro porter. For fully two years thereafter he fantasied that he was a porter, and complained bitterly that he was not colored so that he could qualify for the position.

Linguistic Tags: Symbols of Power and Rejection

Earlier we discussed the immensely important role of language in building fences for our mental categories and our emotional responses. This factor is so crucial that we return to it again—as it bears on childhood learning.

In Goodman's study it turned out that fully half the nursery school children knew the word "nigger." Few of them understood what the epithet culturally implies. But they knew that the word was potent. It was forbidden, taboo, and always fetched some type of strong response from the teachers. It was therefore a "power word." Not infrequently in a temper tantrum a child would call his teacher (whether white or colored) a "nigger" or a "dirty nigger." The term expressed an emotion—nothing more. Nor did it always express anger—sometimes merely excitement. Children wildly racing around, shrieking at play might, in order to enhance their orgies, yell "nigger, nigger, nigger." As a strong word it seemed fit to vocalize the violent expenditure of energy under way.

One observer gives an interesting example of aggressive verbalization during wartime play:

Recently, in a waiting room, I watched three youngsters who sat at a table looking at magazines. Suddenly the smaller boy said: "Here's a soldier and an airplane. He's a Jap." The girl said: "No, he's an American." The little fellow said: "Get him, soldier. Get the Jap." The older boy added, "And Hitler too." "And Mussolini," said the girl. "And the Jews," said the big boy. Then the little fellow started a chant, the others joining in: "The Japs, Hitler, Mussolini, and the Jews! The Japs, Hitler, Mussolini, and the Jews!"[8] It is certain that these children had very little understanding of their bellicose chant. The names of their enemies had an expressive but not a denotative significance.

One little boy was agreeing with his mother, who was warning him never to play with niggers. He said, "No, Mother, I never play with niggers. I only play with white and black children." This child was developing aversion to the term "nigger," without having the slightest idea what the term meant. In other words, the aversion is being set up prior to acquiring a referent.

Other examples could be given of instances where words appear strong and emotionally laden to the child (goy, kike, dago). Only later does he attach the word to a group of people upon whom he can visit the emotions suggested by the word.

We call this process "linguistic precedence in learning." The emotional word has an effect prior to the learning of the referent. Later, the emotional effect becomes attached to the referent.

Before a firm sense of the referent is acquired, the child may go through stages of puzzlement and confusion. This is particularly true because emotional epithets are most likely to be learned when some exciting or traumatic experience is under way. Lasker gives the following example:

Walking across the playground, a settlement worker found a little Italian boy crying bitterly. She asked him what was the matter. "Hit by Polish boy," the little man repeated several times. Inquiry among the bystanders showed that the offender was not Polish at all. Turning again to her little friend, she said, "You mean, hit by a big naughty boy." But he would not have it thus and went on repeating that he had been hit by a Polish boy. This struck the worker as so curious that she made inquiries of the little fellow's family. She learned that it lived in the same house with a Polish family and that the Italian mother, by constantly quarreling with her Polish neighbor, had put into the heads of her children the notion that "Polish" and "bad" were synonymous terms.[9]

When this lad finally learns who Poles are, he already will have a strong prejudice against them. Here is a clear case of linguistic precedence in learning.

Children sometimes confess their perplexity concerning emotional tags. They seem to be groping for proper referents. Trager and Radke, from their work with kindergarten, first and second grade children, give several examples:[10]

Anna   When I was coming out of the dressing room, Peter called me a dirty Jew.

Teacher   Why did you say that, Peter?

Peter (earnestly)   I didn't say it for spite. I was only playing.

Johnny (helping Louis pull off his leggings)   A man called my father a goy.

Louis   What's a goy?

Johnny   I think everybody around here is a goy. But not me. I'm Jewish.

> On being called a "white cracker" by a Negro boy in the class, the teacher said to her class, "I am puzzled by the meaning of two words. Do you know what 'white cracker' means?"
> A number of vague answers were received from the children, one being "You're supposed to say it when you're mad."

Even while the child is having difficulty with words, they have a great power over him. To him they are often a type of magic, of verbal realism. . . .

> A little boy in the South was playing with the child of the washerwoman. Everything was going smoothly until a neighbor white child called over the fence, "Look out, you'll catch it."
> "Catch what?" asked the first white child.
> "Catch the black. You'll get colored too."
> Just this assertion (reminding the child, no doubt, of expressions such as "catch the measles") frightened him. He deserted his colored companion then and there, and never played with him again.

Children often cry if they are called names. Their self-esteem is wounded by any epithet: naughty, dirty, harum-scarum, nigger, dago, Jap, or what not. To escape this verbal realism of early childhood, they often reassure themselves, when they are a little older, with the self-restorative jingle: Sticks and stones may break my bones, but names can never hurt me. But it takes a few years for them to learn that a name is not a thing-in-itself. As we saw earlier verbal realism may never be fully shaken off. The rigidity of linguistic categories may continue in adult thinking. To some adults "communist" or "Jew" is a dirty word—and a dirty thing—an indissoluble unity, as it may be to a child.

The First Stage in Learning Prejudice

Janet, six years of age, was trying hard to integrate her obedience to her mother with her daily social contacts. One day she came running home and asked, "Mother, what is the name of the children I am supposed to hate?"

Janet's wistful question leads us into a theoretical summary of the present chapter.

Janet is stumbling at the threshold of some abstraction. She wishes to form the right category. She intends to oblige her mother by hating the right people when she can find out who they are.

In this situation we suspect the preceding stages in Janet's developmental history:

1. She identifies with the mother, or at least she strongly craves the mother's affection and approval. We may imagine that the home is not "permissive" in atmosphere, but somewhat stern and critical. Janet may have found that she must be on her toes to please her parent. Otherwise she will suffer rejection or punishment. In any event, she has developed a habit of obedience.
2. While she has apparently no strong fear of strangers at the present time, she has learned to be circumspect. Experiences of insecurity with people outside the family circle may be a factor in her present effort to define her circle of loyalties.
3. She undoubtedly has gone through the initial period of curiosity and interest in racial and ethnic differences. She knows now that human beings are clustered into groups—that there are important distinctions if only she can identify them. In the case of Negro and white the visibility factor has helped her. But then she discovered that subtler differences were also important; Jews somehow differed from gentiles; wops from Americans; doctors from salesmen. She is now aware of group differences, though not yet clear concerning all the relevant cues.
4. She has encountered the stage of linguistic precedence in learning. In fact, she is now in this stage. She knows that group X (she knows neither its name nor its identity) is somehow hate-worthy. She already has the emotional meaning but lacks the referential meaning. She seeks now to integrate the proper content with the emotion. She wishes to define her category so as to make her future behavior conform to her mother's desires. As soon as she has the linguistic tag at her command, she will be like the little Italian boy for whom "Polish" and "bad" were synonymous terms.

Up to the present, Janet's development marks what we might call the first stage of ethnocentric learning. Let us christen it the period of *pregeneralized* learning. This label is not altogether satisfactory, but none better describes the potpourri of factors listed above. The term draws attention primarily to the fact that the child has not yet generalized after the fashion of adults. He does not quite understand what a Jew is, what a Negro is, or what his own attitude toward them should be. He does not know even what *he* is—in any consistent sense. He may think he is an American only when he is playing with his toy soldiers (this type of categorizing was not uncommon in wartime). It is not only in ethnic matters that thoughts are prelogical from an adult point of view. A little girl may not think that her mother is her mother when the latter is working at the office; and may not regard her mother as an officeworker when she is at home tending the family.[11]

The child seems to live his mental life in specific contexts. What exists here and now makes up the only reality. The strange-man-who-knocks-at-the-door is something to be feared. It does not matter if he is a delivery man. The Negro boy at school is dirty. He is not a member of a race.

Such independent experiences in concrete procession seem to furnish the child's mind. His pregeneralized thinking (from the adult's point of view) has sometimes been labeled "global," or "syncretistic," or "prelogical."[12]

Now the place of linguistic tags in the course of mental development is crucial. They stand for adult abstractions, for logical generalizations of the sort that mature adults accept. The child learns the tags before he is fully ready to apply them to the adult categories. They prepare him for prejudice. But the process takes time. Only after much fumbling—in the manner of Janet and other children described in this chapter—will the proper categorizing take place.

The Second Stage in Learning Prejudice

As soon as Janet's mother gives a clear answer to Janet, she will in all probability enter a second period of prejudice—one that we may call the period of *total rejection*. Suppose the mother answers, "I told you not to play with Negro children. They are dirty; they have diseases; and they will hurt you. Now don't let me catch you at it." If Janet by now has learned to distinguish Negroes from other groups, even from the dark-skinned Mexican children, or Italians—in other words, if she now has the adult category in mind—she will undoubtedly reject all Negroes, in all circumstances, and with considerable feeling.

The research of Blake and Dennis well illustrates the point.[13] It will be recalled that these investigators studied Southern white children in the fourth and fifth grades (ten- and eleven-year-olds). They asked such questions as, "Which are more musical—Negroes or white people?" "Which are more clean?"—and many questions of a similar type. These children had, by the age of ten, learned to reject the Negro category *totally*. No favorable quality was ascribed to Negroes more often than to whites. In effect, whites had all the virtues; Negroes, none.

While this totalized rejection certainly starts earlier (in many children it will be found by the age of seven or eight), it seems to reach its ethnocentric peak in early puberty. First- and second-grade children often elect to play with, or sit beside, a child of different race or ethnic membership. This friendliness usually disappears in the fifth grade. At that time children choose their own group almost exclusively. Negroes select Negroes, Italians select Italians, and so on.[14]

As children grow older, they normally lose this tendency to total rejection and overgeneralization. Blake and Dennis found that in the 12th grade the white youth ascribed several favorable stereo-types to Negroes. They considered them more musical, more easygoing, better dancers.

The Third Stage

Thus, after a period of *total rejection,* a stage of *differentiation* sets in. The prejudices grow less totalized. Escape clauses are written into the attitude in order to make it more rational and more acceptable to the individual. One says, "Some of my best friends are Jews." Or, "I am not prejudiced against Negroes—I always loved my black Mammy." The child who is first learning adult categories of rejection is not able to make such gracious exceptions. It takes him the first six to eight years of his life to learn total rejection, and another six years or so to modify it. The actual adult creed in his culture is complex indeed. It allows for (and in many ways encourages) ethnocentrism. At the same time, one must give lip service to democracy and equality, or at least ascribe some good qualities to the minority group and some-how plausibly justify the remaining disapproval that one expresses. It takes the child well into adolescence to learn the peculiar double-talk appropriate to prejudice in a democracy.

Around the age of eight, children often *talk* in a highly prejudiced manner. They have learned their categories and their totalized rejection. But the rejection is chiefly verbal. While they may damn the Jews, the wops, the Catholics, they may still *behave* in a relatively democratic manner. They may play with them even while they talk against them. The "total rejection" is chiefly a verbal matter.

Now when the teaching of the school takes effect, the child learns a new verbal norm: he must talk democratically. He must profess to regard all races and creeds as equal. Hence, by the age of 12, we may find *verbal* acceptance, but *behavioral* rejection. By this age the prejudices have finally affected conduct, even while the verbal, democratic norms are beginning to take effect.

The paradox, then, is that younger children may talk undemocratically, but behave democratically, whereas children in puberty may talk (at least in school) democratically but behave with true prejudice. By the age of 15, considerable skill is shown in imitating the adult pattern. Prejudiced talk and democratic talk are reserved for appropriate occasions, and rationalizations are ready for whatever occasions require them. Even conduct is varied according to circumstances. One may be friendly with a Negro in the kitchen, but hostile to a Negro who comes to the front door. Double-dealing, like double-talk, is hard to learn. It takes the entire period of childhood and much of adolescence to master the art of ethnocentrism.

Notes and References

1. D. B. Harris, H. G. Gough, W. E. Martin. Children's ethnic attitudes: II, Relationship to parental beliefs concerning child training. *Child Development,* 1950, **21,** 169–181.

2. These two contrasting styles of child training are described more fully by D. P. Ausubel in *Ego Development and the Personality Disorders.* New York: Grune & Stratton, 1952.

3. The most extensive evidence is contained in researches conducted at the University of California. See: T. W. Adorno, Else Frenkel-Brunswik, D. J. Levinson, R. N. Sanford, *The Authoritarian Personality,* New York: Harper, 1950; also, Else Frenkel-Brunswik, Patterns of social and cognitive outlook in children and parents, *American Journal of Orthopsychiatry,* 1951, **21**, 543–558.

4. N. W. Ackerman and Marie Jahoda. *Anti-Semitism and Emotional Disorder.* New York: Harper, 1950, 45.

5. *Ibid.,* 85.

6. H. Bonner. Sociological aspects of paranoia. *American Journal of Sociology,* 1950, **56**, 255–262.

7. Mary E. Goodman. *Race Awareness in Young Children.* Cambridge: Addison-Wesley, 1952. Other studies have confirmed the fact that Negro children are race-aware before white children: e.g., Ruth Horowitz, Racial aspects of self-identification in nursery school children, *Journal of Psychology,* 1939, **7**, 91–99.

8. Mildred *M. Eakin. Getting Acquaintea with Jewish Neighbors.* New York: Macmillan, 1944.

9. B. Lasker. *Race Attitudes in Children.* New York: Henry Holt, 1929, 98.

10. Helen G. Trager and Marian Radke. Early childhood airs its views. *Educational Leadership,* 1947, **5**, 16–23.

11. E. L. Hartley, M. Rosenbaum, and S. Schwartz. (Children's perceptions of ethnic group membership. *Journal of Psychology,* 1948, **26**, 387–398.

12. *Cf.* H. Werner. *Comparative Psychology of Mental Development.* Chicago: Follett, 1948. J. Piaget. *The Child's Conception of the World. New* York: Harcourt, Brace, 1929, 236. G. Murphy. *Personality.* New York: Harper, 1947, 336.

13. R. Blake and W. Dennis. The development of stereotypes concerning the Negro. *Journal of Abnormal and Social Psychology,* 1943, **38**, 525–531.

14. J. H. Criswell. A sociometric study of race cleavage in the classroom. *Archives of Psychology,* 1939, No. 235.

POSTSCRIPT

Is Race Prejudice a Product of Group Position?

Clearly, there is no one theory that offers a complete explanation of prejudice. However, when we consider theories together or debate differing positions advanced in this issue, we gain insight and understanding. The basic dilemma is whether or not prejudice results from personality traits best revealed through psychological theories, or whether prejudice is more social and cultural, reflecting Blumer's idea of group position. Utilizing both approaches will help us see how social learning takes place. At this point we can ask another question concerning the relationship between attitudes and behavior.

To study race prejudice is to consider the role of attitudes and individual feelings in one's life. Still unclear to us is the relationship of attitudes to behavior. Does race prejudice lead to discriminatory practice? Does the prejudiced person behave differently from the non-prejudiced person? Sociologist Robert Merton suggests that prejudice and discrimination are linked in ways that are determined by different social environments. He developed categories to demonstrate that one can be prejudice and not discriminate, or one is not prejudice but nevertheless discriminates.

Blumer's position shifts the investigation of prejudice away from the psychological to something more sociological, which looks at the relationship of racial groups to each other. His theory is illustrated in the educational videos *Ethnic Notions* and *Color Adjustment* by Marlon Riggs (California Newsreel). They show how racial images of blacks after the Civil War were formed in the white community. In the late nineteenth century the media, largely newspapers and silent movies, depicted blacks as savages or brutes for which freedom from slavery was not a good thing. The movie, *The Birth of a Nation*, directed by D. W. Griffith, presented to the country's dominant white population an image of free-from-slavery blacks with exaggerated physical features associated with negative behavior patterns. The stereotyped images of black men included an alleged desire for white women, and they were to be feared. In the Jim Crow America that evolved after Reconstruction, many whites formed such images of blacks derived from available popular cultural images.

Both Blumer and Allport associate prejudice with attitudes of individuals, whether the cause is personality or social. Beyond individual prejudice is institutional prejudice, which along with institutional discrimination, cannot be ignored in the study of prejudice. For example, institutional racism was the law of the land before the 1954 *Brown* decision. The "separate but equal" doctrine stemming from the landmark *Plessy* case enabled institutions such as schools to discriminate. Institutional prejudice was a "normal" part of American culture and reflected the negative stereotyping of blacks. One of the consequences of institutional prejudice led to self-segregation. Although the country has moved away from legal segregation, the latent effect of institutional prejudice today leads to self-segregation. Students will find Issue 8 ("Do Minorities Engage in Self-Segregation?") closely related to this discussion of prejudice.

For a historical account of the psychological understanding of prejudice, see "Psychology and Prejudice: A Historical Analysis and Integrative Framework," by John Duckett in *American Psychologist* (October 1992). Readers are encouraged to consult the entire classic, *The Nature of Prejudice* (Perseus, 1979), by Gordon Allport. It is a comprehensive and detailed account of prejudice. Another detailed account of the prejudiced personality appears in *The Authoritarian Personality* (Harper & Row, 1950) by Theodor Adorno. Also recommended is "Prejudice" by Thomas Pettigrew in *Harvard Encyclopedia of Ethnic Groups* (Harvard University Press, 1980) edited by Stephen Thornstrom.

Several important videos to further one's understanding of prejudice are available to the student. *The Color of Fear* (Stir-Fry Productions, 1994) by L. M. Wah shows an intense dialogue about race, prejudice, and racism. Jane Elliot's *Blue-Eyed* (California Newsreel) depicts the learning and unlearning process of prejudice for a class of elementary school children. Marlon Riggs' two videos, *Ethnic Notions* and *Color Adjustment* (California Newsreel, 1986), trace the stereotyping of blacks over the nineteenth and twentieth centuries.

To build upon the study of prejudice and look at theories of racism, Christopher Bates Doob's book, *Racism: An American Cauldron* (HarperCollins, 1996) offers a cross-cultural comparison of race relations. Students interested in the politics of race prejudice may find *The Racial Attitudes of American Presidents: From Abraham Lincoln to Theodore Roosevelt* (Anchor, 1972) by George Sinkler informative. He analyzes the role of the presidency in relation to racial problems. *The First R: How Children Learn Race and Racism* by Debra Van Ausdale and Joe Feagin argues that children learn racial attitudes at a very young age. *Race Manners: Navigating the Minefield Between Black and White Americans* (Arcade, 1999) by Bruce A. Jacobs provides a contemporary look at prejudice, racism, and discrimination. A lively feminist perspective is offered by Patricia Williams' *The Rooster's Egg: On the Persistence of Prejudice* (Harvard University Press, 1995).

ISSUE 7

Are Definitions of Race *Just* Political?

YES: Lawrence Wright, "One Drop of Blood," *The New Yorker,* July 12, 1993 (Wendy Weil Agency, Inc.)

NO: Clara Rodriguez and Hector Cordero-Guzman, "Placing Race In Context," *Ethnic and Racial Studies* 15, 4, pp. 523–541, October, 1992 (Routledge)

ISSUE SUMMARY

YES: Lawrence Wright, a writer for *The New Yorker,* demonstrates the influence of politics upon census categories of race and ethnicity. In the 1990s, multiracial groups who did not fit into the government's traditional categories of race and ethnicity began to challenge them as too narrow and inaccurate.

NO: Clara Rodriguez, a professor of sociology at Fordham University, and Hector Cordero-Guzman, an associate professor and chair of the Department of Black and Hispanic Studies at Baruch College of the City University of New York, suggest that race is a much more complex concept. Using responses by Puerto Ricans to questions about racial identity, they argue that racial identity is "more contextually influenced, determined and defined."

Historically, since race in the U.S. has been divided into black or white—one had to be either—a black person was defined as someone having black ancestors. The "one-drop rule," more accurately understood as "one-drop of black blood," refers to racial classification of blacks in the United States. Although race status in America is the product of descent, there are no U.S. Census categories for mixed race persons. The increasing diversity of our population has rendered traditional race and ethnic categories, regardless of how familiar they are, inadequate. Expanded populations of Asians, Hispanics, Middle Easterners, for example, challenge the traditional black-white dichotomy. The politics of how these racial and ethnic groups become categorized is the essence of this issue.

Lawrence Wright discusses the Sawyer hearings of 1993 conducted by the House Subcommittee on the Census, Statistics and Postal Personnel. The hearings were concerned with changing demographics and census categorization.

Essentially there is a dilemma at large concerning race classification. On one hand, we have the traditional categories of race that are reflected in the census. Census data is critical in terms of public policy and the distribution of resources to groups within society. In effect, the established categories protect minority interests. Further, measures of political redistricting that have implication for voting as well as school district formation are based on traditional categories of race and ethnicity. On the other hand, the rapidly increasing number of people who are of mixed race and mixed ethnicity are forced to ignore part of their identity. What is their social cost? What is the political cost of a mixed race category?

Rodriguez and Cordero-Guzman emphasize the social and historical determinants of and categories of race. After Europeans arrived, peoples mixed throughout the Americas and the Caribbean. The historical mixing of people that occurred in the United States resulted in the rule of hypo-decent, or the "one drop rule" and a rigidly enforced black and white dichotomy. Anyone with known African ancestry was classified as "Black." In Puerto Rico, and throughout Latin America, somewhat different racial constructions resulted. Slavery existed and was abominable throughout North America, the Caribbean, and Latin America. However, racial classifications appear to have been more varied and fluid outside of the United States. In other areas, a spectrum of color and types came to be recognized, with class, politics, language, and other social-economic variables also influencing classifications. They remind us of the fact that "popular definitions of 'race' vary from culture to culture." This suggests the importance of historical events, political-economic forces, and context in determining "race."

Why, in the American experience, did mixed race people become categorized as black? Why did the Puerto Rican experience lead to multiple social categories of race? Students have the opportunity to consider the significant role of politics in racial categorization, and contrast it to historical and social context that other cultures employ. Is racial identity simply an individual choice? Or, are there structural and cultural factors that determine race classification? Students should consult the previous two issues (Is skin color a proper determinant of race? Is race prejudice a product of group position?) along with Issue #16 (Should 21st century public policy be class conscious rather than race conscious?) to explore further the complex dimensions of race.

Lawrence Wright  **YES**

One Drop of Blood

Washington in the millennial years is a city of warring racial and ethnic groups fighting for recognition, protection, and entitlements. This war has been fought throughout the second half of the twentieth century largely by black Americans. How much this contest has widened, how bitter it has turned, how complex and baffling it is, and how far-reaching its consequences are became evident in a series of congressional hearings that began last year in the obscure House Subcommittee on Census, Statistics, and Postal Personnel, which is chaired by Representative Thomas C. Sawyer, Democrat of Ohio, and concluded in November, 1993.

Although the Sawyer hearings were scarcely reported in the news and were sparsely attended even by other members of the subcommittee, with the exception of Representative Thomas E. Petri, Republican of Wisconsin, they opened what may become the most searching examination of racial questions in this country since the sixties. Related federal agency hearings, and meetings that will be held in Washington and other cities around the country to prepare for the 2000 census, are considering not only modifications of existing racial categories but also the larger question of whether it is proper for the government to classify people according to arbitrary distinctions of skin color and ancestry. This discussion arises at a time when profound debates are occurring in minority communities about the rightfulness of group entitlements, some government officials are questioning the usefulness of race data, and scientists are debating whether race exists at all.

Tom Sawyer, forty-eight, a former English teacher and a former mayor of Akron, is now in his fourth term representing the Fourteenth District of Ohio. It would be fair to say that neither the House Committee on Post Office and Civil Service nor the subcommittee that Sawyer chairs is the kind of assignment that members of Congress would willingly shed blood for. Indeed, the attitude of most elected officials in Washington toward the census is polite loathing, because it is the census, as much as any other force in the country, that determines their political futures. Congressional districts rise and fall with the shifting demography of the country, yet census matters rarely seize the front pages of home-town newspapers, except briefly, once every ten years. Much of the subcommittee's business has to do with addressing the safety concerns of postal workers and overseeing federal statistical measurements. The subcommittee has an additional responsibility: it reviews the executive branch's policy about which racial and ethnic groups should be officially recognized by the United States government.

"We are unique in this country in the way we describe and define race and ascribe to it characteristics that other cultures view very differently," Sawyer, who is a friendly man with an open, boyish face and graying black hair, says. He points out that the country is in the midst of its most profound demographic shift since the eighteen-nineties—a time that opened "a period of the greatest immigration we have ever seen, whose numbers have not been matched until right now." A deluge of new Americans from every part of the world is overwhelming our traditional racial distinctions, Sawyer believes. "The categories themselves inevitably reflect the temporal bias of every age," he says. "That becomes a problem when the nation itself is undergoing deep and historic diversification."

Looming over the shoulder of Sawyer's subcommittee is the Office of Management and Budget, the federal agency that happens to be responsible for determining standard classifications of racial and ethnic data. Since 1977, those categories have been set by O.M.B. Statistical Directive 15, which controls the racial and ethnic standards on all federal forms and statistics. Directive 15 acknowledges four general racial groups in the United States: American Indian or Alaskan Native; Asian or Pacific Islander; Black; and White. Directive 15 also breaks down ethnicity into Hispanic Origin and Not of Hispanic Origin. These categories, or versions of them, are present on enrollment forms for schoolchildren; on application forms for jobs, scholarships, loans, and mortgages; and, of course, on United States census forms. The categories ask that every American fit himself or herself into one racial and one ethnic box. From this comes the information that is used to monitor and enforce civil-rights legislation, most notably the Voting Rights Act of 1965, but also a smorgasbord of set-asides and entitlements and affirmative-action programs. "The numbers drive the dollars," Sawyer observes, repeating a well-worn Washington adage.

The truth of that statement was abundantly evident in the hearings, in which a variety of racial and ethnic groups were bidding to increase their portions of the federal pot. The National Coalition for an Accurate Count of Asian Pacific Americans lobbied to add Cambodians and Lao to the nine different nationalities already listed on the census forms under the heading of Asian or Pacific Islander. The National Council of La Raza proposed that Hispanics be considered a race, not just an ethnic group. The Arab American Institute asked that persons from the Middle East, now counted as white, be given a separate, protected category of their own. Senator Daniel K. Akaka, a Native Hawaiian, urged that his people be moved from the Asian or Pacific Islander box to the American Indian or Alaskan Native box. "There is the misperception that Native Hawaiians, who number well over two hundred thousand, somehow 'immigrated' to the United States like other Asian or Pacific Island groups," the Senator testified. "This leads to the erroneous impression that Native Hawaiians, the original inhabitants of the Hawaiian Islands, no longer exist." In the Senator's opinion, being placed in the same category as other Native Americans would help rectify that situation. (He did not mention that certain American Indian tribes enjoy privileges concerning gambling concessions that Native Hawaiians currently don't enjoy.) The National Congress of American Indians would like the Hawaiians to stay where they are. In every case, issues of money, but also of identify, are at stake.

In this battle over racial turf, a disturbing new contender has appeared. "When I received my 1990 census form, I realized that there was no race category for my children," Susan Graham, who is a white woman married to a black man in Roswell, Georgia, testified. "I called the Census Bureau. After checking with supervisors, the bureau finally gave me their answer: the children should take the race of their mother. When I objected and asked why my children should be classified as their mother's race only, the Census Bureau representative said to me, in a very hushed voice, 'Because, in cases like these, we always know who the mother is and not always the father.' "

Graham went on to say, "I could not make a race choice from the basic categories when I enrolled my son in kindergarten in Georgia. The only choice I had, like most other parents of multiracial children, was to leave race blank. I later found that my child's teacher was instructed to choose for him based on her knowledge and observation of my child. Ironically, my child has been white on the United States census, black at school, and multiracial at home—all at the same time."

Graham and others were asking that a "Multiracial" box be added to the racial categories specified by Directive 15—a proposal that alarmed representatives of the other racial groups for a number of reasons, not the least of which was that multiracialism threatened to undermine the concept of racial classification altogether.

According to various estimates, at least seventy-five to more than ninety per cent of the people who now check the Black box could check Multiracial, because of their mixed genetic heritage. If a certain proportion of those people—say, ten per cent—should elect to identify themselves as Multiracial, legislative districts in many parts of the country might need to be redrawn. The entire civil-rights regulatory program concerning housing, employment, and education would have to be reassessed. School-desegregation plans would be thrown into the air. Of course, it is possible that only a small number of Americans will elect to choose the Multiracial option, if it is offered, with little social effect. Merely placing such an option on the census invites people to consider choosing it, however. When the census listed "Cajun" as one of several examples under the ancestry question, the number of Cajuns jumped nearly two thousand per cent. To remind people of the possibility is to encourage enormous change.

Those who are charged with enforcing civil-rights laws see the Multiracial box as a wrecking ball aimed at affirmative action, and they hold those in the mixed-race movement responsible. "There's no concern on any of these people's part about the effect on policy—it's just a subjective feeling that their identity needs to be stroked," one government analyst said. "What they don't understand is that it's going to cost their own groups"—by losing the advantages that accrue to minorities by way of affirmative-action programs, for instance. Graham contends that the object of her movement is not to create another protected category. In any case, she said, multiracial people know "to check the right box to get the goodies."

Of course, races have been mixing in America since Columbus arrived. Visitors to Colonial America found plantation slaves who were as light-skinned as their masters. Patrick Henry actually proposed, in 1784, that the State of Virginia encourage intermarriage between whites and Indians, through the use of tax incentives and cash stipends. The legacy of this intermingling is that Americans who are descendants of early settlers, of slaves, or of Indians often have ancestors of different races in their family tree.

Thomas Jefferson supervised the original census, in 1790. The population then was broken down into free white males, free white females, other persons (these included free blacks and "taxable Indians," which meant those living in or around white settlements), and slaves. How unsettled this country has always been about its racial categories is evident in the fact that nearly every census since has measured race differently. For most of the nineteenth century, the census reflected an American obsession with miscegenation. The color of slaves was to be specified as "B," for Black and "M," for mulatto. In the 1890 census, gradations of mulattoes were further broken down into quadroons and octoroons. After 1920, however, the Census Bureau gave up on such distinctions, estimating that three-quarters of all blacks in the United States were racially mixed already, and that pure blacks would soon disappear. Hence-forth anyone with any black ancestry at all would be counted simply as black.

Actual interracial marriages, however, were historically rare. Multiracial children were often marginalized as illegitimate half-breeds who didn't fit comfortably into any racial community. This was particularly true of the offspring of black-white unions. "In my family, like many families with African-American ancestry, there is a history of multiracial offspring associated with rape and concubinage," G. Reginald Daniel, who teaches a course in multiracial identity at the University of California at Los Angeles, says. "I was reared in the segregationist South. Both sides of my family have been mixed for at least three generations. I struggled as a child over the question of why I had to exclude my East Indian and Irish and Native American and French ancestry, and could include only African."

Until recently, people like Daniel were identified simply as black because of a peculiarly American institution known informally as "the one-drop rule," which defines as black a person with as little as a single drop of "black blood." This notion derives from a long-discredited belief that each race had its own blood type, which was correlated with physical appearance and social behavior. The antebellum South promoted the rule as a way of enlarging the slave population with the children of slaveholders. By the nineteen-twenties, in Jim Crow America the one-drop rule was well established as the law of the land. It still is, according to a United States Supreme Court decision as late as 1986, which refused to review a lower court's ruling that a Louisiana woman whose great-great-great-great-grandmother had been the mistress of a French planter was black—even though that proportion of her ancestry amounted to no more than three thirty-seconds of her genetic heritage. "We are the only country in the world that applies the one-drop rule, and the only group that the one-drop rule applies to is people of African descent," Daniel observes.

People of mixed black-and-white ancestry were rejected by whites and found acceptance by blacks. Many of the most notable "black" leaders over the last century and a half were "white" to some extent, from Booker T. Washington and Frederick Douglass (both of whom has white fathers) to W. E. B. Du Bois, Malcolm X, and Martin Luther King Jr. (who had an Irish grandmother and some American Indian ancestry as well.) The fact that Lani Guinier, Louis Farrakhan, and Virginia's former governor Douglas Wilder are defined as black, and define themselves that way, though they have light skin or "European" features, demonstrates how enduring the one-drop rule has proved to be in America, not only among whites but among blacks as well. Daniel sees this as "a double-edged sword." While the one-drop rule encouraged racism, it also galvanized the black community.

"But the one-drop rule is racist," Daniel says. "There's no way you can get away from the fact that it was historically implemented to create as many slaves as possible. No one leaped over to the white community—that was simply the mentality of the nation, and people of African descent internalized it. What this current discourse is about is lifting the lid of racial oppression in our institutions and letting people identify with the totality of their heritage. We have created a nightmare for human dignity. Multiracialism has the potential for undermining the very basis of racism, which is its categories."

But multiracialism introduces nightmares of its own. If people are to be counted as something other than completely black, for instance, how will affirmative-action programs be implemented? Suppose a court orders a city to hire additional black police officers to make up for past discrimination. Will mixed-race officers count? Will they count wholly or partly? Far from solving the problem of fragmented identities, multiracialism could open the door to fractional races, such as we already have in the case of the American Indians. In order to be eligible for certain federal benefits, such as housing-improvement programs, a person must prove that he or she either is a member of a federally recognized Indian tribe or has fifty per cent "Indian blood." One can envision a situation in which nonwhiteness itself becomes the only valued quality, to be compensated in various ways depending on a person's pedigree.

Kwame Anthony Appiah, of Harvard's Philosophy and Afro-American Studies Departments says, "What the Multiracial category aims for is not people of mixed ancestry, because a majority of Americans are actually products of mixed ancestry. This category goes after people who have parents who are socially recognized as belonging to different races. That's

O.K.—that's an interesting social category. But then you have to ask what happens to their children. Do we want to have more boxes, depending upon whether they marry back into one group or the other? What are the children of these people supposed to say? I think about these things because— look, my mother in English; my father is Ghanaian. My sisters are married to a Nigerian and a Norwegian. I have nephews who range from blond-haired kids to very black kids. They are all first cousins. Now, according to the American scheme of things, they're all black—even the guy with blond hair who skis in Oslo. That's what the one-drop rule says. The Multiracial scheme, which is meant to solve anomalies, simply creates more anomalies of its own, and that's because the fundamental concept—that you should be able to assign every American to one of three or four races reliably—is crazy."

These are sentiments that Representative Sawyer agrees with profoundly. He says of the one-drop rule, "It is so embedded in our perception and policy, but it doesn't allow for the blurring that is the reality of our population. Just look at—What are the numbers?" he said in his congressional office as he leafed through a briefing book. "Thirty-eight per cent of American Japanese females and eighteen per cent of American Japanese males marry outside their traditional ethnic and nationality group. Seventy per cent of American Indians marry outside. I grant you that the enormous growth potential of multiracial marriages starts from a relatively small base, but the truth is it starts from a fiction to begin with; that is, what we think of as black-and-white marriages are not marriages between people who come from anything like a clearly defined ethnic, racial, or genetic base."

The United States Supreme Court struck down the last vestige of anti-miscegenation laws in 1967, in Loving v. Virginia. At that time, interracial marriages were rare; only sixty-five thousand marriages between blacks and whites were recorded in the 1970 census. Marriages between Asians and non-Asian Americans tended to be between soldiers and war brides. Since then, mixed marriages occurring between many racial and ethnic groups have risen to the point where they have eroded the distinctions between such peoples. Among American Indians, peoples are more likely to marry outside their group than within it, as Representative Sawyer noted. The number of children living in families where one parent is white and the other is black, Asian, or American Indian, to use one measure, has tripled— from fewer than four hundred thousand in 1970 to one and a half million in 1990—and this doesn't count the children of single parents of children whose parents are divorced.

Blacks are conspicuously less likely to marry outside their group, and yet marriages between blacks and whites have tripled in the last thirty years. Matthijs Kalmijn, a Dutch sociologist, analyzed marriage certificates filed in this country's non-Southern states since the Loving decision and found that in the nineteen-eighties the rate at which black men were marrying white women had reached approximately ten per cent. (The rate for black women marrying white men is about half that figure.) In the 1990 census, six per cent of black householders nationwide had nonblack spouses—still a small percentage, but a significant one.

Multiracial people, because they are now both unable and unwilling to be ignored, and because many of them refuse to be confined to traditional racial categories, inevitably undermine the entire concept of race as an irreducible difference between peoples. The continual modulation of racial differences in America is increasing the jumble created by centuries of ethnic intermarriage. The resulting dilemma is a profound one. If we choose to measure the mixing by counting people as Multiracial, we pull the teeth of the civil-rights laws. Are we ready for that? Is it even possible to make changes in the way we count Americans, given the legislative mandates already built into law? "I don't know," Sawyer concedes. "At this point, my purposes is not so much to alter the laws that underlie these kinds of questions as to raise the question of whether or not the way in which we currently define who we are reflects the reality of the nation we are and who we are becoming. If it does not, then the policies underlying the terms of measurement are doomed to be flawed. What you measure is what you get."

Science has put forward many different racial models, the most enduring being the division of humanity into three broad groupings: the Mongoloid, the Negroid, and the Caucasoid. An influential paper by Masatoshi Nei and Arun K. Roychoudhury, entitled "Gene Differences between Caucasian, Negro, and Japanese Populations," which appeared in *Science*, in 1972, found that the genetic variation among individuals from these racial groups was only slightly greater than the variation within the groups.

In 1965, the anthropologist Stanley Garn proposed hundreds, even thousands, of racial groups, which he saw as gene clusters separated by geography or culture, some with only minor variations between them. The paleontologist Stephen Jay Gould, for one, has proposed doing away with all racial classifications and identifying people by clines—regional divisions that are used to account for the diversity of snails and of songbirds, among many other species. In this Gould follows the anthropologist Ashley Montagu, who waged a lifelong campaign to rid science of the term "race" altogether and never used it except it quotation marks. Montagu would have substituted the term "ethnic group," which he believed carried less odious baggage.

Race, in the common understanding draws upon differences not only of skin color and physical attributes but also of language, nationality, and religion. At times, we have counted as "races" different national groups, such as Mexicans and Filipinos. Some Asian Indians were counted as members of a "Hindu" race in the censuses from 1920 to 1940; then they became white for three decades. Racial categories are often used as ethnic intensifiers, with the aim of justifying the exploitation of one group by another. One can trace the ominous example of Jews in prewar Germany, who were counted as "Israelites," a religious group, until the Nazis came to power and turned them into a race. Mixtures of first- and second-degree Jewishness were distinguished, much as quadroons and octoroons had been in the United States. In fact, the Nazi experience ultimately caused a widespread reëxamination of the idea of race. Canada dropped the race question from its census in 1951 and has so far resisted all attempts to reinstitute it.

People who were working in the United States Bureau of the Census in the fifties and early sixties remember that there was speculation that the race question would soon be phased out in America as well. The American Civil Liberties Union tried to get the race question dropped from the census in 1960, and the State of New Jersey stopped entering race information on birth and death certificates in 1962 and 1963. In 1964, however, the architecture of civil-rights laws began to be erected, and many of the new laws—particularly the Voting Rights Act of 1965—required highly detailed information about minority participation which could be gathered only by the decennial census, the nation's supreme instrument for gathering demographic statistics. The expectation that the race question would wither away surrendered to the realization that race data were fundamental to monitoring and enforcing desegregation. The census soon acquired a political importance that it had never had in the past.

Unfortunately, the sloppiness and multiplicity of certain racial and ethnic categories rendered them practically meaningless for statistical purposes. In 1973, Caspar Weinberger, who was then Secretary of Health, Education and Welfare, asked the Federal Interagency Committee on Education (FICE) to develop some standards for classifying race and ethnicity. An ad-hoc committee sprang into being and proposed to create an intellectual grid that would sort all Americans into five racial and ethnic categories. The first category was American Indian or Alaskan Native. Some members of the committee wanted the category to be called Original Peoples of the Western Hemisphere, in order to include Indians of South American origin, but the distinction that this category was seeking was so-called "Federal Indians," who were eligible for government benefits; to include Indians of any other origin, even though they might be genetically quite similar, would confuse the collecting of data. To accommodate the various, highly diverse peoples who originated in the Far East, Southeast Asia, and the Pacific Islands, the committee proposed a category called Asian or Pacific Islander, thus sweeping into one massive basket Chinese, Samoans, Cambodians, Filipinos, and others—peoples who had little or nothing in common, and many of whom were, indeed, traditional enemies. The fact that American Indians and Alaskan Natives originated from the same Mongoloid stock as many of these peoples did not stop the committee from putting them in a separate racial category. Black was defined as "a person having origins in any of the black racial groups of Africa," and White, initially, as "a person having origins in any of the original peoples of Europe, North Africa, the Middle East, or the Indian subcontinent"—everybody else, in other words. Because the Black category contained anyone with any African heritage at all, the range of actual skin colors covered the entire spectrum, as did the White category, which included Arabs and Asian Indians and various other darker-skinned peoples.

The final classification, Hispanic, was the most problematic of all. In the 1960 census, people whose ancestry was Latin-American were counted as white. Then people of Spanish origin became a protected group, requiring the census to gather data in order to monitor their civil rights. But how to define them? People who spoke Spanish? Defining the population that way would have included millions of Americans who spoke the language but had no actual roots in Hispanic culture, and it excluded Brazilians and children of immigrants who were not taught Spanish in their homes. One approach was to count persons with Spanish surnames, but that created a number of difficulties: marriage made some non-Hispanic women into instant minorities, while stripping other women of their Hispanic status. The 1970 census inquired about people from "Central or South America," and more than a million people checked the box who were not Hispanic; they were from Kansas, Alabama, Mississippi—the central and southern United States, in other words.

The greatest dilemma was that there was no conceivable justification for calling Hispanics a race. There were black Hispanics from the Dominican Republic, Argentines who were almost entirely European whites, Mexicans who would have been counted as American Indians if they had been born north of the Rio Grande. The great preponderance of Hispanics are mestizos—a continuum of many different genetic backgrounds. Moreover, the fluid Latin-American concept of race differs from the rigid United States idea of biologically determined and highly distinct human divisions. In most Latin cultures, skin color is an individual variable—not a group marker—so that within the same family one sibling might be considered white and another black. By 1960, the United States census, which counts the population of Puerto Rico, gave up asking the race question on the island, because race did not carry the same distinction there that it did on the mainland. The ad-hoc committee decided to dodge riddles like these by calling Hispanics an ethnic group, not a race.

In 1977, O.M.B. Statistical Directive 15 adopted the FICE suggestions practically verbatim, with one principal exception: Asian Indians were moved to the Asian or Pacific Islander category. Thus, with little political discussion, the identities of Americans were fixed in five broad groupings. Those racial and ethnic categories that were dreamed up almost twenty years ago were not neutral in their effect. By attempting to provide a way for Americans to describe themselves, the categories actually began to shape those identities. The categories became political entities, with their own constituencies, lobbies, and vested interests. What was even more significant, they caused people to think of themselves in new ways—as members of "races" that were little more than statistical devices. In 1974, the year the ad-hoc committee set to work, few people referred to themselves as Hispanic; rather, people who fell into that grouping tended to identify themselves by nationality—Mexican or Dominican, for instance. Such small categories, however, are inconvenient for statistics and politics, and the creation of the meta-concept "Hispanic" has resulted in the formation of a peculiarly American group. "It is a mixture of ethnicity, culture, history, birth, and a presumption of language," Sawyer contends. Largely because of immigration, the Asian or Pacific Islander group is considered the fastest-growing racial group in the United States, but it is a "racial" category that in all likelihood exists nowhere else in the world. The third-fastest-growing category is

Other—made up of the nearly ten million people, most of them Hispanics, who refused to check any of the prescribed racial boxes. American Indian groups are also growing at a rate that far exceeds the growth of the population as a whole: from about half a million people in 1960 to nearly two million in 1990—a two-hundred-and-fifty-nine-per-cent increase, which was demographically impossible. It seemed to be accounted for by improvements in the census-taking procedure and also by the fact that Native Americans had become fashionable, and people now wished to identify with them. To make matters even more confounding, only seventy-four per cent of those who identified themselves as American Indian by race reported having Indian ancestry.

Whatever the word "race" may mean elsewhere in the world, or to the world of science, it is clear that in America the categories are arbitrary, confused, and hopelessly intermingled. In many cases, Americans don't know who they are, racially speaking. A National Center for Health Statistics study found that 5.8 per cent of the people who called themselves Black were seen as White by a census interviewer. Nearly a third of the people identifying themselves as Asian were classified as White or Black by independent observers. That was also true of seventy per cent of people who identified themselves as American Indians. Robert A. Hahn, an epidemiologist at the Centers for Disease Control and Prevention, analyzed deaths of infants born from 1983 through 1985. In an astounding number of cases, the infant had a different race on its death certificate from the one on its birth certificate, and this finding led to staggering increases in the infant-mortality rate for minority populations—46.9 per cent greater for American Indians, 48.8 per cent greater for Japanese-Americans, 78.7 per cent greater for Filipinos—over what had been previously recorded. Such disparities cast doubt on the dependability of race as a criterion for any statistical survey. "It seems to me that we have to go back and reëvaluate the whole system," Hahn says. "We have to ask, 'What do these categories mean?' We are not talking about race in the way that geneticists might use the term, because we're not making any kind of biological assessment. It's closer to self-perceived membership in a population—which is essentially what ethnicity is." There are genetic variations in disease patterns, Hahn points out, and he goes on to say, "But these variations don't always correspond to so-called races. What's really important is, essentially, two things. One, people from different ancestral backgrounds have different behaviors—diets, ideas about what to do when you're sick—that lead them to different health statuses. Two, people are discriminated against because of other people's perception of who they are and how they should be treated. There's still a lot of discrimination in the health-care system."

Racial statistics do serve an important purpose in the monitoring and enforcement of civil-rights laws; indeed, that has become the main justification for such data. A routine example is the Home Mortgage Disclosure Act. Because of race questions on loan applications, the federal government has been able to document the continued practice of redlining by financial institutions. The Federal Reserve found that, for conventional mortgages, in

1992 the denial rate for blacks and Hispanics was roughly double the rate for whites. Hiring practices, jury selection, discriminatory housing patterns, apportionment of political power—in all these areas, and more, the government patrols society, armed with little more than statistical information to insure equal and fair treatment. "We need these categories essentially to get rid of them," Hahn says.

The unwanted corollary of slotting people by race is that such officially sanctioned classifications may actually worsen racial strife. By creating social-welfare programs based on race rather than on need, the government sets citizens against one another precisely because of perceived racial differences. "It is not 'race' but a *practice* of racial classification that bedevils the society," writes Yehudi Webster, a sociologist at California State University, Los Angeles, and the author of "The Racialization of America." The use of racial statistics, he and others have argued, creates a reality of racial divisions, which then require solutions, such as busing, affirmative action, and multicultural education, all of which are bound to fail, because they heighten the racial awareness that leads to contention. Webster believes that adding a Multiracial box would be "another leap into absurdity," because it reinforces the concept of race in the first place. "In a way, it's a continuation of the one-drop principle. Anybody can say, 'I've got one drop of *something*—I must be multiracial.' It may be a good thing. It may finally convince Americans of the absurdity of racial classification."

In 1990, Itabari Njeri, who writes about interethnic relations for the Los Angeles *Times*, organized a symposium for the National Association of Black Journalists. She recounts a presentation given by Charles Stewart, a Democratic Party activist: "If you consider yourself black for political reasons, raise your hand." The vast majority raised their hands. When Stewart then asked how many people present believed they were of pure African descent, without any mixture, no one raised his hand. Stewart commented later, "If you advocate a category that includes people who are multiracial to the detriment of their black identification, you will replicate what you saw—an empty room. We cannot afford to have an empty room."

Njeri maintains that the social and economic gap between light-skinned blacks and dark-skinned blacks is as great as the gap between all blacks and all whites in America. If people of more obviously mixed backgrounds were to migrate to a Multiracial box, she says, they would be politically abandoning their former allies and the people who needed their help the most. Instead of draining the established categories of their influence, Njeri and others believe, it would be better to eliminate racial categories altogether.

That possibility is actually being discussed in the corridors of government. "It's quite strange—the original idea of O.M.B. Directive 15 has nothing to do with current efforts to 'define' race," says Sally Katzen, the director of the Office of Information and Regulatory Affairs of O.M.B., who has the onerous responsibility of making the final recommendation on revising the racial categories. "When O.M.B. got into the business of establishing categories, it was purely statistical, not programmatic—purely for the purpose of data gathering, not for defining or protecting different categories. It was certainly never meant to *define* a race." And yet for more than twenty years Directive 15 did exactly that, with relatively little outcry. "Recently, a question has been raised about the increasing number of multiracial children. I personally have received pictures of beautiful children who are part Asian and part black, or part American Indian and part Asian, with these letters saying, 'I don't want to check just one box. I don't want to deny part of my heritage.' It's very compelling."

This year, Katzen convened a new interagency committee to consider how races should be categorized, and even whether racial information should be sought at all. "To me it's *offensive*—because I think of the Holocaust—for someone to say what a Jew is," says Katzen. "I don't think a government agency should be defining racial and ethnic categories—that certainly was not what was ever intended by these standards."

Is it any accident that racial and ethnic categories should come under attack now, when being a member of a minority group brings certain advantages? The white colonizers of North America conquered the indigenous people, imported African slaves, brought in Asians as laborers and then excluded them with prejudicial immigration laws, and appropriated Mexican land and the people who were living on it. In short, the nonwhite population of America has historically been subjugated and treated as second-class citizens by the white majority. It is to redress the social and economic inequalities of our history that we have civil-rights laws and affirmative-action plans in the first place. Advocates of various racial and ethnic groups point out that many of the people now calling for a race-blind society are political conservatives, who may have an interest in undermining the advancement of nonwhites in our society. Suddenly, the conservatives have adopted the language of integration, it seems, and the left-leaning racial-identity advocates have adopted the language of separatism. It amounts to a polar reversal of political rhetoric.

Jon Michael Spencer, a professor in the African and Afro-American Studies Curriculum at the University of North Carolina at Chapel Hill, recently wrote an article in *The Black Scholar* lamenting what he calls "the postmodern conspiracy to explode racial identity." The article ignited a passionate debate in the magazine over the nature and the future of race. Spencer believes that race is a useful metaphor for cultural and historic difference, because it permits a level of social cohesion among oppressed classes. "To relinquish the notion of race—even though it's a cruel hoax—at this particular time is to relinquish our fortress against the powers and principalities that still try to undermine us," he says. He sees the Multiracial box as politically damaging to "those who need to galvanize peoples around the racial idea of black."

There are some black cultural nationalists who might welcome the Multiracial category. "In terms of the African-American population, it could be very, very useful, because there is a need to clarify who is in and who is not," Molefi Kete Asante, who is the chairperson of the Department of African-American Studies at Temple University, says. "In fact, I would think they should go further than that—identify those people who are in interracial marriages."

Spencer, however, thinks that it might be better to eliminate racial categories altogether than to create an additional category that empties the others of meaning. "If you had who knows how many thousands or tens of thousands or millions of people claiming to be multiracial, you would lessen the number who are black," Spencer says. "There's no end in sight. There's no limit to which one can go in claiming to be multiracial. For instance, I happen to be very brown in complexion, but when I go to the continent of Africa, blacks and whites there claim that I would be 'colored' rather than black, which means that somewhere in my distant past—probably during the era of slavery—I could have one or more white ancestors. So does that mean that I, too, could check Multiracial? Certainly light-skinned black people might perhaps see this as a way out of being included among a despised racial group. The result could be the creation of another class of people, who are betwixt and between black and white."

Whatever comes out of this discussion, the nation is likely to engage in the most profound debate of racial questions in decades. "We recognize the importance of racial categories in correcting clear injustices under the law," Representative Sawyer says. "The dilemma we face is trying to assure the fundamental guarantees of equality of opportunity while at the same time recognizing that the populations themselves are changing as we seek to categorize them. It reaches the point where it becomes an absurd counting game. Part of the difficulty is that we are dealing with the illusion of precision. We wind up with precise counts of everybody in the country, and they are precisely wrong. They don't reflect who we are as a people. To be effective, the concepts of individual and group identity need to reflect not only who we have been but who we are becoming. The more these categories distort our perception of reality, the less useful they are. We act as if we knew what we're talking about when we talk about race, and we don't."

NO ↰

**Clara E. Rodriguez and
Hector Cordero-Guzman**

Placing Race in Context

Introduction

By the 1960s a consensus had been reached that race as a biological concept was useless (Alland 1971; Harris 1968; Mead et al. 1968; Montagu 1964). There was only one human race and it had infinite variation and some population clusters. Yet, race, as people experience it, is a cultural construct (Sanjek 1990). Thus, how "races" or racial paradigms are determined also varies from culture to culture, as does the meaning of the term "race."

For example, in the United States of America race is conceived as being biologically or genetically based. The White race was defined by the absence of any non-White blood, and, the Black race was defined by the presence of any Black blood. This cultural conception of race differed from that which evolved in Latin America. In Latin America, race may have had blood lines as a referent, but there were also other dimensions brought into "racial classification": for example, class, physical type, and ethnic background. Thus, in the US and in Latin America, two different cultural definitions of "race" arose, each of which took different referents. Each system of racial classification was seen, by those who utilized it, to be the only correct way of viewing individuals.

The fact that popular definitions of "race" vary from culture to culture suggests the importance of historical events, developments or context in determining "race." That there are different systems of racial classification in different countries (and sometimes within countries) is quite counter to the usual perception that most White Americans hold of race in the United States. This is because of the particular way in which race is popularly viewed in the US where race is seen to be genetically based and therefore unchanging. In the words of American sociologists, it is an ascribed characteristic.

An example of how race changes from context to context is the description of the man who, in travelling from Puerto Rico to Mexico to the United States, changes his race from "White to Mulatto to Black" (Mintz 1971). Then there is the case of the Japanese who were accorded the status of honorary Whites in South Africa because of the changing business context. Again, there is the example of the Jews in Europe, who were classified by the

Excerpted from *Ethnic and Racial Studies*, October 1992, pp. 523–529. Copyright © 1992 by International Thomson Publishing, Ltd. Reprinted by permission.

Germans as a race apart from other Europeans, despite the fact that they were a group with highly varied phenotypes and quite diverse genetic strains. In nineteenth-century US and in the early twentieth-century immigration laws, race was used to describe not only Blacks and Whites, but also Slavs, Italians, Anglo-Saxons, etc. A basic white-non-white dichotomous categorization was present, but many European groups were also viewed as subraces, different from Anglo-Saxon stock.

Given the significance of context in determining popular conceptions of race, it is also important to understand what happens to the conceptions of race and racial self-identity of individuals when they move from a country with one racial paradigm to a country with another. Are dual racial paradigms maintained? Do individuals adhere to their own perceptions of race? What determines whether they adopt or maintain their own perceptions of race? Are responses to questions of racial identity altered depending on how respondents interpret the question and its context?

These issues are brought into sharp relief when studying Puerto Ricans, a group with a history of contact with the US but with a different racial paradigm. In this article we study the way in which Puerto Ricans, who have been exposed to both cultures, identify themselves racially, how they are identified by interviewers and how they think that they would be viewed by North Americans. This research sheds light on these two racial paradigms—that of the US and Puerto Rico—and what happens when they come into contact with each other.

Race in Historical Perspective

Although both the United States and Latin America relied on the importation of African slaves to meet labour needs, the conception and incorporation of peoples of African-descent as a "race" took different directions in the two areas (Denton and Massey 1989; Pitt-Rivers 1975; Wagley 1965). Of special interest is the case of the Spanish Caribbean and, in particular, Puerto Rico. In Puerto Rico race came to be seen as a continuum of categories, with different gradations and shades of colour as the norm. In the US race was conceived as a dichotomous concept in which individuals were envisaged, and legally defined, as being either White or Black. Although both areas had instituted slavery and both had clear demarcations between free whites and slaves, the category "White" included more people in Puerto Rico than it would have done in the United States. In addition, there was a variety of race categories in Puerto Rico and many were fluid.[1]

The population of Puerto Rico is mostly descended from the original Taino Indian settlers, white Spanish colonizers, black slaves brought from Africa, and countless other immigrants. The variety of phenotypes in Puerto Rico, then, is mostly the result of a relatively unexamined history of racial mixing and diverse migratory flows. A number of works have touched on the issue of racial mixing in the island, but there is no real consensus on its extent. Puerto Rican and American researchers at different times have discussed or found Puerto Rico to be everything from a mulatto country to a predominantly white country with small subgroups of blacks and mulattos. Compare, for example, the accounts of Seda Bonilla (1961) with those of Gordon (1949), Mills, Senior and Goldsen (1950), and Senior (1965).

The historical formation of race relations in Puerto Rico was accompanied by the development of a distinct nomenclature to describe the different groups. This nomenclature and the racial discourse in Puerto Rico reflected the fact that race was seen to be multidimensional. This was quite distinct from the conception of race that developed in the United States, where new "racial" categories and terms were not developed. On some occasions the US census did separately count mulattos and other mixtures of European and African peoples, but this practice fluctuated and by 1930 the census used only the "Negro" category to describe those with any trait of African descent (Martin 1990). Thus, the offspring of Native American Indians, Asians or Europeans who intermarried with Blacks would simply be counted as Negro.

The 1896 decision of the US Supreme Court in the *Plessy v Ferguson* case legitimated the more dichotomous black/white view of "race." In this case, the petitioner averred that since he was ". . . seven eighths Caucasian and one eighth African blood; and that the mixture of colored blood was not discernible in him . . . ," he was entitled to the rights and privileges of citizens of the white race. The Supreme Court, however, decided against the plaintiff, thus further legitimating the genetic or blood quantum definition of race and sanctioning Jim Crow legislation (Blaustein and Zangrando 1968). The "separate but equal" doctrine elaborated in *Plessy v Ferguson* regulated the level of contact between White and Black Americans and went so far as to define as "Black" any individual who had even a small fraction of "Black" ancestry (Chang 1985, p. 52).

In Puerto Rico and in other parts of Latin America, race was based more on phenotypic and socio-economic definitions of the person rather than on genotypic definitions. Thus, in the US race is generally seen as a fact of biology, while in many parts of Latin America—particularly in the Spanish Caribbean—a more socio-economic conception of race has been the norm. This more socio-economic conception of race has emphasized dimensions that are freely varying, such as physical appearance (as opposed to genetic make-up), social class, and cultural modes of behaviour. For example, Sanjek (1971, p. 1128) notes that in Brazil classification is affected by contextual variables, that is, by situational and sociological variables that would include

> economic class, the dress, personality, education, and relation of the referent to the speaker; the presence of other actors and their relations to the speaker and referent; and contexts of speech, such as gossip, insult, joking, showing affection, maintenance of equality or of differential social status, or pointing out the referent in a group.

This perspective of race is opposed to the US conception, which relies mainly on genetic inheritance. In the United States race is an ascribed characteristic that does not change after birth, or from country to country. It is more dependent on a person's supposed genetic make-up and physical appearance than on socio-economic characteristics. The US conception of race with its emphasis on genetic or biological inheritance privileges a static conception of race. One is and always will be the race into which one was born, one is one's blood. This conception also disallows or ignores more contextual definitions.

In many Latin American countries, race is not a meta-concept based on biological categories, but rather a classification dependent on time and context. According to this more fluid view of race, the determination and relative salience of race categories depend not on their "inherent" nature as physical characteristics but on the historical development of the contexts in which these categories are valued. Within this frame-work, the points of social reference in which a given individual operates are important determinants of racial identity.

A number of arguments seek to account for the different racial conceptions that evolved in the United States and in Puerto Rico. For example, Denton and Massey (1989) cite three elements of the Spanish colonial system that contributed to a greater blending of the peoples in the Spanish Caribbean. First, they argue that the Spanish history of contact with northern African populations made them more tolerant of different colour groups than were northeastern Europeans. Hence, groups of Mediterranean origin, in contrast to northeastern Europeans, tend to see darker people as white. Second, they maintain that the Spanish conceived of slaves and Indians as being subjects or vassals of the crown and as having certain rights. This differed from the North American conception of slaves as being property. (That is not to say, however, that the Spanish treatment of slaves was necessarily more benevolent, merely that it was sanctioned and conceived of differently.) The third factor that Denton and Massey (1989) discuss is the Spanish Catholic Church. They argue that the Church had a central role in the conquest and promoted the conversion, baptism, and attendance of slaves at integrated religious services. Thus, the role of the Church was analogous to that of the Spanish legal code. It promoted ". . . a positive cultural attitude towards persons of color in theory" but failed "to implement the idea in practice."

The history of a country's economic development has also been seen as an important determinant of race relations and racial conceptions. Duany (1985), for example, has argued that Puerto Rico's economy was less dependent on slaves than was that of other countries in the Caribbean. Thus, there was less commitment to slavery as an institution and there were fewer slaves in Puerto Rico, both absolutely and proportionately. This, together with substantial immigration into the island of Europeans and former slaves in the nineteenth century, made for a conception of race that was rather fluid as opposed to strictly dichotomous. Lastly, the greater migration of European women and families to North America as compared with Latin America— where men predominated and European women were scarce—may also have influenced the relations between races and the consequent conceptions of race that evolved.

The differences between these two conceptions of race have been accentuated and made more apparent with the increasing number of Latinos in the

United States. In this article, we explore responses by Puerto Ricans to questions about racial identity. We contend that these responses reflect a conception of race that is different from that generally found in the classical social science literature and from that conventionally held in the US. We also argue that racial identity is contextually influenced, determined and defined.

Race and the United States Census

In the 1980 decennial census results the Puerto Rican conception of race appears to have been manifested. In response to the race item, which asked respondents to identify themselves as White, Black, or Other, 48 per cent of Puerto Ricans living in New York City replied that they were "Other" and wrote in a Spanish descriptor. Another 4 per cent replied that they were "Other" but did not write in any additional comment, 44 per cent said they were "White," and 3.9 per cent said they were "Black." This unique distribution of responses to the race item ran parallel with the national level where a full 40 per cent of all Hispanics (or 7.5 million) replied that they were "Other."

On the national level, where over 60 per cent of the nation's Hispanics are of Mexican origin and Puerto Ricans constitute about 12 per cent, there were similar results. The distribution of Latinos on the race item is particularly surprising in the light of the fact that in no state, including Hawaii, did more than 2 per cent of the general population indicate that they were of "other race" (Rodriguez 1991). See also Denton and Massey (1989) for a detailed discussion of racial identity among Mexican-Americans and Telles and Murguia (1990) for an interesting discussion of the effects of phenotype on the incomes of Mexicans in the United States.

It has been well documented (Denton and Massey 1989; Martin et al. 1988; Tienda and Ortiz 1986) that the Hispanic responses to the race item differed considerably from those of the general population. It is less clear why this is so. One interpretation stresses that the format of the race question may have led to misinterpretation. The question did not include the word race, but rather asked, "Is this person . . . ?" and provided tick-off categories. Included as possible answers were various Asian groups. This may have induced some Latino respondents to respond culturally, namely, to say that they were "Other" and write in "Mexican," "Dominican," etc. (Tienda and Ortiz 1986). In addition, the fact that the race question preceded the Hispanic identifier may have caused a cultural response to the race item. However, Martin et al. (1988) altered the sequence of the race and Hispanic identifier items and found that this affected the responses only of those Hispanics born in the US; it did not affect the tendency of foreign-born Hispanics to report that they were "Other."

Other research also suggests that there are contextual factors that affect the way in which Latinos respond to questions about race. A Content Reinterview Study by census personnel found that of those who reported that they were "Other" in the census, only 10 per cent were similarly classified in the reinterviewing (McKenney, Fernandez and Masamura 1985). Martin et al. (1988, p. 8) conclude: "[I]t appears that many Hispanic people will report themselves as 'Other race' on a self-administered questionnaire, but will be classified as 'White' by enumerators." Chevan (1990) reports on a Current Population Survey in March 1980 in which Hispanics identified themselves overwhelmingly as "White." Thus, in the presence of an interviewer who presented them with four non-Hispanic choices, 97 per cent of Hispanics identified themselves as "White," while "one month later in filling out the Census form in the privacy of their home, almost 40 per cent of Hispanics chose 'Other' and were prompted to write in the meaning of 'Other' on the form." Of those who specified a meaning 90 per cent wrote in a Hispanic identifier (Chevan 1990, p. 8). . . .

Our results also provide insight into the racial responses by Hispanics reported in the 1980 Census. The findings indicate that, regardless of how the "race" question was asked, many Puerto Ricans chose *not* to use the conventional racial categories of White and Black. The "Other" response did not represent a misunderstanding. Nor did it represent self-classification as a racially intermediate person in all cases. These results suggest a more complex reality than that which assumes that this "Other" response simply represented a misunderstanding of the question, or that it represented a homogeneous middle category of mestizos or mulattos.

The findings indicate that we cannot automatically assume that because Puerto Ricans choose to identify as "Other" they are placing themselves in a racially intermediate situation. For some Puerto Ricans a cultural response also carries a racial implication, that is, they see race and culture as being fused. They emphasize the greater validity of ethnic or cultural identity. Culture is race, regardless of the physical types within the culture.

Others see their culture as representing a "mixed" people. Still others view these concepts as independent, and a cultural response does not imply a racial designation for them. In this latter case, a respondent may identify as "Other-Puerto Rican" because he or she is not culturally or politically like White Americans or Black Americans, regardless of his or her particular race. In essence, the United States of America may choose to divide its culture into White and Black races, but a Puerto Rican will not (Rodriguez et al. 1991).

The findings suggest that race can be viewed in more than one way. For many of our respondents, race was something more than phenotype and genotype and was influenced by contextual factors such as class, education, language, and birthplace. These findings challenge the hegemonic and more static biological view of race prevalent in the US and its data-collection agencies. They challenge the arrogance behind the biological view of race implying, as it does, that there is no other view of race. These findings also raise questions about the extent to which culture, class and race are inextricably tied together even within a classification system that purports to be "biologically" anchored. Thus, "race" in the US may also, in practice, be more of a social construction than is generally admitted.

Note

1.   Clearly, the fact that there are different conceptions of race in Puerto Rico and in the US is not meant to imply that there is no racism in Puerto Rico.

References

Alland, Alexander. 1971. *Human Diversity*. New York: Columbia University Press.

Blaustein, Albert P., and Robert L. Zangrando. 1968. *Civil Rights and the American Negro: A Documentary History*. New York: Washington Square Press.

Chang, Harry. 1985. "Toward a Marxist Theory of Racism: Two Essays by Harry Chang." *Review of Radical Political Economics*," 17(3):34–45.

Chevan, Albert. 1990. "Hispanic Racial Identity: Beyond Social Class." Paper presented at the American Sociological Association meetings, Washington, DC, 14 August 1990.

Denton, Nancy, and Douglas S. Massey. 1989. "Racial Identity Among Caribbean Hispanics: The Effect of Double Minority Status on Residential Segregation." *American Sociological Review* 54:790–808.

Duany, Jorge. 1985. "Ethnicity in the Spanish Caribbean: Notes on the Consolidation of Creole Identity in Cuba and Puerto Rico, 1762–1868." *Ethnic Groups* 6:99–123.

Gordon, Maxine W. 1949. "Race Patterns and Prejudice in Puerto Rico," *American Sociological Review* 14:294–301.

Harris, Marvin. 1968. *Patterns of Race in the Americas*. New York: Walker.

Martin, Elizabeth, Theresa J. DeMaio, and Pamela C. Campanelli. 1990. "Context Effects for Census Measures of Race and Hispanic Origin." *Public Opinion Quarterly* 54(4):551–66.

McKenney, Nampeo R., Edward W. Fernandez, and Wilfred T. Masamura. 1985. "The Quality of the Race and Hispanic Origin Information Reported in the 1980 Census," Proceedings of the Survey Research Methods Section (American Statistical Association), pp. 46–50.

Mead, Margaret, Theodosius Dobzhansky, Ethel Tobach, and Robert Light, eds. 1968. *Science and the Concept of Race*. New York: Columbia University Press.

Mills, C. Wright, Clarence Senior, and Rose Goldsen. 1950. *The Puerto Rican Journey: New York's Newest Migrants*. New York: Harper & Row.

Mintz, Sidney W. 1971. "Groups, Group Boundaries and the Perception of Race." *Comparative Studies in Society and History* 13(4):437–50.

Montagu, Ashley, ed. 1964. *The Concept of Race*. New York: Free Press.

Pitt-Rivers, Julian. 1975. "Race, Color and Class in Central America and the Andes." In *Majority and Minority*, edited by Norman Yetman and C. Hoy Steele. Boston: Allyn & Bacon.

Rodriguez, Clara E. 1974. "Puerto Ricans: Between Black and White." *New York Affairs* I(4):92–101.

———. 1991. *Puerto Ricans: Born in the USA*. Boulder, CO: Westview Press.

Rodriguez, Clara E., Aida Castro, Oscar Garcia, and Analisa Torres. 1991. "Latino Racial Identity: In the Eye of the Beholder?" *Latino Studies Journal* 2(3):33–48.

Sanjek, Roger. 1971. "Brazilian Racial Terms: Some Aspects of Meaning and Learning." *American Anthropology* 73(5):1126–43.

———. 1990. "Conceptualizing Caribbean Asians: Race, Acculturation, Creolization." Asian/American Center Working Papers, Queens College/City University of New York.

Seda Bonilla, E. 1961. "Social Structure and Race Relation." *Social Forces* 40:141–48.

Senior, Clarence. 1965. *Strangers, Then Neighbors: From Pilgrims to Puerto Ricans*. Chicago: Quadrangle.

Telles, Edward, and Edward Murguia. 1990. "Phenotypic Discrimination and Income Differences Among Mexican Americans." *Social Science Quarterly* 71(4):682–96.

Tienda, Marta, and Vilma Ortiz. 1986. "'Hispanicity' and the 1980 Census." *Social Science Quarterly* 67:3–20.

Wagley, Charles. 1965. "On the Concept of Social Race in the Americas." In *Contemporary Cultures and Societies of Latin America: A Reader in the Social Anthropology of Middle and South America and the Caribbean*, edited by Dwight B. Heath and Richard N. Adams. New York: Random House.

POSTSCRIPT

Are Definitions of Race *Just* Political?

These two selections illuminate the complex issues of racial classification. America is becoming increasingly diverse and Americans are becoming increasingly aware of it. The appearance of new groups with different views on race within the U.S. and other societies challenges the traditional black-white dichotomy, which has dominated the American classification of race. Do we have the language and vocabulary to talk about the increasing diversity? Increased intermarriage along with the arrival of immigrants of various colors has led to a re-examination of race classification. What are the political implications of changing racial and ethnic classifications?

Rodriguez and Cordero-Guzman would agree that race definitions are political but they also observe that, "in Puerto Rico and in other parts of Latin America, race was based more on phenotypic and socio-economic definitions of the person rather than on genotypic definitions . . . as a fact of biology . . . and genetic inheritance." Thus, the American reliance on biology and ancestry for racial classifications ignores these "more contextual definitions," which also exist in the United States. Wright's article stresses the politics of race classification as reflected in the Census, while Rodriguez and Cordero-Guzman's article explores how the context of the question alters responses to the race question, and how Latino responses to questions of race categories of the Census differ substantially from those of non-Latinos because of different historical contexts. Wright, on the other hand, argues that for political purposes in the United States, "the one-drop of blood rule" determines one's choices.

Although the most recent census in 2000 gave people the option of choosing more than one racial category, there is still no "mixed-race" category. Wright contends that a multiracial category has been met with opposition from many different groups for different reasons. For example, traditional minority groups such as blacks may experience a decrease in official population numbers. At the same time there is not likely to be a decrease in the white category. So, the opposition to a mixed race category is highly politically charged. "The resulting dilemma is a profound one. If we choose to measure the mixing by counting people as Multiracial, we pull the teeth of the civil-rights laws." And this in turn can lead to new forms of racism and discrimination. Hence, race neutral programs, while on the surface appear to be fair and equitable, in reality ignore important racial issues. Without guarantees of legal protection and just representation, will the interests of black and other minority voters be represented?

For an expanded discussion on race, social structure and power, see *Racial Transformation in the United States: From the 1960s to the 1990s* (Routledge, 1994) by Michael Omi and Howard Winant. A classic study of the relationship of race to class, caste and politics is *Caste, Class and Race* (Monthly Review Press, 1948) by Oliver Cromwell Cox. *From Black to Biracial: Transforming Racial Identity Among Americans* (Praeger, 1999) by Kathleen Odell Korgen examines the political and cultural transitions of race since the civil rights movement. *Are Italians White?: How Race is Made in America* (Routledge, 2003) is a collection of essays about race, ethnicity and politics edited by Jennifer Guglielmo and Salvatore Salerno.

Changing Race: Latinos, the Census and the History of Ethnicity in the United States (Critical American Series) (New York University Press 2000) by Clara Rodriguez further develops points made in her selection in Issue #7. Further, she discusses the evolution of race categories in the U.S. "Race, Identity, and 'Box Checking': The Hispanic Classification of OMB Directive No. 15," by Luis Angel Toro in the *Texas Tech Law Review* (1219, 1995) argues that the federal law of racial and ethnic classification is locked into a biological view. "Re-imagining the Latino/a Race" in the *Harvard Blackletter Law Journal* (93, 1995) by Angel R. Oquendo looks at racial dualism and Latino classification. Jon Michael Spencer's "article" in *The Black Scholar* (1993) argues that there is a "postmodern conspiracy to explode racial identity. *Who Is White? Latinos, Asians and the New Black/White Divide* (Lynne Rienner Publishers 2003) by George Yancey explores the changing racial identification process that reflects America's changing demographics. The book contains an interesting questionnaire about race and attitudes.

"The Liberal Retreat From Race," in *Turning Back* (Pantheon Books 1997) by Stephen Steinberg, addresses the post-1960s public policy that moves away from race. This selection and many others dealing with the politics of race appear in Steinberg's *Race and Ethnicity in the United States: Issues and Debates* (Blackwell Publishers 2000).

A discussion of the political effect of voting and redistricting appears in the conclusion, "Why Race Will Continue to Rule," of Michael Eric Dyson's *Race Rules: Navigating the Color Line* (Addison Wesley 1996).

ISSUE 8

Do Minorities Engage in Self-Segregation?

YES: Beverly Daniel Tatum, "Identity Development in Adolescence" in *Why are All the Black Kids Sitting Together in the Cafeteria?* (Basic Books, 1977)

NO: Peter Beinart, "Degree of Separation at Yale," *The New Republic* (November 3, 1997)

ISSUE SUMMARY

YES: Beverly Daniel Tatum, an African-American psychologist, examines identity development among adolescents, especially black youths, and the behavioral outcomes of this phenomenon. She argues that black adolescents' tendency to view themselves in racial terms is due to the totality of personal and environmental responses that they receive from the larger society, and self-segregation is a coping mechanism.

NO: Peter Beinart, Senior Editor for *The New Republic*, in contrast, examines the complexity of the issues of multiculturalism and diversity on the nation's campuses and he asserts that one examine how a broad spectrum of groups responds to the challenges of identity and "fitting in" within increasingly multicultural and diverse communities.

T he continuing legacy of racial segregation and the Jim Crow lifestyles mandated within this system of intergroup relations poses significant challenges to the development of contemporary race relations within the United States. In the wake of the civil rights movement, out of which came a vision of a desegregated and equalitarian nation, many Americans are perplexed by the persistence of racial and ethnic separation.

American colleges and universities are major institutional domains in which the isolation of African-American students and other ethnic groups is a reality that has generated interest, concern, and controversy. African-American students tend to be the primary focus of such concerns on our campuses, though they are not the only group involved in what many

Americans, both scholars and others, characterize as "self-segregation." The focal concern of this social issue is often stated within the question: "Why are all the black kids sitting together in the cafeteria?"

Beverly Daniel Tatum notes that the quest for personal identity is a fundamental aspect of human experience. As black youth proceed in their development from childhood through adolescence, the question of identity evolves and grows, according to Tatum and other psychologists.

This identity development of black youth is influenced by an evolving racial consciousness within their perceptions of self. According to Tatum, these racially focused self-perceptions and identities that black youth develop in response to their experiences within an environment intensify due to messages and treatments they receive in interacting with white America. The challenges facing black youth in their attempts to engage this dominant white world range from having to confront and effectively deal with prejudice and discrimination to resisting stereotypes and affirming other more positive definitions of themselves. In response to these challenges, Tatum examines significant coping strategies that are developed by these youth including self-segregation.

Tatum maintains that black youth develop strategies to affirm and protect themselves from the deleterious effects of their involvement within a society with embedded stereotypes concerning blacks. So, Tatum answers the question, "Why all the black kids are sitting together in the cafeteria?" She does so by exploring the responses of black youth to the stresses of race in our society, and their need to seek meaning, sensitivity, understanding, and support from their black peers.

Peter Beinart examines the concerns with multiculturalism, diversity, and self-segregation on the campuses of colleges and universities. Beinart asserts that African-American students are not the only ones to engage in overt and voluntary disassociation from whites and other ethnic groups in various social settings within these institutions. In addition to African-American and Latino students who seek separate dorms and cultural centers to foster their group identities, there are other groups who desire to be accorded similar sensitivity and accommodation of their needs and desires for separation from others within residential or other social settings. Beinart is critical of America's political/social conservatives who decry separatism among secular black or Latino students, while supporting such tendencies among Orthodox Jewish students and other religious conservatives. To Beinart, this is a clear example of the selectivity, hypocrisy, and significant contradictions within the thinking and policies advocated by America's conservatives with regard to this issue.

Although Beinart recognizes that many groups seek accommodation on campus in support of the maintenance of their identities and cultures, he views such separatist arrangements as undermining society's quest to build a nation of common core values, principles, and goals that identify and unify us as citizens with an American identity.

Both Beinart and Tatum offer the reader insight into the complex problem of race and American identity. Is self-segregation truly voluntary? To what extent is self-segregation on campuses a threat to a common America? Do the social psychological factors cited by Tatum outweigh Beinart's concern with self-segregation? Are the views of these two writers mutually exclusive?

Beverly Daniel Tatum

YES

Identity Development in Adolescence

Walk into any racially mixed high school cafeteria at lunch time and you will instantly notice that in the sea of adolescent faces, there is an identifiable group of Black students sitting together. Conversely, it could be pointed out that there are many groups of White students sitting together as well, though people rarely comment about that. The question on the tip of everyone's tongue is "Why are the Black kids sitting together?" Principals want to know, teachers want to know, White students want to know, the Black students who aren't sitting at the table want to know.

How does it happen that so many Black teenagers end up at the same cafeteria table? They don't start out there. If you walk into racially mixed elementary schools, you will often see young children of diverse racial backgrounds playing with one another, sitting at the snack table together, crossing racial boundaries with an ease uncommon in adolescence. Moving from elementary school to middle school (often at sixth or seventh grade) means interacting with new children from different neighborhoods than before, and a certain degree of clustering by race might therefore be expected, presuming that children who are familiar with one another would form groups. But even in schools where the same children stay together from kindergarten through eighth grade, racial grouping begins by the sixth or seventh grade. What happens?

One thing that happens is puberty. As children enter adolescence, they begin to explore the question of identity, asking "Who am I? Who can I be?" in ways they have not done before. For Black youth, asking "Who am I?" includes thinking about "Who am I ethnically and/or racially? What does it mean to be Black?"

As I write this, I can hear the voice of a White woman who asked me, "Well, all adolescents struggle with questions of identity. They all become more self-conscious about their appearance and more concerned about what their peers think. So what is so different for Black kids?" Of course, she is right that all adolescents look at themselves in new ways, but not all adolescents think about themselves in racial terms.

From WHY ARE ALL BLACK KIDS SITTING TOGETHER IN THE CAFETERIA? 1997, pp. 52–74.

The search for personal identity that intensifies in adolescence can involve several dimensions of an adolescent's life: vocational plans, religious beliefs, values and preferences, political affiliations and beliefs, gender roles, and ethnic identities. The process of exploration may vary across these identity domains. James Marcia described four identity "statuses" to characterize the variation in the identity search process: (1) *diffuse,* a state in which there has been little exploration or active consideration of a particular domain, and no psychological commitment; (2) *foreclosed,* a state in which a commitment has been made to particular roles or belief systems, often those selected by parents, without actively considering alternatives; (3) *moratorium,* a state of active exploration of roles and beliefs in which no commitment has yet been made; and (4) *achieved,* a state of strong personal commitment to a particular dimension of identity following a period of high exploration.

An individual is not likely to explore all identity domains at once, therefore it is not unusual for an adolescent to be actively exploring one dimension while another remains relatively unexamined. Given the impact of dominant and subordinate status, it is not surprising that researchers have found that adolescents of color are more likely to be actively engaged in an exploration of their racial or ethnic identity that are White adolescents.

Why do Black youths, in particular, think about themselves in terms of race? Because that is how the rest of the world thinks of them. Our self-perceptions are shaped by the messages that we receive from those around us, and when young Black men and women enter adolescence, the racial content of those messages intensifies. A case in point: If you were to ask my ten-year-old son, David, to describe himself, he would tell you many things: that he is smart, that he likes to play computer games, that he has an older brother. Near the top of his list, he would likely mention that he is tall for his age. He would probably not mention that he is Black, though he certainly knows that he is. Why would he mention his height and not his racial group membership? When David meets new adults, one of the first questions they ask is "How old are you?" When David states his age, the inevitable reply is "Gee, you're tall for your age!" It happens so frequently that I once overheard David say to someone, "Don't say it, I know. I'm tall for my age." Height is salient for David because it is salient for others.

When David meets new adults, they don't say, "Gee, you're Black for your age!" If you are saying to yourself, of course they don't, think again. Imagine David at fifteen, six-foot-two, wearing the adolescent attire of the day, passing adults he doesn't know on the sidewalk. Do the women hold their purses a little tighter, maybe even cross the street to avoid him? Does he hear the sound of the automatic door locks on cars as he passes by? Is he being followed around by the security guards at the local mall? As he stops in town with his new bicycle, does a police officer hassle him, asking where he got it, implying that it might be stolen? Do strangers assume he plays basketball? Each of these experiences conveys a racial message. At ten, race is not yet salient for David, because it is not yet salient for society. But it will be.

Understanding Racial Identity Development

Psychologist William Cross, author of *Shades of Black: Diversity in African American Identity,* has offered a theory of racial identity development that I have found to be a very useful framework for understanding what is happening not only with David, but with those Black students in the cafeteria. According to Cross's model, referred to as the psychology of nigrescence, or the psychology of becoming Black, the five stages of racial identity development are *pre-encounter, encounter, immersion/emersion, internalization,* and *internalization-commitment.* For the moment, we will consider the first two stages as those are the most relevant for adolescents.

In the first stage, the Black child absorbs many of the beliefs and values of the dominant White culture, including the idea that it is better to be White. The stereotypes, omissions, and distortions that reinforce notions of White superiority are breathed in by Black children as well as White. Simply as a function of being socialized in a Eurocentric culture, some Black children may begin to value the role models, lifestyles, and images of beauty represented by the dominant group more highly than those of their own cultural group. On the other hand, if Black parents are what I call race-conscious—that is, actively seeking to encourage positive racial identity by providing their children with positive cultural images and messages about what it means to be Black—the impact of the dominant society's messages are reduced. In either case, in the pre-encounter stage, the personal and social significance of one's racial group membership has not yet been realized, and racial identity is not yet under examination. At age ten, David and other children like him would seem to be in the pre-encounter stage. When the environmental cues change and the world begins to reflect his Blackness back to him more clearly, he will probably enter the encounter stage.

Transition to the encounter stage is typically precipitated by an event or series of events that force the young person to acknowledge the personal impact of racism. As the result of a new and heightened awareness of the significance of race, the individual begins to grapple with what it means to be a member of a group targeted by racism. Though Cross describes this process as one that unfolds in late adolescence and early adulthood, research suggests that an examination of one's racial or ethnic identity may begin as early as junior high school.

In a study of Black and White eighth graders from an integrated urban junior high school, Jean Phinney and Steve Tarver found clear evidence for the beginning of the search process in this dimension of identity. Among the forty-eight participants, more than a third had thought about the effects of ethnicity on their future, had discussed the issues with family and friends, and were attempting to learn more about their group. While White students in this integrated school were also beginning to think about ethnic identity, there was evidence to suggest a more active search among Black students, especially Black females. Phinney and Tarver's research is consistent with my own study of Black youth in predominantly White communities, where the environmental cues that trigger an examination of racial identity often become evident in middle school or junior high school.

Some of the environmental cues are institutionalized. Though many elementary schools have self-contained classrooms where children of varying performance levels learn together, many middle and secondary schools use "ability grouping," or tracking. Though school administrators often defend their tracking practices as fair and objective, there usually is a recognizable racial pattern to how children are assigned, which often represents the system of advantage operating in the schools. In racially mixed schools, Black children are much more likely to be in the lower track than in the honors track. Such apparent sorting along racial lines sends a message about what it means to be Black. One young honors student I interviewed described the irony of this resegregation in what was an otherwise integrated environment, and hinted at the identity issues it raised for him.

> It was really a very paradoxical existence, here I am in a school that's 35 percent Black, you know, and I'm the only Black in my classes. . . . That always struck me as odd. I guess I felt that I was different from the other Blacks because of that.

In addition to the changes taking place within school, there are changes in the social dynamics outside school. For many parents, puberty raises anxiety about interracial dating. In racially mixed communities, you begin to see what I call the birthday party effect. Young children's birthday parties in multiracial communities are often a reflection of the community's diversity. The parties of elementary school children may be segregated by gender but not by race. At puberty, when the parties become sleepovers or boy-girl events, they become less and less racially diverse.

Black girls, especially in predominantly White communities, may gradually become aware that something has changed. When their White friends start to date, they do not. The issues of emerging sexuality and the societal messages about who is sexually desirable leave young Black women in a very devalued position. One young woman from a Philadelphia suburb described herself as "pursuing White guys throughout high school" to no avail. Since there were no Black boys in her class, she had little choice. She would feel "really pissed off" that those same White boys would date her White friends. For her, "that prom thing was like out of the question."

Though Black girls living in the context of a larger Black community may have more social choices, they too have to contend with devaluing messages about who they are and who they will become, especially if they are poor or working-class. As social scientists Bonnie Ross Leadbeater and Niobe Way point out,

> The school drop-out, the teenage welfare mother, the drug addict, and the victim of domestic violence or of AIDS are among the most prevalent public images of poor and working-class urban adolescent girls. . . . Yet, despite the risks inherent in economic disadvantage, the majority of poor urban adeolescent girls do not fit the stereotypes that are made about them.

Resisting the stereotypes and affirming other definitions of themselves is part of the task facing young Black women in both White and Black communities.

As was illustrated in the example of David, Black boys also face a devalued status in the wider world. The all too familiar media image of a young Black man with his hands cuffed behind his back, arrested for a violent crime, has primed many to view young Black men with suspicion and fear. In the context of predominantly White schools, however, Black boys may enjoy a degree of social success, particularly if they are athletically talented. The culture has embraced the Black athlete, and the young man who can fulfill that role is often pursued by Black girls and White girls alike. But even these young men will encounter experiences that may trigger an examination of their racial identity.

Sometimes the experience is quite dramatic. *The Autobiography of Malcolm X* is a classic tale of racial identity development, and I assign it to my psychology of racism students for just that reason. As a junior high school student, Malcolm was a star. Despite the fact that he was separated from his family and living in a foster home, he was an A student and was elected president of his class. One day he had a conversation with his English teacher, whom he liked and respected, about his future career goals. Malcolm said he wanted to be a lawyer. His teacher responded, "That's no realistic goal for a nigger," and advised him to consider carpentry instead. The message was clear: You are a Black male, your racial group membership matters, plan accordingly. Malcolm's emotional response was typical—anger, confusion, and alienation. He withdrew from his White classmates, stopped participating in class, and eventually left his predominately white Michigan home to live with his sister in Roxbury, a Black community in Boston.

No teacher would say such a thing now, you may be thinking, but don't be so sure. It is certainly less likely that a teacher would use the word *nigger,* but consider these contemporary examples shared by high school students. A young ninth-grade student was sitting in his homeroom. A substitute teacher was in charge of the class. Because the majority of students from this school go on to college, she used the free time to ask the students about their college plans. As a substitute she had very limited information about their academic performance, but she offered some suggestions. When she turned to this young man, one of few Black males in the class, she suggested that he consider a community college. She had recommended four-year colleges to the other students. Like Malcolm, this student got the message.

In another example, a young Black woman attending a desegregated school to which she was bussed was encouraged by a teacher to attend the upcoming school dance. Most of the Black students did not live in the neighborhood and seldom attended the extracurricular activities. The young woman indicated that she wasn't planning to come. The well-intentioned teacher was persistent. Finally the teacher said, "Oh come on, I know you people love to dance." This young woman got the message, too.

Coping with Encounters: Developing an Oppositional Identity

What do these encounters have to do with the cafeteria? Do experiences with racism inevitably result in so-called self-segregation? While certainly a desire to protect oneself from further offense is understandable, it is not the only factor at work. Imagine the young eighth-grade girl who experienced the teacher's use of "you people" and the dancing stereotype as a racial affront. Upset and struggling with adolescent embarrassment, she bumps into a White friend who can see that something is wrong. She explains. Her White friend responds, in an effort to make her feel better perhaps, and says, "Oh, Mr. Smith is such a nice guy, I'm sure he didn't mean it like that. Don't be so sensitive." Perhaps the White friend is right, and Mr. Smith didn't mean it, but imagine your own response when you are upset, perhaps with a spouse or partner. He or she asks what's wrong and you explain why you are offended. Your partner brushes off your complaint, attributing it to your being oversensitive. What happens to your emotional thermostat? It escalates. When feelings, rational or irrational, are invalidated, most people disengage. They not only choose to discontinue the conversation but are more likely to turn to someone who will understand their perspective.

In much the same way, the eighth-grade girl's White friend doesn't get it. She doesn't see the significance of this racial message, but the girls at the "Black table" do. When she tells her story there, one of them is likely to say, "You know what, Mr. Smith said the same thing to me yesterday!" Not only are Black adolescents encountering racism and reflecting on their identity, but their White peers, even when they are not the perpetrators (and sometimes they are), are unprepared to respond in supportive ways. The Black students turn to each other for the much needed support they are not likely to find anywhere else.

In adolescence, as race becomes personally salient for Black youth, finding the answer to questions such as, "What does it mean to be a young Black person? How should I act? What should I do?" is particularly important. And although Black fathers, mothers, aunts, and uncles may hold the answers by offering themselves as role models, they hold little appeal for most adolescents. The last thing many fourteen-year-olds want to do is to grow up to be like their parents. It is the peer group, the kids in the cafeteria, who hold the answers to these questions. They know how to be Black. They have absorbed the stereotypical images of Black youth in the popular culture and are reflecting those images in their self-presentation.

Based on their fieldwork in U.S. high schools, Signithia Fordham and John Ogbu identified a common psychological pattern found among African American high school students are this stage of identity development. They observed that the anger and resentment that adolescents feel in response to their growing awareness of the systematic exclusion of Black people from full participation in U.S. society leads to the development of an oppositional social identity. This oppositional stance both protects one's identity from the psychological assault of racism and keeps the dominant group at a distance. Fordham and Ogbu write:

> Subordinate minorities regard certain forms of behavior and certain activities or events, symbols, and meanings as *not appropriate* for them because those behaviors, events, symbols, and meanings are characteristic of white Americans. At the same time they emphasize other forms of behavior as more appropriate for them because these are *not* a part of white Americans' way of life. To behave in the manner defined as falling within a white cultural frame of reference is to "act white" and is negatively sanctioned.

Certain styles of speech, dress, and music, for example, may be embraced as "authentically Black" and become highly valued, while attitudes and behaviors associated with Whites are viewed with disdain. The peer groups's evaluation of what is Black and what is not can have a powerful impact on adolescent behavior.

Reflecting on her high school years, one Black woman from a White neighborhood described both the pain of being rejected by her Black classmates and her attempts to conform to her peer's definition of Blackness:

> "Oh you sound White, you think you're White," they said. And the idea of sounding White was just so absurd to me. . . . So ninth grade was sort of traumatic in that I started listening to rap music, which I really just don't like. [I said] I'm gonna be Black, and it was just that stupid. But it's more than just how one acts, you know. [The other Black women there] were not into me for the longest time. My first year there was hell.

Sometimes the emergence of an oppositional identity can be quite dramatic, as the young person tries on a new persona almost overnight. At the end of one school year, race may not have appeared to be significant, but often some encounter takes place over the summer and the young person returns to school much more aware of his or her Blackness and ready to make sure that the rest of the world is aware of it, too. There is a certain "in your face" quality that these adolescents can take on, which their teachers often experience as threatening. When a group of Black teens are sitting together in the cafeteria, collectively embodying an oppositional stance, school administrators want to know not only why they are sitting together, but what can be done to prevent it.

We need to understand that in racially mixed settings, racial grouping is a developmental process in response to an environmental stressor, racism. Joining with one's peers for support in the face of stress is a positive coping strategy. What is problematic is that the young people are operating with a very limited definition of what it means to be Black, based largely on cultural stereotypes.

Oppositional Identity Development and Academic Achievement

Unfortunately for Black teenagers, those cultural stereotypes do not usually include academic achievement. Academic success is more often associated with being White. During the encounter phase of racial identity development, when the search for identity leads toward cultural stereotypes and away from anything that might be associated with Whiteness, academic performance often declines. Doing well in school becomes identified as trying to be White. Being smart becomes the opposite of being cool.

While this frame of reference is not universally found among adolescents of African descent, it is commonly observed in Black peer groups. Among the Black college students I have interviewed, many described some conflict or alienation from other African American teens because of their academic success in high school. For example, a twenty-year-old female from a Washington, D.C., suburb explained:

> It was weird, even in high school a lot of the Black students were, like, "Well, you're not really Black." Whether it was because I became president of the sixth-grade class or whatever it was, it started pretty much back then. Junior high, it got worse. I was then labeled certain things, whether it was "the oreo" or I wasn't really Black.

Others described avoiding situations that would set them apart from their Black peers. For example, one young woman declined to participate in a gifted program in her school because she knew it would separate her from the other Black students in the school.

In a study of thirty-three eleventh-graders in a Washington, D.C., school, Fordham and Ogbu found that although some of the students had once been academically successful, few of them remained so. These students also knew that to be identified as a "brainiac" would result in peer rejection. The few students who had maintained strong academic records found ways to play down their academic success enough to maintain some level of acceptance among their Black peers.

Academically successful Black students also need a strategy to find acceptance among their White classmates. Fordham describes one such strategy as *racelessness,* wherein individuals assimilate into the dominant group by de-emphasizing characteristics that might identify them as members of the subordinate group. Jon, a young man I interviewed, offered a classic example of this strategy as he described his approach to dealing with his discomfort at being the only Black person in his advanced classes. He said, "At no point did I ever think I was White or did I ever want to be White. . . . I guess it was one of those things where I tried to de-emphasize the fact that I was Black." This strategy led him to avoid activities that were associated with Blackness. He recalled, "I didn't want to do anything that was traditionally Black, like I never played basketball. I ran cross-country. . . . I went for distance running instead of sprints." He felt he had to show his White classmates that there were "exceptions to all these stereotypes." However, this strategy was of limited usefulness. When he traveled outside his home community with his White teammates, he sometimes encountered overt racism. "I quickly realized that I'm Black, and that's the thing that they're going to see first, no matter how much I try to de-emphasize my Blackness."

A Black student can play down Black identity in order to succeed in school and mainstream institutions without rejecting his Black identity and culture. Instead of becoming raceless, an achieving Black student can become an *emissary,* someone who sees his or her own achievements as advancing the cause of the racial group. For example, social scientists Richard Zweigenhaft and G. William Domhoff describe how a successful Black student, in response to the accusation of acting White, connected his achievement to that of other Black men by saying, "Martin Luther King must not have been Black, then, since he had a doctoral degree, and Malcolm X must not have been Black since he educated himself while in prison." In addition, he demonstrated his loyalty to the Black community by taking an openly political stance against the racial discrimination he observed in his school.

It is clear that an oppositional identity can interfere with academic achievement, and it may be tempting for educators to blame the adolescents themselves for their academic decline. However, the questions that educators and other concerned adults must ask are, How did academic achievement become defined as exclusively White behavior? What is it about the curriculum and the wider culture that reinforces the notion that academic excellence is an exclusively White domain? What curricular interventions might we use to encourage the development of an empowered emissary identity?

An oppositional identity that disdains academic achievement has not always been a characteristic of Black adolescent peer groups. It seems to be a post-desegregation phenomenon. Historically, the oppositional identity found among African Americans in the segregated South included a positive attitude toward education. While Black people may have publicly deferred to Whites, they actively encouraged their children to pursue education as a ticket to greater freedom. While Black parents still see education as the key to upward mobility, in today's desegregated schools the models of success—the teachers, administrators, and curricular heroes—are almost always White.

Black Southern schools, though stigmatized by legally sanctioned segregation, were often staffed by African American educators, themselves visible models of academic achievement. These Black educators may have presented a curriculum that included references to the intellectual legacy of other African Americans. As well, in the context of a segregated school, it was a given that the high achieving students would all be Black. Academic achievement did not have to mean separation from one's Black peers.

The Search for Alternative Images

This historical example reminds us that an oppositional identity discouraging academic achievement is not inevitable even in a racist society. If young people are exposed to images of African American academic achievement in their early years, they won't have to define school achievement as something for Whites only. They will know that there is a long history of Black intellectual achievement.

This point was made quite eloquently by Jon, the young man I quoted earlier. Though he made the choice to excel in school, he labored under the false assumption that he was "inventing the wheel." It wasn't until he reached college and had the opportunity to take African American studies courses that he learned about other African Americans besides Martin Luther King, Malcolm X, and Frederick Douglass—the same three men he had heard about year after year, from kindergarten to high school graduation. As he reflected on his identity struggle in high school, he said:

> It's like I went through three phases. . . . My first phase was being cool, doing whatever was particularly cool for Black people at the time, and that was like in junior high. Then in high school, you know, I thought being Black was basically all stereotypes, so I tried to avoid all of those things. Now in college, you know, I realize that being Black means a variety of things.

Learning his history in college was of great psychological importance to Jon, providing him with role models he had been missing in high school. He was particularly inspired by learning of the intellectual legacy of Black men at his own college:

> When you look at those guys who were here in the Twenties, they couldn't live on campus. They couldn't eat on campus. They couldn't get their hair cut in town. And yet they were all Phi Beta Kappa. . . . That's what being Black really is, you know, knowing who you are, your history, your accomplishments. . . . When I was in junior high, I had White role models. And then when I got into high school, you know, I wasn't sure but I just didn't think having White role models was a good thing. So I got rid of those. And I basically just, you know, only had my parents for role models. I kind of grew up thinking that we were on the cutting edge. We were doing something radically different than everybody else. And not realizing that there are all kinds of Black people doing the very things that I thought we were the only ones doing. . . . You've got to do the very best you can so that you can continue the great traditions that have already been established.

This young man was not alone in his frustration over having learned little about his own cultural history in grade school. Time and again in the research interviews I conducted, Black students lamented the absence of courses in African American history or literature at the high school level and indicated how significant this new learning was to them in college, how excited and affirmed they felt by this newfound knowledge. Sadly, many Black students never get to college, alienated from the process of education long before high school graduation. They may never get access to the information that might have helped them expand their definition of what it means to be Black and, in the process, might have helped them stay in school. Young people are developmentally ready for this information in adolescence. We ought to provide it.

Not at the Table

As we have seen, Jon felt he had to distance himself from his Black peers in order to be successful in high school. He was one of the kids *not* sitting at the Black table. Continued encounters with racism and access to new culturally relevant information empowered him to give up his racelessness and become an emissary. In college, not only did he sit at the Black table, but he emerged as a campus leader, confident in the support of his Black peers. His example illustrates that one's presence at the Black table is often an expression of one's identity development, which evolves over time.

Some Black students may not be developmentally ready for the Black table in junior or senior high school. They may not yet have had their own encounters with racism, and race may not be very salient for them. Just as we don't all reach puberty and begin developing sexual interest at the same time, racial identity development unfolds in idiosyncratic ways. Though my research suggests that adolescence is a common time, one's own life experiences are also important determinants of the timing. The young person whose racial identity development is out of synch with his or her peers often feels in an awkward position. Adolescents are notoriously egocentric and assume that their experience is the same as everyone else's. Just as girls who have become interested in boys become disdainful of their friends still interested in dolls, the Black teens who are at the table can be quite judgmental toward those who are not. "If I think it is a sign of authentic Blackness to sit at this table, then you should too."

The young Black men and women who still hang around with the White classmates they may have known since early childhood will often be snubbed by their Black peers. This dynamic is particularly apparent in regional schools where children from a variety of neighborhoods are brought together. When Black children from predominantly White neighborhoods go to school with Black children from predominantly Black neighborhoods, the former group is often viewed as trying to be White by the latter group. We all speak the language of the streets we live on. Black children living in White neighborhoods often sound White to their Black peers from across town, and may be teased because of it. This can be a very painful experience, particularly when the young person is not fully accepted as part of the White peer group either.

One young Black woman from a predominantly White community described exactly this situation in an interview. In a school with a lot of racial tension, Terri felt that "the worst thing that happened" was the rejection she experienced from the other Black children who were being bussed to her school. Though she wanted to be friends with them, they teased her, calling her an "oreo cookie" and sometimes beating her up. The only close Black friend Terri had was a biracial girl from her neighborhood.

Racial tensions also affected her relationships with White students. One White friend's parents commented, "I can't believe you're Black. You don't seem like all the Black children. You're nice." Though other parents made similar comments, Terri reported that her White friends didn't start making them until junior high school, when Terri's Blackness became something to be explained. One friend introduced Terri to another White girl by saying, "She's not really Black, she just went to Florida and got a really dark tan." A White sixth-grade "boyfriend" became embarrassed when his friends discovered he had a crush on a Black girl. He stopped telling Terri how pretty she was, and instead called her "nigger" and said, "Your lips are too big. I don't want to see you. I won't be your friend anymore."

Despite supportive parents who expressed concern about her situation, Terri said she was a "very depressed child." Her father would have conversations with her "about being Black and beautiful" and about "the union of people of color that had always existed that I needed to find. And the pride." However, her parents did not have a network of Black friends to help support her.

It was the intervention of a Black junior high school teacher that Terri feels helped her the most. Mrs. Campbell "really exposed me to the good Black community because I was so down on it" by getting Terri involved in singing gospel music and introducing her to other Black students who would accept her. "That's when I started having other Black friends. And I thank her a lot for that."

The significant role that Mrs. Campbell played in helping Terri open up illustrates the constructive potential that informed adults can have in the identity development process. She recognized Terri's need for a same-race peer group and helped her find one. Talking to groups of Black students about the variety of living situations Black people come from and the unique situation facing Black adolescents in White communities helps to expand the definition of what it means to be Black and increases intragroup acceptance at a time when that is quite important.

For children in Terri's situation, it is also helpful for Black parents to provide ongoing opportunities for their children to connect with other Black peers even if that means traveling outside the community they live in. Race-conscious parents often do this by attending a Black church or maintaining ties to Black social organizations such as Jack and Jill. Parents who make this effort often find that their children become bicultural, able to move comfortably between Black and White communities, and able to sit at the Black table when they are ready.

Implied in this discussion is the assumption that connecting with one's Black peers in the process of identity development is important and should be encouraged. For young Black people living in predominantly Black communities, such connections occur spontaneously with neighbors and classmates and usually do not require special encouragement. However, for young people in predominantly White communities hey may only occur with active parental intervention. One might wonder if this social connection is really necessary. If a young person has found a niche among a circle of White friends, is it really necessary to establish a Black peer group as a reference point? Eventually it is.

As one's awareness of the daily challenges of living in a racist society increase, it is immensely helpful to be able to share one's experiences with others who have lived it. Even when White friends are willing and able to listen and bear witness to one's struggles, they cannot really share the experience. One young woman came to this realization in her senior year of high school:

> [The isolation] never really bothered me until about senior year when I was the only one in the class. . . . That little burden, that constant burden of you always having to strive to do your best and show that you can do just as much as everybody else. Your White friends can't understand that, and it's really hard to communicate to them. Only someone else of the same racial, same ethnic background would understand something like that.

When one is faced with what Chester Pierce calls the "mundane extreme environmental stress" of racism, in adolescence or in adulthood, the ability to see oneself as part of a larger group from which one can draw support is an important coping strategy. Individuals who do not have such a strategy available to them because they do not experience a shared identity with at least some subset of their racial group are at risk for considerable social isolation.

Of course, who we perceive as sharing our identity may be influenced by other dimensions of identity such as gender, social class, geographical location, skin color, or ethnicity. For example, research indicates that first-generation Black immigrants from the Caribbean tend to emphasize their national origins and ethnic identities, distancing themselves from U.S. Blacks, due in part to their belief that West Indians are viewed more positively by Whites than those American Blacks whose family roots include the experience of U.S. slavery. To relinquish one's ethnic identity as West Indian and take on an African American identity may be understood as downward social mobility. However, second-generation. West Indians without an identifiable accent may lose the relative ethnic privilege their parents experienced and seek racial solidarity with Black American peers in the face of encounters with racism. Whether it is the experience of being followed in stores because they are suspected of shoplifting, seeing people respond to them with fear on the street, or feeling overlooked in school, Black youth can benefit from seeking support from those who have had similar experiences.

An Alternative to the Cafeteria Table

The developmental need to explore the meaning of one's identity with others who are engaged in a similar process manifests itself informally in school corridors and cafeterias across the country. Some educational institutions have sought to meet this need programmatically. Several colleagues and I recently evaluated one such effort, initiated at a Massachusetts middle school participating in a voluntary desegregation program known as the Metropolitan Council for Educational Opportunity (METCO) program. Historically, the small number of African American students who are bussed from Boston to this suburban school have achieved disappointing levels of academic success. In an effort to improve academic achievement, the school introduced a program, known as Student Efficacy Training (SET) that allowed Boston students to meet each day as a group with two staff members. Instead of being in physical education or home economics or study hall, they were meeting, talking about homework difficulties, social issues, and encounters with racism. The meeting was mandatory and at first the students were resentful of missing some of their classes. But the impact was dramatic. Said one young woman,

> In the beginning of the year, I didn't want to do SET at all. It took away my study and it was only METCO students doing it. In the beginning all we did was argue over certain problems or it was more like a rap session and I didn't think it was helping anyone. But then when we looked at records. . . . I know that last year out of all the students, sixth through eighth grade, there was, like, six who were actually good students. Everyone else, it was just pathetic, I mean, like, they were getting like Ds and Fs. . . . The eighth grade is doing much better this year. I mean, they went from Ds and Fs to Bs and Cs and occasional As. . . . And those seventh-graders are doing really good, they have a lot of honor roll students in seventh grade, both guys and girls. Yeah, it's been good. It's really good.

Her report is borne out by an examination of school records. The opportunity to come together in the company of supportive adults allowed these young Black students to talk about the issues that hindered their performance—racial encounters, feelings of isolation, test anxiety, homework dilemmas—in the psychological safety of their own group. In the process, the peer culture changed to one that supported academic performance rather than undermined it, as revealed in these two students' comments:

> Well, a lot of the Boston students, the boys and the girls, used to fight all the time. And now, they stopped yelling at each other so much and calling each other stupid.

> It's like we've all become like one big family, we share things more with each other. We tease each other like brother and sister. We look out for each other with homework and stuff. We always stay on top of each other 'cause we know it's hard with African American students to go to a predominantly White school and try to succeed with everybody else.

The faculty, too, were very enthusiastic about the outcomes of the intervention, as seen in the comments of these two classroom teachers:

> This program has probably produced the most dramatic result of any single change that I've seen at this school. It has produced immediate results that affected behavior and academics and participation in school life.

> My students are more engaged. They aren't battling out a lot of the issues of their anger about being in a White community, coming in from Boston, where do I fit, I don't belong here. I feel that those issues that

often came out in class aren't coming out in class anymore. I think they are being discussed in the SET room, the kids feel more confidence. The kids' grades are higher, the homework response is greater, they're not afraid to participate in class, and I don't see them isolating themselves within class. They are willing to sit with other students happily. . . . I think it's made a very positive impact on their place in the school and on their individual self-esteem. I see them enjoying themselves and able to enjoy all of us as individuals. I can't say enough, it's been the best thing that's happened to the METCO program as far as I'm concerned.

Although this intervention is not a miracle cure for every school, it does highlight what can happen when we think about the developmental needs of Black adolescents coming to terms with their own sense of identity. It might seem counterintuitive that a school involved in a voluntary desegregation program could improve both academic performance and social relationships among students by *separating* the Black students for one period every day. But if we understand the unique challenges facing adolescents of color and the legitimate need they have to feel supported in their identity development, it makes perfect sense.

Though they may not use the language of racial identity development theory to describe it, most Black parents want their children to achieve an internalized sense of personal security, to be able to acknowledge the reality of racism and to respond effectively to it. Our educational institutions should do what they can to encourage this development rather than impede it. When I talk to educators about the need to provide adolescents with identity-affirming experiences and information about their own cultural groups, they sometimes flounder because this information has not been part of their own education. Their understanding of adolescent development has been limited to the White middle-class norms included in most textbooks, their knowledge of Black history limited to Martin Luther King, Jr., and Rosa Parks. They sometimes say with frustration that parents should provide this kind of education for their children. Unfortunately Black parents often attended the same schools the teachers did and have the same informational gaps. We need to acknowledge that an important part of interrupting the cycle of oppression is constant re-education, and sharing what we learn with the next generation.

NO ↵

Peter Beinart

Degree of Separation at Yale

For decades at Cornell University, minority students have opted out of regular dorms and into ethnic theme houses. Last year, Cornell's president proposed changing that slightly: students should wait to enter the Ujamaa house or the Latino Living Center until after their freshman year. The response? Fifteen undergrads went on a hunger strike, hundreds laid down in the street, and Reverend Al Sharpton dropped in to accuse the administration of trying to make black and Latino students "merge in with everyone else so we don't know they're here."

This is the kind of thing that gives conservative critics of political correctness a reason to get up in the morning. And it occasioned the usual shoutfest about diversity, forced integration, and self-segregation—followed by a weak-kneed administration compromise.

So far, so predictable. But right-wing outrage separatism at Cornell raises an interesting question: Why on Earth are conservatives supporting the five Orthodox Jewish students who won't live in the regular dormitories at Yale? The answer is one of the ironies of the culture war: when it comes to religion, the real multiculturalists are all on the Right.

The Yale case and the Cornell case are essentially the same. It's true that the Yalies are asking to move off campus, but that's only because Yale doesn't have specialty houses. If it had a single sex dorm, or a "no-premarital sex" dorm, the Orthodox five would live there. And it's true that the Cornell radicals say they're fleeing racism while the Yale faithful say they're fleeing condoms. But it amounts to the same thing. Yale freshman Elisha Dov Hack's older brother told him that dorm life has made previous Orthodox students less observant. Hunger-striking black senior Dana Miller told *The New York Times* last year that Cornell's proposed change was "an attempt to socialize students into a homogeneous group." Hack and Miller are both really fleeing assimilation.

That's why it's so remarkable that champions of the melting pot like Charles Krauthammer, William Buckley, Kate O'Beirne, and the editors of *The Weekly Standard* have risen to the Yale Five's defense. This, after all, is the same Charles Krauthammer who recently decried "the tragic turn towards black separatism," and the same *Standard* which in September coined the phrase, "diversity gulag."

Conservative views about separatism, it turns out, depend on who's doing the separating. Consider these words, written in September by frequent *National Review* contributor Jacob Neusner: "cripples have their ramps, homosexuals their K-Y dispensers and double beds, blacks their ghettos, Hispanics their barrios, voyeurs their unisex toilets, all courtesy of university housing directors. But rather than extend the same 'sensitivity' to scarcely a minyan—a quorum—of Orthodox Jews, Yale would rather humiliate itself." This tasteful nugget gets to the heart of the issue. All this time everyone thought conservatives opposed "ghettos" and "barrios" on principle. But now it turns out they're just mad that P.C. radicals get them and prudish believers do not.

A good example of this multicultural me-tooism is the Right's support for charter schools. On August 16, 1996, *The Washington Times* called the accreditation of charter schools in the District of Columbia a "ray of hope." Three and a half months later, the principal of the Afrocentric Marcus Garvey Public Charter School assaulted a *Washington Times* reporter. A *Times* commentator, Ernest Lefever, called the attack "the latest in a long string of outrages committed in the name of multiculturalism."

He's right, but the *Times* was asking for it. Multiculturalism isn't just the ideology of the Marcus Garvey charter school, it's the ideology of charter schools, period. Charter schools are based on the idea that communities should be able to fashion their own institutions with minimal interference from outsiders. They represent a rejection of the principle that public schools educate all students in a common curriculum or a common culture. That is why Michael Kelly wrote in this space last December that charter schools "take from the pluribus to destroy the unum." In their mania for local autonomy, conservative educational reformers have recreated the publicly funded black nationalist schools that arose in late 1960s New York under radical chic Mayor John Lindsey—most notoriously in Ocean Hill-Brownsville, Brooklyn.

Their motivation, of course, is different. For liberals, multiculturalism offered emancipation from racial oppression; for conservatives, it's about religion. Charter schools, combined with vouchers for private and parochial schools, and subsidies for home schooling, constitute the multiculturalist Right's assault on a common school system. Many Christian conservatives believe that regular public schools promote an immoral, godless ideology. Like the Orthodox Jews at Yale, they want to separate—and take their money with them. And just as liberals are instinctively (sometimes mindlessly) sympathetic to demands made in the name of anti-racism, secular conservatives jump to defend the beleaguered faithful. In so doing, they end up supporting a multiculturalism of their own. Once upon a time, liberals and conservatives believed in Norman Podhoretz's "brutal bargain." Assimilation was hard and even demeaning, but it bought you entrance into a common American culture. That didn't mean the culture was static; over time it might absorb a bit of your particular ethos. But you pushed from the inside, conscious that you could not both reject assimilation and expect its fruits.

In the 1960s, the Left decided this model wouldn't work for blacks. It believed, naively, that African Americans could remain separate from whites while making ever greater moral claims on them. The result, of course, was a tremendous backlash, as working-class whites learned how to stake the claims of identity themselves.

As conservatives line up behind their own brand of separatism, they should take care not to be similarly naive. The options are these: you either commit to common institutions, and accept the old, painful disjuncture between home and school, or you accept marginality. It is a far different thing to call for prayer in public schools than it is to demand that the citizenry fund religious schools. And it is a far different thing to participate fully in a university while maintaining your identity than it is to expect a university to accept you fully while refusing to give yourself fully to it. If conservatives really cared about the Yale Five, they would tell them what they told the hunger-strikers at Cornell: assimilation is the American way.

POSTSCRIPT

Do Minorities Engage in Self-Segregation?

The separation of blacks from whites within American society is the prevailing context within which race relations develop throughout history. There is a long-standing tradition of segregated schools, neighborhoods, and even churches in the United States. Segregation and racial stereotyping are parts of the American experience, and African-Americans have had to resist racist stereotypes throughout history.

The issue of self-segregation is linked to Issue 1, "Do We Need a Common American Identity?", in that it extends the assimilation-pluralism debate. The debate here is compounded by voluntary segregation in contrast to exclusion. Given the goal of equality, what are the functions of self-segregation? On one hand, as Tatum points out, it offers a means to cope with rejection. However, as Beinart points out, it can undermine the goal of assimilation. Beinart's argument against self-segregation raises further questions about multiculturalism. Does self-segregation contribute to a common American identity, or does it lead to disunity?

The United States has a legacy of conflict-ridden race and ethnic relations rooted in such institutions as slavery, segregation, and related policies and practices of discrimination. Despite this legacy, the idea of assimilation is very strong in America. To Beinart, assimilation is beneficial to a common culture. His concern with self-segregation is that it threatens the *unum*. Beinart's argument is based on social categories such as American cultural identity, viable institutions, and social cohesion. In contrast, Tatum addresses the issue from a social psychological perspective.

Many of the nation's campuses have not achieved multicultural sensitivity. We still have hate crimes and other manifestations of race and ethnic conflict. Confederate flags and other incendiary symbols of American racist tradition are still able to penetrate communities of higher learning. Given such realities, the black "table in the cafeteria" is expected to persist within the educational institutions of the United States. Essentially, Tatum describes black students congregating around these tables as engaging in positive identity formation. Their peers provide them with the reaffirmation and support that they need to affirm that their blackness is a positive quality. The immersion of these youth within the circle of their peers around the black table can facilitate their development of positive senses of self-esteem and self-worth to serve as effective antidotes to the negativity that they often encounter in dealing with the dominant society. Thus Tatum argues that self-segregation is a social adaptation by blacks and other youth in order to function effectively on campus.

Issues 1 ("Do We Need a Common American Identity?"), 4 ("Does White Identity Define America?"), and 13 ("Is a Multicultural Curriculum Essential for Advancing Education?") all share an important theme with this issue of self-segregation. In each case, one side challenged the other of threatening American unity, the *unum,* with some form of multiculturalism. So, whether it's curriculum, or a hyphenated identity, or immigrants of color, or the lunch table, the concern remains. To what extent do differing degrees of multiculturalism affect our common American identity?

Readers will find a discussion regarding the self-segregation issue in *The Rage of a Privileged Class* (HarperCollins, 1993) by Ellis Cose.

ISSUE 9

Are Asian Americans
a Model Minority?

YES: David A. Bell, "America's Greatest Success Story: The Triumph of Asian-Americans," *The New Republic* (July 15 & 22, 1985)

NO: Frank H. Wu, "The Model Minority: Asian American 'Success' as a Race Relations Failure," in *Yellow: Race in America Beyond Black and White* (Basic Books, 2002)

ISSUE SUMMARY

YES: David A. Bell, journalist and historian, agrees that Asian Americans are a "model minority" and expresses a great appreciation for the progress and prominence they have achieved within the nation.

NO: Frank H. Wu, Howard University law professor, rejects the characterization of Asian Americans as a "model minority" based on the belief that this characterization tends to obscure problems facing Asians in America.

T he labeling of Asian Americans as a model minority group emerged in a nation with long experience with conflict-ridden intergroup relations. As a model minority, the Asian Americans are viewed as industrious, frugal, and possessing a strong achievement orientation. These are among the values that are promoted within the dominant white culture. Asian Americans also tend to be associated with the promotion of a success ethic and achievement at much higher levels in significant areas of American life than other minority groups, especially African Americans and Latinos.

The Asian-American population of the United States is rapidly expanding as the nation becomes more diverse. There is great ethnic diversity among these Asian ethnic peoples whose demographic composition extends from the Hmong immigrants of the highlands of Vietnam to Bengali people of the Indian subcontinent. Thus, Asian peoples are contributing to the ongoing expansion of the ethnic composition of the United States.

Although written in 1985, David Bell's selection presents the standard argument in support of Asian Americans for the model minority thesis. Bell is impressed with the fact that Asians have become prominent out of all proportion to their share of the U.S. population. He presents an examination of data gleaned from the Census Bureau and the State Department to demonstrate that the rapid expansion of the Asian-American population will likely intensify in the future.

Bell draws our attention to the new prominence of Asian Americans in business and the professions. He presents evidence of progress that these model citizens have achieved in areas of business, such as the ownership of grocery stores, motels, fishing boats, and the computer industry, and in the professions of medicine and architecture.

It is important to note that Asian Americans have not always been embraced by American society. Throughout most of their history, Asians have experienced prejudice, discrimination, exclusion, and violence at the hands of whites and other groups. Bell provides us with a significant examination of these aspects of Asian-American social history in order to provide a proper social context for understanding these developments. Thus, the "spectacular" success that they have achieved that has earned them the status of America's "model minority" has come at a substantial cost.

Education tends to be viewed as a key factor in achieving socioeconomic progress in America. Asian Americans have embraced this "education ethic," and Bell views this development as a major contributor to the "spectacular" success that he claims they have achieved. Wu, however, is concerned with the disparity between Asians' educational achievements and their institutional success. The claim that Asian Americans have succeeded in certain fields is beyond dispute. However, Wu is wary of the facile tendency of the post–civil rights era to label Asian Americans as a "model minority." For Wu, this label has been employed to promote an exaggerated image of Asian-American "success," and it fails to account for significant inequalities within their lives. He notes "that the only good Asian American is a genius workaholic, not an average or normal man or woman."

The economic achievements of Asians are less than those promoted within the "model minority" imagery according to Wu. There are a number of additional reasons why Wu challenges the "model minority" imagery. The utilization of this label by America's leaders to criticize or inspire other racial and ethnic groups can foster resentment from members of these outgroups, thus undermining the security of Asian Americans.

Lastly, Asian Americans have been subjected to stereotyping throughout the nation's history, and Wu views this "model minority" image as the latest of that line. So Wu has concluded that the "model minority" claim as applied to Asian Americans is a myth that tends to obscure much more than it illuminates in the lives of Asians in America.

David A. Bell

➡ **YES**

America's Greatest Success Story: The Triumph of Asian-Americans

It is the year 2019. In the heart of downtown Los Angeles, massive electronic billboards feature a model in a kimono hawking products labeled in Japanese. In the streets below, figures clad in traditional East Asian peasant garb hurry by, speaking to each other in an English made unrecognizable by the addition of hundreds of Spanish and Asian words. A rough-mannered policeman leaves an incongruously graceful calling card on a doorstep: a delicate origami paper sculpture.

This is, of course, a scene from a science-fiction movie, Ridley Scott's 1982 *Blade Runner*. It is also a vision that Asian-Americans dislike intensely. Hysterical warnings of an imminent Asian "takeover" of the United States stained a whole century of their 140-year history in this country, providing the back-drop for racial violence, legal segregation, and the internment of 110,000 Japanese-Americans in concentration camps during World War II. Today integration into American society, not transformation of American society, is the goal of an overwhelming majority. So why did the critics praise *Blade Runner* for its "realism"? The answer is easy to see.

The Asian-American population is exploding. According to the Census Bureau, it grew an astounding 125 percent between 1970 and 1980, and now stands at 4.1 million, or 1.8 percent of all Americans. Most of the increase is the result of immigration, which accounted for 1.8 million people between 1973 and 1983, the last year for which the Immigration and Naturalization Service has accurate figures (710,000 of these arrived as refugees from Southeast Asia). And the wave shows little sign of subsiding. Ever since the Immigration Act of 1965 permitted large-scale immigration by Asians, they have made up over 40 percent of all newcomers to the United States. Indeed, the arbitrary quota of 20,000 immigrants per country per year established by the act has produced huge backlogs of future Asian-Americans in several countries, including 120,000 in South Korea and 336,000 in the Philippines, some of whom, according to the State Department, have been waiting for their visas since 1970.

The numbers are astonishing. But even more astonishing is the extent to which Asian-Americans have become prominent out of all proportion to their share of the population. It now seems likely that their influx will have as important an effect on American society as the migration from Europe of 100 years ago. Most remarkable of all, it is taking place with relatively tittle trouble.

The new immigration from Asia is a radical development in several ways. First, it has not simply enlarged an existing Asian-American community, but created an entirely new one. Before 1965, and the passage of the Immigration Act, the term "Oriental-American" (which was then the vogue) generally denoted people living on the West Coast, in Hawaii, or in the Chinatowns of a few large cities. Generally they traced their ancestry either to one small part of China, the Toishan district of Kwantung province, or to a small number of communities in Japan (one of the largest of which, ironically, was Hiroshima). Today more than a third of all Asian-Americans live outside Chinatowns in the East, South, and Midwest, and their origins are as diverse as those of "European-Americans." The term "Asian-American" now refers to over 900,000 Chinese from all parts of China and also Vietnam, 800,000 Filipinos, 700,000 Japanese, 500,000 Koreans, 400,000 East Indians, and a huge assortment of everything else from Moslem Cambodians to Catholic Hawaiians. It can mean an illiterate Hmong tribesman or a fully assimilated graduated of the Harvard Business School.

Asian-Americans have also attracted attention by their new prominence in several professions and trades. In New York City, for example, where the Asian-American population jumped from 94,500 in 1970 to 231,500 in 1980, Korean-Americans run an estimated 900 of the city's 1,600 corner grocery stores. Filipino doctors—who outnumber black doctors—have become general practitioners in thousands of rural communities that previously lacked physicians. East Indian-Americans own 800 of California's 6,000 motels. And in parts of Texas, Vietnamese-Americans now control 85 percent of the shrimp-fishing industry, though they only reached this position after considerable strife (now the subject of a film, *Alamo Bay*).

Individual Asian-Americans have become quite prominent as well. I. M. Pei and Minoru Yamasaki have helped transform American architecture. Seiji Ozawa and Yo Yo Ma are giant figures in American music. An Wang created one of the nation's largest computer firms, and Rocky Aoki founded one of its largest restaurant chains (Benihana). Samuel C. C. Ting won a Nobel prize in physics.

◦◦◦

Most spectacular of all, and most significant for the future, is the entry of Asian-Americans into the universities. At Harvard, for example, Asian-Americans ten years ago made up barely three percent of the freshman class. The figure is now ten percent—five times their share of the population. At Brown, Asian-American applications more than tripled over the same period, and at Berkeley they increased from 3,408 in 1982 to 4,235 only three years later. The Berkeley student body is now 22 percent Asian-American, UCLA's is 21 percent, and MIT's 19 percent. The Julliard School of Music in New York is currently 30 percent Asian and Asian-American. American medical schools had only 571 Asian-American students in 1970, but in 1980 they had 1,924, and last year 3,763, or 5.6 percent of total enrollment. What is more, nearly all of these figures are certain to increase. In the current, largely foreign-born Asian-American community, 32.9 percent of people over 25 graduated from college (as opposed to 16.2 percent in the general population). For third-generation Japanese-Americans, the figure is 88 percent.

By any measure these Asian-American students and outstanding. In California only the top 12.5 percent of high school students qualify for admission to the uppermost tier of the state university system, but 39 percent of Asian-American high school students do. On the SATs, Asian-Americans score an average of 519 in math, surpassing whites, the next highest group, by 32 points. Among Japanese-Americans, the most heavily native-born Asian-American group, 68 percent of those taking the math SAT scored above 600—high enough to qualify for admission to almost any university in the country. The Westinghouse Science Talent search, which each year identified 40 top high school science students, picked 12 Asian-Americans in 1983, nine last year, and seven this year. And at Harvard the Phi Beta Kappa chapter last April named as its elite "Junior Twelve" students five Asian-Americans and seven Jews.

۔ۆﺮ

Faced with these statistics, the understandable reflex of many non-Asian-Americans is adulation. President Reagan has called Asian-Americans "our exemplars of hope and inspiration." *Parade* magazine recently featured an article on Asian-Americans titled "The Promise of America," and *Time* and *Newsweek* stories have boasted headlines like "A Formula for Success," "The Drive to Excel," and "A 'Model Minority.'" However, not all of these stories come to grips with the fact that Asian-Americans, like all immigrants, have to deal with a great many problems of adjustment, ranging from the absurd to the deadly serious.

Who would think, for example, that there is a connection between Asian-American immigration and the decimation of California's black bear population? But Los Angeles, whose Korean population grew by 100,000 in the past decade, now has more than 300 licensed herbal-acupuncture shops. And a key ingredient in traditional Korean herbal medicine is *ungdam,* bear gallbladder. The result is widespread illegal hunting and what *Audubon* magazine soberly called "a booming trade in bear parts."

As Mark R. Thompson recently pointed out in *The Wall Street Journal,* the clash of cultures produced by Asian immigration can also have vexing legal results. Take the case of Fumiko Kimura, a Japanese-American woman who tried to drown herself and her two children in the Pacific. She survived but the children did not, and she is now on trial for their murder. As a defense, her lawyers are arguing that parent-child suicide is a common occurrence in Japan. In Fresno, California, meanwhile, 30,000 newly arrived Hmong cause a different problem. "Anthropologists call the custom 'marriage by capture,' " Mr. Thompson writes, "Fresno police and prosecutors call it 'rape.' "

A much more serious problem for Asian-Americans is racial violence. In 1982 two unemployed whites in Detroit beat to death a Chinese-American named Vincent Chin, claiming that they wanted revenge on the Japanese for hurting the automobile industry. After pleading guilty to manslaughter, they paid a $3,000 fine and were released, More recently, groups of Cambodians and Vietnamese in Boston were beaten by white youths, and there have been incidents in New York and Los Angles as well.

ASIANS AND JEWS

Comparing the social success of Asian-Americans with that of the Jews is irresistible. Jews and Asians rank number one and number two, respectively, in median family income. In the Ivy League they are the two groups most heavily "over-represented" in comparison to their shares of the population. And observers are quick to point out all sorts of cultural parallels. As Arthur Rosen, the chairman of (appropriately) the National Committee on United States–China Relations, recently told *The New York Times,* "There are the same kind of strong family ties and the same sacrificial drive on the part of immigrant parents who couldn't get a college education to see that their children do."

In historical terms, the parallels can often be striking. For example, when Russian and Polish Jews came to this country in the late 19th and early 20th centuries, 60 percent of those who went into industry worked in the garment trade. Today thousands of Chinese-American women fill sweatshops in New York City doing the same work of stitching and sewing. In Los Angeles, when the Jews began to arrive in large numbers in the 1880s, 43 percent of them became retail or wholesale proprietors, according to Ivan Light's essay in *Clamor at the Gates.* One hundred years later, 40 percent of Koreans in Los Angeles are also wholesale and retail proprietors. The current controversy over Asian-American admission in Ivy League colleges eerily recalls the Jews' struggle to end quotas in the 1940s and 1950s.

In cultural terms, however, it is easy to take the comparison too far. American Jews remain a relatively homogeneous group, with a common religion and history. Asian-Americans, especially after the post-1965 flood of immigrants, are exactly the opposite. They seem homogeneous largely because they share some racial characteristics. And even those vary widely. The label "Chinese-American" itself covers a range of cultural and linguistic differences that makes those between German and East European Jews, or between Reform and Orthodox Jews, seem trivial in comparison.

The most important parallels between Jews and the various Asian groups are not cultural. They lie rather in the sociological profile of Jewish and Asian immigration. The Jewish newcomers of a hundred years ago never completely fit into the category of "huddled masses." They had an astonishing high literacy rate (nearly 100 percent for German Jews, and over 50 percent for East European Jews), a long tradition of scholarship even in the smallest shtetls, and useful skills. More than two-thirds of male Jewish immigrants were considered skilled workers in America.

Box continued on next page.

Less than three percent of Jewish immigrants had worked on the land. Similarly, the Japanese, Korean, Filipino, and Vietnamese immigrants of the 20th century have come almost exclusively from the middle class. Seventy percent of Korean male immigrants, for example, are college graduates. Like middle-class native-born Americans, Asian and Jewish immigrants alike have fully understood the importance of the universities, and have pushed their children to enter them from the very start.

Thomas Sowell offers another parallel between the successes of Asians and Jews. Both communities have benefited paradoxically, he argues, from their small size and from past discrimination against them. These disadvantages long kept both groups out of politics. And, as Sowell writes in *Race and Economics:* "those American ethnic groups that have succeeded best politically have not usually been the same as those who succeeded best economically . . . those minorities that have pinned their greatest hopes on political action—the Irish and the Negroes, for example—have made some of the slower economic advances." Rather than searching for a solution to their problems through the political process, Jewish, Chinese, and Japanese immigrants developed self-sufficiency by relying on community organizations. The combination of their skills, their desire for education, and the gradual disappearance of discrimination led inexorably to economic success.

D.A.B.

Is this violence an aberration, or does it reflect the persistence of anti-Asian prejudice in America? By at least one indicator, it seems hard to believe that Asian-Americans suffer greatly from discrimination. Their median family income, according to the 1980 census, was $22,713, compared to only $19,917 for whites. True, Asians live almost exclusively in urban areas (where incomes are higher), and generally have more people working in each family. They are also better educated than whites. Irene Natividad, a Filipino-American active in the Democratic Party's Asian Caucus, states bluntly that "we are under-paid for the high level of education we have achieved." However, because of language difficulties and differing professional standards in the United States, many new Asian immigrants initially work in jobs for which they are greatly overqualified.

Ironically, charges of discrimination today arise most frequently in the universities, the setting generally cited as the best evidence of Asian-American achievement. For several years Asian student associations at Ivy League universities have cited figures showing that a smaller percentage of Asian-American students than others are accepted. At Harvard this year, 12.5 percent of Asian-American applicants were admitted, as opposed to 16 percent of all applicants; at Princeton, the figures were 14 to 17 percent. Recently a Princeton professor, Uwe Reinhardt, told a *New York Times* reporter that Princeton has an unofficial quota for Asian-American applicants.

The question of university discrimination is a subtle one. For one thing, it only arises at the most prestigious schools, where admissions are the most subjective. At universities like UCLA, where applicants are judged largely by their grades and SAT scores, Asian-Americans have a higher admission rate than other students (80 percent versus 70 percent for all applicants). And at schools that emphasize science, like MIT, the general excellence of Asian-Americans in the field also produces a higher admission rate.

Why are things different at the Ivy League schools? One reason, according to a recent study done at Princeton, is that very few Asian-Americans are alumni children. The children of alumni are accepted at a rate of about 50 percent, and so raise the overall admissions figure. Athletes have a better chance of admission as well, and few Asian-Americans play varsity sports. These arguments, however, leave out another admissions factor: affirmative action. The fact is that if alumni children have a special advantage, at least some Asians do too, because of their race. At Harvard, for instance, partly in response to complaints from the Asian student organization, the admissions office in the late 1970s began to recruit vigorously among two categories of Asian-Americans: the poor, often living in Chinatowns; and recent immigrants. Today, according to the dean of admissions, L. Fred Jewett, roughly a third of Harvard's Asian-American applicants come from these groups, and are included in the university's "affirmative action" efforts. Like black students, who have a 27 percent admission rate, they find it easier to get in. And this means that the *other* Asian-Americans, the ones with no language problem or economic disadvantage, find things correspondingly tougher. Harvard has no statistics on the two groups. But if we assume the first group has an admissions rate of only 20 percent (very low for affirmative action candidates), the second one still slips down to slightly less than nine percent, or roughly half the overall admissions rate.

Dean Jewett offers two explanations for this phenomenon. First, he says, "family pressure makes more marginal students apply." In other words, many Asian students apply regardless of their qualifications, because of the university's prestige. And second, "a terribly high proportion of the Asian students are heading toward the sciences." In the interests of diversity, then, more of them must be left out.

⁘

It is true that more Asian-Americans go into the sciences. In Harvard's class of 1985, 57 percent of them did (as opposed to 29 percent of all students) and 71 percent went into either the sciences or economics. It is also true that a great many of Harvard's Asian-American applicants have little on their records except scientific excellence. But there are good reasons for this. In the sciences, complete mastery of English is less important than in other fields, an important fact for immigrants and children of immigrants. And scientific careers allow Asian-Americans to avoid the sort of large, hierarchical organization where their unfamiliarity with America, and management's resistance to putting them into highly visible positions, could hinder their advancement. And so the admissions problem comes down to a problem of clashing cultural standards. Since the values of Asian-American applicants differ from the universities' own, many of those applicants appear narrowly focused and dull. As Linda Matthews, an alumni recruiter for Harvard in Los Angeles, says with regret, "We hold them to the standards of white suburban kids. We want them to be cheerleaders and class presidents and all the rest."

The universities, however, consider their idea of the academic community to be liberal and sound. They are understandably hesitant to change it because of a demographic shift in the admissions pool. So how can they resolve this difficult problem? It is hard to say, except to suggest humility, and to recall that this sort of thing has come up before. At Harvard, the admissions office might do well to remember a memorandum Walter Lippmann prepared for the university in 1922. "I am fully prepared to accept the judgment of the Harvard authorities that a concentration of Jews in excess of fifteen per cent will produce a segregation of cultures rather than a fusion," wrote Lippmann, himself a Jew and a Harvard graduate. "They hand on unconsciously and uncritically from one generation to another many distressing personal and social habits. . . .

◦◦◉◦◦

The debate over admissions is abstruse. But for Asian-Americans, it has become an extremely sensitive issue. The universities, after all, represent their route to complete integration in American society, and to an equal chance at the advantages that enticed them and their parents to immigrate in the first place. At the same time, discrimination, even very slight discrimination, recalls the bitter prejudice and discrimination that Asian-Americans suffered for their first hundred years in this country.

Few white Americans today realize just how pervasive legal anti-Asian discrimination was before 1945. The tens of thousand of Chinese laborers who arrived in California in the 1850s and 1860s to work in the goldfields and build the Central Pacific Railroad often lived in virtual slavery (the words kuli, now part of the English language, mean "bitter labor"). Far from having the chance to organize, they were seized on as scapegoats by labor unions, particularly Samuel Gompers's AFL, and often ended up working as strikebreakers instead, thus inviting violent attacks. In 1870 Congress barred Asian immigrants from citizenship, and in 1882 it passed the Chinese Exclusion Act, which summarily prohibited more Chinese from entering the country. Since it did this at a time when 100,600 male Chinese-Americans had the company of only 4,800 females, it effectively sentenced the Chinese community to rapid decline. From 1854 to 1874, California had in effect a law preventing Asian-Americans from testifying in court, leaving them without the protection of the law.

Little changed in the late 19th and early 20th centuries, as large numbers of Japanese and smaller contingents from Korea and the Philippines began to arrive on the West Coast. In 1906 San Francisco made a brief attempt to segregate its school system. In 1910 a California law went so far as to prohibit marriage between Caucasians and "Mongolians," in flagrant defiance of the Fourteenth Amendment. Two Alien Land Acts in 1913 and 1920 prevented noncitizens in California (in other words, all alien immigrants) from owning or leasing land. These laws, and the Chinese Exclusion Act, remained in effect until the 1940s. And of course during the Second World War, President Franklin Roosevelt signed an Executive Order sending 110,000 ethnic Japanese on the West Coast, 64 percent of whom were American citizens, to internment camps. Estimates of the monetary damage to the Japanese-American community from this action range as high as $400,000,000, and Japanese-American political activists have made reparations one of their most important goals. Only in Hawaii, where Japanese-Americans already outnumbered whites 61,000 to 29,000 at the turn of the century, was discrimination relatively less important. (Indeed, 157,000 Japanese-Americans in Hawaii at the start of the war were *not* interned, although they posed a greater possible threat to the war effort than their cousins in California.)

⚜

In light of this history, the current problems of the Asian-American community seem relatively minor, and its success appears even more remarkable. Social scientists wonder just how this success was possible, and how Asian-Americans have managed to avoid the "second-class citizenship" that has trapped so many blacks and Hispanics. There is no single answer, but all the various explanations of the Asian-Americans' success do tend to fall into one category: self-sufficiency.

The first element of this self-sufficiency is family. Conservative sociologist Thomas Sowell writes that "strong, stable families have been characteristic of . . . successful minorities," and calls Chinese-Americans and Japanese-Americans the most stable he has encountered. This quality contributes to success in at least three ways. First and most obviously, it provides a secure environment for children. Second, it pushes those children to do better than their parents. As former Ohio state demographer William Petersen, author of *Japanese-Americans* (1971), says "They're like the Jews in that they have the whole family and the whole community pushing them to make the best of themselves." And finally, it is a significant financial advantage. Traditionally, Asian-Americans have headed into family businesses, with all the family members pitching in long hours to make them a success. For the Chinese, it was restaurants and laundries (as late as 1940, half of the Chinese-American labor force worked in one or the other), for the Japanese, groceries and truck farming, and for the Koreans, groceries. Today the proportion of Koreans working without pay in family businesses is nearly three times as high as any other group. A recent *New York* magazine profile of one typical Korean grocery in New York showed that several of the family members running it consistently worked 15 to 18 hours a day. Thomas Sowell points out that in 1970, although Chinese median family income already exceeded white median family income by a third, their median personal income was only ten percent higher, indicating much greater participation per family.

Also contributing to Asian-American self-sufficiency are powerful community organizations. From the beginning of Chinese-American settlement in California, clan organizations, mutual aid societies, and rotating credit associations gave many Japanese-Americans a start in business, at a time when most banks would only lend to whites. Throughout the first half of this century, the strength of community organizations was an important reason why Asian-Americans tended to live in small, closed communities rather than spreading out among the general population. And during the Depression years, they proved vital. In the early 1930s, when nine percent of the population of New York City subsisted on public relief, only one percent of Chinese-Americans did so. The community structure has also helped keep Asian-American crime rates the lowest in the nation, despite recently increasing gang violence among new Chinese and Vietnamese immigrants. According to the 1980 census, the proportion of Asian-Americans in prison is one-fourth that of the general population.

The more recent immigrants have also developed close communities. In the Washington, D.C., suburb of Arlington, Virginia, there is now a "Little Saigon." Koreans also take advantage of the "ethnic resources" provided by a small community. As Ivan Light writes in an essay in Nathan Glazer's new book, *Clamor at the Gates,* "They help one another with business skills, information, and purchase of ethnic commodities; cluster in particular industries; combine easily in restraint of trade; or utilize rotation credit associations." Light cites a study showing that 34 percent of Korean grocery store owners in Chicago had received financial help from within the Korean community. The immigrants in these communities are self-sufficient in another way as well. Unlike the immigrants of the 19th century, most new Asian-Americans come to the United States with professional skills. Or they come to obtain those skills, and then stay on. Of 16,000 Taiwanese who came to the U.S. as students in the 1960s, only three percent returned to Taiwan.

◦◦◦

So what does the future hold for Asian-Americans? With the removal of most discrimination, and with the massive Asian-American influx in the universities, the importance of tightly knit communities is sure to wane. Indeed, among the older Asian-American groups it already has: since the war, fewer and fewer native-born Chinese-Americans have come to live in Chinatowns. But will complete assimilation follow? One study, at least, seems to indicate that it will, if one can look to the well-established Japanese-Americans for hints as to the future of other Asian groups. According to Professor Harry Kitano of UCLA, 63 percent of Japanese now intermarry.

But can all Asian-Americans follow the prosperous, assimilationist Japanese example? For some, it may not be easy. Hmong tribesmen, for instance, arrived in the United States with little money, few valuable skills, and extreme cultural disorientation. After five years here, they are still heavily dependent on welfare. (When the state of Oregon cut its assistance to refugees, 90 percent of the Hmong there moved to California.) Filipinos, although now the second-largest Asian-American group, make up less than ten percent of the Asian-American population at Harvard, and are the only Asian-Americans to benefit from affirmative action programs at the University of California. Do figures like these point to the emergence of a disadvantaged Asian-American underclass? It is still too early to tell, but the question is not receiving much attention either. As Nathan Glazer says of Asian-Americans, "When they're already above average, it's very hard to pay much attention to those who fall below." Ross Harano, a Chicago businessman active in the Democratic Party's Asian Caucus, argues that the label of "model minority" earned by the most conspicuous Asian-Americans hurt less successful groups. "We need money to help people who can't assimilate as fast as the superstars," he says.

Harano also points out that the stragglers find little help in traditional minority politics. "When blacks talk about a minority agenda, they don't include us," he says. "Most Asians are viewed by blacks as whites." Indeed, in cities with large numbers of Asians and blacks, relations between the communities are tense. In September 1984, for example, *The Los Angeles Sentinel,* a prominent black newspaper, ran a four-part series condemning Koreans for their "takeover" of black businesses, provoking a strong reaction from Asian-American groups. In Harlem some blacks have organized a boycott to Asian-American stores.

Another barrier to complete integration lies in the tendency of many Asian-American students to crowd into a small number of careers, mainly in the sciences. Professor Ronn Takaki of Berkeley is a strong critic of this "maldistribution," and says that universities should make efforts to correct it. The extent of these efforts, he told *The Boston Globe* last December, "will determine whether we have our poets, sociologists, historians, and journalists. If we are all tracked into becoming computer technicians and scientists, this need will not be fulfilled."

Yet it is not clear that the "maldistribution" problem will extend to the next generation. The children of the current immigrants will not share their parents' language difficulties. Nor will they worry as much about joining large institutions where subtle racism might once have barred them from advancement. William Petersen argues, "As the discrimination disappears, as it mostly has already, the self-selection will disappear as well. . . . There's nothing in Chinese or Japanese culture pushing them toward these fields." Professor Kitano of UCLA is not so sure. "The submerging of the individual to the group is another basic Japanese tradition," he wrote in an article for *The Harvard Encyclopedia of American Ethnic Groups.* It is a tradition that causes problems for Japanese-Americans who wish to avoid current career patterns: "It may only be a matter of time before some break out of these middleman jobs, but the structural and cultural restraints may prove difficult to overcome."

⟡

In short, Asian-Americans face undeniable problems of integration. Still, it takes a very narrow mind not to realize that these problems are the envy of every other American racial minority, and of a good number of white ethnic groups as well. Like the Jews, who experienced a similar pattern of discrimination and quotas, and who first crowded into a small range of professions, Asian-Americans have shown an ability to overcome large obstacles in spectacular fashion. In particular, they have done so by taking full advantage of America's greatest civic resource, its schools and universities, just as the Jews did 50 years ago. Now they seem poised to burst out upon American society.

᙮᙮᙮

The clearest indication of this course is in politics, a sphere that Asian-Americans traditionally avoided. Now this is changing. And importantly, it is *not* changing just because Asian-Americans want government to solve their particular problems. Yes, there are "Asian" issues: the loosening of immigration restrictions, reparations for the wartime internment, equal opportunity for the Asian disadvantaged. Asian-American Democrats are at present incensed over the way the Democratic National Committee has stripped their caucus of "official" status. But even the most vehement activists on these points still insist that the most important thing for Asian-Americans is not any particular combination of issues, but simply "being part of the process." Unlike blacks or Hispanics, Asian-American politicians have the luxury of not having to devote the bulk of their time to an "Asian-American agenda," and thus escape becoming prisoners of such an agenda. Who thinks of Senator Daniel Inouye or former senator S. I. Hayakawa primarily in terms of his race? In June a young Chinese-American named Michael Woo won a seat on the Los Angeles City Council, running in a district that is only five percent Asian. According to *The Washington Post,* he attributed his victory to his "links to his fellow young American professionals." This is not typical minority-group politics.

Since Asian-Americans have the luxury of not having to behave like other minority groups, it seems only a matter of time before they, like the Jews, lose their "minority" status altogether, both legally and in the public's perception. And when this occurs, Asian-Americans will have to face the danger not of discrimination but of losing their cultural identity. It is a problem that every immigrant group must eventually come to terms with.

For Americans in general, however, the success of Asian-Americans poses no problems at all. On the contrary, their triumph has done nothing but enrich the United States. Asian-Americans improve every field they enter, for the simple reason that in a free society, a group succeeds by doing something better than it had been done before: Korean grocery stores provide fresher vegetables; Filipino doctors provide better rural health care; Asian science students raise the quality of science in the universities, and go on to provide better medicine, engineering, computer technology, and so on. And by a peculiarly American miracle, the Asian-Americans' success has not been balanced by anyone else's failure. Indeed, as successive waves of immigrants have shown, each new ethnic and racial group adds far more to American society than it takes away. This Fourth of July, that is cause for hope and celebration.

NO

Frank H. Wu

The Model Minority: Asian American "Success" as a Race Relations Failure

Student   "Asians are threatening our economic future. . . . We can see it right here in our own school. Who are getting into the best colleges, in disproportionate numbers? Asian Kids! It's not fair."

Teacher   "Uh . . . That certainly was an unusual essay. . . . Unfortunately, it's racist."

Student   "Um . . . are you sure? My parents helped me."

—Garry Trudeau
Recycled Doonesbury: Second Thoughts on a Gilded Age

Revenge of the Nerds

I am not the model minority. Before I can talk about Asian American experiences at all, I have to kill off the model minority myth because the stereotype obscures many realities. I am an Asian American, but I am not good with computers. I cannot balance my checkbook, much less perform calculus in my head. I would like to fail in school, for no reason other than to cast off my freakish alter ego of geek and nerd. I am tempted to be very rude, just to demonstrate once and for all that I will not be excessively polite, bowing, smiling, and deferring. I am lazy and a loner, who would rather reform the law than obey it and who has no business skills. I yearn to be an artist, an athlete, a rebel, and above all, an ordinary person.

I am fascinated by the imperviousness of the model minority myth against all efforts at debunking it. I am often told by nice people who are bewildered by the fuss, "You Asians are all doing well. What could you have to complain about anyway? Why would you object to a positive image?" To my frustration, many people who say with the utmost conviction that they would like to be color blind revert to being color conscious as soon as they look at Asian Americans, but then shrug off the contradiction. They are nonchalant about the racial generalization, "You Asians are all doing well," dismissive in asking "What could you have to complain about anyway?," and indifferent to the negative consequences of "a positive image."

Even people who are sympathetic to civil rights in general, including other people of color, sometimes resist mentioning civil rights and Asian Americans together in the same sentence. It is as if Asian American civil rights concerns can be ruled out categorically without the need for serious consideration of the facts, because everyone knows that Asian Americans are prospering. . . .

And so it is with Asian Americans. "You Asians are all doing well anyway" summarizes the model minority myth. This is the dominant image of Asians in the United States. Ever since immigration reforms in 1965 led to a great influx of Asian peoples, we have enjoyed an excellent reputation. As a group, we are said to be intelligent, gifted in math and science, polite, hard working, family oriented, law abiding, and successfully entrepreneurial. We revere our elders and show fidelity to tradition. The nation has become familiar with the turn-of-the-century Horatio Alger tales of "pulling yourself up by your own bootstraps" updated for the new millennium with an "Oriental" face and imbued with Asian values.

This miracle is the standard depiction of Asian Americans in fact and fiction, from the news media to scholarly books to Hollywood movies. From the 1960s to the 1990s, profiles of whiz kid Asian Americans became so common as to be cliches. . . .

Conservative politicians especially like to celebrate Asian Americans. President Ronald Reagan called Asian Americans "our exemplars of hope." President George Bush, California Governor Pete Wilson, House Speaker Newt Gingrich—all have been unduly awed by the model minority myth. In a brief for the *Heritage Foundation Policy Review,* California politician Ron Unz said that Asian Americans come from an "anti-liberal Confucian tradition" that "leaves them a natural constituency for conservatives." In the *National Review,* author Willian McGurn made the model minority myth a partisan parable: "Precisely because Asian Americans are making it in their adoptive land, they hold the potential not only to add to Republican rolls but to define a bona-fide American language of civil rights."

According to the model minority myth, Asian immigrants have followed the beacon of economic opportunity from their homes in China, Japan, Korea, the Philippines, India, Vietnam, and all the other countries on the Asian continent and within the Pacific Rim. They might be fleeing despotism or Communism, backwardness or the deprivations or war and famine, but whatever the conditions of their past they know that the legend of Golden Mountain, to use the Cantonese phrase, guides their future.

They arrive in America virtually penniless. They bring barely more than the clothes on their backs. Their meager physical possessions are less important than their mental capacity and work ethic. Thanks to their selfless dedication to a small business or an advanced degree in electrical engineering—or both—they are soon achieving the American Dream. . . .

They were doctors, nurses, engineers, scientists, professors, and librarians, but they have problems pursuing their professions because the requisite license is denied to them owing to their foreign education, or they are discriminated against because they have a heavy accent. Even if they are reduced to the drudgery of jobs for which they are overqualified, they are earning what they could never have in conditions of a developing country. Although they may be sweating as a janitor despite holding a doctorate, the toil is only temporary, until they can secure the patent for their discovery. In the interim, they can save enough to send remittances home to kinfolk who want very much to come here, too.

Whatever endeavor they pursue, Asian Americans are astonishing for their gung-ho enthusiasm. They remain busy with the chores called for by their enterprise twenty-four hours a day, seven days a week, through the holidays. After they sweep out their storefront entryway, they wash down the public sidewalk.

They come to dominate their trades after less than a decade, reducing their competition to the verge of bankruptcy and then buying up their warehouse stocks. Their associations become monopolies, lending money cooperatively among their own members to preserve their collective advantage. In some cities, they hold more than half the commercial licenses and operate a majority of the downtown "mom and pop" retail outlets. Hospitals and universities have departments wholly staffed by Asian immigrants. Private industries ranging from automobile manufacturers to software developers to government agencies, such as the Defense Department, depend on them for research and development.

In turn, their American-born progeny continue the tradition with their staggering academic prowess. They start off speaking pidgin, some of them even being held back a grade to adjust. They are willing to do as they are told, changing their given names to Anglicized Christian names chosen with the help of their teachers and their friends and told matter of factly to their parents. Above all, they study, study, study. . . .

The no-nonsense regimen works wonders. A parade of prodigies named Chang, Nguyen, and Patel takes the prizes at piano recitals and proceeds to graduate from high school with honors as valedictorian, salutatorian, and the rest of the top ten of the class, receiving full scholarships to the Ivy League colleges en route to graduate school and advanced professional training.

In any course on campus, Asian Americans are the best (or worst) classmates. In a physics class, they wreck the grade curve, idly twirling their pens back and forth with thumb and forefinger during lectures, solving problem sets late into the night with their peers, breaking for fried rice seasoned with pungent fish sauce and accompanied by smelly kim chee. In the laboratory, they are polishing up projects begun when they were adolescents, making breakthroughs in biology and chemistry, and publishing papers that make the faculty envious as they strive toward a Nobel prize. If they engage in frivolous activities after hours, as they rarely do, they are betrayed by their telltale red faces, which they develop after drinking just half a glass of beer.

Eventually, they land a job at a high-tech company or they start their own. Making millions, they buy big houses in the suburbs or build monstrosities right up to the property line on vacant lots. They bring their relatives over, starting the cycle over again.

In the view of other Americans, Asian Americans vindicate the American Dream. A publicity campaign designed to secure the acceptance of Asian Americans could hardly improve perceptions. They have done better here than they ever could have dreamed of doing in their homelands. They are living proof of the power of the free market and the absence of racial discrimination. Their good fortune flows from individual self-reliance and community self-sufficiency, not civil rights activism or government welfare benefits. They believe that merit and effort pay off handsomely and justly, and so they do. Asian Americans do not whine about racial discrimination; they only try harder. If they are told that they have a weakness that prevents their social acceptance, they quickly agree and earnestly attempt to cure it. If they are subjected to mistreatment by their employer, they quit and found their own company rather than protesting or suing.

This caricature is the portrait of the model minority. It is a parody of itself. . . .

Cartoonist Garry Trudeau satirized the model minority myth while recognizing its continuity with the earlier treatment of Jewish immigrants. In an installment of his "Doonesbury" comic strips devoted to the subject, another excerpt from which serves as the epigraph to this chapter, he portrays the following exchange between a white boy and an Asian American girl:

> "Hey, good goin' on the National Merit Scholarship, Kim! Fairly awesome."
> "Thanks, Sean."
> "Must be easier to be a grind if you grow up in an Asian family, huh?"
> "I wouldn't know."
> "Huh?"
> "I'm adopted. My parents are Jewish."
> "Jewish? Yo! Say no more!"
> "I wasn't planning to."

Non-Asian American college students have been similarly sarcastic about the model minority myth. On campuses at the end of the twentieth century, non-Asian American students joke that "MIT" stands for "Made In Taiwan" rather than "Massachusetts Institute of Technology"; "UCLA" (pronounced "UCRA" to mock the reputed Asian inability to enunciate a proper "R") means "United Caucasians Lost Among Asians"; and the initials of University of California at Irvine, "UCI," mean "University of Chinese Immigrants." The University of California-Berkeley Engineering school has been spray-painted with graffiti calling on school authorities to "Stop the Asian Hordes."

The model minority myth is daunting. The white president of Stanford University related an apocryphal story about a professor who asked a white student about a poor exam answer in an engineering course, only to receive the comeback, "What do you think I am, Chinese?" The student body president of Berkeley has said, "Some students say that if they see too many Asians in a class, they are not going to take it because the curve will be too high." A Yale student has said, "If you are weak in math or science and find yourself assigned to a class with a majority of Asian kids, the only thing to do is transfer to a different section."

The model minority myth appears to have the twin virtues of being true and being benevolent. It seems to be more benefit than burden for its subjects. It is unlike theories that array human beings in racial hierarchies. On its face, it is neither outlandish nor objectionable. It does not depend on allegations that Asian blood is better or even different than European blood. It relies more on acquired behavior than on inborn biology. It is not presented as some sort of tortured justification for outright oppression, such as incredible stories about African Americans told to legitimize the "peculiar institution" of chattel slavery.

The model minority myth also looks modern. It seems to be the product of scientific research rather than reflexive superstition. It cancels out prejudices of only a generation ago. It is ostensibly founded on empirical findings of social science, primarily Census tabulations. Since the 1980s, the figures have suggested that some Asian ethnic groups, notably Japanese Americans, have attained household incomes equal to or greater than those of white Americans. The numbers are averages, but they seem about as adequate a foundation as could be found for a racial proposition.

For all these reasons, it is a considerable challenge to explain how an apparent tribute can be a dangerous stereotype and why it presents a problem to be overcome. A person who demurs to praise seems to be "politically correct." Yet declining the laudatory title of model minority is fundamental to gaining Asian American autonomy. The model minority myth deserves a thoughtful critique. It would be foolish to condemn it as wrong or racist, without discussion. It is too complex, as well as too common.

Regrettably, the model minority myth embraced by the pundits and the public alike is neither true nor truly flattering. Instead, it is a stock character that plays multiple roles in our racial drama. Like any other myth forming our collective narrative of race, it is ultimately more revealing than reassuring. Complimentary on its face, the model minority myth is disingenuous at its heart.

As well-meaning as it may be, the model minority myth ought to be rejected for three reasons. First, the myth is a gross simplification that is not accurate enough to be seriously used for understanding 10 million people. Second, it conceals within it an invidious statement about African Americans along the lines of the inflammatory taunt: "They made it; why can't you?" Third, the myth is abused both to deny that Asian Americans experience racial discrimination and to turn Asian Americans into a racial threat.

Germs of Truth Within the Myth

Like many racial stereotypes, the model minority myth has a germ of truth. The problem, however, is that the germ becomes exaggerated and distorted. On its own terms, the myth is not even persuasive as a description of the status of Asian Americans. In earning power, for example, the evidence points toward a disparity between what individual white Americans and what individual Asian Americans are paid—and not for lack of trying on the part of Asian Americans.

To figure out the facts, University of Hawaii sociology professor Herbert Barringer led a team that conducted the most comprehensive review of the research literature ever done. Barringer concludes that with respect to income, "in almost every category . . . whites showed advantages over most Asian Americans." . . .

That interpretation, however, is most favorable to white Americans and not Asian Americans. Translated into practical terms, it means that white Americans are paid more than Asian Americans who are equally qualified. Either Asian Americans are not hired for the higher-paying jobs, or they are hired but are still paid less. . . .

The fact that Asian Americans are better educated than white Americans on average undermines rather than supports the model minority myth. The gap between Asian Americans and white Americans that appears with income reverses itself with education. It was consistent throughout the 1980s and 1990s. In 1980, approximately 36 percent of foreign-born Asian Americans had finished college compared with 16 percent of native-born citizens. In 1990, about 42 percent of Asian Americans had finished college compared with 25 percent of the general population. . . . As of 1993, Asian Americans made up 5.3 percent of the college student body but approximately 2.9 percent of the general population. Their desire for education is increasing even as that of other groups is decreasing. Between 1979 and 1989, Asian Americans increased their numbers of Ph.D. recipients by 46 percent while whites and blacks decreased their numbers by 6 and 23 percent, respectively. By 1997, Asian Americans were receiving 12 percent of the doctorates conferred by U.S. universities, and they received more than one-quarter of the doctorates in engineering disciplines.

Although the average educational levels of Asian Americans might be taken as substantiating the model minority myth, the more plausible reading is that Asian Americans have had to overcompensate. Asian Americans receive a lower return on their investment in education. They gain less money than white Americans on average for each additional degree. They are underrepresented in management, and those who are managers earn less than white Americans in comparable positions. . . .

Moreover, Asian immigrants start off relatively privileged. This admission must be made gingerly, so that it will not be taken as corroboration of the model minority myth. In actuality, it undercuts the myth. Most Asian Americans are not rich. But some Asian immigrants are relatively fortunate compared to the many Asians who reside in Asia, and some of them are relatively fortunate compared to native-born Americans (including, incidentally, native-born Asian Americans), even though they have not had an easy time of it in coming to the United States and even though they experience prejudice. A major study of diversity in the power elite found that almost none of the Chinese Americans who served on the boards of directors for Fortune 1000 companies were "authentic bootstrappers."

Almost all of them had come from well-to-do families in China, Taiwan, and Hong Kong.

University of California at Santa Cruz sociologist Deborah Woo examined more closely the media coverage of "a Korean-born immigrant who once worked the night shift at 7-Eleven to put himself through school" and who sold his company for $1 billion, as well as another Korean-born immigrant, a Silicon Valley entrepreneur who lived on ramen noodles and had to pawn his belongings to pay his phone bill, but gave $15 million to the San Francisco Asian Art Museum, "mak[ing] Horatio Alger look like a slacker." Woo delved into the backgrounds of these examples of the model minority myth. In the former instance, the individual was able to start his company because he had received a government contract through a minority set-aside program. In the latter, the man was descended from the royal family that ruled Korea until the Japanese takeover of 1905, and he had been a university professor and an executive in the family business in Korea before emigrating. They are still impressive people, but they have not come from the ghetto. The sheen comes off the model minority myth once the real stories are revealed. . . .

Asian Americans are more likely than white Americans to be self-employed. Self-employed individuals with the same income as corporate employees tend to put in longer hours, with fewer benefits and increased risks of bankruptcy and other setbacks. The average employee of an Asian-owned enterprise is paid less than $10,000 per year. . . .

The model minority myth also masks great disparities among Asian ethnic groups. Japanese Americans and Chinese Americans are closest to equality with whites, but Vietnamese Americans and other Southeast Asian refugees languish at the bottom of the economic pyramid, along with blacks. In the 1980 Census, for example, Vietnamese Americans were below African Americans on average. According to the 1990 Census, 25 percent of Vietnamese Americans and 45 percent of other Southeast Asians lived in poverty. Those poverty rates were higher than the rates for Africans (21 percent) and Hispanics (23 percent).

Finally, the figures for Asian Americans are rendered unreliable by the careless inclusion of Asians who reside in the United States but who are not Asian Americans at all. Hundreds of business executives with Japanese-based multinational companies spend stints of up to a few years here. Their upper-management salaries add to the average Asian American income, but they are no more representative of either Asians overseas or Asian immigrants than a white American vice-president of a Fortune 500 company who was an expatriate manager in Europe would be either average of Americans or of Europeans themselves. They are part of a transnational overclass. . . .

The model minority myth persists, despite violating our societal norms against racial stereotyping and even though it is not accurate. Dozens of amply documented and heavily annotated government studies and scholarly papers, along with a handful of better magazine and newspaper articles supplemented by television segments and public speeches, all intended to destroy the myth, have had negligible effect on popular culture. In the latest college textbook on Asian Americans, professors Lucie Cheng and Philip Q. Yang comment, "despite an unending barrage of attacks, the model minority image has persisted into the 1990s, quite alive if not entirely unscathed."

The myth has not succumbed to individualism or facts because it serves a purpose in reinforcing racial hierarchies. Asian Americans are as much a "middleman minority" as we are a model minority. We are placed in the awkward position of buffer or intermediary, elevated as the preferred racial minority at the expense of denigrating African Americans. Asian American writers and scholars have not hesitated to call the phenomenon what it is. Novelist Frank Chin has described it as "racist love," contrasting it with "racist hate" of other people of color. DePaul University law professor Sumi Cho has explained that Asian Americans are turned into "racial mascots," giving right-wing causes a novel messenger, camouflaging arguments that would look unconscionably self-interested if made by whites about themselves. University of California at Irvine political scientist Claire Kim has argued that Asian Americans are positioned through "racial triangulation," much as a Machiavellian would engage in political triangulation for maximum advantage. Law professor Mari Matsuda famously declared, "we will not be used" in repudiating the model minority myth.

Whatever the effects are called, Asian Americans become pawns. We are not recognized in our own right but advanced for ulterior motives. Michael S. Greve, a leading advocate against racial remedies, said that the controversy over anti-Asian discrimination could be used to attack affirmative action: It presented "an opportunity to call, on behalf of a racial minority (i.e., the Asian applicants), for an end to discrimination. It was an appeal that, when made on behalf of whites, is politically hopeless and, perhaps, no longer entirely respectable."

The model minority myth is resilient because it is a "meme." Scientist Richard Dawkins's concept of a "meme"—a piece of cultural material that can be passed on from person to person, society to society, and generation to generation—advises us that any information and any image can survive and evolve. Dawkins posits that memes are to culture what genes are to biology, replicating themselves in an evolutionary process that selects the bits most likely to survive. Whether they are information or rumor, stereotypes take on their own social life. The longevity and propagation of information depends on its usefulness, not necessarily its truth. The myth is useful, even if it is not true. Its content assuages the conscience and assigns blame, a function that is psychologically needed and socially desired. It tells a comforting narrative of America as having progressed to become a place where race does not matter anymore, and it offers a cautionary parable about the good minority and the bad minority. Author Michael Lind has written that "in addition to fulfilling their immediate functions—selling egg rolls, measuring blood sugar—Vietnamese vendors and Filipino lab technicians serve an additional function for the white overclass: they relieve it of guilt about the squalor of millions of native-born Americans, not only ghetto blacks and poor Hispanics but poor whites." To condemn the myth is not the same as to condemn the individual who has lived it or repeated it. We all like fables with happy endings, especially when we are the actors in the story. . . .

Backlash from the Myth

The model minority myth hurts Asian Americans themselves. It is two-faced. Every attractive trait matches up neatly to its repulsive complement, and the aspects are conducive to reversal. If we acquiesced to the myth in its favorable guise, we would be precluded from rejecting its unfavorable interpretations. We would already have accepted the characteristics at issue as inherent. . . .

Upside down or right side up, the model minority myth whitewashes racial discrimination. "People don't believe it," as one Asian American leader told the *L.A. Times* in 1991, in discussing the prevalence of anti-Asian bias. An Asian American student leader said that, like whites, other people of color doubt claims about attacks: "Some simply didn't see us as minorities. . . . They think if you're Asian you're automatically interning at Merrill Lynch and that you're never touched by racism." The myth implies that bigotry has been brought on by the victims, who must defeat it, rather than that it is the responsibility of the perpetrators, who could be compelled to eliminate it. Senator Alan Simpson, an opponent of immigration, coined the term "compassion fatigue" to describe his sense that Americans were tired of hearing about other peoples' problems (as if those other people weren't tired of their problems). Under Simpson's concept, even if Asian Americans press complaints about bias for which they have evidence, the incidents should be treated as inconsequential or written off as the cost of being a newcomer. The reasoning seems to be that because Asian Americans have theoretically surmounted the deleterious effects of racial discrimination, we cannot be actually aggrieved even if real wrongs are done to us. . . .

The model minority myth does more than cover up racial discrimination; it instigates racial discrimination as retribution. The hyperbole about Asian American affluence can lead to jealousy on the part of non-Asian Americans, who may suspect that Asian Americans are too comfortable or who are convinced by . . . others telling them Asian American gains are their losses. Through the justification of the myth, the humiliation of Asian Americans or even physical attacks directed against Asian Americans become compensation or retaliation. . . .

It would be bad enough if the model minority myth were true. Everyone else would resent Asian Americans for what Asian Americans possess. It is worse that the model minority myth is false. Everyone else resents Asian Americans for what they believe Asian Americans possess. Other Americans say that their resentment is about riches and not race, but they assume that Asian Americans are rich on the basis of race; there is no escaping that the resentment is racial. Above all, the model minority myth is a case study in the risks of racial stereotypes of any kind. It is the stereotyping itself, not the positive or negative valence it assumes temporarily, that is dangerous.

A stereotype confines its subjects. The myth was neither created by nor is it controlled by Asian Americans. It is applied to but not by Asian Americans.

The model minority myth tells us that the only good Asian American is a genius workaholic, not an average or normal man or woman. The expectations of being a supergeek can be debilitating. Asian American children are not allowed to be like other children. They must be superstudents, because their parents, their teachers, and society overall expect nothing less. They become misfits to their classmates. Their rarified upbringing is like that of John Stuart Mill, the great utilitarian philosopher whose father was determined to produce a polymath of the first order. Mill's homeschooling routine, sitting at a desk opposite his father for the entirety of the day except during walks when he would recite his lessons, worked brilliantly, producing a formidable scholar who was publishing learned papers as an adolescent but who also underwent a grave emotional breakdown at an early age. Other than through the model minority myth, few Americans today wish to force their children to endure the box of psychologist B. F. Skinner, with its positive and negative reinforcements to condition behavior as if we were rats to be rewarded for running a maze. Asian American adults are directed into specific occupations. Yet Asian Americans cannot sustain communities in which we all are engineers, no matter how good a profession it is. If we are not to be stunted as communities, we must have artists, journalists, lawyers, crafts-people, police officers, firefighters, social workers, and the myriad others with contributions to make to our civic culture. We should have communities that contain the spectrum of human pursuits, or we will live down to our stereotype. . . .

POSTSCRIPT

Are Asian Americans a Model Minority?

When one examines Asian American's "success" within the United States, it is important to be more specific concerning the group or groups that are the focus of analysis. Such specificity is required because all Asian ethnic groups have not achieved the same levels of success based on traditional measures that are employed in such assessments.

Asian Americans have been involved in the development of the nation for approximately one and a half centuries. This diverse aggregation of immigrant peoples brought cultures to the New World from some of the oldest civilizations to evolve in human history. The tendency to lump such culturally disparate minority groups into a singular macro-level category does not provide an adequate basis for understanding the distinctions that exist among the Asian-American ethnic groups that are impacting their life chances and prospects for advancement within society.

The two selections chosen for this issue present positions on opposite sides of the question: Is the glass half empty, or is it half full? Bell views Asian Americans as Americans "greatest success story." Though he recognizes that all of the problems facing Asians in the quest for acceptance and advancement in society have not been resolved, he chooses to down play such concerns. Bell is certain that Asian Americans are poised to achieve even greater success in a future America where they will become fully assimilated to the extent that they will lose their minority status within society.

Wu is cognizant of the real successes that some Asians have achieved, but he does not endorse the "model minority" notion. He is concerned that this imagery is being attached to Asian Americans at a time when they have not achieved equality with whites in important areas of economic life, and that they are lagging behind on significant indices of success, especially administration and other areas of leadership. And he is seriously concerned about the backlash against Asians that is expressed through stereotyping, hostile sentiments, and violence. Wu feels that the "model minority" rhetoric of U.S. leaders and their supporters tends to obscure these issues and concerns, thus mitigating the prospects of developing meaning and effective strategies for their resolution.

Among the Asian-American ethnic groups, Koreans have achieved more then the Hmong people or other boat people who arrived on America's shores in the wake of the Vietnam War. So, it is important to engage in an analysis of the stratification that exists, both among the various Asian ethnicities and within each of these groups, in order to gain a clearer and more meaningful assessment of their socioeconomic status and the success that they are experiencing in the society.

One question that arises is whether it is possible to establish a scientifically acceptable method to establish a meaningful comparison of the "successes" achieved by different minority groups? For example, how does the fact that African Americans have established over 100 black colleges and universities figure into the determination of success? The creation of these institutions is a major demonstration of the embrace of an ethic of self-reliance an educational achievement by African Americans.

Wu notes that the pitting of one ethnic group against another by American leaders, such as President Ronald Reagan, is dangerous and irresponsible. Such conservative leaders have employed the "model minority" rhetoric to delegitimize the demands of other ethnic groups for the government to be active and effective in resolving social problems. The message to groups such as blacks and Latinos emanating from these leaders is: Why can't you be like them (i.e., quiet and self-reliant)? The countervailing question that such leaders must address, is: What would be the quality of race and ethnic relations today if African Americans had been in the vanguard of the civil rights movement, and what would be the nature of Asian Americans' successes if the movement had not achieved the more open society that exists in the United States today? What value should be accorded African Americans for their Herculean contributions that they have exerted on behalf of freedom and justice for all minorities in America?

For an overview of Asian-American groups, see *Asian Americans: Emerging Minorities* (Prentice-Hall, 1988) by Harry Kitano and Roger Daniels. The June 1998 issue of the *Population Bulletin* was devoted to "Asian-Americans: Diverse and Growing." The volume, written by Sharon M. Lee, is a good introduction to the study of Asian Americans. An article that deals with Asians and assimilation is "In Asian America," by Tamar Jacoby in *Commentary* (July–August 2000). *Everybody Was Kung Fu Fighting: Afro-Asian Connections and the Myth of Cultural Purity* (Beacon Press, 2001) by Vijay Prashad discusses links between black and South Asian experiences. Eric Liu, in *The Accidental Asian: Notes of a Native Speaker* (Random House, 1998), articulates a vision of Asian-American identity.

Stanford Lyman's *The Asian in the West* (Western Studies Center, Desert Research Institute, 1970) is a little known but important discussion on Asians and the beginnings of American institutional racism. Critical of the model minority notion is Won Moo Hurh and Kwang Chung Kim's "The 'Success' Image of Asian Americans: Its Validity, and Its Practical and Theoretical Implications" in *Ethnic and Racial Studies* (1989). *Asian American Dreams: The Emergence of an American People* (Farrar, Straus, 2000) by Helen Zia is a book about the transformation of Asian Americans from "aliens" into Americans with dreams of equality.

Are Hispanics Making Economic Progress?

YES: Linda Chavez, from *Out of the Barrio: Toward a New Politics of Hispanic Assimilation* (Basic Books, 1991)

NO: Robert Aponte, "Urban Hispanic Poverty: Disaggregations and Explanations," *Social Problems* (November 1991)

ISSUE SUMMARY

YES: Linda Chavez, writer and former political candidate, argues that Hispanics are making economic progress in America. She also claims that Hispanic leaders exaggerate the rate of poverty for their own ends.

NO: Robert Aponte, a social scientist, argues that Hispanics are not making economic progress. He presents significant disaggregated data to show that certain Hispanic groups are becoming increasingly poor.

T he fact that Hispanics had surpassed African Americans in 2002 as the nation's largest minority group garnered substantial media attention last summer and served to illuminate the ongoing dynamic of diversification of the American population. This development was based on data released by the Census Bureau that indicated that Hispanics now comprise 13.4% of the U.S. population and African Americans 13.1% in 2002. The Hispanic portion of the U.S. population is growing faster than that of all other groups except Asians.

It should be noted that Hispanics themselves are a very diverse aggregate of peoples. Today's Hispanics represent the progeny of the descendents of the initial colonial encounter of Spanish explorers/adventurers/conquistadors and the New World peoples, cultures, and civilizations that were overtaken and subjugated by these European colonizers. The New World Hispanic is a creation of this imperialistic experience and the cultural and genetic mixing that resulted from it. So, there is very substantial diversity that is reflected in the varieties of skin color and the different cultures of the Hispanic peoples of the United States.

Given the diversity of Hispanic Americans, it is difficult to assess whether they are achieving significant progress in society or not. Some Hispanic groups may be achieving significant progress while others lag on important indices that are employed to determine the socio-economic status that is being achieved by these minority Americans.

As, Robert Aponte points out in the article presented here, Mexican Americans and Puerto Ricans together constitute approximately 80% of the Hispanic population of the United States. Significant numbers of Dominicans, Cubans, Salvadorans, and others complete their ranks within society. It is difficult to "disaggregate" the socioeconomic data in order to determine whether Hispanics, overall, are achieving progress in the United States.

Aponte does not support the contention that Hispanics are achieving significant progress within the United States. To the contrary, he claims that if one disaggregates available data, one will find that Hispanics are experiencing increasing poverty with society.

Linda Chavez focuses on Puerto Ricans and Mexican-Americans, and does not present disaggregated data on the socio-economic status of other Hispanic groups. Citing increasing home ownership and migration from central cities, she notes that Hispanics are progressing. She also notes progress with the increasing number of Hispanics working in white-collar jobs that are managerial, professional, or technical in nature. She examines such categories as work, earnings, education, occupational status, and poverty in order to make the case for Hispanic progress. Further, Chavez argues that "too much government attention" has harmed Puerto Ricans. In spite of this, Puerto Ricans hold up well when compared to other Hispanic groups in educational achievement.

After students evaluate these two articles, they may want to ask why some Hispanic groups are making progress, while others are not. To what extent is language a barrier to Hispanic progress? How stratified is the Hispanic community? How much prejudice and discrimination is directed against Hispanics? Have government social welfare programs harmed some Hispanics? Can economic progress be made without social and political progress?

Linda Chavez  **YES**

Out of the Barrio

In the Beginning

Before the affirmative action age, there were no *Hispanics,* only Mexicans, Puerto Ricans, Cubans, and so on. Indeed, few efforts were made to forge an alliance among the various Hispanic subgroups until the 1970s, when competition with blacks for college admissions, jobs, and other rewards of affirmative action made it advantageous for Hispanics to join forces in order to demand a larger share of the pie. In addition to having no common history, these groups were more or less geographically isolated from one another. Mexican Americans lived in the Southwest, Puerto Ricans in the Northeast, mostly in New York, and Cubans in Florida; . . .

The Second World War marked a turning point for Hispanic activism. Hispanics served with great distinction in the war, earning more Congressional Medals of Honor per capita than any other group. Moreover, unlike blacks, Hispanics served in integrated military units, which brought them into contact with other Americans and introduced them, for the first time, to Americans who lived outside the Southwest. More than 100,000 Puerto Ricans served in the military during the war; later, many of these men and their families decided to migrate from the island in search of greater economic opportunity in the United States. Hispanics returned from the war expecting better treatment than was the standard fare for Mexican Americans and Puerto Ricans in most places. Hispanics wanted to increase their earnings and social standing, live where they wanted, and send their children to better schools. Indeed, there was significant upward mobility for Mexican Americans in the period, especially in California and other areas outside Texas, and for the Puerto Ricans who migrated to New York City. . . .

⌁

"Each decade offered us hope, but our hopes evaporated into smoke. We became the poorest of the poor, the most segregated minority in schools, the lowest paid group in America and the least educated minority in this nation." This view of Hispanics' progress by the president of the National Council of La Raza, one of the country's leading Hispanic civil rights groups, is the prevalent one among Hispanic leaders and is shared by many outside the Hispanic community as well. By and large, Hispanics are perceived to be a disadvantaged minority—poorly educated, concentrated in barrios, economically impoverished; with little hope of participating in the American Dream. This perception has not changed substantially in twenty-five years. And it is wrong.

Hispanics have been called the invisible minority, and indeed they were for many years, largely because most Hispanics lived in the Southwest and the Northeast, away from the most blatant discrimination of the Deep South. But the most invisible Hispanics today are those who have been absorbed into the mainstream. The success of middle-class Hispanics is an untold—and misunderstood—story perhaps least appreciated by Hispanic advocates whose interest is in promoting the view that Latinos cannot make it in this society. The Hispanic poor, who constitute only about one-fourth of the Hispanic population, are visible to all. These are the Hispanics most likely to be studied, analyzed, and reported on and certainly the ones most likely to be read about. A recent computer search of stories about Hispanics in major newspapers and magazines over a twelve-month period turned up more than eighteen hundred stories in which the word *Hispanic* or *Latino* occurred within a hundred words of the word *poverty.* In most people's minds, the expression *poor Hispanic* is almost redundant.

Has Hispanics' Progress Stalled?

Most Hispanics, rather than being poor, lead solidly lower-middle- or middle-class lives, but finding evidence to support this thesis is sometimes difficult. Of course, Hispanic groups vary one from another, as do individuals within any group. Most analysts acknowledge, for example, that Cubans are highly successful. Within one generation, they have virtually closed the earnings and education gap with other Americans. (For a broad range of social and economic indicators for each of the major Hispanic groups, see table 1.) Although some analysts claim that the success of Cubans is due exclusively to their high socioeconomic status when they arrived, many Cuban refugees—especially those who came after the first wave in the 1960s—were in fact skilled or semiskilled workers with relatively little education. Their accomplishments in the United States are attributable in large measure to diligence and hard work. They established enclave economies, in the traditional immigrant mode, opening restaurants, stores, and other émigré-oriented services. . . . But Cubans are as a rule dismissed as the exception among Hispanics. What about other Hispanic groups? Why has there been no "progress" among them?

The largest and most important group is the Mexican American population. . . . [I]ts leaders have driven much of the policy agenda affecting all Hispanics, but the importance of Mexican Americans also stems from their having a longer history in the United States than does any other Hispanic group. If Mexican Americans whose families have lived in the United States for generations are not yet making it in this society, they may

Table 1

Characteristics of Hispanic Subgroups and Non-Hispanics

	Mexican-Origin*	Puerto Rican	Cuban	South/Central American	Other Hispanic	Non-Hispanic
Total population (in millions)	13.3	2.2	1.0	2.8	1.4	246.2
Median age	24.1	27.0	39.1	28.0	31.1	33.5
Median years of schooling (1988)	10.8	12.0	12.4	12.4	12.7	12.7
Percentage in labor force Male	81.2%	69.2%	74.9%	83.7%	75.3%	74.2%
Female	52.9%	41.4%	57.8%	61.0%	57.0%	57.4%
Percentage of unemployed	9.0%	8.6%	5.8%	6.6%	6.2%	5.3%
Median earnings (1989) Male	$12,527	$18,222	$19,336	$15,067	$17,486	$22,081
Female	$8,874	$12,812	$12,880	$10,083	$11,564	$11,885
Percentage of married-couple families	72.5%	57.2%	77.4%	68.7%	69.8%	79.9%
Percentage of female-headed families	19.6%	38.9%	18.9%	25.0%	24.5%	6.0%
Percentage of out-of-wedlock births	28.9%	53.0%	16.1%	37.1%	34.2%	23.9%**
Percentage of families in poverty	25.7%	30.4%	12.5%	16.8%	15.8%	9.2%

*Mexican-origin population includes both native- and foreign-born persons.
**Includes black out-of-wedlock births, 63.1% and white births, 13.9%.

Source: Bureau of the Census, *The Hispanic Population in the United States: March 1990,* Current Population Reports, ser. P-20, no. 449; median years of schooling are from *The Hispanic Population of the United States: March 1988,* Current Population Reports, ser. P-20, no. 438; out-of-wedlock births are from National Center for Health Statistics, *Advance Report of Final Natality Statistics, 1987.*

have a legitimate claim to consider themselves a more or less permanently disadvantaged group, like blacks. That is precisely what Mexican American leaders suggest is happening. Their proof is that statistical measures of Mexican American achievement in education, earnings, poverty rates, and other social and economic indicators have remained largely unchanged for decades. In 1959 the median income of Mexican-origin males in the Southwest was 57 percent that of non-Hispanics. In 1989 it was still 57 percent of non-Hispanic income. If Mexican Americans had made progress, it would show up in improved education attainment and earnings and in lower poverty rates, so the argument goes. Since it doesn't, progress must be stalled.

In the post-civil rights era, the failure of a minority to close the social and economic gap with whites is assumed to be the result of persistent discrimination. Progress is perceived not in absolute but in relative terms. The poor may become less poor over time, but so long as those on the upper rungs of the economic ladder are climbing even faster, the poor are believed to have suffered some harm, even if they have made absolute gains and their lives are much improved. However, in order for Hispanics (or any group on the lower rungs) to close the gap, they must progress at an even greater rate than non-Hispanic whites; their apparent failure to do so in recent years causes Hispanic leaders and the public to conclude that Hispanics are falling behind. Is this a fair way to judge Hispanics' progress? In fact, it makes almost no sense to apply this test today (if it ever did), because the Hispanic population itself is changing so rapidly. This is most true of the Mexican-origin population.

In 1959 the overwhelming majority of persons of Mexican origin living in the United States were native-born, 85 percent. Today only about two-thirds of the people of Mexican origin were born in the United States, and among adults barely one in two was born here. Increasingly, the Hispanic population, including that of Mexican origin, is made up of new immigrants, who, like immigrants of every era, start off at the bottom of the economic ladder. This infusion of new immigrants is bound to distort our image of progress in the Hispanic population, if each time we measure the group we include people who have just arrived and have yet to make their way in this society.

. . . In 1980 there were about 14.6 million Hispanics living in the United States; in 1990, nearly 21 million, an increase of about 44 percent in one decade. At least one-half of this increase was the result of immigration, legal and illegal. . . . [T]his influx consists mostly of poorly educated persons, with minimal skills, who cannot speak English. Not surprisingly, when these Hispanics are added to the pool being measured, the achievement levels of the whole group fall. It is almost inconceivable that the addition of two or three million new immigrants to the Hispanic pool would not seriously distort evidence of Hispanics' progress during the decade. Yet no major Hispanic organization will acknowledge the validity of this reasonable assumption. Instead, Hispanic leaders complain, "Hispanics are the population that has benefitted least from the economic recovery." "The Myth of Hispanic Progress" is the title of a study by a Mexican American professor, purporting to show that "it is simply wrong to assume that Hispanics are making gradual progress toward parity with Anglos." "Hispanic poverty is now comparable to that of blacks and is expected to exceed it by the end of this decade," warns another group.

Hispanics wear disadvantage almost like a badge of distinction, as if groups were competing with each other for the title "most disadvantaged." Sadly, the most frequently heard complaint among Hispanic leaders is not that the public ignores evidence of Hispanics' achievement but that it underestimates their disadvantage. "More than any group in American political history, Hispanic Americans have turned to the national statistical system as an instrument for advancing their political and economic interests, by making visible the magnitude of social and economic problems they face," says a Rockefeller Foundation official. But gathering all Hispanics together under one umbrella obscures as much information as it illuminates, and may make Hispanics—especially the native-born—appear to suffer greater social and economic problems than they actually do.

In fact, a careful examination of the voluminous data on the Hispanic population gathered by the Census Bureau and other federal agencies shows that, as a group, Hispanics have made progress in this society and that most of them have moved into the social and economic mainstream. In most respects, Hispanics—particularly those born here—are very much like other Americans; they work hard, support their own families without outside assistance, have more education and higher earnings than their parents, and own their own home. In short, they are pursuing the American Dream—with increasing success.

Work

Hispanic men are more likely to be members of the labor force—that is, working or looking for work—than non-Hispanic whites. Among all Mexican-origin men sixteen years old or older in 1990, for example, participation in the labor force was substantially higher than it was for non-Hispanic males overall—81 percent compared with 74 percent. This fact bodes well for the future and is in marked contrast to the experience of black men, whose labor force participation has been steadily declining for more than twenty years. Most analysts believe that low attachment to the labor force and its correlate, high dependence on welfare, are prime components of underclass behavior. As the political scientist Lawrence Mead writes in his book *Beyond Entitlement: The Social Obligations of Citizenship,* for many persons who are in the underclass, "the problem is not that jobs are *unavailable* but that they are frequently *unacceptable,* in pay or condition, given that some income is usually available from families or benefit programs." In other words, persons in the underclass frequently choose not to work rather than to take jobs they deem beneath them. . . . The willingness of Hispanic men to work, even at low-wage jobs if their skills qualify them for nothing better, suggests that Hispanics are in no immediate danger of forming a large underclass.

. . . During the 1980s, 3.3 million new Hispanic workers were added to the work force, giving Hispanics a disproportionate share of the new jobs. Hispanics benefited more than any other group in terms of employment growth in the last decade. By the year 2000, they are expected to account for 10 percent of the nation's work force.

Earnings

. . . Hispanic leaders charge that Hispanics' wages have failed to keep pace with those of non-Hispanics. Statistics on average Hispanic earnings during the decade appear to bear this out, but they should be viewed with caution. The changing composition of the Hispanic population, from a predominantly native-born to an increasingly immigrant one, makes an enormous difference in how we interpret the data on Hispanic earnings. Since nearly half of all Hispanic workers are foreign-born and since many of these have immigrated within the last ten years, we should not be surprised that the average earnings of Hispanics appear low. After all, most Hispanic immigrants are semi-skilled workers who do not speak English, and their wages reflect these deficiencies. When huge numbers of such workers are added to the pool on which we base average-earnings figures, they will lower the mean. . . .

When earnings of native-born Mexican American men are analyzed separately from those of Mexican immigrants, a very different picture emerges. On the average, the weekly earnings of Mexican American men are about 83 percent those of non-Hispanic white men—a figure that cuts in half the apparent gap between their earnings and those of non-Hispanics. Even this gap can be explained at least in part. Schooling, experience, hours worked, and geographical region of residence are among several factors that can affect earnings. When we compensate for these variables, we find that Mexican American men earn about 93 percent of the weekly earnings of comparable non-Hispanic white men. English-language proficiency also plays an important role in the earnings of Hispanics; some economists assert that those who are proficient in English experience "no important earnings differences from native-born Anglos." . . .

Education

Contrary to popular opinion, most Mexican American young adults have completed high school, being nearly as likely to do so as other Americans. But the popular press, the federal government, and Hispanic organizations cite statistics that indicate otherwise. They claim that about 60 percent of all Mexican-origin persons do not complete high school. The confusion stems, as it does with earnings data, from lumping native-born Hispanics with immigrants to get statistical averages for the entire group. . . .

Traditionally, Hispanics, like blacks, were more likely to concentrate in fields such as education and the social sciences, which are less remunerative than the physical sciences, business, engineering, and other technical and professional fields. Recently this trend has been reversed; in 1987 (the last year for which such statistics are available), Hispanics were almost as likely as non-Hispanic whites to receive baccalaureate degrees in the natural sciences and were more likely than they to major in computer sciences and engineering.

Occupational Status

Fewer Hispanic college graduates will mean fewer Hispanics in the professions and in higher-paying occupations, but this does not translate into the doomsday predictions about their achievement that advocacy organizations commonly voice. It does not mean, for example, that there will be a "a permanent Hispanic underclass" of persons "stuck in poverty because of low wages and deprived of upward mobility," as one Hispanic leader suggested in a *New York Times* article. It may mean, however, that Hispanics will be more likely to hold jobs as clerks in stores and banks, as secretaries and other office support personnel, as skilled workers, and as laborers. . . . Only in the managerial and professional and the service categories are there very large differences along ethnic lines: 11 percent of all Hispanic males are employed in managerial or professional jobs compared with 27 percent of all non-Hispanics; conversely, 16 percent of the Hispanic males compared with only 9 percent of the non-Hispanic males are employed in service jobs. But these figures include large numbers of immigrants in the Hispanic population, who are disproportionately represented in the service industry and among laborers.

An increasing number of Hispanics are self-employed, many in owner-operated businesses. According to the economist Timothy Bates, who has done a comprehensive study of minority small businesses, those owned by Hispanics are more successful than those owned by blacks. Yet Mexican business owners, a majority of whom are immigrants, are less well educated than any other group; one-third have completed less than twelve years of schooling. One reason why Hispanics may be more successful than blacks in operating small businesses, according to Bates, is that they cater to a nonminority clientele, whereas blacks operate businesses in black neighborhoods, catering to black clients. Hispanic-owned businesses are concentrated in the retail field; about one-quarter of both Mexican and non-Mexican Hispanic firms are retail businesses. About 10 percent of the Mexican-owned firms are in construction.

Poverty

Despite generally encouraging economic indicators for Hispanics, poverty rates are quite high; 26 percent of all Hispanics live below the poverty line. Hispanics are more than twice as likely to be living in poverty than are persons in the general population. Two factors, however, distort the poverty data: the inclusion of Puerto Ricans, who make up about 10 percent of Hispanics, one-third of whom live in poverty; and the low earnings of new immigrants. The persistence of poverty among Puerto Ricans is one of the most troubling features of the Hispanic population. . . .

An exhaustive study of the 1980 census by Frank Bean and Marta Tienda, however, suggests that nativity plays an important role in poverty data, as it does in earnings data generally. Bean and Tienda estimate that the poverty rate among U.S.-born Mexican Americans was nearly 20 percent lower than that among Mexican immigrants in 1980. Their analysis of data from the 1970 census, by contrast, shows almost no difference in poverty rates between Mexican Americans and Mexican immigrants, with both groups suffering significantly greater poverty in 1970 than in 1980. This implies that while poverty was declining among immigrants and the native-born alike between 1970 and 1980, the decline was greater for Mexican Americans.

The Public Policy Implications of Such Findings

For most Hispanics, especially those born in the United States, the last few decades have brought greater economic opportunity and social mobility. They are building solid lower-middle- and middle-class lives that include two-parent households, with a male head who works full-time and earns a wage commensurate with his education and training. Their educational level has been steadily rising, their earnings no longer reflect wide disparities with those of non-Hispanics, and their occupational distribution is coming to resemble more closely that of the general population. They are buying homes—42 percent of all Hispanics owned or were purchasing their home in 1989, including 47 percent of all Mexican Americans—and moving away from inner cities. . . .

There is much reason for optimism about the progress of Hispanics in the United States. . . . Mexican Americans, the oldest and largest Hispanic group, are moving steadily into the middle class, with the majority having established solid, working- and middle-class lives. Even Mexican immigrants and those from other Latin American countries, many of whom have very little formal education, appear to be largely self-sufficient. The vast majority of such immigrants—two-thirds—live above the poverty line, having achieved a standard of living far above that attainable by them in their countries of origin.

There is no indication that any of these groups is in danger of becoming a permanent underclass. If Hispanics choose to (and most *are* choosing to), they will quickly join the mainstream of this society. . . . [T]he evidence suggests that Hispanics, by and large, are behaving much as other ethnic groups did in the past. One group of Hispanics, however, appears not to be following this pattern. Puerto Ricans occupy the lowest rung of the social and economic ladder among Hispanics, and a disturbing number of them show little hope of climbing higher.

. . . Puerto Ricans are not simply the poorest of all Hispanic groups; they experience the highest degree of social dysfunction of any Hispanic group and exceed that of blacks on some indicators. Thirty-nine percent of all Puerto Rican families are headed by single women; 53 percent of all Puerto Rican children are born out of wedlock; the proportion of men in the labor force is lower among Puerto Ricans than any other group, including blacks; Puerto Ricans have the highest welfare participation rate of any group in New York, where nearly half of all Puerto Ricans in the United States live. Yet, on the average, Puerto Ricans are better educated than Mexicans and nearly as well educated as Cubans, with a median education of twelve years. . . .

Some Hopeful Signs

Despite the overall poor performance of Puerto Ricans, there are some bright spots in their achievement—which make their poverty seem all the more stark. While the median family earnings of Puerto Ricans are the lowest of any Hispanic groups, *individual* earnings of both male and female Puerto Ricans are actually higher than those of any other Hispanic subgroup except Cubans. In 1989 Puerto Rican men had median earnings that were 82 percent of those of non-Hispanics; Puerto Rican women's median earnings were actually higher than those of non-Hispanic women. Moreover, the occupational distribution of Puerto Ricans shows that substantial numbers work in white-collar jobs: nearly one-third of the Puerto Rican males who are employed work in managerial, professional, technical, sales, or administrative support jobs and more than two-thirds of the Puerto Rican females who work hold such jobs.

Moreover, Puerto Ricans are not doing uniformly poorly in all parts of the country. Those in Florida, Texas, and California, for example, perform far better than those in New York. . . .

In fact, as their earnings attest, Puerto Ricans who hold jobs are not doing appreciably worse than other Hispanics, or non-Hispanics, once their lower educational attainment is taken into account. The low overall achievement of Puerto Ricans is simply not attributable to the characteristics of those who work but is a factor of the large number of those—male and female—who are neither working nor looking for work. . . .

Where Do Puerto Ricans Go From Here?

Many Puerto Ricans are making it in the United States. There is a thriving middle class of well-educated professionals, managers, and white-collar workers, whose individual earnings are among the highest of all Hispanic groups' and most of whom live in married-couple families. These Puerto Ricans have done what other Hispanics and, indeed, most members of other ethnic groups have: they have moved up the economic ladder and into the social mainstream within one or two generations of their arrival in the United States. . . .

The crisis facing the Puerto Rican community is not simply one of poverty and neglect. If anything, Puerto Ricans have been showered with too much government attention. . . . The fact that Puerto Ricans outside New York succeed proves there is nothing inevitable about Puerto Rican failure. Nor does the existence of prejudice and discrimination explain why so many Puerto Ricans fail when so many other Hispanics, including those from racially mixed backgrounds, are succeeding.

So long as significant numbers of young Puerto Rican men remain alienated from the work force, living by means of crime or charity, fathering children toward whom they feel no responsibility, the prospects of Puerto Ricans in the United States will dim. So long as so many Puerto Rican women allow the men who father their babies to avoid the duties of marriage and parenthood, they will deny their children the promise of a better life, which has been the patrimony of generations of poor immigrants' children. The solution to these problems will not be found in more government programs. Indeed, government has been an accomplice in enabling fathers to abandon their responsibility. Only the Puerto Rican community can save itself, but the healing cannot begin until the community recognizes that many of its deadliest wounds are self-inflicted.

. . . Hispanics have not always had an easy time of it in the United States. Even though discrimination against Mexican Americans and Puerto Ricans was not as severe as it was against blacks, acceptance has come only with struggle, and some prejudices still exist. Discrimination against Hispanics, or any other group, should be fought, and there are laws and a massive administrative apparatus to do so. But the way to eliminate such discrimination is not to classify all Hispanics as victims and treat them as if they could not succeed by their own efforts. Hispanics can and will prosper in the United States by following the example of the millions before them.

Robert Aponte   ↩ **NO**

Urban Hispanic Poverty: Disaggregations and Explanations

Nearly a quarter century since the passage of the Civil Rights Act and the initiation of the massive War on Poverty effort, substantial proportions of inner city minorities appear more hopelessly mired in poverty than at any time since these efforts were undertaken (Tienda 1989, Wacquant and Wilson 1989b, Wilson 1987). The poverty rate among central city blacks, for example, stood at about one person in three in 1989, having risen from a rate of one in four two decades earlier (U.S. Bureau of the Census 1980, 1990). Equally ominous is the poverty rate of central city Latinos (Hispanics), some three in ten, which exceeds that of central city whites by a factor of nearly two and one half (U.S. Bureau of the Census 1990). Associated with these indicators of deprivation among urban minorities have been other signs of potential distress. Available evidence indicates that minorities are experiencing rates of joblessness, welfare receipt, and female headship substantially in excess of the rates prevailing among whites (Tienda 1989, Tienda and Jensen 1988, Wacquant and Wilson 1989b, Wilson and Neckerman 1986).

These important issues have not escaped research attention, but until the 1980s, this research focused almost exclusively on blacks among the minority groups and how they compared to whites (Wilson and Aponte 1985). Indeed, prior to the 1980s, empirical research on the poverty of Hispanics in the United States beyond small scale studies was difficult to perform for lack of data. Hence, as we enter the 1990s, far too little is known about the complex configuration of factors underlying Latino poverty. In addition, while the various reports from the Current Population Survey began producing detailed information on "Hispanics" in the 1970s, often presenting the trends alongside those of blacks and whites, it was not until the mid 1980s that we began to consistently receive detailed, individualized data on the major ethnic groups within the hybrid category of "Hispanic." What little systematic research has been done on the topic has far too often treated the hybrid category as a single group.

From *Social Problems*, vol. 38, no. 4, November 1991, pp. 516–525. Copyright © 1991 by The Society for the Study of Social Problems. All rights reserved. Reprinted with permission.

Any reliance on the aggregate category "Hispanic" is fraught with a high potential to mislead. For analytic purposes beyond the most superficial generalizations, it is crucial that social and economic trends among Hispanics studied be as fully disaggregated as possible if an inquiry is to reveal rather than obscure the dynamics underlying the statistical indicators.* The major current streams of research on minority poverty have produced precious few paradigms with relevance to the Latino population, in part because of the lack of research directed toward the group as a whole, but also because of the failure to consider the individual national groupings separately. Even those analyses incorporating disaggregated indicators need to be interpreted with careful attention paid to the appropriate historic and contemporary circumstances surrounding the various Hispanic groups' incorporation into the mainland United States society.

In the relatively short period that the detailed data have been available, much of significance has been revealed that is consistent with the perspective advanced here. It has been shown, for example, that poverty among Puerto Ricans, the most urban and second largest Latino group, has hovered at a rate averaging over 40 percent in the last several years—a rate second to none among the major ethnic or racial groups for which there is data, and one substantially higher than that of the other Hispanic groups (cf. U.S. Bureau of the Census 1985a, 1986, 1987b, 1988, 1989b). In addition, the rate of poverty for all Hispanics has grown far more rapidly in recent years than that of whites or blacks, as dramatically shown in an important recent report by the Center on Budget and Policy Priorities (Greenstein et al. 1988).

The report notes that the 1987 Hispanic poverty rate of slightly greater than 28 percent is less than 5 percentage points lower than that of blacks, traditionally the poorest group, and nearly three times that of whites, despite the fact that the labor force participation rate of Hispanics is somewhat higher than that of these other groups. Moreover, the increase in Hispanic poverty over the 1980s shown in the Policy Center Report has been fueled largely by increases in poverty among two parent families. Thus, it cannot be blamed on the relatively modest rise in Hispanic single parent families over this particular period, nor can it easily be pinned on sagging work efforts, given the higher than average participation in the workforce of the group.

Importantly, the patterns outlined above appear to defy common sense interpretations. For example, the idea that discrimination can account for the patterning of such indicators falls short of explaining why Puerto Ricans are poorer than blacks even though they almost certainly experience far less discrimination (Massey and Bitterman 1985). Likewise, a human capital perspective by itself cannot explain why Mexicans, who speak poorer English than Puerto Ricans and are less educated than whites and blacks as well as Puerto Ricans, are more often employed than persons of the other three groups (U.S. Bureau of Labor Statistics 1990). . . .

---

*[Disaggregation is the process of breaking data down into smaller, more meaningful parts to better understand the information.—Ed.]

Disaggregations and Context

To speak of Hispanic poverty in urban America at present is to speak of the two largest groups, those of Mexican and those of Puerto Rican extraction, who together account for roughly three-fourths of all U.S. Hispanics. Together these two groups accounted for over 80 percent of all 1987 Hispanic poor within metropolitan areas, their central cities taken separately, or the continental United States as a whole (U.S. Bureau of the Census 1989a). Cubans, the next largest group, have accounted for only about five to six percent of all Hispanics during the 1980s and have significantly lower rates of poverty (U.S. Bureau of the Census 1987a, 1989b; see also U.S. Bureau of the Census 1989b). Hence, this article focuses on Latinos of Mexican or Puerto Rican extraction.

While the diverse groups that comprise the remainder of the Latino population have not yet been numerous enough to have a great impact on the indicators for all Hispanics, it does not follow that their experiences have been trouble free. As noted by the Policy Center Report (Greenstein et al. 1988), available data suggests that many of these other groups are experiencing substantial poverty. . . .

Contrasting sharply with the Cuban experience, the processes whereby Mexicans and Puerto Ricans entered the mainstream urban economy entailed a number of common features. Characteristics shared by these incoming groups include mother tongue, economic or labor migrant status, relatively low levels of skill, inadequate command of English, and little formal education. In addition to their relatively modest social status upon entry, these groups generally received no special government assistance, and each sustained a fair amount of discrimination.

Though the urban settlement of Puerto Ricans on the mainland occurred rapidly, was highly concentrated in a major northern city, and began largely after the Second World War, among Mexicans the process transpired throughout much of the 20th century, was far more gradual and diffuse, and was contained largely within the southwest section of the country. Indeed, in only a few midwestern cities—notably Chicago—where small proportions of each group have settled, do Mexicans and Puerto Ricans maintain any substantial coresidence. In addition, the Puerto Ricans entered as citizens and were thereby entitled to certain rights that were available to only some Mexicans.

From less than 100,000 at the end of the Second World War, the Puerto Rican population on the mainland grew to well over 1 million by 1970, at which time a solid majority were residents of New York City (Moore and Pachon 1985). Although by 1980 the city no longer contained a majority of the nearly two million members of the group, most of those living elsewhere still resided in large metropolitan cities, and mainly in the Northeast. . . .

While rapid immigration by Puerto Ricans is no longer evident, Mexican immigration into both urban and rural areas has continued in recent years. The estimated population of nearly 12 million Mexican-origin Hispanics in 1988 accounted for nearly 63 percent of all mainland Latinos and was about five times the size of the estimated 2.3 million Puerto Ricans (U.S. Bureau of the Census 1989b). If present trends continue, the gap in population size separating these groups will further widen.

These settlement differences may affect social mobility in several ways. First, the economic well-being of Puerto Ricans can be expected to hinge heavily on economic conditions *inside* the major cities of the eastern end of the snowbelt, especially New York, and be particularly dependent on the opportunity structure confronting the less skilled in those areas. Such conditions have not been favorable in recent decades due to the widely documented decline in manufacturing, trade, and other forms of low skilled employment that was most evident in northern *inner cities* beginning with the 1950s and accelerating during the 1970s (Kasarda 1985, Wacquant and Wilson 1989b). Moreover, such jobs have not returned to these places, even where sagging economies have sharply rebounded (as in New York and Boston), since the newer mix of jobs in such areas still tend to require more skills or credentials than previously (Kasarda 1983, 1988).

By contrast, Mexican Hispanics are more dependent upon the opportunity structures confronting less skilled labor in southwestern cities and their suburbs but without heavy reliance on only one or two such areas or on *central city* employment. These areas are believed to have better job prospects for the less skilled than northern cities because of the continued employment growth in low skilled jobs throughout the entire postwar period (Kasarda 1985, Wacquant and Wilson 1989b).

A second important distinction concerns social welfare provisions. Specifically, Puerto Ricans have settled into the *relatively* more generous states of the North, while their counterparts populate a band of states with traditionally low levels of assistance. A notable exception to this is California—the state with the largest number of Mexican Hispanics. However, many among the group in that state are ineligible for assistance due to lack of citizenship. At the same time, many eligible recipients likely co-reside with undocumented immigrants subject to deportation if caught. No doubt many of the impoverished among both such groups will not apply for assistance for fear of triggering discovery of the undocumented in their families or households.

As of 1987, *no state* in the continental U.S. provided enough AFDC [Aid to Families with Dependent Children] benefits to bring families up to the poverty line. . . . Recent research by Jencks and Edin (1990) demonstrates conclusively that very few AFDC families can survive in major cities on just the legally prescribed income; most are forced to cheat, many turn to petty crimes for supplementary income, and some even slip into homelessness (cf. Ellison 1990, Rossi and Wright 1989).

However, this was not always so (Tobier 1984, National Social Science and Law Center 1987). For example, in New York city during the late 1960s, the maximum AFDC benefit package for a family of three, discounting food stamps, could raise the family's income to *97 percent* of the poverty line (Tobier 1984). The payment levels declined gradually during the first part of the 1970s. . . .

The statistical indicators on these groups are consistent with such expectations. For example, among men aged 20 years and over, Puerto Ricans had a labor force participation rate 10 percentage points lower than that of Mexican origin men in 1987 (U.S. Bureau of Labor Statistics 1988), representing a widening of the respective 1977 gap of only five percentage points. The employment-to-population ratios exhibited a similar gap, but they remained unchanged over the ten year period, with the Puerto Rican ratio trailing that of the Mexican origin group by 10 percentage points (Newman 1978), suggesting that the Mexican unemployment rate is catching up to the Puerto Rican rate (Greenstein et al. 1988). Although these are national level trends, they should reflect urban conditions since both groups have become highly urbanized. As expected, Puerto Ricans are also poorer than Mexicans. The central city poverty rate for Puerto Ricans in 1987 was 46 percent, with the corresponding rate for Mexicans 30 percent. The metropolitan area rates were similarly distributed. Likewise, the proportion of families headed by women among central city Puerto Ricans was 49 percent, while only about 21 percent of the Mexican origin families were so headed (U.S. Bureau of the Census 1989a).

Finally, the Current Population Survey reveals that employed Puerto Ricans, on average, earn more than employed Mexicans (U.S. Bureau of the Census 1989b). The survey also reveals that many more Mexican families in poverty have members in the work force than do poor Puerto Rican families, while a substantially higher proportion of the latter group receive government assistance. For example, in 1987, 72 percent of all Mexican origin families in poverty had at least one member in the work force compared to only 24 percent of the Puerto Rican families. Conversely, 72 percent of Puerto Rican families in poverty that year received all of their income from some form of assistance or transfer compared to 25 percent of the Mexican families (U.S. Bureau of the Census 1989a). In spite of the "assistance," not one of these needy families was brought over the poverty line, and many were left with incomes well below the designated level!

It seems likely that the kind of approach urged here, one that maximizes sensitivity to the varying conditions of the individual Latino groups' plights, can help in interpreting trends among data that are largely aggregated. For example, the Policy Center Report reached a number of findings that can be pushed further. The report concluded that recent increases in Hispanic poverty are associated only weakly, if at all, with recent increases in female headship or joblessness within the group. Rather, the poverty increases were strongly associated with declining real wages. The report also noted that the increase in poverty occurred mainly among Mexicans and in the Sunbelt and Midwest. However, the report did *not* make a connection between these factors.

Attending to Latino subgroup differences provides an explanation. We would expect declining real wages to bring more Mexicans into poverty than Puerto Ricans because proportionately more Mexicans hold very low wage jobs. In turn, Mexican dominance in the three regions outside of the Northeast helps explain why those regions, but *not* the Northeast, were more affected by the rise in poverty traceable to real wage declines, even as the Puerto Rican dominated northeastern region maintained the highest level of poverty.

Finally, consideration of the continuation of Mexican immigration leads to a second hypothesis about their vulnerability to falling real wages: Mexicans are employed in regions plagued by labor market crowding resulting from continued immigration, especially since much of it consists of "undocumenteds," a group that clearly constitutes cheaper labor. This especially hurts those with lower levels of education, since they are most likely to compete directly with the latest newcomers. Indeed, the Report singles out the lesser educated Hispanics as the group sustaining the most increased hardship. . . .

Explanations of Urban Poverty

Most current popular theories about urban poverty fall short of fully accounting for the plight of the Hispanic poor because of a narrow focus on blacks. In spite of the apparent deficit, disaggregating the Hispanic figures allows us to apply some of this work to at least one of the two major groups under study.

The culture of poverty.   The idea of a "culture of poverty" generally traces back to the work of Oscar Lewis (1959, 1966) who coined the phrase, although others have advanced similar notions. Lewis developed the core ideas of the argument while studying Mexican and Puerto Rican families. The work suggests that culturally-based attitudes or predispositions such as "present mindedness" and "obsessive consumption" are the major barriers to economic mobility for many of the poor, implying that providing opportunities to the poor will not be enough: some will need "cultural uplifting" as well. The major strength of the idea for my purposes is that it can apply equally well to the poor of any of the Latino groups.

However, the theory is largely discredited within academic circles. . . . In fact, numerous subsequent studies of poor people's values and attitudes have found little support for the theory (Corcoran et al. 1985, Goodwin 1972, Irelan et al. 1969). . . .

The welfare-as-cause argument.   In his book *Losing Ground,* Charles Murray (1984) argues that the liberalization of welfare during the late 1960s and early 1970s made work less beneficial than welfare and encouraged low-income people to avoid work and marriage, in order to reap the benefits of welfare, and that this is a primary source of the rise in female headship and, indirectly, poverty itself. . . .

We might ask if welfare payments were so lucrative, why did the poor fail to escape poverty, at least while "on the dole," but Murray does not address this issue. . . . Moreover, studies on the effects of welfare availability to changes in family structure have produced few results supporting a connection, the overall consensus being that such effects as they exist are relatively weak (Wilson and Neckerman 1986. U.S. General Accounting Office 1987). . . . Thus, welfare appears unlikely to be a major cause of female headship or joblessness among Hispanics, as among blacks. However, it may properly be seen as a major cause of Latino poverty insofar as so many of the Hispanic impoverished who are legally entitled to assistance are left destitute by miserly benefit levels while many other equally needy Hispanics are denied benefits altogether.

The mismatch thesis.   This explanation . . . focuses mainly on older, northern, industrial towns. It finds recent urban poverty rooted in the movement of manufacturing and other blue-collar employment away from snowbelt central cities where blacks and Hispanics make up increasingly larger proportions of the population. As blue-collar industry moved from the cities to the suburbs and from the Snow Belt to the Sun Belt, central city job growth occurred primarily in white-collar jobs for which the black and Hispanic central city residents often did not qualify for lack of skills or credentials.

. . . While studies based on data for 1970 or earlier have tended to disconfirm the hypothesis, work on more recent periods has largely produced supporting results (Holzer 1991). Hence, the argument remains a viable hypothesis about joblessness in northern central cities. Once again, however, the idea offers no explanation for the poverty of Mexicans since relatively few live in those areas. . . .

Labor market segmentation theories (dual labor market theory).   According to early versions of labor market segmentation theories, racial and ethnic minorities were intentionally relegated to the "secondary" sector of the labor market characterized by highly unstable work with low pay and little room for advancement (Cain 1976). More recent versions often suggest that disadvantaged native workers all but openly shun such jobs because of their undesirable characteristics and that immigrants are therefore "imported" to fill the positions (Piore 1979). . . .

Though clearly of important explanatory potential, the segmentation theory falls short of providing a complete explanation for the patterns in question. . . . Thus, the argument would appear to operate better in cities such as New York which have received large numbers of immigrants in recent years than in places such as Buffalo, Cleveland, Philadelphia, or Rochester with proportionately fewer such persons (Waldinger 1989). Yet, Puerto Ricans in these cities appear as plagued by poverty and joblessness as those in New York (U.S. Bureau of the Census 1985b). . . .

The underclass hypothesis.   The underclass argument, proposed by William Julius Wilson (1987, 1988), begins with the observation that declining housing discrimination and rising incomes among some blacks have enabled many to leave the older central city ghettos. Their departure from the highly segregated and traditionally underserviced areas, characterized by higher than average rates of physical deterioration, exacerbates the purely economic problems confronted by the remaining population. . . .

Ghetto residents subjected to the described conditions constitute Wilson's underclass. The combined material and environmental deprivation confronted by the group anchors them firmly to prolonged poverty, welfare dependence, and assorted illicit enterprises. . . . Once again, among Hispanics, only the Puerto Rican poor are as geographically isolated as poor blacks and, therefore, appear to be the only Hispanic population for which this explanation can hold.

Conclusion

. . . The data and discussions presented here, while far from providing a definitive analysis of Hispanic poverty, provide support to a number of generalizations about the problems and potential solutions. Decreased employment opportunities for the less skilled and educated, severely depressed wages among the employed, and restricted or nonexistent welfare benefits comprise the major causes of urban Hispanic poverty. Expanding employment, increasing wages, providing a better living to those unable to work, and promoting higher levels of human capital attainment are major public policy imperatives if these problems are ever to be adequately addressed.

POSTSCRIPT

Are Hispanics Making Economic Progress?

A number of issues extend to the question of Hispanic progress including bilingual education, Latino identity and assimilation, immigration and demographic trends, and politics. Consider that according to the 2000 U.S. Census, 12.5% of the population or approximately 35 million Americans are of Hispanic origin. Hispanics are a very diverse population that includes Mexicans, Puerto Ricans, Cubans, Dominicans, and South and Central Americans, plus others of Caribbean origin. To consider the issue of economic progress of Hispanics as a whole is misleading. This diversity needs to be considered. Both Chavez and Aponte recognize this in their opinions.

A good source dealing with the Hispanic community in America is *The Latino/a Condition: A Critical Reader* (New York University Press, 1998) edited by Richard Delgado and Jean Stefancic. Another is *Latinos in New York: Communities in Transition* (University of Notre Dame Press, 1996) edited by Gabriel Haslip Viera and Baver L. Sherrie. *Hispanics in the United States: An Agenda for the Twenty-First Century* (Transaction Publishers, 2000), edited by Pastora San Juan Cafferty and David Engstrom, provides a comprehensive look at Latino identity. Also dealing with identity is *Hispanic/Latino Identity* (Blackwell Publishers, 2000) by Jorge Gracia.

Sources that document Hispanic progress include "El Millonario Next Door," by Tyce Palmaffy in *Policy Review* (July 1998). It shows that Hispanics represent the United States' fastest-growing pool of business owners. Linda Chavez's *Out of the Barrios: Toward a New Politics of Hispanic Assimilation* (Basic Books, 1991) argues that Hispanics are making significant progress. "Strength in Numbers," an article by Lori Robinson, Paul Cuadros, and Alysia Tate, compares economic progress of Latinos with Blacks in *The Crisis* (Jan./Feb. 2004). A book that demonstrates ethnic conflict between Latinos and Blacks is *The Presumed Alliance: The Unspoken Conflict Between Latinos and Blacks and What It Means for America* (HarperCollins Publishers, 2003), by Nicolas C. Vaca. Hispanic progress in higher education is reflected in *The Leaning Ivory Tower: Latino Professors in American Universities* (State University of New York Press, 1995), edited by Raymond V. Padilla and Rudolfo C. Chavez.

Hispanic community political formation is explored in *Latinos and the Political System* (University of Notre Dame Press, 2000), edited by Chris F. Garcia. An interesting article about the political formation of Hispanics and Jews is "New Bedfellows," (*The New Republic,* August 11, 1997) by Peter Beinart. An additional study of Latinos in New York is *Between Two*

Nations: The Political Predicament of Latinos in New York City (Cornell University Press, 1998) by Michael Jones-Correa.

Rosalie Pedalino Porter argues against bilingualism in "The Case Against Bilingual Education" (*The Atlantic Monthly,* May 1998). She argues that bilingualism retards progress for Hispanics. A balanced account of the bilingualism debate can be found in "Debate Over Bilingualism," by Craig Donegan in *The CQ Researcher* (Jan. 19, 1996). A stand in favor of cultural pluralism including bilingualism as an expansive concept of American is argued in "Demography and Distrust: An Essay on American Languages, Cultural Pluralism, and Official English," in the *Minnesota Law Review* (269, 1962) by Juan F. Perea.

On the Internet . . .

The Civil Rights Project: Harvard University

The Civil Rights Project helps to renew the civil rights movement by "bridging the worlds of ideas and action, and by becoming a preeminent source of intellectual capital and a forum for building consensus within that movement." It is an excellent source of information and research findings in the field of race relations.

http://www.civilrightsproject.harvard.edu/

Social Science Data Analysis Network (SSDAN)

The Social Science Data Analysis Network (SSDAN) runs this site to research segregation in local communities across the country. It offers students a chance to do original quantitative research on segregation by selecting neighborhoods in cities and then analyzing the data on race. This site is recommended for a wide range of research possibilities.

http://www.censusscope.org/segregation.html

Urban Institute

The Urban Institute is a nonpartisan economic and social policy research organization. The Institute includes social scientists and public policy analysts, and the site blends qualitative and quantitative analyses to interpret data without an ideological agenda. Primarily concerned with welfare and its reform, other areas of interest include immigration trends and additional urban issues dealing with minority populations.

http://www.urban.org/welfare/overview.html

American Studies: Georgetown University

This site contains the largest bibliography of Web-based resources in the field of American Studies. The "Race, Ethnicity and Identity" section offers reference and research opportunity for students.

http://cfdev.georgetown.edu/endls/asw/

Library of Congress (LOC)

This Web site offers an extensive online collection including areas of interest to students of race and ethnicity. The section titled "American Memory: U.S. History and Culture" presents a good deal of information to the student including an online exhibit of African American history. The LOC also offers an extensive collection in its Hispanic division.

http://memory.loc.gov/ammem/aaohtml
/exhibit/aointro.html

PART 3

Social and Political Issues of Education and Multiculturalism

The struggles for civil rights and social justice and the increasing immigration of Asians and Hispanics has lead to an increased emphasis on diversity and multiculturalism within American society. Recent census data have confirmed that significant immigration of Asians and Hispanics is altering the demographic composition of the American population. How are these various groups consisting of peoples of color to be included within the prevailing institutions of the nation? What are the appropriate strategies for achieving policies of institutional inclusion? Are multiculturalism and racial diversity contributing to the strength of American institutions and social life, or are these phenomena contributing to racial polarization and disunity within the nation?

- Are America's Schools and Neighborhoods Resegregating?

- Should Race Be a Consideration in College Admissions?

- Is a Multicultural Curriculum Essential for Advancing Education?

- Is Affirmative Action Necessary to Achieve Racial Equality in the United States?

ISSUE 11

Are America's Schools and Neighborhoods Resegregated?

YES: Gary Orfield and Susan E. Eaton, "Turning Back to Segregation," in *Dismantling Desegregation* (New York: The New Press, 1996)

NO: Ingrid Gould Ellen, "Welcome Neighbors?" *The Brookings Review* (Winter 1997)

ISSUE SUMMARY

YES: Gary Orfield, professor of education and social policy at the Harvard Graduate School of Education, and Susan E. Eaton, author, demonstrate that America's public schools are resegregating. Their argument is based on a series of legal decisions beginning in the 1970s that have successfully reversed the historic *Brown* decision.

NO: Ingrid Gould Ellen, writer for *The Brookings Review,* argues that neighborhood racial integration is increasing. She thinks researchers must balance their pessimistic findings of resegregation with increased integration. Although integrated communities are a statistical minority, they are growing.

After the Civil War and the Reconstruction Era, segregation replaced slavery as the primary basis for defining and developing race relations within the United States. In the wake of the *Plessy v. Ferguson* decision of the U.S. Supreme Court in 1896, segregation became the official policy of the U.S. government. Before and after 1896, segregation took shape and form almost as if designed by an architect. The *Plessy* case, a public transportation issue, led to the "separate but equal" doctrine that extended to most areas of life including transportation, public accommodations, housing, employment, marriage, and education. Blacks who challenged the architecture of segregation risked losing jobs, places to live, and worse of all—especially for young black men—lynching. Countless "forced acts of humiliation" kept blacks separate from whites.

It was with the *Brown v. Board of Education* decision of 1954 that legal segregation was reversed. In actuality, there were two *Brown* decisions rendered by the Court. In *Brown I*, the Court ruled that segregated schools are "inherently unequal," and *Plessy* was reversed. In *Brown II*, the Court challenged the school systems of the states to proceed to desegregate public schools "with all deliberate speed." The latter ruling was sufficiently vague and without a time line, so that it provided those who were opposed to integration the social and legal room to stay segregated.

The issues of American public education and residence are inextricably linked. Segregated schools are created through a variety of circumstances. Schools can be segregated because the community is segregated. Within "mixed" communities, schools may be segregated as the result of district mapping practices or neighborhood "redlining." This is known as *de jure* segregation and is illegal. However, *de facto* segregation, or school segregation resulting from housing patterns, is pervasive across the country today. And, the *Brown* decision has had little impact on those communities that practice *de facto* segregation.

Gary Orfield and Susan E. Eaton point out that in recent years, the Supreme Court has reversed itself and authorized school districts to return to segregation. Though little media attention has been given to the decisions, the cases have led to new school resegregation policies. Perhaps the best known of the cases, *Milligan v. Bradley,* in 1974, blocked desegregation plans that would have integrated Detroit with its suburbs. Orfield and Eaton trace the origins of the shift from *Brown* to President Richard Nixon's "southern strategy," which attacked school desegregation policies. Orfield and Eaton point a finger at Justice William Rehnquist and his steadfast refusal to vote in favor of desegregation.

Ingrid Gould Ellen argues that integrated neighborhoods are growing in number and will most likely remain racially mixed in the future. Using census data that link household to neighborhoods, she found that certain demographic groups are more likely to move into racially mixed neighborhoods. Whites who more likely to move into racially mixed neighborhoods are young and single. Thus, she argues that communities with a larger proportion of rental housing are more likely to be integrated. Further, Ellen sees no evidence of white flight. Lastly, she points out that stability is an important factor in maintaining integrated neighborhoods and schools. In other words, the longer a community has been integrated, the more likely that it will remain integrated.

To understand resegregation, students must connect patterns of residential neighborhood formation to public education. Ellen's optimistic argument about the possibility of racial integration could be seen as a new way of looking at housing patterns. At the same time, Orfield and Eaton point to a number of Court decisions that have contributed to an increasing trend of segregation. They call this trend resegregation. What kinds of neighborhoods remain integrated? Segregated? What factors cause neighborhoods to change from integrated to segregated? How has the Court reversed school integration?

**Gary Orfield and
Susan E. Eaton**

 **YES**

Turning Back to Segregation

Four decades after the civil rights revolution began with the Supreme Court's unanimous 1954 school desegregation decision, *Brown v. Board of Education,* the Supreme Court reversed itself in the 1990s, authorizing school districts to return to segregated and unequal public schools. The cases were part of a general reversal of civil rights policy, which included decisions against affirmative action and voting rights. After decades of bitter political, legal, and community struggles over civil rights, there was surprisingly little attention to the new school resegregation policies spelled out in the Court's key 1990s decisions in *Board of Education of Oklahoma City v. Dowell,*[1] *Freeman v. Pitts,*[2] and *Missouri v. Jenkins.*[3] The decisions were often characterized as belated adjustments to an irrelevant, failed policy. But in fact, these historic High Court decisions were a triumph for the decades-long powerful, politicized attacks on school desegregation. The new policies reflected the victory of the conservative movement that altered the federal courts and turned the nation from the dream of *Brown* toward accepting a return to segregation.

Dowell, Pitts, and Jenkins spelled out procedures for court approval of the dismantling of school desegregation plans—plans that, despite the well-publicized problems in some cities, have been one of the few legally enforced routes of access and opportunity for millions of African American and Latino schoolchildren in an increasingly polarized society. Though now showing clear signs of erosion, the school desegregation *Brown v. Board of Education* made possible had weathered political attacks better than many had predicted it would.

But *Dowell, Pills,* and *Jenkins* established legal standards to determine when a local school district had repaid what the Court defined as a historic debt to its black students, a debt incurred during generations of intentional racial segregation and discrimination by state and local policies and practices. Under these decisions, districts that, in the eyes of a court, had obeyed their court orders for several years could send students back to neighborhood schools, even if those schools were segregated and inferior. With the 1995 *Jenkins* decision, the Court further narrowed educational remedies.

From DISMANTLING SEGREGATION, 1996, Chapter 1. Copyright © 1996 by New York Press. Reprinted with permission.

This is a troubling shift. *Brown* rested on the principle that intentional public action to support segregation was a violation of the U.S. Constitution. Under *Dowell and Pitts,* however, public decisions that re-create segregation, sometimes even more severe than before desegregation orders, are now deemed acceptable. These new resegregation decisions legitimate a deliberate return to segregation. As long as school districts temporarily maintain some aspects of desegregation for several years and do not express an intent to, discriminate, the Court approves plans to send minority students back to segregation.

Dowell and *Pitts* embrace new conceptions of racial integration and school desegregation. These decisions view racial integration not as a goal that segregated districts should strive to attain, but as a merely temporary punishment for historic violations, an imposition to be lifted after a few years. After the sentence of desegregation has been served, the normal, "natural" pattern of segregated schools can be restored. In just two years in the early 1990s, *Dowell* and *Pitts* had reduced the long crusade for integrated education to a formalistic requirement that certain rough indicators of desegregation be present briefly.

These resegregation decisions received little national attention, in part because their most dramatic impact was on the South, the region that became the most integrated after *Brown.* The Supreme Court's 1974 *Milliken* decision had already rendered *Brown* almost meaningless for most of the metropolitan North by blocking desegregation plans that would integrate cities with their suburbs. Resegregation decisions made no difference to Washington and New York City since there were no desegregation plans in place.

In this chapter, we analyze the effects of the *Dowell, Pitts,* and *Jenkins* decisions and describe the social and political forces that shaped their underlying philosophy. These three cases largely displace the goal of rooting out the lingering damage of racial segregation and discrimination with the twin goals of minimizing judicial involvement in education and restoring power to local and state governments, whatever the consequences.

The Supreme Court handed down the first of the three resegregation decisions in 1991. *Board of Education of Oklahoma City v. Dowell* outlined circumstances under which courts have authority to release school districts from their obligation to maintain desegregated schools.[4] A previously illegally segregated district whose desegregation plan was being supervised by a court could be freed from oversight if the district had desegregated its students and faculty, and met for a few years the other requirements laid out in the Supreme Court's 1968 *Green v. School Board of New Kent County* decision.[5] *Green* ordered "root and branch" eradication of segregated schooling and specified several areas of a school system—such as students, teachers, transportation, and facilities—in which desegregation was mandatory. Under *Dowell*, a district briefly taking the steps outlined in *Green* can be termed "unitary" and is thus freed from its legal obligation to purge itself of segregation. Unitary might best be understood as the opposite of a "dual" system, in which a school district, in essence, operates two separate systems, one black and one white. A unitary district is assumed to be one that has repaired the damage caused by generations of segregation and overt discrimination.

Under *Brown*, proof of an intentionally segregated dual system triggers desegregation mandates. But once the formerly dual system becomes unitary, according to the decisions of the 1990s, minority students no longer have the special protection of the courts, and school districts no longer face any requirement to maintain desegregation or related education programs.

In 1992, a year after *Dowell*, the *Freeman v. Pitts*[6] decision went even further; holding that various requirements laid out in *Green* need not be present at the same time. This meant, for example, that a once-segregated system could dismantle its student desegregation plan without ever having desegregated its faculty or provided equal access to educational programs.

The Court's 5–4 decision in the 1995 case, *Missouri v. Jenkins*, found the Court's majority determined to narrow the reach of the "separate but equal" remedies provided in big cities after the Supreme Court blocked city-suburban desegregation in 1974. Its 1995 decision prohibited efforts to attract white suburban and private school students *voluntarily* into city schools through excellent programs. Kansas City spent more than a billion dollars upgrading a severely deteriorated school system. The goal here was to create desegregation by making inner city schools so attractive that private school and suburban students would choose to transfer to them. Because possible desegregation was limited within the city system by a lack of white students, the emphasis was put on upgrading the schools. When the district court said that it would examine test scores to help ensure that the remedy actually helped the black children who had been harmed by segregation, the Supreme Court said no, emphasizing the limited role of the courts and the need to restore state and local authority quickly, regardless of remaining inequalities. Ironically, the conservative movement that claimed it would be more productive to emphasize choice and "educational improvement" over desegregation, won a constitutional decision in *Jenkins* that pushed desegregation in big cities toward simple, short-term racial balancing within a city, even where the African American and Latino majority is so large that little contact with whites is possible.

Under *Dowell, Pitts*, and *Jenkins*, school districts need not prove actual racial equality, nor a narrowing of academic gaps between the races. Desegregation remedies can even be removed when achievement gaps between the races have widened, or even if a district has never fully implemented an effective desegregation plan. Formalistic compliance for a time with some limited requirements was enough, even if the roots of racial inequality were untouched.

This profound shift of judicial philosophy is eerily compatible with philosophies espoused by the Nixon, Reagan, and Bush administrations. This should not be much of a surprise, since the Supreme Court appointees of these presidents generally shared conservative assumptions about race, inequality, and schooling with the presidents who appointed them. Furthermore, under the Reagan and Bush administrations, even the federal civil rights agencies actively undermined desegregation while embracing a "separate but equal" philosophy. Clarence Thomas, first named by President Reagan to begin dismantling enforcement activities in the civil rights office at the Education Department, was appointed by President Bush to the

Supreme Court and became the deciding vote on the Supreme Court in the 1995 *Jenkins* decision.

Civil rights groups, represented by only a handful of lawyers, had little money to resist powerful dismantling efforts by local school districts and their legal teams. The fiscal and organizational crises that in the 1990s plagued the NAACP, the most visible and important civil rights organization, compounded the problem. Local school boards seeking to dismantle their desegregation plans were allied in court not only with powerful state officials but also, in the 1980s, with the U.S. Department of Justice.

After *Dowell* and *Pitts,* many educational leaders thought that, with courts out of the way, racial issues might be set aside and attention would shift from the divisiveness of imposed desegregation plans to educational improvement for all children. With this idea in mind, many school systems, including some of the nation's largest, have filed or are now considering filing motions for unitary status that will make it easier for them to return to neighborhood schools. Living under antidesegregation rhetoric and loosening desegregation standards, still other school districts have adopted policies based on "separate but equal" philosophies. Such policies pledge to do what *Brown* said could not be done—provide equality within segregated schools. Some have tried new and fashionable approaches that focused less and less on desegregation and incorrectly view segregation and its accompanying concentration of poverty as irrelevant to educational quality.

Development of Law Before the Resegregation Cases

The school desegregation battle was for a lasting reconstruction of American education, not for desegregation as a temporary punishment for the quickly absolved sin of racial segregation. The significance of the *Dowell, Pitts,* and *Jenkins* decisions, in fact, is best understood within the historical context of this long, difficult and yet unfinished post-*Brown* struggle toward desegregated schooling. The quiet, gradual movement from the holdings of *Brown* to those of *Dowell, Pitts,* and *Jenkins,* expressed allegiance to *Brown* while chipping away at its spirit and its power. In many communities, *Brown* is left intact today in theory only.

The path toward *Brown* and the movement away from it reflect the larger social and political contexts in which the Supreme Court makes its decisions. It handed down the *Brown* decision less than a decade after the end of a world war against a racist Nazi dictatorship. Both the Truman and Eisenhower administrations had explicitly urged the High Court to act against racial segregation in the South.

Harry Truman, in fact, was the first president since Reconstruction to propose a serious civil rights program. In 1947, the Truman-appointed Committee on Civil Rights issued "To Secure These Rights," which called for ending segregation in American life. The report offered forty suggestions for eliminating segregation, among them a proposal for the Justice Department to enter the legal battle against segregation and discrimination in housing. Later that year, Truman called on Congress to prohibit lynching, the poll tax, and segregation in all interstate transportation.[7]

Dwight D. Eisenhower desegregated the military. His Justice Department urged the Supreme Court to end school segregation in the South, and he appointed a chief justice, Earl Warren, who wrote the Brown decision.[8] Although Eisenhower never publicly endorsed the *Brown* decision, the civil rights tradition of the party of Abraham Lincoln still had important echoes in his administration.

The Supreme Court justices who handed down the *Brown* decision were appointed by Presidents Franklin D. Roosevelt, Truman, and Eisenhower. The Court that later expanded and crystallized *Brown's* mandate through the 1968 *Green* decision and the *Keyes* and *Swann* decisions of the early 1970s, which expanded desegregation requirements to the North and approved student transportation as a means for integration, had been changed by the appointments made by Presidents John F. Kennedy and Lyndon B. Johnson.

After 1968, however, no Democratic president would make a Supreme Court appointment for nearly twenty-five years; all appointees in the 1970s and 1980s were chosen by presidents whose campaigns had promised a more conservative judiciary and weaker civil rights policies. Perhaps the starkest symbol of reversal was the appointment of Clarence Thomas, a staunch critic of civil rights policy, to the chair of Justice Thurgood Marshall, who had argued *Brown* as an NAACP Legal Defense Fund lawyer.

Amid all the changes, the central constitutional provision of the Fourteenth Amendment—the guarantee of "equal protection of the laws"— remained unaltered. The broad policy changes generally reflected the political views of the presidents who appointed the justices.

Brown and Its Unanswered Questions

The *Brown* decision had tremendous impact upon the consciousness of the country and was an important catalyst and support for the civil rights movement. It challenged the legitimacy of all public institutions embracing segregation. The decision established a revolutionary principle in a society that had been overtly racist for most of its history. But the statement of principle was separated from the commitment to implementation, and the implementation procedures turned out not to work. For this reason, *Brown* and its implementation decision, *Brown II,* might most accurately be viewed as flawed compromises that combined a soaring repudiation of segregation with an unworkable remedy.

Brown announced, in no uncertain terms, that intentional segregation was unconstitutional; unanimity was obtained, however, by putting off the decision about how to enforce the new constitutional requirement.[9] In order to win a unanimous vote, the High Court diluted the subsequent 1955 *Brown II* decision on enforcement. The enforcement decision was so weak that it could not overcome resistance from the Southern political leaders who were prepared to close public education to resist desegregation.

The 1955 decision on enforcement, *Brown II,* ordered desegregation with "all deliberate speed." The Court did not define what either "desegregation" or "all deliberate speed" meant. *Brown II's,* ambiguity left decisions about implementing *Brown* to the federal district courts in the South, which were without clear guidance from either the High Court or the federal government for more than a decade.[10]

Under fierce local political pressure, most Southern federal courts reacted to the vague mandates by delaying desegregation cases for long periods and then, in the end, ordering limited changes. Often these plans amounted to allowing a few black schoolchildren to attend a few grades in white schools, while maintaining a school district's essentially segregated character. Sometimes this meant that no whites were ever transferred to the previously all-black schools, faculties remained segregated, and black-and-white schools offered educational programs that differed in content and quality.[11]

The Southern segregated school system remained largely intact a full decade after *Brown.* By 1964, only one-fiftieth of Southern black children attended integrated schools. Northern segregation, meanwhile, was virtually untouched until the mid-1970s. Most Northern districts even refused to provide racial data that could be used to measure segregation. For nearly two decades following *Brown,* the Supreme Court denied hearings to school desegregation cases from the North.

After the rise of the civil rights movement, Congress passed the 1964 Civil Rights Act, the first major civil rights law in ninety years. It was only when serious executive enforcement was tied to the principles of *Brown* that the revolutionary potential of the constitutional change became apparent. The 1964 law, which barred discrimination in all schools and other institutions receiving federal dollars, forced rapid and dramatic changes on the South. Under President Johnson, the federal government vigorously enforced desegregation. Federal rules and sanctions took hold in 1965, backed by cutoffs of federal aid to school districts and extensive litigation by Justice Department civil rights lawyers.[12] This commitment lasted for only about three years, dying shortly after Richard Nixon was elected president in 1968.

Just a few years of intensive enforcement was enough to transform Southern schools and create much stricter and clearer desegregation standards. Following the enactment of the 1964 Civil Rights Act and the issuance of executive branch desegregation standards, the Supreme Court established a clear obligation for rapid and thorough desegregation of the South. The guiding principle here was that far-reaching desegregation must be accomplished by immediate change in an unequal opportunity structure. Finally, districts were told what they must do to eliminate segregation, how their progress toward a unitary, nonsegregated system would be measured, and what would be done to force change if they resisted.[13] By 1970, the schools in the South, which had been almost totally segregated in the early 1960s, were far more desegregated than those in any other region. The few years of active enforcement had had huge impacts.

Even when the mandates for action were clear, some key questions remained unanswered. No one really knew how long it would take to repair the corrosive damage caused by many generations of segregation or when the courts' responsibility for oversight would be fulfilled. By the late 1970s, lawyers, educators, and politicians were asking when a court order would cease and what obligations to desegregate would continue once judicial supervision ended. In what would become an increasingly important question well into the 1990s, they asked: Would courts view a return to neighborhood schools, a move with the foreseeable effect of recreating segregation, as a "neutral" act, or as another constitutional violation? Through the 1980s, the Supreme Court justices left these questions unanswered.

A Turn to the Right: Nixon and His Court

Civil rights politics turned sharply to the right following the triumph of Nixon's "Southern strategy" in the 1968 presidential election, a strategy that wooed the Southern vote by attacking early busing policies and other targets of Southern conservatives.[14]

Following Nixon's election, H. R. Haldeman, Nixon's chief of staff, recorded in his diary the President's directives to staff to do as little as possible to enforce desegregation. An excerpt from early 1970 is typical of comments found throughout Haldeman's diary:

> Feb. 4 . . . he plans to take on the integration problem directly. Is really concerned about situation in Southern schools and feels we have to take some leadership to try to reverse Court decisions that have forced integration too far, too fast. Has told Mitchell [Attorney General] to file another case, and keep filing until we get a reversal.[15]

Early on in his first term, Nixon had fired Leon Panetta, then director of the Department of Health, Education, and Welfare's civil rights office, because Panetta had enforced school desegregation requirements. Nixon supported strong congressional action, even a constitutional amendment, to limit urban desegregation.[16]

Against the strong opposition of the Nixon administration, the Supreme Court's 1971 *Swann* decision ruled that busing was an appropriate means of achieving desegregation. That same year, President Nixon named the deeply conservative Justice Department lawyer, William Rehnquist, to the Supreme Court. During his tenure, Nixon appointed four Supreme Court justices. Rehnquist, elevated to chief justice by Ronald Reagan fifteen years later, became the member of the Supreme Court most hostile to desegregation issues. In Rehnquist's first twelve years on the Court, a law review analysis concluded, he had "never voted to uphold a school desegregation plan."[17] When the Rehnquist Court was firmly installed by the end of the 1980s, the stage would be set for dismantling desegregation.

Rehnquist had been a clerk at the Supreme Court during the *Brown* case, and he wrote a memo expressing approval for the "separate but equal" doctrine established by the 1896 *Plessy v. Ferguson* decision, which was the very doctrine that *Brown v. Board of Education* overturned. (Rehnquist later claimed that the memo did not express his views, but was actually an expression of Justice Jackson's early views on the *Brown* case.)[18]

The Rehnquist memo said:

> I realize that it is an unpopular and unhumanitarian position, for which I have been excoriated by "liberal" colleagues, but I think *Plessy* v. *Ferguson* was right and should be reaffirmed.[19]

Professor Sue Davis's analysis of Rehnquist's actual decisions on the Supreme Court in the 1970s and early 1980s showed that, although Rehnquist accepted *Brown* in theory, he gave it a narrow interpretation and disagreed with many of the later Supreme Court decisions that spelled out *Brown's* mandate.[20] Rehnquist was the first clear dissenter on school desegregation in the eighteen years after *Brown*. In the 1973 *Keyes* decision, Rehnquist argued against extending desegregation law to the North, calling the decision a "drastic extension of *Brown*." In a 1975 dissent, he attacked a decision from Wilmington, Delaware, which provided a metropolitan-wide desegregation remedy, calling it "more Draconian than any ever approved by this Court" and accused his colleagues of "total substitution of judicial for popular control of local education."[21]

In a 1979 case in which the Court decided to continue to desegregate entire urban districts rather than just individual schools, Rehnquist accused the majority of favoring a policy of "integration *über alles*," suggesting a parallel with the Nazi anthem, *"Deutschland über alles."*[22] By the time of the resegregation decisions of the 1990s, Rehnquist's views, long expressed in lonely dissents, would become the majority view of the Supreme Court. Rehnquist himself wrote the 1995 *Jenkins* decision.

Accepting Segregation in the North: The Turning Point in Detroit

The impetus of *Brown* and the civil rights movement for desegregating American schools hit a stone wall with the 1974 *Milliken v. Bradley* decision. The metropolitan Detroit decision, known as *Milliken I*, represented the first major Supreme Court blow against school desegregation. With *Milliken*, the Supreme Court was forced to grapple with the basic barrier to achieving urban school desegregation. After the Second World War, the pattern of white suburbanization in Northern cities intensified; many districts were left with too few white students to achieve full and lasting desegregation. In response to this demographic pattern, lower courts hearing the *Milliken* case approved a desegregation plan that would include not only Detroit's central city, but the predominantly white suburbs around it. But, in the face of intense opposition from the Nixon administration and many state governments, the High Court rejected the metropolitan remedy by a 5–4 vote.

This decision was particularly devastating to civil rights advocates, because only the year before, the Court in *Rodriguez* had ruled that children had no constitutional right to equal school expenditures.[23] Taken together,

Rodriguez and *Milliken* meant that illegally segregated minority students in school districts with high numbers of minority students had a right to neither equalization nor desegregation.

Milliken viewed desegregation as unfairly punishing the suburbs. The Court ruled that unless it could be shown either that suburban communities or discriminatory state action created the pattern of all-white suburbs and heavily black city schools, Detroit would have to desegregate by mixing its dwindling white enrollment with its huge and rapidly growing black majority. Chief Justice Warren Burger cited the "deeply rooted tradition" of local control of public schools as the legal rationale for denying a metropolitan remedy and allowing segregated schools to persist. Since the minority population in the industrial North is much more concentrated in a few big cities than it is in the South, this decision guaranteed that segregation would be limited and temporary in much of the North.

In his dissent, Justice Byron White challenged Burger, noting that school districts and municipal governments are not sovereign. State governments and state law created and empowered these districts; thus states have the power to change or dissolve them, White said. The basic tradition of U.S. law is not the independence of local government and school systems, but their existence as subdivisions of state government. He argued that the Supreme Court had ample authority to order the state to craft an interdistrict remedy. Justice William O. Douglas argued in his dissent that "metropolitan treatment" of various problems, such as sewage or water, is "commonplace" and that regional approaches could be used to accomplish the basic constitutional mandate of desegregation.[24]

Justice Thurgood Marshall challenged his colleagues about what he thought was the Court's real reason for denying the suburban-city remedy: suburban political and racial resistance.

The Court did not even consider the ways in which suburban governments around Detroit had perpetuated and contributed to the segregation of housing that led to the segregated schools across Detroit's metropolitan area.

Three years later, in the second Detroit case, *Milliken II*, the Court approved a plan ordering the state to pay for compensatory programs to redress the harms of segregation. But as the judge who later presided over the monetary remedies in Detroit said in 1993, *Milliken II* has been a "limited form of reparations." In Detroit and other cities . . . , the *Milliken II* remedy has not been implemented successfully.[25]

Rejection of city-suburban desegregation brought an end to the period of rapidly increasing school desegregation for black students, which began in 1965. No longer was the most severe segregation found among schools within the same community; the starkest racial separations occurred between urban and suburban school districts within a metropolitan area. But *Milliken* made this segregation almost untouchable. By 1991, African Americans in Michigan were more segregated than those in any other state. When the Supreme Court, through *Milliken I*, slammed the door on the only possible desegregation strategy for cities with few whites, it shifted the attention of urban educators and civil rights lawyers away from desegregation and toward other approaches for helping minority children confined to segregated and inferior city schools.

The outcome in *Milliken v. Bradley* reflected Nixon's goal of weakening desegregation requirements. His four appointees made up four of the five votes to protect the suburbs. *Milliken* was consistent with Nixon's fervent attacks on busing and on efforts to open up suburban housing to black families. He had derided suburban housing initiatives as "forced integration of the suburbs" just before firing the leading advocate for the initiatives, Housing and Urban Development Secretary George Romney. John Ehrlichman, Nixon's top domestic policy advisor, said the strategy was based on politics and on Nixon's conviction that blacks were *genetically inferior* to whites.[26]

Writing to his chief of staff early in 1972, the year of his reelection campaign, Nixon called for emphasis on three domestic issues in the campaign: inflation, the drug problem, and his opposition to busing.[27] Writing two months later to Ehrlichman, Nixon said it was time for the administration to abandon "the responsible position" on desegregation and "come to a Constitutional Amendment" in order to express a clear difference with the Democrats.[28] "We are not going to gain any brownie points whatsoever by being so responsible that we appear to be totally ineffective," he wrote.[29]

Nixon repeatedly declared that mandatory measures to achieve desegregation were unnecessary, and that Congress must stop courts from imposing "complicated plans drawn up by far-away officials in Washington, D.C." Fearing a constitutional crisis if Congress tried to override the authority of the Supreme Court to interpret the Constitution, the Senate narrowly blocked Nixon's attempt to limit judicial power by statute.[30] After he was reelected, the Watergate crisis diverted his attention from the desegregation issue.

By the mid-1970s, the United States had become an increasingly suburban country with a corresponding powerful suburban political perspective. Presidential elections were largely about the suburban vote, reapportionment was about expanding suburban representation, and older suburbs themselves were struggling with the problems of aging facilities and an antitax, antigovernment mood.

After the sudden changes of the civil rights era, the country denied the need to deal with race and income differences. White suburbanites were increasingly isolated from, and more fearful of, rapidly declining central cities. Between the mid-1960s and the early 1970s, Gallup Polls showed that racial inequality and race relations fell from the top concern of Americans to one of their lowest priorities.[31]

But although Nixon's triumph in the *Milliken* case did lock millions of minority schoolchildren into inferior, isolated schools, it did not resegregate the South. In a handful of cases outside the South—in Louisville, Wilmington, and Indianapolis—federal courts found grounds to mandate city-suburban desegregation in spite of *Milliken*. Civil rights advocates crushed by the *Milliken* defeat could at least celebrate the fact that millions of African American and Latino schoolchildren were enrolled in Southern school districts where desegregation was feasible and an increasingly accepted part of community life. This enduring desegregation was the special target of the 1990s resegregation decisions.

The South's Comparative Success in Desegregation

The South was the target of the most aggressive and persistent desegregation enforcement. In the late 1960s, the Justice Department had launched a fullscale attack on Southern segregation under *Green's* "root and branch" mandate. In the early 1970s, after the Supreme Court's *Swann* decision rejected the Nixon administration's efforts to ban busing, the Justice Department reluctantly enforced urban desegregation. In a compromise between Congress and the Nixon administration, a substantial federal aid program for desegregated schools—the Emergency School Aid Act—was passed in 1972.[32] After the Nixon White House halted administrative enforcement of urban school desegregation, federal courts in Washington found the administration in violation of the 1964 Civil Rights Act, which mandated cutoff of federal funds to school districts not complying with desegregation law, and ordered that enforcement resume. As a result, scores of Southern school districts were required to end local desegregation.[33]

The *Green* and *Swann* decisions, which required full and immediate desegregation, had more impact on the South than they did in the North. First of all, there were already hundreds of school districts in the South that had been required, by *Brown* and the 1964 Civil Rights Act, to adopt some kind of desegregation plan. Even though many of these strategies were inadequate—they often consisted of "freedom of choice" transfer options that did not lead to desegregation—there was at least some plan in existence. This was not the case in much of the North. In the South, plans were already on the books and districts were under court jurisdiction or federal administrative supervision. Thus it was a simple matter to file motions or issue regulations to have a plan updated to the newer standards required by *Green* and *Swann*. After *Swann,* more than a hundred districts rapidly implemented new desegregation plans, imposing a move to districtwide orders for immediate and total desegregation of students, faculties, and transportation.

It had been easy to find school districts in the South guilty of segregation, but the question of guilt in the North was always more ambiguous. The South had overt segregation laws requiring separate schools; reading the state laws was enough to prove that government had imposed segregation, which itself was linked to many government actions. Northern segregation was compounded by many complex school policies such as the drawing of attendance zones or the construction of schools serving residentially segregated areas. This meant that civil rights lawyers in the North often had a more arduous task and a less certain outcome in their school desegregation cases. It would take years to prove guilt before anyone even began to talk about a remedy. By the time a plan could be drawn up, shifting demographics often made full, lasting desegregation within the city school system impossible.

Where a northeastern or midwestern metropolitan area had dozens of separate school districts, many metropolitan areas in some Southern states were contained within a single school district. Therefore, the South was much better equipped to institute long-term desegregation within single districts. Florida was an excellent example of this, with countrywide districts including cities and suburbs across the state. The Supreme Court's decision against crossing district lines was much more damaging to Northern desegregation.

Many areas of the booming Sunbelt were experiencing white immigration from the North. This trend was in stark contrast to the declining cities and some metropolitan areas of the North that were losing white residents rapidly.

After *Milliken I,* desegregation law remained relatively stable through the 1980s, and the South maintained the relatively high levels of school integration achieved under *Green, Swann,* and civil rights regulations through 1988. The struggle over the meaning of the law was ongoing. In two 1970s cases originating in the Ohio cities of Dayton and Columbus, Justice Rehnquist failed in his attempt to roll back the citywide desegregation requirements laid out in *Keyes,* which had ruled that once intentional segregation was found in one part of a school system, lower courts should presume that segregation found in other parts of that system was also unconstitutional. This presumption meant that desegregation plans would be drawn for entire districts rather than for just a few schools. Trying to reverse the *Keyes* requirement, Rehnquist, on his own initiative, blocked the desegregation of 43,000 Columbus students just before school opened in 1978. The next year, in the Ohio cases, however, the Supreme Court reaffirmed its citywide desegregation stand.[34]

President Jimmy Carter expressed reservations about busing policies both as governor of Georgia and during his presidential campaign. Griffin Bell, Carter's attorney general, also had a record of opposition.[35] Once Carter was in office, however, he appointed civil rights officials who favored school desegregation, and a few important cases were filed by the Justice Department. These included the Indianapolis case, resulting in a metropolitan-wide desegregation remedy despite the *Milliken* constraints. In fact, the first successful lawsuit to link school and housing desegregation in a single city (Yonkers, N.Y.) was filed under Carter's presidency.

During this time, though, Congress voted to limit mandatory desegregation by prohibiting the use of the federal fund cutoff sanction in the 1964 Civil Rights Act to enforce civil rights compliance if busing was needed. Without this enforcement power, there was no potential for a nationwide executive branch desegregation policy. By the end of its term, however, the Carter administration was trying to craft coordinated school and housing desegregation policies. But the belated effort was aborted by President Reagan's election. Carter did not have the opportunity to appoint a Supreme Court justice.

The Reagan Era and the Movement to Dismantle

Opposition to mandatory desegregation reached a new intensity during the Reagan administration. Although desegregation orders were still sufficiently well-rooted to prevent a clear trend toward resegregation, the shift toward a "separate but equal" philosophy manifested itself at the end of the 1980s. Not even the South's favorable demographics and enforcement history could withstand the dismantling policies and court appointments of the Reagan administration.

In its first months, the administration won congressional action to rescind the Emergency School Aid Act of 1972, cutting off the only significant source of public money earmarked for the educational and human relations dimensions of desegregation plans. This was the largest federal education program deleted in the vast Omnibus Budget Reconciliation Act, which slashed hundreds of programs with a single vote.[36] Only the part that provided funds to specialized "magnet schools" was later restored. This restoration reflected the administration's desire to focus on choice. (Magnet schools relied upon parent's choosing to send their children to a particular school in an effort to achieve desegregation.) The Reagan administration also tried to eliminate Desegregation Assistance Centers, the only federally funded organizations that provide even limited assistance to desegregating school districts. Congress refused wholesale elimination, but funding cuts meant that the number of centers declined by three-fourths during this time.

During President Reagan's administration, the Justice Department, under the direction of Assistant Attorney General for Civil Rights William Bradford Reynolds, supported some of the school districts the Justice Department had once sued for intentional segregation, but failed to file any new desegregation lawsuits.[37] The administration proposed reliance on voluntary parental "choice" measures, like those the Supreme Court had rejected as inadequate in 1968 in *Green*. The administration also shut down research on ways to make desegregation more effective, took control of the formerly independent U.S. Civil Rights Commission, and used it to assail urban desegregation and other civil rights policies.

In 1981, Assistant Attorney General Reynolds told a congressional committee that "compulsory busing of students in order to achieve racial balance in the public schools is not an acceptable remedy." This position, Reynolds said, "has been endorsed by the President, the Vice President, the Secretary of Education, and me." At that time, however, Reynolds said that the administration would not try to apply the anti-desegregation principle to end desegregation plans already in force. He said: "Nothing we have learned in the 10 years since *Swann* leads to the conclusion that the public would be well-served by reopening wounds that have long since healed."[38] This resolve was quickly abandoned. Soon Reynolds and others intervened in older cases in an effort to dismantle settled desegregation plans.

As early as 1982, the administration called on the Supreme Court to restrict busing in metropolitan Nashville.[39] The Justice Department also supported an ultimately successful move in Norfolk, Virginia, to dismantle desegregation and become the first district to get court approval to return to segregated neighborhood schools. The department actively encouraged similar moves toward dismantling in other cities.

By the mid-1980s, educators and policymakers in a number of cities were actively discussing the option of dismantling their desegregation plans. This discussion picked up steam in 1986, soon after the Rehnquist Supreme Court refused to hear the Norfolk case, thus allowing a federal court to permit a return to racially segregated schools.

During this period, the Justice Department insisted that the plans were failures, unfair to whites and to local school systems. The plans should be seen as temporary punishments only, and districts should be allowed to return to segregated neighborhood schools. The department supported neighborhood schools, even in cities with no history of neighborhood schools, where the pre-desegregation policy had sent students to black or white schools, often well outside their neighborhoods.

For most of the 1980s, however, desegregation was surprisingly persistent. In contrast to the widespread belief that desegregation was a fragile, self-destructing policy, school desegregation endured year after year of attacks. Although the Reagan administration continually denounced desegregation as a failure, segregation levels for black students declined slightly during the Reagan years, showing the durability of many local plans, even in the face of opposition from Washington. Public opinion became more supportive of desegregation, even of busing. As the notion that widespread desertion of public schools was caused by integration won favor, the proportion of U.S. students attending public schools actually rose during the decade. Between 1984 and 1991, public school enrollment rose 7.1 percent, while enrollment in private schools dropped 8.9 percent.[40] The political leadership had succeeded in creating the false impression that desegregation policy had failed and families were deserting public education.

The Reagan administration's campaign against desegregation was successful after Reagan left because it was built upon appointments to the Supreme Court and the lower federal courts. Presidents Reagan and Bush appointed a new majority in the Supreme Court, and President Reagan elevated Justice William Rehnquist, the Court's leading opponent of school desegregation, to chief justice. With this new elevation, Rehnquist gained power to assign opinions, thereby gaining tremendous influence within the Court, and became the nation's leading legal figure. A full 60 percent of sitting federal judges in 1995 had been appointed by Presidents Reagan and Bush.[41] They had been screened for ideology to an unprecedented degree with elaborate investigations by the Justice Department and the White House.[42] This is significant because lower federal court judges have extensive power to decide whether a school district is unitary, whether it has complied "in good faith" with the desegregation order, and, finally, whether the district can return to segregated schooling.

The impact of the conservative agenda was finally clear when the Supreme Court handed down the 1991 *Dowell* decision that spelled out the process by which districts could resegregate schools. *Dowell,* and then *Pitts* in 1992, created the means by which even the South might return to segregated education. *Milliken* had blocked desegregation in the North and Midwest; now the South, where rigorous enforcement had led to better levels of desegregation, was vulnerable.

The 1990s' Definition of Unitary Status

The Court expressed its philosophical shift away from *Brown*'s principles most clearly by redefining the legal term "unitary status." In doing so, the Court managed to invent a kind of judicial absolution for the sins of segregation. Under the new resegregation decisions, if a court declared a school district "unitary," that school district could knowingly re-create segregated schools with impunity.

This new use of unitary status represented an important change. Ironically, unitary status had been first used by the Court in its 1968 *Green* decision as a standard that segregated school districts should strive to attain. *Green* posited a unitary school system with equitable interracial schools as a long-term, permanent goal, viewing any school board action that worked against or ignored the goal of total desegregation to be impermissible.

By 1990, unitary status in that sense—discrimination-free, racially integrated education—was no longer the objective; it became merely a method of getting out of racial integration. The Court rejected not only the ideal of lasting integration, but also the idea that elements of a desegregation plan were part of an inseparable package necessary to break down the dual school system and create desegregated education.

Thus unitary status decisions now have profound consequences for racial integration in U.S. schools. A court-supervised district that has never been declared unitary is obligated under the law to avoid actions that create segregated and unequal schools. But after a declaration of unitary status, the courts presume any government action creating racially segregated schools to be innocent, unless a plaintiff proves that the school officials intentionally decided to discriminate. This burden of proof is nearly impossible to meet, as contemporary school officials can easily formulate plausible alternative justifications. They certainly know better than to give overtly racist reasons for the policy change. With local authorities expressing innocence and the courts inclined to accept any professed educational justification regardless of consequences, minority plaintiffs face overwhelming legal obstacles when they try to prevent resegregation and other racial inequalities. Many of the very same actions that were illegal prior to a unitary status declaration become perfectly legal afterward.

The unitary status ruling assumes two things: that segregation does not have far-reaching effects and that a few years of desegregation, no matter how ineffective, could miraculously erase residual "vestiges" or effects of segregation. In this way, the courts implied that generations of discrimination and segregation could be quickly overcome through formal compliance with *Green* requirements for just one-tenth or one-twentieth as much time as the segregation and discrimination had been practiced.

Many courts do not even investigate whether or not vestiges of segregation are ever remedied. For example, under *Pitts*, *Dowell*, and *Jenkins*, school districts do not need to show that education gains or opportunities are equal between minority and white children. Nor do courts require solid evidence that discriminatory attitudes and assumptions growing out of a history of segregation have been purged from the local educational system.

In practice, the shift in the burden of proof that results from the unitary status declaration may be the key difference that allows a system to resegregate its schools. For example, after an Austin, Texas Independent School District was declared unitary in 1983, the federal district court relinquished jurisdiction completely in 1986; one year later, the school board redrew attendance zones to create segregated neighborhood schools. By 1993, nearly one-third of the elementary schools had minority enrollments of more than 80 percent non-white in a district that still had a white majority.[43] The judge allowed this segregation, though the student reassignments created the segregation in fourteen of the nineteen imbalanced schools.[44] Since the school district had been officially proclaimed unitary, actions that created segregation were assumed to be nondiscriminatory as long as the school leaders claimed an educational justification for the new plans. In contrast, an attendance plan in Dallas, then a nonunitary system, was rejected because it would have created too many one-race schools.[45] (Dallas has since been declared unitary.)

After the *Dowell* and *Pitts* decisions of 1991 and 1993, the road to resegregation seemed to be wide open. Teams of lawyers and experts were available, usually at steep fees, to help school districts fight for a return to segregated schools.

By the mid-1990s, several large systems had already moved to reinstitute segregated neighborhood schools, at least for the elementary school grades, by going into court to win unitary status. In some cases, civil rights lawyers, desperate to hang on to whatever remedies they could, simply settled these cases for fear that a trial would result in courts ending all desegregation immediately.

By 1995, courts had granted unitary status in a number of cases. Oklahoma City had been allowed to operate segregated neighborhood schools with only perfunctory consideration of the issues in the Supreme Court guidelines. Austin, Texas, had been allowed to reinstate segregated elementary schools. In Savannah-Chatham County, the district was declared unitary after implementing a purely voluntary plan that failed to meet the guidelines of a 1988 order. In that case, District Judge B. Avant Edenfield's language expressed the views of many judges now supervising desegregation cases. He praised the district's "momentous efforts," claiming that requiring more would be "imposing an exercise in futility." His ruling terminated all supervision of the system.[46] Older central city desegregation plans were closed with settlement agreements. Such agreements were adopted in such cities as Cincinnati and Cleveland.[47] In September 1995, the plan that produced the first Supreme Court decision in the North (Denver) was dissolved and the plan that had made metropolitan Wilmington the most integrated urban center on the east coast was dropped the month before.[48]

Today, a great many school districts remain under desegregation orders and have not filed motions to dissolve their plans. Some, including many in Florida, have plans that are increasingly ineffective because of the tremendous growth of white suburbs and the expansion of city ghettos without any adjustment of attendance areas set up in the old court order.

Many communities are on the brink of initiatives to dissolve plans that had provided an important, if imperfect, route of access for minority schoolchildren. Even in the regions that integrated most successfully and stably in the decades following the *Brown* decision, school systems were debating a return to segregation.

Themes about the "failure" or irrelevance of desegregation echo in public debates in city after city. Proposals for resegregation and attacks on desegregation often sail smoothly through school boards without objection, not because they will produce gains or because they represent the goals of the public, but because the civil rights side has been weakened, poorly funded, and struggling for survival in an increasingly conservative society with deepening racial and economic divisions.

The NAACP, by far the largest civil rights organization and the one with the most influential local chapters, has been in decline during the mid-1990s. It has experienced bitter internal struggles, the removal of its executive director and board chairman, division, and bankruptcy, all of which threaten its viability. With all of the major civil rights programs and many substantive programs crucial to the black community under political and legal attack, weakened civil right groups have been overwhelmed.

Does It Matter?

All this might be of only academic interest if it really were true that school desegregation had "failed," or had already been dismantled, or if the country had learned how to make separate institutions truly equal in a racially divided and extremely unequal society.

The truth, however, is that although urban desegregation has never been popular with whites, it is viewed as a success by both white and minority parents whose children experienced it. In the 1990s, there remains a widely shared preference in the society for integrated schools, though there is deep division about how to get them. Meanwhile, there is simply no workable districtwide model that shows that separate schools have actually been made equal in terms of outcomes or opportunities. A return to "separate but equal" is a bet that some unknown solution will be discovered and successfully implemented, and that local politics will now be sufficiently responsive to the interests of African American and Latino students that they can safely forgo the protection of the courts before ever actually experiencing equal education.

Notes

1. *Bd. of Educ. of Oklahoma City v. Dowell,* 498 U.S. 237 (1991).
2. *Freeman v. Pitts,* 112 S. Ct. 1430 (1992).
3. *Missouri v. Jenkins,* 115 S. Ct. 2038 (1995).
4. *Bd. of Educ. of Oklahoma City v. Dowell,* 498 U.S. 237 (1991).

5. *Green v. Sch. Bd. of New Kent County,* 391 U.S. 430 (1968).

6. *Freeman v. Pitts,* 112 S. Ct. 1430 (1992).

7. Richard Kluger, *Simple Justice* (New York: Vintage Books, 1975), p. 253.

8. Herbert Brownell with John P. Burke, *Advising Ike: The Memoirs of Attorney General Herbert Brownell* (Lawrence: University of Kansas Press, 1993); Mark Stern, "Presidential Strategies and Civil Rights: Eisenhower, the Early Years, 1952–54," *Presidential Studies Quarterly* 19, no. 4 (Fall 1989), pp. 769–95.

9. G. Edward White, *Earl Warren: A Public Life* (New York: Oxford University Press, 1982), pp. 166–8.

10. J. W. Peltason, *58 Lonely Men: Southern Federal Judges and School Desegregation* (New York: Harcourt, Brace and World, 1961).

11. Ibid.; Reed Sarratt, *The Ordeal of Desegregation* (New York: Harper and Row, 1966).

12. Gary Orfield, *The Reconstruction of Southern Education: The Schools and the 1964 Civil Rights Act* (New York: John Wiley, 1969).

13. *Green v. Sch. Bd. of New Kent County,* 391 U.S. 430 (1968).

14. Harry S. Dent, *The Prodigal South Returns to Power* (New York: John Wiley & Sons, 1978).

15. H. R. Haldeman, *The Haldeman Diaries: Inside the Nixon White House* (New York: G. P. Putnam's Sons, 1994), p. 126.

16. Ibid., pp. 126–30, 142, 183–4, 276; Leon Panetta and Peter Gall, *Bring Us Together: The Nixon Team and the Civil Rights Retreat* (Philadelphia: Lippincott, 1971).

17. Sue Davis, "Justice Rehnquist's Equal Protection Clause: An Interim Analysis," *University of Nebraska Law Review* 63 (1984), pp. 288, 308.

18. Senate Committee on the Judiciary, *Hearings on the Nomination of Justice William Hobbs Rehnquist,* 99th Cong. 2d. Sess., 1986, pp. 161–2.

19. Ibid., p. 325.

20. Davis, "Equal Protection," pp. 308–9.

21. *Delaware State Bd. of Educ. v. Evans,* 446 U.S. 923 (1975).

22. *Columbus Bd. of Educ. v. Penick,* 443 U.S. 449 (1979).

23. *San Antonio Indep. Sch. Dist. v. Rodriguez,* 541 U.S. 1 (1973).

24. *Milliken v. Bradley,* 94 S. Ct. 3112, 3134–41 (1974).

25. Judge Avram Cohn, letter to author, May 4, 1994.

26. Bruce Oudes, ed., *From: The President: President Nixon's Secret Files* (New York: Harper and Row, 1989), p. 399.

27. Oudes, *From: The President, Nixon to John Ehrlichman,* May 19, 1972, p. 451.

28. Ibid.

29. Ibid.

30. Gary Orfield, *Congressional Power: Congress and Social Changes* (New York: Harcourt Brace Jovanovich, 1975), pp. 182–4; G. Orfield, *Must We Bus? Segregated Schools and National Policy* (Washington, D.C.: Brookings Institution, 1978), pp. 247–54.

31. George H. Gallup, *The Gallup Poll: Public Opinion 1935–1971* (New York: Random House, 1972), pp. 1934, 2009.

32. Orfield, "Desegregation Aid and the Politics of Polarization," *Congressional Power,* ch. 9.

33. *Adams v. Richardson,* 356 F. Supp. 92 (D.D.C. 1973), was the first of many orders.

34. *Columbus Bd. of Educ. v. Penick,* 443 U.S. 449 (1979); *Dayton Bd. of Educ. v. Brinkman,* 443 U.S. 526 (1979).

35. "What Carter Believes: Interview on the Issues," *U.S. News & World Report,* May 24, 1976, pp. 22–3; Bell record is summarized in 95th Cong. 1st sess., *Congressional Record* daily ed., (January 25, 1977), pp. S1301–6.

36. See John Ellwood, ed., *Reductions in U.S. Domestic Spending* (New Brunswick, N.J.: Transaction Books, 1982), pp. 191–8.

37. Ibid., p. 35.

38. House Committee on the Judiciary, Subcommittee on Civil and Constitutional Rights, *Hearings on School Desegregation,* 97th Cong. 1st sess., 1981, pp. 614, 619.

39. *Education Week,* November 24, 1982.

40. U.S. National Center for Education Statistics, *The Condition of Education* (Washington, D.C.: U.S. Government Printing Office, 1993), p. 100. The trends had shown falling public and rising private enrollment in the 1970–84 period. (Ibid.)

41. Herman Schwartz, *Packing the Courts: The Conservative Campaign to Rewrite the Constitution* (New York: Charles Scribner's Sons, 1988); *New York Times,* November 30, 1995.

42. Edwin Meese III, *With Reagan: The Inside Story* (Washington, D.C.: Regnery Gateway, 1992), pp. 316–17.

43. P. Karatinos, *"Price v. Austin Indep. Sch. Dist.:* Desegregation's Unitary Tar Baby," 77 W. *Educ. L. Rep.* 15 (1992); see also *Price v. Austin Indep. Sch. Dist.,* 729 F. Supp. The Austin Independent School District, Planning and Development Office, March 1994.

44. Karatinos, *"Price v. Austin."*

45. *Tabsy v. Wright,* 713 F. *2d* 90 (5th Cir. 1993).

46. *Stell v. Board of Public Education,* 860 F. Supp. 1563 (S.D. Ga. 1994).

47. *Cleveland Plain Dealer,* August 25, 1994, p. 6-B.

48. Patrice M. Jones, "School District Seeks Release From Edict on Cross-Town Busing," *Cleveland Plain Dealer,* January 5, 1995, p. 1-B; "Court Oversight of Denver Schools Is Ended," *New York Times,* September 13, 1995, p. B7; Peter Schmidt, "U.S. Judge Releases Wilmington Districts from Court Oversight," *Education Week,* September 6, 1995, p. 9.

NO ↩

Ingrid Gould Ellen

Welcome Neighbors? New Evidence on the Possibility of Stable Racial Integration

The conventional wisdom on racial integration in the United States is that there are three kinds of neighborhoods: the all-white neighborhood, the all-black neighborhood, and the exceedingly rare, highly unstable, racially mixed neighborhood. The only real disagreement is about why so few neighborhoods are successfully integrated. Some attribute it to white discrimination pure and simple: whites, that is, have consciously and determinedly excluded blacks from their communities. Others contend that it is a matter of minority choice. Like Norwegians in Brooklyn's Bay Ridge and Italians in Manhattan's Little Italy, African Americans, they explain, prefer to live among their own kind. Finally, others maintain that segregation is driven mainly by income differences across racial groups. But almost all agree that when African Americans do manage to gain a foothold in a previously all-white community, the whites move away in droves—a phenomenon well known as "white flight." Integration is no more than, in the words of Saul Alinsky, the "time between when the first black moves in and last white moves out."

But while there is no denying that the United States remains a remarkably segregated country, such views are too pessimistic. Racially mixed neighborhoods are not as rare as people think. In 1990, according to nationwide census tract data, nearly 20 percent of all census tracts—which generally include a few thousand residents, roughly the size of the typical neighborhood—were racially integrated, defined as between 10 percent and 50 percent black. (Defining an "integrated" neighborhood is inevitably somewhat arbitrary. The 10–50 percent range takes into account both that African Americans make up just 12 percent of the total U.S. population and that most people consider integration to involve a fairly even racial split.) In 1990 more than 15 percent of the non-Hispanic white population and nearly one-third of the black population lived in these mixed neighborhoods. And the proportion is increasing. The number of households, both white and black, living in integrated communities grew markedly between

From *Brookings Review*, Winter 1997, pp. 18–21. Copyright © 1997 by The Brookings Institution Press. Reprinted with permission.

1970 and 1980 and even faster between 1980 and 1990. Most strikingly, the share of white residents living in overwhelmingly white census tracts—those in which blacks represent less than 1 percent of the total population—fell from 63 percent in 1970 to 36 percent in 1990.

Not only are racially mixed neighborhoods more numerous than people think, they are also more stable. An examination of a sample of 34 large U.S. metropolitan areas with significant black populations reveals that more than three quarters of the neighborhoods that were racially mixed in 1980 were still mixed in 1990. And in more than half, the share of non-Hispanic whites remained constant or grew. Most significantly, perhaps, a comparison with data from the 1970s suggests that neighborhoods are becoming more stable over time. The mean white population loss in integrated neighborhoods was lower in the 1980s than in the 1970s; a greater share of integrated tracts remained steady in the 1980s; and fewer tracts experienced dramatic white loss. In sum, neighborhood racial integration appears to be becoming both more widespread and more stable. Again, this is not to claim that America's neighborhoods are no longer dramatically segregated. But it may no longer be accurate to describe them, as have some, as a system of "American Apartheid."

How is it that certain neighborhoods seem to turn rapidly from white to black as soon as a few black households move in, while others hardly seem to change at all? The conventional account of racial mixing has, I think, discouraged people from seriously investigating this question—either by theorizing about what might be different about the more stable areas or by examining matters empirically. Because all mixed neighborhoods are presumed to be highly unstable, explaining the variance in the rate of racial change has hardly seemed pressing. But examining the conditions under which integration seems to thrive offers considerable insight not only into the causes of our nation's racial segregation, but also into the prospects for mitigating it.

Why Are Some Mixed Neighborhoods Stable?

It is possible to devise a variety of theories to explain why some mixed neighborhoods remain integrated. One theory is simply that neighborhoods with fewer minority residents are more likely to be stable. The argument is that white households basically dislike living with minorities and that once the minority population of a given community reaches a concentration greater than they can tolerate, whites abandon the community, which quickly becomes all black. But while this argument has some intuitive appeal in light of our nation's long history of racism, the degree of integration in a mixed community appears to have no bearing on its future racial mix. Whether a community is 10 percent black or 50 percent black, the likelihood of white loss is the same.

A second theory is that communities are more stable when black and white residents have similar incomes and education levels. This theory has an intuitive appeal to those who think that our country has gotten beyond race. But it is not borne out by the data either. Indeed, neighborhoods where blacks and whites are more equal in status are, if anything, less stable.

A third theory—and the one that best fits the evidence—is that residential decisions, especially those of white households, are indeed heavily shaped by negative racial attitudes. But it is not a simple matter of racial animus, of white households being unwilling to live, at any particular moment in time, in neighborhoods with moderately sized black populations. Rather, it is a matter of white households tending to assume that all mixed neighborhoods quickly and inevitably become predominantly black and being uncomfortable with the prospect of living in such an environment in the future.

As for the sources of this discomfort, I would emphasize two. First, whites may simply fear being "left behind" as a racial minority as the community becomes largely black. Second, and more important, white households (and potentially black households as well) may have negative preconceptions about what an all-black neighborhood will be like. Specifically, black neighbors may be thought to bring with them, or at least to portend, a deterioration in what Richard Taub and others have called the "structural position," or strength, of a neighborhood: the aggregate of school quality, public safety, property values, and the like. In other words, white households may not necessarily dislike living next to blacks per se; but many white households, rightly or wrongly, associate blacks with decreasing structural strength. Whether such stereotyped associations should be distinguished from simple racial prejudice on moral grounds deserves lengthy discussion, but certainly they are analytically distinct and have distinct policy implications.

This proposed hypothesis—call it the "racial neighborhood stereotyping" hypothesis—generates some powerful predictions that can be tested empirically. First, it suggests that households who are less invested in the structural strength of the community—renters and households with no children, for instance—will be more open to racial mixing and thus more likely to live in mixed communities. Significantly, if whites simply dislike living near blacks, the opposite should hold true. For white renters—who can enter and exit neighborhoods more easily than homeowners—will be less likely to live in mixed communities.

Second, this hypothesis suggests that—contrary to the conventional view that racial transition is caused by "white flight"—racial concerns are more influential in decisions whether to move into a community than whether to move out. For residents of a community should be fully aware of its structural strength and therefore have less need to rely on race as a signal of this strength. Consequently, entry decisions should be far more important to racial change than exit decisions.

Third, racial mixing should be more stable in communities that seem sheltered in some way from further black growth (either because they are distant from the central area of black residence or because they have been racially stable in the past) or in which school quality, property values, and other neighborhood attributes seem particularly secure.

Testing the Theory

Using a unique census data set that links households to the neighborhoods in which they live, I have tested each of these predictions. The data generally bear them out. First, as predicted, households who are likely to be less invested in the structural strength of a neighborhood appear to be far more open to racial mixing. White households moving into racially mixed areas tend, for instance, to be younger than those opting for predominantly white areas. They also tend to be single rather than married and not to have children. Significantly, childless black households are similarly more open to increasingly black communities than their counterparts with children. Finally, white renters are considerably more willing to move into and remain in racially mixed areas than homeowners are. Thus, communities with relatively larger proportions of rental housing are more likely to remain integrated. Again, this finding runs counter to the pure-prejudice view of neighborhood choice, since renters can leave much more quickly than homeowners.

The data support the second prediction as well. Indeed, there is virtually no evidence of white flight or accelerated departure rates in the face of racial mixing. White households are no more likely to leave a community that is 80 percent black than one that is 2 percent black. And the moving decisions of black households appear insensitive to racial composition as well. Thus, to the extent that integrated neighborhoods do tip, or become increasingly black, entry decisions, rather than exit decisions, appear to be the cause. The point is, residents living in a community are far less likely to consider race as a signal of neighborhood quality than outsiders considering moving in.

As for the third prediction, the evidence confirms that mixed neighborhoods that seem sheltered from further black growth are more stable. In fact, the most crucial determinant of a community's future course of racial change is its past racial stability. The longer a community has been integrated, the more likely it is to remain so. And analysis of individual decision-making confirms this. Controlling for present racial composition, white households are both less likely to leave a mixed community and more likely to enter one if its black population has been fairly steady in the past and thus seems likely to remain steady in the future. Moreover, integrated neighborhoods located farther from black inner-city communities are more likely to remain stable. Of course, the added distance may discourage blacks from entering these communities as quickly, but it seems likely that white expectations play a role too. For white households may view communities closer to the core black area as both more apt to gain black population and more vulnerable to the social dislocation that whites associate with such gain.

Furthermore, mixed neighborhoods in which the housing market is thriving and in which neighborhood amenities seem particularly secure are more likely to remain stable. For example, the data appear to show that communities with large stabilizing institutions, such as universities or military bases, that promise to provide a continual source of people, both white and black, who desire to live in the area provide just such strength and security.

Policy Implications, Big and Small

To the extent the racial neighborhood stereotyping hypothesis is sound, the obvious question arises: what light does it shed on the moral and economic justification for government intervention to maintain mixed neighborhoods or to promote integration generally, and what kinds of policies would most effectively promote integration consistent with this justification? This is not the place to address such a grand question. Suffice it here simply to point out a few salient implications of the hypothesis for existing government policies designed to maintain mixed communities.

One policy that is occasionally used is the setting of an explicit quota on the number of blacks or minorities who may move into a particular mixed community or development where black or minority demand is high. For example, several years back, the owners of Starrett City, a large middle-income apartment complex in Brooklyn built with substantial government subsidies, set a quota on the number of blacks and Hispanics who could live there. In 1987 a federal court found that the quota violates the Fair Housing Act of 1968. But such quotas may also not make much sense as a matter of policy, since, as noted, no specified level of minority representation triggers white departure from a community.

Mixed communities have also tried to stem panic-selling by restricting realtors' unsolicited efforts to encourage homeowners to sell and by banning the display of "For Sale" signs. But if exit decisions are less sensitive than entry decisions to racial composition and less critical to long-run stability, such strategies are poorly targeted. Integration, my results show, would be more effectively promoted by encouraging outsiders to move in, not discouraging insiders from leaving.

Some communities have tried to do just this. For example, some have tried to attract outsiders by public relations campaigns that advertise their particular strengths: their housing stock, their parks, their community solidarity. Such efforts also directly counter white households' fears about the structural decline they associate with predominantly black neighborhoods.

Efforts in mixed communities to raise amenity levels also address white households' fears of community decline. For example, programs to improve the appearance of a community—restoring local playgrounds, cleaning up commercial strips, repairing broken windows—can build social capital and bolster people's faith in a neighborhood's strength.

Finally, the racial neighborhood stereotyping hypothesis has important implications for government policies that have nothing to do with promoting racial integration. For example, policies designed to increase homeownership, such as the homeowner mortgage interest deduction, may have the unintended consequence of exacerbating racial segregation.

Unwarranted Pessimism

The real story about America's neighborhoods, though far from revealing anything close to a color-blind society, is less pessimistic and more dynamic than we have tended to believe. Integrated neighborhoods may be a minority, but their numbers are growing, and many appear likely to remain racially mixed for many years. Researchers must not overlook them. For the question of when and where households seem content to live in racially mixed environments is in many ways the flip side of the ultimate question of why our nation's residential neighborhoods are as segregated as they are. And any progress toward answering the first question is progress toward answering the second. More important, white households should not overlook the facts either, for their overly pessimistic assumption that rapid racial transition is inevitable has helped, by its self-fulfilling nature, to undermine racial mixing.

In hindsight, the optimism of many people during the civil rights era that integration was just around the corner seems hopelessly naive. But the pessimism that has replaced it in recent years does not seem appropriate either. It seems based more on weariness in the face of an endlessly daunting challenge than on the facts, and it has, in my view, slowed our progress toward understanding neighborhood racial segregation.

POSTSCRIPT

Are America's Schools and Neighborhoods Resegregated?

With the increase of suburbanization in the 1970s, America has gradually become more segregated. Segregation is generally imposed by a dominant group on a minority racial or ethnic group. Historically, housing practices in the United States have forced minorities into certain specific neighborhoods. At the same time, members of ethnic groups may seek the safety of a community of racial and ethnic peers. Typically, segregated minority neighborhoods are less desirable. Often poverty, poor government services and low achieving, segregated schools characterize them. On the other hand, all-white neighborhoods—indeed, they too are segregated—must be recognized as a significant factor in racial isolation today.

According to the Civil Rights Project at Harvard, as of 1999, "more than 70% of all Blacks attended schools that were predominantly Black," while white student were even more segregated with the vast majority attending schools "with few or no students of any other race." The Project points out that changes in segregation patterns are taking place in the general context of "an increasingly diverse public schools enrollment." Latinos, for example, have become increasingly segregated. Today more than 7 million Latinos attend public schools. Thus, two interesting trends are developing in the public schools—rising segregation and increasing diversity.

The example of Detroit illustrates the segregation issue. As one of the country's most segregated cities, almost 90% of its residents would have to move from segregated neighborhoods to achieve integration. Further, the vast majority of the residents of Buffalo, Chicago, Cincinnati, St. Louis, New York, Atlanta, Boston, Los Angeles, Houston, Dallas, and Washington, D.C. would also have to move for their cities to achieve racial integration. So, despite magnet schools, charter schools, and voucher programs, the school systems of these cities are becoming increasingly segregated.

Public schools have contributed to racial inequities. The embrace of education as a basis for social advancement is a core value of American culture. So long as blacks, Latinos, and other students of color are subjected to low-quality, poor-performing schools, their prospects for economic advancement and achieving equity with whites will continue to lag. Indeed, the Civil Rights Project points out that "patterns of segregation by race are strongly linked to segregation by poverty, and poverty concentrations are strongly linked to unequal opportunities and outcomes."

To address the issue of resegregation is to assess public education in America. School populations reflect the ethnic and racial composition of the community. Clearly, if the neighborhoods are all-white, then the schools will be too. No policies exist to remedy *de facto* segregation in the schools. Ellen's finding that stable mixed neighborhoods are increasing obscures the fact that many white neighborhoods are segregated.

It is possible that the student will find that both positions articulated here reflect contradictory twenty-first century trends. Large cities may reflect increasing diversity. At the same time, the communities and local neighborhoods in those cities continues to remain racially and ethnically isolated. This is a major paradox.

A general historical background of the imposition of legal segregation in the South following Reconstruction is in *The Strange Career of Jim Crow* (Oxford University Press, 1974) by C. Vann Woodward. For an extensive collection of maps and illustrations of slavery, Reconstruction, and segregation, see *The Atlas of African-American History and Politics: From the Slave Trade to Modern Times* (McGraw-Hill, 1998) by Arwin D. Smallwood. Andrew Hacker's *Two Nations: Black and White, Separate, Hostile, Unequal* (Charles Scribner's Sons, 1992) examines different forms of segregation. For a study of race and class, see Douglas S. Massey and Nancy A. Denton, *American Apartheid: Segregation and the Making of the Underclass* (Harvard University Press, 1993). William Julius Wilson's *The Truly Disadvantaged: The Inner City, the Underclass and Public Policy* (University of Chicago Press, 1987) looks at the economic effects of segregation. Students will find chapters 1 and 6 of *The American Civil Rights Movement: Readings and Interpretations* (McGraw/Dushkin, 2000) by Raymond D'Angelo helpful in this area.

A study of the historic *Brown* decision can begin with *Simple Justice: A History of Brown v. Board of Education and Black America's Struggle for Equality* (Vintage, 1975) by Richard Kluger. It is considered the definitive study of Brown. *Brown v. Board of Education: A Brief History with Documents* (Bedford, 1998) by Waldo Martin offers near complete versions of the important legal briefs and court decisions. A recent issue of *Teaching Tolerance* (Spring 2004) featured a special section entitled "50 Years Later: Brown v. Board of Education." The *Magazine of History* (January 2004, vol. 18, no. 2) is devoted to research on Jim Crow.

Hartford, Connecticut's effort to reverse the resegregation trend is examined by Monte Piliawsky in "Remedies to De Facto School Segregation: The Case of Hartford," in *Black Scholar* (Summer 1998).

Recent data on resegragation can be found in "Race in American Public Schools: Rapidly Resegregation School District" (August 2002) by Erica Frankenberg and Chungmei Lee. They are part of The Civil Rights Project at Harvard University. In contrast, Abigail and Stephan Thernstorm, in *America in Black and White: One Nation, Indivisible* (Simon & Schuster, 1997) defend the laissez-faire progress of U.S. race relations. They attack liberals and civil rights activists who seek to promote legislation to promote desegregation. For a critique of the Thernstroms' position, see Peter Schrag's "How the Other Half Learns," in *The Nation* (November 10, 2003).

ISSUE 12

Should Race Be a Consideration in College Admissions?

YES: William G. Bowen and Neil L. Rudenstine, "Race-Sensitive Admissions: Back to Basics," in *The Chronicle of Higher Education* (February 7, 2003)

NO: Dinesh D'Souza, "A World Without Racial Preferences," *The Weekly Standard* (November 30/December 7, 1998)

ISSUE SUMMARY

YES: William G. Bowen, former President of Princeton University, and Neil L. Rudenstine, former president of Harvard University, make the case for race-sensitive admissions in higher education. With a focus on selective colleges, they cite empirical data that demonstrate the success of beneficiaries of race-sensitive admission policies. In their opinion, both public and private selective colleges should continue such policies.

NO: Dinesh D'Souza, John M. Olin Scholar at the American Enterprise Institute, questions the racial preference argument and argues that merit should decide admission to any organization. His example is the National Basketball Association (NBA) where African Americans make up 79% of the players despite being only 13% of the population. D'Souza contends that since unequal performance determines the racial breakdown of the NBA, the same merit standard should apply to college admission.

Among the many issues considered in this edition of *Taking Sides,* that of college admissions may be the most interesting for students. The highly competitive quest to gain admission to the college of one's choice is perhaps the most important decision high school seniors have to face. Hence, the intense focus on the process of selection to elite colleges and universities. Annual college ratings and long-standing reputations weigh heavily on college-bound seniors. In this context alone, admissions policies face scrutiny from potential applicants. This scrutiny has illuminated the issue of race in college admissions. Recalling Supreme Court decisions including *Bakke, Milligan,* and most recently, *Bollinger,* race remains a factor—among many others—to be considered in admissions, and debated in the early part of the twenty-first century.

The position of William G. Bowen and Neil L. Rudenstine, both of whom have spent many years in higher education at two of America's most selective colleges, is that race-sensitive admissions policies are both necessary and good. Behind their position is the argument that race matters profoundly in America. To consider race as "just another" dimension of diversity is to trivialize the African-American experience and to diminish American history. The aftermath of this history is "to place racial minorities in situations in which embedded perceptions and stereotypes limit opportunities and create divides that demean us all." In effect, they recognize the persistence of race prejudice and racism. Thus, institutional racism along with subtle and complex stereotyping exists in ways that belie the notion of equality.

Bowen and Rudenstine incorporate data from *The Shape of the River: Long Term Consequences of Considering Race in College and University Admissions,* written by Bowen and Derek Bok, which demonstrates the success of race-preference programs. They address the "reverse discrimination" claim often advanced by some whites. Merely to proclaim that a school is an affirmative action institution does not insure admission to an elite college to a reasonably qualified minority. The research of Bowen and Bok tells us that among the elite colleges they studied, "a very considerable number of high-scoring minority students were turned down." For example, they cite, "At the very top of the SAT distribution (in the 1400-plus range), nearly two out of five [minority applicants] were not admitted."

Dinesh D'Souza suggests that race preferences insult the legacy of Martin Luther King. He argues that King came down "on the side of merit in opposition to racial nepotism." Choosing to deny the persistence of racial discrimination, D'Souza introduces the controversial and flawed "bell curve" position of Charles Murray and Richard Herrnstein, which implies that possibly genetics explains why whites and blacks have performance differences. In spite of D'Souza's claim to have a cultural view of racial inequality, he suggests otherwise. Basically, he states that cultural and behavioral differences explain academic achievement and economic performance. D'Souza does not view racism as a significant problem for racial minorities today. Thus, he is against racial preferences.

Using an argument from Shelby Steele, an African-American professor, affirmative action is popular among black and white elites because whites feel morally superior and, at the same time, blacks gain unearned privileges. D'Souza carves out a critique of the race-sensitive position that leads to a color-blind or race-neutral position.

William G. Bowen
and Neil L. Rudenstine

↱ **YES**

Race-Sensitive Admissions:
Back to Basics

The controversy (and confusion) surrounding the White House's recent statements on the use of race in college and university admissions indicate the need for careful examination of the underlying issues. The Justice Department has filed a brief with the U.S. Supreme Court urging it to declare two race-sensitive policies at the University of Michigan unconstitutional; however, the brief does not rule out ever taking race into account, but argues that institutions should first exhaust all "race-neutral" alternatives. Secretary of State Colin Powell has publicly said that he supports not just affirmative action, but also the Michigan policies. National Security Advisor Condoleezza Rice says she opposes the specific methods used by Michigan, but recognizes the need to take race into account in admissions.

As the Supreme Court prepares to hear oral arguments in a case that will shape college admissions processes in the coming decades, those of us who believe that such processes should be permitted to include a nuanced consideration of race must speak out clearly as well as forcefully. Too often, we fear, the key issues have been oversimplified or overlooked. Having been personally involved with this highly contentious subject for more than 30 years, we would like to try to frame the discussion by offering a set of nine connected propositions about race and admissions that derive from core human values and substantial empirical research.

1. The twin goals served by race-sensitive admissions remain critically important.

The debate over race-sensitive admissions has relevance only at public and private institutions of higher education that have to choose among considerably more qualified candidates than they can admit. Essentially all of these "academically selective" colleges and universities have elected to take race into account in making admissions decisions, a fact that, in itself, has considerable import. Race-sensitive admissions programs are intended

From *Chronicle of Higher Education*, February 2003, pp. B7–B10. Copyright © 2003 by William Bowen and Neil Rudenstine. Reprinted with permission.

to serve two important purposes:

- To enrich the learning environment by giving *all* students the opportunity to share perspectives and exchange points of view with classmates from varied backgrounds. The recognition of the educational power of diversity led many colleges and universities—well before the mid-1960s, when the term affirmative action began to be used—to craft incoming classes that included students representing a wide variety of interests, talents, backgrounds, and perspectives. *The Shape of the River,* written by William G. Bowen and Derek Bok, provides abundant evidence that graduates of these institutions value educational diversity and, in general, are strong supporters of race-sensitive admissions. Survey responses from more than 90,000 alumni of selective colleges and universities show that nearly 80 percent of those who enrolled in 1976 and 1989 felt that their alma mater placed the right amount of emphasis—or not enough—on diversity in the admissions process. That same survey also found that there is much more interaction across racial lines than many people suppose. In the 1989 entering cohort, 56 percent of white matriculants and 88 percent of black matriculants indicated that they "knew well" two or more classmates of the other race.
- To serve the needs of the professions, of business, of government, and of society more generally by educating larger numbers of well-prepared minority students who can assume positions of leadership—thereby reducing somewhat the continuing disparity in access to power and responsibility that is related to race in America. Since colonial days, colleges and universities have accepted an obligation to educate individuals who will play leadership roles in society. Today, that requires taking account of the clearly articulated needs of business and the professions for a healthier mix of well-educated leaders and practitioners from varied racial and ethnic backgrounds. Professional groups like the American Bar Association and the American Medical Association, and businesses like General Motors, Microsoft, and American Airlines (among many others), have explicitly endorsed affirmative-action policies in higher education. Leading law firms, hospitals, and businesses depend heavily on their ability to recruit broadly trained individuals from many racial backgrounds who are able to perform at the highest level in settings that are themselves increasingly diverse. A prohibition on the consideration of race in admissions would drastically reduce minority participation in the most selective professional programs. Does it make any sense to resegregate, de facto, many of the country's most respected professional schools and to slow the progress that has been made in achieving diversity within the professions? We don't think so.

2. Private colleges and universities are as likely as their public counterparts to be affected by the outcome of this debate.

The fact that litigation over affirmative action has, thus far, centered on public universities should not lead us to believe that private institutions will be unaffected. The 1996 federal-court ruling in *Hopwood v. Texas,* banning race-sensitive admissions policies in Texas, Louisiana, and Mississippi, has been understood to cover Rice University as well as public universities such as the University of Texas, Title VI of the Civil Rights Act of 1964 subjects all institutions that receive federal funds to any court determinations as to what constitutes "discrimination." Because many private colleges and universities have invested substantial resources in creating diverse entering classes, they might well be *more* dramatically affected by any limitation on their freedom to consider race than would most public institutions. That is especially true because they are, in general, smaller and more selective in admissions than their public counterparts.

It matters that minority applicants have access to the most selective programs, at both undergraduate and graduate levels, in both private and public institutions. The argument that they will surely be able to "get in somewhere" rings hollow to many people. As one black woman quoted in *The Shape of the River* observed wryly to a white parent: "Are you telling me that all those white folks fighting so hard to get their kids into Duke and Stanford are just ignorant? Or are we supposed to believe that attending a top-ranked school is important for their children but not for mine?" That interchange was not just about perceptions. Various studies show that the short-term and long-term gains associated with attending the most selective institutions are, if anything, greater for minority students than for white students, and that academic and other resources are concentrated increasingly in the top tier colleges and universities.

3. Race-sensitive admissions policies involve much "picking and choosing" among individual applicants; they need not be mechanical, are not quota systems, and involve making bets about likely student contributions to campus life and, subsequently, to the larger society.

Contrary to what some people believe, admissions decisions at academically selective public and private colleges and universities are much more than a "numbers game." They involve considerations that extend far beyond test scores and GPAs. Analysis of new data from leading private research universities for the undergraduate class entering in 1999 (reported in the forthcoming *Reclaiming the Game,* by William G. Bowen and Sarah A. Levin) indicates that a very considerable number of high-scoring minority students were turned down. For instance, among male minority applicants with combined SAT scores in the 1200 to 1299 range (which put them well within the top 10 percent of minority test-takers and the top 20 percent of all test-takers, regardless of race), the odds of admission were about 35 percent: That is, roughly two out of three of these minority applicants were denied admission. At the very top of the SAT distribution (in the 1400-plus range), nearly two out of five were *not* admitted. Public universities are larger and somewhat less selective, but they also turn down very high-scoring minority candidates. At two public universities for which detailed data are available, one out of four minority candidates in the 1200 to 1399 SAT range was rejected.

In short, admissions officers at both private and public universities have been doing exactly what Justice Powell, in the landmark 1978 decision. *Regents of the University of California v. Bakke,* said that they should be allowed to do: pursuing "race-sensitive" admissions policies that entail considering race among other factors. They have been weighing considerations that are both objective (advanced-placement courses taken in high school, for example) and subjective (indications of drive, intellectual curiosity, leadership ability, and so on). And they have been selecting very well. According to all the available evidence, minority students admitted to academically selective colleges and universities as long ago as the mid-1970s have been shown to be successful in completing rigorous graduate programs, doing well in the marketplace, and, most notably, contributing in the civic arena out of all proportion to their numbers.

Minority candidates are, of course, by no means the only group of applicants to receive special consideration. Colleges and universities have long paid special attention to children of alumni, to "development cases," to applicants who come from poor families or who have otherwise overcome special obstacles, to applicants who will add to the geographic (including international) diversity of the student body, to students with special talents in fields such as music, and, especially in recent years, to athletes. Some readers may be surprised to learn from *Reclaiming the Game* that recruited athletes at many selective colleges are far more advantaged in the admissions process (that is, are much more likely to be admitted at a given SAT level) than are minority candidates.

A related topic deserves some emphasis, and that is the issue of "quotas." There is not space here to discuss the subject in detail, but one point is important to clarify. The fact that the percentage of minority students in many colleges and universities does not fluctuate substantially from year to year is in no sense prima facie evidence that quotas are being used. Anyone familiar with admissions processes—and with their basic statistics—knows that percentages for virtually all subgroups of any reasonable size are remarkably consistent from year to year. That is because the size of the college going population does not change significantly on an annual basis, nor do the number and quality of secondary schools from which institutions draw applications, nor does the number of qualified candidates. All of these numbers are very stable, and it is therefore not at all surprising that incoming college classes should change very little in their composition from year to year. (For example, we suspect that the fraction of an entering class wearing eyeglasses is remarkably consistent from year to year, but that would hardly persuade us that an eyeglass quota is being imposed.)

4. Selectivity and "merit" involve predictions about on-campus learning environments and future contributions to society.

One of the most common misconceptions is that candidates who have scored above some level or earned a certain grade-point average "deserve" a place in an academically selective institution. That "entitlement" notion is squarely at odds with the fundamental principle that, in choosing among a large number of well-qualified applicants, all of whom are over a high threshold, colleges and universities are making bets on the future, not giving rewards for prior accomplishments. Institutions are meant to take well-considered risks. That can involve turning down candidate "A" (who is entirely admissible but does not stand out in any particular way) in favor of candidate "B" (who is expected to contribute more to the educational milieu of the institution and appears to have better long-term prospects of making a major contribution to society). All applicants, of course, deserve to be evaluated fairly, which means treating them the same way as other similarly situated candidates; but, in the words of Lee Bollinger, president of Columbia University and former president of the University of Michigan, "there is no right to be admitted to a university without regard to how the overall makeup of the student body will affect the educational process or without regard to the needs of the society. . . ." "Merit" is not a simple concept. It has certainly never meant admitting all the valedictorians who apply, or choosing students strictly on the basis of test scores and GPAs.

An elaborate admissions process, which focuses on the particular characteristics of individuals within many subgroups—and on those of the entire pool of applicants—is designed to craft a class that will, in its diversity, be a potent source of educational vitality. Colleges use a variety of procedures to take account of race, and it is essential that differences of opinion concerning the wisdom (or even the legality) of any single approach not lead to an outcome that precludes other approaches.

5. Paying special attention to any group in making admissions decisions entails costs; but the costs of race-sensitive admissions have been modest and well-justified by the benefits.

The "opportunity cost" of admitting any particular student is that another applicant will not be chosen. But such choices are rarely "head-to-head" decisions. For example, there is no reason to believe—as reverse-discrimination lawsuits generally assume—that if a particular minority student had not been accepted, his or her place would have been given to a complainant with comparable or better test scores or grades. The choice might, instead, have been an even higher-scoring minority student who had not been admitted, a student from a foreign country, or a lower-scoring white student from one of several subgroups that are given extra consideration in the admissions process. Making hard choices on the margin is never easy and always—fortunately—involves human judgments made by experienced admissions officers. It is, in any case, wrong to assume that race-sensitive admissions policies have significantly reduced the chances of well-qualified white students to gain admission to the most selective colleges. Findings reported in *The Shape of the River*, based on data for a subset of selective colleges and universities, demonstrate that elimination of race-sensitive policies would have increased the admission rate for white students by less than two percentage points: from roughly 25 percent to 26.5 percent.

It should be emphasized that taking race into account in making admissions decisions does *not* appear to have two kinds of costs often mentioned by critics of these policies.

- First, there is no systemic evidence that race-sensitive admissions policies tend to "harm the beneficiaries" by putting them in settings in which they are overmatched intellectually or "stigmatized" to the point that they would have been better off attending a less selective institution. On the contrary, extensive analysis of data reported in *The Shape of the River* shows that minority students at selective institutions have, over all, performed well. The more selective the institution that they attended, the more likely they were to graduate and earn advanced degrees, the happier they were with their college experience, and the more successful they were in later life.

- Second, the available evidence disposes of the argument that the substitution of "race-sensitive" for "race-neutral" admissions policies has led to admission of many minority students who are not well-suited to take advantage of the educational opportunities they are being offered. Examination of the later accomplishments of those students who would have been "retrospectively rejected" under race-neutral policies shows that they did just as well as a hypothetical reference group that might have been admitted if GPAs and test scores had been the primary criteria (which is, itself, a questionable assumption). There are no significant differences in graduation rates, advanced-degree attainment, earnings, civic contributions, or satisfactions with college. In short, the abandonment of race-sensitive admissions would not have removed from campuses a marginal group of mediocre students. Rather, it would have deprived campuses of much of their diversity and diminished the capacity of the academically selective institutions to benefit larger numbers of talented minority students.

6. Progress has been made in narrowing test-score gaps between minority students and other students, but gaps remain.

A frequently asked question is: Are we getting anywhere? Data on average test scores in *Reclaiming the Game* are encouraging. At a group of liberal-arts colleges and universities examined in 1976 and 1995, average combined SAT test scores for minority students rose roughly 130 points at the liberal-arts colleges and roughly 150 points at the research universities. Test scores for other students rose, too, but by much smaller amounts (roughly 30 points at the liberal-arts colleges and roughly 70 points at the research universities). Test-score gaps narrowed over this period, and the average rank-in-class of minority students on college graduation improved even more than one would have predicted on the basis of test scores alone. As anyone who has studied campus life can attest, there are also many impressionistic signs of progress. Minority students are more involved in a wide range of activities, and increasing numbers of children of minority students of an earlier day are now reaching the age where they are beginning to enroll as "second generation" college students. Graduates are also increasingly making their presence known in the professions and business world.

Still, test-score gaps remain (of roughly 100 to 140 points in the private colleges and universities for which we have data), and so there is still more progress to be made. That is hardly surprising, given the deep-seated nature of the factors that impede academic opportunity and achievement among minority groups—including the fact that a very large proportion of such students continue to attend primary and secondary schools that are underfinanced, insufficiently challenging, and often segregated. It would be naive to expect that a problem as long in the making as the racial divide in educational preparation could be eradicated in a generation or two.

7. There are alternative ways of pursuing diversity, but all substitutes for race-sensitive admissions have serious limitations.

Many of us have a strong appetite for apparently painless alternatives, and it is natural to look for ways to achieve "diversity" without directly confronting the emotion-laden issue of race. Several alternatives to race-sensitive admissions have been suggested. For example, colleges and universities have been urged to:

- Focus on the economically disadvantaged. The argument is that, since racial minorities are especially likely to be poor, racial diversity could be promoted in this way (an approach sometimes referred to as "classbased affirmative action"). The results, however, would not be what some people might expect. Several studies have shown that there are simply very few minority candidates for admission to academically selective institutions who are *both* poor and academically qualified.
- Adopt a "percentage plan" whereby all high-school students in a state who graduate in the top X percent of their classes are automatically guaranteed a place in one of the state's universities. In states like Texas, where the secondary-school system is highly segregated, that approach can yield a significant number of minority admissions at the undergraduate level (although the actual effects, even at the undergraduate level, have been shown by the social scientists Marta Tienda and John F. Kain to be more limited than many have suggested). Moreover, the process is highly mechanical. Students in the top X percent are not simply awarded "points," as the undergraduate program at the University of Michigan does. Rather, they are given automatic admission without any prior scrutiny, and without any consideration of the fact that some high schools are much stronger academically than others.

Even if one considered the top-X-percent plan to be viable at state institutions, it could not work at all at private institutions, which admit from national and international pools of applicants and are so selective that they must turn down the vast majority who apply—including very large numbers of students who graduate at or near the top of their secondary-school classes.

Private institutions could not conceivably adopt a policy that would automatically give admission to students in the top X percent of their class at the hundreds and hundreds of schools—worldwide—from which they attract applicants.

The top-X-percent plan is also entirely ineffective at the professional and graduate-school level, because (like selective undergraduate colleges) these schools have national and international applicant pools, with no conceivable "reference group" of colleges to which they could possibly give such an admission guarantee. Even if there were a set of undegraduate colleges whose top graduates would be guaranteed admission to certain professional schools, the result would not represent any marked degree of racial diversity. For example, if the top 10 percent of students in the academically selective colleges and universities studied in *Reclaiming the Game* were offered admission to a professional school (an unrealistically high percentage given the intensely competitive nature of the admissions process), only 3 percent of the students included in that group would be underrepresented minorities—and, of course, only some modest fractions of those students would be interested even in applying to such programs. If we are examining a top-5-percent plan, the minority component of the pool would be about *one-half of 1 percent.* Without some explicit consideration of race, professional schools (and Ph.D. programs) that ordinarily admit a significant number of their students from selective colleges would simply not be able to enroll a diverse student body.

Other troubling questions include: Do we really want to endorse an admissions approach that depends on de facto segregation at the secondary-school level? Do we want to impose an arbitrary and mechanical admissions standard—based on fixed rank-in-class—on a process that should involve careful consideration of all of an applicant's qualifications as well as thoughtful attention to the overall characteristics of the applicant pool?

- Place heavy weight on "geographic distribution" and so-called "experiential" factors, such as a student's ability to overcome obstacles and handicaps of various kinds, or the experience of living in a home where a language other than English is spoken. The argument here is that, if special attention were given to those and analogous criteria, then a sizable pool of qualified minority students would automatically be created.

But, as we have mentioned, colleges have been using precisely such criteria for many decades, and they have discovered—not surprisingly—that there are large numbers of very competitive "majority" candidates in all of the suggested categories. For example, if a student's home language is Russian, Polish, Arabic, Korean, or Hebrew, will that be weighted by a college as strongly as Spanish? If not, then the institutions will clearly be giving conscious preference to a group of underrepresented minority students—Hispanic students—in a deliberate way that explicitly takes ethnicity (or, in other cases, race) into account.

Similar issues arise with respect to other experiential categories, as well as geographic distribution. There is no need to speculate about (or experiment with) such approaches, because colleges have already had nearly a half-century of experience applying them, and there is ample evidence that the hoped-for results, in terms of minority representation, are not what many people now suggest or claim. Moreover, insofar as such categories were to become surreptitious gateways for minority students, they would soon run the risk of breeding cynicism, and probably inviting legal challenges.

All of the indirect approaches just described pose serious problems. Nor can they be accurately described as "race-neutral." "They have all been conceived with the clear goal (whether practicable or not) of producing an appreciable representation of minority students in higher education. In some cases, they involve the conscious use of a kind of social engineering decried by critics of race-sensitive admissions.

Surely the best way to achieve racial diversity is to acknowledge candidly that minority status is one among many factors that can be considered in an admissions process designed to judge individuals on a case-by-case basis. We can see no reason why a college or university should be compelled to experiment with—and "exhaust"—all suggested alternative approaches before it can turn to a carefully tailored race-sensitive policy that focuses on individual cases. The alternative approaches are susceptible to systematic analysis, based on experience and empirical investigation. A preponderance of them have been tested for decades. All can be shown to be seriously deficient. Indeed, if genuinely race-neutral (and educationally appropriate) methods were available, colleges and universities would long ago have gladly embraced them.

8. Reasonable degrees of institutional autonomy should be permitted—accompanied by a clear expectation of accountability.

As the courts have recognized in other contexts (for example, in giving reasonable deference to administrative agencies), a balance has to be struck between Judicial protection of rights guaranteed to all of us by the Constitution and the desirability of giving a presumption of validity to the judgements of those with special knowledge, experience, and closeness to the actual decisions being made. The widely acclaimed heterogeneity of the American system of higher education has permitted much experimentation in admissions, as in other areas, and has discouraged the kinds of government-mandated uniformity that we find in many other parts of the world. Serious consideration should be given to the disadvantages of imposing too many "dos" and "don'ts" on admissions policies.

The case for allowing a considerable degree of institutional autonomy in such sensitive and complex territory is inextricably tied, in our view, to a clear acceptance by colleges and universities of accountability for the policies they elect and the ways such policies are given effect. There is, to be sure, much more accountability today than many people outside the university world recognize. Admissions practices are highly visible and are subject to challenge by faculty members, trustees and regents, avid investigative reporters, disappointed applicants, and the public at large. Colleges and universities operate in more of a "fishbowl" environment than the great majority of other private and public entities. Nonetheless, we favor even stronger commitments by colleges and universities to monitor closely how specific admissions policies work out in practice. Studies of outcomes should be a regular part of college and university operations, and if it is found, for example, that minority students (or other students) accepted with certain test scores or other qualifications are consistently doing poorly, then some change in policy—or some change in the personnel responsible for administering the stated policy—may well be in order.

That point was made with special force by a very conservative friend of ours, Charles Exley, former chairman and CEO of NCR Corporation and a onetime trustee of Wesleyan University. In a pointed conversation that one of us (Bowen) will long remember, Exley explained that he held essentially the same view that we hold concerning who should select the criteria and make admissions decisions. "I would probably not admit the same class that you would admit, even though I don't know how different the classes would be," he said. "You will certainly make mistakes," he went on, "but I would much rather live with your errors than with those that will inevitably result from the imposition of more outside constraints, including legislative and judicial interventions." And then, with the nicest smile, he concluded: "And, if you make *too* many mistakes, the trustees can always fire you!"

9. Race matters profoundly in America; it differs fundamentally from other "markers" of diversity, and it has to be understood on its own terms.

We believe that it is morally wrong and historically indefensible to think of race as "just another" dimension of diversity. It is a critically important dimension, but it is also far more difficult than others to address. The fundamental reason is that racial classifications were used in this country for more than 300 years in the most odious ways to deprive people of their basic rights. The fact that overt discrimination has now been outlawed should not lead us to believe that race no longer matters. As the legal scholar Ronald Dworkin has put it, "the worst of the stereotypes, suspicions, fears, and hatreds that still poison America are color-coded. . . .

The aftereffects of this long history continue to place racial minorities (and especially African-Americans) in situations in which embedded perceptions and stereotypes limit opportunities and create divides that demean us all. This social reality, described with searing precision by the economist Glenn C. Loury in *The Anatomy of Racial Inequality,* explains why persistence is required in efforts to overcome, day by day, the vestiges of our country's "unlovely racial history." We believe that it would be perverse in the extreme if, after many generations when race was used in the service of blatant discrimination, colleges and universities were now to be prevented from considering race at all, when, at last, we are learning how to use nuanced forms of race-sensitive admissions to improve education for everyone and to diminish racial disparities.

The former Attorney General Nicholas Katzenbach draws a sharp distinction between the use of race to exclude a group of people from educational opportunity ("racial discrimination") and the use of race to enhance learning for all students, thereby serving the mission of colleges and universities chartered to serve the public good. No one contends that white students are being excluded by any college or university today simply because they are white.

NO

Dinesh D'Souza

A World Without
Racial Preferences

If color-blind admissions policies are put into effect," I was warned at a recent debate on the topic, "the number of black students at the most selective colleges and universities would plummet to around 2 percent. Should we as a society be willing to live with such an outcome?"

I hesitated, and in that moment of hesitation, my interlocutor saw his opportunity. "Well, should we?" he pressed.

The answer, it turns out, is yes. But it is an answer that supporters of the current system consider outrageous. They take for granted that the only possible response is "Of course not." So, for example, two pillars of the education establishment, former Princeton president William Bowen and former Harvard president Derek Bok, have just published a widely reviewed defense of affirmative action, *The Shape of the River: Long-Term Consequences of Considering Race in College and University Admissions.* They insist that some form of preferential recruitment is inevitable to avoid the unthinkable outcome of very few African Americans at top-ranked universities. "The adoption of a strict race-neutral standard would reduce black enrollment at . . . academically selective colleges and universities by between 50 and 70 percent," Bowen and Bok observe. "The most selective colleges would experience the largest drops in black enrollment."

These numbers are more or less correct. But what they actually illustrate is not the unacceptable future but the unconscionable present: the magnitude of racial preferences currently in effect. Affirmative action in practice does not mean—as its supporters claim—considering two equally qualified applicants and giving the minority candidate the nod. It has instead come to mean admitting Hispanic and African-American students with grade-point averages of 3.2 and SAT scores of 1100, while turning away white and Asian-American applicants with GPAs of 4.0 and SAT scores of 1300. Far from waging a war against discrimination, advocates such as Bowen and Bok find themselves waging a war against merit. And far from vindicating idealism and promoting social justice, they find themselves cynically subverting the principle of equal rights under the law to the detriment of society as a whole.

From *The Weekly Standard,* November 30/December 7, 1998, pp. 37–38, 40–42. Copyright © 1998 by Weekly Standard. Reprinted with permission.

Before we can decide whether it is simply too embarrassing to permit elite institutions to enroll a very small percentage of blacks or other minorities, we must first ask the question of what produces the racial disparities that so unsettle us and that seem to require affirmative action to counteract. Consider the example of the National Basketball Association. It is no secret that the NBA does not "look like America": African Americans, who are 12 percent of the population, make up 79 percent of the players, while Jews and Asian Americans are conspicuously scarce.

Of course, one never hears demands that the NBA establish a preferential recruitment program for Jews or Asians. But before the notion is dismissed as simply silly, it is instructive to ask why. The answer is presumably that it is merit and not discrimination that produces the racial imbalance on the basketball court. If the coaches hire the best passers and shooters, we tend to think, it shouldn't matter if some ethnic groups dominate and others are hardly represented.

The lesson to be drawn from this example is that inequalities in racial outcomes that are produced by merit are far more defensible than inequalities produced by favoritism or discrimination. And when we turn from the NBA to America's elite colleges and universities, we discover a similar result. Ethnic inequalities are the result not of biased selection procedures but of unequal performance on the part of different groups.

Affirmative action has traditionally been defended as necessary to fight discrimination. But has anyone demonstrated that the blacks and Hispanics preferentially admitted to the best universities were in fact victims of discrimination? Has anyone uncovered at Berkeley or Princeton bigoted admissions officers seeking to exclude minorities? And is there any evidence that the white and Asian-American students refused admission were discriminating against anyone? The answer to these questions is no, no, and no. No one has even alleged unfairness of this sort.

There was, at one time, an attempt by advocates of affirmative action to argue for racial and cultural bias in the SAT and other standardized tests that most elite universities require their applicants to take. This argument, however, has collapsed in recent years, and even Bowen and Bok admit that it is no longer possible to claim that the SAT discriminates against blacks or other minorities. In *The Shape of the River,* they try to confuse the issue by insisting on the obvious point that standardized-test scores "do not predict who will be a civic leader or how satisfied individuals will be with their college experience or with life." But they are at last forced to the chagrined confession: "Almost all colleges have found that when they compare black and white undergraduates who enter with the same SAT scores, blacks earn *lower* grades than whites, not just in their first year but throughout their college careers. . . . Tests like the SAT do not suffer from prediction bias."

This is not to say that the test describes genetic or biological ability. It merely measures differences in academic preparation, and Bowen and Bok acknowledge that the low black enrollments at elite universities that affirmative action policies seek to remedy are primarily produced by "continuing disparities in pre-collegiate academic achievements of black and white students." On those measures of merit that selective colleges use to decide who gets in, not all groups perform equally.

For the civil-rights leadership, these results have come as a nasty surprise. The movement led by Martin Luther King Jr. originally placed itself on the side of merit in opposition to racial nepotism. If laws and public policies were allowed to judge solely on the basis of individual merit, King repeatedly promised, we would see social rewards in America widely dispersed among groups.

In the generation since King's death, it is this premise—that equality of rights for individuals would invariably produce equality of results for groups—that has proved false. The dismaying truth is that even merit sometimes produces ethnic inequality. Consequently it is hardly surprising that some who manned the barricades alongside King now insist that merit is the new guise in which the old racism manifests itself. It is now fashionable for advocates of affirmative action to place the term "merit" in quotation marks or to speak sarcastically of "so-called merit." Their main objection is that merit selection is not producing the outcomes they desire, and their enthusiasm for affirmative action can be attributed to their rediscovery of the blessings of nepotism.

⋰⟨⊙⟩⋱

Meanwhile, behind the scenes, there has been underway a fascinating debate about why merit produces such ethnic inequality. Two views have dominated the debate. The first is the "bell-curve" position, put forward most publicly in recent years by Charles Murray and Richard Herrnstein, which implies that there may be natural or biological differences between groups that would account for their unequal performance on indices of merit. The second is the traditionally liberal position, which insists that when group differences in academic achievement and economic performance exist, they have been artificially created by social deprivation and-racism.

⋰⟨⊙⟩⋱

These two views have functioned like a see-saw: When one goes up, the other goes down. In the early part of this century, most people took for granted that there were natural differences between the races and that these accounted for why some groups were advanced and others relatively backward. This view was fiercely attacked in the middle of this century by liberals who argued that it was unreasonable and unconscionable to contend that natural deficiencies were the cause of blacks' doing poorly when blacks were subjected to so much legal and systematic discrimination, especially in the South.

The liberal view was entirely plausible, which is why the biological explanation was largely discarded. But the liberal view has begun to collapse in recent years, precisely as it proved unable to explain the world that resulted from its triumph. Consider a single statistic: Data from the college board show that, year after year, whites and Asian Americans who come from families earning less than $15,000 a year score higher on both the verbal and math sections of the SAT than African Americans from families earning more than $60,000 a year.

This stunning statistic, whose accuracy is unquestioned by anyone in this debate, is sufficient by itself to destroy the argument of those who have repeated for years that the SAT is a mere calibration of socioeconomic privilege. But it is equally devastating to the liberal attribution of black disadvantage to racial discrimination. Even if discrimination were widespread, how could it operate in such a way as to make poor whites and Asians perform better on math tests than upper-middle-class blacks?

On this question, most advocates of affirmative action do not know how to react. Some simply refuse to discuss the implications of the evidence. Others, like Nathan Glazer, seem to adopt a private conviction of the veracity of the bell-curve explanation. A few years ago, in a review of Murray and Herrnstein in the *New Republic,* Glazer seemed to accept the existence of intrinsic differences in intelligence between the races—while objecting to any mention of the fact in public.

In more recent articles, Glazer has reversed his longtime criticism of affirmative action and said he is now willing to bend admissions standards to avoid the distressing outcome of very few blacks in the best universities. Glazer's second thoughts about affirmative action point to something often missed in such debates, for if the bell-curve thesis is correct, then it in fact constitutes the strongest possible argument *in favor* of affirmative action.

If there are natural differences in ability between ethnic groups that cannot easily be eradicated, then it makes sense for those of us who do not want America to be a racial caste society to support preferential programs that would prevent the consolidation of enduring group hierarchies. Forced, by the collapse of the liberal view, to accept natural inequality, Glazer unsurprisingly now treats blacks as a handicapped population that cannot be expected to compete against other groups.

⚜

But there is, in fact, a third possible view of racial inequality—a view advanced by Thomas Sowell and me and others who find profoundly condescending and degrading the notion that blacks require a "special Olympics" of their own. Basically, we contend that there are cultural or behavioral differences between groups. These differences can be observed in everyday life, measured by the techniques of social science, and directly correlated with academic achievement and economic performance. Even *The Black-White Test Score Gap,* a recent study by two noted liberal scholars, Christopher Jencks and Meredith Phillips, proves upon careful reading to implicitly endorse this cultural view. Jencks and Phillips make all the appropriate genuflections to racial pieties, but they are courageously seeking to make the cultural argument more palatable to liberals.

A few years ago, a Stanford sociologist named Sanford Dornbusch was puzzled at claims that Asian Americans do especially well in math because of some presumed genetic advantage in visual and spatial ability. Dornbusch did a comparative study of white, black, Hispanic, and Asian-American students in San Francisco and concluded that there was a far more obvious reason for the superior performance of Asian Americans: They study harder. Asian Americans simply spend a lot more time doing homework their peers.

~◉~

Of course, this sort of finding leaves unanswered the question of why they study harder. The causes are no doubt complex, but one important factor seems to be family structure. It is obvious that a two-parent family has more time and resources to invest in disciplining children and supervising their study than does a single-parent family. For Asian Americans, the illegitimacy rate in this country is approximately 2 percent. For African Americans, it's nearly 70 percent.

Such a huge difference cannot easily be corrected. Indeed, in a free society, public policy is limited in its ability to transform behavior in the private sphere. Still, while not reverting to the discredited liberal position, the cultural view of racial inequality is at least more hopeful than the bell-curve acceptance of ineradicable difference: We cannot change our genes, but we can change our behavior.

One thing is clear: Racism is no longer the main problem facing blacks or any other group in America today. Even if racism were to disappear overnight, this would do nothing to improve black test scores, increase black entrepreneurship, strengthen black families, or reduce black-on-black crime. These problems have taken on a cultural existence of their own and need to be confronted in their own terms.

The difficult task is rebuilding the cultural capital of the black community, and the role of black scholars, black teachers, black parents, and black entrepreneurs is crucial. The rest of us cannot be leaders, but we can be cheerleaders. Rather than try to rig the numbers to make everyone feel better, we are better off focusing our collective attention on developing the skills of young African Americans at an early age so that they can compete effectively with others in later life.

~◉~

So why doesn't this obvious solution win broad support? In his new book, *A Dream Deferred: The Second Betrayal of Black Freedom in America,* Shelby Steele argues that affirmative action is popular with black and white elites because it serves the purposes of both groups. White elites get to feel morally superior, thus recovering the ethical high ground lost by the sins of the past, and black elites enjoy unearned privileges that they understandably convince themselves they fully deserve. (In *The Shape of the River,* Bowen and Bok devote several chapters to proving the obvious point that blacks who go to Ivy League schools derive financial benefits in later life as a result and are generally satisfied with attending Yale instead of a community college.)

Steele's book bristles with the psychological insights that are his distinctive contribution to the race debate. White liberals, Steele argues (and he might as well be speaking directly of Bowen and Bok), are quite willing to assume general blame for a racist society causing black failures—so long as it's the careers of other people, all the qualified Asian-American and white students rejected from Harvard and Princeton, that are sacrificed in order to confer benefits on blacks and win for liberals recognition as the white saviors of the black race.

⚬⟨◈⟩⚬

What Steele is doing—and it has drawn considerable criticism from reviewers—is something that advocates of affirmative action have always done: questioning the motives of the other side. For years, conservatives have treated liberals as well meaning in their goals though mistaken in their means. And during that same period, liberals have treated conservatives as greedy, uncaring racists. By asking advocates of preferences what's in it for them, Steele unmasks the self-interest that frequently hides behind the banners of equality, diversity, and social uplift.

Steele's main objective is to show that neither the black nor the white elites have an interest in asking fundamental questions: Isn't color-blindness the only principle that is consistent with the fundamental principles of American society? Isn't equality of rights under the law the only workable basis for a multiracial society? Is the black community well served in the long term by a public policy that treats them as an inferior people incapable of competing with others?

Advocates of racial preferences "offer whites moral absolution for their sins and blacks concrete benefits that are hard to turn down," Steele observed to me a few weeks before the recent electoral victory of a referendum abolishing affirmative action in Washington state. "I think we are going to lose because our side has only one thing to offer, and that is moral principle." I ruefully agreed that the scales were tipped in precisely that way. But the astonishing triumph of the referendum in Washington by a comfortable majority—like the triumph of a similar measure two years ago in California—shows that we should not underestimate the power of moral principle in American politics.

When the issue is posed in the basic vocabulary of right and wrong—a lexicon that is utterly incomprehensible to Bowen and Bok—the tortured rationalizations of affirmative-action advocates collapse and the common-sense moral instinct of the American people tends to prevail. There is no cause for conservatives to lose their nerve. The election in 2000 could be the moment when color-blindness is at last the issue on the ballot in many states and at the center of the Republican party's agenda.

POSTSCRIPT

Should Race Be a Consideration in College Admissions?

When we reduce the admissions issue to "well, if it comes down to the admissions committee having to choose between a white student and a black student with identical records, then the black student will be admitted," we lose sight of the larger picture of race-sensitive admissions. That picture is best understood in light of all preferences. Colleges and universities "select" students based on many criteria to insure a diverse student body. Both white parents and minority parents want the best opportunities for their children. Clearly, race has become a contentious college admissions issue for whites. Historically, it has been an issue of exclusion for blacks. Whites have now been forced to examine an advantage previously taken for granted. That privilege was not examined before affirmative action programs.

Preferential treatment in college admissions is not limited to racial minorities. Indeed, there is a long history of preference for children of alumni ("legacies") and athletes. The selection process of qualified applicants leads many colleges to admit lesser-qualified men (at former woman's schools), and lesser-qualified women at traditionally men's colleges. A recent *Princeton Review Guide to the 331 Best Colleges (2001 edition)* makes reference to a selective college known from engineering, "Underrepresented minorities and women are high on the list of desirables in the applicant pool here, and go through the admissions process without any hitches if reasonably well qualified." Clearly middle-class white women, along with underrepresented minorities, benefit directly from this admissions policy. Is there a lack of outcry dealing with white women? Does the argument for merit in these cases exist? Are the public reactions concerning "reverse discrimination" used only to contest race-sensitive policies?

Further reading about race and selective college admissions can be found in *The Wall Street Journal* (April 25, 2003) "College Ties: For Groton Grads, Academics Aren't Only Keys to Ivies," by Daniel Golden. "The Birth of a New Institution," by Geoffrey Kabaservice in the Yale alumni magazine, *Yale* (December 1999) looks at how two Yale presidents utilized minority admissions to strengthen the school. There are numerous guides to colleges and universities that are available to students. They can be used for data on race and higher education. Routinely, journals including *The Chronicle of Higher Education* and *Journal of Blacks in Higher Education* offer data and contemporary accounts of race and college admissions.

ISSUE 13

Is a Multicultural Curriculum Essential for Advancing Education?

YES: Gary B. Nash, "The Great Multicultural Debate," in *Contention* (1992)

NO: Diane Ravitch, "Multiculturalism: E Pluribus Plures," *The American Scholar* (59, no. 3, Summer 1990)

ISSUE SUMMARY

YES: Gary B. Nash, a historian, sketches the development of American history over the past century, as the research of a new generation of historians sheds light on issues such as class conflict, labor relations, gender roles, and race relations. Nash views the teaching of history with a multicultural emphasis as a positive step in American education.

NO: Diane Ravitch, historian of education, fears the incipient weakening of a common knowledge base in American history that is taught in American public schools. This is caused by a particularistic multiculturalism, not the pluralistic multiculturalism that promotes a broad interpretation of a common American culture. Particularists deny the existence of a common American culture, and this sentiment, which now has political influence, has had an adverse impact on the curriculum of public schools.

Given the racial and ethnic diversity of American society, it is inevitable that the value conflicts and cultural pressures of daily life find their way into the classroom. Indeed, the curriculum of public schools has become the early twenty-first century litmus test of the assimilation versus pluralism debate discussed in the first section of this book. Today, multiculturalism plays host to another form of the debate. No one denies that America is a multicultural society, but how, when, and to what extent multiculturalism can and should be taught is controversial.

Gary Nash pushes for a multicultural curriculum that confronts racial and ethnic conflicts of America's past. Older conceptualizations of history are now being reexamined because of four developments, including the increasing diversity of scholars, the influences of the civil rights and other social movements, the internationalization of economics, politics, and cultural affairs, and the continued diversification of the classroom that reflects the surge of late twentieth century new immigrants.

Mutual respect is at the heart of genuine multiculturalism for Nash. Clearly, he does not see multiculturalism as a threat to national unity. His view is thoroughly inclusive. For Nash, a multicultural curriculum is absolutely necessary for a complete education in American society.

Diane Ravitch recognizes the importance of multiculturalism in American education, and, in the context of the search for truth, finds it necessary. While she argues that public schools should primarily concentrate on values and ideas that promote national unity, she believes that an overemphasis on multicultural curricula can lead to a Balkanization of American culture. History, Ravitch writes, is a search for truth. Nevertheless, local and sometimes national interest groups have always affected the history we teach our children. Her caution with multiculturalism today reflects the view that Afrocentrism along with other perspectives that recognize diversity undermine our national unity.

To examine this issue closely, readers may want to incorporate some of the themes from Issue 1, "Do We Need a Common American Identity?" The belief in assimilation forces one to recognize a dominant culture that accommodates subordinate groups and subordinate cultures. We could represent it as $A + B + C = A$. Ravitch's fear is that too much teaching of multiculturalism will result in $A + B + C = A + B + C$. Thus, a common identity will be lost in the education process. While the assimilationist perspective helps us to gain insight into the attempt that many experience to become part of American culture, it may slight or even ignore critical areas of the American experience. So, readers should look to organize their thoughts on a multicultural curriculum around the question. How should racial and ethnic diversity and national identity be taught?

Consistently, students will encounter the terms "diversity" and "multiculturalism" throughout their education. Essentially, diversity is a representation of people that exemplifies cultural and social differences. Multiculturalism, as used in this issue, is the inclusion in scholarship, including theory, analytical perspectives, and data of groups that have been historically underrepresented in educational arenas.

What areas of agreement do you find between Nash and Ravitch? Where do they disagree with regard to multicultural curriculum? Why is this an important educational issue today? To what extent has your education included the study of multiculturalism and diversity? What influence has this exposure had on your idea of American culture? Students interested in further research may investigate the process of how curricular policy is determined.

Gary B. Nash

 **YES**

The Great Multicultural Debate

T he civil rights battles of the '50s and '60s were fought in the courtroom, says David Nicholson of the *Washington Post*, "but in the '90s the struggle for cultural parity will take place in the classroom as blacks and other minorities seek to change what their children are taught."[1] Now, only two years into the decade, the swirling multicultural debate around the country is proving Nicholson correct. But the debate has gone far beyond the subject of what is taught and has led to some remarkable—and troubling—notions of what we are as a people and a society.

Often lost in the present furor is even an elementary sense of how far the writing and teaching of history have moved away from the male-oriented, Eurocentric, and elitist approaches that had dominated for so long at all levels of the American educational system. It is important to understand this because new calls for change often ignore what has already occurred in the rethinking and rewriting of history and, in so doing, sometimes prescribe new formulae that contain hidden dangers.

Reimagining the Past

Among academic historians, agreement is widespread today that history has been presented in a narrow and deeply distorted way, not just in the United States but in every country. In the 1930s, when he was writing *Black Reconstruction,* W. E. B. Du Bois wrote: "I stand at the end of this writing, literally aghast at what American historians have done to this field. . . . [It is] one of the most stupendous efforts the world ever saw to discredit human beings, an effort involving universities, history, science, social life, and religion."[2] Few white historians would have agreed with Du Bois at the time, for in fact he was attacking their work. But a half-century later, the white president of the Organization of American Historians, Leon Litwack, agreed with this assessment. In his presidential address in 1987, Litwack charged that "no group of scholars was more deeply implicated in the miseducation of American youth and did more to shape the thinking of generations of Americans about race and blacks than historians."[3]

From *Contention,* 59, no. 3, Summer 1990, pp. 337–354. Copyright © 1990 by Gray Nash. Reprinted with permission of the Author.

The narrow and distorted lenses through which historians looked for years—which in the main reflected the dominant biases of white, Protestant America—extended far beyond the history of black Americans. Du Bois would surely have been equally dismayed if he had read one of the most widely used books in Western Civilization courses in the 1960s, where the much honored British historian, Hugh Trevor-Roper, magisterially proclaimed that it was useless to study African history because this would only be to inquire into "the unrewarding gyrations of barbarous tribes . . . whose chief function in history . . . is to show to the present an image of the past from which, by history, it has escaped."[4]

Similar mental constructions prevailed in regard to Native American history. In introducing Douglas Leach's history of King Philip's War in 1676, the bloodiest Indian war of the seventeenth century in North America, Samuel Eliot Morison, writing in 1958, instructed readers how to view both colonial—Indian relations and the decolonization movements in the Third World after World War II: "In view of our recent experiences of warfare, and of the many instances today of backward peoples getting enlarged notions of nationalism and turning ferociously on Europeans who have attempted to civilize them, this early conflict of the same nature cannot help but be of interest."[5]

The paradigmatic shift in the writing of history is far from complete, but some of those who currently protest about Eurocentric or racist history take little account of how resolutely the present generation of historians—scholars and teachers alike—have come to grips with older conceptualizations of history. Academic historians, most of them detached from what is going on in the primary and secondary schools of the country unless they have school age children enrolled in public schools, are often puzzled by the furor over the question of "whose history shall we teach" because they have watched—and participated in—wholesale changes in their own discipline in the last thirty years or so. African American history, women's history, and labor history are taught in most colleges and universities; Asian American, Hispanic American, and Native American history are taught in many. These courses are built on an outpouring of scholarship in this generation.

African American history can be taken as an instructive example. Even fifteen years ago, John Hope Franklin, author of the leading textbook in African American history, wrote of "a most profound and salutary change in the approach to the history of human relations in the United States," and he noted that in the process of this change "the new Negro history has come into its own."[6] Since 1977, this blossoming of black history has continued unabated. In compiling a bibliography of African American history for just the period from 1765 to 1830 for the forthcoming *Harvard Guide to Afro-American History,* I tracked down over 200 books and more than 400 articles published since 1965. The proliferation of scholarship for the period after 1830 is even greater. When the *Harvard Guide* is completed, it will detail thousands of books, articles, and doctoral dissertations—an enormous flowering of scholarship.

In women's history, the amount and range of scholarship—and sophisticated courses built upon it—is equally impressive. So too, younger scholars are building on the work of a few old hands to create the knowledge for a thorough understanding of the history, literature, art, music and values of Native Americans, Asian Americans, and other groups. In fact, among professional historians, the big debate is not about the need to recapture the lost past of so many groups and so many struggles over power and wealth in American society and so many neglected parts of world history but about whether this quest, in going so far, has shattered the coherence and usability of history.

In the current atmosphere of heated debate, it is worth some reflection on why and how change has occurred in the writing of history. Four developments have intersected to cause a major transformation. First—and largely forgotten in the current debates—is the wholesale change in the recruitment of professional historians, the people who do historical scholarship, teach at the collegiate level, and, ultimately, are responsible for the textbooks used in the schools. Before World War II, professional historians were drawn almost exclusively from the ranks of white, male, Protestant, and upper-class society. From their perspective, it was entirely fitting that they should be the keepers of the past because they believed that only those of the highest intellect, the most polished manners, and the most developed aesthetic taste could stand above the ruck and look dispassionately at the annals of human behavior. Such a view conformed precisely to the centuries-old view of the elite that ordinary people were ruled by emotion and only the wealthy and educated could transcend this state and achieve disinterested rationality. Pitted against this thoroughly dominant group since the early nineteenth century was a small number of women, African Americans, and white radicals who worked without much recognition as they tried to create alternative histories.

Small cracks in the fortress of the historical profession began to appear in the 1930s as Jews struggled for a place in the profession. Peter Novick's book on the historical profession, *That Noble Dream: The "Objectivity Question" and the American Historical Profession,* gives a vivid picture of the way the profession grudgingly yielded to Jewish aspirations. When applying for his first teaching job, Richard Leopold—who would emerge as a major historian of diplomacy—was described by a graduate mentor at Harvard as "of course a Jew, but since he is a Princeton graduate, you may be reasonably certain he is not of the offensive type." Bert Lowenberg was described in a letter of recommendation as "by temperament and spirit . . . [he] measures up to the whitest Gentiles I know."[7]

Not until after World War II would more than a handful of Jews gain admission to the historical profession. By that time, the GI bill was opening the doors of higher education to broad masses of Americans. This rapidly enlarged and diversified the historians' guild. Religious barriers continued to fall and class barriers began to fall as well, though not without creating consternation in many quarters. At Yale, George Pierson, the chairman of the history department, wrote the university's president in 1957—in a period when the growth of American universities demanded thousands of newly trained professors—that while the doctoral program in English "still draws to a degree from the cultivated, professional, and well-to-do classes . . . by contrast, the subject of history seems to appeal on the whole to a lower social stratum." Pierson complained that "far too few of our history candidates are sons of professional men; far too many list their parent's occupation as janitor, watchman, salesman, grocer, pocketbook cutter, bookkeeper, railroad clerk, pharmacist, clothing cutter, cable tester, mechanic, general clerk, butter-and-egg jobber, and the like." Five years later, Carl Bridenbaugh, the president of the American Historical Association, lamented what he called "The Great Mutation" that he believed was undermining the profession. "Many of the younger practitioners of our craft, and those who are still apprentices, are products of lower middle-class or foreign origins, and their emotions not infrequently get in the way of historical reconstructions."[8]

The notion that lower-class and foreign-born backgrounds disabled apprentice historians by conditioning them to substitute emotion for reason was revived when racial and gender barriers began to fall in the 1960s. The historical profession had for many decades included a small number of notable women and African Americans, and an occasional Native American, Hispanic American, and Asian American. But women began to enter the profession in substantial numbers only in the 1960s, while members of racial minority groups have increased since that time only slowly. Charges that emotions outran analytic insight were again heard from members of the old guard, none of its members more vocal than Oscar Handlin, whose Jewish background had nearly stopped him from entry into the profession a generation before.[9] But by this time, the old guard had been swamped, and social history had surged forward to displace the traditional emphasis on male- and elite-centered political and institutional history and on intellectual history that rarely focused on the thought and consciousness of people who were not of European descent.

Given these changes in the composition of the profession, it is not surprising that new questions have been posed about the past—questions that never occurred to a narrowly constituted group of historians. The emphasis on conflict rather than consensus, on racism and exploitation, on history from the bottom up rather than the top down, on women as well as men, is entirely understandable as people whose history had never been written began recovering it for themselves. Step by step, new historians (including many white males) have constructed previously untold chapters of history and have helped to overcome the deep historical biases that afflicted the profession for many generations.

Sustaining and strengthening the transformation that was beginning to occur because of the different background of historians was the dramatic period of protest and reform that occurred in American society in the 1960s and 1970s. The struggles of women, people of color, and religious minorities to gain equal rights spurred many historians (many of whom were involved in these movements) to ask new questions about the role of race and gender relations in the nation's history and to examine racial minorities, women, and working people as integrally involved in the making of American society. They were not breaking new ground altogether; for many decades, reaching back to the early nineteenth century, individual scholars had tilled the fields of women's and minority history, and the events of the 1930s spurred interest in labor history. But their colleagues in the profession had offered little appreciation of their work, and certainly their efforts to recover the history of women and people of color rarely found its way into textbooks used at the primary, secondary, or even collegiate level.

A third development fueling the change in the writing and teaching of history has been the growing interdependence of the nations of the world. Especially in the public schools this has increased the awareness of the importance of studying the histories of many cultures and of teaching world history rather than simply the history of western civilization. The internationalization of economic, political, and cultural affairs has driven home the point to historians and teachers that a Eurocentric history that measures all progress and renders all historical judgments on the basis of the experience of one part of the world will not equip students for satisfactory adult lives in the twenty-first century.

Lastly, and crucially, teachers have seen the composition of their own classrooms change dramatically in the last two decades. The public schools especially have been repopulated with people of different skin shades, different native languages, different accents, and different cultures of origin. More than two thirds of the children in public schools in New York City, Houston, Dallas, Baltimore, San Francisco, Cleveland, and Memphis are not white. In Los Angeles, Chicago, Philadelphia, Detroit, San Antonio, Washington, D.C., El Paso, and New Orleans children of color occupy more than three quarters of all classroom seats in the public schools and in a few of these cities comprise more than 90 percent of all public schoolchildren.

Such a demographic revolution—accounted for by the century-long migration of rural southern African Americans to the cities and by the Immigration acts of 1965 and 1990 which have opened the doors especially to people from Asia and Latin America—reminds us that this nation has always been a rich mosaic of peoples and cultures. It reminds us also that we cannot begin to understand our history without recognizing the crucial role of racial and religious prejudice and exploitation in our past as well as the vital roles of people from many different ethnic, racial, and religious backgrounds in building American society and making American history. The more usable past that a new generation of historians had been creating since World War II became all the more imperative in the schools as new immigrants and people of color became numerically dominant in most of the large urban public school systems.

To what extent, then, has the presentation of history changed in the public schools? In 1979, reviewing American history textbooks as they had been written for schoolchildren from the early twentieth century forward, Frances FitzGerald concluded that "The texts of the sixties contain the most dramatic rewriting of history ever to take place in American schoolbooks."[10] In FitzGerald's view, one of the largest changes was in the textbooks' new presentation of the United States as a multiracial society—a signal revision brought about, in her view, more because of the pressure of school boards in cities with a high percentage of black and Hispanic students—Newark, New Jersey, and Detroit particularly—than because of the influence of new historical scholarship on writers of textbooks for the schools. Yet FitzGerald admitted that by the late 1970s, textbooks were far from cleansed of Eurocentric bias and represented a "compromise ... among the conflicting demands of a variety of pressure groups, inside and outside the school systems"—a compromise "full of inconsistencies." (Among which, she noted, was an almost absolute ban on any discussion of economic life, social and economic inequality, and violence and conflict in American life.)

Why was it that the flowering of social history in the universities that made such important gains in breaking through Eurocentric conceptualizations of American history and world history made only limited gains for the teaching of a less nationalistic, white-centered, hero-driven, and male-dominated history in the schools? In theory, the schools might have been expected to reflect the remarkable changes in historical scholarship. This proved not to be the case for several reasons. First, most teachers who ended up teaching social studies had only a smattering of history in their Bachelor of Arts education—a few courses or a minor for the large majority of them. Second, most teachers were trained at schools where the new scholarship was only palely represented because the 1970s were years in which new faculty appointments were few, especially in the state universities where most teachers are trained. Third, the books used in the schools, though often produced by professional historians, only cautiously incorporated the new social history of women, laboring people, and minorities because publishers who catered to a national market were far more timid than university presses about publishing history that radically revised our understanding of the past, especially the American past. Thus, by the early 1980s, the textbooks in United States history for the secondary schools reflected far less of the new scholarship than textbooks written for college survey classes.

If the 1960s and 1970s brought only a partial transformation of the curriculum, the 1980s have been a period in which the reconceptualization of history, as presented in the schools, has made impressive gains, even though it has had to struggle against a resurgent conservatism, inside and outside the historical profession, that opposes even the partial reforms of the last generation. The barrage of responses to the rewriting of history in the last generation confirms J. H. Plumb's remark that the "personal ownership of the past has always been a vital strand in the ideology of all ruling classes."[11]

The conservative opposition, growing out of the white backlash to the liberal programs of the Kennedy-Johnson era, was led from the top but it reverberated deep into the ranks of white blue-collar America. In the early 1970s, Jules Feiffer captured the disgruntlement of the man in the streets in a cartoon about the white hard-hat worker who complained: "When I went to school I learned that George Washington never told a lie, slaves were happy on the plantation, the men who opened the West were giants, and we won every war because God was on our side. But where my kid goes to school he learns that Washington was a slaveowner, slaves hated slavery, the men who opened the West committed genocide, and the wars we won were victories for U.S. imperialism. No wonder my kid's not an American. They're teaching him some other country's history." Feiffer's cartoon captured the essence of Plumb's observation that history is a powerful weapon traditionally in the arsenal of the upper class: even an elitist, male-dominated, Eurocentric history appealed to the white working class because, while they were largely excluded from it, they were also the beneficiaries of it relative to women and people of color.

In the last decade, some members of the historical profession have taken stands much like Feiffer's blue-collar white parent. Articles began to appear about 1980 complaining about the "crisis in history"—a crisis, it was argued, caused by the rise of the new social history that traced the historical struggles and contributions of the many groups that had attracted little notice from most historians. C. Vann Woodward called for a return to narrative history because, he maintained, historians had lost their way in the welter of narrow quantitative and technical monographs that could not be synthesized into a broad interpretation of American history suitable for schoolchildren. Henry Steele Commager, Page Smith, and Bernard Bailyn similarly, advised their colleagues to get back to what historians were once noted for—absorbing narrative history. "The sheer disarray and confusion in the proliferation of analytical historiography" and the consequent loss of coherence in the master lessons of history was ruining the profession, Bailyn claimed in his American Historical Association address in 1981.[12] Most of these attacks, while genuinely concerned with how the enormous output of specialized scholarship could be digested and synthesized, were also seen by some as veiled attacks on the writing of the history of race, class, and gender relations in the history of the United States, Europe, and other parts of the world.

Thus, unlike in the period from the 1930s through the 1950s, when opposition to a reconceptualized history was expressed in terms of the unsuitability of the "outsiders" entering the profession, the current debates within the historical profession focus on the kind of history that is being written. The former outsiders are now within the academic gates, and it will not do any longer to attack them as sociologically and temperamentally unsuited for the work they do; rather, it is the history they write that has come under fire.

Opponents see the new history of women, laboring people, religious and racial minorities—sometimes lumped together under the rubric "social history"—as creating a hopelessly chaotic version of the past in which no grand synthesis or overarching themes are possible to discern and all coherence is lost. Of course, the old coherence and the old overarching themes were those derived from studying mostly the experiences of only one group of people in American society or in grounding all the megahistorical constructs in the Western experience. The contribution of the social historians is precisely to show that the overarching themes and the grand syntheses promulgated by past historians will not hold up when we broaden our perspectives and start thinking about the history of all the people who constituted American society, French society, or any other society. If the rise of women's history, African American history, labor history, and other group histories has created a crisis, we must ask "whose crisis?" For example, it is not a crisis for those interested in women's history because students of women's history know they have been vastly enriched by the last generation's scholarship. Moreover, they know that they have not only gained an understanding of the history of women and the family but in the process have obliged all historians to rethink the allegedly coherent paradigms for explaining the past that were derived from studying primarily the male experience. Nor is the current state of scholarship a crisis for those interested in African American history. With our knowledge so vastly enlarged in this area, we can see how correct Du Bois was in his assessment of a viciously distorted history presented to his generation, and we can go on with the work of reconstructing our history. The crisis, in fact, is the crisis of those whose monopolistic hold on the property of history has been shattered. The democratization of the study of history has undermined the master narratives of those who focused on the history of elites and particularly on grandiose syntheses of "the rise of American democracy" or the majestic "rise of Western civilization"—syntheses that, in spite of claims of objectivity, have been highly subjective and selective in the organizing questions asked, the evidence consulted, and the conclusions drawn.[13]

Joan Wallach Scott has argued that what is most disturbing to those who oppose the transformation of the historical profession in the last generation is that the new social history "has exposed the politics by which one particular viewpoint established its predominance."[14] Perhaps even more threatening, however, is the fact that the new history that pays close attention to gender, race, and class—and in so doing demonstrates that historical experiences varied with the position and power of the participants—promises to end forever any single interpretation or completely unified picture of American history (or the history of any society). By showing that different groups experienced a particular era or movement in starkly different ways, such terms as "The Jacksonian Age of the Common Man," the "Westward Movement," the "Progressive Era," or the post-1945 "Affluent Society" become only the tell-tale labels of a narrowly conceived history. What is not new is historians arguing over a particular movement or era. They have always argued—for example, about how radical or conservative the American Revolution was, about the profitability of slavery, or about the character of Progressivism. But these arguments took place within certain conceptually defined spaces where race and gender—and often class—were hardly regarded as usable categories.

Many traditional historians have found it painful to watch time-worn labels and characterizations of staple chapters of history vaporize under the impact of the new social history. To a historical profession dominated by white males, it was fun to argue, for example, about the origins of capitalism or about Turner's frontier thesis—whether the frontier truly was a crucible of democratic ideas and institution-creating behavior, a place where democratic values were continuously replenished. But to these historians, it is painfully unsettling—little fun at all—to consider the westward movement from the perspectives of Native Americans watching the wagon trains appearing from the east, Mexican ranchers and miners of the Southwest who found themselves demographically overwhelmed by the arriving Euroamericans, and Chinese contract laborers brought to the Pacific slope in the 1870s. For each of these groups the "frontier movement" was anything but heroic, anything but the westward "march of democracy." The deepest threat of a new history built upon a consideration of alternative experiences and perspectives is that it goes beyond incorporating notable figures who were women or people of color into the traditional storyline and searches for an altogether new storyline based on the historical experiences of the entire society under investigation.

Notwithstanding the sharp attacks on social history in recent years, multiculturalism—defined as the integration of the histories of both genders and people of all classes and racial or ethnic groups—has proceeded rapidly in the last few years. Multicultural curricula, "stressing a diversity of cultures, races, languages, and religions," and eliminating "ethnocentric and biased concepts and materials from textbook and classroom" have been adopted by school systems throughout the United States.[15] California has implemented an explicitly multicultural history-social science curriculum and many other states and individual school districts are following the same path, though with many variations.

Afrocentrism and Multiculturalism

How do these debates among professional historians connect with and affect the current debates over multiculturalism in the schools? And how do they allow us to appraise the rise of the Afrocentric perspective—a powerful movement within the public schools of the nation's largest cities? Perhaps it is not surprising, given how long it has taken for textbooks and school curricula to change that, while some members of the historical profession were resisting the movement toward a history that pays attention to gender, race, and class, some school reformers, especially those who were not part of the while majority, would find the reforms of the last two decades too slow and too fragmentary. For some educators, particularly a group of African Americans, the reforms were altogether wrongheaded, so that greater speed and thoroughness toward a multicultural approach was not at all desirable.

〜◉〜

Designed primarily to nurture self-esteem in black children by teaching them of the greatness of ancestral Africa and the contributions that Africans of the diaspora have made in many parts of the world, the Afrocentric approach is mostly the work of non-historians. Its most widely visible and vocal leaders are Molefi Kete Asante, whose degree is in rhetoric and communications; Asa Hilliard, whose degree is in education; and Leonard Jeffries, City College in the City University of New York, whose degree is in political science. Such educators surely cannot be faulted for regarding the dropout rates, low achievement scores, and lives blighted by drugs, violence, and early pregnancies of young African Americans as a national tragedy—and one that white America is largely uninterested in addressing. For these educators an Afrocentric curriculum that sees all knowledge and values from an African perspective is a cure. "The only issue for us," says Jeffrey Fletcher, who is part of the Black United Front for Education Reform in Oakland, California, "is how we can get out of this plight. It's like if you have someone around your throat choking you. It's nice to know about the baseball scores and other cultures, but the only thing you need to know is how to get those fingers off your neck."[16]

Afrocentrism is both an intellectual construction and a social-psychological remedy, and the two parts of it deserve separate discussion. As an intellectual construction, Molefi Kete Asante explains, Afrocentricity means "literally placing African ideals at the center of any analysis that involves African culture and behavior."[17] If this means homogenizing all of the many distinct African cultures and blending the entire gamut of religious, moral, and political ideals from Muslim Africa to Christian Africa to the animist rain forest dwellers and blurring the many distinct historical experiences over many centuries of culturally distinct peoples, then most scholars would have much to discuss with Asante. But if Afrocentrism means simply that any consideration of African history or the history of Africans of the diaspora must take account of the culture of the homeland and the way it was transmitted and maintained, at least partially, outside of Africa, then a great many scholars of the black experience—historians, ethnomusicologists, cultural anthropologists, art historians, linguistic scholars, and so forth—have been Afrocentrist for a long time. Certainly I was an Afrocentrist in this sense twenty years ago when I wrote *Red, White, and Black: The Peoples of Early America* because the main thrust of that book was to demonstrate that eastern North America in the seventeenth and eighteenth century was a merging ground for distinct cultures—European, African, and Indian (each distinctly divided within itself)—and that each culture had to be understood on its own terms if the interaction among them was to be fully comprehended.

Hence, Afrocentrists, in insisting on appreciating the integrity of African cultures and the persistence of many of their elements during and beyond the diaspora are building on a decades-old movement to overturn the European colonizers' mindset—a movement to which people of many ethnic and racial identities of the last generation have contributed in sometimes separate and sometimes intersecting ways. In this sense, the claim of Asante that "Few whites have ever examined their culture critically" and his claim that those who have, such as the British historian of Africa, Basil Davidson, have "been severely criticized by their peers," is discouragingly uninformed.[18] Asante's account of what he believes is stubbornly Eurocentric scholarship on African and African American history ignores the work of two generations of African and African American historians, including those who are English, French, Caribbean, and American and who are of various racial inheritances.

In building on a tradition of ridding ourselves of a Eurocentric approach, Afrocentrism as practiced by some of its proponents, virtually none of whom are historians, has produced some notable contradictions and ironies and a great many oversimplifications. For example, though striving to undermine the significance of Western culture, its most trumpeted message is that Egypt was black and African (a distortion and oversimplification in itself) and that black Egyptians taught the ancient Greeks most of what they knew, which is to presume that what the Greeks knew was significant. An irony in Afrocentrism is that its proponents take great pains to find great figures of Western culture, such as Alexander Dumas and Aleksandr Pushkin, who had an African ancestor, and claim them as evidence of the superiority of African culture. Since white America, for more than two centuries, defined anyone with any small portion of African ancestry as black, the Afrocentrists can chortle as they discover that Beethoven's great-grandfather may have been a Moorish soldier in the Spanish army (an assertion, first made by J. A. Rogers, a black journalist a generation ago but still far from proved).[19] But if Beethoven had a black ancestor, the Afrocentrists still have to live with the contradiction of celebrating someone who has been thoroughly a part of western culture while downgrading that culture in the interest of claiming the superiority of African culture as the place where modern science, mathematics, and other disciplines had their origin.

In its treatment of Egypt, Afrocentrists such as Asante and Hilliard are out of touch with most reputable scholarship on the ancient world and give precedence to a part of Africa with which most African Americans had little cultural connection. For Asante, the "Afrocentrist analysis reestablishes the centrality of the ancient Kemetic (Egyptian) civilization and the Nile Valley cultural complex as points of reference for an African perspective."[20] It is certainly true that most 19th- and 20th-century scholars in the West have taken Africans out of Egypt and taken Egypt out of Africa, relocating it in the Middle East. But in correcting this, following the work of the Senegalese Africanist Chiekh Anta Diop and more recently by using very selectively Martin Bernal's *Black Athena: The Afroasiatic Roots of Classical Civilization,* Afrocentrists have tried to turn all of the mixed-race Egyptians into African blacks and to make most of European civilization derivative from black Africa. Moreover, in arguing that the cultures of ancient Egypt and the Nile Valley are the main reference points for an African perspective, such Afrocentrists defy most of the scholarship of the last generation on most of the Africans of the diaspora, whose cultures in West Africa were hardly the same as the culture of the Nile. The *Portland African-American Baseline Essays,* the most comprehensive attempt to set forth an Afrocentric curriculum, clearly follow this misleading path, urging teachers to "identify Egypt and its civilization as a distinct African creation" (that is without Asian or European influences). The Social Studies essay devotes more than three times as much space to the history and culture of ancient Egypt as to the history and culture of West Africa in the period before the beginning of the Atlantic slave trade.[21]

The non-scholarly form of Afrocentrism, drawing on a long-established movement to stop measuring all things by the European cultural yardstick, has moved perilously close to holding up a new yardstick which measures all things by how nearly they approach an African ideal. When we get beyond labels and cultural yardstick waving, what will be enduringly important for those who wish to study the interaction of African peoples and Europeans, in whatever part of the world, is an ability to look through several sets of lenses. Most of us learned a long time ago that this was what good history and good anthropology are all about. It is hardly arguable that to understand African literature or African American history or Afro-Brazilian music one must have an understanding of African culture as well as the cultures with which Africans were interacting. Nor is it deniable that the stigmatizing of African culture and its derivative cultures of the diaspora has been an essential part of white supremacist thought and that it has been institutionalized in our culture and in the cultures of all societies where Europeans were the cultural arbiters. But Afrocentrism becomes a new and dangerous ethnocentrism of its own when it adopts the colonizers' old trick of arranging cultures on a continuum ranging from inferior to superior. It is this aspect of Afrocentrism that disturbs black scholars such as Henry Louis Gates, Jr., who decries such "ethnic fundamentalism" and attempts "to reduce the astonishing diversity of African cultures to a few simple-minded shibboleths."[22] As long ago as 1945, Emery Reves wrote in *The Anatomy of Peace:* "Nothing can distort the true picture of conditions and events in this world more than to regard one's own country [or culture] as the center of the universe and to view all things solely in their relationship to this fixed point."[23] We seem destined to relearn this lesson.

When Afrocentrism makes the leap from theory and scholarly perspective to a curricular prescription for the schools, its problems and dangers multiply. Asante believes that "most African-American children sit in classrooms yet are outside the information being discussed." If he means this statement to apply to modern mathematics, science, and computer skills, or even to reading and writing skills, and if the remedy is to learn about ancient Egyptian concepts of science and magic, then black children taught in an Afrocentric curriculum will not acquire the skills and knowledge without which they can move forward in modern society. In social studies classrooms, knowledge of African history and of the many rich and complex traditions in the period before contact with Europeans, can certainly awaken the interest of African American children (and other children too, one assumes) and can stimulate their sense of how African peoples, interacting with other societies, have been an essential part of the history of humankind. But getting beyond romantic notions of African history will require that they learn that ethnic and national identities have been stronger than pan-Africanism on the African continent, both before and after the long era of the slave trade and European colonization. Equally important, African American children, as much as any other children, need to learn about the history of many cultures and historical experiences. The ultimate goal of a multicultural education is to create mutual respect among students of different religions, races, and ethnic backgrounds by teaching them that rich cultural traditions have existed for centuries in every part of the world. "The natural inclination in people to fear and distrust what they find alien and strange," writes Robert K. Fullinwider, "is tempered by an education that makes students' religions, languages, customs, and values familiar to each other, thereby encouraging in students a sympathetic imagination, a generosity of spirit, and an openness to dialogue."[24]

Perhaps too much emphasis has been placed, in the Afrocentrist educators' program, on the power of pride in African ancestry. In itself, of course, ancestral pride and group pride, when kept in bounds, are conducive to a healthy sense of one's potential. For example, there is little doubt, as Roger Wilkins has written, that it was of great importance to the Civil Rights activists to assert "a human validity that did not derive from whites" and to understand that "the black experience on this continent and in Africa was profound, honorable, and a source of pride."[25] But ancestral and group pride cannot solve the deep social and economic problems that confront so many youth who live in black communities today. If the most radical black educators devote their energies to refashioning children's self-image through an oversimplified and often invented history, what energy will go toward fighting for structural reforms that provide jobs, equal opportunities, decent housing, and a more stable family life for millions of people trapped in poverty and despair? The black historian John Bracey describes the "glories of Ancient Africa" as a understandable but sadly insufficient response "to the harsh realities of the West Side of Chicago, or BedStuy, or the gang mayhem of Los Angeles."[26]

⋅◦⊙◦⋅

Still other explosives infest the minefield of extreme Afrocentrism. If the Afrocentrists are correct that their curriculum will raise self-esteem, and therefore performance levels—a disputed point with little solid evidence—then it is logical to suppose that what is sauce for the goose is sauce for the gander. The logical extension of their reasoning is that a Hispanocentrist approach ought to be instituted for children of Hispanic backgrounds; children of Chinese ancestry in this country ought to receive a Sinocentrist education; a Khmercentrist approach is the best road ahead for the thousands of immigrant children from Cambodia; and so forth. Indeed, logic would require the reinstitution of a Eurocentric approach for low-achieving white children, or a series of nation-specific or European ethnic group-specific approaches to help underachieving children of these backgrounds overcome their disadvantages. But what approach would be employed in thousands of classrooms in large cities across the country where children of a great variety of ethnic, racial, and religious backgrounds mingle? Which ethnically specific curriculum should be taught to the growing number of mixed-race children in a society where miscegenation laws, after a long struggle, no longer exist and the rate of interracial marriage is at an all-time high and is increasing yearly?

Separate Ground and Common Ground

Except among the David Dukes and Pat Buchanans, who so far have had little influence on curricular change, there is little argument about the desirability of including people of all classes, colors, and conditions in our accounts of how history unfolds—indeed, this is simply sound historical analysis. Nor is there much doubt that children will find history more compelling and relevant when they recognize that people of their religion, color, region, ethnic background, or class played active roles in the making of American society. But students also need to discover through history the common humanity of all individuals while discovering the historical relevance of gender, race, religion, and other categories that help shape their identity. And whatever our origins and characteristics, we should hope that all students will find inspiring figures of different colors, genders, and social positions. Harriet Tubman and Ida B. Wells should inspire all students, not simply African American females. Likewise, all students can gain wisdom from studying the trial of Anne Hutchinson or the Lincoln-Douglass debates and draw inspiration from the courage and accomplishments of Black Hawk, John Brown, Elizabeth Blackwell, A. Philip Randolph, Louis Brandeis, Dolores Huerta, and a thousand more. W. E. B. Du Bois knew that the history he was taught was wildly distorted and used as an instrument of white supremacy. But he also understood that he benefitted greatly from reading the great writers of many cultures. "I sit with Shakespeare and he winces not. Across the color line I move arm in arm with Balzac and Dumas, where smiling men and welcoming women glide in gilded halls . . . I summon Aristotle and Aurelius and what soul I will, and they come all graciously with no scorn nor condescension. So, wed with Truth, I live above the veil."[27]

The veil of which Du Bois wrote was the color line, of course, and he is only one of a long line of brilliant black scholars who drew sustenance from all parts of humanity. Ralph Ellison, growing up in Macon County, Alabama, remembered that he "read Marx, Freud, T. S. Eliot, Pound, Gertrude Stein, and Hemingway. Books which seldom, if ever, mentioned Negroes were to release me from whatever 'segregated' idea I might have had of my human possibilities."[28] C. L. R. James, the Trinidadian historian and author of *Black Jacobins,* still after forty years the most important book on the Haitian Revolution, writes movingly of his education in the classics of English literature in the schools of Trinidad. As an adult, James came to understand "the limitation of spirit, vision, and self-respect which was imposed on us by the fact that our masters, our curriculum, our Code of morals, *everything* began from the basis that Britain was the source of all light and leading, and our business was to admire, wonder, imitate, learn." But he went on to read and learn from French and Russian literary greats and to find an authentic voice of his own, much enriched by his cosmopolitan education.[29] His accomplishments are a reminder that a curriculum organized around only one vantage point for learning, whether English, European, or African, will limit the vision of students and therefore keep them from being all that they can be.

Thirteen years ago, looking at the way multiculturalism was proceeding in its earlier stage, Frances FitzGerald worried that the rise of the new social history that concerned the forgotten elements of the population would lead to a history that was a bundle of fragmented group histories. This, she said, would teach that "Americans have no common history, no common culture and no common values, and that membership in a racial cultural group constitutes the most fundamental experience of each individual. The message would be that the center cannot, and should not, hold."[30]

Today, FitzGerald's question about what holds us together, whether we have a common culture, is all the more relevant. If multiculturalism is to get beyond a promiscuous pluralism that gives every thing equal weight and adopts complete moral relativism, it must reach some agreement on what is at the core of American culture. The practical goal of multiculturalism is to foster mutual respect among students by teaching them about the distinct cultures from which those who have come to the United States derive and the distinctive historical experiences of different racial, ethnic, religious, and gender groups in American history. Multicultural education, writes Robert Fullinwider, is "the conscious effort to be sensitive, both in teacher preparation and in curriculum construction, to the cultural, religious, ethnic, and racial variety in our national life in order to (1) produce an educational environment responsive to the needs of students from different backgrounds and (2) instill in students mutual understanding and respect."[31] But nurturing this mutual respect and an appreciation of cultural diversity can only be maintained if parents, teachers, and children reach some basic agreement on some core set of values, ways of airing disputes, conducting dialogue—in short, some agreement on how to operate as members of a civic community, a democratic polity. For a democratic polity to endure, the people of a society made up of many cultures must both "be willing to forbear from forcing onto fellow citizens one proper and approved way of life, . . . must possess a certain amount of respect for one another and a certain amount of understanding of one another's beliefs, . . . and [must] want to participate in a common 'civic culture'."[32]

If the mutual respect that is at the heart of genuine multiculturalism cannot live "in isolation of specific cultural forms and supports," what are these forms and supports?[33] They are, in essence, the central, defining values of the democratic polity. The pluribus in e pluribus unum can be upheld in all manner of cultural, religious, and aesthetic forms—from the clothes an individual or group chooses to wear, to their cuisine, their artistic preferences and styles, the dialect and linguistic constructions of their internal social life, their religious beliefs and practices, and so forth. But pluribus can flourish in these ways only if unum is preserved at the heart of the polity—in a common commitment to core political and moral values. Chief among these values is the notion that under our founding political principles government is derived from the people, that we live under a government of laws, that certain basic rights as spelled out in the first ten amendments to the Constitution are a precious heritage, and that all citizens—apart from whatever group attachments they claim—have a common entitlement as individuals to liberty, equal opportunity, and impartial treatment under the law. This, of course, is a system of political ideals, not a description of political or social reality. But the ideals are clearly stated in the founding documents and have been reference points for virtually every social and political struggle carried out by women, religious minorities, labor, and people of color. Our entire history can be read as a long, painful, and often bloody struggle to bring social practice into correspondence with these lofty goals. But it is the political ideals that still provide the path to unum. In his classic study of race relations, Gunnar Myrdal focused on the central contradiction of a democracy that would not extend equal rights to Jews, black Americans, and other "outsiders" and thereby engaged in a massive hypocrisy. But at the same time, Myrdal recognized that such disadvantaged groups "could not possibly have invented a system of political ideals which better corresponded to their interests."[34] That a struggle has occurred—and is still occurring—is no argument against the ideal of a common core culture. It is only a reminder of an agenda still waiting to be completed, of what the African American historian Vincent Harding has poignantly called "wrestling toward the dawn."[35]

Notes

1. David Nicholson, "Afrocentrism and the Tribalization of America," *Washington Post,* September 23, 1991, p. B1.

2. W. E. B. Du Bois, *Black Reconstruction: An Essay toward a History of the Part Which Black Folk Played in the Attempt to Reconstruct Democracy in America, 1860–1880* (New York: Harcourt, Brace, and Co., 1935), pp. 725, 727.

3. Leon Litwack, "Trouble in Mind: The Bicentennial and the Afro-American Experience," *Journal of American History* 74 (1987), p. 326.

4. Hugh Trevor-Roper, *The Rise of Christian Europe* (New York: Harcourt, Brace & World, 1965), p. 9.

5. Douglas Edward Leach, *Flintlock and Tomahawk: New England in King Philip's War* (New York: Macmillan, 1958), p. ix.

6. John Hope Franklin, "The New Negro History," in John Hope Franklin, *Race and History: Selected Essays, 1938–1988* (Baton Rouge: Louisiana State University Press, 1989), p. 46.

7. Peter Novick, *That Noble Dream: The "Objectivity Question" and the American Historical Profession* (Cambridge: Cambridge University Press, 1988), p. 173.

8. Ibid., pp. 366, 339.

9. Oscar Handlin, *Truth in History* (Cambridge, Mass.: Harvard University Press, 1979), passim.

10. Frances FitzGerald, *America Revised: History Schoolbooks in the Twentieth Century* (Boston: Little, Brown & Co., 1979), p. 58.

11. Quoted in Gary B. Nash, *Race, Class, and Politics: Essays on American Colonial and Revolutionary Society* (Urbana and Chicago: University of Illinois Press, 1986), p. xviii.

12. Bernard Bailyn, "The Challenge of Modern Historiography," *American Historical Review* 87 (1982), p. 3.

13. On these points, see also Joan W. Scott, "Liberal Historians: a Unitary Vision," *Chronicle of Higher Education,* September 11, 1991, pp. B1–2.

14. Joan W. Scott, "History in Crisis? The Others' Side of the Story," *American Historical Review* 94 (1989), p. 690; equally pertinent is Lawrence W. Levine, "The Unpredictable Past: Reflections on Recent American Historiography," *American Historical Review* 94 (1989), pp. 671–9.

15. Robert K. Fullinwider, "The Cosmopolitan Community," unpublished mss, pp. 2–3.

16. Quoted in David L. Kirp, "The Battle of the Books," *San Francisco Chronicle,* "Image" section, February 24, 1991.

17. Molefi Kete Asante, *The Afrocentric Idea* (Philadelphia: Temple University Press, 1987), p. 6.

18. Molefi Kete Asante, "Multiculturalism: An Exchange," *American Scholar,* Spring 1991, p. 268.

19. J. A. Rogers, *100 Amazing Facts About the Negro: With Complete Proof: A Short Cut to the World History of the Negro* (New York: F. Hubner, n.d.), pp. 5, 21–2.

20. Asante, *The Afrocentric Idea,* p. 9.

21. John Henrik Clarke, "Social Studies African-American Baseline Essay" (Portland: Portland Public Schools, 1989), pp. SS-12–13 and passim.

22. Henry Louis Gates, Jr., "Beware of the New Pharoahs," *Newsweek,* September 23, 1991, p. 47.

23. Emery Reves, *The Anatomy of Peace* (New York: Harper & Brothers, 1945), p. 1.

24. Robert K. Fullinwider, "Multicultural Education," *The University of Chicago Legal Forum,* 1991, p. 80.

25. Roger Wilkins, *A Man's Life: An Autobiography* (New York: Simon and Schuster, 1982), p. 184.

26. John Bracey, in *African Commentary,* November 1989, p. 12.

27. W. E. B. Du Bois, *Souls of Black Folk: Essays and Sketches* (Chicago: A. C. McClurg & Co., 1903), p. 82.

28. Ralph Elison quoted in Jim Sleeper, *The Closest of Strangers: Liberalism and the Politics of Race in New York* (New York: W. W. Norton, 1990), p. 234.

29. C. L. R. James, *Beyond a Boundary* (London: Hutchinson & Co., 1963), pp. 38–9, 70, and passim.

30. FitzGerald, *America Revised,* p. 104.

31. Fullinwider, "Multicultural Education," p. 77.

32. Ibid., p. 81.

33. Fullinwider, "Cosmopolitan Community," p. 21.

34. Gunnar Myrdal, *An American Dilemma: The Negro Problem and Modern Democracy* (New York: Harper & Brothers, 1944), p. 13.

35. Vincent Gordon Harding, "Wresting toward the Dawn: The Afro-American Freedom Movement and the Changing Constitution," *Journal of American History* 74 (1987), p. 31.

NO ↵

Multiculturalism:
E Pluribus Plures

Questions of race, ethnicity, and religion have been a perennial source of conflict in American education. The schools have often attracted the zealous attention of those who wish to influence the future, as well as those who wish to change the way we view the past. In our history, the schools have been not only an institution in which to teach young people skills and knowledge, but an arena where interest groups fight to preserve their values, or to revise the judgments of history, or to bring about fundamental social change. In the nineteenth century, Protestants and Catholics battled over which version of the Bible should be used in school, or whether the Bible should be used at all. In recent decades, bitter racial disputes—provoked by policies of racial segregation and discrimination—have generated turmoil in the streets and in the schools. The secularization of the schools during the past century has prompted attacks on the curricula and textbooks and library books by fundamentalist Christians, who object to whatever challenges their faith-based views of history, literature, and science.

Given the diversity of American society, it has been impossible to insulate the schools from pressures that result from differences and tensions among groups. When people differ about basic values, sooner or later those disagreements turn up in battles about how schools are organized or what the schools should teach. Sometimes these battles remove a terrible injustice, like racial segregation. Sometimes, however, interest groups politicize the curriculum and attempt to impose their views on teachers, school officials, and textbook publishers. Across the country, even now, interest groups are pressuring local school boards to remove myths and fables and other imaginative literature from children's readers and to inject the teaching of creationism in biology. When groups cross the line into extremism, advancing their own agenda without regard to reason or to others, they threaten public education itself, making it difficult to teach any issues honestly and making the entire curriculum vulnerable to political campaigns.

For many years, the public schools attempted to neutralize controversies over race, religion, and ethnicity by ignoring them. Educators believed,

Excerpts from *The American Scholar*, vol. 59, no.3, Summer 1990, pp. 337–354. Copyright © 1990 by Diane Ravitch. Reprinted with permission.

or hoped, that the schools could remain outside politics; this was, of course, a vain hope since the schools were pursuing policies based on race, religion, and ethnicity. Nonetheless, such divisive questions were usually excluded from the curriculum. The textbooks minimized problems among groups and taught a sanitized version of history. Race, religion, and ethnicity were presented as minor elements in the American saga; slavery was treated as an episode, immigration as a sidebar, and women were largely absent. The textbooks concentrated on presidents, wars, national politics, and issues of state. An occasional "great black" or "great woman" received mention, but the main narrative paid little attention to minority groups and women.

With the ethnic revival of the 1960s, this approach to the teaching of history came under fire, because the history of national leaders—virtually all of whom were white, Anglo-Saxon, and male—ignored the place in American history of those who were none of the above. The traditional history of elites had been complemented by an assimilationist view of American society, which presumed that everyone in the American melting pot would eventually lose or abandon those ethnic characteristics that distinguished them from mainstream Americans. The ethnic revival demonstrated that many groups did not want to be assimilated or melted. Ethnic studies programs popped up on campuses to teach not only that "black is beautiful," but also that every other variety of ethnicity is "beautiful" as well; everyone who had "roots" began to look for them so that they too could recover that ancestral part of themselves that had not been homogenized.

As ethnicity became an accepted subject for study in the late 1960s, textbooks were assailed for their failure to portray blacks accurately; within a few years, the textbooks in wide use were carefully screened to eliminate bias against minority groups and women. At the same time, new scholarship about the history of women, blacks, and various ethnic minorities found its way into the textbooks. At first, the multicultural content was awkwardly incorporated as little boxes on the side of the main narrative. Then some of the new social historians (like Stephan Thernstrom, Mary Beth Norton, Gary Nash, Winthrop Jordan, and Leon Litwack) themselves wrote textbooks, and the main narrative itself began to reflect a broadened historical understanding of race, ethnicity, and class in the American past. Consequently, today's history textbooks routinely incorporate the experiences of women, blacks, American Indians, and various immigrant groups.

Although most high-school textbooks are deeply unsatisfactory (they still largely neglect religion, they are too long, too encyclopedic, too superficial, and lacking in narrative flow), they are far more sensitive to pluralism than their predecessors. For example, the latest edition of Todd and Curti's *Triumph of the American Nation,* the most popular high-school history text, has significantly increased its coverage of blacks in America, including profiles of Phillis Wheatley, the poet; James Armistead, a revolutionary war spy for Lafayette; Benjamin Banneker, a self-taught scientist and mathematician; Hiram Revels, the first black to serve in the Congress; and Ida B. Wells-Barnett, a tireless crusader against lynching and racism. Even better as a textbook treatment is Jordan and Litwack's *The United States,* which skillfully synthesizes the historical experiences of blacks, Indians, immigrants, women, and other groups into the mainstream of American social and political history. The latest generation of textbooks bluntly acknowledges the racism of the past, describing the struggle for equality by racial minorities while identifying individuals who achieved success as political leaders, doctors, lawyers, scholars, entrepreneurs, teachers, and scientists.

As a result of the political and social changes of recent decades, cultural pluralism is now generally recognized as an organizing principle of this society. In contrast to the idea of the melting pot, which promised to erase ethnic and group differences, children now learn that variety is the spice of life. They learn that America has provided a haven for many different groups and has allowed them to maintain their cultural heritage or to assimilate, or—as is often the case—to do both; the choice is theirs, not the state's. They learn that cultural pluralism is one of the norms of a free society; that differences among groups are a national resource rather than a problem to be solved. Indeed, the unique feature of the United States is that its common culture has been formed by the interaction of its subsidiary cultures. It is a culture that has been influenced over time by immigrants, American Indians, Africans (slave and free) and by their descendants. American music, art, literature, language, food, clothing, sports, holidays, and customs all show the effects of the commingling of diverse cultures in one nation. Paradoxical though it may seem, the United States has a common culture that is multicultural.

Our schools and our institutions of higher learning have in recent years begun to embrace what Catherine R. Stimpson of Rutgers University has called "cultural democracy," a recognition that we must listen to a "diversity of voices" in order to understand our culture, past and present. This understanding of the pluralistic nature of American culture has taken a long time to forge. It is based on sound scholarship and has led to major revisions in what children are taught and what they read in school. The new history is—indeed, must be—a warts-and-all history; it demands an unflinching examination of racism and discrimination in our history. Making these changes is difficult, raises tempers, and ignites controversies, but gives a more interesting and accurate account of American history. Accomplishing these changes is valuable, because there is also a useful lesson for the rest of the world in America's relatively successful experience as a pluralistic society. Throughout human history, the clash of different cultures, races, ethnic groups, and religions has often been the cause of bitter hatred, civil conflict, and international war. The ethnic tensions that now are tearing apart Lebanon, Sri Lanka, Kashmir, and various republics of the Soviet Union remind us of the costs of unfettered group rivalry. Thus, it is a matter of more than domestic importance that we closely examine and try to understand that part of our national history in which different groups competed, fought, suffered, but ultimately learned to live together in relative peace and even achieved a sense of common nationhood.

Alas, these painstaking efforts to expand the understanding of American culture into a richer and more varied tapestry have taken a new turn, and not for the better. Almost any idea, carried to its extreme, can be made pernicious, and this is what is happening now to multiculturalism. Today, pluralistic multiculturalism must contend with a new, particularistic multiculturalism. The pluralists seek a richer common culture; the particularists insist that no common culture is possible or desirable. The new particularism is entering the curriculum in a number of school systems across the country. Advocates of particularism propose an ethnocentric curriculum to raise the self-esteem and academic achievement of children from racial and ethnic minority backgrounds. Without any evidence, they claim that children from minority backgrounds will do well in school *only* if they are immersed in a positive, prideful version of their ancestral culture. If children are of, for example, Fredonian ancestry, they must hear that Fredonians were important in mathematics, science, history, and literature. If they learn about great Fredonians and if their studies use Fredonian examples and Fredonian concepts, they will do well in school. If they do not, they will have low self-esteem and will do badly.

At first glance, this appears akin to the celebratory activities associated with Black History Month or Women's History Month, when schoolchildren learn about the achievements of blacks and women. But the point of those celebrations is to demonstrate that neither race nor gender is an obstacle to high achievement. They teach all children that everyone, regardless of their race, religion, gender, ethnicity, or family origin, can achieve self-fulfillment, honor, and dignity in society if they aim high and work hard.

By contrast, the particularistic version of multiculturalism is unabashedly filiopietistic and deterministic. It teaches children that their identity is determined by their "cultural genes." That something in their blood or their race memory or their cultural DNA defines who they are and what they may achieve. That the culture in which they live is not their own culture, even though they were born here. That American culture is "Eurocentric," and therefore hostile to anyone whose ancestors are not European. Perhaps the most invidious implication of particularism is that racial and ethnic minorities are not and should not try to be part of American culture; it implies that American culture belongs only to those who are white and European; it implies that those who are neither white nor European are alienated from American culture by virtue of their race or ethnicity; it implies that the only culture they do belong to or can ever belong to is the culture of their ancestors, even if their families have lived in this country for generations.

The war on so-called Eurocentrism is intended to foster self-esteem among those who are not of European descent. But how, in fact, is self-esteem developed? How is the sense of one's own possibilities, one's potential choices, developed? Certainly, the school curriculum plays a relatively small role as compared to the influence of family, community, mass media, and society. But to the extent that curriculum influences what children think of themselves, it should encourage children of all racial and ethnic groups to believe that they are part of this society and that they should develop their talents and minds to the fullest. It is enormously inspiring, for example, to learn about men and women from diverse backgrounds who overcame poverty, discrimination, physical handicaps, and other obstacles to achieve success in a variety of fields. Behind every such biography of accomplishment is a story of heroism, perseverance, and self-discipline. Learning these stories will encourage a healthy spirit of pluralism, of mutual respect, and of self-respect among children of different backgrounds. The children of American society today will live their lives in a racially and culturally diverse nation, and their education should prepare them to do so.

The pluralist approach to multiculturalism promotes a broader interpretation of the common American culture and seeks due recognition for the ways that the nation's many racial, ethnic, and cultural groups have transformed the national culture. The pluralists say, in effect, "American culture belongs to us, all of us; the U.S. is us, and we remake it in every generation." But particularists have no interest in extending or revising American culture; indeed, they deny that a common culture exists. Particularists reject any accommodation among groups, any interactions that blur the distinct lines between them. The brand of history that they espouse is one in which everyone is either a descendant of victims or oppressors. By doing so, ancient hatreds are fanned and recreated in each new generation. Particularism has its intellectual roots in the ideology of ethnic separatism and in the black nationalist movement. In the particularist analysis, the nation has five cultures: African American, Asian American, European American, Latino/Hispanic, and Native American. The huge cultural, historical, religious, and linguistic differences within these categories are ignored, as is the considerable intermarriage among these groups, as are the linkages (like gender, class, sexual orientation, and religion) that cut across these five groups. No serious scholar would claim that all Europeans and white Americans are part of the same culture, or that all Asians are part of the same culture, or that all people of Latin-American descent are of the same culture, or that all people of African descent are of the same culture. Any categorization this broad is essentially meaningless and useless.

Several districts—including Detroit, Atlanta, and Washington, D.C.—are developing an Afrocentric curriculum. *Afrocentricity* has been described in a book of the same name by Molefi Kete Asante of Temple University. The Afrocentric curriculum puts Africa at the center of the student's universe. African Americans must "move away from an [sic] Eurocentric framework" because "it is difficult to create freely when you use someone else's motifs, styles, images, and perspectives." Because they are not Africans, "white teachers cannot inspire in our children the visions necessary for them to overcome limitations." Asante recommends that African Americans choose an African name (as he did), reject European dress, embrace African religion (not Islam or Christianity) and love "their own" culture. He scorns the idea of universality as a form of Eurocentric arrogance. The Eurocentrist, he says, thinks of Beethoven or Bach as classical, but the Afrocentrist thinks of Ellington or Coltrane as classical; the Eurocentrist lauds Shakespeare or Twain, while the Afrocentrist prefers Baraka, Shange, or Abiola. Asante is critical of black artists like Arthur Mitchell and Alvin Ailey who ignore Afrocentricity. Likewise, he speaks contemptuously of a group of black university students who spurned the Afrocentrism of the local Black Student Union and formed an organization called Inter-race: "Such madness is the direct consequence of self-hatred, obligatory attitudes, false assumptions about society, and stupidity."

The conflict between pluralism and particularism turns on the issue of universalism. Professor Asante warns his readers against the lure of universalism: "Do not be captured by a sense of universality given to you by the Eurocentric viewpoint; such a viewpoint is contradictory to your own ultimate reality." He insists that there is no alternative to Eurocentrism, Afrocentrism, and other ethnocentrisms. In contrast, the pluralist says, with the Roman playwright Terence, "I am a man: nothing human is alien to me." A contemporary Terence would say "I am a person" or might be a woman, but the point remains the same: you don't have to be black to love Zora Neale Hurston's fiction or Langston Hughes's poetry or Duke Ellington's music. In a pluralist curriculum, we expect children to learn a broad and humane culture, to learn about the ideas and art and animating spirit of many cultures. We expect that children, whatever their color, will be inspired by the courage of people like Helen Keller, Vaclav Havel, Harriet Tubman, and Feng Lizhe. We expect that their response to literature will be determined by the ideas and images it evokes, not by the skin color of the writer. But particularists insist that children can learn only from the experiences of people from the same race.

Particularism is a bad idea whose time has come. It is also a fashion spreading like wildfire through the education system, actively promoted by organizations and individuals with a political and professional interest in strengthening ethnic power bases in the university, in the education profession, and in society itself. One can scarcely pick up an educational journal without learning about a school district that is converting to an ethnocentric curriculum in an attempt to give "self-esteem" to children from racial minorities. A state-funded project in a Sacramento high school is teaching young black males to think like Africans and to develop the "African Mind Model Technique," in order to free themselves of the racism of American culture. A popular black rap singer, KRS-One, complained in an op-ed article in the *New York Times* that the schools should be teaching blacks about their cultural heritage, instead of trying to make everyone Americans. "It's like trying to teach a dog to be a cat," he wrote. KRS-One railed about having to learn about Thomas Jefferson and the Civil War, which had nothing to do (he said) with black history.

◦❀◦

The efficacy of particularist proposals seems to be less important to their sponsors than their value as ideological weapons with which to criticize existing disciplines for their alleged Eurocentric bias. In a recent article titled "The Ethnocentric Basis of Social Science Knowledge Production" in the *Review of Research in Education,* John Stanfield of Yale University argues that neither social science nor science are objective studies, that both instead are "Euro-American" knowledge systems which reproduce "hegemonic racial domination." The claim that science and reason are somehow superior to magic and witch-craft, he writes, is the product of Euro-American ethnocentrism. According to Stanfield, current fears about the misuse of science (for instance, "the nuclear arms race, global pollution") and "the power-plays of Third World nations (the Arab oil boycott and the American–Iranian hostage crisis) have made Western people more aware of nonscientific cognitive styles. These last events are beginning to demonstrate politically that which has begun to be understood in intellectual circles: namely, that modes of social knowledge such as theology, science, and magic are different, not inferior or superior. They represent different ways of perceiving, defining, and organizing knowledge of life experiences." One wonders: If Professor Stanfield broke his leg, would he go to a theologian, a doctor, or a magician?

❧

It is hardly surprising that America's schools would recognize strong cultural ties with Europe since our nation's political, religious, educational, and economic institutions were created chiefly by people of European descent, our government was shaped by European ideas, and nearly 80 percent of the people who live here are of European descent. The particularists treat all of this history as a racist bias toward Europe, rather than as the matter-of-fact consequences of European immigration. Even so, American education is not centered on Europe. American education, if it is centered on anything, is centered on itself. It is "Americentric." Most American students today have never studied any world history; they know very little about Europe, and even less about the rest of the world. Their minds are rooted solidly in the here and now. When the Berlin Wall was opened in the fall of 1989, journalists discovered that most American teenagers had no idea what it was, nor why its opening was such a big deal. Nonetheless, Eurocentrism provides a better target than Americentrism.

In school districts where most children are black and Hispanic, there has been a growing tendency to embrace particularism rather than pluralism. Many of the children in these districts perform poorly in academic classes and leave school without graduating. They would fare better in school if they had well-educated and well-paid teachers, small classes, good materials, encouragement at home and school, summer academic programs, protection from the drugs and crime that ravage their neighborhoods, and higher expectations of satisfying careers upon graduation. These are expensive and time-consuming remedies that must also engage the larger society beyond the school. The lure of particularism is that it offers a less complicated anodyne, one in which the children's academic deficiencies may be addressed—or set aside—by inflating their racial pride. The danger of this remedy is that it will detract attention from the real needs of schools and the real interests of children, while simultaneously arousing distorted race pride in children of all races, increasing racial antagonism and producing fresh recruits for white and black racist groups.

❧

The rising tide of particularism encourages the politicization of all curricula in the schools. If education bureaucrats bend to the political and ideological winds, as is their wont, we can anticipate a generation of struggle over the content of the curriculum in mathematics, science, literature, and history. Demands for "culturally relevant" studies, for ethnostudies of all kinds, will open the classroom to unending battles over whose version is taught, who gets credit for what, and which ethno-interpretation is appropriate. Only recently have districts begun to resist the demands of fundamentalist groups to censor textbooks and library books (and some have not yet begun to do so).

The spread of particularism throws into question the very idea of American public education. Public schools exist to teach children the general skills and knowledge that they need to succeed in American society, and the specific skills and knowledge that they need in order to function as American citizens. They receive public support because they have a public function. Historically, the public schools were known as "common schools" because they were schools for all, even if the children of all the people did not attend them. Over the years, the courts have found that it was unconstitutional to teach religion in the common schools, or to separate children on the basis of their race in the common schools. In their curriculum, their hiring practices, and their general philosophy, the public schools must not discriminate against or give preference to any racial or ethnic group. Yet they are permitted to accommodate cultural diversity by, for example, serving food that is culturally appropriate or providing library collections that emphasize the interests of the local community. However, they should not be expected to teach children to view the world through an ethnocentric perspective that rejects or ignores the common culture. For generations, those groups that wanted to inculcate their religion or their ethnic heritage have instituted private schools—after school, on weekends, or on a full-time basis. There, children learn with others of the same group—Greeks, Poles, Germans, Japanese, Chinese, Jews, Lutherans, Catholics, and so on—and are taught by people from the same group. Valuable as this exclusive experience has been for those who choose it, this has not been the role of public education. One of the primary purposes of public education has been to create a national community, a definition of citizenship and culture that is both expansive and *inclusive.*

The curriculum in public schools must be based on whatever knowledge and practices have been determined to be best by professionals—experienced teachers and scholars—who are competent to make these judgments. Professional societies must be prepared to defend the integrity of their disciplines. When called upon, they should establish review committees to examine disputes over curriculum and to render judgment, in order to help school officials fend off improper political pressure. Where genuine controversies exist, they should be taught and debated in the classroom. Was Egypt a black civilization? Why not raise the question, read the arguments of the different sides in the debate, show slides of Egyptian pharoahs and queens, read books about life in ancient Egypt, invite guest scholars from the local university, and visit museums with Egyptian collections? If scholars disagree, students should know it. One great advantage of this approach is that students will see that history is a lively study, that textbooks are fallible, that historians disagree, that the writing of history is influenced by the historian's politics and ideology, that history is written by people who make choices among alternative facts and interpretations, and that history changes as new facts are uncovered and new interpretations win adherents. They will also learn that cultures and civilizations constantly interact, exchange ideas, and influence one another, and that the idea of racial or ethnic purity is a myth. Another advantage is that students might once again study ancient history, which has all but disappeared from the curricula of American schools. (California recently introduced a required sixth grade course in ancient civilizations, but ancient history is otherwise *terra incognita* in American education.)

The multicultural controversy may do wonders for the study of history, which has been neglected for years in American schools. At this time, only half of our high school graduates ever study any world history. Any serious attempt to broaden students' knowledge of Africa, Europe, Asia, and Latin America will require at least two, and possibly three years of world history (a requirement thus far only in California). American history, too, will need more time than the one-year high-school survey course. Those of us who have insisted for years on the importance of history in the curriculum may not be ready to assent to its redemptive power, but hope that our new allies will ultimately join a constructive dialogue that strengthens the place of history in the schools.

As cultural controversies arise, educators must adhere to the principle of "E Pluribus Unum." That is, they must maintain a balance between the demands of the one—the nation of which we are common citizens—and the many—the varied histories of the American people. It is not necessary to denigrate either the one or the many. Pluralism is a positive value, but it is also important that we preserve a sense of an American community—a society and a culture to which we all belong. If there is no overall community with an agreed-upon vision of liberty and justice, if all we have is a collection of racial and ethnic cultures, lacking any common bonds, then we have no means to mobilize public opinion on behalf of people who are not members of our particular group. We have, for example, no reason to support public education. If there is no larger community, then each group will want to teach its own children in its own way, and public education ceases to exist.

History should not be confused with filiopietism. History gives no grounds for race pride. No race has a monopoly on virtue. If anything, a study of history should inspire humility, rather than pride. People of every racial group have committed terrible crimes, often against others of the same group. Whether one looks at the history of Europe or Africa or Latin America or Asia, every continent offers examples of inhumanity. Slavery has existed in civilizations around the world for centuries. Examples of genocide can be found around the world, throughout history, from ancient times right through to our own day. Governments and cultures, sometimes by edict, sometimes simply following tradition, have practiced not only slavery, but human sacrifice, infanticide, cliterodectomy, and mass murder. If we teach children this, they might recognize how absurd both racial hatred and racial chauvinism are.

What must be preserved in the study of history is the spirit of inquiry, the readiness to open new questions and to pursue new understandings. History, at its best, is a search for truth. The best way to portray this search is through debate and controversy, rather than through imposition of fixed beliefs and immutable facts. Perhaps the most dangerous aspect of school history is its tendency to become Official History, a sanctified version of the Truth taught by the state to captive audiences and embedded in beautiful mass-market textbooks as holy writ. When Official History is written by committees responding to political pressures, rather than by scholars synthesizing the best available research, then the errors of the past are replaced by the politically fashionable errors of the present. It may be difficult to teach children that history is both important and uncertain, and that even the best historians never have all the pieces of the jigsaw puzzle, but it is necessary to do so. If state education departments permit the revision of their history courses and textbooks to become an exercise in power politics, then the entire process of state-level curriculum-making becomes suspect, as does public education itself.

The question of self-esteem is extraordinarily complex, and it goes well beyond the content of the curriculum. Most of what we call self-esteem is formed in the home and in a variety of life experiences, not only in school. Nonetheless, it has been important for blacks—and for other racial groups—to learn about the history of slavery and of the civil rights movement; it has been important for blacks to know that their ancestors actively resisted enslavement and actively pursued equality; and it has been important for blacks and others to learn about black men land women who fought courageously against racism and who provide models of courage, persistence, and intellect. These are instances where the content of the curriculum reflects sound scholarship, and at the same time probably lessens racial prejudice and provides inspiration for those who are descendants of slaves. But knowing about the travails and triumphs of one's forebears does not necessarily translate into either self-esteem or personal accomplishment. For most children, self-esteem—the self-confidence that grows out of having reached a goal—comes not from hearing about the monuments of their ancestors but as a consequence of what they are able to do and accomplish through their own efforts.

As I reflected on these issues, I recalled reading an interview a few years ago with a talented black runner. She said that her model is Mikhail Baryshnikov. She admires him because he is a magnificent athlete. He is not black; he is not female; he is not American-born; he is not even a runner. But he inspires her because of the way he trained and used his body. When I read this, I thought how narrow-minded it is to believe that people can be inspired *only* by those who are exactly like them in race and ethnicity.

POSTSCRIPT

Is a Multicultural Curriculum Essential for Advancing Education?

The eminent historian Eric Foner points out that "the study of history today looks far different than it did a generation ago." To Foner, Nash, and many others, a multicultural curriculum is essential for all students to understand the American experience. However, to some, the "new histories," or emphasis on the "multi" part of American culture, seem to have "fragmented historical scholarship and impeded the attempt to create a unified vision of the American experience."

In higher education, countless faculty debates on core curriculum requirements often reflect the tensions of multiculturalism. What general knowledge should we require all our students to know? What is needed to thrive, much less survive in a multicultural society? Who decides? It would be interesting to find out how curriculum decisions are made. In higher education, it is faculty-based. In contrast, curriculum in public schools must consider the interests of state and local residents. An example is in the adoption of textbooks, which varies not only from state to state, but also often from district to district. In some states, one standard curriculum is mandated including the text. In others, these decisions are left to the district level. Should parents play a role in setting curriculum standards? What role should the teachers play in setting curriculum?

The multicultural curriculum issue is one of America's many examples of how and to what extent the dominant culture responds to new cultures and new interpretations of history. Further, it exposes the importance of public school education and the politics of decision making required to address the issue.

A comprehensive reader that addresses many themes in multiculturalism is *Multiculturalism in the United States: Current Issues, Contemporary Voices* (Pine Forge Press, 2000) edited by Peter Kivisto and Georganne Rundblad. Nathan Glazer argues in *We Are All Multiculturalists Now* (Harvard University Press, 1997) that multiculturalism is well entrenched in American culture, and it is no longer a threat to the status quo. Ronald Takaki cites the potential political divisiveness of multiculturalism along with an explanation of how multiculturalism can help the country deal with diversity in "Multiculturalism: Battleground or Meeting Ground?" from *Annals of the American Academy* (November 1993).

ISSUE 14

Is Affirmative Action Necessary to Achieve Racial Equality in the United States?

YES: Robert Staples, "Black Deprivation-White Privilege: The Assault on Affirmative Action." *The Black Scholar* (vol. 25, no. 3, Summer 1995)

NO: Patrick A. Hall, "Against Our Best Interests: An Ambivalent View of Affirmative Action," *Blacks in Higher Education* (October 1991)

ISSUE SUMMARY

YES: Robert Staples, an African-American sociologist, views affirmative action as a positive policy designed to provide equal economic opportunities for women and other minorities.

NO: Patrick A. Hall, an African-American librarian, is opposed to affirmative action based on the belief that it promotes negative stereotypes of African Americans and other minorities, and that it perpetuates the perception that minorities are not advancing based on merit.

Affirmative action emerged as a primary policy of government to remedy prevailing racial discrimination and to promote equal opportunity consistent with the requirements of the Civil Rights Act of 1964. Yet, despite its noble intentions, the application of this policy in attempts to end bias and promote racial diversity has provoked much controversy.

Those who favor affirmative action programs such as Professor Robert Staples, reject the premise that the United States has achieved the status of a color-blind society, thus obviating the need for the preferences that they provide for members of the "protected classes." Rather, he views American society as one afflicted with an embedded racism that persists today. So, Staples is concerned that the attack on affirmative action is part of a plan designed to maintain white privilege at the expense of the continued suffering and subordination of African Americans and other minorities to include women within society.

Staples points out that affirmative action is not a "black" program. Rather, he concludes that affirmative action programs were initiated to provide equal economic opportunities for minorities and women. Thus, Staples is very critical of politicians and others who play the "race card" by promoting the myth that most of the benefits of affirmative action programs accrue to blacks, when in fact the primary beneficiaries are white females. To Staples, the targeting of blacks in such a fashion reflects a historical tradition of scapegoating blacks within a strategy of "divide and conquer" politics.

Racial politics are a significant aspect of American political life. Staples locates the attack on affirmative action policies as a significant manifestation of the white backlash against civil rights advancement of 1990's politics. He decries the tendency of the opponents of these policies to use them to target African Americans, a group that represents a relatively small minority (12.5%) among the potential beneficiaries of affirmative action, while ignoring the fact that white women are the majority of those targeted for the assistance, which they provide. So, Staples has concluded that the opponents of affirmative action will have accomplished the elimination of an "innocuous" remedial program that has achieved some progress in the pursuit of society's diversity goals if their efforts to abolish such programs are successful.

Opponents of affirmative action view such reforms as bad public policy. Those who tend to view the policy negatively, such as Patrick Hall, believe that affirmative action programs violate the principle of equal opportunity and promote the untenable notion that a group is entitled to a guarantee of success. Hall believes that this evolutionary orientation of affirmative action is divisive and contributes significantly to the perpetuation of racial intolerance within the nation.

Another concern expressed by Hall and others opposed to this issue is the claim that affirmative action reinforces feelings of self-doubt and stifles individual initiatives among blacks and other minorities, thus causing them to miss opportunities that are available to them. They also deny blacks and others the full opportunity to promote the perception within the dominant culture that their hiring was based on merit rather than quotas or preferential hiring.

Hall maintains that affirmative action policies tend to promote stereotypes of blacks. He believes that racial preferences or quotas provide support for those who claim that such policies provide clear evidence that blacks and others cannot advance based on their qualifications and abilities. Hall states that racial preferences, rather than merit-based hiring policies, sometimes lead to the hiring of "vastly unqualified" personnel. Such an outcome of affirmative action policies can only serve to contribute to the controversy and racial polarization that surround these policies. According to Hall and other critics, such programs fail to sort out who is truly disadvantaged. Even though some better-educated and positioned minorities have benefited from these initiatives, they have not provided uplift for the black masses.

Robert Staples ➡ **YES**

Black Deprivation-White Privilege: The Assault On Affirmative Action

The current furor over affirmative action has many of us perplexed. Somehow, black Americans have shifted, in image, from being violent criminals, drug dealers, wife beaters, sexual harassers, welfare cheaters and underclass members to privileged members of the middle-class, who acquired their jobs through some racial quota system at the expense of white males who had superior qualifications for those same jobs. It is a testament to the ingenuity of white male politicians, using the race card, that they can exploit the historically ingrained prejudice against black Americans in the direction of the small black middle-class. For the last twenty-five years, the use of racial code issues, such as law and order, revising the welfare system and the tax revolt has served to transform the southern states from a Democratic stronghold to a Republican majority among its white population.

However, Republicans are increasingly becoming victims of their own success. White Democratic candidates have become as vigilantly anti-crime and welfare as their Republican opponents. In the Louisiana gubernatorial race of 1995, even the black candidates reached out to those whites seeking harsher sentences for criminals, the overwhelming majority of offenders being black in that particular state. While this situation illustrates that there is no honor among thieves, i.e. politicians, it also demonstrates that the diminishing returns of the racial code issues have created a dilemma among the Republican right. Into this void steps the issue of affirmative action, an innocuous program devised more than thirty years ago by President John F. Kennedy to increase the employment of blacks in the public sector. It was expanded by President Richard M. Nixon, who personally believed blacks were intellectually inferior, to include other people of color and white women.

All this occurred at a time when white males held an almost total monopoly of all top and mid-level professional and managerial jobs in the US. Blacks and women who were qualified could not penetrate the barriers to white collar employment except in very special niches for white women (e.g. nursing, home economics or teaching) and a small number of

Reprinted from *Black Scholar*, volume 25, number 3 (summer 1995), pp. 2–6, by permission of the University of Nebraska Press © 1995.

professional blacks who serviced the black community. Subsequently, there was some reduction in the exclusive white male monopoly in the white collar occupations and affirmative action was only one of the reasons for the change. The shift from a manufacturing to a service based economy was a big factor in increasing female employment. And the racial violence of the late 1960s convinced the ruling elites that some blacks had to be brought into white dominated institutions to bring about racial tranquility.

As for affirmative action, there is no consensus on what it is, who are its beneficiaries or what it has achieved. I will not try to define it, since the practice runs the gamut from including people of color and women in the pool of applicants for vacant positions to establishing explicit racial and gender quotas in some institutional spheres. The beneficiaries are generally blacks, Latinos, American Indians, sometimes Asians and women, the disabled, and military veterans. It is estimated that as many as five million people of color have gotten their jobs directly through affirmative action. However, such figures cannot be validated because affirmative action operates in such a complex and convoluted way.

What we do know is that there has been a small shift in the number of blacks who can be regarded as middle-class. Most estimates are generally in the range of one-third of the Afro-American population. The progress for black women has been greater, as recent census figures show that among young black college graduates, women earn more than men. The progress for white women is more complicated to measure, because the majority of them are married to white men and share the same standard of living. Nonetheless, there has been some economic and educational progress for all affected groups and affirmative action is, at least, partly responsible for this progress because it requires employers to be racial and gender inclusive. What has been overshadowed in this debate is that these groups make up about 70 percent of the American population. White males, the alleged victims of affirmative action compose about 30 percent of the population and still hold about 75 percent of the highest earning occupations in this country, and 95 percent at the very top.

Somehow, some way, this whole issue has been distorted into a prevailing belief that white men are the victims of affirmative action and that their rights have been trampled on. Underlying this belief is the assumption that white males are entitled to 100 percent of the high paying occupations, as they had prior to 1965, because they are intellectually superior to people of color and women. That such a notion could have any credence should be absurd on the face of it. Still, it will be upheld in an initiative on the California ballot in 1996, as it was in July of 1995, when the University of California Regents abolished affirmative action in admissions and employment. And this occurred in a state where half the population are people of color and white, non-Hispanic, males compose twenty percent of the state's population.

I will now address the issue of affirmative action in the state of California and at the University of California, where I have lived and taught for the last three decades. About the state: it is a mosaic of geographic, cultural, social and political elements. Its borders house both the radicals of Berkeley and the John Birch Society of Orange County. Not only is California the most populous of the 50 states, it is one of the most racially diverse. Latinos, Asians, blacks and American Indians make up one half of the state's population. Politically it can be a progressive state, since blacks and women have held a higher number of elective offices there than in any other state. Yet, in the last thirty years the state has experienced (1) the passage of a state proposition to legalize racial discrimination in housing, which was declared unconstitutional by the courts, (2) the uprooting of every black person, by white groups, from their homes in the town of Taft, (3) the election of a member of the Ku Klux Klan as the Democratic candidate for a US Congressional seat and (4) the passage of proposition 187, which denies medical treatment and education to undocumented aliens and their children, most of whom are considered people of color.

With this historical backdrop, the Board of Regents of the University of California met in San Francisco on July 20, 1995 to vote on the issue of abolishing affirmative action in admissions and employment. Until this date, there had been no ground swell of public desire to end a program that had existed for 25 years, in a state where blacks and Latinos compose 40 percent of the pool of potential students. But, the Governor, Pete Wilson, who is running for the Republican nomination for president, was way behind in the polls and needed to show he could actually do something about this "wedge issue" that the Republican party discovered in 1995. Typical of 1990s politics, Wilson has a black man, Ward Connerly, himself a beneficiary of affirmative action, to lead the fight to abolish affirmative action. All those involved in the university—the faculty, administration, student groups and alumni were opposed to its abolishment. The vote was a mere formality, as almost all the white male regents were Republican appointees, and by a vote of 15-10, became the first public university to abolish affirmative action.

One would think it a risky political move in a state where people of color make up 50 percent of the population. However, because many Latinos and Asians are recent immigrants, some undocumented, the voting population is 80 percent white. As Mark Di Camillo, of the California Poll commented, "when you do public opinion polling, you see that whites are much more sensitive to issues that relate to the future of California and the position of whites. They probably have greater concern about their own self-interest." Of course, a substantial number of Asians and some Latinos were also opposed to affirmative action at the University of California. The issue is often framed as a black/white one, though blacks make up only 8 percent of the state's population, less than 6 percent of the UC student body and 2 percent of the faculty. By far, the greatest beneficiaries of affirmative action, due to their larger numbers, are white women. Yet they are hardly mentioned in this debate, partly because they are also 52 percent of white voters and their husbands depend on them for their standard of living. The polls show that about two-thirds of white women would vote to abolish affirmative action.

It is not clear what effect the UC Regents' votes will have on the racial and gender balance of the UC campuses. The president of the University of California, Jack Petalson, issued a statement saying, "Few significant changes are likely because UC's employment and contracting programs are governed by state and federal laws, regulations, executive orders and the US Constitution." Because affirmative action is such an innocuous program, it has created strange political bedfellows. Richard Butler, a leading white supremacist and head of the Church of Jesus Christ Christian Aryan Nation hailed Governor Wilson for his support of the UC Regents' decision. He said that "Wilson is beginning to wake up to Aryan views." At the same time, arch conservatives such as Jack Kemp and William Bennett, who are not running for public office, have reaffirmed their support for affirmative action.

This whole debate tends to obscure some of the real issues for the black community. As Jesse Jackson has noted, "There is substantial evidence that affirmative action is inadequately enforced and too narrowly applied." Blacks hold only 4 percent of professional and managerial positions in the US and are a fraction of 1 percent of senior managers in America's major corporations. At the same time, almost a majority of black males are not in the civilian labor force. About 25 percent of young black males are in prison, on probation or parole. Even if white males can reclaim that 4 percent of the executive positions, it will do little to restore them to the 100 percent monopoly they once held.

An essential piece of the attack on affirmative action is that it unfairly discriminates against white males. To accept this premise is to assume that every white male is superior to every woman and person of color. Why else should they control 100 percent of the top positions in the society: for example, in the government contract set asides about 25 percent of the work is often delegated to people of color and women. Presumably, the other 75 percent is held by "deserving" white males. If that aspect of affirmative action is eliminated, white males will get all the hundreds of billions of dollars in taxpayer funds that go to private companies. As for how white males have achieved such an advantage in this one sphere, far in excess of their percentage of the population, it may have more to do with the fact that other white males are making the decisions on whom to award those contracts—not on the merits of a true competition for them.

The center of the white male argument is that they possess skills other groups do not have, particularly as measured by their performance on standardized tests. Thus, they pretend that those tests are valid measures of merit and use them to exclude all but white males from the top paying occupations. It is, indeed, true that they are better test takers than women and people of color—in part because they created and administer the tests. Other research, also by white males, suggests that many of those exams have no relevance to job performance, contain a cultural bias that favors middle-class Anglo males and are not required for most jobs in the US. In many cases, affirmative action was a tool to consider other—often more relevant—measures to evaluate job applicants. And the opponents of affirmative action is hard pressed to name many cases where individuals, hired under affirmative action, lack the necessary skills to do a job for which they are hired.

In reality, most people in this country are capable of performing well at a variety of occupations, because most of what they learn, in performing occupational tasks, is on the job itself. Since there are not enough "desirable and high paying jobs for all the qualified applicants, the system devises arbitrary screening devices such as educational requirements and standardized tests to weed out people. Because white males in the US are socialized into a sense of entitlement to the most prestigious and highest paying positions, they are generally better positioned to take advantage of the those arbitrary screening devices. Moreover, studies over the years have found that between 35–65 percent Americans find their jobs through contacts made via the friends and kinship network, a practice that partly accounts for the white male dominance of senior positions in both the private and public sector.

Affirmative action has experienced some abuses. Why people of color and women are held responsible for the abuses is a mystery, since white males are chiefly responsible for administering affirmative action programs. The greatest abuses seem to occur in the contract set asides, where a few black and Latinos have served as fronts to get government contracts that actually go to Anglo contractors. Another problem has been the classification of racial minorities. Because people with a small percentage of Indian ancestry can live as white Americans, they face no disadvantage different from other whites in this society. Yet, they have often qualified for affirmative action treatment. The problem of white usurpation of Indian identity was so prevalent that American Indians wanted to retain their original name, albeit a misnomer, because so many whites were claiming the title of Native Americans and receiving benefits designed for oppressed American Indians.

Some opponents of affirmative action have suggested replacing its racial/gender components with that of socioeconomic status, which would also include poor whites. Of course poor whites are already included in university recruitment and admission of students as well as being part of the disabled and military veteran category. However it is unfair to equate a low socioeconomic status with the disadvantages of race and gender. A poor white male who gets a college education and a middle-class job simply increases the number of white males in the ruling elite. His problems are over, while women and people of color will continue to encounter glass ceilings in education and employment. And blacks who are middle-class do not escape anything but the economic problems associated with being black. Because the oppression is aimed at the entire group, the political remedies should go to all visible members of the black population.

Finally, this attack on affirmative action is nothing more than a replay of history for Afro-Americans. Slavery was defended with a variety of rationalizations, including the inferiority of blacks, the need to make blacks Christians and the slaveowners' property rights. Racial segregation in schools was defended by the separate but equal doctrine. Southern apartheid was maintained politically under the states' rights defense.

Now, we have the anomaly of having white males, a third of the population who make up 95 percent of those who run America, control and distribute 90 percent of the nation's wealth, trying to portray themselves as victims because women and people of color finally broke their grip on all the society's resources. Their attack on affirmative action can only be characterized as political and economic overkill.

However, despite its absurdity, the assault has the potential to succeed. Politicians have had the wisdom to target blacks as the main recipients of affirmative action, while ignoring the fact that white women make up as much as 80 percent of the beneficiaries. This allows them to get the votes of white women, who may act on their interests as whites and ignore their interests as women. To the degree that they empathize and share households with white males, they have less to lose. Single white women, female heads-of-households and lesbians, will be sacrificed on the altar of larger white interests. Blacks, historically, make a convenient scapegoat for the decline of capitalism and the whites who are casualties of that decline. While they comprise a small percentage of those subject to affirmative action, they remain a national target of prejudice and stereotyping in every corner of the nation.

The notion of a color blind society, with no need for affirmative action, is a fantasy at this point. Race is the most divisive variable extant in the US. Whites commonly betray their class interests on its behalf and individual life chances for both blacks and whites are a direct function of it. Affirmative action is but one tool—not a very effective one—to mitigate its effect. The attack on it is part of a white plan to make people of color their servants again, while they continue to obligate them to pay taxes to subsidize white privilege. What whites may find is they may not want to live in the world they are creating.

Patrick A. Hall  **NO**

Against Our Best Interests: An Ambivalent View of Affirmative Action

Thomas Sowell, a black economist and social critic, wrote these words in his 1984 *Civil Rights: Rhetoric or Reality,* referring to the policies of affirmative action as they have evolved over the last 18 years. As a black man in my 40s, I have in some ways benefited from such entitlement programs, so perhaps I should be the last person to initiate negative discourse toward them. But as I look back over the past decade since I left teaching and entered the library profession, the gains that others like myself have secured appear to be costing us much in the way of societal cohesion and racial tolerance. In retrospect, such pivotal events as the Civil Rights Act of 1964 and the Supreme Court's 1959 *Brown vs. Board of Education* decision provided blacks with the opportunity (stress *opportunity*) to achieve; but they did not guarantee any class, sex, or race the right to succeed.

I argue that the ideals of the civil rights movement were largely betrayed when equal opportunity was transformed into equal group results via evolutionary distortions in entitlement programs. This may be hard for many blacks, including myself, to accept, but the opportunities that have been in place for the past 20 years don't grant the right to guaranteed success, as entitlement programs seek to foster. In short, the civil rights movement gave us the right to vote, not the right to win.

A Historical Brief on Affirmative Action

Like most controversial topics, affirmative action is one of those creatures that everyone has an opinion on; but most people's understanding of its historical antecedents is limited to 60-second sound bites or an occasional segment on "60 Minutes." Honestly, prior to preparing this essay my own knowledge wasn't much better. But as I read through materials tracing its development, it became clear that affirmative action and equal opportunity have evolved into something today that bears very little resemblance to what was originally intended during the civil rights era.

Reprinted from *Black Scholar,* volume 22, number 9 (October 1991), pp. 898–903, by permission of the University of Nebraska Press © 1991.

Prior to the passage of the Civil Rights Act of 1964, President Kennedy first used the term "affirmative action" in 1961 in his Executive Order No. 10,925. Its original intent was not to set up quotas, preferential treatment, or that Darwinian misnomer "protected classes." Kennedy's order sought to use the power of the executive branch and the federal government to monitor and intervene, if necessary, in cases of blatant racial inequalities and discriminatory practices. Even with the passage of the Civil Rights Act of 1964, which gave rise to affirmative action and equal opportunity as distinct legislative philosophies, quotas and preferential treatment were not intrinsic to its application. It was in May 1968 that the Labor Department's Office of Federal Construction Compliance put out guidelines containing the fateful expressions of goals, timetables, and representations. In other words, entitlement was the next logical step, and the malformation of an otherwise good piece of legislation had begun.

The irony in all of this is that affirmative action and equal opportunity originally intended people to be judged on their qualifications as individuals without regard to race, sex, or age. However, the policy as it has evolved requires that blacks, women, and so-called "protected classes" be judged with such differences in mind. I am deeply aware that racism and sexism are still part of the American landscape, and that blacks are especially underrepresented in a variety of job classifications, including librarianship. But the use of quotas and preferential hiring is extremely problematic, and at best represents only a Pyrrhic victory. Some minorities have benefited, but even their achievements are tainted with the asterisk "special hire."

Legislating Fairness

In the fall of 1989, I attended a conference sponsored by the Oregon and Washington chapters of the Association of College and Research Libraries. During one of the sessions the issue of affirmative action and preferential hiring was raised, and some of the conferees commented on how it was causing a rift in staff morale at their various libraries. Several administrators suggested that we should try to point out to our staff how they as whites are privileged and enjoy unseen advantages. As discussion continued, those present seemed to accept this overused piece of hyper-explanation as a defense of affirmative action. I was especially troubled by the great deal of ambiguity that I sensed over this answer.

Talking with several people later during dinner, I discovered that most of them didn't favor affirmative action, but they feared being labeled racist if they said anything against it. This sort of fear can generate resentment; and if history has taught us anything, we should realize that resentments eventually have consequences. To tell people—especially many lower-class whites—that they are privileged "ain't gonna play" in Peoria.

Although this notion of who is and who isn't privileged is a favorite polemic of insulated academics and many "professional blacks" (not to be confused with black professionals), it just doesn't wash with the majority of Americans. We can, as is often the case, write off anyone who objects to affirmative action as a racist—or in my case, "an Uncle Tom suck-up." But it doesn't change the fact that these policies are counterproductive for blacks, whites, and most importantly, our nation, because they threaten to repoliticize race. The recent North Carolina senatorial race between Jesse Helms and Harvey Gantt was just an indication of the racial polarization that many had fought and died to reduce during the civil rights era. It is clear to any social observer that such politically chauvinistic policies as affirmative action inevitably provoke counter-chauvinism; and in a multicultural society such as ours, this could be a deadly scenario.

The Asterisk

I recently had the privilege to talk with historian Shelby Steele, the author of *The Content of Our Character*. Several weeks earlier, I had seen him on the "Today" show discussing his book, and I called to congratulate him on this thought-provoking work, which calls for blacks to look to themselves and not to government entitlements for any lasting socioeconomic progress. Throughout his book, Steele stresses individual initiative as the key to any real progress for blacks.

As we finished our conversation, I felt extremely ambivalent about my own achievements, since affirmative action has always placed an asterisk next to them. After talking with other individuals, both minorities and females, I discovered that many of them harbor the same type of self-doubt, whether it is justified or not. This is only one of the negative consequences of affirmative action despite the so-called gains: No matter how hard one works, or how many master's or doctorate degrees one possesses, the special-hire asterisk—that small star of omission used to indicate doubtful matter—is ever-present.

Affirmative action has really only benefited individuals already in a position to take advantage of it, and has seldom touched the truly disadvantaged—those men and women who lack the education and skills needed to begin careers. As a librarian, I often recommend *The Truly Disadvantaged*, by William Julius Wilson, a book that I feel does an excellent job of illustrating the lack of impact entitlement programs and other forms of social engineering have had on the poor. One of Wilson's most salient comments is that those minorities and women with education and skills have benefited disproportionately from entitlement programs because they were educationally, socially, and most importantly, motivationally disposed to do so.

One has to wonder whether individuals like myself would have achieved success anyway, even without affirmative action. Prior to the preference-based affirmative action of the early 1970s, blacks and women were making considerable strides on their own without the burden of the extra stigma of "protected-class hire," a stigma that indirectly continues to propagate the stereotypes of black inferiority.

Even my own family background suggests that motivation, individual initiative, and perseverance can overcome the most abhorrent situations.

I am the 11th of 12 children, and many of my older brothers and sisters, who are now in their middle and late 50s, negotiated their professional careers in a world without entitlement programs. The blatant discrimination they experienced did not deter them from success.

With the passage of the equal opportunity laws mentioned earlier, minorities were provided with the necessary environment to take their best shot. The current dogma among many in the black community that present-day racism is more subtle but just as insidious speaks more to our mind-sets as helpless victims. This attitude breeds in far too many blacks the inability to seize opportunities that are readily apparent to other minorities. The operative word here is opportunities, not guarantees. With the transition of affirmative action from equal opportunity to preference, from development via individual initiative to the numbers game of representation, we are setting our society and its people against one another. Preference in any circumstance will breed backlash, because it inevitably sets up an "I-win-you-lose" scenario based on race or gender with little concern for the atmosphere it creates in the workplace.

This point was graphically brought home to me while working in the library at a small alternative college in Washington State. Like most academic institutions, the library was pushing racial and gender representation through affirmative action, and on the surface the cherished goal of proportionate representation was being realized. Administrators and various academic deans made sure departments actively sought minority or other protected-class hires. In the library, minority representation was being pushed by individuals with very little concern for staff morale or about qualifications. There existed a largely unspoken rift between the administrators and the staff—both librarians and paraprofessionals—because many staff members felt representation was being rammed down their throats by the administrators.

Although individuals on the staff were quite nice to me, it was apparent to anyone who cared to notice that socially engineered fairness wasn't going to work. Whether they are black, white, red, or whatever, people don't like their concerns to go unnoticed. Administrators and other higher-ups either ignored this growing resentment, hoping it would subside, or simply labeled people who raised objections to blatant quota hires as racist, sexist, or whatever convenient term that could be used to censor discourse about preference policies.

Although most liberal whites at this college would never admit it, many of the hires, especially among the teaching faculty, were "vastly unqualified." People with PhDs from mail-order institutes were hired over colleagues who possessed credentials from places like Berkeley, Northwestern, or Yale. In one instance our library was so desperate to have a so-called "person of color" in technical services that a foreign national was hired. This individual happened to be "highly qualified"; but if the goal of affirmative action was to provide opportunities to historically oppressed minorities, giving the jobs to people from privileged classes from other countries is hardly what the framers of these policies had in mind. We simply cannot allow ourselves to sidestep the difficult goal of developing a formerly oppressed people, like African Americans, to the point where we can achieve proportionate representation on our own. This is the real challenge that faces blacks and other minority groups, a challenge that echoes from the basic belief of the civil rights movement that we should not be judged by our skin color or gender, but by our character. Two decades ago, preference policies offered politicians, both black and white, a cheap and easy way out of this dilemma. Now in the 1990s the balloon payment of socially engineered programs is coming due in the form of racial and ethnic discordance.

Some Unspoken Assumptions

As a black man who grew up in the 1950s and 1960s and witnessed many of the triumphs and tragedies of the civil fights movement, my anxiety about speaking up against entitlement programs is very acute. Affirmative action started off well enough, but it has evolved into a legislative beast that threatens all of us by gradually undermining the very delicate intercultural rapport of our nation. As a reference librarian, I am constantly being exposed to a myriad of ideas that often lead me to explore areas and ideology that I might not otherwise have been exposed to. Along with some of the experiences I have outlined earlier, they have caused me to question some key assumptions underlying race- and gender-specific entitlement policies.

Despite the current economic downturn, I believe an equitable society is still possible, but not in the hyper-race-sensitive mind-set of affirmative action. First, I ask that proponents of affirmative action examine their underlying assumption that statistical disparities in the job market "imply discrimination." Secondly, I question the assumption that large statistical differences between groups do not usually arise, and more importantly persist, without discrimination.

Although a thorough discussion of these two assumptions is well beyond the scope of this article, proponents of entitlement philosophies need to consider (if not admit to) other factors that impede upward mobility, especially among blacks. A negative family background, lack of personal motivation and initiative, and a lack of values that emphasize effort and sacrifice are all factors that will hinder one's chances for success in this society.

The U.S. has also seen a marked shift in the industrial/manufacturing paradigm, which has greatly affected blacks but has produced disparities that have little or nothing to do with blatant discrimination. In the past three decades, people who were heavily represented in the "smokestack" industries (i.e., autoworkers, machinists) have seen their jobs disappear because of automarion, foreign competition, companies moving to foreign countries, and just plain bad management. Blacks as well as working-class whites who depended on this employment were, of course, hurt the most and continue to be so. It could be argued that the reason blacks were so overrepresented in these disappearing industries was because of past discrimination. This has its validity, but doesn't negate the fact that these shifts resulting in massive unemployment have little or nothing to do with race or discrimination, as proponents of affirmative action claim.

The defining of middle-class values as "white" by both less-educated and educated blacks (who should know better) is perhaps the most insidious factor that continues to hamstring the progress of blacks as a group. If someone is reasonably articulate, motivated, and focused on success, the black community often brings forth a particularly nasty reflex response that interprets this as "being white"; the corresponding "black identity" implicitly preferred by many in the community is ephemeral at best and counterproductive to our socio-economic progress. It is no accident that so many black youths chastise their studious peers with the indictment that "it's not cool to study," or "you think you're white." Black adults continue this "racial navel-gazing" by labeling black spokespersons who disagree with this traditional dogma as "white" or "Uncle Toms."

In many ways the greatest obstacle to our progress as a people has been ourselves and many of our so-called leaders. In our single-minded focus on racism and discrimination as "the" factor in our lack of upward mobility, we continue to foster a victim mentality often disguised as a "black identity." This victim mentality consistently leads us to sacrifice the lamb of individual initiative at the altar ol government entitlements.

No Easy Solutions

If not affirmative action, then what? I repeat that it is not affirmative action per se that I object to, but rather its perversion by those who continue to equate it with the civil rights movement. In actuality, the movement ended decades ago, and what has existed for the last 18 years has been the scramble for privileges, turf, and just plain power politics by black opportunists who see profit in maintaining their "wards of the state" status. The painful reality is that society can never repay blacks for their past suffering, but can provide a chance for advancement in today's world. Affirmative action, with its emphasis on representation, circumvents the most difficult ingredient in true individual and group empowerment— development. As Shelby Steele said, representation can be manufactured; development is always hard-earned.

Affirmative action should therefore return to its original purpose of monitoring inequalities and discriminatory practices that still exist. In addition, policymakers should abandon with all haste any racespecific public policies in favor of policies that benefit all the disadvantaged of our nation, regardless of race or gender.

As argued earlier, I can no longer accept the liberal dogma that all whites are somehow privileged, and all blacks are innocent victims. This belief is not only counterproductive to societal cohesion, giving the David Dukes and Louis Farrakhans of our society more fuel for racial polarization, but it also ignores the increasing role that class differences play as significant variables in an individual's chances for upward mobility.

I would like to direct my final comments to black professionals, especially those of us over 40 who can remember the ideals of the black power movement of the 1960s, which preached empowerment through self-determination. We need to tell our young people over and over again to work hard and not use race as an excuse for failure. The effects of historic racism have left us behind in the race for success; but as Martin Luther King, Jr., put it, this only means we have to run a little harder and not equate our salvation as a people with entitlement programs or other outside arbiters. We need to mentor "positively," and not focus on the usual victim litany that inhibits our ability as a people to see opportunities outside the blinders of affirmative action.

POSTSCRIPT

Is Affirmative Action Necessary to Achieve Racial Equality in the United States?

Fortuitously, this postscript is being written on the day that the U.S. Supreme Court rendered its highly anticipated ruling on *Grutter v. Bollinger* concerning the University of Michigan Law School's affirmative action policy. The justices ruled that race may be employed as one factor among others in the decision-making processes of college admissions. Thus the Court upheld the "Bakke standard" that was enunciated by Justice Powell within the ruling on that case in 1978. Since that earlier decision, a standard that permits the use of race as one factor among others has prevailed within the admission policies of the nation's colleges and universities.

Sociologist Orlando Patterson argues "no issue better reveals the American tension between principle and pragmatism than the debate over affirmative action." The principles of fairness, equality, and meritocracy all inform this debate. The discourse on affirmative action policies contains significant misconceptions. There is a tendency to view such programs as remedies for past racism and sexism. It is difficult to comprehend or accept a claim that a limited policy of affirmative action is an adequate response to the legacy of slavery and racial segregation that continues to challenge the nation. In this context, Issue 17 deals with reparations. On the other hand, any racial preferences call into question the prevailing commitment to equal opportunity.

Patrick Hall and other opponents of affirmative action think that such programs are no longer necessary because African Americans and other members of the "protected classes" have made sufficient progress. He and others raise questions about merit in employment and education. Further, Hall expresses concern that the recognition of black achievement will be undermined by such policies. Legitimate concerns about divisiveness and a backlash against such policies are also raised.

Robert Staples and proponents of affirmative action policies must confront the fact that these programs are not applied properly in certain situations. In its 1978 ruling in the *Bakke* case and the recent *Bollinger* case, the court found that racial or gender-based quotas are impermissible applications of affirmative action policies. So, gender or racial preferences that are based on some numerical scheme that utilizes a point system to give protected class members a boost are unconstitutional and must be changed. Quotas, therefore, are unacceptable in affirmative action policy.

Supporters of affirmative action programs embrace the proposition that the goal of achieving racial diversity within the institutions of society is a compelling national interest. They believe that social institutions should reflect the diverse composition of America's population within the profile of their employees. Those who affirm support for such programs are concerned that they will not be able to meet their diversity goals if affirmative action is curtailed or abolished. It is not just the traditional membership of the civil rights community who express such concerns. Leaders of the military establishment and the private corporate world have expressed such concerns, and they were the basis for the *amicus curae* briefs that were filed in support of the University of Michigan's affirmative action policies before the U.S. Supreme Court. Their concern is based on a clear understanding that education and life experiences garnered within diverse environments are vital preparation for one to meet the challenges and function effectively in an increasingly global and multicultural social reality. The achievement of racial and other diversity within educational settings, from preschool to graduate school, is a critical component of any meaningful response to these concerns.

Further reading that supports affirmative action can be found in "Racism Has Its Privileges," by Roger Wilkins in *The Nation* (March 22, 1995). Stephen Carter's *Reflections of an Affirmative Action Baby* (HarperCollins, 1991) furthers the case for affirmative action. An argument in support of affirmative action as a redistributive measure in American society is made by Cornel West in "Equality and Identity," in *The American Prospect* (Spring 1992). Orlando Patterson's op-ed piece "Affirmative Action: The Sequel" (*The New York Times,* June 6, 2003) written just before the *Bollinger* decision, argues "using diversity as a rationale for affirmative action also distorts the aims of affirmative action." Ronald Dworkin in "Is Affirmative Action Doomed?" (*New York Review of Books* November 5, 1998) makes the case for the constitutionality of affirmative action. The entire Fall/Winter edition of *The Black Scholar* (2003) is devoted to an analysis of the rulings on admissions policy at the University of Michigan, June 16, 2003.

A critique of affirmative action by a Shelby Steele, an African American educator is developed in *The Content of Our Character* (St. Martin's Press, 1990). Charles Murray attacks affirmative action programs in his article "Affirmative Racism," which appeared in *The New Republic* (December 31, 1984). Carl Cohen, in "Race Preference and the Universities—A Final Reckoning," in a *Commentary* (September 2001) article, argues that the most recent Supreme Court case will end quotas in college admissions. In another *Commentary* (February 1999) article, Stephan and Abigail Thernstrom argue against racial preferences in admissions in "Racial Preferences: What We Now Know." Clarence Thomas argues against numerical measures of affirmative action in "Affirmative Action Goals and Timetables: Too Tough? Not Tough Enough!" in the *Yale Law and PolicyReview* (Summer 1987).

The Affirmative Action Debate (Perseus Books Group, 1996) edited by George E. Curry and Cornel West includes several different perspectives of the subject. Another anthology on affirmative action is *Debating Affirmative Action: Race, Gender, Ethnicity, and the Politics of Inclusion* (Delta, 1994) edited by Nicholaus Mills.

On the Internet . . .

American Civil Liberties Union

This site covers current information on immigrants' rights and issues of civil rights, including voting rights. It reviews Supreme Court decisions and other legislative action. The archives section offers a wealth of information on race and ethnic legal cases throughout American history. There is an interesting section on racial profiling.

http://www.aclu.org

U.S. Department of State

The U.S. Department of State Web site will enable students to read official texts and speeches dealing with race and immigration issues such as racial profiling, affirmative action, black colleges, racism, voting rights, and immigrant labor.

http://usinfo.state.gov/usa/civilrights/homepage.htm

The Sociological Imagination: Race and Ethnicity

This is the "race and ethnicity" part of the "Exercising the Sociological Imagination Tour" from the Trinity University Department of Sociology and Anthropology Web site. Helpful to students is the "Sociological Tour Through Cyberspace," which offers links to resources in race and ethnicity along with brief reports on American minority groups.

http://www.trinity.edu/~mkearl/index.html#in

Race in the 21st Century

This is the Web site of a political science professor at Michigan State University. Among the many offerings dealing with multiculturalism, education, civil rights, standardized tests, and citizenship is William B. Allen's "Race in the 21st Century" (3/22/99), dealing with race as a consideration in college admissions. Allen represents a conservative perspective.

http://www.msu.edu/~allenwi/presentations
/Race_in_21st_Century_America.htm

Human Rights Watch

This is the Web site of Human Rights Watch, an organization dedicated to protecting the rights of people around the world with offices in Europe and the United States. It contains a general statement on reparations.

http://www.hrw.org/campaigns/race/reparations.htm

PART 4

Issues for the Twenty-First Century

T *wenty-first century America is truly a nation of diverse ethnicities. As indicated earlier, the Asians and Hispanics are the fastest growing groups within the American population. Within the past year, the media have highlighted the fact that Hispanics have passed African Americans as the leading minority group within the American population. Yet, despite the continued darkening of the skin color of the American population, issues of color continue to confront this nation. Among the issues to be resolved in twenty-first century America are racial profiling, reparations, and race-conscious public policies, among other concerns. These issues continue to generate conflict within the American population and its political and economic elites.*

- Is Racism a Permanent Feature of American Society?

- Should Twenty-First Century Public Policy Be Class Conscious Rather than Race Conscious?

- Is Now the Time for Reparations for African Americans?

- Is Racial Profiling Defensible Public Policy?

ISSUE 15

Is Racism a Permanent Feature of American Society?

YES: Derrick Bell, "Divining Our Racial Themes," in *Faces at the Bottom of the Well: The Permanence of Racism* (Basic Books, 1992)

NO: Dinesh D'Souza, "The End of Racism" in *The End of Racism: Principles for a Multiracial Society* (Free Press, 1995)

ISSUE SUMMARY

YES: Derrick Bell, a prominent African-American scholar and authority on civil rights and constitutional law, argues that the prospects for achieving racial equality in the United States are "illusory" for blacks.

NO: Dinesh D'Souza, media commentator and writer, believes that racial discrimination against blacks has substantially eroded within American society and that lagging progress among them is due to other factors, such as culture, rather than racism.

$\mathbf{R}$acist ideology has been employed throughout the nation's history in attempts to justify institutional policies and practices such as slavery and segregation. Despite the substantial efforts of supporters of a racially egalitarian society, the reification of racism is a continuing reality of this nation.

The persistence of ideological and institutional racism within the United States has given rise to a debate over the prospects for ridding our society of this glaring contradiction. On one side of this debate are those who believe that a proper examination of the American experience and the treatment of African Americans and other peoples of color throughout history leads to the conclusion that racism is unlikely to be eroded in this country and will continue to challenge the American creed. The other side is comprised of those who advance the more optimistic view concerning race relations within the United States. Members of this camp claim that the destructive impact of racism is declining in this country, and that any lagging progress of African Americans is due to factors other than racial discrimination.

Derrick Bell is a proponent of the thesis that racism is a permanent feature of American society. His now classic thesis is supported by an analysis of some of the most important aspects of African Americans' historical development. Bell reminds us that despite the fact of significant progress for some blacks of the United States, the legacy of slavery has left a significant portion of the race "with life-long poverty and soul-devastating despair . . .".

Bell believes that race consciousness is so imbedded in whites that it is virtually impossible to rise above it. He argues that "few whites are able to identify with blacks as a group" and tend to view them through "comforting racial stereotypes." Bell cites a number of examples of the destructive impact of racial bonding among whites upon blacks' efforts to progress within society. He points out that even poor whites have tended to support institutions such as slavery and segregation rather than coalescing with blacks to fight against common social disadvantages such as unemployment and poverty. Given this record of race relations, it is impossible for Bell to accept the claim that racism has been largely overcome in these United States. To the contrary, he is strongly of the view that a critical and proper examination of the history of black-white relations supports the conclusion that racism is a permanent feature of American society.

Dinesh D'Souza does not agree with Bell that racism is a permanent strain of the fabric of American society. D'Souza distinguishes between racial discrimination that is "irrational, motivated by bigotry" and that which is "rational from the point of view of the discriminator." While admitting that such discrimination may be harmful to individual blacks, D'Souza rejects any causal linkage between the lagging indicators of blacks' overall progress with racial discrimination. Since he believes that racism is a diminishing force within American life, D'Souza argues that factors other than racial discrimination are the sources of lagging progress toward the American dream. He is strongly supportive of the view that cultural factors contribute to social pathology, including crime, unwed motherhood, and others, and are the primary causes of the prevailing and persistent gap in socioeconomic achievement between blacks and whites.

D'Souza argues that the failure of blacks to observe and embrace certain of the cultural norms of the dominant American society is a major reason why the race is not achieving more in America. He argues that those blacks who are successful exhibit cultural values that promote success. Those who are not achieving are immersed in a defective culture that is antithetical to success. Thus, D'Souza would argue that blacks need to place a much greater emphasis on overcoming cultural barriers rather than continuing to assert that the race is being held back by a persistent racism that afflicts America.

The reader would benefit from expanding his or her perspective to include ideas and concepts dealing with social and cultural values. This is a debate in itself. That is, do structural conditions such as racism, discrimination, and lack of opportunity lead to inequality and poverty? Or, is poverty attributed to individual factors including socialization and value formation? Bell makes the structural argument while D'Souza offers a culture of poverty thesis.

Derrick Bell  **YES**

Faces at the Bottom of the Well: The Permanence of Racism

Divining Our Racial Themes

In these bloody days and frightful nights when an urban warrior can find no face more despicable than his own, no ammunition more deadly than self-hate and no target more deserving of his true aim than his brother, we must wonder how we came so late and lonely to this place.

—Maya Angelou

When I was Growing up in the years before the Second World War, our slave heritage was more a symbol of shame than a source of pride. It burdened black people with an indelible mark of difference as we struggled to be like whites. In those far-off days, survival and progress seemed to require moving beyond, even rejecting slavery. Childhood friends in a West Indian family who lived a few doors away often boasted—erroneously as I later learned—that their people had never been slaves. My own more accurate—but hardly more praiseworthy—response was that my forebears included many free Negroes, some of whom had Choctaw and Blackfoot Indian blood.

In those days, self-delusion was both easy and comforting. Slavery was barely mentioned in the schools and seldom discussed by the descendants of its survivors, particularly those who had somehow moved themselves to the North. Emigration, whether from the Caribbean islands or from the Deep South states, provided a geographical distance that encouraged and enhanced individual denial of our collective, slave past. We sang spirituals but detached the songs from their slave origins. As I look back, I see this reaction as no less sad, for being very understandable. We were a subordinate and mostly shunned portion of a society that managed to lay the onus of slavery neatly on those who were slaves while simultaneously exonerating those who were slaveholders. All things considered, it seemed a history best left alone.

Then, after the Second World War and particularly in the 1960s, slavery became—for a few academics and some militant Negroes—a subject of fascination and a sure means of evoking racial rage as a prelude to righteously repeated demands for "Freedom Now!" In response to a resurrection of interest in our past, new books on slavery were written, long out-of-print volumes republished. The new awareness reached its highest point in 1977 with the television version of Alex Haley's biographical novel, *Roots*. The highly successful miniseries informed millions of Americans—black as well as white—that slavery in fact existed and that it was awful. Not, of course, as awful as it would have been save for the good white folks the television writers had created to ease the slaves' anguish, and the evil ones on whose shoulders they placed all the guilt. Through the magic of literary license, white viewers could feel revulsion for slavery without necessarily recognizing American slavery as a burden on the nation's history, certainly not a burden requiring reparations in the present.

Even so, under pressure of civil rights protests, many white Americans were ready to accede to if not applaud Supreme Court rulings that the Constitution should no longer recognize and validate laws that kept in place the odious badges of slavery.

As a result, two centuries after the Constitution's adoption, we did live in a far more enlightened world. Slavery was no more. Judicial precedent and a plethora of civil rights statutes formally prohibited racial discrimination. Compliance was far from perfect, but the slavery provisions in the Constitution[1] did seem lamentable artifacts of a less enlightened era.

But the fact of slavery refuses to fade, along with the deeply embedded personal attitudes and public policy assumptions that supported it for so long. Indeed, the racism that made slavery feasible is far from dead in the last decade of twentieth-century America; and the civil rights gains, so hard won, are being steadily eroded. Despite undeniable progress for many, no African Americans are insulated from incidents of racial discrimination. Our careers, even our lives, are threatened because of our color. Even the most successful of us are haunted by the plight of our less fortunate brethren who struggle for existence in what some social scientists call the "underclass." Burdened with life-long poverty and soul-devastating despair, they live beyond the pale of the American Dream. What we designate as "racial progress" is not a solution to that problem. It is a regeneration of the problem in a particularly perverse form.

According to data compiled in 1990 for basic measures of poverty, unemployment, and income, the slow advances African Americans made during the 1960s and 1970s have definitely been reversed. The unemployment rate for blacks is 2.5 times the rate for whites. Black per-capita income is not even two thirds of the income for whites; and blacks, most of whom own little wealth or business property, are three times more likely to have income below the poverty level than whites. If trends of the last two decades are allowed to continue, readers can safely—and sadly—assume that the current figures are worse than those cited here.[2]

Statistics cannot, however, begin to express the havoc caused by joblessness and poverty: broken homes, anarchy in communities, futility in the public schools. All are the bitter harvest of race-determined unemployment in a society where work provides sustenance, status, and the all-important sense of self-worth. What we now call the "inner city" is, in fact, the American equivalent of the South African homelands. Poverty is less the source than the status of men and women who, despised because of their race, seek refuge in self-rejection. Drug-related crime, teenaged parenthood, and disrupted and disrupting family life all are manifestations of a despair that feeds on self. That despair is bred anew each day by the images on ever-playing television sets, images confirming that theirs is the disgraceful form of living, not the only way people live.

Few whites are able to identify with blacks as a group—the essential prerequisite for feeling empathy with, rather than aversion from, blacks' self-inflicted suffering, as expressed by the poet Maya Angelou in this introduction's epigraph. Unable or unwilling to perceive that "there but for the grace of God, go I," few whites are ready to actively promote civil rights for blacks. Because of an irrational but easily roused fear that any social reform will unjustly benefit blacks, whites fail to support the programs this country desperately needs to address the ever-widening gap between the rich and the poor, both black and white.

Lulled by comforting racial stereotypes, fearful that blacks will unfairly get ahead of them, all too many whites respond to even the most dire reports of race-based disadvantage with either a sympathetic headshake or victim-blaming rationalizations. Both responses lead easily to the conclusion that contemporary complaints of racial discrimination are simply excuses put forward by people who are unable or unwilling to compete on an equal basis in a competitive society.

For white people who both deny racism and see a heavy dose of the Horatio Alger myth as the answer to blacks' problems, how sweet it must be when a black person stands in a public place and condemns as slothful and unambitious those blacks who are not making it. Whites eagerly embrace black conservatives' homilies to self-help, however grossly unrealistic such messages are in an economy where millions, white as well as black, are unemployed and, more important, in one where racial discrimination in the workplace is as vicious (if less obvious) than it was when employers posted signs "no negras need apply."

Whatever the relief from responsibility such thinking provides those who embrace it, more than a decade of civil rights setbacks in the White House, in the courts, and in the critical realm of media-nurtured public opinion has forced retrenchment in the tattered civil rights ranks. We must reassess our cause and our approach to it, but repetition of time-worn slogans simply will not do. As a popular colloquialism puts it, it is time to "get real" about race and the persistence of racism in America.

To make such an assessment—to plan for the future by reviewing the experiences of the past—we must ask whether the formidable hurdles we now face in the elusive quest for racial equality are simply a challenge to our commitment, whether they are the latest variation of the old hymn "One More River to Cross." Or, as we once again gear up to meet the challenges posed by these unexpected new setbacks, are we ignoring a current message with implications for the future which history has already taught us about the past?

Such assessment is hard to make. On the one hand, contemporary color barriers are certainly less visible as a result of our successful effort to strip the law's endorsement from the hated Jim Crow signs. Today one can travel for thousands of miles across this country and never see a public facility designated as "Colored" or "White." Indeed, the very absence of visible signs of discrimination creates an atmosphere of racial neutrality and encourages whites to believe that racism is a thing of the past. On the other hand, the general use of so-called neutral standards to continue exclusionary practices reduces the effectiveness of traditional civil rights laws, while rendering discriminatory actions more oppressive than ever. Racial bias in the pre-*Brown* era was stark, open, unalloyed with hypocrisy and blank-faced lies. We blacks, when rejected, knew who our enemies were. They were not us! Today, because bias is masked in unofficial practices and "neutral" standards, we must wrestle with the question whether race or some individual failing has cost us the job, denied us the promotion, or prompted our being rejected as tenants for an apartment. Either conclusion breeds frustration and alienation—and a rage we dare not show to others or admit to ourselves.

Modern discrimination is, moreover, not practiced indiscriminately. Whites, ready and willing to applaud, even idolize black athletes and entertainers, refuse to hire, or balk at working with, blacks. Whites who number individual blacks among their closest friends approve, or do not oppose, practices that bar selling or renting homes or apartments in their neighborhoods to blacks they don't know. Employers, not wanting "too many of them," are willing to hire one or two black people, but will reject those who apply later. Most hotels and restaurants who offer black patrons courteous—even deferential—treatment, uniformly reject black job applicants, except perhaps for the most menial jobs. When did you last see a black waiter in a really good restaurant?

Racial schizophrenia is not limited to hotels and restaurants. As a result, neither professional status nor relatively high income protects even accomplished blacks from capricious acts of discrimination that may reflect either individual "preference" or an institution's bias. The motivations for bias vary; the disadvantage to black victims is the same.

Careful examination reveals a pattern to these seemingly arbitrary racial actions. When whites perceive that it will be profitable or at least cost-free to serve, hire, admit, or otherwise deal with blacks on a nondiscriminatory basis, they do so. When they fear—accurately or not—that there may be a loss, inconvenience, or upset to themselves or other whites, discriminatory conduct usually follows. Selections and rejections reflect preference as much as prejudice. A preference for whites makes it harder to prove the discrimination outlawed by civil rights laws. This difficulty, when combined with lackluster enforcement, explains why discrimination in employment and in the housing market continues to prevail more than two decades after enactment of the Equal Employment Opportunity Act of 1965 and the Fair Housing Act of 1968.

Racial policy is the culmination of thousands of these individual practices. Black people, then, are caught in a double bind. We are, as I have said, disadvantaged unless whites perceive that nondiscriminatory treatment for us will be a benefit for them. In addition, even when nonracist practices might bring a benefit, whites may rely on discrimination against blacks as a unifying factor and a safety valve for frustrations during economic hard times.

Almost always, the injustices that dramatically diminish the rights of blacks are linked to the serious economic disadvantage suffered by many whites who lack money and power. Whites, rather than acknowledge the similarity of their disadvantage, particularly when compared with that of better-off whites, are easily detoured into protecting their sense of entitlement vis-à-vis blacks for all things of value. Evidently, this racial preference expectation is hypnotic. It is this compulsive fascination that seems to prevent most whites from even seeing—much less resenting—the far more sizable gap between their status and those who occupy the lofty levels at the top of our society.

Race consciousness of this character, as Professor Kimberlè Crenshaw suggested in 1988 in a pathbreaking *Harvard Law Review* article, makes it difficult for whites "to imagine the world differently. It also creates the desire for identification with privileged elites. By focusing on a distinct, subordinate 'other,' whites include themselves in the dominant circle—an arena in which most hold no real power, but only their privileged racial identity."

The critically important stabilizing role that blacks play in this society constitutes a major barrier in the way of achieving racial equality. Throughout history, politicians have used blacks as scapegoats for failed economic or political policies. Before the Civil War, rich slave owners persuaded the white working class to stand with them against the danger of slave revolts—even though the existence of slavery condemned white workers to a life of economic privation. After the Civil War, poor whites fought social reforms and settled for segregation rather than see formerly enslaved blacks get ahead. Most labor unions preferred to allow plant owners to break strikes with black scab labor than allow blacks to join their ranks. The "them against us" racial ploy—always a potent force in economic bad times—is working again: today whites, as disadvantaged by high-status entrance requirements as blacks, fight to end affirmative action policies that, by eliminating class-based entrance requirements and requiring widespread advertising of jobs, have likely helped far more whites than blacks. And in the 1990s, as through much of the 1980s, millions of Americans—white as well as black—face steadily worsening conditions: unemployment, inaccessible health care, inadequate housing, mediocre education, and pollution of the environment. The gap in national incomes is approaching a crisis as those in the top fifth now earn more than their counterparts in the bottom four fifths combined. The conservative guru Kevin Phillips used a different but no less disturbing comparison: the top two million income earners in this country earn more than the next one hundred million.

Shocking. And yet conservative white politicians are able to gain and hold even the highest office despite their failure to address seriously any of these issues. They rely instead on the time-tested formula of getting needy whites to identify on the basis of their shared skin color, and suggest with little or no subtlety that white people must stand together against the Willie Hortons, or against racial quotas, or against affirmative action. The code words differ. The message is the same. Whites are rallied on the basis of racial pride and patriotism to accept their often lowly lot in life, and encouraged to vent their frustration by opposing any serious advancement by blacks. Crucial to this situation is the unstated understanding by the mass of whites that they will accept large disparities in economic opportunity in respect to other whites as long as they have a priority over blacks and other people of color for access to the few opportunities available.

This "racial bonding" by whites means that black rights and interests are always vulnerable to diminishment if not to outright destruction. The willingness of whites over time to respond to this racial rallying cry explains—far more than does the failure of liberal democratic practices (re black rights) to coincide with liberal democratic theory—blacks' continuing subordinate status. This is, of course, contrary to the philosophy of Gunnar Myrdal's massive midcentury study *The American Dilemma*. Myrdal and two generations of civil rights advocates accepted the idea of racism as merely an odious holdover from slavery, "a terrible and inexplicable anomaly stuck in the middle of our liberal democratic ethos." No one doubted that the standard American policy making was adequate to the task of abolishing racism. White America, it was assumed, *wanted* to abolish racism.[3]

Forty years later, in *The New American Dilemma*, Professor Jennifer Hochschild examined what she called Myrdal's "anomaly thesis," and concluded that it simply cannot explain the persistence of racial discrimination. Rather, the continued viability of racism demonstrates "that racism is not simply an excrescence on a fundamentally healthy liberal democratic body, but is part of what shapes and energizes the body." Under this view, "liberal democracy and racism in the United States are historically, even inherently, reinforcing; American society as we know it exists only because of its foundation in racially based slavery, and it thrives only because racial discrimination continues. The apparent anomaly is an actual symbiosis."

The permanence of this "symbiosis" ensures that civil rights gains will be temporary and setbacks inevitable. Consider: In this last decade of the twentieth century, color determines the social and economic status of all African Americans, both those who have been highly successful and their poverty-bound brethren whose lives are grounded in misery and despair. We rise and fall less as a result of our efforts than in response to the needs of a white society that condemns all blacks to quasi citizenship as surely as it segregated our parents and enslaved their forebears. The fact is that, despite what we designate as progress wrought through struggle over many generations, we remain what we were in the beginning: a dark and foreign presence, always the designated "other." Tolerated in good times, despised when things go wrong, as a people we are scapegoated and sacrificed as distraction or catalyst for compromise to facilitate resolution of political differences or relieve economic adversity.

We are now, as were our forebears when they were brought to the New World, objects of barter for those who, while profiting from our existence, deny our humanity. It is in the light of this fact that we must consider the haunting questions about slavery and exploitation contained in Professor Linda Myers's *Understanding an Afrocentric World View: Introduction to an Optimal Psychology,* questions that serve as their own answers.

We simply cannot prepare realistically for our future without assessing honestly our past. It seems cold, accusatory, but we must try to fathom with her "the mentality of a people that could continue for over 300 years to kidnap an estimated 50 million youth and young adults from Africa, transport them across the Atlantic with about half dying unable to withstand the inhumanity of the passage, and enslave them as animals."

As Professor Myers reminds us, blacks were not the only, and certainly not America's most, persecuted people. Appropriately, she asks about the mindset of European Americans to native Americans. After all, those in possession of the land were basically friendly to the newcomers. And yet the European Americans proceeded to annihilate almost the entire race, ultimately forcing the survivors onto reservations after stealing their land. Far from acknowledging and atoning for these atrocities, American history portrays whites as the heroes, the Indian victims as savage villains. "What," she wonders, "can be understood about the world view of a people who claim to be building a democracy with freedom and justice for all, and at the same time own slaves and deny others basic human rights?"

Of course, Americans did not invent slavery. The practice has existed throughout recorded history, and Professor Orlando Patterson, a respected scholar, argues impressively that American slavery was no worse than that practiced in other parts of the world.[4] But it is not comparative slavery policies that concern me. Slavery is, as an example of what white America has done, a constant reminder of what white America might do.

We must see this country's history of slavery, not as an insuperable racial barrier to blacks, but as a legacy of enlightenment from our enslaved forebears reminding us that if they survived the ultimate form of racism, we and those whites who stand with us can at least view racial oppression in its many contemporary forms without underestimating its critical importance and likely permanent status in this country.

To initiate the reconsideration, I want to set forth this proposition, which will be easier to reject than refute: *Black people will never gain full equality in this country. Even those herculean efforts we hail as successful will produce no more than temporary "peaks of progress," short-lived victories that slide into irrelevance as racial patterns adapt in ways that maintain white dominance. This is a hard-to-accept fact that all history verifies. We must acknowledge it, not as a sign of submission, but as an act of ultimate defiance.*

We identify with and hail as hero the man or woman willing to face even death without flinching. Why? Because, while no one escapes death, those who conquer their dread of it are freed to live more fully. In similar fashion, African Americans must confront and conquer the otherwise deadening reality of our permanent subordinate status. Only in this way can we prevent ourselves from being dragged down by society's racial hostility. Beyond survival lies the potential to perceive more clearly both a reason and the means for further struggle.

In this book, Geneva Crenshaw, the civil rights lawyer—protagonist of my earlier *And We Are Not Saved: The Elusive Quest for Racial Justice*, returns in a series of stories that offer an allegorical perspective on old dreams, long-held fears, and current conditions. The provocative format of story, a product of experience and imagination, allows me to take a new look at what, for want of a better phrase, I will call "racial themes." Easier to recognize than describe, they are essentials in the baggage of people subordinated by color in a land that boasts of individual freedom and equality. Some of these themes—reliance on law, involvement in protests, belief in freedom symbols—are familiar and generally known. Others—the yearning for a true homeland, the rejection of racial testimony, the temptation to violent retaliation—are real but seldom revealed. Revelation does not much alter the mystique of interracial romance or lessen its feared consequences. Nor does the search ever end for a full understanding of why blacks are and remain this country's designated scapegoats. . . .

The goal of racial equality is, while comforting to many whites, more illusory than real for blacks. For too long, we have worked for substantive reform, then settled for weakly worded and poorly enforced legislation, indeterminate judicial decisions, token government positions, even holidays. I repeat. If we are to seek new goals for our struggles, we must first reassess the worth of the racial assumptions on which, without careful thought, we have presumed too much and relied on too long.

Let's begin.

Notes

1. According to William Wiecek, ten provisions in the Constitution directly or indirectly provided for slavery and protected slave owners.

2. Not all the data are bleak. While the median family income for black families declined in the 1970s and 1980s, the proportion of African-American families with incomes of $35,000 to $50,000 increased from 23.3 to 27.5 percent. The proportion with incomes above $50,000 increased by 38 percent, from 10.0 to 13.8 percent. The overall median income for blacks declined though: while the top quarter made progress, the bottom half was sliding backward, and the proportion of blacks receiving very low income (less than $5,000) actually increased.

3. According to Myrdal, the "Negro problem in America represents a moral lag in the development of the nation and a study of it must record nearly everything which is bad and wrong in America. . . . However, . . . not since Reconstruction has there been more reason to anticipate fundamental changes in American race relations, changes which will involve a development toward the American ideals."

4. He suggests: "The dishonor of slavery . . . came in the primal act of submission. It was the most immediate human expression of the inability to defend oneself or to secure one's livelihood. . . . The dishonor the slave was compelled to experience sprang instead from that raw, human sense of debasement inherent in having no being except as an expression of another's being."

NO ◁

Dinesh D'Souza

The End of Racism

Racism undoubtedly exists, but it no longer has the power to thwart blacks or any other group in achieving their economic, political, and social aspirations. It cannot be denied that African Americans suffer slights in terms of taxidrivers who pass them by, pedestrians who treat them as a security risk, banks that are reluctant to invest in black neighborhoods, and other forms of continued discrimination. Some of this discrimination is irrational, motivated by bigotry or faulty generalization. Much of it, as we have seen, is behavior that is rational from the point of view of the discriminator and at the same time harmful for black individuals who do not conform to the behavioral pattern of their peers. Such incidents undoubtedly cause pain, and invite legitimate public sympathy and concern. But they do not explain why blacks as a group do worse than other groups in getting into selective colleges, performing well on tests, gaining access to rewarding jobs and professions, starting and successfully operating independent businesses, and maintaining productive and cohesive communities.

Racism cannot explain most of the contemporary hardships faced by African Americans, even if some of them had their historical roots in oppression. Activists like Derrick Bell may deny it, but America today is not the same place that it was a generation ago. African Americans now live in a country where a black man, Colin Powell, who three decades ago could not be served a hamburger in many Southern restaurants, became chairman of the Joint Chiefs of Staff; where an African American, Douglas Wilder, was elected governor of Virginia, the heart of the Confederacy; where a former Dixiecrat like Senator Strom Thurmond supported the nomination of Clarence Thomas, a black man married to a white woman, for the Supreme Court; and where an interracial jury convicted Byron De La Beckwith for killing civil rights activist Medgar Evers a generation after two all-white juries acquitted him.

Many scholars and civil rights activists continue to blame racism for African American problems; yet if white racism controls the destiny of blacks today, how has one segment of the black community prospered so much over the past generation, while the condition of the black underclass has deteriorated? Since black women and black men are equally exposed to white bigotry, why are black women competitive with white women in the workplace, while black men lag behind all other groups? In major cities in which blacks dominate the institutions of government, is it realistic to assume that white racism is the main cause of crime, delinquency, and dilapidation? It also is not at all clear how racism could prevent the children of middle-class blacks from performing as well as whites and Asians on tests of mathematical and logical reasoning. Black pathologies such as illegitimacy, dependency, and crime are far more serious today than in the past, when racism was indisputably more potent and pervasive. "No one who supports the contemporary racism thesis," William Julius Wilson acknowledges, "has provided adequate or convincing answers to these questions."[1]

Even if racism were to disappear overnight, the worst problems facing black America would persist. Single parenthood and welfare dependency among the black underclass would not cease. Crack and AIDS would continue to ravage black communities. The black crime rate, with its disproportionate impact on African American communities, would still extract a terrible toll.[2] Indeed drugs and black-on-black crime kill more blacks in a year than all the lynchings in U.S. history. Racism is hardly the most serious problem facing African Americans in the United States today. Their main challenge is a civilizational breakdown that stretches across class lines but is especially concentrated in the black underclass. At every socioeconomic level, blacks are uncompetitive on those measures of achievement that are essential to modern industrial society. Many middle-class African Americans are, by their own account, distorted in their social relations by the consuming passion of black rage. And nothing strengthens racism in this country more than the behavior of the African American underclass, which flagrantly violates and scandalizes basic codes of responsibility, decency, and civility. As far as many blacks are concerned, as E. Franklin Frazier once wrote, "The travail of civilization is not yet ended."[3]

Racism began in the West as a biological explanation for a large gap of civilizational development separating blacks from whites. Today racism is reinforced and made plausible by the reemergence of that gap within the United States. For many whites the criminal and irresponsible black underclass represents a revival of barbarism in the midst of Western civilization. If this is true, the best way to eradicate beliefs in black inferiority is to remove their empirical basis. As African American scholars Jeff Howard and Ray Hammond argue, if blacks as a group can show that they are capable of performing competitively in schools and the work force, and exercising both the rights and the responsibilities of American citizenship, then racism will be deprived of its foundation in experience.[4] If blacks can close the civilization gap, the race problem in this country is likely to become insignificant. African Americans in particular and society in general have the daunting mission to address the serious internal problems within black culture. That is the best antiracism now.

In private, some activists like Jesse Jackson will tentatively acknowledge black pathologies. Yet it is difficult for liberal whites and mainstream black leaders to confront these problems publicly because of the deep-rooted ideology of cultural relativism. If all cultures are equal, on what grounds can the standards of mainstream society be applied to evaluate the performance and conduct of African Americans? If such standards are entirely relative and culture-bound, on what basis can blacks who are productive and law-abiding establish valid norms for blacks who are not? As Elijah Anderson argues, the inner city is characterized by two rival cultures: a hegemonic culture of pathology and a besieged culture of decency. By refusing to acknowledge that one culture is better than another—by erasing the distinction between barbarism and civilization—cultural relativism cruelly inhibits the nation from identifying and working to ameliorate pathologies that are destroying the life chances of millions of African Americans. Thus we arrive at a singular irony: cultural relativism, once the instrument of racial emancipation for blacks, has now become an obstacle to confronting real problems that cannot be avoided. One may say that today the most formidable ideological barrier facing blacks is not racism but antiracism.

Rethinking Relativism

As we have seen, liberals in the twentieth century embraced relativism because it offered a basis for affirming and working to secure racial equality. Undoubtedly the relativist proclamation of the equality of all cultures provided liberals with a powerful rationale to reject the classic racist assertion of white civilizational superiority. But as often happens, the solution to an old problem becomes the source of a new one. Relativism has now imprisoned liberals in an iron cage that prevents them from acknowledging black pathology, makes it impossible for them to support policies that uphold any standard of responsibility, and compels them to blame every problem faced by blacks on white racism or its institutional legacy. This explains the interminable liberal rhetoric about the "root causes" of poverty, the "bitter hoax" of the American dream, the mysterious disappearance of "meaningful" jobs, the prospect of a "resurgence" of "hate," the danger of "imposing one's morality," the need to avoid "code words," and how we should all "understand the rage." Pondering what he concedes are the shocking behavior patterns of the black underclass, columnist Michael Massing can only ask, "what has driven these people to engage in such excesses?"[5] By denying that blacks can fail on their own, cultural relativism denies them the possibility of achieving success. Seeking to cover up black failure, relativism suppresses cultural autonomy, refusing to grant blacks control over their destiny.

Modern liberals are well aware of the differences in academic achievement, economic performance, family structure, and crime rates between blacks and other groups. Given that these differences persist at all socioeconomic levels, there are three possible explanations: genes, culture, and racial discrimination (or some combination of these factors). Since many liberals are committed to the precept that all cultures are or should be equal, it follows that observable group differences are the product of either discrimination or genes. If discrimination cannot fully explain why blacks do not perform as well as whites on various measures of performance, then the conclusion cannot be escaped: according to the liberal paradigm, blacks must be genetically inferior. Arthur Jensen and Charles Murray wait in the wings.

Since relativism makes it impossible for liberals to confront the issue of black cultural pathology—to do so is seen as "blaming the victim"—the desire to avoid a genetic explanation forces liberals to blame group differences on racism. At first glance it seems difficult, if not impossible, to argue that African Americans as a group perform substantially worse in intellectual and economic ventures than whites and Asians of similar background because they are passed up by racist cabdrivers or because shopkeepers follow them around in stores. Yet despite their absurdity, such suggestions are required by a liberal ideology that requires white racism to explain black failure. If racism cannot be located in individuals, it must be diagnosed in institutional structures. The charge of racism becomes a kind of incantation intended to ward off the demons of black inferiority. It offers a bewitched understanding that makes nonsense of everyday perception and empirical reality by alleging the subtle workings of unfriendly ghosts. In this Ptolemaic universe, the idea of racism serves the function of corrective epicycles that need to be invoked constantly to preserve the liberal edifice of cultural relativism and liberal confidence in black capacity. Raising the question of "why so many young men are engaging in what amounts to self-inflicted genocide," Andrew Hacker provides the prescribed answer. "It is white America that has made being black so disconsolate an estate."[6]

Thus begins the liberal project to offer an elaborate and shifting rationale for black incapacity. If African Americans do not do well on tests, that is because the tests are biased, and because white society has deprived them of the necessary skills. If they drop out of school, they have been driven out by racism which injures black self-esteem. If they have illegitimate children, this is because society refuses to provide black males with steady jobs. If they are convicted of a disproportionate number of violent crimes, this is because the police, judges, and juries are racist. Those who have committed crimes have been pressured to do so by undeserved economic hardship. Riots are automatically attributed to legitimate outbursts of black rage. In short, the liberal position on black failure can be reduced to a single implausible slogan: Just say racism. Yet liberals recognize that old forms of segregation and overt discrimination have greatly eroded, so where is this racism that is supposedly holding African Americans back at every juncture? Bull Connor does not serve in the Princeton admissions office, where he keeps blacks out with hoses and dogs; Bull Connor is dead. The main obstacle to more blacks getting into Princeton is the university's selective admissions standards. Consequently many liberals find that they must now treat merit itself as a mere cover for racism. In case after case, liberals are destroying legitimate institutions and practices in order to conceal the embarrassing reality of black failure.

In the view of its founders, such as Locke, liberalism is a philosophy that seeks to establish fair rules so that people with different interests have the freedom to pursue their goals within a framework of state neutrality. In modern liberal society, democratic elections, free markets, and civil liberties are all instruments that aim at maximizing freedom without dictating results. Liberalism does not tell you who to vote for, what to buy, or how to exercise your freedom of religion and speech. Liberal procedures such as the jury system and the presumption of innocence are intended to secure basic rights. Yet in order to compel the relativist outcome of substantive racial equality, liberals are forced to subvert these very principles. The easiest way to ensure that more blacks enter selective colleges and receive well-paying jobs is to lower admissions and hiring standards. If companies prove recalcitrant, the civil rights laws invert the premise of Western justice and treat defendants who fail to hire a proportional number of blacks as "guilty until proven innocent." In order to ensure that blacks are elected to represent blacks, voting districts are drawn in such a way as to virtually foreordain the result. In some cases, free speech is subordinated to the goals of sensitivity and diversity, as in so-called hate speech and hate crimes laws. At every stage, fundamental liberal principles are being sacrificed at the altar of cultural relativism. In its fanatical commitment to the relativist ideology of group equality, liberalism is inexorably destroying itself.

In the 1960s, many liberals supported civil rights because of a deep confidence in color-blind rules that would give blacks a fair chance to compete on their merits. The results of the last few decades have eroded this faith, so that now many of these same white liberals mainly produce alibis for black failure. These apologies take on a ritualistic and sometimes comic aspect, and there is some question about whether they are even believed by their advocates. Shelby Steele points out that many of the same activists who offer extensive arguments for why grades and standardized aptitude and achievement tests are meaningless nevertheless demonstrate intense private concern about how their own sons and daughters do on such measures of performance. If this double standard exists, it shows that many activists don't want to get rid of standards altogether, they want to get rid of standards *for blacks*. Eventually such self-deception becomes corrosive; many liberals may cease to believe in their own ingenious excuses and become like lawyers who suspect, finally, that their client may be guilty. Indeed before the moral tribunal of liberalism, blacks seem to stand publicly exculpated but privately convicted. White liberals do not want blacks to fail but many seem to behave as though, in every competition that is not rigged, they expect them to do so. Moreover, the routine abridgment of standards for blacks makes it more likely that blacks will fail at tasks for which they are inadequately prepared. Liberalism, which began as an ideology of equal rights, has degenerated into the paternalism of rigged results.

While contemporary liberalism destroys its principles, it clears the pathway for various species of illiberalism. Ironically liberalism which has for much of this century been the ideology of antiracism is now establishing the foundation for a new racism, black and white. Today's invocations of white power are based upon an appeal to cultural integrity and racial pride; on what grounds can liberal relativists criticize groups like Jared Taylor's "American Renaissance" which assert the right to defend their own cultural norms? Similarly white liberals find it difficult to condemn Afrocentric extremism and black racism because those ideologies are also constructed on the foundation of Boasian relativism. Instead, all the threats and actions of black racists must be blamed on societal racism or on liberalism itself: "Look what we made them do."[7] Not only does liberal relativism legitimate white and black racism, but it also concedes the high ground to the forces of bigotry: white racists become the unchallenged custodians of Western civilization, and black racists become the most clear-eyed diagnosticians of our social problems. . . .

Rethinking Racism

So what about racism? . . . [Racism] is not reducible to ignorance or fear. Not only is the liberal remedy for racism incorrect; the basic diagnosis of the malady is wrong. Racism is what it always was: an opinion that recognizes real civilizational differences and attributes them to biology. Liberal relativism has been based on the denial of the differences. Liberals should henceforth admit the differences but deny their biological foundation. Thus liberals can continue to reject racism by preserving the Boasian distinction between race and culture. This is not a denial of the fact that individuals do differ or even the possibility that there are some natural differences between groups. Yet liberals can convincingly argue that whatever these may be, they are not significant enough to warrant differential treatment by law or policy. In other words, intrinsic differences are irrelevant when it comes to the ability of citizens to exercise their rights and responsibilities. Liberals can explain group differences in academic and economic performance by pointing to cultural differences, and acknowledging that some cultures are functionally superior to others. The racist fallacy, as Anthony Appiah contends, is the act of "biologizing what is culture."[8]

Yet this new liberal understanding should not make the present mistake—duplicated in thousands of sensitivity classes—of treating racism the way a Baptist preacher considers sin. Rather, it should recognize racism as an opinion, which may be right or wrong, but which in any case is a point of view that should be argued with and not suppressed. Antiracist education is largely a waste of time because it typically results in intellectual and moral coercion. Heavy-handed bullying may produce public acquiescence but it cannot compel private assent. Increasingly it appears that it is liberal antiracism that is based on ignorance and fear: ignorance of the true nature of racism, and fear that the racist point of view better explains the world than its liberal counterpart.

For a generation, liberals have treated racism as a form of psychological dementia in need of increasingly coercive forms of enlightenment. But liberal societies should not seek to regulate people's inner thoughts, nor should they outlaw ideas however reprehensible we find them. Hate speech and hate crime laws that impose punishment or enhanced penalties for proscribed motives and viewpoints are inherently illiberal and destructive of intellectual independence and conscience. Americans should recognize that racism is not what it used to be; it does exist, but we can live with it. This is not to say that racism does not do damage, only that the sorts of measures that would be needed to eradicate all vestiges of racist thought can only be totalitarian. Efforts to root out residual racism often create more injustice than they eliminate.

The crucial policy issue is what to do about discrimination. Irrational discrimination of the sort that inspired the civil rights laws of the 1960s is now, as we have seen, a relatively infrequent occurrence. Although such discrimination continues to cause harm, it is irrelevant to the prospects of blacks as a group because it is selective rather than comprehensive in scope. For a minority like African Americans, discrimination is only catastrophic when virtually everyone colludes to enforce it. Consider what would happen if every baseball team in America refused to hire blacks. Blacks would suffer most, because they would be denied the opportunity to play professional baseball. And fans would suffer, because the quality of games would be diminished. But what if only a few teams—say the New York Yankees and the Los Angeles Dodgers—refused to hire blacks? African Americans as a group would suffer hardly at all, because the best black players would offer their services to other teams. The Yankees and the Dodgers would suffer a great deal, because they would be deprived of the chance to hire talented black players. Eventually competitive pressure would force the Yankees and Dodgers either to hire blacks, or to suffer losses in games and revenue.[9] As Gary Becker has pointed out, in a free market, selective discrimination imposes the heaviest cost on the discriminator, which is where it should be. Some people will undoubtedly continue to eschew blacks because of their "taste for discrimination," but most will continue to deal with them because of their taste for profit.[10] Rational discrimination, on the other hand, is likely to persist even in a fully competitive market. . . .

What we need is a long-term strategy that holds the government to a rigorous standard of race neutrality, while allowing private actors to be free to discriminate as they wish. In practice, this means uncompromising color blindness in government hiring and promotion, criminal justice, and the drawing of voting districts. Yet individuals and companies would be allowed to discriminate in private transactions such as renting an apartment or hiring for a job. Am I calling for a repeal of the Civil Rights Act of 1964? Actually, yes. The law should be changed so that its nondiscrimination provisions apply only to the government.

The End of Racism

Once we have set aside the false remedies premised on relativism—proportional representation and multiculturalism—it is possible to directly address America's real problem, which is partly a race problem and partly a black problem. The solution to the race problem is a public policy that is strictly indifferent to race. The black problem can be solved only through a program of cultural reconstruction in which society plays a supporting role but which is carried out primarily by African Americans themselves. Both projects need to be pursued simultaneously; neither can work by itself. If society is race neutral but blacks remain uncompetitive, then equality of rights for individuals will lead to dramatic inequality of result for groups, liberal embarrassment will set in, and we are back on the path to racial preferences. On the other hand, if blacks are going to reform their community, they have a right to expect that they will be treated equally under the law. Although America has a long way to go, many mistakes have been made, and current antagonisms are high, still there are hopeful signs that the nation can move toward a society in which race ceases to matter, a destination that we can term "the end of racism."

Notes

1.   William Julius Wilson, *The Truly Disadvantaged: The Inner City, the Underclass, and Public Policy,* University of Chicago, Chicago, 1987, p. 11.

2.   "If all racial discrimination were abolished today, the life prospects facing many poor blacks would still constitute major challenges for public policy." Gerald David Jaynes and Robin M. Williams, *A Common Destiny: Blacks and American Society,* National Academy Press, Washington, DC, 1989, p. 4.

3.   E. Franklin Frazier, *The Negro Family in the United States,* University of Chicago Press, Chicago, 1939, p. 487.

4.   "When we react to the rumor of inferiority by avoiding intellectual engagement, and when we allow our children to do so, black people forfeit the opportunity for intellectual development which could extinguish the debate about our capacities, and set the stage for group progress." Jeff Howard and Ray Hammond, "Rumors of Inferiority," *The New Republic,* September 9, 1985.

5.   Michael Massing, "Ghetto Blasting," *New Yorker,* January 16, 1995, p. 36.

6.   Andrew Hacker, *Two Nations: Black and White, Separate, Hostile, Unequal,* Ballantine Books, New York, 1992, p. 218.

7.   An example of this rhetoric is Joe Feagin and Hernan Vera's assertion that despite her incendiary rhetoric, "Sister Souljah is not the problem—she is only a messenger with bad news about the state of white racism." Joe Feagin and Hernan Vera, *White Racism: The Basics,* Routledge, New York, 1995, p. 131.

8.   Anthony Appiah, *In My Father's House: Africa in the Philosophy of Culture,* Oxford University Press, New York, 1992, p. 45.

9.   Jencks, *Rethinking Social Policy,* p. 41.

10. Gary S. Becker, *The Economics of Discrimination,* University of Chicago Press, Chicago, 1971.

POSTSCRIPT

Is Racism a Permanent Feature of American Society?

Racism has played a major role in the formation and ongoing development of the American society. Given this existential reality, it is not difficult to understand that some observers and analysts of American race relations, when confronted with the inequality that persists between blacks and whites in society would blame this phenomenon on racial discrimination. Those who support this argument view racism as a continuing and permanent reality of American society.

Derrick Bell is a proponent of this view. In the selection, Bell argues that "Black people will never gain full equality in this country." For him the legacy of institutional discrimination that was reflected in slavery continues through the exclusionary policies of racial segregation that has left blacks "at the bottom of the well." Additionally, Bell views certain roles that blacks play in the society, such as the scapegoat, as contributing to the permanence of racism. Who will play these roles? He also views the color-coded perceptions and behaviors that dominate social interaction between the "races" as so culturally imbedded as to be virtually impossible to overcome.

It is interesting to note that in the America of today there is substantial support, especially within the white population, for the goal of achieving a color-blind society as the proper response to the deleterious influences of an endemic and pervasive racism on the people and institutions of the nation. Such a policy recommendation is based on a clear recognition that white racism within the nation and throughout the world is reflective of a profound and entrenched color consciousness that has manifested itself in long-standing practices and policies of discrimination and exclusion, a sorting-out process that is primarily based on the color of one's skin. However, the debate over such a policy goal within society serves to illuminate the salience of "race" and the establishment of distinct color-coded racial categories in influencing the development of social relations within modern societies such as these United States and South Africa.

D'Souza, in contrast, argues that blacks who do not conform to the destructive behavior of their peers are making significant progress in the United States. So, he firmly believes that the blacks who are lagging in their pursuit of the American dream are afflicted by destructive impacts of black culture (i.e., the wrong values). The culture he refers to is that of the black underclass. D'Souza believes that the social pathology that it produces within African-American life is the primary source of the lagging progress of the race.

A comprehensive reader entitled *Racism* (Oxford, 1999), edited by Martin Bulmer and John Solomos, offers students both classical and contemporary selections on racism. Gunnar Myrdal's *An American Dilemma* (Harper, 1944) is a classic that deconstructs post–World War II race relations. In agreement with Bell is Eduardo Bonilla-Silva's *Racism Without Racists: Color-Blind Racism and the Persistence of Racial Inequality in the United States* (Rowman & Littlefield, 2003). He argues that the emphasis on "color-blindness" is a new form of racism. Also, for an extended argument, see Bonilla-Silva's *White Supremacy and Racism in the Post Civil Rights Era* (Rienner, 2001). William Julius Wilson's *The Declining Significance of Race: Blacks and Changing American Institutions* (University of Chicago Press, 1978) emphasizes issues of class although it does not deny the existence of racism.

For literature dealing with cultural values and poverty, see *La Vida: A Puerto Rican Family in the Culture of Poverty, San Juan and New York* (Random House, 1966) by Oscar Lewis. Edward Banfield, in *The Unheavenly City* (Little, Brown, 1970) argues that cultural values are the major cause of urban poverty. Lawrence E. Harrison promotes the culture of poverty thesis in *Who Prospers? How Cultural Values Shape Economic and Political Success* (Basic Books, 1992). A critique of the culture of poverty perspective can be found in *Yo' Mama's Disfunktional: Fighting the Culture Wars in Urban America* (Beacon, 1997) by Robin Kelly. A structural explanation of poverty can be found in *The Truly Disadvantaged* (University of Chicago Press, 1990), written by William Julius Wilson, the leading authority on the black underclass.

ISSUE 16

Should Twenty-First Century Public Policy Be Class Conscious Rather than Race Conscious?

YES: Richard Kahlenberg, "Class, Not Race," in *The New Republic* (April 3, 1995)

NO: Amy Gutmann, "Should Public Policy Be Class Conscious Rather than Color Conscious?" from *Color Conscious* (Princeton University Press, 1996)

ISSUE SUMMARY

YES: Richard Kahlenberg, fellow at the Center for National Policy, argues that class-based policies would provide a basis for attacking the problems of poverty and disadvantage that are experienced by members of all groups within society, thus ameliorating the resentment among whites who are not included in race-based policy initiatives.

NO: Amy Gutmann, a political scientist, believes that racial injustices are a continuing reality of society and that class-based preferences tend to dilute their necessary focus on racism and their effects on society.

Poverty and racism are enduring paradoxes of the American experience, and they have exerted a profound impact on the nation. As the 1960s emerged, both race and poverty became significant issues within the nation's politics. In the wake of the election of 1960, the U.S. government launched a war against poverty. Yet, poverty persists in the United States, as does the debate over the content and direction of government policy devised to deal with this social problem. At the same time, the civil rights movement led to important policies involving race. One of the prevailing dichotomies that informs our national discourse on this issue today is whether public policy dealing with disadvantage should be based on considerations of class or race.

Richard Kahlenberg provides us with an illuminating presentation in support of a class-based public policy. Such a policy would be based on a race-neutral principle. He argues that a class-based emphasis could serve to unify African Americans and the white working class, two groups often involved in social conflict. Kahlenberg argues that the race-based focus of affirmative action does not provide for equality of opportunity for all Americans in any meaningful sense, but rather "it merely creates a self-perpetuating Black elite along with a white one."

Kahlenberg believes that as mainstream public opinion turns increasingly hostile to race-based public policies, class-based policies may be the only meaningful alternative. He is strongly supportive of the view that class-based public policies in this sphere possess significant social and political utility in a nation where issues of race are still highly contentious and resistance to racial preferences continues to grow.

Amy Gutmann presents an alternative view. She endorses race-based initiatives within the public policy domain and disagrees with Kahlenberg's contention that the Civil Rights Act of 1964 affirmed that class was the "central impediment" to equal opportunity in the United States. Gutmann is concerned that class-based public policies tend to obscure the fact that racial injustice is a continuing reality of American life and that blacks of all social strata must contend with racism. She is not prepared to embrace the notion that the United States is becoming color-blind. To Gutmann, class-based policies have less potential for overcoming the racial divisions that continue to plague this nation than Kahlenberg contends.

Gutmann focuses much of her attention on an examination of the debate over whether class preferences should supplant race preferences in college admissions. She notes that while advocates of such a shift in policy claim that it would provide black Americans with a fair opportunity for admission because their group is disproportionately poor, such an alternative policy does not consider factors other than poverty. Gutmann supports a policy orientation that recognizes both class-based initiatives and color-conscious programs. And, she insists that racial injustice must be retained at the center of our deliberations about social justice and the policies advocated to confront these vexing issues in order to progress and achieve the vision of a racially egalitarian society.

The reader should expect that the class-race policy debate will take many different forms and continue to be with us for the foreseeable future. For example, race and college admissions (Issue 12) and affirmative action (Issue 14) are two relevant and pressing social issues. Readers should note some similarity between Kahlenberg and Gutmann. Nevertheless, Gutmann emphasizes race-based policy. How does her basic argument for race depart from her class argument? If policy moves in a class-based direction, will race issues tend to be ignored? What do you make of the color-blind policy argument? Have these issues influenced your life chances?

Richard Kahlenberg  **YES**

Class, not Race

In an act that reflected panic as much as cool reflection, Bill Clinton said recently that he is reviewing all federal affirmative action programs to see "whether there is some other way we can reach [our] objective without giving a preference by race or gender." As the country's mood swings violently against affirmative action, and as Republicans gear up to use the issue to bludgeon the Democratic coalition yet again in 1996, the whole project of legislating racial equality seems suddenly in doubt. The Democrats, terrified of the issue, are now hoping it will just go away. It won't. But at every political impasse, there is a political opportunity. Bill Clinton now has a chance, as no other Democrat has had since 1968, to turn a glaring liability for his party into an advantage—without betraying basic Democratic principles.

There is, as Clinton said, a way "we can work this out." But it isn't the "*Bakke* straddle," which says yes to affirmative action (race as a factor) but no to quotas. It isn't William Julius Wilson's call to "emphasize" race-neutral social programs, while downplaying affirmative action. The days of downplaying are gone; we can count on the Republicans for that. The way out—an idea Clinton hinted at—is to introduce the principle of race neutrality and the goal of aiding the disadvantaged into affirmative action preference programs themselves: to base preferences, in education, entry-level employment and public contracting, on class, not race.

Were Clinton to propose this move, the media would charge him with lurching to the right. Jesse Jackson's presidential campaign would surely soon follow. But despite its association with conservatives such as Clarence Thomas, Antonin Scalia and Dinesh D'Souza, the idea of class-based affirmative action should in fact appeal to the left as well. After all, its message of addressing class unfairness and its political potential for building cross-racial coalitions are traditional liberal staples.

For many years, the left argued not only that class was important, but also that it was more important than race. This argument was practical, ideological and politic. An emphasis on class inequality meant Robert Kennedy riding in a motorcade through cheering white and black sections of racially torn Gary, Indiana, in 1968, with black Mayor Richard Hatcher on one side, and white working-class boxing hero Tony Zale on the other.

Ideologically, it was clear that with the passage of the Civil Rights Act of 1964, class replaced caste as the central impediment to equal opportunity. Martin Luther King Jr. moved from the Montgomery Boycott to the Poor People's Campaign, which he described as "his last, greatest dream," and "something bigger than just a civil rights movement for Negroes." RFK told David Halberstam that "it was pointless to talk about the real problem in America being black and white, it was really rich and poor, which was a much more complex subject."

Finally, the left emphasized class because to confuse class and race was seen not only as wrong but as dangerous. This notion was at the heart of the protest over Daniel Patrick Moynihan's 1965 report, *The Negro Family: The Case for National Action,* in which Moynihan depicted the rising rates of illegitimacy among poor blacks. While Moynihan's critics were wrong to silence discussion of illegitimacy among blacks, they rightly noted that the title of the report, which implicated all blacks, was misleading, and that fairly high rates of illegitimacy also were present among poor whites—a point which Moynihan readily endorses today. (In the wake of the second set of L.A. riots in 1992, Moynihan rose on the Senate floor to reaffirm that family structure "is not an issue of race but of class. . . . It is class behavior.")

The irony is that affirmative action based on race violates these three liberal insights. It provides the ultimate wedge to destroy Robert Kennedy's coalition. It says that despite civil rights protections, the wealthiest African American is more deserving of preference than the poorest white. It relentlessly focuses all attention on race.

In contrast, Lyndon Johnson's June 1965 address to Howard University, in which the concept of affirmative action was first unveiled, did not ignore class. In a speech drafted by Moynihan, Johnson spoke of the bifurcation of the black community, and, in his celebrated metaphor, said we needed to aid those "hobbled" in life's race by past discrimination. This suggested special help for disadvantaged blacks, not all blacks; for the young Clarence Thomas, but not for Clarence Thomas's son. Johnson balked at implementing the thematic language of his speech. His Executive Order 11246, calling for "affirmative action" among federal contractors, initially meant greater outreach and required hiring without respect to race. In fact, LBJ rescinded his Labor Department's proposal to provide for racial quotas in the construction industry in Philadelphia. It fell to Richard Nixon to implement the "Philadelphia Plan," in what Nixon's aides say was a conscious effort to drive a wedge between blacks and labor. (Once he placed racial preferences on the table, Nixon adroitly extricated himself, and by 1972 was campaigning against racial quotas.)

The ironies were compounded by the Supreme Court. In the 1974 case *DeFunis* v. *Odegaard,* in which a system of racial preferences in law school admissions was at issue, it was the Court's liberal giant, William O. Douglas, who argued that racial preferences were unconstitutional, and suggested instead that preferences be based on disadvantage. Four years later, in the *Bakke* case, the great proponent of affirmative action as a means to achieve "diversity" was Nixon appointee Lewis F. Powell Jr. Somewhere along the line, the right wing embraced Douglas and Critical Race Theory embraced Powell.

Today, the left pushes racial preferences, even for the most advantaged minorities, in order to promote diversity and provide role models for disadvantaged blacks—an argument which, if it came from Ronald Reagan, the left would rightly dismiss as trickle-down social theory. Today, when William Julius Wilson argues the opposite of the Moynihan report—that the problems facing the black community are rooted more in class than race—it is Wilson who is excoriated by civil rights groups. The left can barely utter the word "class," instead resorting to euphemisms such as "income groups," "wage earners" and "people who play by the rules."

For all of this, the left has paid a tremendous price. On a political level, with a few notable exceptions, the history of the past twenty-five years is a history of white, working-class Robert Kennedy Democrats turning first into Wallace Democrats, then into Nixon and Reagan Democrats and ultimately into today's Angry White Males. Time and again, the white working class votes its race rather than its class, and Republicans win. The failure of the left to embrace class also helps turn poor blacks, for whom racial preferences are, in Stephen Carter's words, "stunningly irrelevant," toward Louis Farrakhan.

On the merits, the left has committed itself to a goal—equality of group results—which seems highly radical, when it is in fact rather unambitious. To the extent that affirmative action, at its ultimate moment of success, merely creates a self-perpetuating black elite along with a white one, its goal is modest—certainly more conservative than real equality of opportunity, which gives blacks and whites and other Americans of all economic strata a fair chance at success.

The priority given to race over class has inevitably exacerbated white racism. Today, both liberals and conservatives conflate race and class because it serves both of their purposes to do so. Every year, when SAT scores are released, the breakdown by race shows enormous gaps between blacks on the one hand and whites and Asians on the other. The NAACP cites these figures as evidence that we need to do more. Charles Murray cites the same statistics as evidence of intractable racial differences. We rarely see a breakdown of scores by class, which would show enormous gaps between rich and poor, gaps that would help explain the differences in scores by race.

On the legal front, it once made some strategic sense to emphasize race over class. But when states moved to the remedial phrase—and began trying to address past discrimination—the racial focus became a liability. The strict scrutiny that struck down Jim Crow is now used, to varying degrees, to curtail racial preferences. Class, on the other hand, is not one of the suspect categories under the Fourteenth Amendment, which leaves class-based remedies much less assailable.

If class-based affirmative action is a theory that liberals should take seriously, how would it work in practice? In this magazine, Michael Kinsley has asked, "Does Clarence Thomas, the sharecropper's kid, get more or fewer preference points than the unemployed miner's son from Appalachia?" Most conservative proponents of class-based affirmative action have failed to explain their idea with any degree of specificity. Either they're insincere—offering the alternative only for tactical reasons—or they're stumped.

The former is more likely. While the questions of implementation are serious and difficult, they are not impossible to answer. At the university level, admissions committees deal every day with precisely the type of apples-and-oranges question that Kinsley poses. Should a law school admit an applicant with a 3.2 GPA from Yale or a 3.3 from Georgetown? How do you compare those two if one applicant worked for the Peace Corps but the other had slightly higher LSATS?

In fact, a number of universities already give preferences for disadvantaged students in addition to racial minorities. Since 1989 Berkeley has granted special consideration to applicants "from socioeconomically disadvantaged backgrounds . . . regardless of race or ethnicity." Temple University Law School has, since the 1970s, given preference to "applicants who have overcome exceptional and continuous economic deprivation." And at Hastings College of Law, 20 percent of the class is set aside for disadvantaged students through the Legal Equal Opportunity Program. Even the U.C.-Davis medical program challenged by Allan Bakke was limited to "disadvantaged" minorities, a system which Davis apparently did not find impossible to administer.

Similar class-based preference programs could be provided by public employers and federal contractors for high school graduates not pursuing college, on the theory that at that age their class-based handicaps hide their true potential and are not at all of their own making. In public contracting, government agencies could follow the model of New York City's old class-based program, which provided preferences based not on the ethnicity or gender of the contractor, but to small firms located in New York City which did part of their business in depressed areas or employed economically disadvantaged workers.

The definition of class or disadvantage may vary according to context, but if, for example, the government chose to require class-based affirmative action from universities receiving federal funds, it is possible to devise an enforceable set of objective standards for deprivation. If the aim of class-based affirmative action is to provide a system of genuine equality of opportunity, a leg up to promising students who have done well despite the odds, we have a wealth of sociological data to devise an obstacles test. While some might balk at the very idea of reducing disadvantage to a number, we currently reduce intellectual promise to numbers—SATS and GPAS—and adding a number for disadvantage into the calculus just makes deciding who gets ahead and who does not a little fairer.

There are three basic ways to proceed: with a simple, moderate or complex definition. The simple method is to ask college applicants their family's income and measure disadvantage by that factor alone, on the theory that income is a good proxy for a whole host of economic disadvantages (such as bad schools or a difficult learning environment). This oversimplified approach is essentially the tack we've taken with respect to compensatory race-based affirmative action. For example, most affirmative action programs ask applicants to check a racial box and sweep all the ambiguities under the rug. Even though African Americans have, as Justice Thurgood Marshall said in *Bakke,* suffered a history "different in kind, not just degree, from that of other ethnic groups," universities don't calibrate preferences based on comparative group disadvantage (and, in the Davis system challenged by Bakke, two-thirds of the preferences went to Mexican-Americans and Asians, not blacks). We also ignore the question of when an individual's family immigrated in order to determine whether the family was even theoretically subject to the official discrimination in this country on which preferences are predicated.

"Diversity" was supposed to solve all this by saying we don't care about compensation, only viewpoint. But, again, if universities are genuinely seeking diversity of viewpoints, they should inquire whether a minority applicant really does have the "minority viewpoint" being sought. Derrick Bell's famous statement—"the ends of diversity are not served by people who look black and think white"—is at once repellent and a relevant critique of the assumption that all minority members think alike. In theory, we need some assurance from the applicant that he or she will in fact interact with students of different backgrounds, lest the cosmetic diversity of the freshman yearbook be lost to the reality of ethnic theme houses.

The second way to proceed, the moderately complicated calculus of class, would look at what sociologists believe to be the Big Three determinants of life chances: parental income, education and occupation. Parents' education, which is highly correlated with a child's academic achievement, can be measured in number of years. And while ranking occupations might seem hopelessly complex, various attempts to do so objectively have yielded remarkably consistent results—from the Barr Scale of the early 1920s to Alba Edwards Census rankings of the 1940s to the Duncan Scores of the 1960s.

The third alternative, the complex calculus of disadvantage, would count all the factors mentioned, but might also look at net worth, the quality of secondary education, neighborhood influences and family structure. An applicant's family wealth is readily available from financial aid forms, and provides a long-term view of relative disadvantage, to supplement the "snapshot" picture that income provides. We also know that schooling opportunities are crucial to a student's life chances, even controlling for home environment. Some data suggest that a disadvantaged student at a middle-class school does better on average than a middle-class student at a school with high concentrations of poverty. Objective figures are available to measure secondary school quality—from per student expenditure, to the percentage of students receiving free or reduced-price lunches, to a school's median score on standardized achievement tests. Neighborhood influences, measured by the concentration of poverty within Census tracts or zip codes, could also be factored in, since numerous studies have found that living in a low-income community can adversely affect an individual's life chances above and beyond family income. Finally, everyone from Dan Quayle to Donna Shalala agrees that children growing up in single-parent homes have a tougher time. This factor could be taken into account as well.

The point is not that this list is the perfect one, but that it *is* possible to devise a series of fairly objective and verifiable factors that measure the degree to which a teenager's true potential has been hidden. (As it happens, the complex definition is the one that disproportionately benefits African Americans. Even among similar income groups, blacks are more likely than whites to live in concentrated poverty, go to bad schools and live in single-parent homes.) It's just not true that a system of class preferences is inherently harder to administer than a system based on race. Race only seems simpler because we have ignored the ambiguities. And racial preferences are just as easy to ridicule. To paraphrase Kinsley, does a new Indian immigrant get fewer or more points than a third-generation Latino whose mother is Anglo?

Who should benefit? Mickey Kaus, in "Class Is In," (TRB, March 27) argued that class preferences should be reserved for the underclass. But the injuries of class extend beyond the poorest. The offspring of the working poor and the working class lack advantages, too, and indeed SAT scores correlate lockstep with income at every increment Unless you believe in genetic inferiority, these statistics suggest unfairness is not confined to the underclass. As a practical matter, a teenager who emerges from the underclass has little chance of surviving at an elite college. At Berkeley, administrators found that using a definition of disadvantaged, under which neither parent attended a four-year college and the family could not afford to pay $1,000 in education expenses, failed to bring in enough students who were likely to pass.

Still, there are several serious objections to class-based preferences that must be addressed.

1. *We're not ready to be color-blind because racial discrimination continues to afflict our society.* Ron Brown says affirmative action "continues to be needed not to redress grievances of the past, but the current discrimination that continues to exist." This is a relatively new theory, which conveniently elides the fact that preferences were supposed to be temporary. It also stands logic on its head. While racial discrimination undoubtedly still exists, the Civil Rights Act of 1964 was meant to address prospective discrimination. Affirmative action—discrimination in itself—makes sense only to the extent that there is a current-day legacy of *past* discrimination which new prospective laws cannot reach back and remedy.

In the contexts of education and employment, the Civil Rights Act already contains powerful tools to address intentional and unintentional discrimination. The Civil Rights Act of 1991 reaffirmed the need to address unintentional discrimination—by requiring employers to justify employment practices that are statistically more likely to hurt minorities—but it did so without crossing the line to required preferences. This principle also applies to Title VI of the Civil Rights Act, so that if, for example, it can be shown that the SAT produces an unjustified disparate impact, a university can be barred from using it. In addition, "soft" forms of affirmative action, which require employers and universities to broaden the net and interview people from all races are good ways of ensuring positions are not filled by word of mouth, through wealthy white networks.

We have weaker tools to deal with discrimination in other areas of life—say, taxi drivers who refuse to pick up black businessmen—but how does a preference in education or employment remedy that wrong? By contrast, there is nothing illegal about bad schools, bad housing and grossly stunted opportunities for the poor. A class preference is perfectly appropriate.

2. *Class preferences will be just as stigmatizing as racial preferences.* Kinsley argues that "any debilitating self-doubt that exists because of affirmative action is not going to be mitigated by being told you got into Harvard because of your 'socioeconomic disadvantage' rather than your race."

But class preferences are different from racial preferences in at least two important respects. First, stigma—in one's own eyes and the eyes of others—is bound up with the question of whether an admissions criterion is accepted as legitimate. Students with good grades aren't seen as getting in "just because they're smart." And there appears to be a societal consensus— from Douglas to Scalia—that kids from poor backgrounds deserve a leg up. Such a consensus has never existed for class-blind racial preferences.

Second, there is no myth of inferiority in this country about the abilities of poor people comparable to that about African Americans. Now, if racial preferences are purely a matter of compensatory justice, then the question of whether preferences exacerbate white racism is not relevant. But today racial preferences are often justified by social utility (bringing different racial groups together helps dispel stereotypes) in which case the social consequences are highly relevant. The general argument made by proponents of racial preferences—that policies need to be grounded in social reality, not ahistorical theory—cuts in favor of the class category. Why? Precisely because there is no stubborn historical myth for it to reinforce.

Kaus makes a related argument when he says that class preferences "will still reward those who play the victim." But if objective criteria are used to define the disadvantaged, there is no way to "play" the victim. Poor and working-class teenagers are the victims of class inequality not of their own making. Preferences, unlike, say, a welfare check, tell poor teenagers not that they are helpless victims, but that we think their long-run potential is great, and we're going to give them a chance—if they work their tails off—to prove themselves.

3. *Class preferences continue to treat people as members of groups as opposed to individuals.* Yes. But so do university admissions policies that summarily reject students below a certain SAT level. It's hard to know what treating people as individuals means. (Perhaps if university admissions committees interviewed the teachers of each applicant back to kindergarten to get a

better picture of their academic potential, we'd be treating them more as individuals.) The question is not whether we treat people as members of groups—that's inevitable—but whether the group is a relevant one. And in measuring disadvantage (and hidden potential) class is surely a much better proxy than race.

4. *Class-based affirmative action will not yield a diverse student body in elite colleges.* Actually, there is reason to believe that class preferences will disproportionately benefit people of color in most contexts—since minorities are disproportionately poor. In the university context, however, class-based preferences were rejected during the 1970s in part because of fear that they would produce inadequate numbers of minority students. The problem is that when you control for income, African American students do worse than white and Asian students on the SAT—due in part to differences in culture and linguistic patterns, and in part to the way income alone as a measurement hides other class-based differences among ethnic groups.

The concern is a serious and complicated one. Briefly, there are four responses. First, even Murray and Richard Herrnstein agree that the residual racial gap in scores has declined significantly in the past two decades, so the concern, though real, is not as great as it once, was. Second, if we use the sophisticated definition of class discussed earlier—which reflects the relative disadvantage of blacks vis-a-vis whites of the same income level—the racial gap should close further. Third, we can improve racial diversity by getting rid of unjustified preferences—for alumni kids or students from underrepresented geographic regions—which disproportionately hurt people of color. Finally, if the goal is to provide genuine equal opportunity, not equality of group result, and if we are satisfied that a meritocratic system which corrects for class inequality is the best possible approximation of that equality, then we have achieved our goal.

5. *Class-based affirmative action will cause as much resentment among those left out as race-based affirmative action.* Kinsley argues that the rejected applicant in the infamous Jesse Helms commercial from 1990 would feel just as angry for losing out on a class-based as a race-based preference, since both involve "making up for past injustice." The difference, of course, is that class preferences go to the actual victims of class injury, mooting the whole question of intergenerational justice. In the racial context, this was called "victim specificity." Even the Reagan administration was in favor of compensating actual victims of racial discrimination.

The larger point implicit in Kinsley's question is a more serious one: that any preference system, whether race- or class-based, is "still a form of zero-sum social engineering." Why should liberals push for class preferences at all? Why not just provide more funding for education, safer schools, better nutrition? The answer is that liberals should do these things; but we cannot hold our breath for it to happen. In 1993, when all the planets were aligned—a populist Democratic president, Democratic control of both Houses of Congress—they produced: what *The New York Times* called "A BUDGET WORTHY OF MR. BUSH." Cheaper alternatives, such as preferences, must supplement more expensive strategies of social spending. Besides, to the extent that class preferences help change the focus of public discourse from race to class, they help reforge the coalition needed to sustain the social programs liberals want.

Class preferences could restore the successful formula on which the early civil rights movement rested: morally unassailable underpinnings and a relatively inexpensive agenda. It's crucial to remember that Martin Luther King Jr. called for special consideration based on class, not race. After laying out a forceful argument for the special debt owed to blacks, King rejected the call for a Negro Bill of Rights in favor of a Bill of Rights for the Disadvantaged. It was King's insight that there were nonracial ways to remedy racial wrongs, and that the injuries of class deserve attention along with the injuries of race.

None of this is to argue that King would have opposed affirmative action if the alternative were to do nothing. For Jesse Helms to invoke King's color-blind rhetoric now that it is in the interests of white people to do so is the worst kind of hypocrisy. Some form of compensation is necessary, and I think affirmative action, though deeply flawed, is better than nothing.

But the opportunity to save affirmative action of any kind may soon pass. If the Supreme Court continues to narrow the instances in which racial preferences are justified, if California voters put an end to affirmative action in their state and if Congress begins to roll back racial preferences in legislation which President Clinton finds hard to veto—or President Phil Gramm signs with gusto—conservatives will have less and less reason to bargain. Now is the time to call their bluff.

NO

Amy Gutmann

Should Public Policy Be Class Conscious Rather than Color Conscious?

We have yet carefully to consider a proposal that promises to go a long way toward securing fair opportunity for black Americans while avoiding the pitfalls of color consciousness by shifting the focus of public policy from race to class. One advocate of "class, not race" argues that "it was clear that with the passage of the Civil Rights Act of 1964, class replaced caste as the central impediment to equal opportunity."[1] If class is the central impediment to equal opportunity, then using class as a qualification may be fairer to individuals than using race. Counting poverty as a qualification—on grounds that it is highly correlated with unequal opportunity, with untapped intellectual potential, and with life experience from which more affluent individuals can learn—would help blacks and non-blacks alike, but only those who are poor. In addition to being fairer, its advocates claim, class preferences would be politically more feasible and therefore potentially more effective in addressing racial as well as class injustice. The apparently rising tide of resentment and distrust between blacks and whites in the United States makes the call to leave race preferences behind all the more appealing.

Advocates most often look to university admissions as the realm in which class should supplant color as a qualification, so it makes sense to focus on the promise of "class, not race" in this extensive and familiar realm. University admissions policies would be fairer if considerations of color were left behind, advocates argue, while considerations of class took their place. Why? Because poverty accompanied by academic accomplishment is, generally speaking, a sign of uncommon effort, untapped intellectual potential, and unusual life experiences from which more affluent students can learn.

One advocate of "class, not race" notes that "we rarely see a breakdown of [SAT] scores by class, which would show enormous gaps between rich and poor, gaps that would help explain differences in scores by race."[2] After breaking down average SAT scores by class and race, we see enormous gaps between rich and poor students. If this were all that we

APPIAH, K. ANTHONY: COLOR CONSCIOUS. © 1996 Princeton University Press, 1998 paperback edition. Reprinted by permission of Princeton University Press.

observed, then the shift from class to race could provide fair opportunity for black Americans, since black Americans are disproportionately poor. But when average SAT scores are broken down by class and race, we also see enormous gaps between black and white students *within* the same income groups. Moreover, the very same argument that "class, not race" advocates invoke for counting poverty as a qualification in admissions also supports the idea that being black is a similarly important qualification. The same evidence of a significant gap in SAT scores between groups—whether identified by class or color—lends support to the idea that both poor students and black students face distinctive educational disadvantages. The educational disadvantages faced by black students are not statistically accounted for by the income differentials between white and black students. This is what we should expect if (and only if) color is an independent cause of injustice in this country.

The evidence from SAT scores alone is of course insufficient to provide a full picture of either class or racial injustice, let alone its causes. But the very same kind of evidence that advocates take as sufficient to support class as a consideration for university admissions also supports color as a consideration. There is a significant gap between the average SAT scores of groups, whether those groups are defined by class, color, or both. The average combined SAT scores for black students whose parents earn between $10,000 and $20,000 is 175 points lower than the average combined score for white students whose parents fall in the same income category. The gap between the average SAT scores of black and white students within this income category narrows by only 21 points out of the 196 point gap between all black and white students taking the test.

As long as such gaps perist, a "class, not race" policy in university admissions will do far less to increase the higher educational opportunity of blacks than nonblacks. If selective colleges and universities reject color in order to adopt class as a consideration in admitting disadvantaged students, their student bodies would become almost entirely nonblack. For colleges and universities committed to educating future leaders, this result should be as alarming as the image of an affluent, multicolored society without well-educated black leaders. It is just as doubtful that nonblack leaders in such a society could be well educated, for their education would have taken place in almost entirely nonblack universities.

Proportional representation by color in selective universities is not an ultimate goal of a just society. Fair equality of opportunity is. The problem in universities' focusing on class considerations to the exclusion of color is not disproportionality of results but unfairness, as indicated by the inconsistency in the reasoning that supports the proposed shift from color to class. The statistical evidence of lower average SAT scores by income categories is taken to indicate that low-income students are disadvantaged in a way that warrants making low income a qualification. But the analogous statistical evidence of lower average SAT scores by the U.S. Census's racial categories is not taken to indicate that black students are disadvantaged in a way that warrants making color a qualification.

The same statistical evidence that is used to establish the case for class as a consideration in admissions is either ignored or discounted when considering color as a consideration, and for no good reason. Some critics say that individual responsibility is undermined when black students who have lower SAT scores than nonblack students are admitted, but precisely the same argument could be made against admitting students from poor families who score lower than their more affluent peers. In both cases, the argument is extremely weak. Holding individuals responsible for their educational achievement is completely consistent with counting class *and* color as qualifications, as long as class and color are not the *only* qualifications, and individuals are not held to be *exclusively* responsible for their educational successes or failures.

The situation is therefore more complex than the "class, not race" perspective admits. In order to be admitted to a selective university, all applicants—whether they be poor, middle-class, rich, black, white, or some other color—must demonstrate unusual educational accomplishment relative to their similarly situated peers. They must also demonstrate the capacity to succeed academically, once admitted. These prerequisites to admission to a selective university ensure that individual applicants are held responsible for educational achievement. But social institutions, including universities, also share responsibility with individuals for overcoming the obstacles associated with color and class in our society. Why? Because to be responsible for accomplishing something entails having the effective power to do so. Individuals often do not have the power to overcome all the obstacles associated with being poor or black. Nor is responsibility a zero-sum quantity. Just because individuals are responsible for working hard does not mean that institutions are not responsible for coming to their aid, when they can thereby help equalize opportunity. It is therefore both unrealistic and unfair to expect individuals alone to overcome all the obstacles that are associated with being black or poor in our society.

The "class, not race" perspective admits half as much by urging universities to consider low income as a qualification for university admission—not the only qualification, to be sure, but a legitimate one that can justify admitting some applicants with lower SAT scores and lower high school grades and passing over other applicants with higher SAT scores and high school grades. Universities fall short of providing fair equality of educational opportunity, according to the "class, not race" perspective, to the extent that their admission policies neglect low income as an obstacle to educational achievement, and therefore refuse to pass over some applicants who score higher on these conventional indices (which do not predict future educational performance past the freshman year, let alone future career success or social leadership). The very same thing can be said about neglecting the extent to which being black is an obstacle to educational achievement in our society. The refusal to count being black as one qualification among many entails falling short of providing fair equality of educational opportunity for black students who demonstrate unusual educational achievement relative to the obstacles that they have faced.

The best available evidence suggests that color and class are both obstacles, with interactive effects in the lives of a majority of black Americans.

Why, then, shift from color to class, rather than use both class and color, as independently important considerations in university admissions? The inconsistency and unfairness in substituting class for color as a qualification becomes vivid when we imagine what universities that adopt the "class, not race" perspective would effectively be saying to their applicants. To the average low-income white student, they would say— "Giving you a boost in admissions is consistent with our expectation that you have worked hard to get where you are and will continue to work hard to earn your future success." To the average low-income black student, they would say—"If we give you an added boost in admissions over the average low-income white student, we will be denying your responsibility for your lower scores and decreasing your incentive to work hard and earn your success." To average middle-income black students, they would say: "We cannot give you any boost in admissions over average middle-income white students because you no more than they have any special obstacles to overcome."

Universities could achieve consistency by refusing to consider any of the educational obstacles faced by applicants, whether they be poor or black or physically handicapped. But the price of this policy would be forsaking fair equality of educational opportunity as well as overlooking the potential for intellectual accomplishment and social leadership of individuals who have faced far greater than average obstacles to academic achievement, as conventionally measured. Yet another price of a policy of "neither class nor color" would be discounting the values—associational as well as educational—of cultural diversity on university campuses. Consistency would also require giving up all the other, nonacademic factors that the most selective universities have traditionally considered relevant in admissions, such as geographical diversity and athletic ability.

Were citizens of this society engaged in designing our system of higher education from scratch, a case might be made for counting only intellectual accomplishment in admissions. But few if any critics of counting color as a consideration in university admissions propose such a radical redesigning of our college and university system. In any case, the fairest way to such radical restructuring would not begin by giving up on color as a consideration in admissions. There are many reasons to doubt whether such a radical redesign would produce a better system of higher education than the one we now have, and there is no reason to believe that this society would democratically support such a restructuring. In this context, we cannot justify rejecting color while accepting class as one among many legitimate considerations for admissions.

What about the critics' claim that when universities give a boost to applicants above and beyond their actual educational achievements, they fostser in that group of applicants a sense of irresponsibility for their (relative lack of) educational achievements? This argument from the value of individual responsibility cannot be sustained for two reasons. First responsibility is not zero-sum. If universities assume some responsibility for helping applicants who have faced unusually great obstacles to educational achievement, they are not denying the responsibility of those applicants to work hard and demonstrate their capacity to succeed once they are admitted. (Perhaps the critics are objecting to universities that admit a high proportion of black students who cannot graduate, in which case the critics are pointing to a correctable problem, and not one that besets the strongest case for counting color as a qualification.) Second, the same argument from responsibility is rarely if ever invoked in opposition to giving a boost to low-income or physically handicapped students, even though it applies with the same (weak) force. The force of the argument is weak because responsibility for educational accomplishment is both institutional and individual. When universities share responsibility for helping students overcome educational obstacles, they do not therefore relieve them of the responsibility to succeed academically. Students who are given a boost in an admissions process still must compete for admissions, work for their grades, and compete for jobs on the basis of their qualifications.

The case for both class *and* color as considerations in university admissions is therefore strong: stronger than either consideration taken to the exclusion of the other. The "class, not race" proposal, by contrast, fails by the color blind test of fairness; it does not treat like cases alike. It discriminates against blacks by giving a boost only to students who score low because of disadvantages associated with poverty, but not to students who score low because of disadvantages that are as credibly associated with their color.

A more complex way of counting class as a qualification, some critics say, would avoid these inequities and thereby obviate the need to take color into account. A "complex calculus of advantage" would take into account not only parental income, education, and occupation but also "net worth, the quality of secondary education, neighborhood influences and family structure." The complex calculus of class is fairer than the simple one, which counts only income, because it considers more dimensions of disadvantage. Since blacks "are more likely than whites to live in concentrated poverty, to go to bad schools and live in single-parent homes," the complex calculus would "disproportionately" benefit blacks.[3] Its advocates say that the complex calculus not only is fair but also has a decisive political advantage over any color conscious policy: it would go almost as far toward fair equality of educational opportunity as would explicit considerations of color without calling attention to the enduring racial divisions in our society.

But the political strength of the complex calculus of disadvantage is also its weakness. By not calling attention to enduring divisions of color in our society, some suggest, we may be better able to overcome them. But it is at least as likely that we will thereby fail to make much progress in overcoming them. It is impossible to say on the basis of available evidence—and the enduring imperfections of our self-understanding—which is more likely to be the case. What we can say with near certainty is that if blacks who live in concentrated poverty, go to bad schools, or live in single-parent homes are also stigmatized by racial prejudice as whites are not, then even the most complex calculus of *class* is an imperfect substitute for also taking color explicitly into account. Perhaps the disadvantages of color can be adequately addressed by remedies that do not explicitly take color into account, but the adequacy of the complex calculus of disadvantage will then be closely related to the intention of its designers to come as close as possible to achieving the justice demanded by color as well as class consciousness.

Fairness speaks in favor of taking both class and color into account as qualifications. If politics precludes considerations of color, then we are far better off, morally speaking, with a complex calculus of class than with a simple one. But we would be better off still with policies that at least implicitly recognize the independent dimension of color as an obstacle to educational achievement in our society. The color blind principle of fairness has these inclusive implications. It encourages employers and universities to consider both class and color dimensions of disadvantage (along with other dimensions, such as gender) and also to consider a wider range of qualifications for jobs and places in a university.

Even color, class, *and* gender considerations, taken together, however, would not adequately address the problem of racial injustice. None of these considerations, as commonly defended, addresses a more urgent problem: the deprivation experienced by the poorest citizens, over 30 percent of whom are black. The poorest citizens are not in a position to benefit from admissions or hiring policies that count either class or color as added qualifications. This is a weakness shared by all kinds of policies that focus on giving a boost to individuals—whatever their skin color and relative advantage to one another—who are already among the more advantaged of our society. Millions of citizens, a vastly disproportionate number of them black, suffer from economic and educational deprivations so great as to elude the admittedly incomplete and relatively inexpensive remedies of affirmative action. Policies aimed at increasing employment, job training, health care, child care, housing, and education are desperately needed for all these individuals, regardless of their color. These policies, like the admissions policies we have been considering, would not give *preferential* treatment to anyone. They would treat the least advantaged citizens as civic equals who should not be deprived of a fair chance to live a good life or participate as equals in democratic politics because of the bad luck of the natural lottery of birth or upbringing.

Social welfare and fair workfare policies—which provide jobs that pay and adequate child care for everyone who can work—are a necessary part of any adequate response to racial injustice. They are also far more expensive than admissions and hiring policies that treat class and color as qualifications, and far more expensive than policies of preferential treatment, at least in the short run. Over time, these policies would in all likelihood more than pay for themselves. They would alleviate the increasingly expensive and widespread problems of welfare dependency, unemployment, and crime in this country. Moreover, without fair workfare and welfare policies, we cannot be a society of civic equals. Citizens will be fighting for their fair share of a social pie that cannot provide fairness for everyone; many men and women who are willing and able to work will not be able to find work that pays, and others will work full-time only to earn less, or little more than they would on welfare, while they are also unable to ensure adequate care for their children.

The political fights in such a context will invariably divide us by groups since effective democratic politics is by its very nature group politics. To build a society in which citizens both help themselves by helping each other and help each other by helping themselves, we must be committed not only to making the economic pie sufficiently large but also to dividing it in such a way that every person who is willing to work can find adequate child care and decent work that pays.

As urgent as social welfare, workfare, and child care policies are they would not by themselves constitute a sufficient response to racial injustice in the short run. We have seen that color conscious programs are also part of a comprehensive response to injustice, although not the most urgent (or most expensive) part. Suppose that a more comprehensive, color conscious perspective is fair. Is it feasible? An eye-opening study entitled *The Scar of Race* shows that mere mention of the words "affirmative action" elicits negative attitudes about black Americans from white Americans. After affirmative action is mentioned in the course of an interview with white citizens, the proportion of respondents who agree with the claim that "blacks are irresponsible" almost doubles, increasing from 26 percent to 43 percent. (The proportions grow from 20 percent to 31 percent for the claim that "blacks are lazy" and from 29 percent to 36 percent for the claim that "blacks are arrogant.") White Americans' "dislike of particular racial policies," the authors conclude, "can provoke dislike of blacks, as well as the other way around."[4]

"Provoking dislike" is importantly ambiguous between *producing* dislike and *triggering* the open expression of it (where the dislike already preceded the mere mention of affirmative action). It is doubtful that the mere mention of affirmative action *creates* racial prejudice. More likely, it *releases greater oral expression* of preexisting racial animosity. Many white Americans seem to take the mention of affirmative action, particularly in a matter-of-fact question that opens up the possibility of their criticizing affirmative action policies, as a signal that it is acceptable to be critical not only of affirmative action but also of blacks. This is cause for concern, but the concern cannot be effectively addressed simply by relabeling affirmative action policies as something else. A good reason to avoid the term "affirmative action" is the massive confusion that surrounds its meaning. An effective and appropriate response to this confusion would be to go beyond simple sound bites, which rarely serve justice well, and distinguish between morally better and worse policies that are color conscious. The negative reaction to the mere mention of the term "affirmative action" surely is not a sufficient reason to abandon affirmative action programs—whatever we call them—that are otherwise fair and beneficial to blacks.

Another finding of this same study suggests why it would be a mistake to oppose affirmative action only on these grounds. The popularity of programs that are perceived to help blacks is highly volatile, shifting with citizens' perception of the state of the law and the moral commitments of political leadership. When white citizens are asked for their views on a set-aside program for minorities—"a law to ensure that a certain number of federal contracts go to minority contractors," 43 percent say they favor it. But when they are told that the set-aside program for minorities is a law passed by both houses of Congress, the support significantly increases to 57 percent.[5]

Not only does the force of law seem to have the capacity to change people's minds on race matters, so does the force of moral argument. When exposed to counterarguments to their expressed positions on various policy responses to racial problems, many people switch their position in the direction of the counterarguments. This tendency is greatest for social welfare policies, such as government spending for blacks, but the tendency is also significant for affirmative action policies, where an even greater proportion of whites shift to favoring a pro–affirmative action position than switch to an anti–affirmative action position when exposed to counterarguments to their original positions. Twenty-three percent of white respondents shift from a negative to a positive position on affirmative action, compared to 17 percent who shift in the opposite direction.[6]

Moral argument and political leadership, as this study vividly indicates, make a significant difference in public opinion on race matters. This is potentially good news for deliberative democracy. Were we to make our politics more deliberative, we would also—in all likelihood—increase the potential for bringing public policy and color consciousness more in line with the force of moral arguments. There are no guarantees, of course, about where the force of argument will lead citizens and public officials on these complex issues. But as long as the potential exists for changing minds through deliberation, citizens and public officials alike have good reason—moral as well as prudential—not to endorse public policies merely because they conform to public opinion polls. "New majorities can be made—and unmade," Paul Sniderman and Thomas Piazza conclude. "The future is not foreordained. It is the business of politics to decide it."[7]

All the more reason to approach the political morality of race with renewed openness, at least as much openness as ordinary citizens evince in extended discussions of racially charged issues, which include most issues of our public life. Unless we keep the aim of overcoming racial injustice at the front of our minds and at the center of our democratic deliberations, we shall not arrive at an adequate response to racial injustice. I do not pretend to be able to provide that response, or even anything close to it in this essay. But there is value in keeping democratic doors open to exploring new possibilities and to changing minds, including our own, as our deliberations on these issues continue. Only if we keep the aim of overcoming racial injustice at the center of our deliberations about social justice can we realistically hope to develop into a democracy with liberty and justice for all.

Notes

1. Richard Kahlenberg, "Class, Not Race," *New Republic,* April 3, 1995, p. 21.
2. Ibid., p. 24.
3. Ibid., p. 25.
4. Paul M. Sniderman and Thomas Piazza, *The Scar of Race* (Cambridge, Mass.: Harvard University Press, 1993), p. 104.
5. Ibid., pp. 131–2.
6. Ibid., p. 148.
7. Ibid., p. 165.

POSTSCRIPT

Should Twenty-First Century Public Policy Be Class Conscious Rather than Race Conscious?

The stratification of society by class and race is a reality that is manifested in significant inequality and poverty within modern nations. As the nation emerged as the dominant economic power in the world, the persistence of poverty and racism became increasing cause for concern. Many people were suffering while living in conditions that were an affront to our national conscience and contrary to the image that the United States desired to project in the world. Significant books concerning America's poor were published, including Evans and Agee, *Now Let Us Sing in Praise of Famous Men,* and Michael Harrington, *The Other America,* to bring attention to this problem. At the same time, most areas of American life, including education, were still segregated.

The European Americans who arrived on these shores seeking a new beginning and expanded life chances were poor by contemporary standards and they eked out a hardscrabble existence as they sought their fortunes in these new lands. Poverty persisted in this new nation, and as capitalism emerged, the system of social stratification that it produced resulted in a lower class and, a more recently identified, underclass that are continuing realities of American life.

Slavery, followed by segregation, defined race relations. In 1896, segregation was legalized by the Supreme Court's *Plessy v. Ferguson* decision. Public policy, "separate but equal," compounded the problem of poverty for blacks. While the *Brown* decision in 1954 overturned *Plessy,* school integration proceeded slowly with great resistance. Race-based policies beginning with *Brown* and the Civil Rights Act of 1964 addressed race discrimination.

The New Deal initiatives of the 1930s including The Social Security Act of 1935 addressed the persistent issue of poverty. Policy dealing with unemployment, retirement compensation, public assistance, and health care followed. These are class-based issues. American politics are adversarial in nature, and fault lines that they expose will continue to resonate within society. Should public policy of the twentieth century be class conscious rather than race conscious?

Advocates of class-based public policies are at their best when they examine comparative disadvantages of whites and African Americans and ask whether an affluent black person should be extended a preference to advance while the white poor are not similarly accommodated. How could anyone suggest that the child of a millionaire black athlete should be granted a preference while the needs of a poor white Appalachian are ignored? Ideally, both race and class are the relevant contemporary issues that underscore much of the public policy debate.

Further reading includes William Julius Wilson, *The Declining Significance of Race: Blacks and Changing American Institutions* (University of Chicago, 1978); James Boggs, in *Racism and the Class Struggle* (Monthly Review Press, 1970), examines the interrelationship between race and class in black struggles against racisms; and *Class, Race and Affirmative Action* (Basic Books, 1996) by Richard D. Kahlenberg makes the argument for class-based remedies for injustices.

ISSUE 17

Is Now the Time for Reparations for African Americans?

YES: Robert L. Allen, "Past Due: The African American Quest for Reparations," *The Black Scholar* (vol. 28, no. 2, Summer 1998)

NO: "Slavery and the Law: Time and Punishment," *The Economist* (vol. 363, no. 8268, April 13, 2002)

ISSUE SUMMARY

YES: Robert L. Allen, professor and senior editor of *The Black Scholar,* argues that reparations for African Americans are necessary to achieve an economically just society within the United States.

NO: Staff writers from *The Economist* oppose reparations and question whether such a policy is appropriate in a nation where the victims of slavery are difficult to identify and the perpetrators of past racial oppressions are no longer among us.

T he debate over the proposal for reparations for African Americans has generated even more controversy than affirmative action policies. Many Americans believe that since the African Americans currently residing in the nation did not experience slavery and racial segregation—the two major components of the society's racist legacy—they are not entitled to such a benefit. Other commentators, including some African Americans, oppose reparations because they believe that the acceptance of such a payout would result in a foreclosure of opportunities to have future racial grievances dealt with by meaningful and effective means. Others are concerned with the financial and budgetary pressures that reparations would place upon the U.S. treasury. Still others strongly believe that reparations are a meaningful and appropriate response to the dilemma of race within the American experience and the legacy of racial inequalities that it has bequeathed to the nation. It is abundantly clear, therefore, that the proposal to grant reparations to African Americans is a significant wedge issue of American society and politics where race relations are concerned.

Robert L. Allen favors reparations for African Americans and employs an historical perspective to support his position. He presents an historical examination of the quest for reparations as African-American leaders and organizations throughout history have advanced it in order to document the strong support that this policy has received within society. Allen proceeds to examine the problems that African Americans have experienced in acquiring property and income, and accumulating wealth in this country throughout history. These inequities/disparities are the direct result of the racist legacy of slavery and segregation. Thus, Robert Allen argues: "Reparations provides a framework for the redistribution of wealth within the existing political economy, and thereby moving towards economic equality between whites and blacks." Finally, Allen presents a significant body of evidence concerning the precedents that are available for supporting reparations for African Americans and the legal principles upon which the claim for such restitution rests.

The authors of the article from *The Economist* are opposed to reparations and begin their disagreement with such a policy by focusing upon the complexity of this issue of American race relations. These authors state the view that identifying the victims and the perpetrators of past oppressions, such as slavery, is so complex that it is virtually impossible to do so. They also claim that the corporations that were involved in the economic exploitation of slave labor have long since mended their ways and should no longer be held responsible for the historical plight of African Americans.

For the reader who has just now been introduced to this topic, a consideration of general related questions may help gain insight into the issue. Historically, what is the justification of reparations for any group? Under what circumstances should a group be granted reparations? Is it possible to "settle" claims of past exploitation and injustice with a lump sum of money? For those in favor of reparations for African Americans, is there a danger that a monetary award will foreclose opportunities for resolving future racial grievances? Will reparations minimize racial prejudice and discrimination? Will reparations contribute to American unity or further racial polarization?

Robert L. Allen

 **YES**

Past Due: The African American Quest for Reparations

In recent years the quest for reparations for Africa and Africa's children in the Diaspora has emerged as an important issue. A growing number of activists, scholars and political leaders, such as British M.P. Bernie Grant and U.S. Congressman John Conyers, have taken up the call for reparations. Organizations have been formed to press the issue, and a foundation for engagement with governments, particularly in Britain and (perhaps) the United States, is being laid. The issue of reparations is truly global and it has many dimensions—moral, cultural, social, psychological, political and economic. In this article, I will focus chiefly on reparations as a matter of social justice for African Americans, but I am cognizant of the fact that the struggle for reparations is a global issue requiring a unified, international mobilization.

History of the Quest for Reparations

The quest for reparations has a long and deeply rooted history in the life and struggles of the African American community. Reparations have been proposed and fought for by individuals and organizations representing a wide range of social and political viewpoints. As early as 1854 a black emigrationist convention called for a "national indemnity" as a "redress of our grievances for the unparalleled wrongs, undisguised impositions, and unmitigated oppression which we have suffered at the hands of this American people."[1] After the Civil War the anti-slavery activist Sojourner Truth organized a petition campaign seeking free public land for the former slaves.[2] In support of her campaign Sojourner Truth said: "America owes to my people some of the dividends. She can afford to pay and she must pay. I shall make them understand that there is a debt to the Negro people which they can never repay. At least, then, they must make amends."[3] Her valiant campaign was unsuccessful.

In the 1890s another black woman, Callie House, filed lawsuits and petitioned Congress for reparations payments to African Americans. Her efforts were endorsed by Frederick Douglass, but again there was no success.[4]

Reprinted from *Black Scholar*, volume 28, number 2 (summer 1998), pp. 2–13, by permission of the University of Nebraska Press © 1998.

Religious leaders have also called for reparations. Bishop Henry McNeal Turner once declared: "We have worked, enriched the country and helped give it a standing among the powers of the earth. . . ." Turner estimated that the United States owed black people $40 billion for unpaid labor.[5] Most recently Rev. Amos Brown, pastor of Third Baptist Church in San Francisco, called for reparations in the form of tax credits and automatic tuition for African American youths who qualify for higher education.[6]

Marcus Garvey's call of "Africa for Africans at home and abroad" echoed the quest for restitution. In the "Declaration of the Rights the Negro People of the World" adopted in 1920 by the Universal Negro Improvement Association, Point 15 declared: "We strongly condemn the cupidity of those nations of the world who, by open aggression or secret schemes, have seized the territories and inexhaustible natural wealth of Africa, and we place on record our most solemn determination to reclaim the treasures and possession of the vast continent of our forefathers."[7]

One of the foremost proponents of reparations was the venerable Queen Mother Moore. An activist in the Garvey movement and many other organizations during a long life spanning nearly a century, she insisted that restitution was required to make amends for the great injustice of slavery.[8]

The Nation of Islam also made a reparations demand. In its program for establishing a separate state the Nation asserted that "our former slave masters are obligated to provide such land and that the areas must be fertile and minerally rich. We believe that our former slave masters are obligated to maintain and supply our needs in this separate territory for the next 20 to 25 years—until we are able to produce and supply our own needs."[9]

The quest for reparations was voiced in the Ten-Point Program of the Black Panther Party. Point Number Three states: "We believe that this racist government has robbed us and now we are demanding the overdue debt of forty acres and two mules. Forty acres and two mules was promised 100 years ago as restitution for slave labor and mass murder of Black people. We will accept payment in currency which will be distributed to our many communities. The Germans are now aiding the Jews in Israel for the genocide of the Jewish people. The Germans murdered six million Jews. The American racist has taken part in the slaughter of over fifty million Black people; therefore, we feel that this is a modest demand that we make."[10]

In the late 1960s, two of the most dramatic demands for reparations were put forward by former SNCC leader James Forman and by the nationalist Republic of New Africa.

In 1969 Forman strode into Riverside Church in New York City and presented a Black Manifesto calling for $500 million in reparations from white Christian Churches and Jewish synagogues. The Manifesto stemmed from a Black Economic Development Conference held in Detroit under the auspices of Christian churches. Commenting on the thinking behind the reparations demand, Forman wrote in *The Making of Black Revolutionaries:* "Reparations did not represent any kind of long-range goal to our minds, but an intermediate step on the path to liberation. We saw it as a politically correct step, for the concept of reparation reflected the need to adjust past wrongs—to compensate for the enslavement of black people by Christians and their subsequent exploitation by Christians and Jews in the United States. Our demands—to be called the Black Manifesto—would not merely involve money but would be a call for revolutionary action, a Manifesto that spoke of the human misery of black people under capitalism and imperialism, and pointed the way to ending these conditions."[11] The Manifesto proposed that reparations be used for helping black farmers, establishing black print and electronic media, funding training, research and community organizing centers, assistance in organizing welfare recipients and black workers, funding research on black economic development and links with Africa, and funding a black university.[12]

The Republic of New Africa (RNA) was founded in 1968 with the purpose of establishing an independent Black Republic in five southern states with large black populations. (South Carolina, Georgia, Alabama, Mississippi and Louisiana) In 1972 the RNA developed what it called an Anti-Depression Program that called for $300 billion in reparations from the U.S. government, part of which would be used to finance establishment of new communities in the proposed black republic.[13] The program featured three "legislative requests" to be presented to the U.S. Congress. One proposal called for the ceding of land to the RNA in areas where black people voted for independence. A second proposal called for reparations of $300 billion. The third proposal called for negotiations between the U.S. Government and the RNA with regard to the details of reparations.

The RNA reparations proposal noted that reparations are commonly paid by one nation to another to compensate for damage caused by unjust acts of war. For example, the document pointed to payments made to various nations by the Federal Republic of Germany for damage caused by the Nazi regime during World War II. The document argued that slavery constituted a form of unjust warfare against the African nation in America, and the damage caused by this warfare provided the basis for a demand for reparations.[14]

In comparing the Black Manifesto and the RNA Anti-Depression Program several things stand out. The Black Manifesto was directed not at the government but at church institutions, and its monetary demands were much more modest. Reparations payments were to be used fund a Southern land bank, independent media, training and organizing efforts, and educational initiatives. The RNA demand was directed to the government and sought reparations to fund new self-sustaining communities as part of an independent black nation. These communities were to develop their own industries, health and educational systems, media, and public infrastructure. Both the Black Manifesto and the RNA program stressed the need for independence from white control. Both the RNA and Forman deployed the concept of domestic colonialism. For the RNA reparations were a means of establishing a separate black nation. For Forman reparations were a step in the process of liberation of an oppressed black community and socialist transformation of America.

Neither program made much headway. The Black Manifesto was ridiculed by most whites, although it did gain a respectful response in journals such as *Commonweal, Christian Century,* and *World Outlook. Christian Century* wrote: "We do not believe the idea of reparations is ridiculous. This generation of blacks continues to pay the price of earlier generations' slavery and subjugation; this generation of whites continues to enjoy the profits of racial exploitation." Nevertheless, the monetary response was minimal; the churches increased their contributions to black organizations by $1 million.[15]

The RNA program was also ridiculed, although the RNA garnered a more dangerous form of attention. In 1971 RNA headquarters in Jackson, Mississippi was the target of a COINTELPRO-type attack by local policemen and FBI agents. In the ensuing shootout a local policeman was fatally wounded. Eleven RNA members, including President Imari Obadele I, were arrested and charged with murder, assault, and treason against the state of Mississippi.[16]

Despite government repression, the RNA pressed its program, lobbying for it at both the Democratic National Convention and the National Black Political Convention held in Gary in 1972.[17]

NBPC Endorses Reparations

The National Black Political Convention (NBPC) endorsed the demand for reparations, which had been raised by a number of delegates. A resolution passed by the NBPC stated: "The economic impoverishment of the Black community in America is clearly traceable to the historic enslavement of our people and to the racist discrimination to which we have been subjected since 'emancipation.' Indeed, much of the unprecedented economic wealth and power of American capitalism has obviously been built upon this exploitation of Black people." The resolution asserted that "we must not rest until American society has recognized our valid, historic right to reparations, to a massive claim on the financial assets of the American economy. At the same time, it is necessary Black people realize that full economic development for us cannot take place without radical transformation of the economic system which has so clearly exploited us these many years."[18] The Convention recommended that a presidential convention be established, with a majority of black members, to determine appropriate reparations and methods of payment.

The Black Manifesto, RNA program and the Black Political Convention resolution brought the issue of reparations into a wider public discourse.

As early as 1970 maverick black businessman Dempsey Travis came up with a proposal for a new homestead act as a form of reparations. Travis calculated that if the government had granted 40 acres to the each of the former slaves the value of this land would have been $21.6 billion (valued at $150 an acre). Travis called for establishing a fund in this amount to assist black people in buying land and homes.[19]

In 1973 white law professor Boris Bitker wrote a book entitled *The Case for Black Reparations*. Noting the "paucity of analysis" that followed Forman's presentation of the Black Manifesto, Bitker offered a narrowly legalistic argument for black reparations. Unlike most black advocates of reparations, Bitker dismissed any reparations demand based on the "ancient injustice" of slavery as largely moot.[20] Instead he argued for reparations that "seek to redress injuries caused by a system of legally imposed segregation that was eventually held in *Brown v. Board of Education* to violate the equal-protection clause of the Fourteenth Amendment."[21]

Bitker's argument made use of the authority of Section 1983, Title 42 of the United States Code. Section 1983, enacted more than a century ago as part of an act to control the Ku Klux Klan, provided that "Every person who, under color of any statute . . . of any State or Territory, subjects . . . any citizen of the United States . . . to the deprivation of any rights . . . secured by the Constitution and laws, shall be liable to the party injured in an action at law, suit in equity, or other proper proceeding for redress."[22] Bitker suggested that a valid claim for reparations could be brought on the grounds that segregation and Jim Crow statutes were found in 1954 to be unconstitutional and therefore subject to a "proceeding for redress" under Section 1983.

In 1974 black economist Robert S. Browne, at the time the director of the Black Economic Research Center, wrote of reparations as requiring "a massive capital transfer of a sizable chunk of America's wealth to the black community."[23] Racial disparities in both economic status and political power could be traced to disparities in ownership of capital assets, according to Browne. Echoing the position that was most widely adopted by black advocates of reparations, Browne said a moral justification for reparations derived from "the debt owed to Blacks for the centuries of unpaid slave labor which built so much of the early American economy, and from the discriminatory wage and employment patterns to which Blacks were subjected after emancipation." Browne also invoked white America's "national self-interest" and desire for racial peace when he further suggested that such "gross inequities" in wealth distribution would exacerbate racial tensions if not redressed.

Following Browne's lead other economists took up serious discussion and advocacy of reparations. They produced a body of work on the economics of slavery, the present value of past labor performed by slaves, the value of black labor since emancipation and racial disparities in distribution of wealth.[24] A good summary statement of this research and its implications for reparations was provided by economist David Swinton: "Discrimination and racism reduced the historic accumulation of capital by blacks and increased the accumulation by whites. The resulting disparities in ownership of capital are transmitted intergenerationally. These capital disparities would prevent attainment of racial equality even if current discrimination ended and blacks and whites had identical tastes and preferences. It would, therefore, be necessary to repair historic damage to the black capital stock in order to ensure attainment of equality."[25]

New Activism Emerges

In the last decade reparations have again become an activist issue with the establishment of the National Coalition of Blacks for Reparations in America (N'COBRA)[26] in the U.S., and the Africa Reparations Movement (ARM)[27] internationally. Founded in 1989 N'COBRA is an umbrella group that sponsors a Reparations Awareness Day each February 25th and holds an annual convention. The organization has done much to create public awareness in the U.S. about the issue of reparations.[28] Similarly, the Africa Reparations Movement, founded in 1993 as an outgrowth of a conference on reparations held in Nigeria, has worked in the international arena to promote the idea of reparations, including cancellation of the external debt of African nations and return of stolen art objects to their home countries. British M.P. Bernie Grant is Chairperson of ARM, and he has taken an active role in pushing the British government to begin to take the issue of reparations seriously.[29]

In the arena of public policy in the U.S. there have been growing efforts to get reparations on the agenda. In 1987 the Republic of New Africa again drafted a reparations bill and circulated it to members of Congress.[30] In 1989, seventeen years after the Gary Black Political Convention, Congressman John Conyers introduced a bill in Congress calling for creation of a presidential commission to study the question of reparations for African Americans. The Conyers bill (originally HR 40, now HR 891) followed the passage of the Civil Liberties Act of 1988 which granted reparations to Japanese Americans who were unjustly interned during World War II. With the success of the reparations effort by Japanese Americans, black activists succeeded in getting several cities, including Detroit, Cleveland, and the District of Columbia to pass resolutions endorsing the tenets of reparations.[31] The Conyers bill, which has been put forward every year since 1989, presents "findings" that "the institution of slavery was constitutionally and statutorily sanctioned by the Government of the United States from 1798 through 1865" and that slavery "constituted an immoral and inhumane deprivation of Africans' life, liberty, African citizenship rights, and cultural heritage, and denied them the fruits of their own labor." So far, every year the Conyers bill has been bottled up in committee and prevented from coming before Congress. Nevertheless, the bill has become a significant rallying point for those individuals and organizations seeking to get a serious hearing for reparations.

The Conyers bill calls for appropriating $8 million to establish a commission to study reparations proposals for African Americans. Specifically the commission would:

1. examine the institution of slavery which existed from 1619 through 1865 within the United States and the colonies that became the United States, including the extent to which the Federal and State governments constitutionally and statutorilysupported the institution of slavery;

2. examine de jure and de facto discrimination against freed slaves and their descendants from the end of the Civil War to the present, including economic, political, and social discrimination;
3. examine the lingering negative effects of the institution of slavery and the discrimination described in paragraph (2) on living African Americans and on society in the United States;
4. recommend appropriate ways to educate the American public of the Commission's findings;
5. recommend appropriate remedies in consideration of the Commission's findings on the matters described in paragraphs (1) and (2); and
6. submit to the Congress the results of such examination, together with such recommendations.[32]

If deemed appropriate, the remedies to be considered include the possibility of a formal apology from the government and payment of compensation to the descendants of African slaves. The commission would recommend what form any compensation should take and who would be eligible.

The commission would have seven members; three to be appointed by the President, three to be appointed by the Speaker of the House of Representatives; and one to be appointed by the President pro tempore of the Senate.

This past year we have seen a maneuver by President Clinton to coopt the Conyers bill by creating a Race Commission with a mandate to conduct a dialogue on race. The Race Commission has not gotten beyond the usual debates over access to jobs and discussion of ways to reduce discrimination. Meanwhile, the *New York Times* reported that over the past two years federal government agencies slashed affirmative action funding and "conducted the most sweeping reductions of [affirmative action] measures since they were instituted."[33] Seen in this light, Clinton's Race Commission is a cynical cosmetic gesture designed to deflect attention from the administration's dismantling of affirmative action programs.

In June 1998 a Black Radical Congress held in Chicago brought together activists from around the country. A draft of a "Black Freedom Agenda for the 21st Century" proposed for the Congress included a demand for reparations. Point number ten of the Freedom Agenda stated: "We demand just compensation and reparations for the systematic brutality and exploitation our people have suffered historically and continue to experience today. We claim the legal and moral right to demand and receive just compensation for oppression which was responsible for the destruction of millions of Black people's lives."

Political Economy and Reparations

With the destruction of affirmative action programs the quest for reparations gains added urgency. However, let me stress that my discussion of reparations is not meant to dismiss issues of access to employment and the necessity of challenging racial discrimination in education and other areas of social life. Social movements and public policies that address racial discrimination in employment, education and elsewhere are clearly important in bringing about any progressive change. However, such remedies do not address the systematic long-term de-capitalization of the African American community. Struggles for civil rights are important, but not sufficient. Transfers of capital resources into the African American community must also occur. Such transfers, to be most effective, must be class-based, aimed at benefitting first and foremost the black workingclass—those who have been most ravaged by the depredations of capitalism and who have benefitted least from the social reforms of the civil rights era.

From the standpoint of political economy I think the *process of underdevelopment* of the African American community and the *role of the state* in this process of underdevelopment are critical in understanding the unfolding of the quest for reparations.

Manning Marable has argued convincingly that capitalism is the fundamental cause of the underdevelopment of black America. At the same time, the wealth produced by slave labor enormously enhanced the economic and political development of North America. In his seminal book, *How Capitalism Underdeveloped Black America,* Marable wrote: "Capitalist development has occurred not in spite of the exclusion of Blacks, but because of the brutal exploitation of Blacks as workers and consumers. Blacks have never been equal partners in the American Social Contract, because the system exists not to develop, but to *underdevelop Black people.*"[34]

He goes on to write:

> The ordeal of slavery was responsible for accelerating the economic and political power of Europe and North America over the rest of the mostly nonwhite world. Since the demise of slavery, and the emergence of modern capitalism, the process of Black underdevelopment has expanded and deepened. To understand this dynamic of degradation, first, is to recognize that development itself is comparative in essence, a relationship of inequality between the capitalist ruling class and those who are exploited. Underdevelopment is not the absence of development; it is the inevitable product of an oppressed population's integration into the world market economy and political system. Once "freed," Black Americans were not compensated for their 246 years of free labor to this country's slave oligarchy. The only means of survival and economic development they possessed was their ability to work, their labor power, which they sold in various forms to the agricultural capitalist. Sharecropping and convict leasing were followed by industrial labor at low wages. . . . Throughout the totality of economic relations, Black workers were exploited—in land tenure, in the ownership of factories shops and other enterprises, in the means of transportation, in energy, and so forth. *The constant expropriation of surplus value created by Black labor is the heart and soul of underdevelopment.*"[35]

Underdevelopment manifests in the restriction of black labor to certain functions: chattel slavery, sharecropping, low-paid industrial work, a reserve army of labor (aka the "underclass"). Underdevelopment manifests in the restricted and distorted development of black landownership, home ownership and black business enterprises. It manifests in chronic impoverishment, the fostering of retrograde political leadership, the destruction of black education, the spread of racist violence, and the wholesale incarceration of black youth.

The role of the state, as Marable and others have noted, was critical to the process of underdevelopment. Specifically, the underdevelopment of Black America occurred not because of the "normal" operation of capitalist economic and property relations, rather the state apparatus was directly and intimately involved in the expropriation of surplus value *from* black workers and the blocking of capital accumulation *by* African Americans.

From the earliest colonial period the passage of laws establishing racial slavery ensured that black labor could be exploited without compensation and in perpetuity. Virginia colony, with a plantation economy based on tobacco, led the way. By the 1640s *de facto* African slavery existed in Virginia colony; in the 1660s slavery became institutionalized in law. This was done in two ways. Laws were passed effectively excluding Africans as non-Christians from limitation of the number of years they could be held in bondage.[36] A Virginia law in 1661 regarding punishment of runaway servants recognized that some black workers were already enslaved for life; it referred to "any Negroes who are incapable of making satisfaction by addition of time."[37] Secondly, the status of slavery was made hereditary. In 1662 the Virginia Assembly decreed that the children of a slave mother shall themselves be slaves, regardless of the status of the father.[38] This law flew in the face of English patriarchal tradition, but it guaranteed that African bondage could be passed down through the generations without interruption.

At the same time European indentured servants were granted privileges based on whiteness. They were protected from enslavement by statutes limiting the period of servitude (typically 4–6 years). Moreover, capital accumulation by whites was privileged. In 1705 in Virginia the colonial assembly passed a law granting white servants 50 acres of land, 30 shillings, a musket and food upon completion of their term of service.[39] No such landstake would be granted to black workers.

Free black people also found their freedom circumscribed by the state. Licensing was used to exclude them from certain occupations. They could not own land in many areas, and they were largely excluded from the franchise. In California and elsewhere they could not testify in court against whites, further undermining their ability to protect themselves.[40] In 1668, Virginia, seemingly always in the forefront of new ways to oppress black people, made free African American women liable to taxes on the ground that black women should not admitted to the "exemptions and impunities of the English."[41]

Theodore Allen, in the second volume of his important work, *The Invention of the White Race,* notes one consequence of such state intervention.

He reports that in Virginia landholding by blacks declined from about 11 percent in 1666 to one-quarter of one percent in 1860. Allen concludes that this precipitous decline was the result not of normal capitalist economic development but due to a system of racial oppression enforced by the state.[42]

Role of U.S. Government

The formation of the U.S. government after the American War for Independence continued the process of state-sanctioned black oppression. The U.S. Constitution itself recognized and approved the existence of slavery. The Constitution declared that the abolition of the slave trade was prohibited for twenty years; that runaway slaves must be returned to the slaveholders; and that, for purposes of determining the number of representatives each state shall have in Congress, slaves were to be counted as three-fifths of a person. After the American Revolution slavery was abolished in many northern states, but the federal government aided the long arm of slavery in reaching into those states. In 1850 Congress passed a Fugitive Slave Law that required all federal marshals to assist slaveholders in capturing fugitive slaves, even in those states where slavery had been abolished. Then in 1857 the U.S. Supreme Court overturned the last limitations on slavery and made it a *national* institution. In the Dred Scott case the Court ruled that even if a slave lives for years in a free territory in the North the slave does not become free. Chief Justice Roger Taney argued that under the U.S. Constitution slaves were property just like any other property, and that therefore a slaveholder had the right to take his slaves to any part of the country and to maintain ownership of them, just as he would any other form of property. Under this ruling it became possible for slaveholding to legally exist even in states that had abolished slavery.

But Taney went even further and argued that no black person, whether slave or free, could ever be a citizen because black people were "a subordinate and inferior class of beings." The Dred Scott decision fixed in law the subordinate *racial* status of black people as an "inferior class" denied citizenship rights and other legal protections. In the words of the Court black people "had no rights which a white man was bound to respect."

The prospects for black economic emancipation were dealt a severe blow after the Civil War. Black people had hoped for land redistribution by the federal government. Land redistribution was justified, as an Alabama black convention put it, on the grounds that "the property which [the planters] hold was nearly all earned by the sweat of *our* brows."[43] The failure of Congress to enact land redistribution guaranteed black economic subservience. Black people would be exploited as sharecroppers and agricultural workers and denied access to land. The original Freedman's Bureau Act, passed by Congress in 1865, assigned 40 acres of land to "every male citizen, whether refugee or freedman," for their use for a term of three years at a nominal rent. This was vetoed by President Andrew Johnson,

Lincoln's successor. In 1867 Thaddeus Stevens introduced a plan to confiscate the lands of the big planters—almost 400 million acres. The families of the former slaves would each receive 40 acres and $50 dollars, and the remaining land was to be sold off for $10 per acre. Stevens' plan would have created one million black landowners in the South, an independent class of small farmers. But Congress rejected the idea of wholesale confiscation of the big plantations.[44] Indeed, the Freedmen's Bureau Act that became law in 1866 provided for the restoration of abandoned and confiscated plantations to former white owners in the South. The property rights of the planter class, now protected by northern capital, took precedence over the claims of black workers without whose labor the plantations would be worthless. Even efforts by blacks to buy land were obstructed so that white planters could continue to exploit their labor.[45] As one white landowner put it bluntly, "Who'd work the land if the niggers had farms of their own?"[46]

Commenting on the significance these developments W.E.B. Du Bois observed that Lincoln even considered compensating the slaveholders for their losses, but not the slaves. "Lincoln was impressed by the loss of capital invested in slaves, but curiously never seemed seriously to consider the correlative loss of wage and opportunity of slave workers, the tangible results of whose exploitation had gone into the planters' pockets for two centuries."[47] In 1864, Lincoln momentarily considered paying the South $400 million as compensation for the loss of slaves. He later abandoned this idea. Regardless of Lincoln's views, black people hoped for land redistribution. "So far as the Negroes were concerned," Du Bois writes, "their demand for a reasonable part of the land on which they had worked for a quarter of a millennium was absolutely justified, and to give them anything less than this was an economic farce. On the other hand, to have given each of the million Negro free families a forty-acre freehold would have made a basis of real democracy in the United States that might easily have transformed the modern world." Du Bois concludes that "The restoration of the lands [to the planters] not only deprived Negroes in various ways of a clear path toward livelihood, but greatly discouraged them and broke their faith in the United States Government."[48]

Black people did seize some abandoned plantations, and some land was parcelled out by General Sherman in the Sea islands off the coast of South Carolina. But the government later sought to regain this land.[49] Meanwhile the Southern Homestead Act of 1866 opened up 46 million acres of land to settlers. The vast majority of this land went to whites, with blacks being excluded by various means including discriminatory court rulings.[50] At the same time the government handed out another 23 million acres of land to the railroads.

The Civil War and its aftermath emancipated black workers from slavery but fixed on them a new subordinate status as propertyless sharecroppers and wage workers. The overthrow of Reconstruction rolled back the political gains blacks had made. In 1883 the U.S. Supreme Court overturned the Civil Rights Law of 1875 which had guaranteed equal access to public accommodations without regard to race, color or previous condition of servitude. This was capped by the Court's decision in 1896 in *Plessy vs. Ferguson* affirming the segregationist doctrine of "separate but equal." Disfranchisement and peonage followed in the wake of these rulings by the nation's highest court.

Landowning by black farmers did increase after the Civil War, despite the absence of widespread land redistribution to the freed people, nevertheless the systematic transfer of black-owned land to white hands, facilitated by state policies with regard to subsidies and loans, would insure that landownership by black farmers would dwindle until today it is negligible.[51] The state assiduously protected the interests of the landed classes and their demand for a propertyless work force that could be bound by debt to the plantations. When this required racially discriminatory laws and practices these were readily put in place. In the modern era, as in the slave era, the state has been the chief instrument shaping the exploitation of black labor and blocking the accumulation of capital assets by black people.

Impact on Wealth Accumulation

While black workers and farmers have been hardest hit by the policies of the state, the black middle class is not exempt. Melvin Oliver and Thomas Shapiro in *Black Wealth/White Wealth* note that the much celebrated progress of the new black middle class that has emerged since World War II is highly deceptive. While it is true, the authors observe, that middle class blacks are approaching middle class whites in terms of annual income, when it comes to wealth and capital assets, the black middle class lags far behind. White families typically have a net worth 8 to 10 times as large as the net worth accumulated by black families.[52] This discrepancy remains even when occupation and income are comparable. Oliver and Shapiro contend that this disparity does not result from the normal operation of a capitalist economy but is the result of what they call the "racialization of the state," by which they mean systematic, state-sanctioned mining of the wealth created by black labor and the blocking of asset accumulation by African Americans. For example, in the period from 1933 to 1978 over 35 million American families benefitted from homeowner equity accumulation as a result of suburban home ownership polices of the federal government. Blacks were largely excluded from this process due to such practices as restrictive covenants and "redlining" (refusing to make loans in certain areas). The Federal Housing Authority endorsed restrictive covenants on the grounds that "if a neighborhood is to retain stability, it is necessary that properties shall continue to be occupied by the same social and racial classes."[53]

"The FHA's actions have had a lasting impact on the wealth portfolios of black Americans," Oliver and Shapiro write. "Locked out of the greatest mass-based opportunity for wealth accumulation in American history, African Americans who desired and were able to afford home ownership found themselves consigned to central-city communities where their investments were affected by the 'self-fulfilling prophecies' of the FHA appraisers: cut off from sources of new investment their homes and communities deteriorated and lost value in comparison to those homes and communities that FHA appraisers deemed desirable."[54]

The difficulty of gaining access to credit has enabled banks and finance companies to strip mine black communities of housing equity through unscrupulous backdoor loans and by charging higher interest rates and points for conventional mortgages. As many as half of borrowers who must opt for high-interest loans end up losing their homes through foreclosure.[55]

Home ownership is the primary means for accumulating capital among middle class Americans. Housing equity can underwrite the cost of college education for children and provide for a comfortable retirement for parents. It is a major form of inheritance passed on to the next generation. Oliver and Shapiro calculated what they called the cost of being black in the housing market in terms of higher interest rates, lost home equity, and mortgages denied to qualified borrowers. That cost came to $82 billion in 1992.

"The main consequence for future generations of current discrimination or past discrimination is that it reduces capital accumulation," commented David Swinton, an economist and president of Benedict College in South Carolina. "If it is desirable to equalize the status of the races in the future, then there must be some make up, some compensation, some reparations . . . for the capital that these groups were prevented from accumulating. Otherwise, the past will continue to perpetuate itself throughout the future."[56]

Most recently Clarence Munford's bold and important new book, *Race and Reparations,* offers a thoughtful and provocative discussion of reparations. Taking civilization as his unit of analysis, Munford argues that racism is deeply embedded in white, Western civilization. The oppression and exploitation of Africa, Africans in the Diaspora and people of color generally, he argues, stems from the racist impulse of white colonialism and imperialism growing out of the Atlantic slave trade.[57] In turn, the racist reality of slavery underlies the demand for reparations. Emancipation and ending of legal segregation were not enough, he writes, because they leave intact a disparity in wealth and resources that will remain for centuries.[58] "Reparations—and its Siamese twin, Black empowerment," Munford writes, "are imperative if the end of formal segregation is ever to amount to anything but a sham leading absolutely nowhere."[59]

Munford calls for a reparations program that "should be broadly construed as encompassing affirmative action, employment equity, race-conscious quotas, parity, minority set-asides, equality of results, free, state-of-the-art health care and, above all, legislated and government-administered remittances of assets and monies."[60] Munford also proposes a family income plan, to be extended to all citizens, to prevent families from falling below a specified income level. He also suggests channeling reparations funds into housing, education and job skills; funding of investments with dividends allocated on a per capita or per household basis; government-funded urban land reform; and financing of the purchase of productive industries.[61]

Interestingly, Munford offers a reason for for whites to support reparations on an international basis. He argues that a massive reparations program in Africa and the western hemisphere could greatly stimulate the global economy much as the Marshall Plan did following World War II. "Reparations could function as the post-Cold War spark plug, helping to keep the world economy from spinning its wheels."[62]

However, Munford is not so sanguine as to think that whites will welcome his reparations program. On the contrary he thinks that what will be required is "a mass political campaign in favor of reparations encompassing all the main components of the Black community."[63] Munford argues that reparations is also an issue for Africa and the Diaspora requiring coordinated action. He cites the 1993 Pan-African Congress on Reparations held in Nigeria, and growing interest in reparations on the part of black people in Brazil, the Caribbean and other areas of the Diaspora, as evidence of an emerging global campaign.

"The cry for reparations on both sides of the Atlantic," Munford concludes, "represents two sides of a single coin, as it were. One side of the coin is white aggression, 550 years of Caucasian assault on the people and continent of Africa. The other side of the coin is history's greatest Diaspora, the scattering of Blacks to live lives of exile outside Mother Africa, in communities of suffering. . . . Both the Diaspora and the continent have irrefutable claims to reparations."[64]

Conclusion: The Cost of Being Black

Much discussion of the plight of African Americans has centered on disparities in access to jobs and income between blacks and whites. Underlying these differences are fundamental disparities in the distribution of wealth and capital. The political economy of white hegemony and black subordination is based on these disparities—disparities that are structured into the functioning of the capitalist economic system and maintained by the political power of the state.

The cost of being black amounts to a tax unfairly imposed solely because of race. It is analogous to the tax that Virginia imposed on free black women in 1668. The state must bear responsibility for abolishing such an unjust tax and making restitution for the period that it was imposed. Not only does the race tax harm the present generation, its effects are cumulative—it deprives the present generation and denies an inheritance to the next. Imposed by the state, the burdensome and unfair race tax can only be remedied by the federal government. More than a matter of individuals or regions, the state must be held accountable to remove the burden and make appropriate restitution for value lost.

The concept of reparations provides a framework for thinking about such restitution. The basic argument I would make is that the African American community has a just claim to compensation for that part of the wealth of the United States that was derived from violating the human rights, citizenship and property rights of black people. In particular, the vast wealth created by slave labor stands as the most egregious example of the expropriation without compensation of black labor's product. But the race tax, the cost of being black, continued after slavery and it continues today. Reparations must address both the human and economic costs of slavery, and the human and economic injustices that have been imposed on African Americans from the end of the Civil War until the present.

The quest for reparations is deeply embedded in the African American experience and black consciousness. It cuts across all ideological lines in the black community, finding advocates among emigrationists, nationalists, integrationists, religious figures, black elected officials, capitalists, socialists, liberals and radicals.

The widespread and frequent recurrence of this quest in African American history suggests that it reflects a deeply felt sense of catastrophic racial injustice—an unconscionable and still unremedied past injustice that continues to be produced and reproduced in new forms in the present.

The issue of reparations also involves critical issues of political economy insofar as it calls our attention to (1) the importance of structured racial inequities of wealth and capital; (2) the role that this structure of inequality has played in the development of U.S. capitalism and the underdevelopment of black America; and (3) the role of the state in structuring racial inequalities of wealth; (4) the fact that elimination of present discrimination is not sufficient to reverse the cumulative and continuing effects of state-sanctioned racial inequities in distribution of wealth and capital.

As many advocates of reparations have argued, if we are seeking a more economically just society, a society in which equality (or parity) is more than rhetoric, then the issue of reparations must be addressed. Reparations provides a framework for the redistribution of wealth within the existing political economy, and thereby moving towards economic equality between whites and blacks. Transfers of wealth in the form of capital assets and resources—black community ownership of national and local economic enterprises, housing and home ownership, educational scholarships—are critical to the success of any effort aimed at reversing the present underdevelopment of the black community. In my view, such transfers must first and foremost benefit the black workingclass and the poor.

I would argue that the quest for reparations also raises questions about the nature and legitimacy of the capitalist political economy, most fundamentally capitalist alienation of labor from ownership of the wealth that labor produces, and the role of the state in this process. At its most radical, the demand for reparations stands as a critique of capitalist property relations. It also underscores the need for *general* redistribution of wealth and resources. Seen in this light, the struggle for racial reparations can be convergent with the struggle for a socialist society in which black people would have full and equal access to the total wealth and resources of society. Only in the presence of such full and equal access to the total wealth and resources of society could we conclude that racial discrimination has been eliminated.

Finally, it must be said again that the issue of reparations is a global issue, for the enslavement of Africans and the colonization of Africa is a global issue. The situation of African Americans cannot be divided from the situation of Africans in Africa and the Diaspora. If civil rights alone are insufficient to assure full equality for black Americans, then national independence alone is insufficient to assure national liberation for the former colonies. As Frantz Fanon commented in *The Wretched of the Earth:*

> We are not blinded by the moral reparation of national independence; nor are we fed by it. The wealth of the imperial countries is our wealth too. . . . Europe is literally the creation of the Third World. The wealth which smothers her is that which was stolen from the under-developed peoples. The ports of Holland, the docks of Bordeaux and Liverpool were specialised in the Negro slave-trade, and owe their renown to millions of deported slaves. So when we hear the head of a European state declare with his hand on his heart that he must come to the help of the poor under-developed peoples, we do not tremble with gratitude. Quite the contrary; we say to ourselves: 'It is a just reparation which will be paid to us.' . . . This help should be the ratification of a double realisation: the realisation by the colonised peoples that *it is their due,* and the realisation by the capitalist powers that in fact *they must pay.* For if, through lack of intelligence . . . the capitalist countries refuse to pay, then the relentless dialectic of their own system will smother them.[65]

The African American quest for reparations is part of a much larger, global reparations movement by black people in Africa, the Caribbean, South America and Britain. This global movement has been gaining strength in recent years. Africa and black people in the Diaspora represent a powerful force, a sleeping giant, that has been drugged by the poisons of colonialism, slavery and racism. But the giant is awakening, fitfully but certainly, from the nightmare, and justice must be served. In the words of Fanon, a just reparation must be paid for the lives that were lost and for the wealth and labor that were stolen.

Notes

1. Mary Frances Berry and John W. Blassingame, *Long Memory: The Black Experience in America* (New York: Oxford University Press, 1982), p. 405.
2. *Ibid,* p. 406; Nell Irvin Painter, *Sojourner Truth: A Life, A Symbol* (New York: W.W. Norton & Co., 1996), p. 244.
3. Quoted in Jeanette Davis-Adeshote, *Black Survival in White America* (Orange, NJ: Bryant and Dillon Publishers, 1995), p. 87.
4. Berry and Blassingame, *Long Memory,* p. 406.
5. *Ibid,* p. 405.

6. *San Francisco Chronicle*, February 10, 1998.

7. William L. Van Deburg (ed.), *Modern Black Nationalism* (New York: New York University Press, 1997), p. 27.

8. Herb Boyd, "Longtime Activist Queen Mother Moore, 98, Dies," in *The Black Scholar*, Vol. 27, No. 2 (Summer 1997), inside front cover.

9. John H. Bracey, Jr., August Meir and Elliot Rudwick (eds.), *Black Nationalism in America* (New York: Bobbs-Merrill Co., 1970), p. 404.

10. Huey P. Newton, *To Die for the People: Selected Writings and Speeches* (New York: Writers and Readers Publishing, 1995), p. 3.

11. James Forman, *The Making of Black Revolutionaries* (Seattle: University of Washington Press, 1997), p. 545.

12. E. Franklin Frazier and C. Eric Lincoln, *The Negro Church in America/The Black Church Since Frazier* (New York: Schocken Books, 1974), p. 184–186.

13. Imari Abubakari Obadele I, *Foundations of the Black Nation* (Detroit: House of Songhay, 1975), p. 68.

14. *Ibid*, 80–89.

15. Berry and Blassingame, *Long Memory*, p. 406.

16. "The Repression of the RNA," in *The Black Scholar*, Vol. 3., No. 2 (October, 1971), p. 57.

17. Obadele, *Foundations*, p. 112–13.

18. Quoted in Boris I. Bitker, *The Case for Black Reparations* (New York: Random House, 1973), p. 79–80.

19. Dempsey J. Travis, "The Homestead Act," in *The Black Scholar*, Vol. 1, No. 6 (April, 1970), p. 15.

20. Bitker, p. 9.

21. *Ibid*, p. 18.

22. Quoted in Bitker, p. 31.

23. Quoted in William Darity, Jr., "Forty Acres and a Mule: Placing a Price Tag on Oppression," in Richard F. America (ed.), *The Wealth of Races: The Present Value of Benefits from Past Injustices* (New York: Greenwood Press, 1990), p. 5.

24. See Richard F. America (ed.), *The Wealth of Races: The Present Value of Benefits from Past Injustices* (New York: Greenwood Press, 1990), Melvin L. Oliver and Thomas M. Shapiro, *Black Wealth/White Wealth: A New Perspective on Racial Inequality* (New York: Routledge, 1995).

25. David H. Swinton, "Racial Inequality and Reparations," in America, *The Wealth of Races*, p. 157.

26. Address: N'COBRA, P.O. Box 62622, Washington, D.C. 20020-2622. Website: http//www.ncobra.com

27. Address: ARM, 3 Devonshire Chambers, 557 High Road, Tottenham, London, N17 6SB, United Kingdom. Website: http//the.arc.co.uk/arm/home.html

28. Lori Robinson, "Righting a Wrong," in *Emerge* magazine, Vol. 8, No. 4 (February, 1997), pp. 44, 46.

29. Interview in *West Africa* magazine, 27 October–9 November, 1997.

30. Van Deburg, *Modern Black Nationalism*, p. 333.

31. *Ibid*.

32. U.S. House of Representatives, H.R. 891.

33. *The New York Times*, March 16, 1998, p. A5.

34. Manning Marable, *How Capitalism Underdeveloped Black America* (Boston: South End Press, 1983), p. 2 (emphasis in original).

35. *Ibid*, p. 7 (emphasis in original).

36. Theodore W. Allen, *The Invention of the White Race (Vol. Two): The Origins of Racial Oppression in Anglo-America* (New York: Verso, 1997), p. 179. The loophole allowing possible freedom for Christian Africans was closed in 1662. Allen, p. 197.

37. *Ibid*, p. 187.

38. *Ibid*, p. 197.

39. Ronald Takaki, *A Different Mirror: A History of Multicultural America* (Boston: Little, Brown & Co., 1993), p. 66.

40. Berry and Blassingame, *Long Memory*, p. 35.

41. Allen, *Invention of the White Race*, p. 187.

42. *Ibid*, pp. 184–85.

43. Quoted in Eric Foner, *Reconstruction: America's Unfinished Revolution, 1863–1877* (New York: Harper & Row, 1988), p. 105.

44. William Z. Foster, *The Negro People in American History* (New York: International Publishers, 1954), p. 300.

45. *The Negro in Virginia* (Winston-Salem, NC: John F. Blair, Publisher, 1994), p. 249.

46. Quoted in Oliver and Shapiro, *Black Wealth/White Wealth*, p. 15.

47. W.E.B. Du Bois, *Black Reconstruction in America* (New York: Atheneum, 1979), p. 150.

48. *Ibid*, pp. 602–3.

49. Foster, *The Negro People in American History*, pp. 302–3.

50. Oliver and Shapiro, *Black Wealth/White Wealth*, p. 14.

51. Marable, *How Capitalism Underdeveloped Black America*, p. 49.

52. Oliver and Shapiro, *Black Wealth/White Wealth*, pp. 116–17.

53. *Ibid*, pp. 16–18.

54. *Ibid*.

55. *Ibid*, pp. 20–21.

56. Quoted in Lori Robinson, "Righting a Wrong," in *Emerge* magazine, p. 45.

57. Clarence J. Munford, *Race and Reparations: A Black Perspective for the 21st Century* (Trenton, NJ: Africa World Press, 1996), pp. 57–58.

58. *Ibid*, pp. 421, 427–28.

59. *Ibid*, p. 414.

60. *Ibid*, pp. 430–31.

61. *Ibid*, pp. 432–34.

62. *Ibid*, p. 416.

63. *Ibid*, p. 431.

64. *Ibid*, p. 439.

65. Frantz Fanon, *The Wretched of the Earth* (New York: Grove Press, 1963), pp. 80–81 (emphasis in original).

Slavery and the Law: Time and Punishment

What would Abraham Lincoln have made of Edward Fagan? In the past few weeks, the New York lawyer has launched a war against firms that he claims profited from slavery, filing legal complaints against FleetBoston, a bank, Aetna, and CSX, a transport company. New York Life, Lehman Brothers, Norfolk Southern, Liggett and Lloyd's of London will follow next week. In all, some 60 companies are in his sights.

The suits are being filed on behalf of all descendants of slaves in America, a 30m-strong group. The defendants are the legal successors of entities that existed when slavery was still legal: FleetBoston, for example, is the present-day incarnation of the Providence Bank of Rhode Island. Economists put the current value of the companies' ill-gotten gains in the trillions. . . . Mr Fagan reckons a settlement would fall somewhere "in the tens of billions." The lawyers will collect a percentage of that.

Calls for reparations date back to the 1960s. In 2000 Mr Fagan was approached by Deadria Farmer-Paellmann, a black activist who has provided much of the research (and is one of the plaintiffs). The current plan seems to rely on two things: a few companies tiring of the lawsuits and agreeing to pay up, and others lobbying the government to shoulder its share.

In 1988 Congress authorised payments to 80,000 Japanese-Americans who had been interned during the second world war. Some $1.6 billion was paid out. But the precedent for the present lawsuits is Nazi slave labour. After the war the German government made big reparations, particularly to Israel, for its role in the Holocaust. In the 1990s Mr Fagan and other lawyers sued German firms on behalf of former slave-labourers. Legally, the case was fiddly: much revolved around whether slave labour was legal under the Nazi regime and whether too much time had passed to prosecute the firms. Two suits, against Degussa and Siemens, were dismissed by a judge who decided that reparations were a matter of foreign policy and politics, not of the law.

But public opinion proved decisive. With New York regulators deeming Deutsche Bank's recalcitrance over the issue to be a barrier to its purchase of Bankers Trust, and with hundreds of local authorities threatening regulatory sanctions, the Germans worried about their ability to do business in America. Bill Clinton assured them that a settlement would protect them against future suits. A fund of $5.2 billion, created by the firms and the German government, is now being disbursed.

The legal merits of slavery lawsuits are even more contentious. Last year a United Nations conference on racism in Durban (from which America walked out) branded slavery "a crime against humanity" which "should have always been so." Mr Fagan argues that there should be no statute of limitations for such a crime. But the legal idea of a crime against humanity was invented decades after slavery was banned in America, so a court will have to define that crime retroactively. The UN conference steered clear of doing that.

The plaintiffs' case may be undermined by the money involved. They say that every dollar a firm should have paid to a slave 150 years ago should be subject to compound interest at a rate tied to the firms' growth. Each dollar could be worth anything from $6,250 to over $400,000. "This is exactly the kind of ridiculous lawsuit that a statute of limitations is designed to prevent," says Richard Epstein, a law professor at the University of Chicago.

Assessing the profits banks and insurers made from slavery is also hard. Fleet-Boston's ancestor, for instance, profited from financing the slave trade when it was already illegal under American law. Its contracts were thus all technically unenforceable, frauds for which the statute of limitations has long since expired. And although slavery itself was certainly profitable, it is less clear whether Aetna made money from insuring it.

When quizzed about such obstacles, Mr Fagan and his clients reply that public opinion will sway the courts again. Mr Fagan predicts boycotts, shareholder lawsuits, even race riots. Local politicians are being urged to hold hearings and create commissions to study the impact of slavery in their jurisdictions. A "Millions for Reparations" march is planned for August in Washington, DC.

Will it work? Cleverly, Mr Fagan will multiply his chances of success not just by suing more companies but by launching complaints in more jurisdictions across the country. In recent years, American juries have often found against big companies in such celebrity cases. John McWhorter, a black conservative at the Manhattan Institute, bets that all three companies sued so far would rather settle out of court.

If they do, they will surely lobby Congress to contribute its share. Until the civil war, the American government was as complicit in slavery as its German equivalent. Mr Fagan reckons a fund like the September 11th victims' compensation fund, where the airlines and the federal government paid in to a government-administered pot, would be a good resolution.

A Nation Decides

But it is not clear that public opinion will rally to Mr Fagan's cause as readily as he hopes. The Germans—foreigners who had committed crimes against Americans, many of whom were still alive—were easier targets. Polls have shown 70% of whites objecting even to a public apology for slavery. Despite a longstanding campaign for reparations by Charles Ogletree, a Harvard professor, black leaders also seem divided on the issue. Jesse Jackson supports the suits. Others think that the government alone should pay up. Some want the money to support a fund devoted to black education; others would prefer a cash payment and a national apology. A few worry that the lawsuits could distract Americans from re-examining the role of slavery. "If a lawsuit does not lead to a general discussion in society about slavery," argues Elazar Barkan, the author of "The Guilt of Nations" (Norton, 2000), "then the lawsuits are not very helpful."

One lawyer who advised the German firms to settle says that their American counterparts should "go to court and fight like hell." Such tough talk may not last long: companies that come under pressure from Mr Jackson's boycotts tend to settle quickly. But it is hard to see how all this will help America understand its past.

POSTSCRIPT

Is Now the Time for Reparations for African Americans?

A significant basis for the movement for reparations resides in the claim that African Americans should receive compensation for the unpaid labor that they provided during the Slave Era and for the ongoing discriminatory and exclusionary policies. The opponents of reparations, in contrast, tend not to accept the alleged connection between the racist past of American social history and the lagging position of blacks today. The anti-reparations advocates are not convinced that the current generation of African Americans hold their white counterparts or other groups accountable for what they consider the sins of America's past. Rather, opponents of reparations tended to view contemporary white Americans as having broken with the racist past of the United States experience and committed themselves to supporting reasonable policies designed to produce a genuine multiracial society in the United States.

Slavery produced wealth, income, and status for whites, while blacks lagged behind. Exploitation of black labor during the era of segregation coupled with the loss of voting rights meant that blacks could not employ their potential political and economic power to alter their condition. In contrast, despite the difficult challenges that immigrant groups such as the Irish had in establishing a footing in the New World, they were able to vote and to use the power of the franchise and government to advance their interests. Due to the loss of political rights, African Americans were virtually foreclosed from opportunities to employ these vehicles to advance in society until the Voting Rights Act was passed in 1965.

Robert L. Allen has identified seven important precedents in support of reparations. In this regard, it should be noted that in addition to the survivors of the Holocaust, Native Americans, Japanese Americans, and aboriginal peoples of Alaska and Canada have all received reparations. It is also noteworthy that compensation is accepted within American jurisprudence as a just award to those who have suffered wrongs. The writers from *The Economist* do not think you can connect today's white population with the injustices of the past. Are today's blacks victims of slavery? Is there a meaningful connection between slavery, segregation, and the contemporary status of African Americans? How do we identify victims of injustice racially?

Reparations is a very difficult issue confronting race relations within the United States. It is an issue that is surrounded by a good deal of controversy and resistance. Clearly, it is a wedge issue within American politics, and despite the arguments in support of reparations, this policy faces significant challenges to its adoption and implementation.

An explanation of the intellectual origins of the global reparations movement in *The Guilt of Nations: Restitution and Negotiating Historical Injustices* (W.W. Norton, 2000) by Elazar Barkan includes the case of Holocaust victims. *CQ Researcher* devoted its June 22, 2001 issue to the reparations movement. It provides a historical overview. The economic benefits of slavery to America are demonstrated in Robert F. Starobin's *Industrial Slavery in the Old South* (Oxford University Press, 1970), and in *Capitalism and Slavery* (Capricorn Books, 1966) by Eric Williams.

For further reading, advocates of reparations will find in *The Debt: What America Owes to Blacks* (Dutton, 2000) by Randall Robinson a strong supportive argument. Wole Soyinka, in *The Burden of Memory, The Muse of Forgiveness* (Oxford University Press, 2003) argues that reparations are a key to real social justice. Another selection in support of reparations is "The Growing Movement for Reparations," in *When Sorry Isn't Enough: The Controversy over Apologies and Reparations for Human Injustice,* edited by Roy L. Brooks (New York University Press, 1999).

Opponents of reparations for African Americans will find support in "The Case Against Reparations" (*Progressive,* December 2000) by Adolph L. Reed. A strong case against reparations appeared in a *St. Petersburg Times* (June 25, 2000) article, "Our Country Has Paid the Bill for Slavery," by Martin Dyckman. Similarly, an article opposing Holocaust reparations can be found in "Holocaust Reparations—A Growing Scandal," by Gabriel Schoenfeld in *Commentary* (September 2000).

The reparations debate is covered in seminal essays collected and edited by Raymond A. Winbush in *Should America Pay? Slavery and the Raging Debate on Reparations* (HarperCollins Publishers, 2003). It is the best treatment of the reparations issue to date.

ISSUE 18

Is Racial Profiling Defensible Public Policy?

YES: John Derbyshire, "In Defense of Racial Profiling," *National Review* (February 19, 2001)

NO: David A. Harris, "Profiles in Injustice: American Life under the Regime of Racial Profiling" in *Profiles in Injustice: Why Racial Profiling Cannot Work* (The New Press, 2002)

ISSUE SUMMARY

YES: John Derbyshire, political commentator for *National Review,* views racial profiling as a "common sense policy" and a valid response to crime control and national security concerns.

NO: David A. Harris, law professor and leading authority on racial profiling, argues that racial profiling is ineffective and damaging to our diverse nation. He believes it hinders effective law enforcement.

The issue of racial profiling has raised many questions concerning the society's commitment to the rule of law and the protection of individual rights as provided within the Constitution of the United States. This issue has gained greater salience in America in the wake of the events of September 11, 2001 that gave impetus to an overwhelming focus on national security both within and outside of government.

John Derbyshire suggests that racial profiling is a reasonable and appropriate response to the challenges that confront the nation in its attempts to prevent crime and to maintain social order effectively. He argues that since blacks, especially young black males, commit a disproportionate share of the crimes, targeting these youth as a strategy of effective crime control is sensible, and it represents an efficient utilization of finite police resources. He offers a similar argument in support of the profiling of Arabs and Muslims for national security purposes.

Derbyshire agrees that racial profiling as a social policy involves the negative stereotyping of African Americans and other targeted populations.

However, he is not concerned about this aspect of racial profiling because "a negative stereotype can be correct, and even useful."

The stereotyping of African Americans is one concern with the policy of racial profiling. Derbyshire is concerned that if the larger American society responds to negative sentiments and curtails or abolishes racial profiling, it will have eliminated one of the most effective policies for crime prevention and control. He believes that such a response to the concerns of blacks and others regarding this social policy represents a failure "to confront our national hysteria about race," and this tendency is contributing to the suspicions and distrust that continue to divide the races.

In addition to viewing racial profiling as morally wrong, David Harris argues that there are other salient reasons for opposing this practice. Thus, he is concerned that the police are targeting persons with dark skins without proper reference to probable cause, an important principle of American law. To Harris, treating an entire group as potential criminals based on the wrongdoing of a small cohort of its members violates the equal protection principle of the XIV Amendment of the Constitution of the United States, a significant value of the nation's political culture.

Harris is also convinced that racial profiling is an ineffective practice of law enforcement, and he presents an empirical argument to support his claim. Additionally, David Harris is concerned that racial profiling is having a corrosive impact on the relationship between the police and the African American, Hispanic, and other minority communities they are responsible to protect and to serve. He believes that such treatment of minority groups can only result in a diminution of respect for law enforcement and a polarization between the police and members of these communities, thus making effective law enforcement more difficult to achieve.

To place this issue in perspective, readers must confront the topics of race, crime, and criminal justice. How does our concern with law enforcement contribute to racial profiling? Does the culture of police contribute to racial profiling? Is racial profiling unequal treatment? Are minority police officers a response to this problem? On the other hand, is there an anti-police culture within the African-American community? Did Timothy McVeigh's actions as the Oklahoma City bomber generate profiling? Are members of anti-government militias who congregate in remote areas and sharpen their military skills with live arms being targeted in accordance with a "white" profile?

John Derbyshire

In Defense of Racial Profiling: Where Is Our Common Sense?

Racial profiling has become one of the shibboleths of our time. Anyone who wants a public career in the United States must place himself on record as being against it. Thus, ex-senator John Ashcroft, on the eve of his confirmation hearings: "It's wrong, inappropriate, shouldn't be done." During the vice-presidential debate last October, moderator Bernard Shaw invited the candidates to imagine themselves black victims of racial profiling. Both made the required ritual protestations of outrage. Lieberman: "I have a few African-American friends who have gone through this horror, and you know, it makes me want to kind of hit the wall, because it is such an assault on their humanity and their citizenship." Cheney: "It's the sense of anger and frustration and rage that would go with knowing that the only reason you were stopped . . . was because of the color of your skin . . ." In the strange, rather depressing, pattern these things always follow nowadays, the American public has speedily swung into line behind the Pied Pipers: Gallup reports that 81 percent of the public disapproves of racial profiling.

All of which represents an extraordinary level of awareness of, and hostility to, and even *passion* against ("hit the wall . . ." a practice that, up to about five years ago, practically nobody had heard of. It is, in fact, instructive to begin by looking at the history of this shibboleth.

To people who follow politics, the term "racial profiling" probably first registered when Al Gore debated Bill Bradley at New York's Apollo Theatre in February 2000. Here is Bradley, speaking of the 1999 shooting of African immigrant Amadou Diallo by New York City police: "I . . . think it reflects . . . racial profiling that seeps into the mind of someone so that he sees a wallet in the hand of a white man as a wallet, but a wallet in the hand of a black man as a gun. And we—we have to change that. I would issue an executive order that would eliminate racial profiling at the federal level."

Nobody was unkind enough to ask Sen. Bradley how an executive order would change what a policeman sees in a dark lobby in a dangerous neighborhood at night. Nor was anyone so tactless as to ask him about the case of LaTanya Haggerty, shot dead in June 1999 by a Chicago policewoman who mistook her cell phone for a handgun. The police-woman was, like Ms. Haggerty, black.

Al Gore, in that debate at the Apollo, did successfully, and famously, ambush Bradley by remarking that: "You know, racial profiling practically began in New Jersey, Senator Bradley." In true Clinton-Gore fashion, this is not true, but it is *sort of* true. "Racial profiling" the *thing* has been around for as long as police work, and is practiced everywhere. "Racial profiling" the *term* did indeed have its origins on the New Jersey Turnpike in the early 1990s. The reason for the prominence of this rather unappeal-ing stretch of expressway in the history of the phenomenon is simple: The turnpike is the main conduit for the shipment of illegal drugs and other contraband to the great criminal marts of the Northeast.

The career of the term "racial profiling" seems to have begun in 1994, but did not really take off until April 1998, when two white New Jersey state troopers pulled over a van for speeding. As they approached the van from behind, it suddenly reversed towards them. The troopers fired eleven shots from their handguns, wounding three of the van's four occupants, who were all black or Hispanic. The troopers, James Kenna and John Hogan, subsequently became poster boys for the "racial profiling" lobbies, facing the same indignities, though so far with less serious consequences, as were endured by the Los Angeles policemen in the Rodney King case: endless investigations, double jeopardy, and so on.

And a shibboleth was born. News-media databases list only a scatter-ing of instances of the term "racial profiling" from 1994 to 1998. In that latter year, the number hit double digits, and thereafter rose quickly into the hundreds and thousands. Now we all know about it, and we are, of course, all against it.

Well, not quite all. American courts—including (see below) the U.S. Supreme Court—are not against it. Jurisprudence on the matter is pretty clear: So long as race is only one factor in a generalized approach to the questioning of suspects, it may be considered. And of course, *pace* Candidate Cheney, it always *is* only one factor. I have been unable to locate any statistics on the point, but I feel sure that elderly black women are stopped by the police much less often than are young white men.

Even in the political sphere, where truth-telling and independent thinking on matters of race have long been liabilities, there are those who refuse to mouth the required pieties. Alan Keyes, when asked by Larry King if he would be angry with a police officer who pulled him over for being black, replied: "I was raised that everything I did represented my family, my race, and my country. I would be angry with the people giving me a bad reputation."

Goodbye to Common Sense

Practically all law-enforcement professionals believe in the need for racial profiling. In an article on the topic for *The New York Times Magazine* in June 1999, Jeffrey Goldberg interviewed Bernard Parks, chief of the

Los Angeles Police Department. Parks, who is black, asked rhetorically of racial profiling: "Should we play the percentages? . . . It's common sense." Note that date, though. This was pretty much the latest time at which it was possible for a public official to speak truthfully about racial profiling. Law-enforcement professionals were learning the importance of keeping their thoughts to themselves. Four months before the Goldberg piece saw print, New Jersey state-police superintendent Carl Williams, in an interview, said that certain crimes were associated with certain ethnic groups, and that it was naïve to think that race was not an issue in policing—both statements, of course, perfectly true. Supt. Williams was fired the same day by Gov. Christie Todd Whitman.

Like other race issues in the U.S., racial profiling is a "tadpole," with an enormous black head and a long but comparatively inconsequential brown, yellow, and red tail. While Hispanic, "Asian-American," and other lesser groups have taken up the "racial profiling" chant with gusto, the crux of the matter is the resentment that black Americans feel toward the attentions of white policemen. By far the largest number of Americans angry about racial profiling are law-abiding black people who feel that they are stopped and questioned because the police regard *all* black people with undue suspicion. They feel that they are the victims of a negative stereotype.

They are. Unfortunately, a negative stereotype can be correct, and even useful. I was surprised to find, when researching this article, that within the academic field of social psychology there is a large literature on stereotypes, and that much of it—an entire school of thought—holds that stereotypes are essential life tools. On the scientific evidence, the primary function of stereotypes is what researchers call "the reality function." That is, stereotypes are useful tools for dealing with the world. Confronted with a snake or a fawn, our immediate behavior is determined by generalized beliefs—stereotypes—about snakes and fawns. Stereotypes are, in fact, merely one aspect of the mind's ability to make generalizations, without which science and mathematics, not to mention, as the snake/fawn example shows, much of everyday life, would be impossible.

At some level, everybody knows this stuff, even the guardians of the "racial profiling" flame. Jesse Jackson famously, in 1993, confessed that: "There is nothing more painful to me at this stage in my life than to walk down the street and hear footsteps and start thinking about robbery, then look around and see somebody white and feel relieved." Here is Sandra Seegars of the Washington, D.C., Taxicab Commission:

> Late at night, if I saw young black men dressed in a slovenly way, I wouldn't pick them up . . . And during the day, I'd think twice about it.

Pressed to define "slovenly," Ms. Seegars elaborated thus: "A young black guy with his hat on backwards, shirttail hanging down longer than his coat, baggy pants down below his underwear, and unlaced tennis shoes." Now *there's* a stereotype for you! Ms. Seegars is, of course, black.

Law-enforcement officials are simply employing the same stereotypes as you, me, Jesse, and Sandra, but taking the opposite course of action. What we seek to avoid, they pursue. They do this for reasons of simple efficiency. A policeman who concentrates a disproportionate amount of his limited time and resources on young black men is going to uncover far more crimes—and therefore be far more successful in his career—than one who biases his attention toward, say, middle-aged Asian women. It is, as Chief Parks said, common sense.

Similarly with the tail of the tadpole—racial-profiling issues that do not involve black people. China is known to have obtained a top-secret warhead design. Among those with clearance to work on that design are people from various kinds of national and racial background. Which ones should investigators concentrate on? The Swedes? The answer surely is: They should first check out anyone who has family or friends in China, who has made trips to China, or who has met with Chinese officials. This would include me, for example—my father-in-law is an official of the Chinese Communist Party. Would I then have been "racially profiled"?

It is not very surprising to learn that the main fruit of the "racial profiling" hysteria has been a decline in the efficiency of police work. In Philadelphia, a federal court order now requires police to fill out both sides of an 8½-by-11 sheet on every citizen contact. Law-enforcement agencies nationwide are engaged in similar statistics-gathering exercises, under pressure from federal lawmakers like U.S. Rep. John Conyers, who has announced that he will introduce a bill to force police agencies to keep detailed information about traffic stops. ("The struggle goes on," declared Rep. Conyers. The struggle that is going on, it sometimes seems, is a struggle to prevent our police forces from accomplishing any useful work at all.)

The mountain of statistics that is being brought forth by all this panic does not, on the evidence so far, seem likely to shed much light on what is happening. The numbers have a way of leading off into infinite regresses of uncertainty. The city of San Jose, Calif., for example, discovered that, yes, the percentage of blacks being stopped was higher than their representation in the city's population. Ah, but patrol cars were computer-assigned to high-crime districts, which are mainly inhabited by minorities. So that over-representation might actually be an under-representation! But then, minorities have fewer cars. . . .

The Core Arguments

Notwithstanding the extreme difficulty of finding out what is actually happening, we can at least seek some moral and philosophical grounds on which to take a stand either for or against racial profiling. I am going to take it as a given that most readers of this article will be of a conservative inclination, and shall offer only those arguments likely to appeal to persons so inclined. If you seek arguments of other kinds, they are not hard to find—just pick up your newspaper or turn on your TV.

Of arguments *against* racial profiling, probably the ones most persuasive to a conservative are the ones from libertarianism. Many of the stop-and-search cases that brought this matter into the headlines were part of the so-called war on drugs. The police procedures behind them were ratified by court decisions of the 1980s, themselves mostly responding to the rising tide of illegal narcotics. In U.S. vs. *Montoya De Hernandez* (1985) for example, Chief Justice Rehnquist validated the detention of a suspected "balloon swallowing" drug courier until the material had passed through her system, by noting previous invasions upheld by the Court:

> [F]irst class mail may be opened without a warrant on less than probable cause . . . Automotive travellers may be stopped . . . near the border without individualized suspicion *even if the stop is based largely on ethnicity* . . .

(My italics.) The Chief Justice further noted that these incursions are in response to "the veritable national crisis in law enforcement caused by smuggling of illegal narcotics."

Many on the political Right feel that the war on drugs is at best misguided, at worst a moral and constitutional disaster. Yet it is naïve to imagine that the "racial profiling" hubbub would go away, or even much diminish, if all state and federal drug laws were repealed tomorrow. Black and Hispanic Americans would still be committing crimes at rates higher than citizens of other races. The differential criminality of various ethnic groups is not only, or even mainly, located in drug crimes. In 1997, for example, blacks, who are 13 percent of the U.S. population, comprised 35 percent of those arrested for embezzlement. (It is not generally appreciated that black Americans commit higher levels not only of "street crime," but also of white-collar crime.)

Even without the drug war, diligent police officers would still, therefore, be correct to regard black and Hispanic citizens—other factors duly considered—as more likely to be breaking the law. The Chinese government would still be trying to recruit spies exclusively from among Chinese-born Americans. (The Chinese Communist Party is, in this respect, the keenest "racial profiler" of all.) The Amadou Diallo case—the police were looking for a rapist—would still have happened.

The best non-libertarian argument against racial profiling is the one from equality before the law. This has been most cogently presented by Prof. Randall Kennedy of Harvard. Kennedy concedes most of the points I have made. Yes, he says:

> Statistics abundantly confirm that African Americans—and particularly young black men—commit a dramatically disproportionate share of street crime in the United States. This is a sociological fact, not a figment of the media's (or the police's) racist imagination. In recent years, for example, victims of crime report blacks as the perpetrators in around 25 per cent of the violent crimes suffered, although blacks constitute only about twelve percent of the nation's population.

And yes, says Prof. Kennedy, outlawing racial profiling will reduce the efficiency of police work. Nonetheless, for constitutional and moral reasons we should outlaw the practice. If this places extra burdens on law enforcement, well, "racial equality, like all good things in life, costs something; it does not come for free."

There are two problems with this. The first is that Kennedy has minimized the black–white difference in criminality, and therefore that "cost." I don't know where his 25 percent comes from, or what "recent years" means, but I do know that in Department of Justice figures for 1997, victims report 60 percent of robberies as having been committed by black persons. In that same year, a black American was eight times more likely than a non-black to commit homicide—and "non-black" here includes Hispanics, not broken out separately in these figures. A racial-profiling ban, under which police officers were required to stop and question suspects in precise proportion to their demographic representation (in what? the precinct population? the state population? the national population?), would lead to *massive* inefficiencies in police work. Which is to say, massive declines in the apprehension of criminals.

The other problem is with the special status that Prof. Kennedy accords to race. Kennedy: "Racial distinctions are and should be different from other lines of social stratification." Thus, if it can be shown, as it surely can, that state troopers stop young people more than old people, relative to young people's numerical representation on the road being patrolled, that is of no consequence. If they stop black people more than white people, on the same criterion, that is of large consequence. This, in spite of the fact that the categories "age" and "race" are both rather fuzzy (define "young") and are both useful predictors of criminality. In spite of the fact, too, that the principle of equality before the law does not, and up to now has never been thought to, guarantee equal outcomes for any law-enforcement process, only that a citizen who has come under reasonable suspicion will be treated fairly.

It is on this special status accorded to race that, I believe, we have gone most seriously astray. I am willing, in fact, to say much more than this: In the matter of race, I think the Anglo-Saxon world has taken leave of its senses. The campaign to ban racial profiling is, as I see it, a part of that large, broad-fronted assault on common sense that our over-educated, over-lawyered society has been enduring for some forty years now, and whose roots are in a fanatical egalitarianism, a grim determination not to face up to the realities of group differences, a theological attachment to the doctrine that the sole and sufficient explanation for all such differences is "racism"—which is to say, the malice and cruelty of white people—and a nursed and petted guilt towards the behavior of our ancestors.

At present, Americans are drifting away from the concept of belonging to a single nation. I do not think this drift will be arrested until we can shed the idea that deference to the sensitivities of racial minorities—however overwrought those sensitivities may be, however over-stimulated by unscrupulous mountebanks, however disconnected from reality—trumps every other consideration, including even the maintenance of social order. To shed that idea, we must confront our national hysteria about race, which causes large numbers of otherwise sane people to believe that the hearts of their fellow citizens are filled with malice towards them. So long as we continue to pander to that poisonous, preposterous belief, we shall only wander off deeper into a wilderness of division, mistrust, and institutionalized rancor—that wilderness, the most freshly painted sign-post to which bears the legend RACIAL PROFILING.

NO ⬅

David A. Harris

Profiles in Injustice: American Life under the Regime of Racial Profiling

Sergeant Rossano Gerald

Sergeant First Class Rossano Gerald, a black man, had made the United States Army his life. He served in Operation Desert Storm in Iraq, winning the Bronze Star, and in Operation United Shield in Somalia. His nineteen-year military career has included postings both in the United States and overseas. Military service runs deep in Sergeant Gerald's family; he describes himself as an "army brat" who grew up on military bases.

One blazing hot August day in 1998, Sergeant Gerald and his twelve-year-old son, Gregory, were on their way to a big family reunion in Oklahoma. Almost as soon as they crossed into Oklahoma from Arkansas, an Oklahoma Highway Patrol officer stopped their car. He questioned them, warning Sergeant Gerald not to follow cars in front of him too closely, then allowed him to leave. (Gerald denies following any other cars too closely; because he had noticed several highway patrol cars as he entered the state, he had been driving with extra caution.) But less than half an hour farther into Oklahoma, another highway patrol officer stopped Sergeant Gerald again, this time accusing him of changing lanes without signaling. Sergeant Gerald denied this, and he told the officer that another officer had just stopped him.

Despite Sergeant Gerald's having produced a valid driver's license, proof of insurance, and army identification, the troopers—several squad cars had arrived by now—asked to search his car. Sergeant Gerald politely refused; after answering numerous questions, Sergeant Gerald asked many times that the officer in charge call his commanding officer at his base. The highway patrol officers refused each request. Instead, the police put Sergeant Gerald and Gregory into a squad car, turned off the air conditioning, and turned on the car's fan, which blew suffocatingly hot air into the vehicle; they warned Sergeant Gerald and Gregory that the police dogs present would attack them if they tried to escape.

When Sergeant Gerald still refused to allow them to search his car, the troopers told him that Oklahoma statutes allowed them to search (a blatant misstatement of the law), and they had a drug-sniffing dog search the vehicle. Sergeant Gerald knew something about these animals; as part of his army duties, he'd worked with military police officers using drug-detection dogs. The dog never gave any signal that it smelled drugs, but the troopers told Sergeant Gerald that the dog had "alerted" to the presence of narcotics and that they were going to search his car.

For what seemed like hours in the oppressive heat, Sergeant Gerald—now in handcuffs in the backseat of a patrol car—watched as officers used a variety of tools to take apart door panels, consoles, even the inside of the car's roof; at one point they announced that they had found a "secret compartment" in the car's floor. (It was actually a factory-installed footrest.) The troopers attempted to block his view of the search by raising the hoods on their vehicles, and one of them deactivated a patrol car video-evidence camera. They went through every item in the luggage, questioning Sergeant Gerald about Gregory's plane tickets home, which they found in one of the suitcases. (Gregory lived with his mother in northern Indiana, and Sergeant Gerald planned to put him on a plane home after the reunion.) Meanwhile, Gregory was moved to another police car against his father's express wishes; he was made to sit in the front while a dog barked and growled at him from the backseat and a police officer asked him about his father's "involvement" in drug trafficking.

After two and a half hours—and no recovery of any drugs—the police released Sergeant Gerald with a warning ticket. When he asked them what they planned to do about the mess they had made of his car and his personal belongings, they gave him a screwdriver. Their parting words to him: "We ain't good at repacking." Damage to the car amounted to more than a thousand dollars.

Sergeant Gerald filed a lawsuit to contest his mistreatment. Although he has little taste or desire for litigation, he felt he owed it to his son, Gregory, to show that people who have power cannot abuse others with impunity. "I'm an authority figure myself," Sergeant Gerald says. "I don't want my son thinking for one minute that this kind of behavior by anyone in uniform is acceptable." The lawsuit ended with a settlement of seventy-five thousand dollars paid to Sergeant Gerald and Gregory, even as state officials still denied any wrongdoing. "I think I serve my country well," Sergeant Gerald said. "I never want my son to see racism like this happen." Gregory, he said, remains "scarred" by the experience.

Judge Filemon Vela

In 1980, President Carter appointed Filemon Vela United States District Judge for the Southern District of Texas. Vela had been an elected state judge for six years before that, following a career in private practice. Judge Vela's chambers are in Brownsville, Texas, just across the Rio Grande from Matamoros, Mexico. Brownsville has a long history of connection with

Mexico; many of its 130,000 citizens are of Mexican descent. Judge Vela's own great-grandfather came to Texas from Mexico in the 1860s. People know Judge Vela not only for what he does in his courtroom, but also for his activities in the community. His bedrock beliefs in education and straight talk led him to help organize and direct a program in which young male and female convicts serving drug sentences come to local high schools to tell the students how involvement with drugs and violence stole their futures. Judge Vela plays the Ted Koppel role in these sessions, asking the inmates about everything from their fear of prison rape to their shame at having embarrassed their families. Judge Vela's wife, Blanca Vela, is the mayor of Brownsville; between their friends, families, and their many personal and professional acquaintances, they know almost everyone in the city who is involved in politics and civic life.

In 1997, the area around Brownsville became the focus of intense immigration enforcement. "Operation Rio Grande" increased the number of agents in the area from seven hundred to twelve hundred by the end of 1999 and poured sophisticated equipment and resources into the effort. The stepped-up activity paralleled similar operations in California, West Texas, and other illegal immigration hot spots. The result was a strong, proactive Border Patrol presence, enough to affect almost everyone of Mexican descent.

During the summer of 1999, Judge Vela and three members of his staff drove to Laredo, one of the cities in south Texas where Judge Vela holds court on a regular basis. The four rode in a Ford Explorer. A Border Patrol agent, who'd been sitting in a vehicle parked next to the side of the road, pulled them over. The agent asked Judge Vela and the others in the car about their citizenship. After they had answered, Judge Vela asked the agent why he had stopped the car. "He said he stopped us because there were too many people in the vehicle," Vela says, though the Explorer could certainly have held more passengers. Only then did Judge Vela tell the agent who he was; he also said that he felt that the agent did not have legal grounds to stop them. Though the agent quickly ended the encounter, telling Judge Vela and his staff they could go, Vela made a complaint to the officer's superiors—not so much about the conduct of the particular officer involved but rather about the practices and policies that led him to make an unjustified stop. As a judge, he was keenly aware that for any search that uncovers contraband to "stand up in court," the stop of the car that led to the search had to be legal. If the stop was illegal, a judge would have to throw out the evidence—and a criminal would go free. It's not at all surprising that Judge Vela's complaint was taken seriously by the Border Patrol; he received assurances that Border Patrol agents would get more training and education to teach them to stop motorists only with a legal basis.

Almost exactly a year after his first encounter with the Border Patrol, Judge Vela was again on his way to Laredo to preside in court, driving on the same road, this time as the passenger of an assistant U.S. attorney. His staff was riding in another vehicle, traveling along with them. Again, a Border

Patrol agent pulled the car over; again, Judge Vela—an American citizen, an attorney, and a federal judge—had to answer questions about his citizenship. Once again, Judge Vela asked why the agent stopped them. The answer this time: the car had tinted windows. Judge Vela filed another complaint, but he was not surprised that a second incident had occurred.

Judge Vela talks about these experiences with candor and a touch of humor. He feels that although it is important to speak out, he cannot allow himself to be defined or embittered by what has happened. "If I ever catch myself being affected by these kinds of things, I should not allow myself to sit [as a judge]," he says. Yet it is clear that these experiences have confirmed for him that everyone in the Hispanic community is a target of immigration enforcement, regardless of whether they are citizens, or of their status or station in life. "If they stop us . . . we who are attorneys, we who study law . . . then my goodness, what will they do to persons who do not have our place?" he wonders. "If they can do it to you and me," he says, referring to himself, his staff, and the assistant U.S. attorney who were with him, "who won't they do it to?" Vela has taught American law and constitutionalism on behalf of the Unites States government to attorneys, judges, and other officials all over the world, particularly in Latin America, and he believes with all his heart that the United States and its Constitution are something special, something unique—something worth preserving. "But if you let these things happen, it will deteriorate." He worries that something is badly out of balance. Another Hispanic judge in Brownsville, who has also experienced the Border Patrol's tactics firsthand, puts it this way: "It feels like occupied territory. It does not feel like we're in the United States of America."

Minhtran Tran and Quyen Pham

With school out for the year, Minhtran Tran and Quyen Pham went shopping one morning at a strip of stores in Garden Grove, a city of approximately 150,000 in Orange County, California. Neither girl, both fifteen-year-old honor students, had a police record or had had any contact at all with law enforcement. When they decided to leave and went to a pay phone outside the stores, police from Garden Grove's gang suppression unit drove up, got out of their cars, and confronted them and a third young Asian girl. The police accused them of making trouble and asked them whether they belonged to a gang, allegedly because they were wearing gang clothing. Officers then put the three girls up against a wall and took photographs of them with a Polaroid camera. None of the girls consented; in fact, the police never asked for their permission, let alone the permission of their parents. The "gang attire" they were alleged to have been wearing could have described the clothing of a million other teenagers that day: form-fitting shirts and oversized baggy pants. The police also took down information from the girls, including height, weight, age, hair and eye color, their home addresses, and the names of the schools they attended.

Minhtran Tran and Quyen Pham may have felt disturbed by their treatment that day, but they received a worse shock later. Other kids they knew who went to the Garden Grove Police Station later that day told the girls that they saw the Polaroid pictures the police had taken of them pinned up on a prominent bulletin board. The girls found this hard to understand; police had not charged or cited them, and they hadn't done anything. They felt that the police had labeled them criminals and treated them as gang members because they were Asians dressed in a certain way. Eventually, along with other young Asian Americans, the two girls became the plaintiffs in a lawsuit against the Garden Grove Police Department.

The photographing of the high school honor students by police did not happen by accident. Rather, it came about as part of a set of practices put in place as a deliberate effort to fight gangs in California. With an influx of Asian immigrants to the West Coast over the last twenty-five years, including refugees from Southeast Asia, the region's Asian population has surged. The growth of any immigrant population typically contributes to the problems one customarily finds in any city or suburban area, including crime and gangs. The Asian population is no different, despite the model minority stereotype, and in the early 1990s southern California communities began to make a concerted effort to combat what they saw as a rising menace.

One of the first examples of the effort came in a thirty-page report, entitled "Asian Gangs in Little Saigon: Identification and Methods of Operation." The document, written by Detective Mark Nye of the Westminster Police Department, explored many aspects of Orange County's Asian youth gangs, from what they did to how they dressed to which cars they drove. The report discussed many different demographic groups, including female gang members. Nye warned that "female gang members in some cases dress very similar to male gang members. They will wear baggy, loose fitting clothing, baggy pants, oversized shirts, usually untucked, and in some cases baseball caps." (Parents will recognize this description of clothing as the nearly ubiquitous uniform of the American teenager—Asian, African American, Hispanic, or white.) Female members of Asian gangs, Nye said, looked enough like their male counterparts that they "can be mistakenly identified as males." And in a catch-22 that makes it difficult to see how any young Asian woman could avoid being labeled as a gang member, Nye said that Asian girls who did not dress in typical gang attire were really just in "disguise."

Robert Wilkins

In the early morning hours of a Monday in May 1992, Robert Wilkins and three members of his extended family were driving to Washington, D.C., from Chicago. The four, all African Americans, had traveled together to Chicago a few days before for the funeral of Wilkins's grandfather, the family patriarch. As they drove along an interstate highway outside of Cumberland, Maryland, a Maryland State Police car pulled them over.

Wilkins's cousin had been at the wheel; when Wilkins noticed that the stop had lasted some time and that the trooper had brought his cousin to the rear of their rental car, where he could not be seen, Wilkins and his uncle got out to see what was happening.

Wilkins's decision to get out of the car and investigate made perfect sense. He had exactly the right training to deal with a situation like this. A graduate of Harvard Law School, Wilkins was himself a criminal defense lawyer. He practiced with Washington, D.C.'s Public Defender Service, one of the most highly regarded public defender offices in the nation. Wilkins had considerable seasoning not only in the ins and outs of criminal and constitutional law, but also in the nuances of police tactics and street stops. He was a skilled trial lawyer, accustomed to speaking his mind in court crisply, authoritatively, and carefully, even though he was a soft-spoken person. He also had considerable experience dealing with police officers.

Wilkins's cousin, who had been driving, told him that the trooper wanted consent to search the car. It was true; the trooper showed Wilkins a consent-to-search form—a piece of paper that, if signed, would indicate that the trooper had obtained voluntary consent to a search of the car. "I explained to him who I was and that I was a public defender in Washington, D.C.," Wilkins said, "and I understood clearly what our rights were and what his rights were, and that we didn't want to have the car searched." The trooper's reply, though perhaps showing a lack of understanding of the law, was just as clear as Wilkins's statement had been. "He looked at me," Wilkins said, "and he said, 'Well, if you don't have anything to hide, then what's the problem?'"

Undoubtedly, most ordinary people would have given in to the officer's demand at this point, but Wilkins was not so easily intimidated. "I thought to myself that this is the exact, most inappropriate response that the law enforcement officer can give," he said. Just asserting your rights "shouldn't make you suspicious." Wilkins held firm; he told the officer that he and his family wanted to be left alone.

The trooper seemed genuinely puzzled and surprised. Giving the trooper credit for frankness, Wilkins remembers his explanation. "He said, 'Well, this is routine, no one ever objects.' I said I don't know what other people do and that may be the case that nobody else does, but we object." The trooper, perhaps sensing that he was not going to get to search the car the easy way, began to play hardball. He told Wilkins that he and his family would have to wait for a drug-sniffing dog. Wilkins continued to stand his ground, calmly but firmly. He told the trooper that *United States* v. *Sharpe*, a U.S. Supreme Court decision, said that he could not detain Wilkins and his family without some fact-based suspicion, and he asserted that there was nothing even remotely suspicious about the family. Though Wilkins clearly had the law on his side, the trooper didn't care to debate the issue. He told Wilkins that these searches were "just routine procedure" because the police had been having "problems with rental cars and drugs." (Wilkins and his family were driving a Virginia-registered rental car; the license plate, with its first letter *R*, showed this.) "He wasn't rude, he was firm," Wilkins recalls. "He just made clear, 'Look, you know, this is procedure. . . . You're gonna have to wait here for this dog.'" Even offering to show the trooper the program from his grandfather's funeral did not change anything. By this time, other troopers had arrived. Though they saw Wilkins begin to write down names and badge numbers on a pad, the troopers were undeterred; in fact, Wilkins remembers that at least one seemed quite amused by his insistence on his rights.

And the way the trooper wanted it was, in the end, the way it went. The family was held until the dog arrived. Despite their strenuous objections, all of them were forced to get out of the car and stand in the dark and the rain by the side of the road as the dog—so reminiscent to Wilkins and his family of the dogs turned loose on blacks in the South by police in civil rights confrontations—sniffed every inch of the exterior of the car. And only after this careful search turned up nothing were they allowed to leave—with a $105 ticket, though the trooper had originally told them they would receive only a warning. It was only later that Wilkins learned he'd been stopped because of a written profile (prepared by the Maryland State Police) that described him perfectly—a black male in a rental car.

⋅◦⟨◉⟩◦⋅

All four of these stories may sound like egregious examples of police run amok, the work of rogue officers. But the truth is that these situations were the result of a well-known, well-used law enforcement technique that has spread all over the country. It has become known as "racial profiling"—and it describes life for millions of Americans who happen to be black, brown, or Asian. What happened to Sergeant Gerald, Judge Vela, Minhtran Tran and Quyen Pham, and Robert Wilkins is not uncommon at all among people like them. They have lived with these practices for many years—even if the rest of the nation has become aware of racial profiling only recently.

Racial profiling grew out of a law enforcement tactic called *criminal* profiling. *Criminal* profiling has come into increasing use over the last twenty years, not just as a way to solve particular crimes police know about but also as a way to predict who may be involved in as-yet-undiscovered crimes, especially drug offenses. *Criminal* profiling is designed to help police spot criminals by developing sets of personal and behavioral characteristics associated with particular offenses. By comparing individuals they observe with profiles, officers should have a better basis for deciding which people to treat as suspects. Officers may see no direct evidence of crime, but they can rely on noncriminal but observable characteristics associated with crime to decide whether someone seems suspicious and therefore deserving of greater police scrutiny.

When these characteristics include race or ethnicity as a factor in predicting crimes, *criminal* profiling can become *racial* profiling. Racial profiling is a crime-fighting strategy—a government policy that treats African Americans, Latinos, and members of other minority groups as criminal suspects on the assumption that doing so will increase the odds of catching criminals. Many in law enforcement argue that it makes sense to use race or ethnicity in criminal profiles because there is a strong statistical association between membership in minority groups and involvement in crime. Having black or brown skin elevates the chances that any given person may be engaged in crime, especially drug crime, the thinking of police and many members of the public goes. The disproportionately large number of minorities reflected in arrest and incarceration statistics is further proof, the argument continues, that skin color is a valid indicator of a greater propensity to commit crime. Supporters of racial profiling arrive, therefore, at the conclusion that focusing police suspicion on blacks, Latinos, Asians, and other minorities makes perfect sense. Racial profiling is nothing more than rational law enforcement.

If racial profiling is what directs police suspicion at minorities, it is high-discretion police tactics that put these suspicions into action, turning profiles into police investigations. These high-discretion methods allow police to detain, question, and search people who have exhibited no concrete evidence of wrongdoing—something the law would almost never otherwise allow. But thanks to the U.S. Supreme Court, which has widened the permissible scope of police discretion and vastly increased law enforcement power at the same time that profiling has come into wide use, these tactics are all perfectly legal. For example, police officers can use traffic enforcement as a legal excuse to "fish" for evidence, even though officers have observed no criminal conduct. Officers can also ask for "voluntary" consent to search, without even a whisper of a reason to think the citizen asked has done anything wrong. And officers can also "stop and frisk" pedestrians without the probable cause they need in other circumstances.

Taken at face value, we could say that racial profiling is morally and ethically wrong. It is clearly unconscionable to treat an individual as a criminal suspect simply because a small number of individuals from the same racial or ethnic group are criminals. But in a society dedicated to equal justice under law, such a practice also undermines our commitment to individual civil rights. Enforcing the law on the basis of racial and ethnic calculations therefore also offends the Constitution. All Americans are guaranteed "the equal protection of the law"; there are few values closer to the core of our political culture. Enforcing the law in a racially or ethnically biased way violates this central principle.

Racial profiling also damages the relationship between police departments and the communities they serve. Almost all police departments today describe themselves as service oriented; community policing, a philosophy of law enforcement that features partnerships between police and the citizens they serve, has become the accepted and applauded orthodoxy everywhere. Yet profiling, which treats all citizens of particular racial and ethnic groups as potential criminals, can do nothing but alienate these same citizens from their police. It breaks down the trust that must be at the heart of any true partnership, and it threatens to defeat community policing's best efforts to fight crime and disorder. Racial profiling reinforces the preexisting fissures of race in our society. By putting citizens in categories by race and ethnicity to determine which ones should be regarded as suspicious and therefore worthy of greater police scrutiny, we divide ourselves into "the good" and "the bad," the citizen and the criminal.

. . . Apart from the moral, ethical, and constitutional arguments against racial profiling, which have increasingly been embraced by Americans of all colors in recent years, new data now offer an irrefutable statistical argument against the practice. Despite the widespread belief that racial profiling, reprehensible though it may be, is an effective and efficient way of catching criminals—a "rational" approach to law enforcement—newly collected information about "hit rates" gives the lie to this assumption: the numbers just don't add up. Data emerging from studies done over the last few years demonstrate conclusively that hit rates—the rates at which police actually find contraband on people they stop—run contrary to long-held "commonsense" beliefs about the effectiveness of racial profiling. The rate at which officers uncover contraband in stops and searches is *not* higher for blacks than for whites, as most people believe. Contrary to what the "rational" law enforcement justification for racial profiling would predict, *the hit rate for drugs and weapons in police searches of African Americans is the same as or lower than the rate for whites*. Comparing Latinos and whites yields even more surprising results. Police catch criminals among Latinos at *far lower rates* than among whites. These results hold true in studies done in New York, Maryland, New Jersey, and other places. We see the same results in data collected by the U.S. Customs Service, concerning the searches it does of people entering the country at airports: the hit rate is lower for blacks than it is for whites, and the hit rate for Latinos is lower still.

Other data also yield startling surprises. For example, while it is true that automobile stops sometimes result in large seizures of drugs, this rarely happens. In fact, police usually find nothing at all; when they do find drugs, it is almost always very small amounts. The quantities discovered seldom exceed enough for personal use and often amount to even less—so-called trace amounts that can be detected but not used. Of course, what we see on the evening news are the big seizures; we seldom hear about the small ones and never about the far more numerous times that officers come up empty-handed. We come away with the mistaken impression that these tactics are not only rational and fair but successful—when nothing could be further from the truth. All of this exposes the rational law enforcement argument as, at best, the product of a set of mistaken assumptions. If blacks and Latinos who are stopped as a result of racial profiling are no more likely or are even less likely to be in possession of drugs or other contraband than whites, it simply doesn't make sense to enforce the law in this way. And if the net results are not a constant parade of big-time seizures of contraband but mostly "dry holes" and tiny amounts, there's no real payoff. If "rational" law enforcement seems to make sense, that is only because we are selective in our interpretations of facts and limited in our vision of what police do and in the effects these actions have.

Even if we were to overlook racial profiling's moral, legal, and social flaws, it simply does not work as a law enforcement tactic. And it is a way of enforcing the law that we almost surely would not accept in other circumstances. Suppose, for example, that profiles focused not on race and ethnicity but on poverty. We can imagine appearance characteristics for poverty that would prove almost as easy to observe as skin color: clothing and personal appearance, the physical condition and age of vehicles, and the neighborhood in which a person lives. Yet we would almost certainly object if police consistently stopped, questioned, and searched almost everyone who looked poor. The assumption that police should treat *all* poor people as criminal suspects because *some* poor people commit crimes would—and should—outrage us. Yet this is precisely what is happening when we police with racial profiles—except, of course, that the burden is likely to be distributed not by poverty but by race and ethnicity.

It would be easy to assume that racial profiling has its roots only in the racism of individual racist police officers—that the officers who engage in this practice are bigots whom we should simply root out of the police force. Surely there are bigots among police officers, but there are also bigots in every other profession. The great majority of police officers are good people who make use of racial profiling unintentionally. They do so not because they are bigoted or bad, but because they think it is the right way to catch criminals. Racial profiling is an institutional practice— a tactic accepted and encouraged by police agencies as a legitimate, effective crime-fighting tool. It is a method full of assumptions that have, for too long, gone untested, unexamined, and unchallenged. And when we do challenge it—push hard on its underlying premises and look at real data—policing with racial profiles cannot be said to be a rational response to crime. It is instead a misdirected attack on a difficult set of problems that causes its own damage to innocent individuals, to policing, to society, and to the law itself. Racial profiling is based not on real evidence but on distorted ideas about crime and an overly narrow view of how to attack it. We can do better; in fact, we must do better. The task of this book is to get us beyond the inaccurate, incorrect, and misleading ways in which we think about crime and how to fight it.

POSTSCRIPT

Is Racial Profiling Defensible Public Policy?

The debate over racial profiling serves to illuminate a major division in American politics between the advocates of human rights and individual liberties and others who are willing to relinquish the protection of certain rights in the interests of law and order and national security. Racial minorities tend to view such policies as unwarranted assaults on their human dignity, and counterproductive to achieving the goals of the wars on drugs, crime, and terrorism. Others are concerned that instead of promoting national security, this policy has alienated minorities and immigrant groups and has raised serious concerns around the world. There is a growing perception within the international community that racial profiling is compromising the U.S. government's commitments to the rule of law and to equal rights and social justice.

The current controversy over racial profiling entered the public consciousness when the issue emerged in New Jersey and other states that were forced to respond to mounting criticisms of law enforcement practices and policies. Due to the vigorous campaign that was launched against this policy by the Black Ministerial Conference of New Jersey, the ACLU, and other black and Latino leaders and organizations, racial profiling appeared to lose some support. However, due to the events of September 11, 2001 and the ensuing declaration of a war on terrorism, public attitudes on this issue seem to have shifted, and many Americans now view it as necessary to secure the nation against a growing threat to national security.

In response to the September 11 terrorist attacks, there has been a perceptible shift in the focus of racial profiling from the war on drugs to a war on terrorism that tends to target Arabs and Muslims, both citizens and immigrants, as suspects. The treatment that members of these groups have received from police, the Immigration and Naturalization Service, and other agents of national security has caused many of their members to reconsider their status and identity within the American society. So, racial profiling is having disconcerting effects on Arabs and Muslims of the United States and is producing negative perceptions of this country within their extended communities throughout the world.

Significant evidence is available to demonstrate the ineffectiveness of racial profiling. Yet, people are standing in the netting of racial profiling based on suspicions derived from racial stereotyping, thus exposing the contradictory nature of this practice.

It is important to note that there was a significant increase in the Hispanic and Asian populations of the United States during the 1990s. As a result of this increase in immigration, the minority population of the nation has continued to grow and now approaches one hundred million. These demographic changes in the United States' population make it clear that managing diversity is one of the most significant challenges facing current and future leadership of the nation. Hence, the issue of racial profiling will become relevant in the future.

More reading critiquing racial profiling can be found in David Harris' *Profiles in Injustice* (The New Press, 2002). Journalist Kenneth Meek discusses racial profiling and incidents on the New Jersey Turnpike in *Driving While Black: What to Do if You Are a Victim of Racial Profiling* (Broadway Books, 2000). *Race, Crime and the Law* (Vintage, 1998) by Randall Kennedy suggests that liberals and conservatives have more in common than expected when it comes to crime. He argues that blacks do not receive adequate police protection. David Cole explains how law enforcement is a two-tiered system in America in *No Equal Justice: Race and Class in the American Criminal Justice System* (New Press, 2000).

A Comprehensive and balanced examination of race, crime, and the criminal justice system is in *The Color of Justice: Race, Ethnicity, and Crime in America* (Wadsworth, 1999) by Samuel Walker, Merian Delone, and Cassia C. Spohn. Images of color and images of crime are addressed in *Race, Crime and Criminal Justice* (Roxbury Publishing Co., 2002) edited by Coramae Richey Mamr and Marjorie Sue Zatz. The March 2004 issue of *American Behavorial Scientist* (Sage Publications) is entitled "Critical Racial and Ethnic Studies: Profiling and Reparations." Six articles deal with examples of racial profiling.

Katheryn K. Rusell discusses crime hoaxes of both blacks and whites in *The Color of Crime: Racial Hoaxes, White Fear, Black Protectionism, Police Harassment, and Other Macroaggressions (Critical America Series)* (New York University Press, 1999). Heather MacDonald justifies police crime-control tactics and methods in *Are Cops Racist?* (Ivan R. Dee Inc., 2003). Students are encouraged to research the growing literature in the area of race, crime, and criminology.

Contributors to This Volume

EDITORS

RAYMOND D ANGELO is a professor of sociology at St. Joseph's College in New York where he serves as Chair of the Department of Social Sciences. He graduated from Duquesne University and received an MA from the New School for Social Research. His Ph.D. is from Bryn Mawr College. He has been involved with teaching and research in race and ethnic studies throughout his academic career. He is a recipient of two fellowships from the National Science Foundation and a research award from the National Institute of Justice, and is a recent recipient of a National Endowment for the Humanities award. D'Angelo is author and editor of *The American Civil Rights Movement: Readings and Interpretations* (McGraw Hill/Dushkin, 2000) and has contributed to the *Arena Review: Journal for the Study of Sport and Sociology* and *Civil Rights in the United States*. He is active in historic preservation.

HERBERT DOUGLAS is a professor of Law and Justice Studies at Rowan University in Glassboro, New Jersey where he also serves as an African American Studies and International Studies faculty member. He graduated from Duquesne University and received his Ph.D. from the University of Toledo. He was a recipient of a Fulbright-Hays Fellowship to study in the Soviet Union in summer 1990. He is involved in social causes including membership on the governing board of the Fair Share Housing Center in Camden, New Jersey, an organization designed to promote the housing needs of low and moderate income families. He was coordinator of a foreign studies program in Ghana in the summer 1979 conducted by the Office of International Studies of SUNY Brockport. Douglas contributed "Migration and Adaptations of African American Families within Urban America," to *Minority Voices: Linking Personal Ethnic History and the Sociological Imagination* (Allyn & Bacon, 2005) edited by John Myers. He has been involved with teaching and research in race and ethnic studies throughout his academic career.

STAFF

Larry Loeppke   Managing Editor
Jill Peter   Senior Developmental Editor
Nichole Altman   Developmental Editor
Beth Kundert   Production Manager
Jane Mohr   Project Manager
Tara McDermott   Design Coordinator
Bonnie Coakley   Editorial Assistant

413

AUTHORS

ROBERT L. ALLEN is senior editor of *The Black Scholar*. A long-time activist and professor, he is author of *The Port Chicago Mutiny* (Amistad Press, 1993) and coeditor with Herb Boyd of *Brotherman: The Odyssey of Black Men in America* (Sagebrush Education Resources, 1996).

GORDON ALLPORT (1897–1967) was a social psychologist and author of *The Nature of Prejudice* (1954).

ROBERT APONTE is a sociologist at Indiana University–School of Liberal Arts and acting chair of the Sociology Department. He helped found the Julian Samora Research Institute at Michigan State University.

PETER BEINART is a Senior Editor to *The New Republic*. He has also written for *The New York Times, The Wall Street Journal, The Financial Times, The Boston Globe, The Atlantic Monthly, Newsweek,* and *Time*.

DAVID A. BELL, journalist and historian, is a former reporter and researcher for *The National Review*.

DERRICK BELL is a visiting professor of law at New York University School of Law. He is author of many books including *Faces at the Bottom of the Well: The Permanence of Racism* (Basic Books, 1992) and the classic *Race, Racism and American Law* (Aspen Publishers Inc., 2000).

HERBERT BLUMER (1900–1987) was a former professional football player who became a sociology professor at the University of Chicago and the University of California, Berkeley. He helped to establish symbolic interactionism as a major paradigm in sociology.

WILLIAM G. BOWEN is president of the Andrew W. Mellon Foundation. He is coauthor, along with Derek Bok, of *The Shape of the River: Long-Term Consequences of Considering Race in College and University Admissions* (Princeton University Press, 1998).

PETER BRIMELOW is senior editor of *Forbes* and *National Review*. He is the author of *Alien Nation: Common Sense About America's Immigration Disaster* (Perennial, 1996).

LINDA CHAVEZ is a syndicated columnist for several newspapers throughout the country. She is author of *Out of the Barrio: Toward a New Politics of Hispanic Assimilation* (Basic Books, 1991) and, most recently, *An Unlikely Conservative* (Basic Books, 2002), which is her autobiography.

DAVID COLE is a professor at the Georgetown University Law Center and author of *Enemy Aliens* and *Terrorism and the Constitution: Sacrificing Civil Liberties in the Name of National Security*.

HECTOR CORDERO-GUZMAN is an associate professor and chair of the Department of Black and Hispanic Studies at Baruch College of the City University of New York.

ELLIS COSE is the author of *The Press, A Nation of Strangers,* and *The Rage of a Privileged Class*. He is now a writer and essayist for *Newsweek*.

JOHN DERBYSHIRE is a critic, commentator and novelist. He is a regular contributor to *The National Review* and author of *Prime Obsession* (Joseph Henry Press, 2003).

DINESH D'SOUZA is the John Olin Research Fellow at the American Enterprise Institute. He is author of *The End of Racism: Principles for a Multicultural Society* (Free Press, 1995) and *Illiberal Education: The Politics of Race and Sex on Campus* (Free Press, 1991).

W.E.B. Du BOIS (1868–1963), author of *Souls of Black Folk,* was a sociologist, writer, scholar, and civil rights activist. He was one of the founders of the NAACP and editor of its publication, the *Crisis.*

INGRID GOULD ELLEN is assistant professor of public policy and urban planning at the New York University Wagner Graduate School of Public Service. She is author of *Sharing America's Neighborhoods: The Prospects for Stable Racial Integration* (Harvard University Press, 2000).

AMY GUTMANN is a professor of politics at Princeton University. She has written many books including *Identity and Democracy* (Princeton University Press, 2003) and *Color Conscious: The Political Morality of Race* (Princeton University Press, 1996) with Kwame Anthony Appiah.

PATRICK A. HALL is the instructional services coordinator of the University Libraries at Notre Dame University.

DAVID A. HARRIS is a professor of law and values at the University of Toledo College of Law and Soros Senior Justice Fellow at the Center of Crime, Communities and Justice in New York City. He is author of *Profiles in Injustice: Why Racial Profiling Cannot Work* (New Press, 2003).

MARVIN HARRIS is an anthropologist and a graduate research professor at the University of Florida. He is author of many books including *Cows, Pigs, Wars and Witches: The Riddles of Culture* (Vintage, 1989).

RICHARD KAHLENBERG is a fellow at the Century Foundation. His most recent book is *America's Untapped Resource: Low Income Students in Higher Education* (Twentieth Century Fund, 2004).

GARY B. NASH is a professor of history at the University of California, Los Angeles, where he is director of the Center for the National for History in the Schools. He was co-chair of the National History Standards Project. He is author of numerous publications.

GARY ORFIELD is a professor of education at Harvard University where he is involved with the Civil Rights Project. He is author of *Dismantling Desegregation: The Quiet Reversal of Brown v. Board of Education* (The New Press, 1996).

DIANE RAVITCH is a professor of history and education at Teachers College, Columbia University. She is author of many books including *Left Back: A Century of Failed School Reforms* (Simon & Schuster, 2000) and *The Language Police: How Pressure Groups Restrict What Students Learn* (Alfred A. Knopf, 2000).

CLARA E. RODRIGUEZ is a professor of sociology in the Division of Social Sciences at Fordham University. She is author of *Latin Looks: Latina and Latino Images in the U.S. Media* (Westview Press, 1997) and *Changing Race: Latinos, the Census and the History of Ethnicity in the United States* (New York University Press, 2000).

LILLIAN B. RUBIN is a sociologist and author of *Worlds of Pain, Just Friends, Intimate Strangers,* and *Families on the Fault Line* (HarperPerennial, 1994), She is also a Senior Research Fellow at the Institute for the Study of Social Change at the University of California at Berkeley.

ARTHUR M. SCHLESINGER, JR., is a historian and former speech writer to President John F. Kennedy. He is the author of many books including *The Disuniting of America: Reflections on a Multicultural Society* (W.W. Norton, 1992).

ROBERT STAPLES is a professor of sociology at the University of California, San Francisco and author of *Black Masculinity: The Black Male's Role in American Society* (Black Scholar Press, 1982) and *Families at the Crossroads: Challenges and Prospects* (Jossey-Bass Inc., 1993), coauthored with Leanor Boulin Johnson.

BEVERLY TATUM is a clinical psychologist and current president of Spelman College. She is author of *Why Are All the Black Kids Sitting Together in the Cafeteria? and Other Conversations About Race* (Basic Books, 1997).

MICHAEL WALZER is a political philosopher and professor at the Princeton University Center for Advanced Study. He is author of *On Toleration* and *Exodus and Revolution* (Basic Books, 2000).

BOOKER T. WASHINGTON (1856–1915) was an educator and reformer who became an important spokesman for African Americans after the turn of the twentieth century. He was the founder of Tuskegee Institute, an industrial school for blacks in Alabama.

LAWRENCE WRIGHT is a staff writer for *The New Yorker*. He is author of *Noriega: God's Favorite* (Simon & Schuster, 2000) and *Twins: And What They Tell Us About Who We Are* (John Wiley & Sons, 1999).

FRANK H. WU is a law professor at the Howard University School of Law. He writes for many publications and is the author of *Yellow: Race in America Beyond Black and White* (Basic Books, 2002).

HOWARD ZINN is a professor emeritus of political science at Boston University, an activist, and author of *SNCC: The New Abolitionists* (South End Press, 2002) and *A Peoples History of the United States* (Perennial, 2003).

Index